The Will to Kill

Fifth Edition

Sara Miller McCune founded SAGE Publishing in 1965 to support the dissemination of usable knowledge and educate a global community. SAGE publishes more than 1000 journals and over 800 new books each year, spanning a wide range of subject areas. Our growing selection of library products includes archives, data, case studies and video. SAGE remains majority owned by our founder and after her lifetime will become owned by a charitable trust that secures the company's continued independence.

Los Angeles | London | New Delhi | Singapore | Washington DC | Melbourne

The Will to Kill

Making Sense of Senseless Murder

Fifth Edition

James Alan Fox

Northeastern University

Jack Levin

Northeastern University

Kenna Quinet

Indiana University–Purdue University Indianapolis

$SAGE

Los Angeles | London | New Delhi
Singapore | Washington DC | Melbourne

FOR INFORMATION:

SAGE Publications, Inc.
2455 Teller Road
Thousand Oaks, California 91320
E-mail: order@sagepub.com

SAGE Publications Ltd.
1 Oliver's Yard
55 City Road
London, EC1Y 1SP
United Kingdom

SAGE Publications India Pvt. Ltd.
B 1/I 1 Mohan Cooperative Industrial Area
Mathura Road, New Delhi 110 044
India

SAGE Publications Asia-Pacific Pte. Ltd.
3 Church Street
#10-04 Samsung Hub
Singapore 049483

Copyright © 2019 by SAGE Publications, Inc.

Printed in the United States of America.

Library of Congress Cataloging-in-Publication Data

Names: Fox, James Alan, author. | Levin, Jack, 1941- author. | Quinet, Kenna, author.

Title: The will to kill : making sense of senseless murder / James Alan Fox, Northeastern University, Jack Levin, Northeastern University, Kenna Quinet, Indiana University-Purdue University Indianapolis.

Description: Fifth Edition. | Thousand Oaks : SAGE Publications, [2017] | Revised edition of the authors' The will to kill, c2012. | Includes bibliographical references and index.

Identifiers: LCCN 2017049053 | ISBN 9781506365961 (pbk. : alk. paper)

Subjects: LCSH: Murder. | Homicide. | Criminal psychology. | Criminal justice, Administration of.

Classification: LCC HV6515 .F69 2017 | DDC 364.152/3—dc23
LC record available at https://lccn.loc.gov/2017049053

Acquisitions Editor: Jessica Miller
Editorial Assistant: Rebecca Lee
Content Development Editor: Laura Kirkhuff
Production Editor: Karen Wiley
Copy Editor: Colleen Brennan
Typesetter: Hurix Digital
Proofreader: Tricia Currie-Knight
Indexer: David Luljak
Cover Designer: Candice Harman
Marketing Manager: Jillian Ragusa

This book is printed on acid-free paper.

MIX
Paper from responsible sources
FSC® C014174
www.fsc.org

18 19 20 21 22 10 9 8 7 6 5 4 3 2 1

BRIEF CONTENTS

DETAILED CONTENTS

ABOUT THE AUTHORS

James Alan Fox is the Lipman Family Professor of Criminology, Law, and Public Policy at Northeastern University. He has published 18 books, dozens of journal and magazine articles, as well as hundreds of freelance columns in newspapers around the country, primarily in the areas of multiple murder, youth crime, school and campus violence, workplace violence, and capital punishment. As a member of its Board of Contributors, his opinion column appears frequently in *USA Today*. Fox often gives keynote talks and testimony before Congress and in criminal and civil court proceedings. He has briefed various leaders in the United States and abroad and has worked on criminal investigations of serial and mass murder cases. He also served as a visiting fellow with the Bureau of Justice Statistics focusing on homicide patterns and trends. He has received several awards and honors for his work, including the Hugo Adam Bedau Award for excellence in capital punishment scholarship.

Jack Levin is the Brudnick Professor Emeritus in the Department of Sociology at Northeastern University, where he codirects its Center on Violence and Conflict. He has authored or coauthored more than 30 books, most recently *The Violence of Hate* and *Hate Crime: A Global Perspective*. Levin has also published more than 250 articles and columns in professional journals, books, magazines, and newspapers, such as the *New York Times, London Sunday Times, Boston Globe, Dallas Morning News, Philadelphia Inquirer, Christian Science Monitor, Chicago Tribune, Washington Post*, and *USA Today*. Levin was honored by the Massachusetts Council for Advancement and Support of Education as its Professor of the Year and by the American Sociological Association for his contributions to the public understanding of sociology. He has also received awards from the Eastern Sociological Society, New England Sociological Association, Association of Clinical and Applied Sociology, and Society for the Study of Social Problems. He has spoken to a wide variety of community, academic, and professional groups, including the White House Conference on Hate Crimes, the Department of Justice, OSCE's Office for Democratic Institutions and Human Rights (a membership of 59 countries), and the International Association of Chiefs of Police.

Kenna Quinet is an associate professor of criminal justice in the School of Public and Environmental Affairs at Indiana University Purdue University Indianapolis (IUPUI). She is also a certified medico-legal death investigator and deputy coroner at the Marion County Coroner's Office. Her research interests include homicide, missing persons, causes of death, and unidentified and unclaimed dead. Quinet teaches homicide courses as well as an animal rights course at IUPUI and has won more than 15 teaching awards. Since 1992 she has worked closely with law enforcement, including the evaluation of community policing initiatives and drug interdiction, and has provided more than 80 media interviews. Since 2010 she has served as an Indiana representative for NamUs, the national missing and unidentified persons system.

PREFACE

We are excited to have this revision of *The Will to Kill* published by SAGE. In this fifth edition, we have done a substantial rewrite and update of the previous version, published in 2012. Indeed, much has changed over the past half dozen years in the landscape of criminal homicide, including heightened concern over mass shootings, hate-motivated homicide, and terrorism; new laws, shifting policies, and U.S. Supreme Court rulings pertaining to gun rights, the punishment of juveniles, and the death penalty; and advances in surveillance technology, computer-aided investigation, and DNA forensic testing. These and other changes guided much of this revision.

Consistent with our long-standing practice of including timely data, all of the tables and charts have been updated to 2016 (and occasionally 2017), relying on the latest available data at the time of this writing. Finally, throughout the chapters, we have added or replaced illustrative cases of the various forms of homicide, focusing particularly on those crimes that drew significant interest from the public and policymakers alike, that provided some unique insight into violent behavior, or that offered a global perspective.

Similar to earlier editions, this book is about the circumstances in which people kill one another. In the pages that follow, we review homicide laws, introduce theories (biological, psychological, and sociological) purporting to explain murderous impulses, and present statistical data depicting patterns and trends in homicide. Then, we cover a range of topics from school and workplace rampages to killings inspired by hate or terrorist ideology; from homicides committed by juveniles or youth gangs to serial slayings and medical murders. In two closing chapters, we examine criminal justice responses to homicide, including the strategies and tactics employed to apprehend, prosecute, and punish killers.

Notwithstanding its broad scope, this book is, by design, not entirely comprehensive (although we strive to be comprehensible in what we do present). As our subtitle, "Making Sense of Senseless Murder," indicates, we purposely concentrate on the extraordinary and seemingly inexplicable cases—those involving large body counts, bizarre crime scenes, elements of sadism, and seemingly irrational motivation. Thus, the reader will hardly find in the pages that follow detailed accounts explaining why a man who loses his temper impulsively shoots his spouse, why a barroom brawl results in a fatal stabbing, or why an impoverished out-of-work father robs and kills a liquor store clerk. The chapters focus much more on family annihilations, fatal romantic attractions, school shootings, mass poisonings by cultists or medical practitioners, serial killers who rape and torture their victims, and disgruntled ex-workers and customers who go on a shooting rampage.

We have accepted the challenge to concentrate on homicides that don't make obvious sense. This is not to suggest, however, that *The Will to Kill* would not be useful for understanding a much broader range of murders. We believe, on the contrary, that the lessons to be learned from examining outrageous or atypical murders can be easily extrapolated to more ordinary and mundane homicides as well. By dissecting extreme cases, we derive a selection of "pure types" against which most murders can be compared and, hopefully, better understood.

The intriguing and sensational circumstances that surround most, if not all, of the cases of homicide presented throughout this book have made them inordinately important in a public policy sense. These are, after all, the murder cases that have typically made the headlines or have gone viral on social media; they are the examples that politicians point to when they seek to change some aspect of criminal law or to secure funding for programs and policies to reduce violence. These are also the murder cases on which public opinion about homicide is often based.

A number of tables and charts are included throughout the book to document or illustrate various homicide patterns and society's response to them. Most of the tabulations and graphs are based on a 1976–2016 cumulative file of the FBI's Supplementary Homicide Reports maintained by James Alan Fox. We also relied on a comprehensive database of mass murders from 2006 through 2016 developed by the research staff at *USA Today* and expanded in scope by Emma E. Fridel of Northeastern University. In addition, we used a significant subset of serial murder cases contained in a database managed by Michael Aamodt of Radford University.

In the process of completing this book, we benefited from the support graciously provided by others. Most critically, Emma E. Fridel, coauthor of our companion book *Extreme Killing*, offered helpful comments through multiple versions of the manuscript. The book is far better for her involvement. We also are grateful for input given by William Krause of the Congressional Research Service and Michael Aamodt of Radford University. Finally, we were fortunate to have a variety of excellent recommendations from reviewers enlisted by the publisher. These reviewers include:

Minna Cirino,
Shenandoah University

Kenneth D. Colburn Jr.,
Butler University

Fatematul Jannat, PhD,
Delta State University

Edward L. Powers,
University of Central Arkansas

Gordana Rabrenovic,
Northeastern University

Alecia Schmidt,
Missouri Valley College

Clete Snell,
University of Houston–Downtown

Emily Strohacker, MA,
University of Central Florida

And speaking of SAGE Publications, we are especially appreciative of the efforts of our editor, Jessica Miller, who was patient and supportive throughout our "summer of revision." Also, we thank our former editor, Jerry Westby, who worked diligently in the process of transferring the book from its former home.

In preparing this new edition of *The Will to Kill*, as well as in our other professional activities, we continue to benefit from our associations with the Lipman and Brudnick families. Finally, we are grateful to our families and friends for being so patient and understanding during the months we were figuratively glued to our computer screens.

James Alan Fox
Jack Levin
Kenna Quinet

CHAPTER ONE

THE LURE AND THE LAW OF HOMICIDE

Homicide intrigues virtually all of us. From the sensational and historic double-murder trial of ex-football star O. J. Simpson to the travails of the elusive yet fictional Hannibal Lecter of Thomas Harris's *The Silence of the Lambs*, we are drawn irresistibly to the drama, mystery, intrigue, and power of murder and murderers, both real and invented.

It would hardly be an overstatement to suggest that within popular culture, murder has become profitable. True crime books exploded in popularity in the late 1980s, detailing the crimes and lives of serial killers, mass murders, killer cults, killer kids, and crimes involving celebrities. Entire television channels devoted to crime stories, and mostly tales of murder and mayhem, now exist. *People* magazine, a yardstick for America's enchantments, frequently places killers on its front cover. Films, books, trading cards, action figures, even artwork, center on murders and murderers, creating a cottage industry in murderabilia.

Although U.S. homicide rates are relatively low compared to previous decades and nowhere near those of the late 1980s and early 1990s, the media focus on homicide can distort our perceptions of the actual risk. A focus on the facts and the science of homicide studies will guide our journey.

FASCINATION WITH MURDER

What is it about homicide that captures our attention? Or perhaps a more fitting question is, what is it about us that explains our captivation? And what kinds of killings are especially appealing to the general public, which seems to have an insatiable appetite for true crime books and films? It is our obsession with murder—both as news and as entertainment—that prompts online sources, print, movies, and television shows to feature infamous killers.

For most of us, a fascination with murder is entirely benign. Ironically, we are drawn to murder, and especially to its most grisly and grotesque examples, as an escape from the mundane problems we face in everyday life, problems such as how to pay the bills, how to avoid being mugged, or how to get a long-awaited promotion at work. Paying the bills, avoiding a mugger, and waiting for an overdue promotion—these are all too real. By contrast, some homicides are so extraordinary that psychologically they might as well be fiction. The killers might as well be characters in a novel or a film. Because they are so unlikely, at least from the point of view of true crime buffs, they are also a form of entertainment and enjoyment. Homicides yielding large body counts, for example, a massacre in a shopping mall or at a school or in the family, may qualify as crossing the line into fantasy. But the most fascinating homicides are those involving extreme forms of sadism: crimes in which victims are tortured, raped, and dismembered. The more grotesque (and therefore removed from ordinary life) a particular killing spree is, the more likely it is to provide an escape from everyday life.

A second source of fascination with murder is not so trivial. In fact, there are many people who feel intensely vulnerable to the effects of violence, so much so that they read true crime stories and watch TV docudramas about murder not because they seek to escape psychologically but in order to learn how to avoid becoming victims of homicide (and hopefully not to learn how to avoid being caught). Going beyond their role as members of the audience for murder, some actually seek to overcome feelings of powerlessness, anxiety, and vulnerability by planning careers as criminologists, crime investigators, or forensic psychologists. They hope to learn the techniques of criminal profiling and DNA analysis. The better they understand the murdering mind and the process of criminal investigation, the more they are able to distance themselves psychologically from the killers they fear and to feel safe.

The third and final source of fascination is also the most troubling. There are some individuals—hopefully, few in number—who live vicariously through the exploits of sadistic killers. Fascinated with power but controlled by normal feelings of conscience, these individuals are psychologically incapable of murdering for pleasure, money, or protection. They can, however, learn every detail of a killer's biography, every detail of a killer's modus operandi, and every detail of the investigation by which a killer is brought to justice.

The most infamous and celebrated killers sometimes attract fan clubs, complete with member organizations, newsletters, and even fund-raisers. At the extreme, we occasionally hear about someone, usually a woman, a so-called killer groupie, who dates or even marries an incarcerated murderer. Among the many possible motivations for her attraction, she may regard her man as an important celebrity, a powerful figure worthy of respect and admiration. Women who are attracted to men who have committed gruesome crimes may actually have a paraphilia, called hybristophilia, a sexual attraction to really bad boys.

The public preoccupation with murder apparently extends to the news media as well, both print and electronic. In a sense, the prime-time news is more like the crime-time news, and the events that are the least common in reality appear to be featured more than the rest.

According to the *Tyndall Report*, the extent of crime coverage in national network news on ABC, CBS, and NBC quadrupled between 2010 and 2016, and a healthy share of it focused on homicide, including mass shootings and deadly acts of terrorism. Moreover, local news programs are especially focused on reporting about murder.

The reality of crime is quite different, however. According to Federal Bureau of Investigation (FBI) tallies, homicide accounts for only 1% of all violent offenses and 0.1% of all serious offenses. Furthermore, the murders that seem particularly exploited are those that involve sex, sadism, or celebrity—hardly the norm in stark reality.

The 1995 criminal trial of O. J. Simpson, who was accused of having stabbed to death his estranged wife Nicole Brown Simpson and her companion Ronald Goldman, provides a prime (and prime-time) example of this excess. The case contained all of the elements required to gain the attention of the nation and achieve top TV ratings—a well-liked, even heroic, celebrity football player and his beautiful wife, an interracial romance gone bad, rumors of spouse abuse, and charges of police racism. Indeed, the television coverage of the trial was so excessive that someone unfamiliar with American popular culture might have thought that O. J. Simpson was a senator or that the trial was a congressional impeachment proceeding. Not only did Court TV (later renamed truTV) televise the entire 195-day trial live, but for a period of time, regular television programming was preempted so that Americans could get their daily dose of courtroom drama. In addition, periodic rundowns of trial proceedings were regularly featured on network newscasts, morning talk shows, and prime-time news magazine shows. Television trials, while entertaining millions of people who subscribed to cable news channels, also gave them access to a nondegree education in U.S. law.

Interest in O. J. Simpson remains strong, even two decades after the jury acquitted him on the murder charges. Three television series aired in 2006–2007 delved into the O. J. case, including an eight-part documentary on ESPN, a 10-part series on FX, and an Investigation Discovery program focusing on the possibility of his innocence. In July 2017, after Simpson served only 9 years of a 33-year sentence for a 2007 armed robbery in Las Vegas, the Nevada Parole Board granted him parole. All major networks interrupted their regular programming to air the hearing. Clearly, this case continues to draw attention, speculation, conspiracy theories, ratings, and pain for the Goldman and Brown families.

SELLING EVIL

In 1985, the *National Lampoon* spoofed the U.S. glorification of murderers by publishing a series of "Mass Murderer Trading Cards," complete with photos, autographs, and statistics on "all your favorite slayers." As a parody, the *Lampoon* had placed despicable multiple killers in a context generally reserved for superstars. What was meant as social satire in 1985 soon become a social reality. In 1991, a California trading card company published its first series of mass and serial killer cards, spotlighting such infamous criminals as Jeffrey Dahmer, Theodore Bundy, and Charles Manson. Selling for $10 per pack (without bubble gum), it was no joke. Several other card makers soon followed suit, hoping to cash in on the celebrity of multiple murderers.

Even comic books have been used as a vehicle for celebrating the exploits of vicious killers like Jeffrey Dahmer, rather than traditional superheroes. By giving him a starring role once held by the likes of Batman and Superman, the killer is unnecessarily glorified, as in Marshall McLuhan's famous adage, "The medium is the message." The victims' memory is trivialized by being placed in a comic book format. In a more respectable context, the coveted cover of *People* magazine has often served as a spotlight for infamous criminals. It was bad enough that Milwaukee's confessed cannibal Jeffrey Dahmer was on the cover of *People* multiple times, an honor usually reserved for Hollywood stars and Washington politicians, but this magazine also chose Dahmer as one of its "25 Most Intriguing People of 1991" and later placed him on its list of the "100 Most Intriguing People of the Century."

Consider how *People* magazine has changed since the 1970s, when celebrities selected for the cover included First Lady Pat Nixon, Barbara Walters, Richard Burton, Joe Namath, Ralph Nader, and Mary Tyler Moore—individuals who were honored for their achievements in politics, industry, sports, and entertainment. By the late 1980s, many of the cover stories had turned negative, covering stories such as JFK and the mob, Robin Williams's love affair with his son's nanny, the troubled life of Christina Onassis, and the scandal behind the Tawana Brawley rape case. *People*'s covers also began to feature rapists, murderers, and other criminals, including preppy murderer Robert Chambers, school shooter Laurie Dann, wife killer Charles Stuart, the parricidal Menendez brothers, "Long Island Lolita" Amy Fisher, cult leader David Koresh, Columbine murderers Dylan Klebold and Eric Harris, and, of course, serial killer Jeffrey Dahmer. Additional *People* magazine covers have included the JonBenét Ramsey case, the Long Island serial killer, Steven Avery, Jodi Arias, Oscar Pistorius, Scott Peterson, and Casey Anthony.

Some folks don't find just information from their murder viewing; they find inspiration. A number of films and television shows may have inspired real killers. The Reelz channel features an entire series on copycat killers that were inspired by, or at least paralleled, the fictional murders in *RoboCop*, *Scream*, *Hannibal*, and other movies. Likewise, other films, including *The Dark Knight*, *Natural Born Killers*, *Saw*, and *American Psycho*, appear to have given some killers gruesome ideas. Troubled people can find messages to mimic almost anywhere they look.

Television and movies have also helped to turn our criminals into celebrities. Docudramas are often biographies of vicious criminals, many of whom are played by leading actors and actresses, for example, Mark Harmon as Theodore Bundy, Brian Dennehy as John Wayne Gacy, and Helen Hunt as Pam Smart. In fact, Charlize Theron won an Oscar for playing serial killer Aileen Wuornos in the film *Monster*. And two forthcoming movies will star Zac Efron as Ted Bundy and Leonardo DiCaprio as H. H. Holmes. Having glamorous actors cast in the roles of vicious killers unfortunately infuses these killers with glamour.

Capitalizing, and profiting, from public fascination with murder, the first ever true crime conference, CrimeCon, was held in Indianapolis in 2017. With their own Facebook page, CrimeCon encourages attendance by prodding, "You know you're dying to go." With 2017 registration fees ranging from $200 to $600, true crime fans were entertained with podcasters, documentary filmmakers, homicide detectives, TV personalities, mock trials, and Nancy Grace as the keynote speaker.

The glorification of serial killers has created a big-money market for almost anything that they say or do: the artwork of John Wayne Gacy, who got the death penalty for killing 33 young men and boys in Des Plaines, Illinois; the paintings of mass murderer Richard Speck, who slaughtered eight nurses in Chicago; the refrigerator in which Jeffrey Dahmer had stored his victims' body parts; songs written or recorded by Charles Manson; the poetry of Danny Rolling, who brutally tortured, killed, and mutilated five college students in Gainesville, Florida; and the writings of Theodore Kaczynski, the Unabomber. The popularity of murderabilia, the collectibles of murder, has inspired a market for various third-party souvenirs and products of questionable taste: aprons, boxer shorts, and thongs with images of serial killers; mass killer T-shirts bearing quips such as "Gardening helps you hide bodies"; and action-figure toys of infamous murderers like Manson and Dahmer. Although murder-based board games like Clue have been around since the 1940s, the murder mystery game trend has seen the development of several different serial killer trivia and board games. For example, Serial Killer: The Board Game comes packaged inside a body bag, features "dead baby" markers, and instructs players to kill as many children and babies as possible before being captured by the FBI.

Son of Sam laws, named after serial killer David Berkowitz, were passed in a number of states in an attempt to prohibit murderers from profiting off royalties from books and movies, but these statutes have been struck down as violations of free speech. Similarly, various state laws designed to halt the distribution of killers' fingernails, dirt from victims' graves, autographed Christmas cards, art work, or clothes have been ruled unconstitutional. The U.S. Congress attempted, unsuccessfully, to stop prisoners from using the mail to send out anything that would garner them a profit.

Although some states have passed laws that prohibit payments to the killers from purchasers and allow for asset forfeiture, the murderabilia industry isn't going away. Assuming a prisoner does not use the mail to share the items with a distributor and does not personally profit from their sale, most states allow an individual to sell items linked to heinous murder cases. The online site eBay may have stopped the sale of murderabilia, but several other websites still offer such items, and what many consider a despicable industry continues to thrive.

HOMICIDE LAW

In everyday usage, the terms *murder*, *homicide*, *kill*, plus a variety of more colorful synonyms such as *slaughter*, *butcher*, *massacre*, *slay*, or even slang terms like *knock off*, *bump off*, and *polish off*, are often used somewhat interchangeably. This practice (except for the slang) will be followed throughout most of this book for the sake of convenience, if not readability. It is important, nevertheless, to understand the distinctions among these concepts.

The term *killing* represents the most general notion of extinguishing life. Although there is nothing inherent in the broad concept of killing that excludes suicide or even animal abuse, our attention will be limited to homicidal acts, those specifically directed against other human beings. We will discuss suicides, but only those that are coupled with a homicide. We also will examine killers who train on animals, but only as a pathway to targeting human prey.

Not all acts of killing are illegal. Most societies authorize agents of the state—police officers and soldiers, for example—to kill under appropriate circumstances. Wartime aggression against an enemy nation as well as state-sanctioned executions of condemned prisoners are not violations of the law, although certain governmental acts of violence can be proscribed by international treaty (e.g., genocide, the attempt to exterminate a racial or ethnic group).

Criminal homicide refers to unlawful and unjustifiable actions or inactions that result in the death of other human beings. The level of homicide charged will be a function of two dimensions, *mens rea* and *actus reus*. *Mens rea* refers to the concept of guilty intent, and *actus reus* refers to the act itself (or omission of an act). Thus, with *mens rea* we must determine the state of mind/guilty mind and with *actus reus*, a guilty act. When a guilty mind concurs with a guilty act, the elements of a crime has occurred. Homicidal acts include such clear-cut misdeeds as shooting a semi-automatic rifle at a crowd of people in a shopping mall or poisoning over-the-counter cold medications. As we will see, stabbing an intruder to death during a burglary is also a homicide but may be legally justifiable (i.e., noncriminal), depending on the particular circumstances.

Failures to act (known in the law as omissions) can also result in criminal charges if such inactivity helps to precipitate a death. Omissions can be subtle yet are nonetheless illegal, such as when a landlord disregards faulty wiring that causes a fatal blaze or a parent neglects a child to the point the youngster starves to death, even if the parent had not intended this tragic outcome.

Although it may seem self-evident, a necessary condition for homicide is that the intended victim of a dangerous act or neglectful omission is indeed a living human being. Thus, shooting at a suitcase hidden underneath bedsheets to look like a sleeping person constitutes attempted murder, but shooting at someone who had just died in bed of a heart attack technically does not. That is, it is factually impossible to kill someone who isn't where he or she is believed to be, but it is legally impossible to kill a corpse. Even though the defense of legal impossibility derives from the English common law origins of our system of jurisprudence, in recent years U.S. courts have been reluctant to recognize it as an excuse.

The often-debated question of when life begins—be it at birth or at conception—has turned into a wider issue for homicide law than just the legality of medically performed abortions. Pregnant mothers who place their unborn babies at risk by using narcotics have been prosecuted for child endangerment, as well as homicide, more specifically feticide, should the fetus fail to survive. In Alabama, a conviction for "using while pregnant" that leads to the death of a newborn can result in a sentence of 10 years to life. In a recent Indiana case, Bei Bei Shuai was charged with murder and feticide after her failed suicide attempt by rat poison resulted in the death of the baby she was carrying. Ten days after ingesting the poison, Shuai's baby was delivered by emergency cesarean section at 33 weeks gestation and lived for only two days. This case triggered international attention and a public outcry, including concern from *The Guardian* news in the United Kingdom regarding the criminalization of pregnancy in the United States. Shuai's case was the first in the history of Indiana in which a woman was prosecuted for murder for a suicide attempt while pregnant. Although originally charged with murder and feticide, in 2013 Shuai pleaded guilty to a misdemeanor charge of criminal recklessness and was released, having been sentenced to time served (433 days).

According to the National Conference of State Legislatures, at least 38 states have on their books laws recognizing unborn children as homicide victims, some states only recognizing the fetus if viable, and at least 23 of those states recognize the fetus at the earliest stages of pregnancy. Some states may charge the fetal death as an involuntary manslaughter. And, in 2004, by the closest of margins (one vote in the Senate), the U.S. Congress passed the Unborn Victims of Violence Act, which recognizes unborn children as victims if injured or killed during the commission of federal or military crimes of violence.

The various situations described here may all constitute homicide, but they do so at varying levels of culpability and, therefore, involve varying levels of punishment. The criminal law recognizes types and degrees of homicide based on such notions as intent, reasonableness, premeditation, gravity, provocation, and foreseeability. The law of homicide is particularly complex and differs somewhat from jurisdiction to jurisdiction. State laws change frequently, moreover, as politically minded legislatures and constitutionally minded courts struggle to fine-tune the definitions and applications of criminal codes.

Additionally, as technological changes occur, homicide investigation techniques and laws change as well. A California woman, Deborah Matis-Engle, was convicted of vehicular manslaughter and sentenced to six years in prison for killing a woman in another vehicle as she was texting and speeding through a construction zone. She was paying her bills by cell phone in the minutes before and up to the horrific car crash. In the weeks after the "accident," Matis-Engle was, on two occasions, spotted by California Highway Patrol continuing to text and drive. Hundreds of deaths have occurred as a result of people recklessly taking selfies, and emergency rooms are filled with "petextrians," pedestrians who are injured or killed as a result of texting while paying little or no attention to passing vehicles. The *New York Post* was right in its June 18, 2016, headline, "Our Cellphones Are Killing Us."

As illustrated by Table 1.1, the sentences can be considerable for using a car as a deadly weapon in the case of drunk driving. The vast majority of states have vehicular homicide and/or vehicular manslaughter laws on the books. Depending on the circumstances (e.g., intoxication, speeding, reckless driving, drag racing, and texting), someone without the intent to kill can be sentenced to prison a long term of years. In many states, the most severe penalties are meted out for distracted motorists who kill a worker in a construction zone. At the 2014 South by Southwest music festival in Austin, Texas, Rashad Owens, 21, drunk and attempting to flee the police, crashed his car through a barricade and accelerated into a group of

Table 1.1   Possible Jail/Prison Sentences for DUI Fatalities by State

State	Sentence	State	Sentence
Alabama	1–10 years	Montana	0–30 years
Alaska	1–99 years	Nebraska	1–50 years
Arizona	1–22 years	Nevada	2–25 years
Arkansas	5–20 years	New Hampshire	0–15 years
California	0–10 years	New Jersey	5–10 years
Colorado	0–24 years	New Mexico	0–6 years
Connecticut	1–10 years	New York	0–15 years
District of Columbia	0–30 years	North Carolina	15–480 months
Delaware	1–5 years	North Dakota	0 to life
Florida	0–15 years	Ohio	1–15 years
Georgia	0–15 years	Oklahoma	0–1 year
Hawaii	0–10 years	Oregon	0–20 years
Idaho	0–15 years	Pennsylvania	0–10 years
Illinois	1–28 years	Rhode Island	5–20 years
Indiana	2–20 years	South Carolina	1–25 years
Iowa	1–25 years	South Dakota	0–15 years
Kansas	0–172 months	Tennessee	8–60 years
Kentucky	0–10 years	Texas	2–20 years
Louisiana	3–30 years	Utah	0–15 years
Maine	6 months–10 years	Vermont	1–15 years
Maryland	0–5 years	Virginia	1–20 years
Massachusetts	30 days–15 years	Washington	31–177 months
Michigan	0–20 years	West Virginia	90 days–10 years
Minnesota	0–10 years	Wisconsin	0–40 years
Mississippi	5–25 years	Wyoming	0–20 years
Missouri	0–15 years		

Source: Mothers Against Drunk Driving.

people, killing 4 and injuring 20 others. Convicted of capital murder, he received an automatic sentence of life without the possibility of parole.

Road rage, clearly a loss of self-control, routinely makes headlines as motorists run each other off the road, engage in high-speed chases, get into fights, and even shoot and kill one another. A 2014 survey of 2,705 licensed drivers taken by the AAA Foundation for Traffic Safety found that 78% admitted to at least one instance of aggressive driving during the previous year—acts such as purposely tailgating, intentionally blocking another car's path, and deliberately cutting someone off. Nearly 4% reported having exited their car to confront another motorist. Also according to the AAA Foundation for Traffic Safety, over one-third (37%) of aggressive driving incidents (the technical term for road rage) involve a firearm. No matter how one feels about gun owners' rights and gun control, hopefully we can all agree on one thing as an immediate fix. When it comes to driving, "gunning it" should be about horsepower, not firepower.

As the nuances of using vehicles to commit murder and mayhem have become codified into law, so, too, are lawmakers scrambling to respond to crimes facilitated by use of the internet, including the well-publicized assaults committed by "Craigslist Killer" Philip Markoff. Taking time from his studies, the 23-year-old medical student selected his victims online through their erotic services listings. Some he robbed in order to pay his gambling debts, and another, 25-year-old "masseuse" Julissa Brisman, he killed in a guest room of an upscale Boston hotel. Months before his trial, Markoff took his own life, writing the name of his ex-fiancé in his own blood on the wall of his jail cell.

In another internet-related homicide case, Thomas Montgomery, 47, of Buffalo, New York, fatally shot his coworker and friend, Brian Barrett, 22, because they were both involved with the same woman in an internet love triangle. The woman was older than 40, but pretended to be 18, as she chatted with the two men and sent gifts to Montgomery through the mail (gifts intercepted by Montgomery's wife). Montgomery's jealousy over the fact that his coworker was talking about having an internet relationship with the same woman led him to fire three shots at Barrett with a .30-caliber rifle. Montgomery pleaded guilty to first-degree manslaughter; he then tried to retract his plea, but the retraction was refused by the judge, and he was sentenced to 20 years in prison.

One blog, craigslistkillings, identifies more than 100 homicides that have occurred as a result of Craigslist transactions. And a number of other online sources, such as backpage.com, have been linked to homicides, including the recent case of serial murderer Darren Vann, who hunted for victims through classified ads for sex for sale. A 2015 *Washington Post* story chronicled the potential horrors of online dating and profiled five murders resulting from love online. Online dating services and apps like Match.com, Tinder, OkCupid, and eHarmony can serve as hunting grounds for killers and other predators. Although these online opportunities for predators are relatively new, classified ads have long been tied to murder cases as offenders hunt for victims who advertise to sell property, sell services, or meet a mate. For virtually as long as classifieds have existed, killers or killer teams have used want ads to find their victims. Raymond Fernandez and Martha Beck killed as many as 20 women in the late 1940s, trolling for women who had placed "lonely hearts" ads, an early version of online dating; these women were tricked out of their life savings and then murdered by Fernandez and Beck, who were eventually executed for their crimes.

Online fantasizing about murder can potentially serve as criminal intent sufficient for a conviction, as Gilberto Valle, a former NYPD cop, found out. Dubbed the "cannibal cop," Valle expressed online his sexual fetishes of kidnapping, raping, murdering, and eating women but never actually kidnapped, raped, murdered, or cannibalized anyone. Finding evidence of his online activities, his wife reported Valle to the police and later testified against him in court. Valle was convicted of conspiracy to commit kidnapping. Many legal scholars argued that he was being prosecuted for thought crimes, and the appeals court agreed, overturning his conviction. According to the appeals court, even though he had done research on methods of torture and abduction, accessed a database for information, and conducted some surveillance on his fantasy victims, the *actus reus* element of the crime was missing. His fantasies of abduction were just role-play. Although he escaped criminal penalties, Valle was fired from the NYPD for illegally accessing a law enforcement database to find information about his fantasy victims. Even after losing his job because of his fantasies, Valle apparently still continued to visit cannibalism fetish websites. Having destroyed his marriage, Valle signed up for a dating website but was forced off when his identity was revealed.

Offenders can exploit the power of the internet to further their crimes, but law enforcement and vigilant cybersleuths can also use the internet to apprehend them. A suspected serial/spree killer was arrested in July 2010 after he became Facebook friends with the sister of one of his victims. Mark Dizon, 28, was charged with killing nine people over the course of three robberies. A family friend of one of the murder victims had looked up Dizon on Facebook, as she thought he matched the description given by witnesses, and saw that the sister of a victim was on Dizon's friend list. Many other crimes have been solved when offenders posted and boasted on social media.

Rather than just boasting about their crimes, some offenders have taken things a step further and actually posted video of their murders. In April 2017, Steve Stephens, dubbed the "Facebook Killer," livestreamed himself killing a random citizen, Robert Godwin, Sr. Two days later, after a nationwide manhunt, an observant citizen tipped off police to Stephens's whereabouts. When confronted by the police, Stephens killed himself.

MURDER

The laws governing homicide vary from state to state, yet all jurisdictions distinguish murder from less serious forms of homicide (e.g., manslaughter). Murder requires malicious intent (or simply "malice"), an aim to cause death or great bodily harm. In addition, malicious intent can extend to acts that are reckless or show "depraved indifference" to human life, such as exploding a bomb inside a school, even if the perpetrator never meant to hurt anyone. Assaults not necessarily designed to be fatal can constitute murder so long as the deadly outcome is a reasonable or foresee-able possibility. Thus, if a victim of an unarmed assault (e.g., a blow to the chest) falls down, bangs his head on the sidewalk, and then dies three days later from the head injury, the assailant can be charged with second-degree murder. A parent, distraught over a crying, colicky baby, who shakes the infant to silence her and does it so vigor-ously as to cause death, can also be charged with second-degree murder (assuming that the parent is aware that this rough form of treatment can be detrimental).

In early English common law, the root of the U.S. legal system, murder was automatically punishable by death. However, wishing to mitigate the law's inflexibility and excessive harshness, legislatures in postrevolutionary America moved to limit capital punishment only to the most grievous acts by establishing degrees of homicide, typically first and second degrees for capital and noncapital murder, respectively.

First-Degree Murder

In contemporary statutes, the degree of murder, first versus second, essentially turns on whether the offender premeditated the act of violence. Premeditation entails some evidence of planning, deliberation, or scheming, although not necessarily over a prolonged time period. In fact, the extent of deliberation can be a matter of minutes or even seconds. A plan to kill one's spouse after doubling the size of her life insurance policy obviously reveals cunning and cold-blooded deliberation. Yet an act of road rage in which a motorist deliberately chases another vehicle, forcing it off the road into a fatal encounter with a concrete pole, can also reflect sufficient deliberation so as to constitute first-degree murder.

Scott Peterson, for example, told his mistress, Amber Frey, that his wife had died two weeks before he actually murdered her (and her unborn son). This and other elements of premeditation clearly showed that Peterson had planned to murder his pregnant wife, Laci. Peterson was convicted and sentenced to death by lethal injection. He currently spends his days in a 4-by-9-foot cell on San Quentin's death row. Jodi Arias's claims of self-defense were rejected by jurors, who found her guilty of the first-degree murder of ex-boyfriend Travis Alexander. Although jurors could not agree on sentencing and she avoided a death penalty verdict, she will spend the rest of her life in prison in Arizona. A rental car, a change in hair color before the trip, and the purchase of three five-gallon gas cans for the nearly 3,000 miles of travel to get to Alexander was evidence enough for premeditation, and the nearly 30 stab wounds, slit throat, and a gunshot wound to the head convinced the jury that Arias was a cold-blooded murderer. Illustrating that hybristophiles aren't just women, Arias received marriage proposals every week before and after her conviction. Thriving on the attention, she has even contemplated a prison wedding to one of her pen pals.

Many states also consider intentional acts of homicide that are especially brutal, cruel, or extreme to be first-degree murder, even if the crime is not premeditated. On the evening of August 28, 1995, for example, Richard Rosenthal and his wife, Laura Jane, argued heatedly in the backyard of their suburban Boston home. The fight began over a burned ziti dinner and escalated quickly. The 40-year-old insurance executive lost all control over his temper and started beating his wife repeatedly with a rock. He then cut open her chest with a six-inch kitchen knife and impaled her heart and lungs on a stake in the backyard. Although Rosenthal may not have planned the fatal attack, the jury convicted him of first-degree murder because of the "extreme atrocity and cruelty" of the crime. Rosenthal mounted an unsuccessful insanity plea at trial but was instead convicted of first-degree murder and received a sentence of life without parole.

The so-called felony-murder rule also grants murder status, typically in the first degree, for any death that results during the commission of a dangerous felony, such as a robbery or arson. Even though the felon may not have planned or intended for someone to die during the crime, the intent and planning surrounding the commission of a reckless act are by law transferred to the homicide. If, for example, a robber fatally shoots a store clerk because the victim is too slow in handing over the contents of the cash register, the charge is "murder one." He may have planned to use the gun only to intimidate but not to kill; however, the deliberation in committing a dangerous felony like robbery translates into premeditation for the homicide.

The felony-murder rule may apply even when the felon does not directly cause the death, so long as the fatality results from an act or conspiracy in which he or she is implicated. If, for example, the police shoot and mistakenly kill a hostage whom the robber has taken as a shield, the offender may be charged with first-degree murder.

Twenty-nine-year-old Aldrin Diaz was charged with murder following a disturbance on January 28, 2000, outside of a Providence, Rhode Island, restaurant, even though he never fired his weapon and dropped it when ordered to do so by the police. During the incident, an off-duty cop, rushing to assist fellow officers with his gun drawn, was fatally shot by a uniformed officer who had mistakenly identified the cop in street clothes as one of the combatants. Because Diaz's use of a gun precipitated the chain of events leading to the officer's death, he could have been held legally responsible under the felony-murder rule, although the charge was ultimately dropped.

The felony-murder rule may appear unreasonably strict when, for example, the person charged with murder takes a fall for the one who directed the crime, or, as in the Diaz case, when a police action results in a death. In an attempt to address this concern, some courts have limited the application of the rule to deaths that were foreseeable during the commission of the dangerous felony. You can be charged with murder without killing anyone.

A North Carolina man, Larry Whitfield, 21, was charged with felony-murder after he robbed a bank and then broke into a home looking for a place to hide. The 79-year-old grandmother living there had a heart attack, being literally scared to death when she saw Whitfield in her home. Whitfield was found not guilty of murder but was convicted of causing her death by kidnapping and received an automatic life sentence. Although the conviction was eventually overturned, the U.S. Supreme Court upheld his bank robbery conviction, for which he was sentenced to 27 years in prison. "Homicide by heart attack" occurs when a victim suffers a fatal heart attack after, for example, being hit on the head by an object, being punched in the face by a robber, being startled awake by a home intruder, or being engaged in a struggle with a purse snatcher. The offender can be arrested for murder for having precipitated a victim's cardiac arrest, without even having touched the deceased.[1]

The "Elkhart Four" case illustrates how felony-murder convictions can result even when the offenders didn't take a weapon to the scene. In 2012, five young men from Elkhart, Indiana, decided to burglarize a house, believing incorrectly that no one was home. Four members of the group broke into the house while another waited across the street as a lookout. The homeowner, awoken by noise, confronted the intruders with a gun, killing one and wounding another. The surviving four would-be burglars were charged with felony-murder. Although they were unarmed, the four defendants were convicted, and all received prison sentences in excess of 45 years. After years of legal wrangling and significant national media exposure, the murder convictions were vacated and all four were resentenced for burglary.

The nature of the crime determines not only how the homicide is charged but also the potential penalty, including death in the majority of states (see Chapter 14 for details). Various aggravating and mitigating factors can be considered in determining the appropriate sentence, but they are required elements for deciding in capital cases between the death penalty or a life sentence. Aggravating factors, such as multiple victims or torture, increase the defendant's culpability, while mitigating factors, such as no prior offenses and acting under extreme duress, may lessen criminal responsibility and, therefore, lighten the sentence. The range of aggravators and mitigators varies by jurisdiction. Table 1.2 lists aggravating and mitigating factors for the imposition of the federal death penalty. Note that the last mitigating factor, "other factors in background, character, or circumstance," is

Table 1.2 Aggravating and Mitigating Factors in the Federal Death Penalty

Aggravating Factors	Mitigating Factors
Death during commission of another crime	Impaired capacity to appreciate wrongfulness of conduct or conform to the requirements of law
Previous conviction of violent felony involving firearm	Substantial duress
Previous conviction of offense with a sentence of death or life imprisonment	Minor participation in commission of crime
Previous conviction of other serious offenses	Equally culpable defendants not being punished by death
Grave risk of death to additional persons	No prior criminal record
Heinous, cruel, or depraved manner of committing offense	Mental or emotional disturbance
Procurement of offense by payment	Victim consented to conduct resulting in death
Offense committed for pecuniary gain	Other factors in background, character, or circumstances
Substantial planning and premeditation	
Conviction for two felony drug offenses	
Victim vulnerability due to old age, youth, or infirmity	
Conviction for serious federal drug offenses	
Continuing criminal enterprise involving drug sales to minors	
Victim was a government official	
Prior conviction of sexual assault or child molestation	
Multiple killings or attempted killings	

basically anything else that your defense attorney can argue that would convince a jury to show leniency.

Second-Degree Murder

Homicides that reflect malicious intent yet lack premeditation, that do not show extreme cruelty, and that are not committed during the course of a dangerous felony are considered murders in the second degree. For example, a man who impulsively stabs his teenage son to death during an argument over a football game has, given the spontaneity of the act, committed second-degree murder. Homicides committed under the influence of alcohol or drugs are also generally considered second-degree murders, if the intoxication is believed to have reduced the drunken person's capacity to act deliberately and premeditate the deadly assault. In some states, the jury can only consider the charges the prosecutor has presented, whereas in other states, the jury has a wide range of choices to make regarding what level of homicide they may convict on. In some cases, jurors may not find that the elements of first-degree murder have been met beyond a reasonable doubt but those of second-degree murder have. But if a prosecutor initially overcharges, hoping for a plea bargain, and the defendant chooses to go to trial, the strategy can backfire.

MANSLAUGHTER

Homicides that lack malicious intent or reckless disregard for life are considered manslaughters, which in turn are divided into voluntary and involuntary forms. Voluntary manslaughter is the intentional killing of another person under extenuating circumstances, such as provocation or emotional duress (the so-called heat of passion) without time or opportunity for cooling off. The action is downgraded to a reaction as a response to some sort of provocation, and thus the malice is somewhat negated and the crime is a manslaughter instead of a murder. A woman who kills her husband on finding him sexually molesting their daughter has committed voluntary manslaughter. If, on the other hand, she deliberately seeks him out in order to avenge his act of incest, she could be charged with murder, although most juries would likely respond sympathetically.

In 1993, a man was on trial for molesting four young boys at a Christian camp, including Ellie Nesler's 6-year-old son. The irate mother took a gun to the courtroom and shot the defendant five times, killing him. She was convicted of voluntary manslaughter and sentenced to 10 years in prison. Nesler became a folk hero to many and had supporters across the United States, although some of her support faded when it was revealed she was high on meth at the time of the shooting and had an extensive criminal history. Her original conviction was overturned as a result of juror misconduct, and she eventually pled guilty to manslaughter, serving a total of three years in prison (she was released early after being diagnosed with breast cancer). But that was not the end of the story. In 2002, Nesler was convicted for selling methamphetamine and went back to prison until 2006.

Also considered acts of manslaughter are deaths that result from fistfights, barroom brawls, or similar conflicts between equal combatants. Of course, a person who picks a fight with someone much smaller can be charged with murder if the disadvantaged victim dies. Voluntary manslaughter also applies when a person uses excessive force in self-defense or wrongly but honestly perceives that self-defense is required given the situation. Thus, for example, shooting a neighbor under a genuine, yet mistaken belief that he was a burglar is not considered murder, but neither is it accidental in the eyes of the law. As the recent case of a couple seeking YouTube fame illustrates, there are also multiple degrees of manslaughter in some states and clearly multiple levels of stupidity. Nineteen-year-old Monalisa Perez, seven months pregnant, shot a gun aimed at a book that her boyfriend, Pedro Ruiz III, was holding at his chest, both expecting that the hardcover volume would stop the projectile. It didn't, and Ruiz died from the gunshot wound. Perez was charged with second-degree manslaughter, which, in Minnesota, equates to involuntary manslaughter as a result of recklessness or gross negligence.

Some cases involving mob mentality cross the line between self-defense and criminal behavior. In 2007, for example, an angry crowd in Austin, Texas, dragged a passenger from a car that had just hit and injured a small girl. The driver of the automobile managed to escape the mob, but the passenger, David Rivas Morales, 40, was beaten to death by eight bystanders. According to witnesses, it was 16-year-old Samuel Byrd who delivered the final blow, resulting in his conviction for manslaughter in juvenile court. Kurtiss Colvin, a 22-year-old boxer, was also charged with manslaughter but was convicted of the lesser included offense of aggravated assault.

In the crime of manslaughter, it is the heat of passion, intense fear, or provocation that negates the malice required for murder. Malicious intent is presumed absent when the killer reacts, understandably yet unjustifiably, to some provocation (such as the discovery of an unfaithful lover or the attack by an inebriated drinking buddy) or duress (such as murdering and cannibalizing another human being in order to stay alive while lost in the wilderness). Although one may use deadly force in self-defense or to survive a perilous attack, the use of excessive force (e.g., shooting an unarmed attacker) also constitutes manslaughter.

The provocation necessary to reduce the crime of murder to that of manslaughter must be reasonable in some objective sense. The fact that an offender feels provoked does not automatically constitute the lesser offense. Vigilantism, for example, may entail a deeply felt emotional reaction to a perceived injustice in society, as in the actions of 36-year-old Michael A. Mullen, but is not recognized as legitimate provocation. In September 2005, Mullen telephoned the Bellingham, Washington, police and confessed to having shot to death two men—Hank Eisses, 49, and Victor Vasquez, 68—whom he had identified from Whatcom County's online registry of sex offenders. Mullen was outraged and upset about a recent widely publicized case involving Joseph E. Duncan III, a repeated sex offender from Washington State who had been arrested in Idaho for kidnapping and murder. Duncan had bludgeoned to death three people inside the Groene family home near Coeur d'Alene, Idaho, in order to kidnap for sex 9-year-old Dylan and 8-year-old Shasta. Dylan eventually became Duncan's fourth murder victim, but Shasta was rescued when an observant Denny's waitress recognized the little girl and called police.

Shasta's rescue hardly assuaged Mullen's anger over the fact that a repeat sex offender was free to commit this heinous act. For Mullen, Duncan's release from custody by Washington State was the final straw—someone had to do something. He explained in a letter sent to the *Seattle Times* that he targeted the two sex offenders, Eisses and Vasquez, as a step toward preventing another tragedy like what had happened in Idaho. It especially galled the vigilante that Duncan had bragged to his female abductee about ending the lives of her siblings and that he had discarded their remains like garbage.

Michael Mullen's decision to target locally accessible sex offenders to avenge Duncan's alleged crimes was in part to dramatize the plight of victims like the Groenes. Mullen also indicated his desire to be executed as soon as possible; he wanted to reach the hereafter in time to welcome Duncan's arrival: "I am not proud of taking two lives . . . but my death alone would have meant nothing," wrote Mullen. While serving a 44-year prison sentence, the convicted vigilante was found dead inside his cell, an apparent suicide.

There are limits to the levels of provocation that can reduce murder to manslaughter. Words, slogans, insults, gestures, or style of dress and appearance may be socially provocative, yet not so in a legal sense. A hot-tempered individual who fatally attacks someone for uttering a racial slur and a homophobic man who kills in reaction to a proposition from another man have committed murder, even though in both cases the victims may have precipitated their own demise.

Jonathan Schmitz of Lake Orion, Michigan, for example, was convicted of second-degree murder for slaying his friend and neighbor Scott Amedure with a

12-gauge shotgun because the victim had publicly humiliated him. Amedure, age 32, had revealed his sexual attraction to Schmitz during a 1995 taped episode of the Jenny Jones television talk show, titled "Same-Sex Secret Crushes." During the program, the host elicited Amedure's whipped cream and strawberries fantasy involving Schmitz. The heterosexual defendant testified that he was embarrassed and mortified in front of a crowd and had been led to believe by the staff of the show that his secret admirer was a woman.

The critical factor in assessing Schmitz's criminal responsibility was the three-day time span separating the defendant's public embarrassment from the subsequent shooting. Because of the "cooling-off" period, the jury rejected Schmitz's claim that he killed during an insane rage provoked by his victim's public admission. Schmitz's conviction was overturned on appeal because of errors in the jury selection process. Yet, in his subsequent retrial, a second jury convicted him of second-degree murder, rejecting his "crime of passion" defense. Schmitz was given a prison sentence of 25 to 50 years but was released in August 2017 after having served 22 years.

A death resulting from negligence is considered involuntary manslaughter. The law punishes those whose recklessness or negligence causes loss of life as well as those who fail in their duty to act in a manner that may prevent someone from dying. For example, on February 20, 2003, a swiftly moving blaze killed 100 people and injured over 200 more at a West Warwick, Rhode Island, club when a pyrotechnic display used by the rock band Great White accidentally ignited soundproofing material behind the stage. Daniel Biechele, Great White's tour manager and the man who set off the pyrotechnics, pled guilty to 100 counts of involuntary manslaughter and was sentenced to four years in prison. Jeffrey and Michael Derderian, the two brothers who owned the Station Nightclub, pled no contest to charges of involuntary manslaughter. Jeffrey Derderian was sentenced to three years of probation and 500 hours of community service, while his brother Michael was ordered to serve four years in a minimum-security prison and three years of probation. All three men are now out of prison and the short prison terms and probation were difficult for many who lost spouses or children to accept, especially in view of the large death toll, yet the absence of malice certainly influenced the legal outcome.

It is also involuntary manslaughter if a physician carelessly writes out a prescription for the wrong medication or the improper dosage, thereby causing the death of a patient, or if a gun owner does not responsibly lock away his weapons. Following the February 29, 2000, fatal shooting of a 6-year-old girl by her first-grade classmate at the Buell Elementary School in Mount Morris Township, Michigan, 19-year-old Jamelle James, who lived with the young perpetrator, was charged with involuntary manslaughter. Although James was not present at the scene of the shooting, court papers alleged that he had carelessly left the murder weapon, a loaded .32-caliber semi-automatic, within easy reach of the 6-year-old shooter. The irresponsible adult was convicted and sentenced to serve a prison term of 2 to 15 years.

The duty to act can extend to some rather dark places, as illustrated by the bizarre "dominatrix trial" of Barbara Asher, aka Mistress Lauren M., following the July 2000 disappearance of 53-year-old Michael Lord. According to the prosecution theory, Lord suffered a heart attack while strapped to a rack in a Quincy, Massachusetts, condominium in which Asher performed her "bondage and discipline" professional services. The prosecutor argued that Asher deliberately chose not to seek medical help for the dying man out of fear that her illicit business would be exposed. It was further alleged that Asher, with the assistance of a friend, dismembered Lord's body, disposing of it in a trash dumpster in Maine. At trial, the state failed to produce any physical evidence to support its argument or even to prove that the victim had visited Asher's dungeon of domination. Despite its distaste for the defendant's trade, the jury acquitted Asher due to lack of proof.

Like the felony-murder doctrine, the misdemeanor-manslaughter rule applies if a death occurs while the offender is engaged in a misdemeanor, an act less serious than a felony. In Worcester, Massachusetts, for example, a homeless man and woman, both marginally disabled intellectually, were charged with involuntary manslaughter following an abandoned 1999 warehouse blaze in which six firefighters perished. Not only had the homeless squatters caused the fire by carelessly burning a candle, but they apparently failed to report the fire as it spread rapidly. Because both defendants were marginally disabled intellectually, a plea bargain was offered and accepted, placing the two on 5 years' probation.

Recently in the United States, five former Michigan state government officials were charged with involuntary manslaughter as a result of deaths associated with the contaminated Flint, Michigan, water supply. Prosecutors have argued that at least 11 people died of tainted water and thousands more were made sick, as officials covered up what they knew to be poisonous drinking water. More than two dozen other state officials were also charged criminally for obstruction of justice and neglect of duty.

All the cases just described involve the crimes and punishments of individuals or groups of individuals. But can corporations have *mens rea*? The United Kingdom passed a corporate manslaughter and homicide act in 2007 that allows corporations, unions, police, and some government agencies to be charged with murder or manslaughter. The sentences handed out include orders to remedy a dangerous condition, orders to publicize the failure, and fines. Hundreds of charges have been brought since the act was passed. Prior to 2007, only individuals could be charged, but now the corporate or governmental agency itself is also liable criminally (as well as civilly). In the United States, by contrast, only individuals or groups of individuals within an organization can be charged for worker deaths from falls, explosions, and machinery malfunction. There is some movement, however, to follow the lead of the Brits in this regard.

DEFENSES TO CRIMINAL HOMICIDE

The law recognizes both justifications and excuses that limit an individual's criminal responsibility for committing homicide. In certain defenses (sometimes referred to as justifications), defendants admit to having carried out the killing but maintain that, under the circumstances (e.g., the exercise of police powers or citizen use of self-defense), what they did was proper under the law and therefore noncriminal. Thus, a claim of self-defense would suggest that an individual committed the act but was justified in doing so. The accused admits being responsible for the act but claims that it was legal. In excuses, by contrast, defendants admit what they did was wrong but maintain that, under the circumstances (e.g., duress, mistake, entrapment, insanity, intoxication, extreme youth or senility, diminished capacity, sleepwalking, and various psychiatric syndromes), they were not fully responsible for the criminal act they perpetrated.

In July 2003, 86-year-old George Russell Weller hit the gas pedal instead of the brake in his 1992 Buick and careened into a crowded farmers market in Santa Monica, killing 10 people ranging in age from 7 months to 78 years. In addition, he injured more than 60 pedestrians. Although Weller had tested negative for drugs and alcohol and had passed a vision and written driving exam three years earlier, evidence came to light that his driving skills had been impaired for some time. Ten years earlier, Weller had crashed his car into a retaining wall. More recently, he damaged his own garage on at least two occasions. Weller's horrendous accident brought the issue of elderly drivers and the law to the forefront of public debate.

Weller never accepted responsibility or showed genuine remorse. Evidence suggested that he had actually been in control of the car and was steering his way through the crowd; perhaps he could have avoided hitting many of the people. On the day of the accident, moreover, he had had a minor accident a short distance away and was possibly fleeing the scene when he crashed into the farmers market. After the carnage, as people lay dead or dying, Weller was heard chastising the victims because they didn't get out of his way and also asking witnesses to imagine how he felt.

Despite his age, Weller was charged and convicted of 10 counts of vehicular homicide with gross negligence. By his November 2006 sentencing date, Weller's health had so deteriorated that Superior Court Judge Michael Johnson ordered the frail defendant to serve 5 years' probation but no jail time, a decision that upset the families of Weller's victims. Judge Johnson noted that Weller's actions and apparent indifference to the suffering he had caused clearly warranted prison time, yet the judge was persuaded against incarceration for practical reasons. Not only would prison life kill the man, but it would burden the state with the cost of his medical care. Thus, in the final analysis, old age and senility did not excuse Weller from responsibility for his actions. Come sentencing time, however, age did play a role in assessing the appropriate punishment. Based on inadequate barrier protection at the farmers market, the City of Santa Monica paid out $21 million to settle dozens of civil lawsuits. Weller died in 2010 at age 94.

More recently, Laura Lundquist, 98, was indicted in 2009 on second-degree murder charges after allegedly strangling and suffocating her 100-year-old nursing home roommate, Elizabeth Barrow. Lundquist had complained about the number of visitors her roommate received, accused Barrow of taking over their room, and wanted Barrow's bed because it was by the window. Lundquist was ruled incompetent to stand trial due to dementia and was placed in a state psychiatric hospital.

Justifiable Homicides by Police and Citizens

In contrast to excuse defenses that lessen or eliminate responsibility for criminal conduct, certain homicides are considered completely legitimate. Killings by public officials in the course of executing their duties and job responsibilities are generally considered justifiable, although in reaction to recent abuses of power, the police have been restricted from using deadly force against unarmed, nondangerous suspects fleeing the scene of a felony. Four white New York City police officers were charged with, but acquitted of, second-degree murder after firing a 41-shot barrage of bullets at an unarmed West African immigrant, 22-year-old Amadou Diallo, on February 4, 1999, during an anticrime sweep through the Bronx. The jury felt that the officers were justified in using deadly force when they mistakenly yet reasonably believed Diallo had reached for a gun. The victim was actually reaching for his wallet, presumably in order to produce some identification.

Police action shootings have come under increased scrutiny, thanks in part to video recordings of the events. Controversial police killings of citizens— including Michael Brown in Ferguson, Missouri; Philando Castile in Falcon Heights, Minnesota; Alton Sterling in Baton Rouge, Louisiana; and Tamir Rice in

Cleveland, Ohio—sparked protests, riots, and debates, as well as the Black Lives Matter movement. Although the Uniform Crime Report of the FBI reports the number of justifiable homicides by police against citizens and citizens against citizens, these statistics, particularly the police action killings, have been found to be grossly inaccurate. The lack of reliable data on police use of deadly force encouraged the *Washington Post* to start tracking all instances of civilians killed by police. The *Post* tallied 991 citizens killed by the police in 2015, 963 in 2016, and 987 for the year 2017. Not surprisingly, black males are overrepresented in these deaths, as are the mentally ill, who account for as many as 25% of persons killed by police.

The vast majority of officers who kill citizens in the line of duty are found to have been acting within the deadly force laws, policies, and procedures of their department. When on rare occasions officers are charged in civilian deaths, they are rarely convicted. Thus, it is not just the death of a citizen that creates community outrage but the lack of convictions at trial when officers are in fact prosecuted.

There has been a recent uptick in the number of police officers killed by civilians. Although the overall number of fatal assaults on the police has remained fairly stable over the past decade (an average of about 50 officers killed annually), there have been clusters of murders of officers, including the five officers killed and nine others injured in a Dallas, Texas, shooting in 2016.[2] The offender was a U.S. Army veteran who was angry over the shootings of black men by police and had stated he wanted to kill white people. There is clearly a need for greater transparency, accountability, and open dialogue regarding the police use of force.

For the civilian actions, homicides are considered justifiable if they are in reaction to a level of provocation so great that deadly force is necessary in defense of self or others, and sometimes home or property. To constitute self-defense, however, only that amount of force sufficient to repel an attack or intrusion is permitted by law. Generally, one cannot fend off a fist with a gun, unless the weapon is required to counterbalance any disadvantage in size or strength. Thus, a child or diminutive adult may be justified when using a gun to defend against a knife assault by a larger assailant. However, if excessive force is in fact used in defense of self or others, then manslaughter charges may result. Media accounts are filled with homeowners killing would-be robbers and burglars. According to FBI data, approximately 300 citizens justifiably kill their fellow citizens every year, and nearly 85% of those are firearm deaths.

Rarely has a citizen-on-citizen killing resulted in more controversy than the February 2012 fatal shooting of Trayvon Martin, a black 17-year-old dressed in a hoodie, at the hands of neighborhood watch coordinator George Zimmerman. Martin was walking back from a convenience store in Sanford, Florida, where he was visiting his father's fiancé. Zimmerman, 28, called the police to report a suspicious person dressed in a hoodie and then started following him. Shortly after the call, Zimmerman shot the youth dead. After questioning him, the police released Zimmerman that same evening, deciding that there was little reason to dispute the claim of self-defense. Even though the victim was not armed, Zimmerman still feared for his safety.

Months later, after a national outcry over an apparent injustice, a special prosecutor charged Zimmerman with second-degree murder. Many legal scholars claimed that this was a case of politically motivated overcharging, as the details did not support the elements of second-degree murder, especially in the poster state for stand your ground laws, which allow citizens to use deadly force when they feel threatened. Zimmerman was acquitted, which would serve as the first straw leading eventually to the Black Lives Matter movement.

The law pertaining to criminal defenses, be they justifications or excuses, is constantly changing in line with various shifts in culture, advances in science, or public responses to high-profile crimes. Historically, self-defense was only justified if no other reasonable means of escape or retreat existed. Known in many states as the retreat doctrine, if the victim of an attack could safely flee, rather than use lethal force, then this opportunity had to be taken. Fewer than 20 states still require retreat or even partial retreat in cases of self-defense. States are allowing homeowners to defend their homes by using deadly force, and juries have typically been sympathetic to this "castle doctrine" over the retreat requirement. Moreover, the "castle" now often includes not only the home but also businesses and vehicles. In addition, many states have passed "shoot first" or "stand your ground" laws that give citizens the right to use deadly force anywhere and anytime they feel themselves, others, or their property being threatened.

Of course, there are limits even to the newer laws expanding the right of self-defense. Once the perceived threat has subsided, citizens must allow the police to take control. A citizen cannot keep a would-be robber or rapist in the basement to mete out his or her own form of justice. Nor can he or she pursue the assailant beyond the reasonable "curtilage" area surrounding the home. In December 2001, Indianapolis resident Michael Clements responded aggressively when Leon Williams Jr., unlawfully entered his home. Clements chased Williams down the street and shot him in the back. Clements was charged and convicted of aggravated battery and of carrying a weapon without a license and was sentenced to six years in prison. In pursuing the intruder beyond his home, Clements had changed roles from victim to assailant.

Even though the law generally permits individuals to use force in the defense of property, it is the element of personal danger (not property rights) that underlies this prescription. Thus, a resident or retailer is not permitted to set a death trap in order to catch a burglar or some other intruder. Even so, the sympathies of jurors often run contrary to the law. In 1986, Prentice Rasheed, a store owner in the Liberty City section of Miami, set a makeshift booby trap to ward off burglars, resulting in the electrocution of a drug-addicted intruder. The grand jury, seeing him more as hero than villain, elected not to indict Rasheed for manslaughter.

The highly controversial stand your ground law in Florida prompted the Brady Campaign to Prevent Handgun Violence to fight the move by impacting the Sunshine State's tourism industry. The Brady Center produced warning cards and distributed them to visitors arriving at Florida airports:

Thinking about a Florida Vacation? Please Ensure Your Family Is Safe.

A new law in the Sunshine State authorizes nervous or frightened residents to use deadly force.

In Florida, avoid disputes. Use special caution in arguing with motorists on Florida roads.

Police and prosecutors are concerned about the potential for unnecessary violence.

TRAVELERS: BE VERY AWARE OF FLORIDA'S SHOOT FIRST LAW.

A one-year follow-up of "shoot first" cases in central Florida published by the *Orlando Sentinel* newspaper identified 13 shootings resulting in six deaths and four injuries.[3] All but one of those shot were unarmed. The reasonableness of the perceived threat apparently has opened a perplexing gray area in the law. In one episode, 43-year-old Michael Brady of Winter Haven was cleared of any responsibility for fatally shooting Justin Boyette, as the 6'2", 270-pound man, who had been drinking at Brady's neighbor's home, approached on his lawn. Brady claimed to have been frightened by Boyette's menacing gestures. Friends of the victim argued that Boyette was just trying to be friendly.

Following Florida's lead and with encouragement from the politically powerful National Rifle Association, several other states passed their own expanded castle doctrine or stand your ground laws. Although the exact details vary considerably, over half the states have some form of stand your ground. The Texas and Oklahoma shoot-first provisions are even more forgiving and broad than Florida's. In those states, citizens can use deadly force in self-defense or in defense of a third person in order to prevent imminent kidnapping, murder, sexual assault, or robbery. Such force may also be used to protect property (if during the night) and to prevent arson, burglary, robbery, theft, or criminal mischief. Time will tell whether this approach to empowering victims results in more innocent lives lost than saved. Research conducted in 2012 found that states with stand your ground laws have actually experienced an increase in homicide, suggesting that these laws have no real deterrent effect.[4] Altercations that otherwise may have resulted in a fistfight, a shouting match, or retreat are now increasingly likely to lead to homicides.

Whatever the specific provisions of a state's stand your ground law, people sometimes perceive personal danger where there is none. In Louisiana in 1994, for example, a 16-year-old Japanese exchange student, Yoshihiro Hattori, was shot and killed by Rodney Peairs. Dressed up like John Travolta in the film *Saturday Night Fever*, Hattori went to the wrong address looking for a Halloween party to which he had been invited. As Mrs. Peairs saw him approach their house, she told her husband to get his gun. Hattori was gesturing wildly and had a camera in his hand, trying to explain to Mr. Peairs that he was there for a party. The Japanese exchange student likely did not understand Mr. Peairs's demand to "Freeze!" Although the case prompted local petitions for tighter gun control and sparked public outcry in the victim's home country of Japan, a jury acquitted Mr. Peairs. It seems that his wife panicked, and he feared for her safety and the safety of their three children. The jury thought this was a reasonable response to a perceived threat, even if the perception was incorrect.

The legitimate use of deadly force as self-defense is also limited to the immediate time frame when danger is imminent. An attempt to fight back, for example, following an assault that occurred the previous day becomes an act of aggression or vengeance and can be punishable as murder. In such instances, we might sympathize with the avenger. We may feel that his or her culpability is limited, even though the act of revenge cannot be tolerated or legitimated in a civilized society. Thus, the law provides a range of excuses that reduce the wrongfulness of the act. Contrary to justifiable homicide, in which the claim is, "I killed him, but it was my responsibility, right, or duty," in excusable killings, the reasoning is, "I did it, but I couldn't help myself."

Excuses for Homicide and Diminished Capacity

Historically, mental illness (being too confused), intoxication (being too drunk), and age (being too young) have been used to negate or reduce culpability, the logic being that these conditions limit or even eliminate criminal responsibility or punishability. More recently, legislatures and courts have grappled with novel theories of how free will may be restricted, including defenses based on such conditions as battered woman syndrome (BWS), premenstrual syndrome (PMS), postpartum depression (PPD), and posttraumatic stress disorder (PTSD). The list of potential defenses is seemingly endless. In recent years, even some defenses, such as black rage, urban survivor syndrome, and gay panic, have been raised in attempts to excuse criminal responsibility, although with very little success.

In one bizarre case, 44-year-old Scott Falater of Phoenix, Arizona, raised a somnambulism (sleepwalking) defense as an excuse for his rather bad night in January 1997 when he stabbed his wife of 20 years with a hunting knife 44 times before holding her head under water until she drowned. The defense argued that lack of consciousness would fail to meet the intent requirement of the law. The jury rejected entirely his explanation and excuse.

Defendants have also raised cultural customs and religious beliefs as excuses for criminal conduct, but also with mixed success. The First Amendment of the Constitution protects the free exercise of religion, yet this right can sometimes come in conflict with another person's rights, including the right to life. Laurie Grouard Walker, a practicing Christian Scientist from Sacramento, California, for example, was convicted of involuntary manslaughter following the 1984 death of her 4-year-old daughter, Shauntay, from meningitis. Consistent with her religious beliefs, Walker had chosen prayer rather than medicine as a means of treating her daughter's flu-like symptoms. Although California, like many other states, provides a statutory exemption to criminal prosecution in the practice of religion, the California Supreme Court held that the rights of the child preempted the exemption. A federal judge later overturned Walker's conviction, but on procedural, not religious, grounds. By contrast, in a similar case in Massachusetts (the home of the Christian Science Church), the state's Supreme Judicial Court, citing religious freedom as a basis, overturned the manslaughter convictions of David and Ginger Twitchell, who also had relied unsuccessfully on faith healing to treat their 2-year-old son, Robyn.

Law and culture sometimes come in conflict, forcing an individual to make a very difficult choice. In January 1985, after learning of her husband's adultery, Fumiko Kimura, a 33-year-old Japanese immigrant, walked with her 4-year-old son and infant daughter into the Pacific Ocean off Santa Monica to save them from the shame that her husband had brought on the family. Kimura was pulled to safety and charged with the deaths of her two children. Although customs of her cultural heritage could not excuse her actions entirely, her lack of malice resulted in a light sentence of one year in jail and five years on probation.

HOMICIDE LAW IN PRACTICE

Homicide levels, types, excuses, and justifications are summarized in Table 1.3. When homicide cases come to trial, however, the jury is typically offered an even wider range of possible verdicts. If a defendant is charged with first-degree murder, for example, jurors are typically presented with the option of convicting on a lesser charge—second-degree murder, manslaughter, or possibly even assault with a deadly weapon. On many occasions, a jury will find a defendant guilty of a lesser charge than the facts would dictate or even not guilty altogether because of their sympathies surrounding the case.

Jury nullification, as it is called, is particularly common when smaller or weaker victims are charged with using excessive force to kill an abusive partner or a feared predator. Even if the facts fall short of self-defense, the jury can still choose to excuse. The infamous subway vigilante Bernhard Goetz was cleared by

Table 1.3 Types of Homicide

Classification	Elements	Example
First-degree murder	Homicide with malicious intent and with premeditation or extreme cruelty	A man decides to kill his wife, rather than divorce her, to ensure that he maintains sole custody of their children.
Second-degree murder	Homicide with malicious intent, indifference, or recklessness, but no premeditation or extreme cruelty	A man kills his wife during an argument over how best to discipline their children.
Felony-murder	Homicide during the course of a dangerous felony	A man commits arson in order to collect insurance, not knowing that his wife is home and will die from smoke inhalation.
Voluntary manslaughter	Willful homicide with provocation, under emotional duress, or from using excessive force in self-defense	A man kills his wife when he finds her spanking their child with a belt.
Involuntary manslaughter	Non-willful homicide resulting from negligence or disregard for safety of others	Driving while dialing his cell phone, a man slams into a tree, killing his wife, who is seated next to him.
Misdemeanor-manslaughter	Homicide during the course of a misdemeanor	As a prank, a man yells "fire" in a crowded theater, and his wife dies in the subsequent rush to escape.
Justifiable homicide	Killing a fleeing felon or in self-defense	A man kills his wife as she attempts to strangle their child.
Excusable homicide	Homicide with diminished capacity based on mental illness, age, or other conditions	A man kills his wife under a delusion that she is demonically possessed.

a New York City jury of homicide charges for his December 22, 1984, shooting of several black youngsters who had accosted him on the train. Even though the teens were unarmed, the jurors apparently identified with Goetz's fear in the situation and excused his quick-on-the-trigger response. Goetz was acquitted of all charges except a minor gun offense.

In the vast majority of criminal prosecutions, the case never reaches a jury. The charges may be dropped without a trial because of insufficient evidence, or the case may be decided by a trial judge. But most often, the defendant accepts a negotiated guilty plea. In such instances, the charge may be reduced from what the facts would indicate in exchange for the defendant's plea. Also, in crimes involving two or more accomplices, one defendant will often plead a lesser charge in exchange for giving testimony against his or her accomplices.

The physician's prescription blunder, which, as noted earlier, would constitute involuntary manslaughter, may also result in a civil action—a malpractice claim or even a wrongful death suit. In fact, virtually all criminal homicides can result in two kinds of trials, which can proceed in succession: criminal prosecutions leading to prison time and civil suits brought by families of the victims to recover financial damages. Unlike the criminal proceedings, the burden of proof in the civil action is far less demanding; guilt must be shown by a preponderance of evidence rather than beyond a reasonable doubt. Thus, for example, it is not inconsistent or even uncommon to encounter defendants like ex-football star O. J. Simpson being found not guilty in criminal court but civilly responsible.

The criminal prosecution of O. J. Simpson, the most watched trial in U.S. history, provides an important lesson for understanding the application of homicide law to real-world cases. As critical as the eyewitness testimony, the DNA evidence, and the credibility of the defendant's alibi were in shaping opinion inside and outside the courtroom, issues of race, class, and gender also had an impact. Some observers speculated that the jury, in acquitting Simpson, had sought to send a message about racism and police misconduct. Others argued that the defendant's wealth had bought him the best defense (the Dream Team) that money could buy; still others claimed that Simpson's celebrity status earned him special treatment.

Notwithstanding the actual rule of law, the political context surrounding a homicide (issues of race, gender, and class, among others) ultimately determines, as Susan Estrich persuasively argued, how the criminal law is applied to the facts, how a case is charged by a prosecutor, how a jury responds to a defendant's strategy, and how an appellate court considers procedural challenges.[5] For these many reasons, therefore, the punishment may not exactly fit the crime.

Recent attention to the deaths of children left in hot cars illustrates that the law is not always applied equally. The parents of a 7-month-old girl who died in St. Louis in August 2007 were never charged. The mother, a pediatrician, and father, a researcher, miscommunicated, so that neither of them remembered the baby was in the car until passersby spotted her hours later and broke out a window. By that time, it was too late to save her life; the baby had died from heat exposure. In this case, the prosecutor decided that poor communication between the parents did not meet the criterion of criminal negligence. Similarly, an Ohio mom who forgot she had left her 2-year-old child in her car was not charged in the child's death. She had thought to stop and pick up doughnuts for her coworkers but did not remember her child in the backseat. The mother had been warned on previous occasions about leaving the child in the car unattended. In a 2001 case, however, a Missouri man who forgot his child in his automobile was charged with involuntary manslaughter, pleaded guilty, and received 5 years of probation. An analysis of 300 cases of children who died in hot vehicles found that there were charges in only about half of the cases.[6]

Whatever the role of gender, race, and class in charging decisions, well-meaning modifications in law sometimes carry unanticipated negative consequences. Parents and laws have moved babies and children to the backseats of cars and put them in backward-facing car seats. A sleeping child may all too easily become a forgotten child. But, although most cases of kids dying in hot cars are judged as tragic accidents or manslaughters as a result of negligence, one recent hot car death was premeditated murder. Justin Ross Harris, 35, of Georgia was recently convicted of murder after his 22-month-old son Cooper died after seven hours in the 120-degree car. Harris's claims of being forgetful were destroyed at trial when evidence showed he had researched child hot car deaths, had sexting relationships with many other women (some underage), and clearly wanted out from under the burdens of being a father. Harris was sentenced to life without parole for the murder and an additional 32 years for cruelty to children, sexual exploitation of children (for trying to get an underage girl to text him photos of her genitalia), and dissemination of harmful material to minors.

ENDNOTES

1. Staci A. Turner, Jeffrey J. Barnard, Sheila D. Spotswood, and Joseph A. Prahlow, "'Homicide by Heart Attack' Revisited," *Journal of Forensic Science* 49 (2004): 598–600.

2. Federal Bureau of Investigation, *Law Enforcement Officers Killed and Assaulted—2016* (Washington, DC: U.S. Department of Justice, 2017).

3. Henry Pearson Curtis, "Gun Law Triggers at Least 13 Shootings," *Orlando Sentinel*, June 11, 2006.

4. Cheng Cheng and Mark Hoetsra, "Does Strengthening Self-Defense Law Deter Crime or Escalate Violence? Evidence From Castle Doctrine" (Working Paper 18134, National Bureau of Economic Research, June 2012); Chandler B. McClellan and Erdal Teskin, "Stand Your Ground Laws, Homicides, and Injuries" (Working Paper 18187, National Bureau of Economic Research, June 2012).

5. Susan Estrich, *Getting Away With Murder* (Cambridge, MA: Harvard University Press, 1998).

6. Jeremy Kohler, "Prosecution or Persecution?" *St. Louis Post-Dispatch*, September 10, 2007.

CHAPTER TWO

THE KILLERS AND THEIR VICTIMS

I f one's view of society were based largely on television programming and the story lines crafted by Hollywood screenwriters, it would surely seem that America is inundated with violent crime, especially murder. However, unlike television and film, where the frequency of murders seems to increase unabatedly, the rate of murder in America has remained relatively low for the past decade or more. A few cities are experiencing recent spikes in murder, especially gun homicide, but these are largely restricted to certain impoverished neighborhoods. Most urban areas are reporting homicide rates that are at a 50-year low, or at least close to it, levels not seen since the early 1960s.[1]

Of course, the murder rate hasn't always been so low. As shown in Figure 2.1, the rate of murder—the number of homicide victims per 100,000 population—rose sharply during the late 1960s and 1970s, reaching a high of 10.2 in 1980. Then, after subsiding through much of the 1980s, the rate surged once again, peaking at 9.8 in 1991, before declining by nearly 50% during the much less violent 1990s.

The end of the 1990s decade, however, also brought an end to the great 1990s slide in murder rates. With the new millennium, the national homicide rate

Figure 2.1   U.S. Homicide Rate, 1950–2016

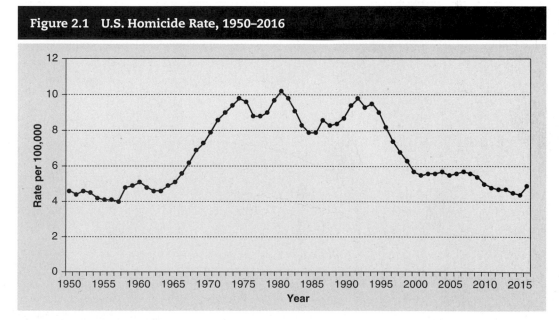

Source: FBI, *Crime in the United States.*

plateaued, seemingly reaching a level that was hard to beat. However, after 2008, the nation's murder rate declined once again, falling to 4.5 per 100,000 population in 2014, the lowest since the 1950s.

In an apparent end to the slide, the homicide rate jumped by more than 10% in 2015 over 2014 (and then almost that much in 2016 over 2015). Although the murder rate is still relatively low and the sudden increase was largely an aberrant spike after several years of improvement, much was made politically about the 2015 crime statistics that were released during the 2016 presidential campaign. Populist candidate and Republican Party nominee Donald Trump repeatedly stated that the double-digit jump in the murder rate was the largest increase in decades, evidence that America needed his heavy law and order platform, which included more control on immigration and less control on guns. Whatever the merits of Trump's position, which certainly appeared to have helped him in winning the White House, the focus on a one-year jump in crime made far too much of very little.

Although the latest increases in murder are disappointing and represent hundreds more victims killed, they should be put in perspective. The 2015 and 2016 homicide rates would not be remarkable were it not for the successes of the previous years. The homicide rate in 2016 was still much lower, nearly half as high, than the peaks in murder that had been witnessed in the 1980s and 1990s.

The relatively low U.S. murder rate in recent years is, of course, still too high, particularly when contrasted with those of other developed nations. Table 2.1 displays homicide rates for 81 nations around the world, each with a population of more than 5 million. Although such comparisons can be affected by variations in the quality of data collection procedures, the table does provide a fairly clear sense of the poor ranking of the United States among reporting nations, especially European allies.

Table 2.1   Homicide Rates in Selected Countries, 2015

Country	Region	Rate	Country	Region	Rate
El Salvador	Americas	108.6	India*	Asia	3.2
Honduras	Americas	63.8	Uzbekistan	Asia	3.0
Venezuela	Americas	57.2	Bangladesh	Asia	2.5
South Africa	Africa	34.3	Libya	Africa	2.5
Guatemala*	Americas	31.2	Azerbaijan*	Asia	2.5
Brazil	Americas	26.7	Myanmar	Asia	2.4
Colombia	Americas	26.5	Nepal*	Asia	2.3
Dominican Republic*	Americas	17.4	Belgium	Europe	2.0
Mexico	Americas	16.4	Sierra Leone	Africa	1.9
Congo	Africa	13.4	Bulgaria	Europe	1.8
Uganda*	Africa	11.8	Canada	Americas	1.7
Russia	Europe	11.3	Finland	Europe	1.6

Country	Region	Rate	Country	Region	Rate
Mali	Africa	10.8	France	Europe	1.6
Iraq*	Asia	10.1	Saudi Arabia	Asia	1.5
Philippines*	Asia	9.8	Romania	Europe	1.5
Nigeria	Africa	9.8	Hungary*	Europe	1.5
Angola	Africa	9.7	Algeria	Africa	1.4
Paraguay	Americas	9.3	Israel	Asia	1.4
Togo	Africa	9.1	Sweden	Europe	1.2
Chad	Africa	9.0	Serbia	Europe	1.1
Guinea	Africa	8.5	Morocco*	Africa	1.1
Ecuador*	Americas	8.2	Denmark	Europe	1.0
Ethiopia	Africa	7.6	Australia	Oceania	1.0
Eritrea	Africa	7.5	Portugal	Europe	1.0
Senegal	Africa	7.3	United Kingdom*	Europe	0.9
Peru	Americas	7.2	Slovakia	Europe	0.9
Argentina	Americas	6.5	Germany	Europe	0.9
Sudan	Africa	6.5	Greece	Europe	0.9
Benin	Africa	6.0	Italy	Europe	0.8
Cameroon	Africa	5.9	China*	Asia	0.7
Kenya	Africa	5.8	Poland	Europe	0.7
Somalia	Africa	5.6	Switzerland	Europe	0.7
Kyrgyzstan	Asia	5.1	Spain	Europe	0.7
United States	Americas	4.9	United Arab Emirates	Asia	0.7
Kazakhstan	Asia	4.8	Netherlands	Europe	0.6
Iran	Asia	4.1	Norway*	Europe	0.6
Burundi*	Africa	4.0	Austria	Europe	0.5
Lebanon	Asia	4.0	Indonesia*	Asia	0.5
Chile*	Americas	3.6	Japan*	Asia	0.3
Belarus*	Europe	3.6	Singapore	Asia	0.3
Thailand	Asia	3.5			

*Rate for 2014 most recent available.

As shown, the United States, even following its post-1990s crime drop, has one of the highest homicide rates among industrialized nations. Heading the list are countries that experience high levels of political turmoil and bloodshed (comparable in the United States only in extraordinary and rare cases such as the 1995 Oklahoma City bombing). America's homicide problem is more a matter of interpersonal rather than political conflict.

A popular explanation for the United States' dubious distinction among nations implicates the country's lax or unenforced gun laws and the easy availability of firearms. There are some 300 million firearms in the United States, almost as many as there are citizens. Even so, the nongun homicide rate for the United States in 2015 (1.6 per 100,000 population) was still higher than the overall murder rate for nearly all European counties as well as Australia, China, and Japan. Thus, guns may be part of the problem, but they are not the entire problem. Because many other countries have relatively high levels of gun ownership and low levels of gun homicide, it seems to be more a function of a willingness in the United States to use a firearm, thus requiring a mind-set change rather than just an access change.

Regardless of weaponry, American society is deeply rooted in violence. From the days of the American Revolution to the Wild, Wild West, the country was developed as a consequence of violent conquests. In modern times, moreover, American society applauds and rewards the victor, almost without regard for who is victimized in the relentless pursuit of success, profit, and power. This selfish drive for personal gain has led some social critics to label American culture as "sociopathic."[2] In popular culture as well, movies, music, and even fashion glorify and glamorize violence of all forms. It is often said that America has a love affair with violence, but it may be more like a marriage.

At the same time that many conditions of U.S. culture and society have encouraged violence, the traditional institutions of social control—family, community, schools, religion—have grown particularly weak. In their place, we have invested heavily in formal institutions of social control, most notably prisons. With prison and jail populations well above 2 million, many times greater than even three decades ago, increasing numbers of dangerous felons are being incarcerated for longer periods of time. Undoubtedly, the downturn in murder rates is partially a result of increased punitiveness for all crimes, yet at a significant price. Each year, some 600,000 offenders are released from U.S. prisons. Unless their incarceration reformed them and their transition back into society is positive, much of the crime reduction gained over the past two decades could be lost.

The most significant drops in homicide during recent years have come in the large U.S. cities, the very locales that had experienced the most precipitous increases in murder during the late 1980s. To borrow on Newton's law of physics, what goes up generally comes down, and the steeper the rise is, the steeper the subsequent descent will be. In fact, as shown in Figure 2.2, most of the change, upward and downward, in U.S. homicide rates during the past three decades can be traced to the larger cities—cities with populations of more than a quarter million. This is especially true of some of the largest metropolitan areas, such as New York and Los Angeles, which were overrun by crack cocaine markets during the late 1980s and responded with smart policing strategies in the 1990s to help reverse the trend. A variety of other factors contributed to the decline, including increased incarceration rates and stiffer sentencing, which kept dangerous felons off the street for longer periods of time, and changes in illegal drug markets. These and other contributors will be discussed in detail in Chapter 5.

Even though the rate of killing moved downward throughout the 1990s and has remained low ever since then, the U.S. public apparently is not fully convinced.

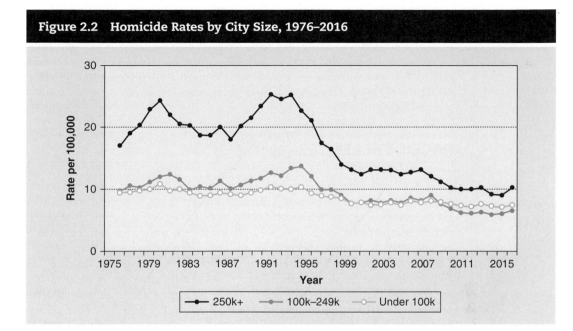

Figure 2.2 Homicide Rates by City Size, 1976–2016

In fact, recent Gallup surveys have found that 7 out of 10 Americans believe that crime is on the rise, despite the compelling statistics showing otherwise.[3]

The media obsession with crime as news and entertainment is likely responsible for this disconnect between perception and reality. Public perceptions of crime trends are based much more on media crime reports than the FBI's *Uniform Crime Reports*. Seeing is believing, it is said, and images of cold and lifeless bodies at a blood-splattered crime scene shown on the nightly news are far more persuasive in shaping public opinion than are cold and lifeless statistics presented in a newspaper report or a government document. Furthermore, news about crime rates coming down simply is not highlighted in the same way as are stories of mini-epidemics in carjackings, hate crimes, child abductions, mass shootings, or whatever the journalist's crime du jour may be. In terms of the mass media, the popular idiom "No news is good news" is reversed, "Good news is no news," and turned inside out, "Bad news is big news." Because of fast-advancing telecommunications technology, news coverage of crime has become more immediate, more graphic, and more pervasive. Even if there are fewer homicides available to reporters today than in the early 1990s, there are still plenty to lead off the news. Furthermore, should a news station not have a nearby tragedy to feature, satellite feeds from other corners of the nation can easily fill the local news void. Many of the nation's major news outlets also feature sections of their website devoted exclusively to coverage of crime stories. More than anything else, the national news picture is about violence, except of course when some other catastrophe, like a plane crash or a hurricane, demands center stage.

The evolution of all-news cable channels, such as MSNBC, CNN, and FOX News, among others, has also altered the way in which homicide and other crime stories are reported. In earlier years, when major television networks controlled most of the programming, local affiliates would not normally interrupt the viewing schedule for anything other than a major breaking story of national significance (e.g., an attempt to assassinate a top political figure) or a local matter of great importance. But by today's practices, the 24-hour cable news channels are drawn to continuing coverage of crimes, investigations, or trials to fill their vacuum of airtime. Thus, events such as the Virginia Tech mass shooting or even the 2017 O. J. Simpson parole hearing, had they occurred decades earlier, would not have been covered live by the major networks. Yet, given that the cable news channels now feature continuing coverage of breaking crime news (with music and graphics fitting the big event), the networks feel pressure to follow suit so as not to lose their audience.

RACE DIFFERENCES

More than just exaggerating the risk of murder, television portrayals of homicide also distort the characteristics of killers and their victims. Because the networks are motivated by ratings, television dramas as well as news programs feature white victims and perpetrators to appeal to a predominantly white audience. For example, in a content analysis of the 2000–2001 season of the hit show *Law & Order*, Eschholz, Mallard, and Flynn found that 75% of the show's violent offenders and 76% of their victims were white as compared to 13% and 19%, respectively, in the actual crime records of the New York Police Department.[4] A similar disconnect was observed for episodes of the crime drama *NYPD Blue*. If script writers were driven more by a desire for realism, homicide offenders and victims would be roughly equally spread between whites and blacks.

Table 2.2 shows demographic patterns—specifically race, sex, and age—of victims and offenders from 2000 through 2016 combined. In terms of race, slightly more than one-half of homicide offenders are black, and slightly less than one-half of victims are black. Because the nation's white and black populations are quite different in size (over the years represented in the table, 79.9% of the population was white, 13.5% was black, and 6.6% other races), the rates of offending and victimization diverge. As indicated in the table, the rate of homicide (per 100,000 population) committed by blacks (23.5) is about seven times that of whites (3.2), and the rate of victimization is about six times higher for blacks (18.9) than for whites (3.1).

The large race difference among homicide victims and perpetrators has much to do with the kinds of killing in which blacks predominate. Table 2.3 shows the racial split among both victims and offenders in various homicide subtypes. At the extreme, blacks are greatly overrepresented among those who commit felony-related homicides (59.3% of offenders) such as robbery, as well as those involved in drug-related incidents (55.1% and 60.6% of victims and perpetrators, respectively). Much of this extreme overrepresentation is related to the geography of homicide, in that violent crime is associated with the heavy concentration of blacks among the urban underclass. The link between race and homicide has been traced to socioeconomic factors such as low income, poor education, and inadequate employment opportunities.[5]

At the other extreme, blacks are far less overrepresented in domestic homicides—those involving intimates, infanticides, and family killings generally—as well as in sex-related murders. Also noteworthy is the lesser extent of overrepresentation of blacks as perpetrators of workplace homicides, which may be, in part, a function of higher black unemployment rates, particularly in the age categories most likely to perpetrate workplace violence. No job means no opportunity for killing coworkers. Many of the workplace shootings have involved civil service positions (e.g., government and post office workers), which may reflect the greater number of whites holding these jobs.

Table 2.2 Homicide Victims and Offenders by Demographic Groups, 2000–2016 Combined

		Percentage Distribution			Rate per 100,000	
		Victims	Offenders	Population	Victims	Offenders
Race						
	White	47.8%	43.3%	79.9%	3.1	3.2
	Black	48.8%	53.8%	13.5%	18.9	23.5
	Other	3.4%	2.9%	6.6%	2.7	2.6
	Total	100.0%	100.0%	100.0%	5.2	5.9
Sex						
	Male	78.6%	90.6%	49.2%	8.3	10.9
	Female	21.4%	9.4%	50.8%	2.2	1.1
	Total	100.0%	100.0%	100.0%	5.2	5.9
Age Group						
	Under 14	5.4%	0.2%	18.7%	1.5	0.1
	14–17	4.7%	7.9%	5.6%	4.4	8.4
	18–24	24.8%	38.5%	9.9%	13.1	23.0
	25–34	26.1%	27.6%	13.5%	10.1	12.1
	35–49	23.4%	17.8%	21.1%	5.8	5.0
	50+	15.7%	8.0%	31.2%	2.6	1.5
	Total	100.0%	100.0%	100.0%	5.2	5.9

In recent years, shootings with undertones of racial bias have received significant attention, especially those involving apparent overresponse by guardians of the law. The 2012 fatal shooting of Trayvon Martin, an unarmed 17-year-old African American, by a white neighborhood watch volunteer in Sanford, Florida, started a national debate about race and justice. However, in a few places the debate turned into angry protest and even rioting following a number of high-profile and controversial killings of young black men by police, including Michael Brown in suburban St. Louis, Tamir Rice in Cleveland, Freddie Gray in Baltimore, and others in cities large and small. Many Americans were left questioning why these police shootings were happening and what could be done to stop them. Sadly, a few individuals did more than demand change and retaliated with violence, including the July 7, 2016, massacre of five police officers in Dallas.

By virtue of the racial makeup of many urban police departments and the racial composition of the communities they patrol, it is not surprising that there are frequent episodes of blacks being fatally shot, justifiably or not, at the hands of

Table 2.3 Race Differences by Homicide Type, 2000–2016 Combined

	Victims			Offenders		
	White	**Black**	**Other**	**White**	**Black**	**Other**
All homicides	47.8%	48.8%	3.4%	43.3%	53.8%	2.9%
Intimate	66.4%	29.1%	4.5%	63.6%	32.7%	3.8%
Family	68.7%	26.4%	4.9%	67.7%	28.0%	4.3%
Infanticide	58.2%	37.8%	4.0%	57.8%	38.5%	3.7%
Eldercide	75.7%	20.7%	3.6%	65.5%	31.4%	3.1%
Felony-murder	49.8%	46.5%	3.7%	38.4%	59.3%	2.3%
Sex-related	65.2%	31.1%	3.7%	53.2%	42.5%	4.4%
Drug-related	42.8%	55.1%	2.1%	37.5%	60.6%	1.9%
Gang-related	50.4%	46.0%	3.6%	51.8%	43.7%	4.5%
Argument	53.0%	43.0%	4.0%	49.8%	46.7%	3.5%
Workplace	79.8%	11.1%	9.1%	74.3%	17.9%	7.8%
Gun homicide	41.0%	56.2%	2.8%	36.7%	61.0%	2.3%
Arson	57.0%	37.3%	5.7%	55.0%	40.1%	4.9%
Poison	75.3%	17.7%	7.0%	76.8%	17.4%	5.8%
Multiple victims	55.6%	39.8%	4.6%	47.6%	48.8%	3.6%
Multiple offenders	47.7%	48.8%	3.5%	39.1%	58.2%	2.6%

white officers. However, when it comes to killings that do not involve the police, the vast majority are intraracial rather than interracial. As shown in Figure 2.3, approximately 81% of white homicide victims are killed by white assailants, and about 90% of black victims are killed by members of their own race.

This similarity between victim and offender race is one of the most consistent patterns over the years. Because homicides typically involve a victim and offender who know each other—often on intimate terms—the similarity of race between homicide participants follows from the similarity of race between individuals in most interpersonal relationships. This likeness of victim and offender race holds even for relationships that are more distant than family. As shown, among homicides involving friends and acquaintances, 81% of white victims and 89% of black victims are slain by someone of the same race. Because of the racial homogeneity of most neighborhoods, moreover, it is even true that most stranger killings are intraracial—67% for white victims and 90% for blacks.

The higher prevalence of blacks killing whites over whites killing blacks should not necessarily be interpreted as a greater propensity toward interracial attacks instigated by blacks. Even if the victim were chosen randomly, blacks

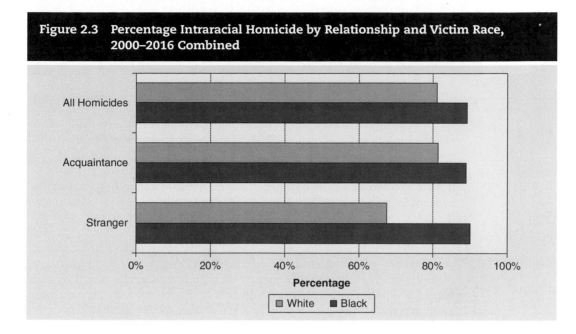

Figure 2.3   Percentage Intraracial Homicide by Relationship and Victim Race, 2000–2016 Combined

would victimize whites more than whites would blacks simply because of the predominance of whites among the potential targets. Because the U.S. population is primarily white, it is more likely for a black assailant to come across a potential white victim than it is for a white assailant to encounter a black victim.

Despite the tendency for most homicides, even those involving strangers, to be intraracial, it is important not to minimize the concern for fatal interracial attacks. The percentage of homicides that cross race lines has increased from less than 10% in the 1970s to about 15% in the past several years. To some extent, this increase reflects growing levels of racial hostility; it could also be a result of greater contact between black and white Americans in everyday activities, including work, school, and romantic relationships.

GENDER DIFFERENCES

In addition to race, media images of gender are also frequently distorted. Pritchard and Hughes examined the factors that affect four measures of print newsworthiness of homicide cases—frequency of coverage, average story length, proportion of front-page placement, and use of photographs.[6] Overall, they found that homicides involving male offenders and female victims receive the most intense coverage.

Gender was a primary force driving the intense media coverage of the February 2006 brutal murder of 24-year-old Imette St. Guillen, who was abducted late at night from a popular bar in the SoHo section of lower Manhattan. Her body was recovered in Brooklyn; she was found naked with her hands bound behind her back with plastic ties and her ankles tied with shoelaces. A gym sock was stuffed down her throat, and her face was wrapped in brown packing tape.

Of course, the brutality of the murder, the location of the crime in the Big Apple, and the fact that the victim was white while the prime suspect, Darryl Littlejohn, was black all added to the potential for sensationalism. Yet it was more the "young, defenseless graduate student" allegedly abducted, tortured, and killed by the "big, bad ex-con bouncer" that made news producers salivate. Three years later, in a closely watched trial, Littlejohn was convicted of first-degree murder.

In the actual pattern of homicide cases over the four decades, the offenders are indeed most often men. Yet, contrary to the media emphasis on crimes against women, most murder victims are also men.

As shown in Table 2.2, men are far more likely than women to kill (90.6% of offenders are men) and to be killed (78.6% of victims are men). In the 1970s, some scholars speculated that changing gender roles would lead to an increased involvement of women in crime.[7] However, murder has remained overwhelmingly a male preoccupation. If anything, the gender ratio among perpetrators has widened in recent years: from six males for every female in the mid-1970s to nine males for every female in the years since 2010.

As with race, most homicides occur in same-sex pairs; since 2000, 72% of all murders involved men killing men. Overall, for the years 2000–2016 combined, just over 90% of offenders were male and 80% of their victims were also male, typically killed in disputes over money, drugs, turf, honor, or pride. Cross-sex homicides predominate only when women kill; that is, not only do most male murderers (81%) kill men, but most female murderers (78%) also kill men.

It is important not to lose sight of the particular physical and situational vulnerability of women in dealings with men. Moreover, the statistical predominance of male victims likely stems from issues of victim precipitation. That is, men are far more likely to start a fight or to place themselves in dangerous or volatile situations resulting in their own death. Yet, the common media focus on "femicide"—female victims, especially of male killers—does not reflect the norm in actual patterns of murder.

When women do commit homicide, the nature of the offense is sharply different from those perpetrated by men. Women tend to kill close intimates (husbands, boyfriends, sons, or daughters), whereas men often attack strangers or mere acquaintances. Over the years 2000 through 2016, specifically, 52% of female assailants murdered intimate partners or family members, whereas 82% of male perpetrators killed acquaintances or strangers. Specifically, as shown in Table 2.4, the gender ratio among murderers narrows considerably in family homicides (22.6% of offenders are female) and especially infanticides (34.7% female offenders). Homicides by women often result from turmoil or stress that may build up over time. Men, by contrast, are often quick to respond violently, killing an acquaintance in a bar who challenges them or even a stranger on the street who insults them. Also shown in Table 2.4, predatory incidents, such as felony-murders, stranger killings, and especially sexual homicides, are overwhelmingly the province of men. Homicides within the family, by contrast, are somewhat more "equal opportunity" by gender, even though most family killings are still committed by men.

The instruments of murder selected by men and women are also very different. Men are better trained in the use of firearms, often feel comfortable with them, and therefore favor a gun when there is some murdering to do. By contrast, women prefer methods that are cleaner and more distant. Whereas fewer than 7% of gun killings are committed by women, nearly 20% of homicides by arson and almost half of murders by poison involve female offenders. Also, women often choose poison or suffocation in cases of family murder, including infanticide.

Unlike guns or brute force, women have more equal access to fire or poison as a means of committing homicide. In fact, because of their traditional role as

Table 2.4 Gender Differences by Homicide Type, 2000–2016 Combined

	Victims		Offenders	
	Male	Female	Male	Female
All homicides	78.6%	21.4%	90.6%	9.4%
Intimate	23.0%	77.0%	77.4%	22.6%
Family	46.1%	53.9%	77.4%	22.6%
Infanticide	57.8%	42.2%	65.3%	34.7%
Eldercide	57.1%	42.9%	84.2%	15.8%
Felony-murder	82.4%	17.6%	92.5%	7.5%
Sex-related	20.4%	79.6%	93.6%	6.4%
Drug-related	90.9%	9.1%	93.1%	6.9%
Gang-related	95.5%	4.5%	96.0%	4.0%
Argument	74.0%	26.0%	89.2%	10.8%
Workplace	78.7%	21.3%	90.2%	9.8%
Gun homicide	84.7%	15.3%	93.5%	6.5%
Arson	56.2%	43.8%	81.1%	18.9%
Poison	53.4%	46.6%	53.3%	46.7%
Multiple victims	67.4%	32.6%	92.6%	7.4%
Multiple offenders	87.4%	12.6%	88.9%	11.1%

homemakers and caretakers, women are often better acquainted than men with the harmful effects of various drugs and poisons. It was not difficult, for example, for 64-year-old Sacramento landlady Dorothea Montalvo Puente to poison her elderly boarders in order to cash in their social security checks. It was also not difficult for Puente to cover up the crimes by burying her victims in the yard of her rooming house—until 1988, that is, when a local social worker discovered that her missing clients' social security checks were being cashed. Despite her claims that all of her boarders had died of natural causes, Puente was convicted of murder and sentenced to life without the possibility of parole. In 2011, the murdering landlady passed away at the age of 82 while still behind the walls of the Central California Women's Facility in Chowchilla. Unlike her victims, however, Puente's death was indeed from natural causes.

Over the past few decades, the United States has endured several instances of product tampering, which not only scared the public but also brought about major changes in the packaging of consumer goods. In 1982, seven Chicago-area residents were fatally poisoned when they unknowingly ingested cyanide-laced Extra-Strength Tylenol capsules. The killer responsible for placing the poisoned analgesics on the shelves of local drug stores and supermarkets was never apprehended, which led to some speculation, based at least on statistical patterns, that the murderer was a woman.

Regardless of the Tylenol poisoner's identity and gender, the case no doubt influenced the thinking of Stella M. Nickell of Auburn, Washington, when she conceived a plan to kill her husband, Bruce, in order to collect the proceeds of a $176,000 life insurance policy. In June 1986, 52-year-old Bruce Nickell died after swallowing a poisoned Extra-Strength Excedrin capsule. Susan Snow, age 40, also of Auburn but unknown to Nickell, died after purchasing a contaminated bottle from a local store. She was the unfortunate victim of Stella Nickell's scheme to make the deaths appear to be the work of a random killer. Nickell was sentenced to a 90-year prison term with parole eligibility beginning in 2018.

Murders for hire are also especially appealing to women who see the death of their spouse as a distasteful but necessary step to resolve a difficult situation. As described more fully in the next chapter, 22-year-old Pamela Smart of Derry, New Hampshire, had grown tired of her marriage of less than a year to her 24-year-old husband, Greg, and was having an affair with her 15-year-old student. She wanted to end the marriage but didn't want the stress and complications of a divorce, not to mention the possibility that her adulterous affair with a minor might come to light in the process. Murder would be quicker, and she had her young lover and his friends do the dirty work.

Reflecting recent thinking in criminology about female offenders, in her book, *When She Was Bad*, Patricia Pearson argues that women are far more violent than most people assume. Much of this violence is explained away by portraying murdering women as mentally ill, hormonally unstable, or victims whose actions are driven by forces beyond their control.[8] But Pearson argues that this is a particularly unfeminist view of females. She discusses how indirect female aggression may look different than direct male aggression but is deadly just the same. In school, girls engage in rumormongering and character assassination and provoke boys to beat up (or even kill) other boys or their female rivals through social manipulation. Or they nonchalantly murder newborns and then go about their social lives of attending proms and parties with their dying babies abandoned in trash bins, coolers, and closets. Women assault and kill their former and current boyfriends and husbands rather than face being dumped for another woman. A scorned woman may run over her husband with his car or abuse her stepchildren as surrogates for her hostility toward her mate.

Notwithstanding these instances of quiet killing using drugs, poisons, or hired guns, there are certainly countless cases of women committing murder in far more brutal ways. In a closely watched 2013 trial, Jodi Ann Arias was convicted of murdering her ex-boyfriend Travis Alexander at his Mesa, Arizona, home. The 30-year-old victim was found dead inside the shower. He had suffered multiple stab wounds, a gunshot wound to the head, and his throat had been slashed from ear to ear. Arias's story of what had taken place changed multiple times, but she insisted she killed Alexander in self-defense after he had become enraged when she dropped his camera. Taking the stand in her own defense, the 32-year-old woman detailed how she and Alexander enjoyed engaging in rough sex, sparing the court none of the lurid details of sexual bondage and anal penetration. According to Arias, their relationship had become increasingly violent, but she insisted that she killed him when he flew into a fit of rage. The jury rejected her claim of self-defense and convicted her of first-degree murder. During the penalty hearing, however, jurors were divided on the question of the death penalty, which resulted in Arias's being sentenced to life without parole.

When women do engage in direct aggression such as hitting, it is often referred to in humorous, nonserious, trivializing terms like "catfight" or "hair-pulling contests." People joke about aggressive women with premenstrual syndrome (PMS). Some people laughed when Clara Harris ran over and murdered her husband in front of his hysterical daughter. Others joked about Lorena Bobbitt excising her abusive husband's penis.

The time may have come to stop portraying violent women as helpless or confused "children" rather than the cold, calculated killers they can be. Women may simply be better than men at hiding their aggression, getting others to do their dirty work, or engaging in less brutal forms of lethal violence.

Certainly Karla Homolka, arrested in Canada in 1993, was convincing as the victim of a battering spouse rather than as a sexual predator. Along with her husband, Paul Bernardo, she participated in the brutal rapes and sadistic murders of three teenage girls—one of whom was her own sister. When police questioned Homolka about Bernardo's possible involvement in the death of one of the girls, they offered her a "sweetheart deal" to talk. What the authorities did not realize was that Karla herself (who admits to performing oral sex on her own unconscious sister and wanting to give her husband her sister's virginity as a Christmas present) was a dangerous sexual sadist who played much more than an ancillary role in the rapes and murders. The deal had already been confirmed by the time police and prosecutors saw videotapes of the murders and heard other evidence about her involvement. Because of this premature negotiation, Homolka was freed from prison on July 4, 2005 (her personal independence day), at the end of her 12-year sentence. Despite widespread outrage, particularly in the province of Ontario, where the crimes had occurred, there was nothing the authorities could do to prolong her incarceration.

AGE DIFFERENCES

A crime time capsule of the 1990s would likely be decidedly slanted toward murders committed by juveniles. In recent years, the mass media have focused heavily on homicides committed by teenagers—not just the most sensationalistic crimes like the April 1999 Columbine High School massacre but also the general problem of armed and dangerous youngsters. On March 25, 1996, the usually understated cover of *U.S. News & World Report*, screamed "Teenage Time Bombs: Violent Juvenile Crime Is Soaring and It's Going to Get Worse." Even *People* magazine devoted its June 23, 1997, issue to the rhetorical query, "Kids Without a Conscience?" The report examined a variety of senseless homicides, including the case of a 15-year-old couple who murdered and disemboweled a 44-year-old drinking buddy in Manhattan's Central Park and the story of an 18-year-old New Jersey girl who delivered a baby in the bathroom during her senior prom, dumped the child in the trash, and then returned to dance with her prom date.

The extensive media attention given to juvenile offenders is well out of proportion with their relative involvement in violence.[9] As shown in Table 2.2, only about 10% of murderers and victims are under 18 years old. By contrast, young adults, ages 18 to 24, represent almost 40% of the offenders and about one-quarter of the victims.

The disconnect between media hype and statistical reality in regard to juvenile homicide has led some observers to allege that journalists as well as politicians have exploited a few highly publicized cases for their own ends. According to attorney and author Peter Elikann, a whole generation of teenagers has been demonized in media and political circles, which cast them as ruthless superpredators.[10]

The superpredator concept was first conceived by John J. DiIulio Jr. In the book *Body Count*, DiIulio and coauthors Bennett and Walters commented that "America is now home to thickening ranks of juvenile 'superpredators'—radically impulsive, brutally remorseless youngsters, including ever more preteen boys, who murder, assault, rape, rob, burglarize, deal deadly drugs, join gun-toting gangs, and create serious communal disorders."[11]

The term *superpredator* may indeed have been inflammatory and unduly sensationalistic. It may even be technically inaccurate, because juvenile violence is typically impulsive rather than predatory (the true superpredators are more accurately serial killers who prey on scores of innocent victims). Notwithstanding such caveats, the frequent attention given to youth violence, and especially murder, may have had much to do with the special character (i.e., the unmitigated senselessness) of youthful killings. When adults kill, it often involves rather commonplace motivations such as jealousy, revenge, or greed. When kids kill, the reasons are often as trivial as a pair of sneakers or a challenging glance.

Juvenile homicides are quite different from adult killings in several other respects. As shown in Table 2.5, the involvement of adolescents is far greater in gang killings, gun killings, and homicides that involve multiple offenders (two or more accomplices working together).

More than their older counterparts, juveniles tend to travel and kill in groups, sometimes tightly organized gangs with a well-defined hierarchy of authority, but often just informal cliques or bands. It is often the strong influence of peers that motivates murder, rather than any particular burning desire of the perpetrator to kill. It is easier psychologically to participate in a horrible crime because your friends are doing it, too.

Despite the limited involvement overall of juveniles in homicide, the intensive focus on young killers, especially during the early 1990s as described earlier, can be understood based on patterns of growth during that era in their rate of murder. Whereas 8.3% of murders during the years 1976–1985 were committed by offenders under age 18, juveniles during the mid-1980s to the mid-1990s were implicated in 12.6% of the killings. Correspondingly, the age of murderers dropped over this time period, from about 31 years old on average in the mid-1980s down to nearly 27 years old on average in the mid-1990s, trending upward slightly since then. A similar pattern of youth movement has occurred among victims, with an average age in the mid-1980s of nearly 35 years old, down to an average victim age of just over 31 years old in the mid-1990s. The parallel trends in the average ages of offenders and victims are understandable because offenders tend to murder victims close to their own age.

It seems that the younger the killer is, the greater the shock people feel. Over the past several years, the nation was clearly shaken when, for example, two boys, ages 10 and 11, dropped a 5-year-old out of a 14th-story window in a Chicago housing project in retaliation for tattling on them; when an 11-year-old and a 13-year-old killed four students and one teacher at their middle school in Jonesboro, Arkansas; and even when a 6-year-old Michigan boy shot and killed his first-grade classmate. Notwithstanding these sensational stories of preteen killers, murder at the hands of younger children—those under age 14—has remained especially rare. Since 2000, on average, about 40 children age 13 and younger and fewer than 5 children age 10 and younger commit homicide each year nationwide, and neither tally has shown any indication of increasing. Thus, despite the special senselessness of kiddie murder, it remains little more than a horrifying aberration.

Table 2.5 Age Differences by Homicide Type, 2000–2016 Combined

	Victims					Offenders				
	Under 18	18–24	25–34	35–49	50+	Under 18	18–24	25–34	35–49	50+
All homicides	10.1%	24.8%	26.1%	23.4%	15.7%	8.2%	38.5%	27.6%	17.8%	8.0%
Intimate	1.2%	12.6%	25.3%	36.7%	24.3%	0.6%	10.7%	24.0%	38.4%	26.3%
Family	26.2%	6.6%	13.4%	23.8%	30.0%	4.4%	20.1%	24.8%	28.7%	22.0%
Infanticide	100.0%	—	—	—	—	5.1%	43.2%	37.6%	12.2%	1.9%
Eldercide	—	—	—	—	100.0%	5.4%	17.3%	18.6%	25.6%	33.1%
Felony-murder	7.1%	23.6%	25.9%	23.6%	19.7%	10.1%	44.4%	27.3%	13.8%	4.4%
Sex-related	18.4%	18.2%	21.1%	25.1%	17.2%	6.5%	32.4%	31.8%	24.0%	5.3%
Drug-related	5.3%	31.3%	33.6%	22.9%	6.9%	8.3%	46.0%	30.2%	12.7%	2.8%
Gang-related	16.7%	45.9%	25.8%	9.6%	2.0%	16.8%	55.3%	20.4%	5.8%	1.7%
Argument	5.9%	22.8%	27.0%	28.2%	16.2%	5.4%	31.1%	28.4%	23.6%	11.4%
Workplace	0.5%	5.6%	13.1%	32.6%	48.2%	1.4%	16.0%	26.6%	34.6%	21.4%
Gun homicide	7.2%	30.1%	29.8%	22.0%	10.9%	9.0%	42.6%	26.9%	14.5%	7.0%
Arson	23.8%	10.1%	13.9%	23.7%	28.6%	7.9%	27.0%	27.0%	26.9%	11.3%
Poison	33.3%	7.5%	5.4%	19.0%	34.8%	5.5%	18.9%	24.1%	28.2%	23.4%
Multiple victims	15.9%	23.1%	23.8%	19.9%	17.2%	7.8%	37.2%	28.4%	19.0%	7.6%
Multiple offenders	11.0%	29.7%	26.7%	20.0%	12.5%	12.4%	49.3%	25.4%	10.4%	2.5%

In terms of the age patterns between victims and offenders, homicide is intragenerational. Adults tend to target other adults (husband, wife, coworkers, friends), and adolescents tend to target their contemporaries as well. The major exception, of course, is in cases of infanticide (victims under the age of 5), in which the perpetrator tends to be a parent or some other caretaker (e.g., Mom's boyfriend) but certainly not a playmate. Figure 2.4 provides perspective on the match between victim and offender age. In this plot, depicting homicides in 2016, the greater the density of points (each representing a separate incident), the more commonplace is the victim–offender age combination. Aside from the sizable left-hand cluster of children killed by adults (infanticides) and the more modest number of elders murdered by younger perpetrators (eldercides), the plot thickens along the diagonal, showing that most offenders and their victims are similar in age.

As frequently described by social scientists, numerous characteristics of lifestyle tend to change dramatically as a person moves through the life course from infancy into adolescence, and from adulthood into retirement age. The same can be said for styles of death by homicide. Figure 2.5 shows that three key homicide characteristics—whether the offender was known to the victim, whether the homicide was felony related, and whether a gun was used—vary considerably by age of the victim.

Firearms are rarely needed in murders of young children, but gun use increases steadily throughout the teenage years, peaks at just over 80% for older adolescents, and then declines steadily with advancing victim age. The vulnerability of elders, as with young children, produces a large proportion of deaths with weapons other than guns. Also, children are almost always murdered by someone they know, in contrast to victims of older ages, who, about three-quarters of the time, are killed by a family member or acquaintance. The percentage of victims killed in the course of a felony increases with age. For victims aged 50 and older, the proportion

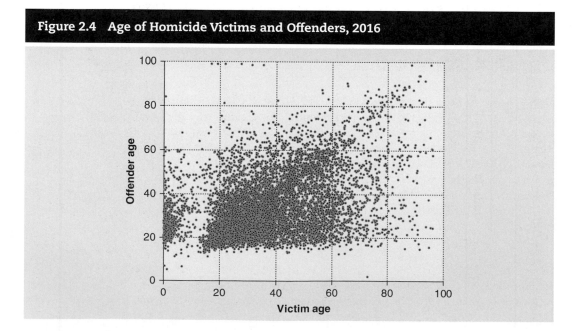

Figure 2.4   Age of Homicide Victims and Offenders, 2016

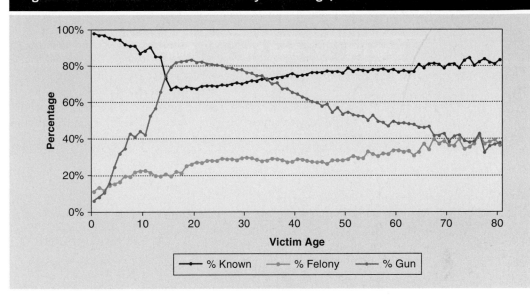

Figure 2.5 Homicide Characteristics by Victim Age, 2000–2016 Combined

of murders resulting from robberies and other attacks by strangers increases, while the number of murders resulting from interpersonal disputes declines.

Some criminologists have noted that the elderly have the highest levels of fear of violence yet the lowest risk of victimization. Their low victimization rate results, however, from the fact that senior citizens are rarely killed by family members and often live alone with few occasions for engaging in deadly disputes. By contrast, elders have relatively high rates of felony-murder victimization (47% of homicide victims over age 65 are killed in felony-related incidents, compared with only 25% of victims younger than 65), often dying in attacks that younger victims would survive. Thus, the fears of elders may not be as irrational as many observers have suggested.[12]

DIFFERENCES BY LOCATION

Besides patterns in terms of race, sex, and age, homicides vary considerably by location, specifically urbanicity and geographic region. As noted earlier, most of the recent shifts (upward and then downward) in homicide rates occurred in larger U.S. cities (those with populations over 250,000) rather than small cities, suburbs, or rural communities. Table 2.6 shows that urban areas also tend to be overrepresented in homicides that are gang related, drug related, and gun related. By contrast, homicides in the family, including infanticides and killings by romantic intimates, as well as murders on the job are spread more evenly across location types, with particular prevalence in the suburbs.

Table 2.7 displays the 2016 homicide rates for the nation's largest municipalities (with at least 25 homicides during the year and populations over 300,000). The list of 48 cities reflects wide variability, from a high of 59.8 per 100,000 for St. Louis to a low of 3.5 per 100,000 for San Diego. Together these cities represent about one-sixth, or 15%, of the U.S. population, yet accounted for 36% of the nation's murders in 2016.

Table 2.6   Location Differences by Homicide Type, 2000–2016 Combined

	Location			
	Large City	**Small City**	**Suburban**	**Rural**
All homicides	54.4%	12.9%	24.5%	8.2%
Intimate	35.1%	14.8%	34.6%	15.4%
Family	32.7%	14.0%	37.1%	16.2%
Infanticide	42.3%	16.2%	30.4%	11.0%
Eldercide	37.3%	13.7%	33.9%	15.2%
Felony-murder	49.2%	13.3%	30.1%	7.4%
Sex-related	46.8%	15.6%	25.1%	12.5%
Drug-related	57.9%	11.5%	22.8%	7.7%
Gang-related	72.0%	11.3%	15.9%	0.7%
Argument	49.8%	13.7%	24.9%	11.6%
Workplace	34.0%	10.1%	38.9%	17.0%
Gun homicide	58.2%	12.0%	22.6%	7.2%
Arson	45.8%	15.7%	26.8%	11.8%
Poison	31.0%	18.1%	37.8%	13.0%
Multiple victims	44.6%	13.1%	30.0%	12.3%
Multiple offenders	54.9%	13.6%	23.5%	8.0%

A certain measure of caution is needed in interpreting the homicide rate of any single jurisdiction for any particular year. Because many cities have homicide counts that are near or below 100 annually, some fluctuation tends to occur over time as a result of various random factors such as how many shooting victims are able to survive their injuries so as not to be among the murder statistics. Table 2.7 is merely a snapshot in time when some cities may have had unusually high murder tolls while others experienced relatively low levels. For example, Kansas City tallied 119 homicides in 2005, a whopping 31% increase over the 91 killings that occurred in 2004. However, such a large one-year change often represents an aberration in local fluctuations rather than a trend. As was predicted, the Kansas City murder tally dropped back to 103 in 2006, a more usual level for the city.[13] The opposite type of statistical swing can also occur. For example, Kansas City enjoyed a 21% drop in homicide from 2013 to 2014 (100 murders down to just 79), but then the tally rebounded to 109 murders in 2015 and 129 in 2016.

In an analysis of city murder trends from 1985 through 2005, Fox showed that whenever a city experiences a sudden spike in murder of 20% or more, there is about a 75% chance that the next year will show an improvement.[14] Called statistical regression to the mean, this phenomenon shows that the more a city's homicide count drifts up or down from its usual level, the more likely it is that the following year will bring a return toward the norm.

In addition to the advised caution in interpreting short-term spikes in local homicide counts, observations concerning city murder statistics need to take into account any special circumstances that might impact significantly on the murder statistics. For example, in 2005, New Orleans was absent from the FBI's city homicide tallies. Notwithstanding the homicides that occurred in the aftermath of Hurricane Katrina, crime statistics were not available for the second half of 2005 for this storm-devastated area. Also experiencing a "Katrina effect" was the city of Houston, which became home to thousands of hurricane evacuees. Houston's homicide tally for 2005 was 23% higher than 2004, largely owing to the nearly 10 killings per month above average that the city experienced in the four months after the catastrophic storm to the east. As a further illustration, in 1995, Oklahoma City ranked at near the top of the list of city homicide rates, but only because its murder toll of 227 included 168 people killed in the bombing at the Alfred P. Murrah Federal Building. By contrast, the FBI decided that the thousands killed on September 11, 2001, in the attack on the World Trade Center would not count toward New York City's murder figures. Regardless of these idiosyncrasies, the data shown in Table 2.7 for 2016 alone do not appear to contain any known irregularities.

Given the extent of variability among cities, many analysts have been tempted to treat crime rankings as measures of comparative safety or dangerousness. The news media, in particular, often attempt to approach these city-by-city rates as indicators of relative security and quality of life. Using homicide rates in this manner, however, is as tricky as it is enticing. These 51 cities vary considerably in terms of both demography (i.e., population characteristics) and geography, making any attempt to identify the safest or deadliest U.S. cities to be problematic, at best.

The most difficult aspect of making sense of city homicide rankings involves the extent to which the municipalities include or exclude suburban communities. New York City, for example, consists of much more than the Manhattan downtown areas; it encompasses residential neighborhoods in Queens and Staten Island. The population in a city like San Antonio may have boomed in recent years, but the million-plus population count is, in large part, a result of sprawling city limits. Cities such as Seattle and Boston are densely populated and urbanized, compared with, for example, Bakersfield. Quite clearly, density and urbanness tend to correlate with crime levels, regardless of overall population count.

In addition to the issue of population density, the use of resident population figures may, in certain cases, distort the homicide victimization rates. Many cities contain large numbers of nonresidents (e.g., commuters, tourists, seasonal visitors, out-of-state college students, and homeless people) who may be at some risk of homicide for certain periods of time yet are excluded from the population base used in calculating the city's homicide rate.

Besides these qualifications, an unusual demographic distribution (by race, sex, or age) can impact a city's murder rate. Most notably, the top 10 cities in Table 2.7 all have high concentrations of black residents. It is not race itself that accounts for this pattern but the socioeconomic conditions that tend to be associated with a sizable minority population. In a study of crime rates in the largest U.S. cities, Cohen, Fox, and Wolfgang found that the strong statistical correlation between violent crime rates and the percentage of blacks in the population vanishes when controlling for the percentage of families below the poverty line, the percentage of children in broken homes, and other dimensions of social disorganization.[15]

Another common approach to analyzing murder rates is to examine variations among states. As shown in Table 2.8, state homicide rates for 2016 ranged from

Table 2.7 City Homicide Rates, 2016

City	Population	Number of Homicides	Homicide Rate
St. Louis	314,507	188	59.8
Baltimore	618,385	318	51.4
Detroit	669,673	303	45.2
New Orleans	397,208	174	43.8
Cleveland	386,227	135	35.0
Memphis	656,434	196	29.9
Chicago	2,725,153	765	28.1
Kansas City	478,364	129	27.0
Milwaukee	600,193	141	23.5
Atlanta	472,579	111	23.5
Washington, D.C.	681,170	138	20.3
Oakland	424,998	85	20.0
Pittsburgh	302,443	57	18.8
Tulsa	405,748	72	17.7
Louisville	683,825	119	17.4
Philadelphia	1,570,826	273	17.4
Indianapolis	866,351	148	17.1
Stockton	308,348	49	15.9
Dallas	1,320,939	171	12.9
Houston	2,334,348	301	12.9
Miami	449,469	55	12.2
Nashville	668,685	81	12.1
Jacksonville	880,557	106	12.0
Oklahoma City	641,681	70	10.9
Albuquerque	561,560	61	10.9
Columbus	862,515	91	10.6
San Antonio	1,498,642	149	9.9
Las Vegas	1,592,178	158	9.9

City	Population	Number of Homicides	Homicide Rate
Phoenix	1,586,611	146	9.2
Bakersfield	378,788	32	8.4
Minneapolis	416,751	35	8.4
Sacramento	495,471	41	8.3
Denver	699,259	57	8.2
Wichita	391,399	31	7.9
Fort Worth	851,849	66	7.7
Tampa	375,904	29	7.7
Charlotte	896,379	67	7.5
Fresno	524,796	39	7.4
Los Angeles	4,007,905	293	7.3
Boston	673,880	49	7.3
Long Beach	476,476	33	6.9
San Francisco	871,155	57	6.5
Omaha	446,163	29	6.5
Tucson	533,663	30	5.6
San Jose	1,041,844	47	4.5
Austin	956,911	39	4.1
New York	8,566,917	335	3.9
San Diego	1,413,414	50	3.5

Source: FBI, *Crime in the United States.*

Note: Includes cities with a population of at least 300,000 and 25 or more homicides.

a high of 11.8 (per 100,000 population) in Louisiana to a low of 1.3 in New Hampshire. As with the city tabulations, these state differences to some extent reflect the degree of urbanness and population density. For example, many of the states near the bottom of the list are fairly rural, sparsely populated, and (with the exception of Hawaii) subject to cold temperatures in the winter months, characteristics that tend to lower the homicide rate. At the same time, some regional differences are fairly significant and hard to miss. For example, 7 of the 10 highest murder-rate states are within the southern region of the nation. As illustrated in Figure 2.6, there are some clearly defined clusters of low and high homicide rate areas within the nation. Specifically, in 2016, the New England, north-central, and northwestern states generally had rates under 3.0 per 100,000,

Table 2.8 State Homicide Rates

State	Population	Homicides	Homicide Rate
Louisiana	4,681,666	554	11.8
Missouri	6,093,000	537	8.8
Alabama	4,863,300	407	8.4
Illinois	12,801,539	1,054	8.2
Maryland	6,016,447	481	8.0
Mississippi	2,988,726	238	8.0
Nevada	2,940,058	224	7.6
South Carolina	4,961,119	366	7.4
Tennessee	6,651,194	486	7.3
Arkansas	2,988,248	216	7.2
Alaska	741,894	52	7.0
North Carolina	10,146,788	678	6.7
New Mexico	2,081,015	139	6.7
Indiana	6,633,053	439	6.6
Georgia	10,310,371	681	6.6
Oklahoma	3,923,561	245	6.2
Michigan	9,928,300	598	6.0
Delaware	952,065	56	5.9
Kentucky	4,436,974	260	5.9
Virginia	8,411,808	484	5.8
Ohio	11,614,373	654	5.6
Arizona	6,931,071	380	5.5
Florida	20,612,439	1,111	5.4
Texas	27,862,596	1,478	5.3
Pennsylvania	12,784,227	661	5.2
California	39,250,017	1,930	4.9
West Virginia	1,831,102	81	4.4
New Jersey	8,944,469	372	4.2
Wisconsin	5,778,708	229	4.0

State	Population	Homicides	Homicide Rate
Kansas	2,907,289	111	3.8
Colorado	5,540,545	204	3.7
Montana	1,042,520	36	3.5
Wyoming	585,501	20	3.4
New York	19,745,289	630	3.2
South Dakota	865,454	27	3.1
Idaho	1,683,140	49	2.9
Oregon	4,093,465	113	2.8
Rhode Island	1,056,426	29	2.7
Washington	7,288,000	195	2.7
Nebraska	1,907,116	49	2.6
Hawaii	1,428,557	35	2.5
Utah	3,051,217	72	2.4
Iowa	3,134,693	71	2.3
Vermont	624,594	14	2.2
Connecticut	3,576,452	78	2.2
North Dakota	757,952	15	2.0
Massachusetts	6,811,779	134	2.0
Minnesota	5,519,952	101	1.8
Maine	1,331,479	20	1.5
New Hampshire	1,334,795	17	1.3

Source: FBI, *Crime in the United States.*

whereas almost all the southern states, especially those in the Deep South, were within the highest rate category (6.0 and higher).

Homicide patterns among states translate, of course, into overall regional differences, as shown in Table 2.9. In relation to population share, homicides are more prevalent in the South, even though the region is not as urbanized as others. Over the 2000–2016 time period, the South was home to 43.8% of all homicides but only 36.8% of the U.S. population. The southern pattern is especially pronounced in gun homicides (44.6%) and is also overrepresented in homicides involving an argument (42.2%) or within the family (43.2%). Figure 2.7 confirms the role of firearms in the higher rate of homicide within the South. As shown, for example, the gun homicide rate for this region (4.3 per 100,000

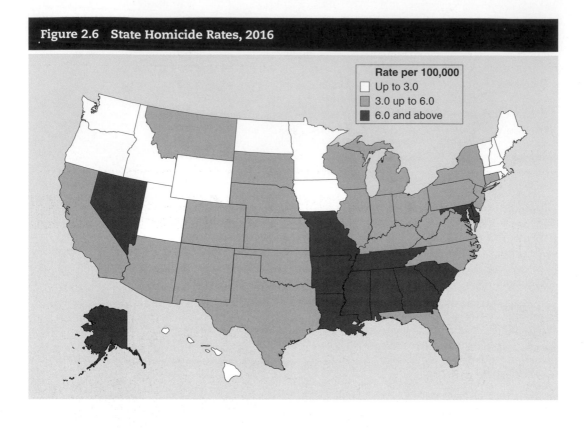

Figure 2.6   State Homicide Rates, 2016

Rate per 100,000
- Up to 3.0
- 3.0 up to 6.0
- 6.0 and above

Table 2.9   Regional Differences by Homicide Type, 2000–2016 Combined

	Region			
	Northeast	**Midwest**	**South**	**West**
All homicides	13.8%	20.6%	43.8%	21.7%
Intimate	13.4%	18.4%	46.2%	22.0%
Family	11.3%	18.1%	48.2%	22.5%
Infanticide	11.8%	22.2%	43.7%	22.4%
Eldercide	13.2%	18.0%	47.0%	21.8%
Felony-murder	15.2%	16.0%	51.8%	16.9%
Sex-related	16.6%	22.5%	33.4%	27.5%
Drug-related	21.7%	22.5%	36.6%	19.2%
Gang-related	5.3%	26.9%	6.9%	60.9%
Argument	15.6%	17.8%	42.2%	24.4%
Workplace	10.5%	21.4%	34.6%	33.5%
Gun homicide	13.0%	21.0%	44.6%	21.3%

	Region			
	Northeast	**Midwest**	**South**	**West**
Arson	20.4%	25.8%	36.8%	17.0%
Poison	21.3%	21.0%	32.6%	25.1%
Multiple victims	11.1%	22.0%	44.9%	22.0%
Multiple offenders	10.5%	23.9%	46.3%	19.2%

Figure 2.7   Homicide Rate by Region and Weapon, 2000–2016 Combined

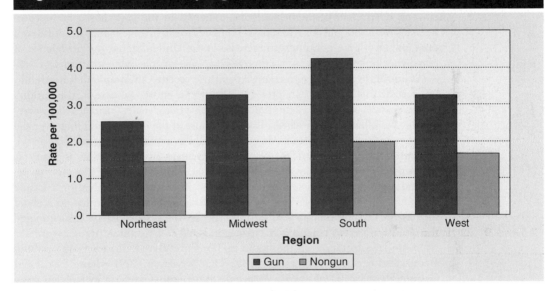

population) is higher than the overall (gun and nongun) rate for the Northeast (4.0 per 100,000 population).

Doerner applied the subculture of violence theory, described earlier, to account for the elevated southern murder rates.[16] That is, in the South where rates of gun ownership are relatively high, violence is often seen as an acceptable way to resolve disagreements. Rather than taking it to court, southern combatants often take it outside, in the long-standing tradition of a duel.

THE ROLE OF FIREARMS

Any discussion of the rate of murder in the United States and how to prevent interpersonal violence must consider the role of guns. Unfortunately, the available gun research is difficult to decipher and is highly charged politically. Regardless of the findings concerning the link between guns and crime and the tone of the debate, few people tend to change their positions.

Do guns cause or at least facilitate homicidal behavior? Are homicidal people more likely to own guns? Should the government limit gun ownership or instead, as John R. Lott Jr. argued in his controversial book, *More Guns, Less Crime*, encourage people to arm themselves? Lott suggested that the loss of lives to gun-involved homicides, suicides, and accidents is not as great as lives saved by the actual use of guns and their deterrent effect. Using many sources of gun data, Lott found no benefits of waiting periods, gun buybacks, or even background checks and suggested that there are clear benefits in states where citizens can carry concealed firearms. Lott's research even suggested that public mass shootings are less likely to occur in places where a citizen victim may be armed.[17] However, Duwe, Kovandzic, and Moody concluded, based on a careful analysis of state-level data for the years 1977–1999, that "right to carry" laws neither increased nor decreased the risk of mass shootings in public places.[18] While there is little agreement about what to do with guns in the United States, there is basic consensus about figures on gun ownership. According to a recent Pew Research Center survey, 42% of adults report having a gun in their home, and two-thirds of them indicate owning multiple firearms.[19] There are as many as 300 million guns in the hands of private citizens, nearly half of them handguns. Whereas in the past most purchases of firearms were shotguns or rifles, most gun sales today involve handguns. Although the number of guns continues to increase in the United States, the prevalence of gun ownership has declined; in other words, fewer people own more guns.

Guns have played a significant role in the recent U.S. homicide rate trends. As discussed in depth in Chapter 5, virtually the entire increase in the nation's homicide rate during the late 1980s involved young males, primarily minority youth, who killed using firearms. Likewise, most of the decline in killing over the past decade or so represented a drop specifically in gun-related incidents.

American gun owners may use their firearms in self-defense as many as thousands of times a year (perhaps hundreds of thousands of times or more, depending on which data source one believes). According to the National Crime Victimization Survey (NCVS), would-be assault victims use guns to defend themselves 110,000 times a year. At the other extreme, Gary Kleck has estimated that guns are used to defend U.S. citizens as many as 2.5 million times a year.[20]

Gun laws formerly on the books in Texas prohibited citizens from carrying a concealed firearm. As a result, on the October day in 1991 when 35-year-old George Hennard Jr. massacred 23 people at a Luby's Cafeteria in Killeen, none of the patrons had possession of a gun. Suzanna Gratia Hupp helplessly watched her mother and father die as Hennard blasted away at a crowd of stunned and helpless customers. In the midst of the carnage, she had a clear shot at the assailant and reached for her purse to get her gun. But Hupp soon realized her gun was appropriately locked safely away in her car.

Believing to this day that she or some other customer might have been able to overtake the gunman, if licensed gun owners had been allowed to have guns in restaurants or other public places, she became an outspoken and forceful advocate for concealed weapons laws. Hupp suggested that gun-free zones, such as schools and day care centers, are especially attractive to mass murderers because there they can kill people "like fish in a barrel." Riding a wave of publicity following the Luby's murders, Hupp became the first Texan to be awarded a lifetime membership in the National Rifle Association. She traveled far and wide to push an anti–gun control agenda and was later elected to the Texas legislature largely based on her visibility on the gun issue.[21]

It is easy to cite cases, like the Luby's mass murder, in which a gun may have prevented enormous bloodshed. On the other hand, research has also shown that the presence of a gun in the home tends to increase the risk of a family-related homicide or suicide.[22] As with most areas of debate in regard to crime control strategies, there are few clear-cut answers.

Public policy recommendations regarding guns run the continuum from a total ban on private ownership to encouraging all adult Americans to carry a firearm. The 1993 Brady Law, which mandated background checks and initial waiting periods, may or may not have had the desired effect on gun crimes; there is evidence on both sides of the argument. Other gun control strategies include reducing the supply and availability of guns, limiting who can own guns (e.g., restricting convicted felons, domestic abusers, and the mentally ill from purchasing guns), and controlling how or where guns may be used (e.g., banning guns in certain places and requiring trigger locks). Such strategies may help to keep guns away from the small proportion of gun owners who choose to use their guns to commit murder.

Even if a jurisdiction maintains and enforces strict gun laws, it may still experience a significant problem related to gun violence. For example, until 2008, when the U.S. Supreme Court ruled (in *District of Columbia v. Heller*) that the Washington, D.C., gun ban was unconstitutional, the nation's capital had had a substantially higher percentage of gun homicides than the country overall (73% vs. 64%). However, although Washington, D.C., tightly restricted gun ownership, the jurisdiction is surrounded by areas with less restrictive gun regulations, specifically Maryland and Virginia. The overriding conclusion of this murky relationship between gun availability and gun crime is that, even though guns increase the lethality of criminal assaults, the nation's high homicide rate is larger than a matter of guns.

Since the early 1980s, Chicago also employed a blanket ban on handguns, although this prohibition was similarly determined by the Supreme Court, in the 2010 *McDonald v. City of Chicago* decision, to violate the Second Amendment right to bear arms for sake of self-protection. Notwithstanding the constitutional question, the ban was estimated to have resulted in anywhere between 677 and 942 fewer gun homicides within the city over the quarter century in which the ban was in force.[23]

The two landmark gun decisions handed down by the nation's highest court may prove to impact the homicide rate in Washington, D.C., Chicago, and potentially elsewhere to the extent that the principles are applied more widely. Some observers expect that the effect will be an increase in murders if more citizens keep a gun in their home, whereas others anticipate a lower death toll if private citizens arm themselves for self-protection. Only time will tell.

CHANGING PATTERNS IN HOMICIDE

The age, race, and gender patterns described thus far are based primarily on the years 2000 through 2016, a time frame when homicide rates were relatively level. Earlier decades, however, had shown some large fluctuations in the murder rate that were associated with significant shifts in the characteristics of victims, perpetrators, and the crimes themselves.

Table 2.10 displays percentage breakdowns of victim and offender demographics and other key factors across several time periods: 1976–1985, 1986–1995 (when the homicide rate was elevated), 1996–2005 (when the homicide rate was declining), and 2006–2016. One of the more noteworthy areas of change involves the age distribution of victims and offenders. As noted earlier, the percentage of juvenile killers peaked during the 1990s (especially the early part of that decade), and the same held true for young victims, particularly in light of the similarity in the ages of murderers and their victims.

Table 2.10 Long-Term Changes in Homicide Patterns

		Years			
		1976–1985	1986–1995	1996–2005	2006–2016
Victim age	<18	6.9%	9.3%	10.3%	9.9%
	18–24	22.5%	24.2%	25.4%	24.4%
	25–34	30.2%	29.6%	25.5%	26.3%
	35–49	22.2%	22.4%	24.6%	22.7%
	50+	18.1%	14.5%	14.1%	16.8%
Offender age	<18	8.3%	12.7%	9.8%	7.8%
	18–24	32.4%	35.7%	39.8%	37.5%
	25–34	31.7%	28.3%	25.7%	28.3%
	35–49	18.6%	17.0%	18.1%	17.6%
	50+	9.0%	6.4%	6.6%	8.8%
Victim sex	Male	77.6%	77.3%	77.3%	79.1%
	Female	22.4%	22.7%	22.7%	20.9%
Offender sex	Male	86.7%	90.2%	90.8%	90.5%
	Female	13.3%	9.8%	9.2%	9.5%
Victim race	White	55.3%	48.6%	49.0%	47.2%
	Black	42.8%	48.7%	47.6%	49.4%
	Other	2.0%	2.7%	3.4%	3.4%
Offender race	White	49.9%	43.6%	44.2%	42.9%
	Black	48.1%	53.8%	52.6%	54.3%
	Other	2.0%	2.6%	3.2%	2.8%
Weapon	Gun	62.3%	65.2%	65.8%	68.5%
	Knife	19.9%	16.5%	13.1%	12.3%
	Other	17.8%	18.3%	21.1%	19.2%
Relationship	Intimate	16.4%	13.7%	13.5%	13.3%
	Family	10.5%	9.5%	10.9%	12.4%
	Acquaintance	48.7%	52.6%	49.8%	48.5%
	Stranger	24.5%	24.3%	25.8%	25.8%
Circumstances	Felony	21.7%	28.0%	27.7%	27.9%
	Argument	54.0%	49.7%	45.7%	39.7%
	Other	24.2%	22.3%	26.6%	32.4%

Also striking is the gradually widening gender gap in terms of perpetrators, with the percentage of male offenders rising from 86.7% in 1976–1985 to 90.5% more recently. Notwithstanding the media focus on increasing levels of violence exhibited by females, at least in terms of lethal violence, males are even more prevalent than ever. In addition, the predominance of blacks among the victims and perpetrators has, for the most part, increased over recent decades.

There have also been shifts in patterns of weapon use, victim–offender relationship, and circumstances. Since 1976, the role of guns has expanded, homicides have involved fewer intimate partners and slightly more strangers, and the percentage of episodes arising spontaneously from an argument has steadily diminished. To a large extent, however, these changes in weapon use, victim–offender relationship, and homicide circumstances have resulted because of trends in the age, sex, and race distribution of murderers.

Chicken Little and the Ferguson Defect

"The sky is falling! The sky is falling!" proclaimed Chicken Little in the classic folktale about mass hysteria. Along her journey to inform the king of the impending doom, the panicky bird convinced her friends Henny Penny, Ducky Lucky, Goosey Loosey, and Turkey Lurkey that their lives were in danger.

A similar story, although one that involved real people and real hysteria, took place in 2015 sparked by an opinion column in the May 29, 2015, edition of the *Wall Street Journal* by conservative political commentator Heather Mac Donald, called "The New Nationwide Crime Wave."[24] Noting increases in shootings and homicides during the first part of 2015 in cities such as Baltimore, New York, and Chicago, Mac Donald speculated that the police had grown gun-shy in the face of "Black Lives Matter" protests in Ferguson, Missouri, and elsewhere following controversial slayings of blacks by officers in blue. Labeling it the "Ferguson Effect," she suggested that the police were becoming passive in carrying out their patrols, less apt to confront situations for fear of reprisal. Better to avoid situations that might lead to suspension from the force or, worse, criminal charges. As a result, according to Mac Donald, criminals were having a field day as the cops were standing down.

As evidence, Mac Donald cited recent crime spikes in various cities around the country, including New York, Baltimore, and Chicago, yet failed to note places where crime levels remained unchanged or were even down. She also relayed comments from the front line, including one NYPD officer who said, "Any cop who uses his gun now has to worry about being indicted and losing his job and family." Whether that sentiment reflected the prevailing view of among all cops in New York and elsewhere remained in doubt.

The theory gathered momentum rather quickly, with an assist from countless newspaper and television journalists. Even James Comey, then FBI director, provided some support during an October 2015 speech in Chicago, the epicenter of the concern for out-of-control lawlessness. When asked directly about the Ferguson Effect, the nation's top law enforcement official responded, "I don't know whether this explains it entirely, but I do have a strong sense that some part of the explanation is a chill wind blowing through American law enforcement over the last year. And that wind is surely changing behavior."[25]

Despite its seductive ring, the Ferguson Effect was based largely on anecdotal evidence, selective testimonials, and cherry-picked statistics. The hard facts, however, failed to provide much support. Although murder rates were up in certain cities, such as New York, the increase was from a level that was significantly lower than years gone by. With murder rates at a 50-year low, it was not unexpected to see some bounce back. In addition, although murder rates were up in some cities, they continued to be low or even lower in many others.

At the end of his journey, Chicken Little encountered Foxy Loxy, who helped his friend to see that it was only an acorn, not the entire sky, that had fallen. Similarly, although New York City had witnessed a 19.5% spike in murder during the first part of 2015, by year's end that increase was only 5.7%. In 2016, moreover, the murder count dropped back down, to just slightly above the record low that had been set in 2014.

The case of New York City is not unique. A July 2017 report from the Vera Institute notes that "over-generalization from partial-year data on homicides in a small sample of major U.S. cities led to premature conclusions being drawn about a nationwide reversal of the general decline in violent crime." The Vera report then concluded, "Violent crime remains near its lowest point in decades and fears of a new violent crime wave are unfounded. Crime rates fluctuate over time and it is important that any discussion of statistics on violent crime takes account of these natural variations."[26]

The Ferguson Effect was very much a speculative overreaction to a short-term bump in crime—more like a Ferguson Defect. The lesson is clear: A one-year increase in crime does not constitute a trend.

BREAKING THE MOLD

Despite all the patterns in murder victimization and offending described in this chapter, many homicides still run counter to the norm (i.e., young black males killing other young males with guns). For example, Philip Markoff, a promising medical student, murdered a call girl he met through a Craigslist ad and later, while awaiting trial, committed suicide with a razor blade, using his own blood to scrawl his ex-fiancé's name on the wall of his jail cell. Aileen Wuornos was executed in October 2002 by the state of Florida because she killed seven strangers in the style of male serial killers such as Theodore Bundy. In the small town of Plainfield, Wisconsin, Edward Gein was in his 50s when he began committing a hideous series of crimes, including murder, cannibalism, grave robbing, and necrophilia. Most of the recent multiple shootings in schools around the country have been committed by white youngsters in suburban or small towns. Incidents like these help to make the study of homicide ever fascinating and challenging. The challenge, and the focus of the chapters to follow, is to make sense out of seemingly senseless acts of murder.

ENDNOTES

1. Matthew Friedman, Ames Grawert, and James Cullen, *Crime Trends: 1990–2016* (New York: Brennan Center for Justice, April 18, 2017).

2. Charles Derber, *The Wilding of America: How Greed and Violence Are Eroding Our Nation's Character* (New York: St. Martin's Press, 1996).

3. Art Swift, "Americans' Perceptions of U.S. Crime Problem Are Steady," *Gallup News*, November 9, 2016.

4. Sarah Eschholz, Matthew Mallard, and Stacey Flynn, "Images of Prime Time Justice: A Content Analysis of 'NYPD Blue' and 'Law & Order,'" *Journal of Criminal Justice and Popular Culture* 10 (2004): 161–180.

5. William Julius Wilson, *The Truly Disadvantaged: The Inner City, the Underclass and Public Policy* (Chicago: University of Chicago Press, 1987).

6. David Pritchard and Karen D. Hughes, "Patterns of Deviance in Crime News," *Journal of Communication* 47 (1997): 49–67.

7. Freda Adler, *Sisters in Crime: The Rise of the New Female Criminal* (New York: McGraw-Hill, 1975); Rita James Simon, *Women and Crime* (Lexington, MA: Lexington Books, 1975).

8. Patricia Pearson, *When She Was Bad: Violent Women and the Myth of Innocence* (New York: Viking Press, 1997).

9. Jessica M. Pollak and Charis E. Kubrin, "Crime in the News: How Crimes, Offenders, and Victims Are Portrayed in the Media," *Journal of Criminal Justice and Popular Culture* 14 (2007): 59–83.

10. Peter Elikann, *Superpredators: The Demonization of Our Children by the Law* (New York: Plenum Press, 1999).

11. William J. Bennett, John J. DiIulio, and John P. Walters, *Body Count: Moral Poverty and How to Win America's War Against Crime and Drugs* (New York: Simon and Schuster, 1996), 27.

12. James Alan Fox and Jack Levin, "Homicide Against the Elderly: A Research Note," *Criminology* 28 (1991): 317–327.

13. Christine Vendel, "You Still Have a Problem," *Kansas City Star*, January 1, 2007, p. A1.

14. James Alan Fox, "Roasting Chicken Little: Epidemic Thinking About Crime" (Paper presented at the 113th Annual Meeting of the International Association of Chiefs of Police, Boston, MA, October 16, 2006).

15. Bernard Cohen, James Alan Fox, and Marvin E. Wolfgang, *The Memphis and Shelby County Crime Report, 1996* (Memphis, TN: Guardsmark, 1996).

16. William G. Doerner, "A Regional Analysis of Homicide Rates in the United States," *Criminology* 13 (1975): 90–101.

17. John R. Lott Jr., *More Guns, Less Crime: Understanding Crime and Gun Control Laws* (Chicago: University of Chicago Press, 1998).

18. Grant Duwe, Tomislav Kovandzic, and Carlisle E. Moody, "The Impact of Right-to-Carry Concealed Firearm Laws on Mass Public Shootings," *Homicide Studies* 6 (2002): 271–296.

19. Pew Research Center, June 2017, "America's Complex Relationship with Guns."

20. Gary Kleck, *Point Blank: Guns and Violence in America* (Hawthorne, NY: Aldine de Gruyter, 1991).

21. Suzanna Gratia Hupp, *From Luby's to the Legislature: One Woman's Fight Against Gun Control* (San Antonio, TX: Privateer Press, 2010).

22. Linda L. Dahlberg, Robin M. Ikeda, and Marcie-Jo Kresnow, "Guns in the Home and Risk of a Violent Death in the Home: Findings From a National Study," *Journal of Epidemiology* 160 (2004): 929–936.

23. James Alan Fox and Jack Levin, Brief and Appendix of Professors of Criminal Justice as Amici Curiae in Support of Respondents, *McDonald et al. v. City of Chicago et al.*, U.S. Supreme Court, No. 08-1521, January 6, 2010.

24. Heather Mac Donald, "The New Nationwide Crime Wave," *Wall Street Journal*, May 29, 2015.

25. David A. Graham, "The FBI Director's Troubling Comments on the 'Ferguson Effect,'" *Atlantic*, October 26, 2015.

26. Bruce Frederick, *Measuring Public Safety: Responsibly Interpreting Statistics on Violent Crime* (New York: Vera Institute of Justice, 2017).

CHAPTER THREE

EXPLAINING THE WILL TO KILL

Whereas legal scholars debate issues of intent and criminal responsibility in homicide cases, criminologists tend to take a different approach. They seek to answer the question: Why do people kill one another?

The major schools of thought regarding the causes of crime, and thus the causes of homicide, have included supernatural, free will, biological, psychological, and sociological explanations. Is violence an inherent aspect of human nature? Do some people have violent genes? Or, do we learn it from others? Is it simply a product of a choice made by the murderer? Is it the result of poor parenting or inferior schooling?

Society cannot make informed policy decisions and create successful violence intervention and prevention programs without first attempting to understand the causes of violent behavior. If homicidal acts are learned and reinforced in social settings such as the family or schools, prevention policies will be very different from those that are appropriate if the primary causes of violence are biological.

Once we begin to explain acts of murder, we come to some inevitable questions: Does explanation translate to justification? At what point, if ever, does the cause of a behavior become an excuse? At what point, for example, does abuse or neglect experienced by the offender actually reduce criminal responsibility? In 2003, the U.S. Supreme Court vacated the death sentence of Kevin Wiggins because of the incompetence of his attorneys. The justices felt that competent attorneys would have presented information regarding Wiggins's "excruciating" childhood. Their decision was that if the lawyers had properly included this information in his defense, Wiggins might not have received a death sentence for his crimes. So, even if an explanation of an individual's behavior does not affect the decision of guilt or innocence, it may still be relevant in determining the severity of the punishment.

Although focused on homicidal behavior, this chapter will include theories that more broadly explain violent behavior rather than just those violent events that end in death. Except for the life or death consequences, there is often little difference between homicide and aggravated assault. One crime ends in death and the other does not, often because of proximity to hospitals or police personnel, choice of weapon, or the presence of bystanders. These two crimes have similar offender and victim race, class, gender, and age characteristics.[1] Therefore, the same theories may be helpful in explaining both types of violent crime.

Also, as you make your way through the various types of theories, consider how these factors explain why American homicide rates continue to be higher than most other democratized countries. In *American Homicide*, Randolph Roth suggests that American crime rates are in large part a function of weak public faith in government and little trust in elected officials. Roth suggests that as public sentiments change over time and place, so does the U.S. homicide rate.[2] Other researchers have tried to explain the American murder phenomenon with historical variables such as population mobility, weak government, the history of violence associated with slavery (particularly in the South), and an American tolerance of murder as illustrated by low conviction rates for U.S. homicides as opposed to European conviction rates.[3] Are Americans less civilized than citizens of other democracies? Were the early American immigrants a particularly violent lineage?

THE DEVIL MADE ME DO IT

Only since the late 1800s has our approach to criminal violence been informed by scientific criminological theories. Before that, there were two major schools of thought about the causes of criminal behavior. For most of human history, society accepted supernatural or spiritual explanations.[4] Whether the crime was stealing a goat or murdering a neighbor, the explanation was the same: demonic possession. The punishments were the same also—both theft and murder and many other crimes were punishable by death.

The supernatural phase of explanation left a legacy of irrationality, resulting in thousands of witch hunts and executions. Some sources report that by the end of the 1600s, hundreds of thousands of people had been executed throughout the world because they were believed to be inhabited by evil spirits. Often these executions included torture, such as burning at the stake or boiling in oil, in part to extract a confession or an admission of consorting with the Devil.

By the mid-eighteenth century, the supernatural phase of explanation and its history of chaos, injustice, and torture gave way to the classical school of thought based on the presumption of free will—in other words, assuming that people are responsible for their decisions and their actions. Yet, to some extent, the Devil or other "evil spirit" explanations of homicidal behavior are still with us. Several recent cases have included claims of evil spirits and exorcism as the justification for a homicide. Rayoung Kim, 18, died after beatings and asphyxiation that occurred during religious prayers to drive out evil spirits. Kim's mother, along with others, allegedly participated in the events leading to her daughter's death. In another case, numerous human bite marks, broken bones, multiple skull fractures, brain injuries, a torn liver, detached retinas, and abrasions covered the body of 13-month-old Amora Carson after her mother and the mother's boyfriend, both 20, allegedly killed the baby during a 2008 exorcism. Little Amora was also allegedly sexually assaulted with a pipe wrench. The defendants apparently decided on a "do-it-yourself" exorcism after they failed to raise the money to hire an exorcist. Due to the extensive nature of the injuries, the medical examiner was unable to determine the exact cause of death, but the manner of death was ruled a homicide. Amora's mother was sentenced to life without parole and her boyfriend was sentenced to death row in Texas. These are only two of many U.S. cases over the past few years where attempted exorcisms of evil spirits resulted in brutal homicides. Claims of satanic influence ("the Devil made me do it") continue to be present in many U.S. murder cases each year and remain a convenient explanation for what we do not understand.

BACK TO THE CLASSICS

In response to the irrationality, anarchy, and injustice of the supernatural phase of explanation and its harsh punishment methods, a school of thought emerged in the eighteenth century that viewed criminal behavior, including homicide, as a product of free will or a rational choice. Marking a return to the principles of early Greek philosophers, the writings of Cesare Beccaria (1738–1794) and Jeremy Bentham (1748–1832) shaped the foundations of the second phase of explanation— classical criminology.[5]

Although the classical school included a number of complexities, its fundamental premise about the cause of criminal behavior was simple: Crime is a rational choice made by the offender, who chooses to kill with free will. Rather than believing that the murderer was a witch or possessed by a demon, classical criminology viewed human beings as possessing mental calculators that they used to determine, "Is this murder worth it? What do I have to lose? And what are the costs versus the gains?" Thus, a murderer would strike when, after evaluating all other options, killing seemed to be the best possible solution, that is, when the crime seemed worth the risk. Government officials believed that in order to prevent crime, criminal codes, laws, and punishments should be created so that each person, knowing the risks, would decide that crime does not pay. For each offense, therefore, there would be a fitting and proportional punishment.

Obviously, many factors such as alcohol, drugs, anger, and mental illness can affect our decisions and choices. The classical school lost favor in part because of its rigid orientation toward punishing the crime and ignoring these individual circumstances. But it also lost momentum when immigration, industrialization, and urbanization during the late 1800s drove crime levels upward. The prevailing view in society was that the classical notions about criminal behavior and punishment were failing.

Although the classical approach was dormant for some time in criminological theory, it made a comeback in the 1970s, retooled as rational choice theory.[6] Are murderers rational? In 1990, 22-year-old Pamela Smart, a media services director at a New Hampshire high school, hired three students (including Billy Flynn, 15, who was her lover) to kill her husband Greg. She was convicted and sentenced to life in prison for this calculated murder. Pamela Smart planned her husband's death in great detail. Her scheme included an affair with a teenage student, a staged burglary, an unlocked front door, disguises, and the decision to use a gun instead of a knife so there would be less blood on her white leather furniture. She even instructed the boys not to kill her husband in front of her beloved Shih Tzu, for fear that it would traumatize the little dog. From Smart's perspective, the murder of her husband was worth about $140,000 in life insurance and the couple's personal property. Smart avoided the death penalty but did receive a life sentence for first-degree murder. Billy Flynn was paroled in 2015 at the age of 41.

Certain parents are so competitive that they are willing to do anything, even commit murder, in order to advance the successes of their children. For 42-year-old Wanda Holloway of Houston, Texas, a murder was worth planning if it meant that her eighth-grade daughter Shanna would get to become a high school cheerleader. Holloway asked Terry Harper, her former brother-in-law, to locate a hit man. Her scheme was to arrange the murder of another girl's mother so that Shanna's chief rival would be too emotionally distraught to try out for the cheerleading squad. For Holloway, a human life was worth trading for a cheerleading spot for her daughter. Fortunately for the intended target, Harper told the police about Wanda

Holloway's devious plot. The "cheerleader mom" was convicted of attempted murder-for-hire but served only 6 months of her 10-year sentence.

Most research on homicides illustrates that they are not planned, premeditated murders but spontaneous, seemingly irrational events. How is it that day-to-day frustration so easily boils over into homicide? Are there factors at work that are not apparent to most of us? In *Seductions of Crime*, Jack Katz suggests that there are benefits of crime, even for what appears to be cold-blooded "senseless" murder.[7] Katz argues that the killers in these cases are often defending their own moral worth and social status, committing murder as a last attempt at gaining respectability in situations where humiliation has turned into rage. These offenders believe they can resolve their humiliation by destroying the source—a wife, a boss, fellow students, or society in general. Katz's research reminds us to consider the emotional benefits of murder that are part of some offenders' crime calculations.

USING SCIENCE TO EXPLAIN VIOLENCE

Emerging in the late nineteenth century, positivism—as reflected in biology, psychology, sociology, and economics—employed scientific observation and measurement to explain criminal behavior. This approach was a shift away from free will and rational choice toward determinism. Positivists believe that external factors cause criminal behavior, including murder. The first positivistic criminological theories were biological, and these were quickly followed by psychological and sociological explanations.

Most of the criminological explanations of homicide are not theories specific to homicide; rather, they are broader, more general explanations of crimes ranging from shoplifting, drug use, and exam cheating to rape and murder. Moreover, even theories that try to explain why people kill aim to address the whole class of events, not just one case. Thus, we do not have a theory about why Ted Bundy was a serial killer (because theories are not designed to explain single cases), but a theory about serial killers, or perhaps, even more broadly, murderers in general, might help to explain the likes of a Ted Bundy.

It is sometimes frustrating that we cannot definitively state what causes crime or violence. Criminology is a "soft" science; there are no certainties, but only likelihoods and probabilities. It is not a certainty that severe child abuse will create a murderer, but abuse is one of many factors that may increase the likelihood that someone will behave violently.

Early Biological Explanations of Criminal Behavior

The earliest biological theories of criminal behavior focused on body constitution, heredity, and intelligence. As early as the eighteenth century, scientific researchers were applying the techniques of physiognomy (the study of facial features) and phrenology (the study of bumps on the head) in search of clues to criminal behavior. Although not noted at the time, phrenology ("skull feeling") presents an interesting causal order problem: Did the bumps on the head cause the homicidal behavior? Or did a history of violent behavior leave the offender with bumps on the head? This "which came first" causal order dilemma haunts a number of early biological studies, including theories about a possible link between violence and testosterone levels or head trauma. But as we will see, more recent, scientifically rigorous studies have been able to study individuals who had no violent history and after sustaining a brain injury subsequently developed antisocial characteristics and behaviors.

The apparent breakthrough to uncovering the secrets of criminal conduct came in 1876, when an Italian physician, Cesare Lombroso, published his famous volume, *The Criminal Man*, advancing the premise of a "born criminal." Lombroso suggested that criminals are atavistic; that is, they are a throwback to an earlier, more primitive evolutionary stage of human development. This notion was influenced heavily by Charles Darwin's 1871 treatise, *The Origins of Man*. Lombroso, in his detailed empirical study of Italian prisoners, noted that criminals show outward signs of their anomalies (known as stigmata), such as long arms, large ears, and sloping foreheads.

Although the theory has long since been discredited, Lombroso's work in criminal anthropology spirited a new tradition of empirical research, in both Europe and the United States, earning him the undisputed title as the father of modern criminology. Many followed Lombroso's lead in trying to expand or refute his theories. Both Richard Dugdale's study of the Jukes family and Henry Goddard's report on the Kallikak clan suggested that criminal tendency, although not necessarily visible from physical characteristics, is an inherited condition that persists through generations of offspring. Even though the work of both Dugdale and Goddard has been rejected as unscientific, the idea that some people "look" like criminals (e.g., profiling) or that some families are genetically predisposed to violence is still part of contemporary thinking about the origin of criminal behavior.

Both Ernst Kretschmer and William Sheldon attempted to use body type and physique as indicators or correlates of various forms of human behavior, including criminality. In the 1940s, Sheldon suggested that the mesomorph somatotype (muscular and athletic) was more likely to be found in populations of violent criminals.

As late as the 1950s, Harvard University researchers Sheldon and Eleanor Glueck were including various body measurements in their multidisciplinary studies of the biological, psychological, and social factors distinguishing delinquents and nondelinquents. Although at the time social scientists sharply criticized the Gluecks for including biological traits among the thousands of variables they examined, years later their work was praised as one of the most significant multidisciplinary efforts ever undertaken to explain crime.[8] The Gluecks did not suffer from disciplinary blinders; they studied biological, psychological, and sociological variables and how they interact to produce criminal behavior.

In another controversial area of biology, researchers in the 1960s purported to demonstrate that inmates in institutions for the criminally insane were significantly more likely to possess the "XYY syndrome." That is, they believed that as many as 100,000 men—so-called Super Males—were inclined to violence by virtue of an extra Y, or male sex, chromosome.[9] The XYY anomaly became a popular explanation for extreme forms of violence after it was erroneously reported that mass murderer Richard Speck possessed the extra Y chromosome. In July 1966, Speck had committed the "crime of the century" when he murdered eight student nurses in their Chicago apartment. Newspaper articles and even some scientific accounts reported that Speck's XYY constitution was apparent in such phenotypical characteristics as facial acne, tallness, long extremities, mild mental retardation, and a history of mental illness.

To this day, high school science teachers occasionally repeat the Richard Speck as Super Male mythology. However, we now know that very few violent criminals possess an extra Y chromosome. Those who actually have this genetic abnormality may be treated more harshly and be more likely institutionalized, often simply because of their abnormally awkward and substantial physical features. Thus, the disproportionate presence of XYYs in institutions for the criminally insane may be more a function of the way they look than the way they act.

This is not to say that chromosomes are unimportant in explaining differences in homicidal proneness. Clearly, males have a far greater propensity for committing senseless and extreme acts of violence than do females, a fact that seems to hold true almost universally across virtually all cultures and time periods. Thus, it is more accurately the normal Y chromosome (the 46th or male chromosome), not the extra Y (the 47th or Super Male chromosome), that might make the vital difference.

Whatever momentum the biological school of criminological theory had retained went on life support during the sociologically dominated, humanistic climate of the 1960s. Actually, for most of the twentieth century, the field of criminology was biophobic. In more contemporary times, however, the biological approach (not nearly as dogmatic and narrow as in Lombroso's day) appears to have been resuscitated with the aid of new ideas and new technologies, allowing us to probe deeply into the bodies and brains of violent criminals. Modern biosocial theories of crime integrate biological variables such as learning disabilities, food allergies, neurological problems, and genetics within the social contexts of family structure, childrearing, abuse, and other factors.

Modern Biosocial Theory and Neurocriminology

In a four-year longitudinal study of antisocial boys, researchers at the University of Chicago Medical School discovered a biological propensity for violence.[10] Boys with histories of starting fights, stealing, carrying weapons, and engaging in forced sexual acts had lower than expected levels of the stress hormone cortisol (a hormone typically released in response to fear) in their saliva. More than one-third of the boys with low cortisol levels were identified by their peers as the "meanest in their class." Some researchers have also connected antisocial criminal behavior with high levels of the male hormone testosterone. Although studies have frequently confirmed this relationship, there is little evidence yet of a strong causal effect of testosterone on the propensity to commit criminal violence.[11] If the findings about testosterone, cortisol, or other important hormones are valid, then at least some violent children may have a biological predisposition for antisocial behavior, even youngsters who grow up in healthy, nonthreatening families. This predisposition may make them less fearful of the possible punishments for their antisocial behavior and also less amenable to counseling or therapy. At the extreme, some of these violent children may be inclined to commit homicide, regardless of the punishment they anticipate. Even if hormones do not have a profound influence on homicidal behavior, there is growing evidence of a biological basis for differences in the propensity for violence.

The Human Brain

Millions of Americans are the victims of some form of brain dysfunction involving epilepsy, learning disabilities, attention-deficit hyperactivity disorder (ADHD), strokes, brain tumors, head injuries, or malnutrition. Clinical studies suggest that certain brain diseases or injuries can result in outbursts of anger and occasionally in episodes of violent behavior. In a Polish study, for example, researchers discovered an organic lesion in the central nervous system in 14 of 24 killers. Gross and Wilson similarly concluded that a large body of evidence points to an association between brain disorders and impulsive violence.[12]

Only days after Richard Speck's mass murder of eight Chicago nurses, Charles Whitman's 1966 University of Texas tower sniper mass murder included 47 gunshot victims, 16 of whom died, including his wife and mother. Whitman's murders are often attributed to a brain tumor that was discovered at autopsy—a brain tumor that supposedly caused him to snap. However, Whitman was not simply the all-American boy who suddenly went berserk. His murders were planned in advance; he had a history of drug abuse, a childhood filled with violence and exposure to guns, and a discharge from the military. Whitman failed in school, at jobs, and in the military. His one major accomplishment was his marksmanship.[13] The extent to which his brain tumor may or may not have played a role in his mass murder plans illustrates the complexities of disentangling biological, psychological, and social sources of homicidal behavior.

Recent work has also illustrated the role of brain-related factors in the histories of homicide *victims*. Swedish researchers compared characteristics of persons killed in homicides to a matched comparison group of people in the general population and found that traumatic brain injury, as well as physical abuse, alcohol dependence, and a criminal lifestyle, for both males and females, increased the risk of being murdered.[14] The study's authors speculated that traumatic brain injury may affect homicide victimization due to behavioral issues such as irritability, agitation, belligerence, and inappropriate social responses on the part of victims. Thus, it appears that traumatic brain injury may play a role in both homicide offending and victimization.

Diana Fishbein's interdisciplinary research illustrates that antisocial behavior, including violence, is a result of various genetic and biological factors but that these factors do not alone cause violence.[15] Rather, they interact with other psychological, environmental, and social conditions to produce aggression. A child born with brain systems that create the need for thrill-seeking and impulsive behavior may, under adverse social conditions, become aggressive. These negative conditions—stressors such as poverty or child abuse—act as triggers for violent behavior. Biological predispositions point to the importance of interdisciplinary work in the study of violence.

Several recent studies have located deficiencies in brain areas that affect impulse control and ethical/moral decision making—factors that could contribute to homicidal impulses.[16] Some important recent biological advancements focus on the amygdala, which plays a significant role in emotional processing. Studies suggest that psychopaths may have abnormal amygdala function. Psychopaths have limited startle responses and are more insensitive to pain. They are less likely to be able to read emotional cues from others (e.g., fear, anger, disgust), and they lack empathy.

Damage in another part of the brain, the orbitofrontal cortex located in the prefrontal cortex, can also influence our ability to control our emotions. Raine's important work on the magnetic resonance imaging (MRI) results of psychopath brains as compared to normal brains found much less gray matter in the prefrontal cortex of the psychopaths. In addition, they have lower heart rates and anxiety and less fear of apprehension and punishment.[17] Thus, whether it is in the amygdala or prefrontal cortex, the decision-making processes and moral compass of psychopaths can be explained, at least in part, by their dysfunctional brains.

This Is Your Brain on Drugs

Presenting a new twist to the "drugs cause crime" argument, various psychiatric drugs widely prescribed to treat depression and attention deficit disorder (ADD) have recently been suspected of triggering murderous behavior by altering the brain's biology. As discussed in greater detail in Chapter 9, Joseph Wesbecker, on the morning of September 14, 1989, went on a 20-minute rampage at the Standard Gravure printing plant in Louisville, Kentucky, where he had worked as a pressman for over two decades. Opening fire with an AK-47 assault weapon, Wesbecker shot to death eight of his coworkers and then took his own life. Some people tried to blame Wesbecker's deadly outburst on his long-standing struggle with depression. Others placed the blame squarely on the antidepressant Prozac, which he had been taking for several weeks prior to the massacre.

Besides Wesbecker, there is a long list of other high-profile killers who were treated with psychiatric medications just before they committed senseless murders. On September 27, 1997, Sam Manzie, a 15-year-old boy from Freehold, New Jersey, who was being treated with the antidepressant Paxil, raped and strangled to death an 11-year-old boy in his neighborhood. On May 20, 1999, T. J. Solomon, a 15-year-old student at Heritage High School in Georgia, who was taking Ritalin, opened fire on his classmates, wounding six of them. On May 21, 1998, Kip Kinkel, a 14-year-old boy from Springfield, Oregon, who took both Ritalin and Prozac, killed his parents and then launched a shooting spree through his high school. On April 20, 1999, 18-year-old Eric Harris of Littleton, Colorado, who was taking the antidepressant Luvox, teamed up with his friend Dylan Klebold to perpetrate a horrific rampage at Columbine High School, killing 12 students and a teacher.

The Citizens Commission on Human Rights International is a nonprofit mental health industry watchdog group concerned about the effects of antidepressants and other drugs. They list nearly 30 cases of murders and murder-suicides committed by individuals on psychiatric drugs.[18] We should therefore be wary of the possible effects on behavior of brain-altering psychiatric medicines. Still, the case might be stronger if it were not for the fact that killers who were being treated at the time they committed murder typically had many of the usual warning signs associated with such crimes.

In some cases, there was good reason why a psychiatrist had prescribed a psychotropic drug: The killer had been profoundly depressed, disappointed, and discouraged about the future. Moreover, the actions of some killers who commit a rampage are typically neither episodic nor spontaneous. Whatever role Prozac may have had in lifting the weight of depression and enabling him to take action, Wesbecker began preparing for mass murder by purchasing guns and making hit lists six months before starting the medication. At most, the drug may have reduced his inhibitions, but it hardly inspired him to kill. The Prozac controversy surrounding cases like Wesbecker's shooting spree affirms the importance of establishing causal order when attempting to explain how various factors may cause a murder. But in other cases, where there was no threat of harm to others or self-harm until after the person began taking psychiatric medicines, we should consider the possible dangerous effects of psychotropic drugs.

Genetics

Barbara Oakley's book *Evil Genes: Why Rome Fell, Hitler Rose, Enron Failed, and My Sister Stole My Mother's Boyfriend* describes the impact of genetics on our neurobiology and how genes affect our tendencies toward selfishness and sociopathy. Oakley's argument suggests that some people may be inclined to take advantage of others or be "born bad" as a result of personality disorders that were present at birth. What does this suggest about the policy implications of preventing the biologically challenged from wreaking havoc on others?[19]

Although the extra Y chromosome theory was mostly media hype, recent research on the genetic influence of chromosomes is promising. Because males only have one X chromosome, if that chromosome has a mutated gene, men are stuck with the dysfunctional copy, whereas women have a back-up copy that protects against this problem. Consider the *MAOA* (monoamine oxidase A) gene, located on the X chromosome. The MAOA protein helps the body metabolize and control chemical messengers called neurotransmitters. Those who are unable to make the MAOA protein can suffer from borderline intellectual disability, a lack of impulse control, aggression, and violent behavior.[20] More commonly, people can inherit a form of the gene that is less effective in producing the MAOA protein and has been linked to violence. For example, one recent study found that a variant of the *MAOA* gene that is less effective in producing protein contributes to an increased likelihood of violent behavior, but only when the person has experienced childhood abuse or maltreatment.[21] And although still in their infancy as a legal defense, genetic influences are now being introduced as mitigating circumstances in murder cases, with varying results.[22] In the first-ever sentence reduction in a European court, an Italian appellate court reduced the sentence of convicted murderer Abdelmalek Bayout due to his low-activity *MAOA* gene. The sentence was reduced from 12 years to 9 years, so, although he was viewed as responsible for his behavior, the mitigating circumstance of having an aggressive gene mattered at sentencing.

Genes are linked to antisocial behavior and empathy, but these traits interact with the environment.[23] Some people's DNA may lead them to seek out dangerous, exciting environments, thus reinforcing the genetic effect. Genes don't determine behavior by themselves; rather, it is the combination of genetics and life events and situations that may contribute to violent behavior.

Killer Instincts?

Combining both biological and psychological approaches, proponents of the field of ethology (the study of animals in their natural environment) also support the existence of an aggressive instinct—a natural urge to be violent and commit murder. Prominent ethologist and Nobel Prize winner Konrad Lorenz presented a large amount of evidence that animals are aggressive by nature.[24] He described, for example, the battles between male animals as they compete for females and the defensive behavior of a group of animals whose territory is invaded by another creature of the same species. He described the massacre that ensues when different colonies of insects or rodents are mixed together: They literally tear one another apart.

Lorenz argued that because humans evolve from violent animals, they must have inherited their destructive dispositions. Denying the possibility that behavior is primarily a reaction to environmental conditions, he asserted instead that it results from internal and spontaneous forces. External stimulation is often unnecessary. Lorenz assumed that aggression gives animals an advantage in the struggle for survival. He assumed further that human violence could be explained in the same way.

The Future of Biological Explanations of Homicidal Behavior

Technological advancements in brain scans and DNA analysis now present scientific evidence that the brains of killers are physically as well as genetically different. Interestingly, the research suggests that even though you may have brain deficiencies and genetic predispositions toward violence, these biological tendencies may not be triggered unless you are exposed to abuse or violence in childhood. This suggests, yet again, that biology is not destiny and highlights the importance of considering biological, psychological, and social factors when trying to understand why offenders kill.

The early policy recommendations of biological sources of crime, including plans for "weeding out the defectives," were immoral and frightening. The early Lombrosian and inheritance theorists supported eugenics—the idea that some people would need to be sterilized or even euthanized because of their biological deficiencies. Although modern biological policy responses to aggression include less offensive treatments, such as drugs and even vitamins, the dangerous notions of preventing violence by selective breeding, sterilization, castration, or euthanasia emphasize the importance of linking theory with sensible public policy. More recent and reasonable biosocial policy interventions include various chemotherapies (e.g., hormones, antidepressants, anticonvulsants), substance abuse treatment, and family and individual therapies. However, even these policy responses come with serious questions: Can we require people to be medicated? Can we medicate them involuntarily?

Another critical policy question spawned by biological theories of violence is that if the offender is a victim of a biological abnormality, to what extent should he or she be held accountable for criminal acts? Although the public may recognize the facilitating role played by various biological predispositions toward aggression, most people still want the offender to be punished, and they still believe the offender made a choice. Some integrated theories of crime are sensitive to these issues by blending various biological, psychological, and sociological variables along with a component of individual choice.[25] Generally, a brain disorder cannot fully explain why a vengeful husband methodically plans the murder of his wife or why the members of an organized hate group commit a series of murders and robberies in the hope of inciting a race war; however, it may help to explain their predisposition toward pursuing violent solutions. As our scientific understanding of the brain increases, we may modify the extent to which we think people have free will. Hopefully, as we accumulate information about the control our genes and brains have over our behavior, we can also discover ethical ways to control our brains.

PSYCHOLOGICAL EXPLANATIONS

Biological, psychological, and sociological theories can be difficult to disentangle. For example, what causes someone to be a psychopath or a sociopath, and what's the difference between the two? What is the role of personality disorders such as narcissism, histrionic, borderline, schizoid, and antisocial personality disorders? Whereas biologists might point to the role of hormones, cortisol, the amygdala, or adrenalin in the development of the antisocial personality disorder (i.e., sociopathy), some psychologists have long argued instead that antisocial behavior, and especially homicidal proneness, has its roots in early childhood.[26] Are most murderers mentally ill? If so, what kinds of mental illnesses do they tend to have? And what are the causes of these illnesses? There is some empirical connection between certain mental illnesses and certain kinds of criminal behavior, but the association is far from clear-cut.

Psychosis

Psychosis is a serious form of mental illness in which the individual is out of touch with reality. He or she may be delusional, experience hallucinations, hear voices, and suffer from a profound thought disorder. Most mentally ill individuals, however, even those who suffer from psychosis, are not violent. Still, in a small number of public massacres, paranoid schizophrenia (a type of psychosis) is present in the psychology of the perpetrator. As suggested in Chapter 9, there is some evidence that mass killers James Holmes (who shot to death 12 people at an Aurora, Colorado, cinema), Jared Loughner (who injured Representative Gabby Giffords and killed six others at a Tucson shopping center), and Sylvia Seegrist (who killed three outside a Springfield, Pennsylvania, shopping mall) were diagnosed as suffering from schizophrenia. Still, it should be emphasized that most people who have schizophrenia never kill anyone. In fact, most forms of mental illness (e.g., depression, bipolar disorders, anxiety, phobias) are not associated with violence. Indeed, most mentally ill people never hurt anyone, and their mental illness may make them more vulnerable to victimization, not offending.

A particular type of psychosis has been found in women after they have given birth. Postpartum psychosis (PPP) has been linked to several cases of mothers who murder their children. Andrea Yates, 36, a mother in Texas, drowned her five children, ranging in age from 6 months to 7 years, because, she said, the voice of the Devil commanded her to do so. Like many cases of PPP, Yates had a history of depression, suicide attempts, and other mental health risk factors. While most women who give birth suffer from some degree of depression, 10% to 15% of these women have the more severe PPP. The risk factors for PPP include a personal or family history of mental health issues, such as depression, anxiety, obsessive-compulsive disorder, panic attacks, bipolar disorder, marital conflicts, previous episodes of postpartum depression or psychosis, hormonal risks, and certain characteristics of the baby, including the infant's health, personality, and disability.[27] The homicides of children as a result of the mother's PPP, as with many other forms of mental illness, appear to draw on biological, psychological, and situational forces that come together at the time of the birth to produce a pathological state of mind. More than 15 years after murdering her five children, Yates remains in a mental institution in Texas.

One possible explanation for the link between mental illness and violent behavior, however weak it may turn out to be, has been offered by the research of Bruce Link and his colleagues.[28] This research proposes that psychotic patients are more likely to feel threatened by others, even if there is no actual threat. In addition, if these patients suffer from delusions that they are being persecuted or controlled by others (e.g., they believe that their minds and thoughts are being dominated by forces beyond their control and that there are people who wish to do them harm), they are more likely to engage in violent, aggressive behavior.[29]

Furthermore, the link between mental illness and crime may be indirect. If people suffering from serious mental illness are more likely to self-medicate with drugs and alcohol, it could be that substance abuse is the key to their violent behavior, rather than the mental illness itself. Also, to the extent that both violent behavior and mental illness are linked to such background factors as child abuse, trauma, and neglect, then the apparent association between homicide and mental illness may be spurious or misleading.

Finally, if mental illness were determined to be a strong predictor of violent behavior, then what should our policy response be? Should it be mandatory psychiatric treatment and medication (e.g., chemical lobotomies) for violent offenders? Should these perpetrators be institutionalized in mental hospitals rather than prisons? Should psychopaths be punished?

Sociopaths, Psychopaths, and Personality Disorders

There are differences in the defining characteristics of psychopaths and sociopaths. *Psychopathy* (the term typically used by psychologists) is usually used to emphasize a condition of innate origin and includes biological and psychological traits present at birth (the nature argument). In contrast, the term *sociopathy* emphasizes an external (nurture) source of personality and behavioral traits. For example, some youngsters are so brutalized—physically or sexually abused, neglected, abandoned, or adopted under extremely harsh circumstances—that they fail to develop a capacity to bond with other human beings.[30] In any case, both of these terms have been replaced by the umbrella term *antisocial personality disorder* (APD). While recognizing the subtle differences between them, we use these terms interchangeably and primarily use the term *sociopath*.

Hare developed the Psychopathy Checklist–Revised (PCL-R) to measure both the personality and case history/behaviors of psychopathy.[31] Although counting for as little as 1% of the population, psychopaths may commit over 50% of crimes.[32] Cleckley and, later, McCord and McCord have characterized psychopaths as possessing superficial charm; low anxiety; a lack of remorse, empathy, and insight; impulsivity; aggression; callous disregard for the suffering of other people; and parasitic manipulation of others.[33] As a result, psychopaths are able to kill without the emotional baggage.

Some killers do not score particularly high on the PCL-R, leading some to suggest it is not psychopathy alone that triggers murder but rather elements of psychopathy combined with other personality disorders. Personality disorders identified in the case histories of those who kill include, but are not limited to, narcissistic personality disorder, borderline personality disorder, schizoid personality disorder, and histrionic personality disorder. The *Diagnostic and Statistical Manual of Mental Disorders* includes the following diagnostic criteria and descriptions.[34]

Persons with **narcissistic personality disorder** have grandiose ideas, need excessive admiration, exploit others, and lack empathy. These sufferers of malignant self-love are often arrogant and envious of others and overreact if they believe they have been slighted. They have a sense of entitlement and are often threatened by the successes or possessions of others.

Borderline personality disorder creates instability in personal relationships. The individual often forms intense relationships and then reacts with rage and extreme anger to any sense of real or perceived abandonment. Unlike the narcissist, those with a borderline personality disorder are often suicidal in word or deed. They tend to suffer from self-loathing and feelings of emptiness, and they may also engage in self-damaging impulsive activities, including promiscuous sex, spending, food, or substance use.

Schizoid personality disorder is characterized by detached relationships with others and restricted emotions. Those who suffer from this disorder are often loners, have little interest in sexual activities, have few friends, seem indifferent to praise or criticism, are emotionally cold, and appear not to take pleasure in almost any activity.

Histrionic personality disorder is characterized by constant attention-seeking, excessive emotions, and inappropriate sexual seductiveness. Those who suffer from histrionic personality disorder consider relationships to be more intimate than they really are. They are uncomfortable unless they are the center of attention and have both exaggerated emotional states as well as rapid shifts in emotion.

Also appearing in the case histories of killers are autism spectrum disorders and dissociative identity disorder. **Autism spectrum disorders** (including Asperger's syndrome) are characterized by poor communication skills across multiple settings; poor emotional connections; abnormalities in body language or eye contact; restricted and repetitive patterns of interest, activities, or behavior; and difficulty in initiating or maintaining relationships.[35] Recent research by Allely and colleagues found autism spectrum disorders in more than 10% of serial and mass killers, much higher than in the general population.[36] Serial and mass killers who were highly suspected to have autism spectrum disorders include Theodore Kaczynski, Jeffrey Dahmer, and Dylan Klebold. Those killers who had evidence of both autism spectrum disorders and head injury were of particular interest to researchers.

Dissociative identity disorder, formerly known as multiple personality disorder, is often overdiagnosed and misunderstood. The formal diagnosis requires the formation of at least two distinct personalities that have different moods, memories, and knowledge. The sufferer will often have big gaps of memory loss when one of the personalities is active. This disorder is very rare (less than 2%) and is often a result of severe childhood trauma, including physical and sexual abuse.[37] The literature is filled with claims of dissociative identity disorder that turn out to be iatrogenic; that is, the multiple personalities are created by the very treatments designed to address them. Moreover, some killers have been known to feign dissociative identity disorder in order to plead not guilty by reason of insanity in court.

Even if a killer is diagnosed with any of the many different types of personality disorders, it may not influence how he or she is charged, convicted, or sentenced. In extreme cases, the killer may spend time in a psychiatric institution instead of a prison, but even cannibal killer Jeffrey Dahmer was viewed by the court as not suffering from insanity.

Freud and Psychoanalysis

Illustrating another perspective that is both biological and psychological, Freud embraced the human nature viewpoint when he proposed that people are born with "an active instinct for hatred and destruction."[38] He proposed, in his concept of the "id," that biological urges were expressed from birth on and that the psychosexual stages of development were universally confined to the first five years of life. The psychoanalytic view of human nature suggests that all human beings are predisposed, given particular circumstances, to lash out at other people. But if we as humans have a "killer instinct," how is it that most individuals never succumb to their "natural" tendencies, especially not in the extreme case of committing murder?

Although few practicing criminologists adhere to Freudian traditions, Freudian theory in the form of "bonding" or "attachment therapy" is still a treatment method for troubled children.[39] As is the case with many therapies, positive outcomes are not always the result. In April 2000, 10-year-old Candace Newmaker was smothered during a "rebirthing" session conducted by therapists and her mother. The Freudian-based therapy was intended to give the troubled child a new bond and new beginning with her adoptive mother via the new birth. In this case, a child was suffocated and asphyxiated by five adults who were acting as a quasi–birth canal by crushing the girl with pillows. Two of Candace's therapists were convicted of reckless child abuse in her death, two other who assisted were sentenced to probation and community service, and her mother, who pled guilty to abuse and neglect, received a suspended sentence. Several other children have died from various applications of this pseudoscience of rebirthing or attachment therapy.

Evolutionary Psychology

The work of evolutionary psychologists Daly and Wilson also blends biological and psychological factors. For these researchers, the psychological processes involved in the homicidal act are as much choice as they are a matter of thousands of years of experiences in human decision making. Why do we like sweets? Because thousands of years ago, our ancestors found out that foods with a sweet taste were rich in nutrients. Why are we so threatened by the infidelity of our mate? Is it perhaps because we don't want to spend our time caring for someone else's gene pool? Even personal ads are filled with the request for "no kids." Daly and Wilson's theory would help explain why the infidelity of a wife has historically been considered more serious than that of a husband. Men could spend resources caring for a child who, unbeknownst to them, was not biologically theirs. It is unlikely women could be tricked into doing the same. Humans with a common goal of survival of their genetic heritage make decisions that they believe will support their self-interests—specifically, their genetic self-interests.[40]

Basing their conclusions about human behavior on animal studies, evolutionary psychologists have similarly contended that human violence is triggered by so-called selfish genes, which are propelled by a biological need to perpetuate themselves in one's offspring. If true, an individual would be less likely to eliminate people who are closely related by heredity—less likely to murder siblings than cousins, and less likely to kill cousins than unrelated strangers. It is self-defeating, according to the evolutionary psychology perspective, for individuals to murder those who share their genetic makeup.

Some researchers have used the sociobiological perspective to explain violence in stepfamilies. Stepparents have absolutely no biological investment in their spouses' children, even if they love them. Thus, we might expect parents to murder their stepchildren at a greater rate than they kill their biological offspring. If the sociobiologists are right, then stepfamilies should be at greater risk of violence than blood relatives. According to Daly and Wilson, the incidence of violence is indeed far greater in stepfamilies than in traditional families where the children are genetically related both to parents and to one another.[41] For example, Daly and Wilson determined that the rate of infanticide (the killing of young children) is 60 times higher in stepfamilies than in biologically connected families.

Daly and Wilson also suggested that homicides perpetrated by stepfathers differ from those by biological fathers not only quantitatively but qualitatively as well. Biological fathers who kill their offspring are more likely to do so as a desperate act of twisted love before committing suicide. Stepfathers, however, rarely kill their children and then themselves. Moreover, stepfathers are more likely to beat their young stepchildren to death, whereas biological fathers are more likely to kill their youngsters with guns or asphyxiation, methods that do not require brute force. Children's fables of wicked stepmothers have occasionally come true. Michelle Gauvin, 34, of Lafayette, Indiana, was sentenced to life without parole for the March 2005 murder of her 4-year-old stepdaughter, Aiyana. With the assistance of Aiyana's biological father, Michelle had repeatedly tied her stepdaughter to a chair, where she was paddled with a broken cutting board and whipped with a belt. After six months of brutal abuse, Aiyana died of trauma to her head.

We should keep in mind that murder is a rare phenomenon, of course, and the members of most stepfamilies do not harm one another. The theoretical task is to pinpoint the factors that increase the probability that rare instances of deadly violence are more likely to occur. Moreover, as is the case with all of our biological variables, there are social and environmental contexts that might explain differences in infanticide between biological families and stepfamilies.

Personality Traits

Is there a violent personality? The psychological perspective considers the relationship between various personality traits and aggressive behavior. Many people have taken the Minnesota Multiphasic Personality Inventory (MMPI) or other personality tests that attempt to measure traits such as introversion, hostility, suspicion, assertiveness, and impulsiveness. There should be no surprise that comparisons of inmate and student population personality inventories often show no significant differences because these are not mutually exclusive categories of people (students can become inmates, and vice versa). Although some researchers, such as the Gluecks, found significant personality differences between offenders and nonoffenders, most research has been far less definitive regarding the violent personality. Rather than just one or two personality traits, more recent research has found that a set of personality traits may cluster together to create "negative emotionality," and this cluster of traits is more likely to be present in juvenile offenders. These traits include stress, cowardice or bullying, approval seeking, jealousy, low self-esteem, fears of abandonment, moodiness, anger, immaturity, and suspicion.[42]

Recent psychological research suggests that sensation-seeking personalities are susceptible to boredom, seek engagement in disinhibitive behaviors (e.g., alcohol use, partying), pursue unconventional lifestyles and experiences (e.g., the use of LSD), and engage in thrill- and adventure-seeking behaviors (e.g., risky sporting activities). More specifically, researchers find that sensation seekers are more likely to engage in aggressive behavior because it relieves their boredom and because these individuals also suffer from increased levels of hostility and anger. The researchers hypothesize a vicious cycle in which behaving aggressively over time causes others to respond negatively to them, which further contributes to the sensation seekers' hostility and anger.[43]

As we have seen, certain personality traits may manifest themselves, at least in part, in the social context. While one person who is an aggressive risk taker grows up in a loving home, another person born with a similar set of personality characteristics may be raised in conditions of abuse or neglect. Additionally, if individuals with a personality or genetic predisposition toward risk taking are born into prosperous families, they may have legitimate ways to satisfy their need for thrill and excitement, for example, by engaging in certain high-risk sports such as skydiving. But if these same people are instead born into poor or dysfunctional families with no legitimate avenues to exercise risk taking, the outcomes could be criminal, even deadly.

Paraphilias

A psychological dimension that does appear to be associated with at least one type of murderer, the serial killer, is the presence of some paraphilias, that is, sexual attractions to unusual or bizarre objects. Paraphilias seem to cluster; in other words, people with one paraphilia (e.g., a sexual attraction to gas masks, fur, amputees, or human excrement) typically have more than one. Obviously, not all paraphilias are linked to murder (e.g., exhibitionism, voyeurism, and cross-dressing). However, several sexual proclivities, such as pedophilia and necrophilia, necessitate criminal behavior that may, in some cases, also lead to murder. Serial killer Jerry Brudos had a shoe fetish by the time he was 5 years old and also developed a fetish for women's underwear and cross-dressing. Eventually Brudos progressed to rape and murder. In his souvenir collection was the foot of one of his victims, which he used to model his shoe collection. Brudos was also found to have amputated breasts in his possession. Having murdered at least four women, Brudos spent nearly 40 years in prison before he died of cancer in 2006. Although paraphilias represent distortions in what a person perceives to be sexually arousing, they are generally not the kind of profound distortions in thinking or perception that would mitigate criminal responsibility.

IQ and Crime

One of the most hotly debated topics related to criminality is whether low intelligence predicts criminal and violent behavior. As early as the 1920s, Goddard and several other psychologists were applying the new Simon–Binet intelligence quotient (IQ) in their studies of criminal populations.[44] In congressional testimony, they argued that Americans needed protection from the "worthless" eastern and southern European immigrants, who scored lower on intelligence tests than their counterparts from western and northern Europe. Based on their relatively low IQ scores, psychologists of the day testified in 1924 in favor of legislation limiting the flow of Italian, Polish, and Jewish newcomers into the country. This work reflected a history of feeblemindedness (low IQ) profiling that lasted at least from 1900 through the 1930s. In 1907, Indiana passed the first eugenics law allowing for state-authorized sterilizations; many other states followed with their own, sometimes even more aggressive, laws. Lasting until the 1960s, many states had mandatory sterilization laws for residents of mental institutions, welfare moms, the intellectually disabled, and epileptics. Not until 2003 did the state of North Carolina abolish its 74-year-old eugenics law that allowed the state (among other things) to sterilize a woman without her consent based on the conclusion that she was feebleminded. Thus, the IQ debate and the frightful social policy that flows from it have a long-checkered past in the annals of criminological theory.

Notwithstanding the questionable policy responses, quality scientific research, such as the work of Sheldon and Eleanor Glueck in *Unraveling Juvenile Delinquency*, has indeed found IQ to be a significant predictor of delinquency. As recently as 1977, criminologists Travis Hirschi and Michael Hindelang observed IQ to be a stronger predictor of delinquency than either social class or race.[45]

The controversy surrounding whether IQ is a significant predictor of violent crime as well as the debate about the factors influencing IQ remain unresolved, even after a half-century of research. Why would we expect IQ to predict violence? Do we believe that people with a low IQ could be more easily convinced by others to kill someone, or that they are too unintelligent to see viable solutions other than murder? Does low IQ leave people with such limited means of earning money that they kill because of the frustration of being poor or as part of their menial job? Perhaps the strongest possible link between IQ and violence would be in the extent to which IQ affects a person's ability to perceive consequences and make informed choices.[46] As with many other biological and psychological variables, IQ also fails to account for significant gender, seasonal, regional, and age variations in homicide and is likely moderated through a number of social context variables (e.g., education, parenting, exposure to violence).

Obviously, very low intelligence can restrict a person's ability to understand right from wrong, but the association between low IQ and the will to kill remains dubious. Studies of IQ and crime are generally performed on convicted offenders. Because more than one-third of murders are unsolved, perhaps it is the more intelligent offenders who are less likely to be caught, convicted, and, therefore, studied.

Whether they be Freudian factors, personality traits and disorders, mental illness, natural aggression, or IQ, the psychological variables reviewed here are characteristics of individuals. Thus, to some extent, criminal justice responses and punishments need to be individually tailored as well. Yet many citizens and policymakers are not comfortable with therapies or sanctions that vary from individual offender to individual offender. However, based on what we know about individual biological and psychological predispositions toward violence, overly rigid punishment responses that treat all offenders in the same way may be questionable in terms of their fairness or appropriateness.

THE SOCIAL SOURCES OF MURDER

Rather than the individual-specific variables of biological and psychological positivism, sociologists often look for the origins of crime and violence in the external world. Sociological variables include macro-level factors or community-level characteristics of neighborhoods such as mobility, poverty, disorder, and inequality. Other sociological theories focus on individual-level variables including peer influence, our bonds to others, strain, or the effects of labeling and stigma.

Sociological positivism began with theories that attempted to explain the high crime rates in lower-class urban areas. From the early 1900s through the 1950s, criminological theory operated on the assumption that crime is predominantly a problem of lower-class areas and their residents. Although these early theories may have been useful in explaining the activities of lower-class boys who joined urban gangs, they were obviously inadequate to explain homicides that did not involve offenders from a lower economic class.

Social Disorganization

Social disorganization theory focuses on the factors that weaken communities—mobility, heterogeneity, and poverty—rather than biological or psychological deficiencies in the residents of those communities. Transience and poverty combine to create conditions such that no matter who lives there, those areas will have higher crime rates.[47] According to social disorganization theory, the causes of violent behavior are the very factors that lead to social disorganization. Clearly, this sort of theory would be most useful for explaining felony-murders or even homicides that result from an argument on the street corner but would fail to explain murder committed by middle- and upper-class offenders.

Some researchers have retooled social disorganization theory to incorporate many area-level variables other than mobility, poverty, and heterogeneity. These so-called social ecology theories still focus on the characteristics of areas and how some areas may be particularly fertile ground for crime and violence. These types of community-level explanations are particularly helpful in understanding why certain areas of cities have a disproportionate share of homicides.

In 2006, many cities across the United States began to see increases in their homicide rates. These increases were typically not citywide, but rather were concentrated in certain parts of the community. The view that bad neighborhoods can foster conditions that lead to violence among residents can be seen in policy responses that mirror the social disorganization perspective. The addition of streetlights in high homicide areas, along with neighborhood cleanups and the destruction of abandoned houses, all point to efforts to reduce the social disorganization of an area. In practice, these theoretical ideas often become the justification for strategies that include increased police presence and more aggressive policing, all strategies intended to fix an area by replacing disorder with order but not the original focus of social disorganization theory's ideas of improving the neighborhood by creating parks and recreational areas, cleaning up trash and abandoned houses, and mentoring juveniles.

Social scientists have long recognized that absolute levels of unemployment or income do not necessarily translate into a subjective feeling of misery. The impact of economic variables on feelings of deprivation or frustration—especially at levels that promote murder—depends at least to some extent on an individual's standards of comparison. On both individual and aggregate levels, criminologists focus on relative deprivation by asking: How much status and salary do individuals enjoy relative to the amount of prestige and money they had 5 or 10 years earlier? How much money do they earn relative to their friends, neighbors, and other significant people in their lives? To what extent has the unemployment rate risen or fallen over time? How wide is the income gap between rich and poor, and how does income inequality across countries and over time correlate with rates of murder?

Downward mobility, the very process of losing economic ground, may contribute to individuals' feelings of deprivation, even if they are millionaires.[48] As a cohort, those baby boomers who entered the labor force during the late 1960s and 1970s may experience a sense of losing economic ground even at a time when the unemployment rate is very low. Since the early 1970s, the income gap between the haves and the have-nots has continued to widen, resulting in a shrinking middle class. At the bottom of the socioeconomic ladder, the level of permanent, intergenerational poverty in major U.S. cities, often referred to as the underclass and the "truly disadvantaged," has not abated.[49]

According to a study by the Economic Policy Institute and the Center on Budget and Policy Priorities, income inequality has been on the rise for decades. The average family in the top 1% of earners now makes 40 times more than the average family in the bottom 90% of households. Families in the top 0.01%—the 1% of the 1%—make, on average, almost 200 times more than those in the bottom 90%.[50] It seems that prosperity has not had the same impact throughout the class structure. Instead, it has pushed rich and poor Americans further and further apart. Downward mobility has been particularly steep for displaced manufacturing workers, who, since the 1970s, have found themselves stuck in service-sector jobs that pay less and have fewer fringe benefits. More recently, a bull market made the wealthy even wealthier and further widened the disparity between rich and poor.

Cross-national comparisons have often failed to uncover any relationship between aggregate rates of unemployment and homicide. At least at the national level, the unemployment rate seems to have little, if anything, to do with differences in murder rates across countries. Comparing income inequality across nations yields quite a different result, however. Specifically, countries with high levels of income inequality, such as the United States, also tend to have high rates of homicide.[51] Still, as income inequality has continued to increase over the past decade in the United States, homicide rates have declined. Thus, income inequality may help explain cross-national differences in homicide rates but does not seem to be a reliable tool for explaining recent fluctuations in homicide rates within the United States.

Principles of psychology and sociology, rather than economics, might explain the differential impact of unemployment and income inequality on murder rates. When joblessness prevails, many citizens feel that everyone is in the same sinking boat. Economic misery may therefore not be tied to feelings of inequity or unfairness (i.e., things are bad, but at least they are bad for everyone). Under conditions of income inequality, however, citizens find themselves in different boats, some much larger and more lavish than others. A few even own luxury yachts while many others have merely rowboats that are rapidly taking on water. Those individuals who are left behind, even if their boats are bigger than ever before, feel as though they are victims of economic injustice. Compared with wealthy segments of their society, they are losing ground and feel relatively deprived.

The recent economic downturns have occurred when homicide rates were relatively low, at levels not seen since the 1960s. The years 2008 and 2009 witnessed a sharp drop in stock prices and surge in unemployment and home foreclosures, prompting many observers to predict a spike in violent crime. To the contrary, trends in violent crime rates, including homicide, do not tend to correlate with shifts in the economy. Generally, those who lose their jobs or homes do not simply turn to violent street crime in order to make ends meet. Notwithstanding the gloomy forecast, homicide rates have remained relatively low and have even declined overall. However, the negative effects of an economic downturn can potentially occur indirectly to the extent that budgets for crime prevention and control measures are slashed. Eventually, such budget cuts can contribute to increases in the murder rates.

Strain, Frustration, and Murder

In 2002, Thomas Junta, the father of a youth hockey player, was sentenced to 6 to 10 years in prison for what has become the latest trend—parents' sports rage. Junta beat another player's father, Michael Costin, to death, because he believed that Costin's son had been unnecessarily rough on the ice against his son. Their sons, as well as other 10-year-olds, witnessed the beating that started inside and ended up outside the rink. Junta claimed self-defense, and there was, in fact, evidence of a violent history for the victim. Yet, clearly the judge and jury thought that Junta's anger had spilled over into unjustified rage and violence. This is but one of the many cases in which we find drivers, airplane passengers, and parents losing control over trivial frustrations and resorting to aggression and violence.

The concept of frustration-aggression has had a powerful influence on the field of criminology. In 1939, a group of Yale University psychologists focused on the effects of frustration—an unpleasant psychological state resulting from the failure to satisfy some need or desire—on aggressive behavior.[52] They proposed that frustration and aggression are inextricably connected. In what became famous as the "frustration-aggression hypothesis," they argued that frustration always causes some form of aggression and that aggression is always preceded by frustration. Thus, anything that interferes with an individual's movement toward a goal—whether it is as minor as waiting for a long red light to change or as major as failing to earn enough money to feed one's children—will inevitably lead to the expression of aggression, including murder.

Notwithstanding the original conceptualization, frustration is not necessarily followed by aggression (or else, few of us would make it home each day). When is frustration followed by aggression? When people think they can get away with it, when there are no police around, when they don't care what parents, teachers, or significant others think, when they are drinking, or when the frustration is extreme. All of these scenarios illustrate the obvious contextual factors that facilitate or limit how the state of frustration manifests itself. Thus, although humans may descend from a long line of aggressors, societal pressures or controls can increase or decrease the expression of those instincts.

Though the original frustration-aggression hypothesis may have been overstated, it is not without some validity. Aggressive behavior does tend to increase when people are prevented from reaching a goal they expect to attain. There are people who yell at their children after a bad day at the office; there are men who punch the wall after being dumped by a girlfriend. At the extreme, some individuals have annihilated their ex-spouse and children because of a nasty divorce and custody battle. Others have murdered their supervisor after being fired from a job. A few students have been so frustrated with school that they have gunned down their teachers and classmates. Clearly, we now know that the progression from frustration to aggression is not inevitable.

The vast majority of people deal with the frustrations of daily life without harming or killing others. Indeed, commuters are much more likely to wait patiently for a long light to change or seek a faster route home than to shout obscenities or shoot another driver, even though some motorists do vent their feelings of road rage. People are more likely to change jobs or seek training for higher-paying work than to stab their boss or a family member. People learn to develop coping skills in responding to the frustrations of everyday life.

Not only does aggression not follow every frustrating episode, but just as clearly, frustration does not precede every aggressive action. There are countless examples of violence that occur in the absence of any especially frustrating circumstances. For example, a soldier engages in combat because he is ordered to do so by his commanding officer. A young child shoots his playmate after seeing a gunfight on television. A hit man for the mob eliminates the leader of a rival "family" because he is paid to do so.

The tendency for frustration to lead to aggression is greatest when the frustration is severe and unexpected—that is, if people are deprived of something important that they were certain of getting such as a promised promotion that falls through at the last moment. The tendency is also greater when people believe they can get away with being aggressive, that is, when they do not anticipate being punished in return or being rejected by their friends and associates. For example, a child is more likely to bully his playmates if he thinks none of them will stand up to him and that his parents will not find out.[53]

Early on, Stuart Palmer studied 51 convicted murderers to determine whether severe frustrations suffered during childhood might have led them to commit murder later in their lives.[54] To provide a comparison group of similar men who had not killed anyone, Palmer also studied the nearest-in-age brother of each murderer. He found that the 51 convicted killers had indeed experienced more intense frustrations than had their brothers who were not convicted of murder. Specifically, the convicted murderers were more likely to have been dissatisfied with their prestige or status, to have suffered physical defects, to have done poorly in school, and to have had fewer friends. In short, they had led "dismal, unprestigious, frustrating lives." Illustrating an extremely deadly response to frustration, a number of the more infamous mass murderers— including Mark Barton, who slaughtered nine and injured a dozen others at two Atlanta investment offices in 1999 after losing a fortune in the stock market—suffered "reward withdrawal" or status loss before their violent rampages.

Strain theory was originally an attempt to explain why certain areas have higher crime rates. In his classic analysis, Robert Merton recognized that strain can be institutionalized in the misalignment of goals and culturally prescribed means.[55] According to U.S. cultural values learned from an early age, all members of society are expected to strive for economic success. Yet, there is far less emphasis in U.S. society on providing the structural opportunities for achieving that success. This disparity invites what Merton refers to as "innovation": when an individual accepts the cultural emphasis on the success goal but rejects the socially acceptable means for its attainment. In some cases, an individual will substitute illegitimate (often illegal) but more effective methods of securing wealth and power. For middle-class deviants, the pressure to innovate might take the form of unethical business practices and white-collar crime. But for members of society lacking in education and economic resources, innovation more frequently becomes street crime, including gang membership, drug dealing, property offenses, and violence.

In the concept of strain, Robert Agnew has transformed the frustration-aggression hypothesis into a much broader concept.[56] In his general strain theory, Agnew proposes that criminal violence is a result of strain—frustration, but also anger, disappointment, fear, or depression—that originates in destructive social ties. He identifies four important sources of strain: (a) the presence of negative stimuli (e.g., child abuse, peer rejection, school failure, and physical punishment); (b) the removal of positive stimuli (e.g., death of a loved one, parents' divorce, and residential mobility); (c) relative deprivation (e.g., peers who make more money or get better grades because they have "connections"); and (d) failure to achieve desired goals (e.g., missing out on success because of a lack of educational opportunities).

Also in the spirit of strain theory, Steve Messner and Richard Rosenfeld, in *Crime and the American Dream*, suggest that the breakdown of social institutions regulating behavior (churches, schools, and families) has contributed to elevated levels of crime in the United States.[57] According to Messner and Rosenfeld, the economy has become the dominant force controlling behavior and has dwarfed any other institution's ability to curb crime. Families are run like businesses, and roles that don't generate income (e.g., stay-at-home moms) are not valued. In a society where the pursuit of material success is valued above all else, we should not be surprised to witness a crime wave like the crack-related homicide epidemic of the late 1980s.

Cultural Deviance

Cultural deviance theories (also called subcultural theories) do not contend that criminals are necessarily strained but that they obey the norms they were taught—rules of behavior that just happen to differ from those of the law. In other words, criminals learn different codes of right and wrong. Wolfgang and Ferracuti long ago proposed that higher homicide rates among young men, in the lower classes, among blacks, and in the South may have a cultural basis. They are a result of a "subculture of violence," in which violent behavior, even murder, is regarded as an appropriate and rewarded response to a menacing situation (e.g., a threatening glance, a jostle, an insulting comment, and the presence of a weapon).[58] In this subculture, violence is a norm to which everyone is expected to comply, and those who do so are accorded high status and respect. According to subculture of violence theorists, under such cultural conditions, murder becomes more likely. The subcultural explanation for southern homicide patterns is supported by evidence showing that murders occurring in the South are more likely than those in other regions to arise from arguments between people who know each other.[59] These confrontations typically escalate when the reputation or honor of an individual is impugned by an insulting remark. Also supporting the subcultural perspective is evidence that Southerners, more than residents of other regions, approve of using defensive violence against people who pose a serious threat to their personal safety rather than seeking nonviolent alternatives.[60]

Media accounts have suggested, irresponsibly, that there is a link between Latino populations and crime. Recent research finds that areas with higher concentrations of legal and illegal immigrant populations not only do not have higher rates of violence but often have lower rates of violence. In addition to Latino homicide rates being lower, homicide rates are also lower for blacks and whites living in these areas. Anti-immigrant legislation that claims a link between Latino populations and increased crime and violence are simply unfounded. Immigrant populations can even strengthen a neighborhood and improve levels of social control, economic development, and neighborhood improvement.[61]

There are many different versions of cultural deviance theory, but they all embrace the argument that homicide offenders have learned a set of values and beliefs that promote the use of violence.[62] These individuals are more willing to use physical force to settle disputes, and, according to the cultural deviance perspective, this response is learned. The idea that someone perceives a verbal slight as "fightin' words" is often used in explanations of gang-related homicides. Although most of the fundamental premises of subcultural theory make sense, these theories have received little empirical support, as the variables associated with violence are more likely to be structural or situational than cultural. Rather than a "southern subculture of violence," the source of higher homicide rates in the South is in part explained by factors such as poverty, income inequality, racial segregation, religiosity, weather, alcohol and drug use, and gun ownership.[63]

Early subcultural theories were highly criticized as racist and class biased. Interestingly, this type of research continues, as is illustrated by Elijah Anderson's *Code of the Streets*.[64] Anderson proposed that the lives of young, inner-city blacks are characterized by a code focused on getting and maintaining respect. In areas of poverty, few jobs, and drug use, the presentation of self in everyday interactions is focused on possessions and body language that command respect and requires a quick and violent response if respect is threatened. Anderson's oppositional culture develops because of racism, little faith in police and the criminal justice system, and a lack of opportunity. In Anderson's streets, everyone has to look out for themselves and use violence to maintain their sense of self.

Although not presented as a full-blown theory, J. D. Vance also describes a subculture in his memoir *Hillbilly Elegy*.[65] This Appalachian culture in crisis is the white, working class who Vance describes as suffering from generations of abuse, poverty, addiction, and violence. Loyalty and love of country are mixed with a poor work ethic, resentment, and a cycle of living on welfare.

Learning to Kill

Some criminologists would argue that it is not primarily the bad neighborhood, strain, or exposure to a subculture that creates the propensity for violence but rather that people learn to kill one another. Forms and levels of violence vary tremendously from culture to culture.

Social learning theory offers another approach to explaining individual and social differences in the propensity to commit acts of extreme violence. According to this theory, most aggressive behavior involves skills that we must learn from others.[66] We learn to be violent not only through rewards and punishments but also through the role models we imitate. Clearly, significant people around us may serve as models of learning in many other areas of life—for example, in acquiring language, using facial expressions, and dressing for various occasions. In a similar fashion, imitation may also occur in learning violent behavior, even behavior as violent as homicide.

Some have suggested that the mass media generally, and television in particular, could provide powerful models for aggressive conduct. After the 1999 Columbine school massacre, there was significant discussion of the role of violent media in the killers' motives. Both were known to play violent video games like *Doom* and be big fans of the movie *Natural Born Killers*. The influence of violent media became a moral panic and convenient scapegoat. Lawsuits brought by the Columbine victims' families against a number of game makers were dismissed by a judge.

Obviously, the vast majority of people exposed to violent media do not behave violently at all. There are clearly some people who seize on this sort of media as a model for their own behavior, yet there are likely a number of other stronger causal factors at work as well. There is less than definitive scientific evidence to support a strong causal link between violent media and violent behavior.[67] However, research does suggest that there is an increase in aggressive attitudes and mood (e.g., hostility, argumentative) and aggressive behavior (choices of play styles in laboratory settings) in people who play violent video games.[68] Clearly, there is no credible evidence to suggest these games turn people into killers, even if they have some influence on the perspective of the already-troubled, at-risk kid.[69]

There has been much hype and irresponsibility regarding the claims of the influence of violent media on violent behavior. Given the recent dramatic declines in violence, including youth violence, we certainly have not seen a reduction in violent media consumption. Some experts suggest that we should not spend money and time researching media violence as a "cause of crime" when evidence that this is the case simply does not exist in the scientific literature. Rather, we should focus on the scientifically established causes of crime, that is, poverty, school failure, and family dysfunction. The ideologues who use issues such as violent video games to further agendas of censorship and a "sky is falling" panic for each generation (e.g., rock and roll, comic books and other books, movies, dancing, and media) should be closely scrutinized, and their claims should be carefully and scientifically tested.[70]

Rather than the media, many learning theories have focused on arguably the stronger influence of the day-to-day interactions that we all have with others. Models for murder can be located in the groups to which an individual belongs. Edwin Sutherland's differential association theory contends that criminal behavior is learned during adolescence from an individual's most intimate social relations—his peers, family, and friends. In addition to learning attitudes supporting violence, individuals acquire criminal skills through these associations (no one is born knowing how to hotwire a car, make a bomb, or use a gun). In addition, individuals learn by observing group members who violate the law, from shoplifting and taking illicit drugs to armed robbery and murder. To the extent that people associate with others who regard criminal behavior in a positive light, they are also excluded from associating with those who reject the criminal lifestyle. Just as they learn a host of important values, individuals adopt the criminal attitudes and behavior of their intimate associates.[71]

In a more recent version of social learning theory, Akers blends differential association with conditioning effects of rewards and punishments to explain the development of criminality.[72] In his differential reinforcement theory, Akers suggests that the acceptance of violence does not come merely from associating with a particular group of intimates but from associating with a group whose members reinforce violent behavior and punish law-abiding behavior. According to Akers, offenders learn violence in several different ways from group members—by observing and imitating the deviant behavior of others, by being rewarded and praised by group members for engaging in deviant behavior, and by acquiring attitudes from group members that support and stimulate deviant behavior. The significant level of empirical support for learning theories should give us pause about the criminogenic effects of incarceration. If prisons aren't schools for crime, then perhaps they are at least study halls.

Lonnie Athens also suggests that criminals are trained and conditioned to be violent through a process he calls violentization. Athens, a criminologist, grew up in a very violent world, and his theory is grounded in his personal experiences as well as extensive, qualitative interviews with violent offenders. According to this theory, offenders experience their own brutalization early in life and are coached into belligerence by others. They learn to use violence to gain respect and frighten others and, finally, to use violence in order to get what they want and bond with others who feel similarly.[73]

Self-Control, Social Control, and Murder

Still another theoretical perspective hypothesizes that virtually all criminal behavior is a result of a lack of control rather than a function of learning. Control theories envision a set of controls or bonds that work to limit involvement in criminal behavior. But control theory also takes account of the fact that not everyone's moral sense prevents him or her from committing acts of criminal violence. Hirschi argued that criminality is often controlled by an individual's commitments and attachments to conventional institutions, beliefs, activities, and groups.[74] Many people refrain from engaging in violent behavior because they fear losing their relationships with significant others—with family, friends, and peers. However, members of society who lack strong social ties may also lack the motivation to become law-abiding citizens. According to this theory, a person would commit violence or murder when he or she had no controlling influence from attachments to others, commitments to conventional behavior, involvements in conventional activities, and belief in the morality of the law—in a sense, nothing left to lose.

An important insight provided by control theory is that commitment or attachment to conventional individuals and institutions inoculates human beings from committing violent offenses. Regrettably, in recent years some Americans have suffered a sharp decline in close bonds with others in their communities. Those areas that have large numbers of individuals lacking in social bonds (e.g., the very poor, the drug addicted, the unemployed, drifters, transients, migrants, and newcomers) also tend to have high rates of crime, including murder.

Years ago, in an early version of control theory, Walter Reckless described the factors that encourage criminal behavior as a set of "pushes and pulls."[75] Consistent with Reckless's perspective, we have discussed in this chapter a number of conditions that can push an individual away from conventional society—for example, being frustrated by poor grades or parental disapproval when not "measuring up" in the conventional sense; having a personality disorder characterized by lack of remorse and empathy; feeling distant from conventional goals, institutions, or individuals; and suffering from repeated head traumas, a disorder that can make everyday functioning difficult. Other factors reviewed in this chapter can pull individuals toward murderous behavior—for example, growing up in a subculture in which violence is seen as a virtue; finding social support with a group of friends who engage in criminal behavior; and finding models (fictional or factual) whose murderous behavior is rewarded. In explaining the will to kill, we might then search for the presence of the forces that both push individuals away from conventional society and pull them toward the crime of murder.

Labeling Theory

Secondary deviance occurs when an individual is stigmatized by his placement in a special program, a special classroom, or a special school. The individual is regarded as special, in only a negative sense. A child is "emotionally disturbed" or "learning disabled" or "a slow learner." An adult may be labeled as a "sex offender" or "a criminal" or "a psychopath." When we think about intervening in the lives of potentially troubled individuals, we should also remember the components of labeling theory. Labeling someone as a problem by putting them in special programs or publicly displaying their record of arrests could in itself cause future problems because of stigma.

Of course, there are many individuals who are in need of a formal program, regardless of whether they are stigmatized as a result. But the loner kid who likes violent video games will most likely never harm anyone. Singling him out with some sort of intervention can suggest to his parents and teachers that he suffers from a major problem when no problem actually exists. Moreover, an unnecessary intervention may waste limited resources on programs that aren't needed. In fact, we may create a problem simply by labeling some people as at risk for future violence. Empirical assessments of labeling theory find mixed or little support for the idea that the label actually causes future deviant behavior. At the same time, we need to be aware that intervention itself might contribute to the very problem we were trying to avoid.[76]

INTEGRATED THEORIES

The last few decades in criminology have seen the birth of integrated theories. Although the Gluecks conducted one of the most interdisciplinary studies ever done in criminology, their findings were not presented as a theoretical model. Fishbein's work as well as the work of Daly and Wilson included variables from multiple disciplines but only fairly recently did scholars develop formal integrated criminological theories. The three major types of integrated criminological theories are multifactor (see Fishbein in biosocial theories), latent trait, and life course or developmental theories. Rather than focus on just one variable, these theories combine several different theoretical perspectives into one model. Some integrated theories combine different disciplines, including biology, psychology, and sociology, whereas other integrated theories combine only one disciplinary perspective (e.g., sociological theories).

One example of an integrated theory includes Gottfredson and Hirschi's *A General Theory of Crime*, which pointed to the importance of parental love, supervision, and consistent discipline in the formation of self-control. This theory not only seeks to explain why someone might be a shoplifter or serial killer (both would primarily be a function of low self-control and opportunity) but can also be used to explain a host of other maladaptive behaviors such as gambling, alcohol and drug use, financial irresponsibility, interpersonal relationship problems, smoking, and eating disorders. Part of the appeal of the Gottfredson and Hirschi perspective is that the theory incorporates biological, psychological, and sociological variables within a context of opportunities. A person with a number of high-risk variables such as brain dysfunction, an impulsive personality, and bad parents might still reject becoming a criminal because of the lack of opportunity for involvement in crime. What is more, engagement in criminal behavior declines and self-control increases with age as a result of many factors, including hormonal changes, socialization, and the increasing cost of losing control.[77]

Gottfredson and Hirschi argue that low self-control is a latent trait, formed early in life and not likely to be modified very profoundly through experience. In contrast, Sampson and Laub's integrated theory is embedded in social control theory but finds that the risks of offending and desistance vary over the life course. Using the Gluecks' data, Sampson and Laub are able to explain not only offending but also desistance from offending, suggesting that the ability of people to form social capital, bonds and connections through stable relationships, and job and career opportunities may protect them from committing criminal acts and even provide a way for criminals to go straight.[78]

A WORD OF CAUTION ABOUT CAUSE

Having reviewed in this chapter a wide range of theories, summarized in Table 3.1, all purporting to explain murderous intentions and other violent behavior, we may have created a rather confusing image of the variables responsible for murder. Certainly, each theory has limitations. Most have been criticized, if not condemned, for their shortcomings and flaws.

Explaining the many different types of murder will likely require a complex theory. As much as we would like to find the magic bullet of explaining murder, the reality is that it is a complex theoretical soup made up of many ingredients that simmer over a period of years or even decades. Mixed in with biological, psychological, and sociological variables are facilitators, including drug and alcohol use and access to guns.

It is wise to keep in mind that even good theories that have been tested and validated with empirical research cannot account for the full variety of human behavior. Good theories can explain some cases of homicide but not all forms of homicidal proneness, no matter which variables are used. The important notion that correlation does not imply causation is virtually a mantra of social science research. For example, blacks have significantly higher rates of committing murder than do whites, but this correlation is not necessarily the impact of race itself; instead, it is likely also a result of a host of socioeconomic conditions associated with race.

In addition, correlation also does not guarantee predictability. Explaining behavior after it has occurred (and not predicting behavior in advance) is the strength of theory. Men have rates of committing homicide many times higher than women. Yet, although most killers are male, most males do not kill. Theories that

Table 3.1   Selected Theories of Violence and Homicide

Theory and Dates	Selected Proponents	Key Concepts	Policy Implications
Supernatural Through late 1600s		Demonic possession, evil spirits, witchcraft, and the Devil cause crime	Torture and execution drive out evil; chaos, cruelty, and anarchy characterize punishments for crime; exorcisms
Classical Mid-1700s–late 1800s	Beccaria and Bentham	Violent behavior is a result of choice and free will, reasoning, decision making, and assessment of pain versus gain	Deterrence through certain, swift, and proportional punishment; utilitarian-based notion of justice
Early Biological 1800s–1960s	Lombroso, Garofalo, Goddard, Dugdale, Sheldon	Criminals have a physical and/or genetic inferiority that predisposes them to criminal behaviors; includes atavism, criminal anthropology, genetics, body types, and XYY chromosome	Eugenics; sterilization; feeblemindedness profiling; psychosurgery
Recent Biology 1970s–present	Fishbein, Brunner, Moffitt & Caspi, Raine	Genetics, MACA, traumatic brain injury, amygdala and prefrontal cortex issues	Medication; surgical interventions; medical implants; therapy
Psychoanalytic 1920s–present	Freud	Unconscious motives and repression drive criminal behavior	Psychoanalysis to relieve overactive id, neurosis, and psychosis
Psychological/ Psychiatric Early 1900s–present	Lorenz, Fromm, Skinner, Bandura, Eysenck, Herrnstein & Murray	Aggression is a response to frustration; aggression is a result of imitation, modeling, and rewards for violence; violence is linked to low IQ	Counseling, drug therapy, and behavior modification to treat violence as an individual-level phenomenon
Personality Disorders 1940s–present	Cleckley, Hare, McCord & McCord, American Psychological Association	Violence linked to mental illness via personality disorders, autism spectrum disorders, dissociative identity disorder	Limited successful interventions; some effect of medication and therapy; prevention is best hope
Rational Choice Mid-1970s–present	Clarke, Cornish, Katz	Classical notions of free will combined with positivistic variables; offenders choose to be violent but certain variables influence the ability to make reasoned choices	Target hardening; situational crime prevention; displacement; classical punishment responses with more focus on severe punishments

(Continued)

Table 3.1 (Continued)

Theory and Dates	Selected Proponents	Key Concepts	Policy Implications
Social Disorganization and Social Ecology 1920s–present	Shaw & McKay, Bursik, Sampson	Disorganized areas breed criminal influences	Employment and educational opportunities; neighborhood revitalization; positive role models; strong families and schools
Cultural Deviance 1920s–present	Wolfgang & Ferracuti, Cohen, Miller, Cloward & Ohlin, Anderson	Some groups/individuals have different value systems; different socialization forms the foundation for subculture or gang support for violence	Positive role models; legitimate educational and economic opportunities
Strain 1930s–present	Merton, Agnew, Messner & Rosenfeld	Frustration results from blocked legitimate opportunities; crime and delinquency are an individual adaptation or coping mechanism in response to strain; economic success is a primary form of institutional control	Focus on values and institutions other than financial success (family, church, and school); provide psychological and structural opportunities for success
Social Learning 1930s–present	Sutherland, Burgess, Akers, Phillips, Athens	People learn to commit violent acts; violence continues if reinforced; peer groups influence modeling; highlights copycat offending and media influences	Positive role models and relearning noncriminal values and strategies
Social and Self Control 1950s–present	Reckless, Hirschi, Gottfredson & Hirschi	People must be socialized to resist pushes and pulls toward crime; delinquency as a result of weakened bonds to society; proper parental supervision, love, and discipline develop self-control in children; self-control as the ability to control natural tendencies	Encourage bonding and attachment to conventional others; increase individual stakes in conformity
Labeling 1960s–present	Lemert, Goffman, Becker	Being labeled leads to deviance; stigmatizing labels create self-fulfilling prophecy	Limited interventions; avoid stigma
Integrated 1950s–present	Gluecks, Fishbein, Gottfredson & Hirschi, Sampson & Laub	Biological predispositions create conditional free will; fixed latent traits; malleable traits, protective factors, developmental and life-course approaches	Combined modalities (drugs, counseling, family intervention); educational opportunities; possibilities for marriage, family, and career to redirect criminals

reduce a murderous response to the impact of a single variable fail to recognize the complexity of the will to kill. Even elaborate models that predict murder based on demographics, family patterns, peer groups, and other factors fail more than they succeed in identifying killers. The best they can do is to pinpoint those at greatest risk, usually after they have already committed serious crimes. What society would do with these high-risk individuals if we could predict their future behavior then becomes an important ethical and policy question.

In this chapter, we have offered a taste of the many perspectives and theoretical traditions that have been invoked in attempts to explain and predict violence in general, and homicide in particular. Any effort to survey completely and in depth the broad array of theories for homicidal proneness would fill volumes, and already has. In 1988, the National Academy of Sciences commissioned an expert panel on violence to describe in some detail the multitude of causal theories.[79] Even after the publication of the panel's four volumes of research findings, our understanding and ability to explain, much less predict, extreme violence is still quite limited. Human behavior is complex, and the linkages between biological, psychological, and sociological stimuli and the subsequent homicidal response are much more complicated and difficult to identify than the movements of laboratory mice in search of a piece of cheese at the finish line of a circuitous maze.

After all that has been researched and written on the topic of homicide, which disciplinary tradition has the most to contribute in explaining why some people kill and others do not? Does the abnormal psychology of the murderer or his physical constitution hold greater insights into the mystery of murder? Are the bad schools, bad parents, and/or bad peers more telling?

The simple answer to these difficult questions is: It depends. It is likely that all of these notions have some merit—not to understand all kinds of murder but perhaps some discrete subset. A focus on head trauma or environmental toxins may help us to comprehend sudden and uncharacteristic outbursts of murderous rage but will do little to account for cold-blooded acts of murder for hire. Learning theories of social psychology and sociological hypotheses pertaining to social class and social structure are valuable for understanding serious gang violence, but they may be inadequate for interpreting infanticide. Violence has many sources, and an integrated theoretical approach that includes an array of biological, psychological, and sociological variables will be best suited to explain it.

Regardless of the theoretical approach, we often think of causation in terms of some form of deficiency, deviation, or defect. A "bad seed," diseased brain, poor parenting, maltreatment, drug side effect, running with a bad crowd, exposure to harmful media, poor opportunities, bad days, and bad breaks are all valuable notions, but none alone is generally sufficient to drive a person to kill. Even a person struggling with a combination of biological, psychological, or sociological abnormalities (such as a learning-disabled child raised by an impoverished and unconcerned single parent, who plays violent video games with his delinquent buddies) has an ability to make a choice, although it may be limited by his various handicaps. Although our options and opportunities in life are impacted by a host of advantages and disadvantages, virtually all of us have some degree of free will. Human beings have choices in how to respond when the rewards we have come to expect are suddenly withdrawn or unavailable. By nature of heredity and nurture of environment, some individuals are more prone to violence than others, yet free will still exists. The will to kill, although governed by numerous internal and external forces, still includes choice and human decision making, and thus accountability and culpability.

1. Marc Reidel and Wayne Welsh, *Criminal Violence: Patterns, Causes and Prevention* (Los Angeles: Roxbury, 2002).

2. Randolph Roth, *American Homicide* (Cambridge, MA: Harvard University Press, 2009).

3. Jill Lepore, "Why Is American History So Murderous?" *New Yorker*, November 9, 2009.

4. George B. Vold, Thomas J. Bernard, and Jeffrey B. Snipes, *Theoretical Criminology* (New York: Oxford University Press, 2002).

5. Cesare Beccaria, *On Crimes and Punishments*, trans. Henry Paolucci (Indianapolis: Bobbs-Merrill, 1963); Jeremy Bentham, *A Fragment on Government and an Introduction to the Principles of Morals and Legislation*, ed. Wilfred Harrison (New York: Oxford University Press, 1967).

6. Derek Cornish and Ronald Clarke, eds., *The Reasoning Criminal: Rational Choice Perspectives on Offending* (New York: Springer-Verlag, 1986).

7. Jack Katz, *Seductions of Crime* (New York: Basic Books, 1990).

8. Robert Sampson and John Laub, *Crime in the Making: Pathways and Turning Points Through Life* (Cambridge, MA: Harvard University Press, 1993); Sheldon Glueck and Eleanor Glueck, *Unraveling Juvenile Delinquency* (Cambridge, MA: Harvard University Press, 1950); Sheldon Glueck and Eleanor Glueck, *Predicting Delinquency and Crime* (Cambridge, MA: Harvard University Press, 1967).

9. Saleem Shah, "The 47, XYY Chromosomal Abnormality: A Critical Appraisal With Respect to Antisocial and Violent Behavior," in W. Lynn Smith and Arthur Kling, eds., *Issues in Brain/Behavior Control* (New York: Spectrum, 1976); Lawrence Taylor, *Born to Crime: The Genetic Causes of Criminal Behavior* (Westport, CT: Greenwood Press, 1984).

10. Keith McBurnett, Benjamin B. Lahey, Paul J. Rathouz, and Rolf Loeber, "Low Salivary Cortisol and Persistent Aggression in Boys Referred for Disruptive Behavior," *Archives of General Psychiatry* 57 (2000): 21–27.

11. Alan Booth and D. Wayne Osgood, "The Influence of Testosterone on Deviance in Adulthood," *Criminology* 31 (1993): 93–117.

12. Mortimer D. Gross and William C. Wilson, *Minimal Brain Dysfunction* (New York: Brunner/Mazel, 1974).

13. Gary M. Lavergne, *A Sniper in the Tower: The Charles Whitman Murders* (Denton, TX: University of North Texas Press, 1997).

14. Christer Allgulander and Bo Nilsson, "Victims of Criminal Homicide in Sweden: A Matched Case-Control Study of Health and Social Factors Among All 1,739 Cases During 1978-1994," *American Journal of Psychiatry* 157 (2000): 244–247.

15. Diana Fishbein, *Biobehavioral Perspectives in Criminology* (Belmont, CA: Wadsworth, 2001).

16. H. G. Brunner, M. Nelen, X. O. Breakefield, H. H. Ropers, and B. A. van Oost, "Abnormal Behavior Associated with a Point Mutation in the Structural Gene for Monoamine Oxidase A," *Science* 262 (1993): 578–580; Avshalom Caspi, Joseph McClay, Terrie E. Moffitt, et al., "Role of Genotype in the Cycle of Violence in Maltreated Children," *Science* 297 (2002): 851–854; Andrea L. Glenn, "The Other Allele: Exploring the Long Allele of the Serotonin Transporter Gene as a Potential Risk Factor for Psychopathy: A Review of the Parallels in Findings," *Neuroscience and Biobehavioral Reviews* 35 (2011): 612–620.

17. Adrian Raine, "From Genes to Brain to Antisocial Behavior," *Current Directions in Psychological Science* 17 (2008): 323–328.

18. Citizens Commission on Human Rights International, "Other Murders/Murder-Suicides Committed by Individuals on Psychiatric Drugs" (no date), https://www.cchrint.org/psychiatric-drugs/drug_warnings_on_violence/recent-murdersmurder-suicides.

19. Barbara Oakley, *Evil Genes: Why Rome Fell, Hitler Rose, Enron Failed, and My Sister Stole My Mother's Boyfriend* (Amherst, NY: Prometheus Books, 2007).

20. Brunner et al., "Abnormal Behavior Associated with a Point Mutation in the Structural Gene for Monoamine Oxidase A."

21. Caspi et al., "Role of Genotype in the Cycle of Violence in Maltreated Children."

22. Emiliano Feresin, "Lighter Sentence for Murderer With 'Bad Genes,'" *Nature*, October 30, 2009.

23. T. E. Moffitt, "The New Look of Behavioral Genetics in Developmental Psychopathology: Gene–Environment Interplay in Antisocial Behaviors," *Psychological Bulletin* 131 (2005): 533–554.

24. Konrad Lorenz, *On Aggression* (New York: Harcourt, Brace and World, 1966).

25. Diana H. Fishbein, "Biological Perspectives in Criminology," *Criminology* 28 (1990): 27–72; James Q. Wilson and Richard J. Herrnstein, *Crime and Human Nature* (New York: Simon and Schuster, 1985).

26. Eric Fidler, "Hormone Level Linked to Antisocial Behavior in Boys," *Boston Globe*, January 14, 2000.

27. Brenda Lane, "How to Manage Postpartum Depression," October 5, 2017, https://www.verywell.com/how-to-manage-postpartum-depression-2759426; Postpartum Support International, "Postpartum Psychosis," http://

www.postpartum.net/learn-more/postpartum-psychosis; Carmen Monzin, "Postpartum Psychosis: Updates and Clinical Issues," *Psychiatric Times*, http://www.psychiatrictimes.com/special-reports/postpartum-psychosis-updates-and-clinical-issues.

28. B. G. Link, J. C. Phelan, M. Bresnahan, A. Stueve, and B. A. Pescosolido, "Public Conceptions of Mental Illness: Labels, Causes, Dangerousness, and Social Distance," *American Journal of Public Health* 89 (1999): 1328–1333.

29. Bruce Link, John Monahan, Ann Stueve, and Francis T. Cullen, "Real in Their Consequences: A Sociological Approach to Understanding the Association Between Psychotic Symptoms and Violence," *American Sociological Review* 64 (1999): 316–332.

30. Ken Magid and Carol A. McKelvey, *High Risk: Children Without a Conscience* (New York: Bantam Books, 1988); Robert D. Hare, *Without Conscience: The Disturbing World of the Psychopaths Among Us* (New York: Guilford Press, 1997).

31. Robert D. Hare, *The Hare Psychopathy Checklist–Revised* (Toronto: Multihealth Systems, 2003).

32. Robert D. Hare, *Without Conscience: The Disturbing World of the Psychopaths Among Us* (New York: Pocket Books, 1993).

33. Hervey M. Cleckley, The Mask of Sanity: An *Attempt to Clarify Some Issues About the So-Called Psychopathic Personality* (New York: Mosby, 1941); William McCord and Joan McCord, *The Psychopath: An Essay on the Criminal Mind* (Princeton, NJ: Van Nostrand).

34. American Psychiatric Association, *Diagnostic and Statistical Manual of Mental Disorders*, 5th ed. (Arlington, VA: American Psychiatric Association, 2013).

35. Ibid.

36. Clare S. Allely, Helen Minnis, Lucy Thompson, Philip Wilson, and Christopher Gillberg, "Neurodevelopmental and Psychosocial Risk Factors in Serial Killers and Mass Murderers," *Aggression and Violent Behavior* 19 (2014): 288–301.

37. American Psychiatric Association, *Diagnostic and Statistical Manual of Mental Disorders*, 5th ed. (Washington, DC; London: American Psychiatric Publishing, 2014).

38. Sigmund Freud, *New Introductory Lectures on Psychoanalysis* (London: Hogarth Press, 1949).

39. See www.therapyinla.com for discussions of successful attachment therapy and other forms of psychotherapy.

40. Martin Daly and Margo Wilson, "An Evolutionary Psychological Perspective on Homicide," in M. Dwayne Smith and Margaret A. Zahn, eds., *Homicide: A Sourcebook of Social Research* (Thousand Oaks, CA: Sage, 1999).

41. Ibid.

42. Caspi et al., "Role of Genotype in the Cycle of Violence in Maltreated Children"; Robert Krueger

and Pamela Schmutte, "Are Some People Crime Prone? Replications of the Personality–Crime Relationship Across Countries, Genders, Races and Methods," *Criminology* 32 (1994): 163–195.

43. Jeff Joireman, Jonathan Anderson, and Alan Strathman, "The Aggression Paradox: Understanding Links Among Aggression, Sensation Seeking, and the Consideration of Future Consequences," *Journal of Personality and Social Psychology* 84 (2003): 1287–1302.

44. Vold, Bernard, and Snipes, *Theoretical Criminology*.

45. Travis Hirschi and Michael Hindelang, "Intelligence and Delinquency: A Revisionist Review," *American Sociological Review* 42 (1977): 471–586.

46. Fishbein, "Biological Perspectives in Criminology."

47. Clifford R. Shaw and Henry D. McKay, *Juvenile Delinquency and Urban Areas* (Chicago: University of Chicago Press, 1972).

48. Katherine S. Newman, *Falling From Grace* (New York: Free Press, 1988).

49. William Julius Wilson, *The Truly Disadvantaged: The Inner City, the Underclass and Public Policy* (Chicago: University of Chicago Press, 1987).

50. Dave Gilson and Edwin Rios, "11 Charts That Show Income Inequality Isn't Getting Better Anytime Soon," *Mother Jones*, December 22, 2016.

51. Gary LaFree, "A Summary and Review of Cross-National Comparative Studies of Homicide," in Smith and Zahn, eds., *Homicide: A Sourcebook of Social Research*.

52. John Dollard, Leonard W. Doob, Neal E. Miller, O. H. Mowrer, and Robert R. Sears, *Frustration and Aggression* (New Haven, CT: Yale University Press, 1939).

53. Jeffrey H. Goldstein, *Aggression and Crimes of Violence* (New York: Oxford University Press, 1986).

54. Stuart H. Palmer, *The Psychology of Murder* (New York: Crowell, 1960).

55. Robert K. Merton, *Social Theory and Social Structure* (Glencoe, IL: Free Press, 1957).

56. Robert Agnew, "Foundation for a General Strain Theory of Crime and Delinquency," *Criminology* 30 (1992): 47–88.

57. Steven F. Messner and Richard Rosenfeld, *Crime and the American Dream*, 5th ed. (Belmont, CA: Wadsworth, 2012).

58. Marvin E. Wolfgang and Franco Ferracuti, *The Subculture of Violence: Towards an Integrated Theory in Criminology* (London: Tavistock, 1967).

59. Richard E. Nisbett, "Violence and U.S. Regional Culture," *American Psychologist* 48 (1993): 441–449.

60. T. W. Rice and C. R. Goldman, "Another Look at the Subculture of Violence Thesis: Who Murders Whom and Under What Circumstances," *Sociological Spectrum* 14 (1994): 371–384.

61. Ramiro Martinez Jr., "Crime and Immigration," *Criminologist* 35 (2010): 16–17.

62. Christopher G. Ellison, "Southern Culture and Firearms Ownership," *Social Science Quarterly* 72 (1991): 267–283; Jay Corzine, Lin Huff-Corzine, and Hugh P. Whitt, "Cultural and Subcultural Theories of Homicide," in Smith and Zahn, eds., *Homicide: A Sourcebook of Social Research*.

63. Albert Cohen, *Delinquent Boys: The Culture of the Gang* (Glencoe, IL: Free Press, 1955); Richard A. Cloward and Lloyd E. Ohlin, *Delinquency and Opportunity: A Theory of Delinquent Gang* (New York: Free Press, 1960); Walter Miller, "Lower Class Culture as Generating Milieu of Gang Delinquency," *Journal of Social Issues* 14 (1958): 5–19; Wolfgang and Ferracuti, *The Subculture of Violence*.

64. Elijah Anderson, *Code of the Street: Decency, Violence, and the Moral Life of the Inner City* (New York: Norton, 2000).

65. J. D. Vance, *Hillbilly Elegy* (New York: HarperCollins, 2016).

66. Albert Bandura, *Social Learning Theory* (Englewood Cliffs, NJ: Prentice Hall, 1977).

67. Jonathan L. Freedman, *Media Violence and Its Effect on Aggression: Assessing the Scientific Evidence* (Toronto: University of Toronto Press, 2002).

68. American Psychological Association, "APA Review Confirms Link Between Playing Violent Video Games and Aggression," Press release, August 13, 2015.

69. Greg Toppo, "Do Violent Video Games Inspire Violent Behavior?" *Scientific American*, July 1, 2015.

70. Christopher J. Ferguson and Cheryl K. Olson, "The Supreme Court and Video Game Violence: Will Regulation Be Worth the Costs to the First Amendment?" *Criminologist* 35 (2010): 18–21.

71. Edwin H. Sutherland, *Principles of Criminology*, 4th ed. (Philadelphia: Lippincott, 1947).

72. Ronald L. Akers, *Criminological Theories: Introduction, Evaluation and Application* (Los Angeles, CA: Roxbury, 2000).

73. Richard Rhodes, *Why They Kill: Discoveries of a Maverick Criminologist* (New York: Knopf, 1999).

74. Travis Hirschi, *Causes of Delinquency* (Berkeley, CA: University of California Press, 1969); Michael Gottfredson and Travis Hirschi, *A General Theory of Crime* (Stanford, CA: Stanford University Press, 1990).

75. Walter C. Reckless, "A New Theory of Delinquency and Crime," *Federal Probation* 25 (1961): 42–46.

76. Edwin Lemert, *Social Pathology* (New York: McGraw-Hill, 1951); Erving Goffman, *Stigma: Notes on the Management of a Spoiled Identity* (Englewood Cliffs, NJ: Prentice Hall, 1963); Howard Becker, *Outsiders: Studies in the Sociology of Deviance* (New York: Free Press, 1973).

77. Gottfredson and Hirschi, *A General Theory of Crime*.

78. Sampson and Laub, *Crime in the Making: Pathways and Turning Points Through Life*.

79. Albert J. Reiss Jr. and Jeffrey A. Roth, eds., *Understanding and Preventing Violence: Panel on the Understanding and Control of Violent Behavior* (Washington, DC: National Academy of Sciences, 1993).

CHAPTER FOUR

INTIMATE AND FAMILY MURDER

The family unit encompasses a wide constellation of relationships, many of which are linked by bloodlines. Understandably yet tragically, the around-the-clock opportunity for conflict and discord within families often causes that same blood to spill. Notwithstanding all the positive and nurturing aspects of family life, it is quite telling that the study of homicide has so many expressions within the family unit—instances when affection turns unhappily to aggression, including spousicide (spouse killings) and intimate partner homicide (spouses, ex-spouses, girlfriends or boyfriends); parricide, patricide, and matricide (the murder of parents, fathers, and mothers, respectively); siblicide, fratricide, and sororicide (the murder of a sibling, brother, and sister, respectively); filicide (murder of children by their parents) and infanticide (murder of young children); and familicide (murder of multiple family members), among other less common forms of intrafamilial homicide. That criminologists have established so many labels to describe killings by and of family members indicates the diversity of this phenomenon. Since different types of domestic homicides may have different patterns and trends, it is important that our discussion disaggregates the various types of domestic homicide.

Most people are immune from certain types of murder, such as drug-related killings, gang-related murders, and even school shootings, by virtue of their lifestyles. However, virtually everyone has some chance, however small, of being the victim of domestic homicide, unless of course they have absolutely no family or romantic connections. That said, intimate partner homicide and family-related murder typically aren't random and tend to occur in troubled relationships or families with histories of mental health, substance abuse, financial troubles, and domestic violence. Occasionally, however, an entire family is wiped out by one of its members with no criminal history and no warning signs.

Although the number of domestic homicides, especially intimate partner homicides, has declined over the past 20 years, as with most types of killing, homicides involving intimate partners or family members are significantly more common in the United States than in Canada, England, France, and other industrialized countries. During the years 2000 through 2016, intimate partners or family members killed 68,000 Americans, translating to an annual average of nearly 4,000 victims. As reflected in the breakdown of intimate partner and family homicides shown in Table 4.1, over half (52.4%) of the domestic homicides involved intimates (spouses, ex-spouses, or boyfriends/girlfriends), and over half of these intimate partner homicides involved current or former spouses as opposed to current boyfriends or girlfriends.

Table 4.1 Intimate Partner and Family Homicide, 2000–2016 Combined

Relationship of Victim to Offender	Sex of Victim		Total
	Male	**Female**	
Spouse	14.4%	37.4%	26.6%
Ex-spouse	1.0%	2.7%	1.9%
Parent	12.9%	8.0%	10.3%
Child	24.6%	12.7%	18.3%
Sibling	9.2%	1.8%	5.3%
Other family	21.0%	7.1%	13.7%
Boyfriend/girlfriend	16.9%	30.2%	23.9%
Total	100.0%	100.0%	100.0%

KILLING FOR PROFIT AND PRACTICALITY

Murder in the family and other intimate relationships spans a wide range of motives, from jealousy to revenge, from attention seeking to mercy. It is one of the most insidious motives, if only for its selfish cold-bloodedness, when the family unit occasionally becomes a vehicle for profit. Murders involving strangers, as we would expect, frequently involve the profit motive. Yet greed knows no limits. Blood may be thicker than water, but not always when cash is involved.

On Halloween 1974, as other Houston residents prepared treats to distribute to the neighborhood children, Ronald Clark O'Bryan replaced the white sugary powder inside several Pixy Stix with cyanide, one of which he placed in his own son's bag of goodies. O'Bryan's dastardly plan was to kill his 8-year-old son and collect on a $20,000 insurance policy. He had hoped that rampant concern (unfounded, as there are no documented cases of children dying from Halloween candy poisoned by strangers) for treat tampering as a form of adolescent Halloween trickery and the discovery of similarly contaminated candy in other children's bags (which fortunately was not eaten) would provide a convenient cover-up to his selfish deed. O'Bryan's plan failed. He was convicted of first-degree murder and was poisoned to death himself 10 years later in the form of lethal injection in a Texas prison.

Another episode of cold, calculating family murder, one that included overtones of racism, sent shockwaves reverberating through Boston, Massachusetts. On October 23, 1989, the police received an urgent call from a man using his car phone to report that he and his pregnant wife had just been shot by a stranger who had jumped into the backseat of their car. The caller, identified as 29-year-old Charles Stuart, claimed that he and his wife had been attacked by a black intruder dressed in a jogging suit as they drove home from a birthing class in a predominantly black section of the city. Charles Stuart survived the attack, but his wife and unborn child were not so fortunate.

Bostonians quickly rushed to support Charles Stuart with an unparalleled outpouring of sympathy. Everyone in Boston had heard the recording of Stuart's heart-wrenching call to 9-1-1 and had seen graphic images of the crime scene showing his wife Carol covered in blood and slumped in the passenger seat of the car. Everyone was shaken by Stuart's sorrowful eulogy to his wife read at the funeral he was too sick to attend. Even the most die-hard cynic was moved when, despite the severity of his injuries, Stuart begged to be taken across town to cradle his dying infant son in his arms. With the skill of a Shakespearean actor, Stuart played the role of a grieving husband and father.

By January 1990, however, as the police investigation into the homicide continued feverishly, Charles Stuart's story started to crumble. It was eventually discovered that he had indeed shot his wife to death after she refused to abort the pregnancy. Stuart had sensed that fatherhood would put a major dent in his ambitious career plans. His wife was a successful tax attorney, and he believed she would quit her job to stay home with their baby. Once the hoax was discovered, Stuart jumped off a bridge to his death rather than face public outrage, not to mention state prison. Stuart's brother, Matthew, confessed to helping him dispose of the gun and jewelry on the night of the murder and served 5 years in prison. Matthew had been led to believe the whole thing was just an insurance scam, and he helped Stuart that night without knowing Stuart had also murdered his wife. After his release, Matthew died from an overdose in a homeless shelter in 2011.

Charles Stuart was far from the only murderous husband who had a profound disdain for fatherhood. In December 2002, another woman in her eighth month of pregnancy was killed by her husband. Initially, Scott Peterson reported the disappearance of his 27-year-old wife Laci while he was on a Christmas Eve fishing trip in San Francisco Bay, some 90 miles from the couple's home in Modesto.

Believing him to be a loving and devoted husband, friends and relatives were initially sympathetic to Scott. As time passed and Laci didn't return, however, Scott's alibi began to fall apart. Massage therapist Amber Frey confessed to having an affair with the missing woman's husband, who denied his extramarital fling until photos of the romantically posed couple were discovered. In addition, several witnesses reported that Scott did not seem to be upset about his missing wife. He did little to further the investigation, when it was still possible that Laci was alive. He minimized media opportunities designed to gain the assistance of the public in locating his wife. Four months later, her decomposed body finally washed up on the shores of San Francisco Bay, in proximity to the area in which her husband claimed he had been fishing. Police investigators suggested that he had probably tied her to a concrete anchor, causing her body to sink to the bottom of the bay.

The motive for the murder was initially unclear. It apparently wasn't Scott's short-term affair: He had hooked up with Amber on only four occasions. It didn't seem like he did it for money: Scott had no financial problems. In fact, if Laci had lived, the couple would have inherited some part of Laci's grandparents' $2.4 million estate. Yet there were credible reports that Scott rejected his own impending fatherhood. He felt trapped and depressed and didn't want a child. He may not have appreciated the added responsibility of childrearing; he may have been unwilling to share the attention he had received from his spouse; he may have thought that fatherhood cramped his style with women. At his trial, Scott's sister-in-law testified that she had asked him whether he was ready for fatherhood. His response was telling: "I was kinda hoping for infertility."

OBSESSION AND JEALOUSY

The killer's desired reward in domestic murder cases is often not a practical matter. Instead, the motive involves securing the love and affection of another person. Tufts University professor William Douglas, a middle-aged family man, had grown so helplessly obsessed with prostitute Robin Benedict that he wanted her all to himself. Embezzling funds from various federal grants, Douglas placed Benedict on his research payroll to compensate her for sexual exclusivity. As time progressed and Douglas's obsession grew deeper, however, Benedict resisted his jealous possessiveness.

On March 5, 1983, Douglas, unable to accept the thought of his beloved Robin sexually entwined with another man, bludgeoned the 21-year-old call girl to death with a sledgehammer and dumped her body in a trash bin off Route 95, south of Boston. Although her body was never recovered by the police, the prosecution forged ahead with murder charges against the disgraced biochemist. Faced with a murder rap, Douglas pled guilty in exchange for a reduced charge of manslaughter.

The figurative romantic triangle has three points, and at each nexus we find a person with sufficient motivation for murder. Occasionally, the triangle's apex—the unfaithful two-timer—is murdered for his or her infidelity by a jealous and spiteful mate or lover. Forty-five-year-old Clara Harris, a dentist, tried everything to keep her husband, David, 41, from leaving her for another woman. She scheduled liposuction and breast augmentation surgery, went to a tanning salon, hired a personal trainer, lost 20 pounds, lightened her hair, and wore more provocative clothing. When none of this worked, Harris got behind the wheel of her car and repeatedly ran over her husband in a hotel parking lot, while his daughter (her stepdaughter) looked on in horror. Harris claimed the whole episode was an accident; however, a videotape of the incident, recorded by the private investigator hired by Harris to follow her philandering husband, showed her running over him multiple (perhaps as many as five) times. Harris was convicted of murder and sentenced to 20 years in prison and fined $10,000. In January 2007, a civil jury also awarded $3.75 million to Harris's in-laws as a result of their wrongful death suit against their son's killer. Denied early release in 2016, Harris was then granted parole in November 2017.

The Texas jury sent a clear message that it is hardly acceptable to kill an unfaithful mate rather than face rejection. Harris, like many rejected spouse killers, seemed to think that by killing her husband, she could preserve their relationship forever. More often, however, it is one of the competing rivals (not the two-timer) who is killed in order to clear the path for romance. On April 29, 1997, 33-year-old Craig Rabinowitz of Merion, Pennsylvania, an affluent suburb outside of Philadelphia, reported to the police that he had discovered his wife, Stefanie, dead in the bathtub, apparently the victim of an intruder. But in the following weeks, his story dissolved in the face of forensic evidence revealing a web of obsession and financial debt that served as a powerful motive for murder. Rabinowitz had secretly fantasized sharing a life with an exotic dancer nicknamed "Summer" and spent more than $100,000 on trips and private couch dances with the object of his desire. Unable to maintain his innocence any longer, Rabinowitz confessed to killing his wife, not only to remove her as an obstacle to romantic bliss but also to receive almost $2 million in life insurance to pay off his personal and business debts.

Romantic triangles can also lead to the violent expulsion of an outside threat to an existing relationship. While money and passion combined to drive Rabinowitz to murder his wife, affairs of the heart are often sufficient in themselves to inspire a homicide. When David Graham, a popular high school student athlete from Mansfield, Texas, confessed to his sweetheart, Diane Zamora, about his sexual tryst with sophomore Adrianne Jones, Zamora flew into an uncontrollable rage. As Graham tried to calm her, Zamora jealously insisted that Jones had to be killed. To prove his remorse and devotion, Graham conspired with Zamora in the

December 1995 beating and shooting death of Jones. The two lovers then went off to become cadets in military academies and vowed to keep the crime as their dark secret. However, Zamora later broke the pact by admitting her involvement to her roommates, leading to the arrest and conviction of the two conspirators for murder.

In 2012, 21-year-old Laura Aceves became the victim of her jealous ex-boyfriend and a justice system that failed to protect her despite clear evidence of an imminent threat. She was murdered by Victor Acuna-Sanchez, 18, while he was out on bail awaiting trial for two previous incidents of domestic assault. Laura had left her abuser and filed for yet another restraining order. Acuna-Sanchez missed meetings with his probation officer with no consequences, bragged about having guns in his possession, and, in the end, violated multiple orders of protection to hunt her down and kill her. For two years, he had beaten her, destroyed her property, and threatened to kill her and her children if she left him. On multiple occasions, he had punched her to the point of unconsciousness, strangled her, poured bleach in her car's gas tank, burned her passport and social security card, and destroyed her clothes and furniture. Multiple gaps in the system allowed Acuna-Sanchez to continue terrorizing her. Laura's murder was the impetus for Arkansas to pass "Laura's Law," which required police to screen domestic abuse cases and assess the risk of homicide.

Heterosexuals do not have the market cornered on domestic violence or homicide. In December 2002, for example, 24-year-old Dorothy Haines of Ocean City, New Jersey, murdered and dismembered her lover, Suzanne Stiehl, 39, and bragged about it afterward. Haines pled guilty to aggravated manslaughter and received the sentence of 27 years in prison. In Norfolk, Virginia, John "Smoke" Davis, 24, also pled guilty to killing his partner, 36-year-old Ronald Luper, during a July 2005 incident that was very much out of character for the couple. Davis and Luper shared a rocky and violent relationship that featured occasional knife fights. However, the level of discord eventually culminated in a final and fatal altercation involving tools—a hammer and a screwdriver. At one point, Luper tore off Davis's lip with his teeth, prompting Davis to grab his gun and shoot his boyfriend twice.

Unfortunately, and in large part due to bias, domestic homicide figures involving the lesbian, gay, bisexual, transgender, and queer (LGBTQ) community are not officially tracked in any systematic way. Although there is a "homosexual relationship" category in the FBI's *Supplementary Homicide Reports*, many of these cases are apparently classified instead as acquaintance killings. With same-sex marriages having been recognized by the U.S. Supreme Court in 2015, advocates are hopeful that additional resources will be made available to monitor and respond to violence in nontraditional relationships. From what data are available, it appears that the LGBTQ community has much higher rates of domestic violence. Based on victimization survey data, lesbian and bisexual women report much higher lifetime prevalence rates of violence than do heterosexual women, and gay and bisexual men report higher lifetime intimate partner violence prevalence rates than heterosexual men.[1] Members of the LGBTQ community are less likely to report their experiences with domestic violence to the authorities for fear of being judged negatively or even outed by service providers, including police. Moreover, stereotypes that fights between women are just "catfights" and won't involve serious harm and that male victims should just "man up" and defend themselves leave LGBTQ victims without the support they need. The lack of intervention in early instances of partner violence increases the likelihood of escalation to domestic homicide.

For the longest time, the social stigma attached to gay relationships could itself serve as the precipitant for murder. In Columbia, Missouri, Jesse Valencia, a 23-year-old openly gay college student, was murdered by his deeply closeted lover, Steven Rios, a married man and a patrolman on the local police force. Apparently, Officer Rios had a history of soliciting sex from both men and women while on duty and had stalked several crime victims while working on their cases. In June 2004, as Valencia tried to end the affair and threatened to expose Rios to the police brass, Rios choked Valencia into unconsciousness and then slashed his throat, dumping the body in an alleyway before returning home to his wife and new baby. Rios's first murder conviction was overturned on appeal, but the second conviction, in 2009, resulted in a life sentence with possibility of parole in 23 years.

Attitudes toward gay and lesbian relationships have, of course, changed for the better since 2004, when Rios felt compelled to kill as means of concealing his sexual activities. Although there may be less of a need now to commit murder as an identity cover-up, it will remain the case that ostensibly loving relationships, gay or straight, will all too often serve as a breeding ground for jealousy, hostility, and murder.

POWER, CONTROL, AND ABUSE

The extraordinary cases of family and intimate homicide described thus far involve a selfish and cold-blooded scheme to commit murder in order to achieve a financial or romantic goal. Most instances of homicide within intimate relationships, however, are more likely to represent an expression of power or a defensive response to it, rather than an instrumental means for satisfying some other personal objective.

More often than not, the use of lethal force by a spouse is not the first violent episode within the relationship (and may even have been preceded by the murder of another spouse). One recent study examined 250 cases of women murdered by their intimate partners and found that nearly two-thirds had been assaulted by their mate in the past. In situations like these, murder is not so much a spontaneous, unpredictable act or a behavior out of character for the perpetrator but the culmination of a consistent and growing pattern of abuse within the relationship.[2]

Although the jury in the criminal trial of ex–football star O. J. Simpson may, for example, have been unconvinced that he had murdered his estranged wife, Nicole Brown, and her friend Ronald Goldman, it was incontrovertible that he had assaulted and terrorized her in the years leading up to her violent death. The jury, like millions of Americans, heard 9-1-1 tapes of her desperate pleas for help while O. J. Simpson stormed her apartment. Notwithstanding his guilt or innocence, the potential for lethal violence had clearly been evidenced.

The most troubling and perplexing cases of domestic violence involve relationships held together not so much by intimacy and affection but by intimidation and aggression. In some marriages, the husband's sense of ego and self-worth depends on his ability to control, dominate, and manipulate his wife and children—not just to be in charge of traditional male responsibilities such as the family finances but to have complete and absolute authority over the household. Should his position of authority be questioned by what he perceives (or misperceives) as insolence or disobedience from his subordinate partner, he may use violence or the threat of violence to enforce his rule and reestablish command. The frequency and level of violence within such a relationship typically escalate as the abuser/controller constantly expands and tests the limits of aggression, possessiveness, and control. His wife may threaten to leave for the sake of the children, if not for herself, and he may try to exploit her needs and feelings of guilt by begging for forgiveness and promising to change. Unfortunately, in some cases, the only change to occur is for the violence to increase in its brutality as he attempts to tighten his control.

Despite widespread efforts in this country to emancipate victims of domestic violence, we have not successfully resolved all the legal, financial, and emotional ties that can strangle a woman as much as her abusive spouse can. Many women remain in a violent and potentially lethal relationship out of emotional or financial dependency or a perception, even if a false one, that staying together is better for the children.

Domestic violence expert Lenore Walker has characterized the response of some abuse victims as "learned helplessness."[3] Frustrated in her ineffectual struggles to repel early episodes of abuse, a woman may come to develop a sense of resignation that she is helpless in controlling her own fate or that of the children. Seeing no way out while perhaps hoping things will improve, she may stay in the abusive marriage, sometimes until the level of violence becomes deadly. Learned helplessness has its origins in the 1965 work of psychologist Martin Seligman's "experiments," which included shocking dogs. Seligman discovered that even when they could escape, the dogs continued to endure the abuse without attempting to do so. Obviously, despite this cruel experiment by an unenlightened scientist with no regard for animal suffering, there is actually very little scientific support for the concept of learned helplessness in most humans. In actuality, certain types of people—often, those suffering from depression, anxiety, and other mental health disorders—are much more likely to endure and not flee from abusive situations.

Similar to the *Stockholm syndrome*, a term used to describe the compliant behavior of hostages, a domestic abuse victim who feels trapped in a violent relationship can become even more closely bonded to her attacker.[4] Initially, she may strive to please and appease her abuser as a means of sheer survival. As she becomes more isolated from others, she may grow increasingly dependent on her abuser for whatever bits of attention and meager rewards he concedes her. In extreme cases, she can identify so closely with her controlling mate that she focuses exclusively on his real or imagined good points, unable psychologically to see him in a more accurate light and even believing that she deserves the abuse she endures.

As an alternative response to sustained abuse, a woman may grow in her determination to survive. Rather than give up hope and give in to their victimizers, many women find the courage and will to fight back—figuratively, if not literally—by seeking help and refuge from friends and family or legal and social services.[5]

Although the survival instinct may be healthier both physically and emotionally, on occasion, attempts to escape and survive can instigate retaliatory acts of lethal violence. A move to terminate the relationship occasionally becomes the innocent precipitant to murder, sparked by what Dutton has called "abandonment rage."[6] For example, in a study of a group of nearly 300 women murdered by their intimates, researchers found that 42% of victims had either separated or threatened to separate from their assailant.[7] It is the fear of this kind of deadly outcome that ultimately keeps many women in violent relationships. The usual question "Why didn't she just leave?" is an uninformed question because leaving is one of the most dangerous things a battered woman can do.

When a woman does attempt to break away from an abusive partner, he may see her effort to take over control of the relationship as nothing less than a capital offense, punishable by death. In 1991, for example, 39-year-old James Colbert of Concord, New Hampshire, killed his estranged wife and three daughters before taking his own life by leaping off a bridge into the water below. Learning that his wife had started a new relationship, Colbert reasoned, "If I can't have her and the kids, then no one can." As an ultimate expression of control, Colbert, and definitely not his wife, would be the one to decide when, where, how, and on what terms their marriage would end.

Although the most typical scenario involves lethal violence as the offensive climax to escalating abuse by a husband, in 23% of domestic murders occurring between 2000 and 2016, it was the woman who dealt the fatal blow. Just like men, the woman may murder in response to her mate's infidelity, or she kills him to collect life insurance, or kills him in order to be with her lover. But, more often than men, intimate partner homicides committed by women are frequently a self-protective response to intimidation, threats, and physical, emotional, or sexual abuse.[8]

In a 1977 murder case made famous in the TV film *The Burning Bed*, starring actress Farrah Fawcett, 30-year-old Francine Hughes of Dansville, Michigan, poured gasoline around the bed where her ex-husband Mickey lay sleeping off his latest drinking binge. After lighting a match and setting her former husband ablaze, she loaded her children into the car and drove straight to the police station, where she confessed. To the detectives, it had seemed like a simple case of domestic homicide. But, after hearing testimony detailing 14 years of battery and death threats, the jury surprised the legal community, if not the nation, by finding Hughes not guilty by reason of temporary insanity.

Ever since the "burning bed" case, the courts have struggled with the battered woman syndrome as a defense to murder.[9] A chronic abuse victim feels trapped as a consequence of her prolonged history of physical, sexual, or psychological punishment. In the tradition of English common law, in order to invoke self-defense, the risk of aggression has to be immediate and with no reasonable means of escape. Yet, increasingly, the courts have excused or at least lessened responsibility when violence was not imminent but a day-to-day, continuing threat. As for the requirement of taking flight, the courts have begun to recognize that legal ties and financial dependencies, if not feelings of sheer terror, often prevent what ordinarily would appear to be opportunities for escape.

Whatever the posture of the courts with regard to women fighting back at their partners, popular culture may send a different message. For example, a recent article in the *Economist* described the changing portrayal of domestic violence in country music.[10] In past decades the lyrics of country music typically referred to domestic violence by men toward women. However, more recent songs describe women fighting back against their abusers by killing them, or what Peterson characterizes as "self-help."[11] Female empowerment is clearly the theme of many Carrie Underwood songs but with lyrics such as "Something in his Tennessee whiskey," "How he died is still a mystery," and "She heard those sirens screaming out / Her daddy laid there passed out on the couch" suggesting murder as an appropriate response.[12] We don't want a generation of women to believe poisoning is a viable solution any more than we approve of the violent messages in gangsta rap songs.

One of the most dramatic and fascinating changes in homicide patterns over the past several decades involves the prevalence of intimate partner homicide. Partially due to the efforts by battered women advocacy groups, the incidence of domestic homicide has fallen nationally over the past quarter century. Overall, as shown in Figure 4.1, the number of homicides of husbands, wives, and boyfriends/girlfriends has declined steadily from 3,268 in 1976 to 2,157 in 2016, a substantial 34% decline.

Dugan and her colleagues found that some resources, such as warrantless arrest provisions and economic assistance for victims, may indeed have reduced the incidence of domestic violence homicides. However, warrantless arrests had a positive effect only for white victims, both married and unmarried.[13] Protective

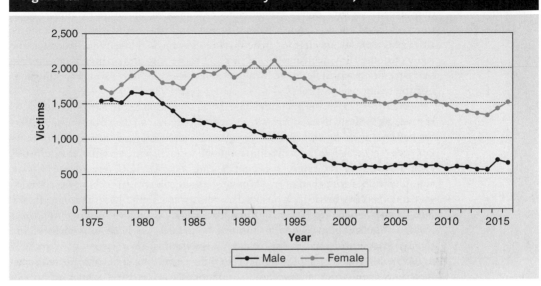

Figure 4.1 Intimate Partner Homicide by Sex of Victim, 1976–2016

orders issued in court, for example, may have increased the risk of homicide for some demographic groups (e.g., unmarried black male and female partners). It is critically important, therefore, when implementing domestic violence reduction policies, that both the protective effects and the potential for backlash/retaliation be considered.

Some critics have suggested that the downturn in spousal homicide is little more than a demographic artifact resulting from changes in domesticity, or living arrangements, rather than any real progress in violence reduction between marital partners. According to this theory, as divorce rates rise and marriage rates decline, fewer men and women are "eligible" to be murdered by their spouses. However, contrary to the popular notion that divorce rates are increasing, analysis shows that both marriage and divorce rates have declined since about 1980. Perhaps reflecting the decline in marriage, the number of unmarried women murdered by boyfriends has increased significantly, from a yearly average of about 320 in the period 1976–1980 to an average of about 470 per year in 2011–2016, an increase of 45%. Over the past four decades, the percentage of intimate partner homicides that involved a boyfriend–girlfriend relationship, as opposed to marital relationship, grew from less than 25% to nearly 50% of the total intimate homicides by 2015.[14] Although this growth is at least in part consistent with the expanded number of unmarried women in the population, it does suggest that declining marriage rates have put fewer women at risk for spousal homicide but more women at risk for "dating" homicide.

Over the latter half of the twentieth century, divorce laws were indeed liberalized. By contrast to an earlier era when the marital ties could not be broken easily without proof of cause, such as mental or physical cruelty or adultery, no-fault divorce laws have permitted couples to split before the level of discord reaches extreme and violent proportions. Yet, for relationships in which violence is indeed a form of control, the easy availability of divorce can be a cruel illusion. The "if I can't have you, no one can" threat would generally prohibit an amicable no-fault divorce. Fortunately, improvement in the economic status of women has eroded the control men have historically had over their spouses.

Another factor behind the decline in intimate homicide is that the social stigma associated with being an abused spouse (as well as a divorcée) has greatly diminished. During a less enlightened era, victims of domestic abuse often internalized blame and guilt for their own victimization. "If only I were a better wife, a better cook, a better lover, he wouldn't get mad and beat me." Today, as the topic of domestic violence has been brought more into the open, victims are less likely to feel responsible for their plight and thus more likely to make a move to exit the relationship.

Besides divorce, more immediate legal and social interventions—such as restraining orders, mandatory police arrest procedures, abuse hotlines, shelters for battered women, and support groups and counseling for victims of domestic violence—have helped provide some abused women with a viable escape route, even though, as indicated, these steps can, on occasion, precipitate violent counteraction. More than ever, a woman has alternatives to picking up a loaded gun and shooting her loaded husband. As shown in Figure 4.1, it is ironically the men who have benefited the most from intervention strategies designed to protect women. The steepest decline in intimate homicides has been in women killing their partners (husbands, ex-husbands, and boyfriends), down from 1,537 in 1976 to 649 in 2016, a remarkable decline. Given the expanding array of legal and social interventions, murder is less often the only or last resort for a woman to protect herself from a current or former intimate who abuses or stalks her.

By contrast, the improvement in the number of women killed by their intimates has been more modest and relatively recent. From 1976 to 1993, the incidents of women killed by intimates increased from about 1,700 to 2,100 per year. Apparently, men were unconcerned about the increasing array of interventions available to victims of domestic violence. In fact, some men were inspired in a decidedly violent way in the face of restraining orders and other initiatives by their wives or girlfriends to escape. It is only since 1993 that the number of men killing wives, ex-wives, and girlfriends has declined as well, from 2,105 in 1993 to 1,508 in 2016. This downturn coincides with passage of the federal Violence Against Women Act as well as the Domestic Violence Offender Gun Ban (often referred to as the "Lautenberg Amendment"), which prohibits gun purchases for anyone convicted of misdemeanor domestic violence.

Although the numbers of men killed by women and women killed by men in domestic homicides had been steady or declining for years, Figure 4.1 shows a recent uptick for both groups. Men were victims of 690 intimate partner homicides in 2015 and 649 in 2016, higher numbers than any year since 2000 (but nowhere near the 1979 number of 1,658) and women were the victims of 1,508 intimate partner homicides in 2016 (versus the high in 1993 of 2,105), a level not seen since 2009. This uptick may signal a disturbing trend and may be a manifestation of the stresses induced by the mortgage crisis, underemployment, a lack of domestic violence shelter space and the opioid epidemic. New York City officials are concerned that as their overall homicide rate has declined for 25 years and declined by as much as 40% since 2002, domestic homicides have remained relatively high.

We read frequently of domestic disputes that escalate rapidly to deadly proportions, especially if a gun is available. In fact, two-thirds of homicides by intimate partners involve a gun. The firearm may have been purchased ostensibly to protect and defend the family from an outside intruder, but ultimately it is fired offensively against a loved one in a moment of rage or revenge. In their analysis of cases in Tennessee, Washington, and Ohio, for example, Arthur Kellermann and his colleagues found that a gun in the home increased the likelihood of domestic homicide by nearly a factor of three.[15]

Figure 4.2 shows the trends in intimate partner homicide by weapon type for male victims. Aside from the uptick in 2016, the number of males killed by their partners with a gun has remained below 400 since 1999, and knife homicides have remained at or below about 200 a year. For female victims of intimate partner homicide, as illustrated by Figure 4.3, we see the same uptick in 2015–2016 and nearly two times the male victim number each year, about 800 women murdered with a gun. Women killed by knives continues to decline, and like male victims, the number of women killed with other methods has remained fairly stable since 1976.

Figure 4.2   Intimate Partner Homicide by Weapon Type, Male Victims, 1976–2016

Figure 4.3   Intimate Partner Homicide by Weapon Type, Female Victims, 1976–2016

The availability of social and legal interventions to abuse victims is, unfortunately, not equally extensive in all parts of the country. The decline in the percentage of homicides involving intimate partners has occurred primarily in urban areas. It is in these same locales where the greatest emphasis has been placed on providing resources such as shelters for battered women. In many suburbs and especially rural areas, a victim of abuse may not have access to such escape routes and may even remain in a dangerous and potentially lethal relationship to avoid the stigma within her small community.

Similar to programs that track sex offenders, some jurisdictions are using global positioning satellite systems (GPS) for domestic violence offenders with restraining orders. When the offender enters the off-limits zone, the victim and police are alerted. In addition, research that found that primary care and other physicians may be a useful source of information regarding possible domestic violence has led to a screening tool used by thousands of doctors across the United States. Most women, and some men, who have recently seen a doctor will recall some version of the question, "Do you feel safe in your home?" particularly if the doctor's visit is a result of some sort of accidental injury but also for people who may be suffering from anxiety or depression.

Most incidents of domestic violence don't become domestic homicides, but which ones do? Although risk assessments for domestic violence have been around for decades, they appear only recently to have been implemented by law enforcement. Taking the woman aside and asking her some simple questions about what is happening in the home, including asking about the extent of injuries, the frequency of abuse, forced sexual activities, substance abuse, and the presence of firearms in the house, can help police determine the potential lethality of the situation and link the woman to important resources. Although departments in at least 33 states are using a lethality risk assessment, most departments across the United States do not appear to measure the risk of a future domestic homicide when they respond to a domestic violence call. Only one state, Arkansas, has passed a law requiring all police to screen domestic violence victims to assess their risk of domestic homicide.

Although most of the media coverage of traumatic brain injury (TBI) has focused on the National Football League (NFL) and returning veterans, we also know that the beatings and concussions sustained by domestic violence victims over the course of years or even decades are doing significant damage to their brains. As many as 20 million women may be exposed to a traumatic brain injury from domestic violence each year. As with a diagnosis of learned helplessness, there is also the potential that a diagnosis of TBI could be used against a woman in custody battles.

In addition to the horrific toll of physical and psychological damage, domestic violence also takes a sometimes devastating financial toll on a survivor. A woman may stagger out of the relationship alive but her credit is ruined, her savings is gone, and she has lost her job. Financial counseling and assistance are now a big part of restoring a survivor's life.

A severe lack of funding and shelter space continues to plague the United States. According to the National Network to End Domestic Violence, as many as 11,000 requests for help every day go unmet. Many women stay in an abusive situation versus facing homelessness for themselves and their children. Even when shelter space is available, the vast majority of shelters do not accept pets. Thus, a woman may have to leave her cat or dog, knowing that her abuser will harm or kill it. We know that women who seek shelter for domestic violence are much more likely to report that their batterers hurt or killed animals than women who are not victims of domestic violence. As many as half of domestic violence victims in shelters left pets with their abusers, and as many as 65% of domestic violence victims are unable to leave because they won't leave their pets. Finally, in response to this critical problem, some shelters now offer foster programs for pets, and a few even offer on-site places for pets.

Do domestic violence programs for abusers work? The court-mandated treatment programs for batterers have never been reliably evaluated and are criticized by many as not effective. The National Institute of Justice (NIJ) in 2003 found most of the intervention programs focused on batterers did not change their likelihood to reoffend, and in 2009 NIJ found that some programs may even make abusers worse.[16] Rather than attempting to intervene in the tangled, controlling minds of abusers, our best bet may be to focus our limited resources on prevention programs and teach boys, and girls, about healthy relationships.

In the final analysis, people often wonder in cases of cold-blooded spousal homicide, "Why didn't he just get a divorce?" For some killers, lethal dissolution of their marriage has far greater benefits—monetary and otherwise—than the legal alternative in divorce court. Clearly, some estranged husbands and wives are motivated to keep all of the marital assets, leaving aside any extra profit from life insurance. Another "asset" they may not want to share is custody of the children. In 2002, for example, 43-year-old Harold Stonier of Concord, Massachusetts, paid a significant sum of money to a hit man who turned out to be an undercover agent. Stonier apparently wanted his wife dead, even if it meant paying a sum greater than what he may have forfeited in a divorce settlement. According to his taped statements, he did not want to lose custody of his son, Jamie. The only way to ensure he got custody, Stonier reasoned, was to eliminate his wife. Liberalized divorce laws may therefore have had a greater impact on husbands killing wives than on wives killing their husbands. And for women who are afraid when they hear about the latest extremist mass murder, the reality of their real risk is domestic homicide, not terrorist homicide. As recently noted by Gloria Steinem, more American women have been killed by their partners since September 11, 2001, than all of the victims from the September 11 attacks plus the deaths in the wars in Iraq and Afghanistan. Time for a real risks versus perceived risks reality check.

FAMILY ANNIHILATION

Most family homicides involve a single perpetrator (usually the husband/father) and a single victim (usually his wife). Even when only one person is attacked, others in the household, typically the children, become secondary victims, suffering indirectly by witnessing violence and by having to live with its consequences, that is, having a murdered mother and an incarcerated father.

Liem and her colleagues found that familicides involving an intimate partner and at least one child occurred approximately 23 times each year in the United States. In these cases, interpersonal problems (threat of divorce, separation, or a rival relationship) were found to be more critical than financial problems. Overall, 96% of perpetrators were male, with ages ranging from 18 to 90. Approximately 44% of offenders had a previous criminal history, including drug offenses, violence, and domestic violence.[17]

On occasion, however, the domestic murderer doesn't stop with just one victim but may extend his carnage through the entire family. Although the children may have little or nothing to do with his grudge or grievance, they may still be linked in his mind with the primary victim—after all, they are her children.

At the extreme in terms of extent of victimization, nearly half the mass murders in the United States involve family members of the perpetrator, a matter to be discussed in Chapter 9. Typically, these mass murders involve a husband and father murdering his wife and children in a single violent episode. However, on occasion, violence can spread to extended family, as well as others caught in the path of destruction.

Although his castle was little more than a ramshackle home in Dover, Arkansas, Ronald Gene Simmons was the king in his kingdom. He ruled the household, his wife, children, and grandchildren with absolute control. Simmons dictated where his family members could go, when, and with whom. By Christmastime 1987, however, he was losing his grip—not on reality but on his family. Simmons's family life seemed to be crumbling around him. Although the kids still obeyed, they now did so without a shred of respect for their father. They had grown rude and insulting toward him. To a former military man like Simmons, this "verbal abuse" was sheer insubordination. But insubordination was nothing compared to desertion. Simmons was aware that his wife was on the verge of leaving him and taking the kids with her. In a final desperate act of control, Simmons executed his entire family, not only his wife, children, and grandchildren who lived with him but also his older children and their families in succession as they came to the house to visit for Christmas. By the end of a five-day siege, Simmons had killed 14 family members in the largest family massacre in U.S. history. Even then, he wasn't quite finished. After annihilating his family, he launched a 45-minute rampage through the nearby town of Russellville, where he killed two and wounded four others. Simmons was executed by lethal injection in 1990.

Family annihilation is usually committed by the husband/father. In murder by proxy, the husband suffers through a nasty separation or divorce, perhaps also a child custody battle, blaming his partner for all of his misfortunes.[18] From the killer's standpoint, she caused the breakup; she will not let him see his own children; she is pure evil. Revenge is the motive.

Angry over a recent divorce, Bruce Pardo, 45, showed up at his former in-laws' house dressed in a Santa suit on Christmas Eve. With more than 25 people present in the house, Pardo began shooting and then set the house ablaze with a flamethrower. Nine people, including his ex-wife, both of her parents, two of her brothers, her sister, and several other relatives, were killed. Evidence suggests Pardo planned to escape (plane tickets and money were later discovered), but the Santa suit caught on fire during the massacre, so he changed his plans from fleeing the country to driving to his brother's house and killing himself in his car.

Familicides are certainly not unique to the United States. In 1985, for example, England's Jeremy Bamber, hoping to inherit the family's estate, killed his adoptive parents, his adoptive sister, and her twin sons. Bamber attempted to frame his adoptive sister, who had struggled with mental health issues, for the murders. In the end, all he received for his efforts was a lengthy prison sentence.

In 2016, Hasnain Warekar, a 32-year-old clerk living in Thane, India, hosted a large family dinner for his wife and two daughters, his parents, four sisters, four nephews, and two nieces. There was little chance of it being a pleasant occasion, as Warekar had lost his family's money in a stock trade gone bad and suspected that his family was also aware of his having sexually abused his intellectually challenged sister. It didn't take long for the guests to fall asleep from the spiked beverage, giving Warekar ample time to slit their throats, after which he took his own life.

One sister managed to flee after hiding in a bedroom, and she provided details of the horrific family slaughter she had witnessed.

Murder for Love

Within families, murder can be an expression of love and compassion. Despite the laws prohibiting euthanasia, occasionally children kill elderly and dying parents or parents kill their sickly children to spare them the misery of living. Sometimes it is a case of assisted suicide in which the victim is too weak to execute the fatal procedure. Other times, a loving family member may make the decision for the victim in a merciful act of homicide.

Family annihilations of perfectly healthy loved ones can also reflect the same notion of love, albeit twisted and inspired by depression. To the murderer, life on earth may be so miserable that he feels his loved ones will be better off dead. In what psychiatrist Shervert Frazier termed *suicide by proxy*, the killer sees his loved ones as an extension of himself.[19] He feels personal responsibility for the well-being of his wife and children and sees no other way out of his predicament. Although less common than murder by proxy, suicide by proxy (also known as extended suicide) involves a perverse sense of altruism, in which the perpetrator decides to kill himself and everyone else in his family, taking them all to a better life in the hereafter, where they will be reunited in eternal bliss. The assailant typically has suffered a financial catastrophe.[20] He may have been fired or may have lost a tremendous amount in the stock market, and he believes that he will never again be capable of supporting his family.

Apparently triggered by looming financial problems, Brian Short, 45, shot his three teenaged children, his wife, and then himself inside their Minnesota home in 2015. The family had recently stopped their weekly housecleaning service and Short's nursing website was embroiled in a federal lawsuit. In a similar case in 2017, after hosting a dinner party for friends, Keith Kroeker shot and killed his twin 10-year-old sons and 7-year-old daughter; killed his wife, Erin, 37, with the use of a blunt instrument; set the house on fire; and then shot and killed himself. The Kroeker family was thought to be a close, religious family in their small Oregon town of about 3,000 people. As it happened, the family remained close through life and death.

Lawrence DeLisle, age 29, of Lincoln Park, Michigan, had become so overwhelmed with despair that he deliberately drove his station wagon straight into the Detroit River in an effort to murder his entire family—his wife, four kids, and himself. After hitting the water, his survival instinct overtook his self-pity, and he successfully swam to safety, as did his wife. The children were not so lucky, however. Unable to extricate themselves from their seat belts, they drowned within minutes. DeLisle's father had killed himself in the same car less than two years before the Detroit River incident, and there were still blood stains in the car from his father's suicide by gun. Despite his claim of innocence (even though he originally confessed to police after hours of interrogation), DeLisle was convicted of four counts of murder and one count of the attempted murder of his wife and received multiple life sentences without parole. DeLisle has continued to proclaim his innocence, and in 2014 on the 25th anniversary of the tragedy he still claimed that the gas pedal stuck and the whole event was an accident. His wife divorced him and remarried.

While it is easy to be suspicious of DeLisle's motives, other family murderers have been better able to follow through on their suicide mission. By May 1990, 37-year-old Hermino Elizalde, described by friends and neighbors in Chicago as a devoted father, had become hopelessly despondent over his recent firing. He was even more concerned about his ex-wife's attempt to exploit his lapse in employment to win custody of their four daughters and one son, after she accused him of mistreating them. Rather than losing his beloved children, he decided to keep them together at any cost . . . at least spiritually. Elizalde doused his sleeping children with gasoline, lit a match, and set them afire one at a time. When he was sure they were dead, he set himself on fire. By killing them all, Elizalde felt assured that they would be reunited in a better life after death.

Many people find it absolutely unfathomable that someone would commit murder in the name of love. Yet, the emotions that motivated George T. O'Leary to shoot his wife and five of his six children to death inside their Boston, Massachusetts, home in 1973 are crystal clear. "I love my wife," O'Leary wrote in his suicide note just before swallowing a lethal dose of sleeping pills. "I love my children. I can't live without them. So I'm going to take them with me. . . . I'm sorry I had to do it."

Familicides, even instances of murder out of love, can occasionally involve multiple perpetrators. In 2012, 54-year-old Sandy Ford, a devout Jehovah's Witness, barricaded herself in the family garage with her three grandchildren and her 32-year-old son Andy, along with two dogs and a cat. Sandy and Andy were upset over the prospect of having to return the children to their mother and father. Instead, they filled the garage with carbon monoxide and died along with the three children, ages 5, 6, and 10.

MURDER-SUICIDE

Murder-suicides typically take one of four forms. The most common type involves spouses or other intimate partners. Most of these situations are motivated by rejection and jealousy, although some are an elderly man (or, more rarely, a woman) who is unable to cope with his spouse's declining health or move to assisted living. The second most common type of murder-suicide involves a parent who murders a child or even multiple children before committing suicide. A third type, as described in the previous section, is associated with a family annihilation, and a final form includes extrafamilial victims (e.g., friends, coworkers).[21]

There is no national tracking system for murder-suicide, and thus most of the data on this type of event are based on a review of coroner and medical examiner records as well as news accounts. Comstock and her colleagues studied cases of murder-suicide in the state of Oklahoma from 1994 to 2001. They found that the typical offender was a white male over 30 years of age who killed a current or former intimate partner.[22] Men were much more likely than women to kill themselves after murdering their partner and/or children. These relationships were characterized as possessive and usually stemmed from divorce or estrangement. Eighty percent of the victims were female, two-thirds were current or former intimate partners, and 20% of victims were children of the perpetrator.

The Violence Policy Center (VPC) began tracking murder-suicides in 2002. Based on analysis of news reports from 2002 to 2014, VPC has found that more than 1,200 Americans die in murder-suicides each year. Because in many cases there is more than one murder victim, the homicide toll exceeds the suicide toll. VPC findings for 2014 showed that 72% of the murder-suicides were intimate partners, 89% involved male perpetrators, 93% involved a gun, and 80% of murder-suicides occurred at home. Similar to patterns in homicide, 90% of murder-suicides were committed by men, but unlike murders generally, 75% of victims in murder-suicide were women. Also unique is the role of age. Whereas individuals over age 55 were rarely implicated in murder, one-third of those who carried out murder-suicide were over age 55.[23] Almost three-quarters of all murder-suicides in the VPC report involved intimate partners, yet some reflected caregiver situations between partners or even an adult child caring for aging, sick parents.

Are murder-suicides more like homicides or more like suicides? Recent research comparing murder-suicide to homicide and to suicide found that murder-suicides are a unique type of event, differing from both homicides and suicides. Perpetrators of homicide-suicides are older, more likely to be male, and more likely to be married than are single-victim homicide offenders or people who only kill themselves. This study also found less of an effect of alcohol use, less history of domestic violence, and less unemployment in homicide-suicides as compared to homicides. Looking globally, these researchers reported the highest rates of murder-suicide in the United States, followed by Switzerland, both countries with the highest rates of gun ownership.[24] The typical warning signs of alcohol use, unemployment, or previous domestic violence history are less likely to characterize murder-suicides, potentially leaving us with fewer known interventions and pointing to the need for detailed study of these events.

What causes some intimate partners to commit suicide after the homicide of a partner? The search for risk factors reveals that a history of perpetrator depression, a previous history of battering, and the presence of a firearm all increase the likelihood of murder-suicide. When a perpetrator threatens to kill the woman and/or other family members, threatens the family with a weapon, engages in stalking behavior, has had orders of protection filed against him, and uses alcohol and drugs, these should be warning signs for the possibility of a murder-suicide.[25]

The death toll is high in some murder-suicides, particularly those involving male perpetrators. In July 2006, Trevor Branscum, 37, killed his four sleeping children with his hunting rifle and then killed himself. The children ranged from 5 to 12 years of age. Branscum had had an argument with his wife. She then left the house, and he killed the children in what appeared to be an attempt to punish his wife over their dispute. But men aren't the only ones to hand out their own death penalty as the punishment for rejection. Jessica Edens of South Carolina allegedly shot and killed her estranged husband's new girlfriend, then killed her two children, ages 5 and 9, and then shot herself. Eden was stalking, harassing, texting, posting online, and calling incessantly in the days before the murders and suicide. Her husband had called the police, and they had checked on the welfare of the children the day before the murders and found them to be watching TV and eating popcorn. The inability to cope with rejection and move on is clearly a skill some people don't have.

Although the media seems to focus its coverage more on the murder-suicide cases that involve younger couples, research by Donna Cohen found the rate of murder-suicide to be twice as high among the over-55 age group than among younger couples.[26] Her research also suggested that this phenomenon (older couple murder-suicides) may be on the rise. In older couples, it is most common for the husband to be the perpetrator and the wife to be the unwitting victim, typically shot while asleep. Many episodes may stem from the husband's inability to cope with a caregiving role. He may rationalize his crime as an act of love or compassion, but often the wife is not terminally ill; he just can't cope with the burdens of caretaking.

PARRICIDE

Family massacres are generally committed by the head of the household who perceives that he has total say over his clan, in life and in death. He feels entitled by his position to determine his family's destiny. Yet, a few family annihilations have also been committed by children as a violent reaction to this same type of parental domination and control. In 1976, for example, 18-year-old Harry De La Roche Jr. methodically executed his mother, father, and two brothers in their beds in order to free himself of his dad's domination. Home from college for Thanksgiving vacation, De La Roche could not bring himself to face his father with his decision to quit school. Murder would be the easier way out. After 40 years, De La Roche is still in prison in New Jersey, having been denied parole on several occasions, in part due to his unwillingness to ever admit that he murdered his family.

Most parricides take the life of a single victim, one parent or guardian, and not an entire family killed by a child. In July 2010, for example, Adruis Ovalles, a 15-year-old boy from New York City, stabbed to death Albert Hartzog, his mother's live-in boyfriend and biological father of his younger brother, a man with whom Adruis had numerous conflicts in the past. Adruis became enraged when he learned that Hartzog had disconnected the cable service, so that he could no longer watch television.

According to Kathleen Heide, the majority of children who kill a parent aren't children at all—at least in terms of chronological age.[27] Adult children who kill are typically males who suffer from a serious mental illness, such as schizophrenia. Danny Green, 40, shot and killed his mother, sister, and his sister's two children because he thought they were keeping him from being with his obsession, Selena Gomez.

Annually, almost 300 parents are slain by their children or stepchildren, and only 17% involve a child or stepchild under the age of 18. As shown in Figure 4.4, the largest number of incidents involve fathers killed by their sons or stepsons (52.1%), followed by mothers slain by sons or stepsons (34.5%), fathers by daughters (6.9%), and mothers by daughters (6.5%). When sons kill, they are more likely to kill the male parent, whereas when daughters kill, they are equally

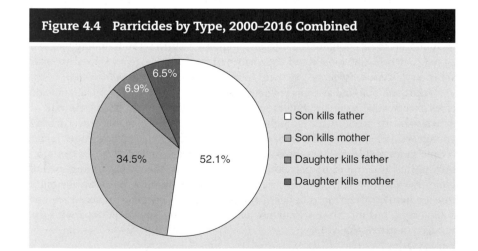

Figure 4.4 Parricides by Type, 2000–2016 Combined

- □ Son kills father
- ▨ Son kills mother
- ▦ Daughter kills father
- ■ Daughter kills mother

likely to kill a male or female parent. When a parent is murdered, the male parent is murdered 60% of the time and the female parent 40% of the time.

Heide has proposed a three-category typology for parricides. In her view, this crime is most frequently committed in response to severe physical or sexual abuse. As with preemptive attacks by battered wives, the act of parricide is more defensive than offensive. The defensive strike can also come on behalf of another person, typically protecting a mother from her abusive husband or boyfriend. On the evening of January 9, 2006, for example, Andrew Taylor, a 16-year-old boy who attended Tohoma High School in Ravensdale, Washington, fatally shot his father, 52-year-old Richard Taylor, in the back, after witnessing him threaten to kill his mother, shove her against a wall, and lunge at her with a broomstick. Andrew's mother later told the juvenile court that her son was "a really good boy" who was "just protecting me." Friends close to the family concurred, characterizing Andrew as a "mellow, nice kid." They also indicated that Andrew's father had become increasingly bad tempered, possibly even abusive, after recently suffering a debilitating back injury in a serious collision with a drunk driver.

Heide's other two parricide categories involve psychological rather than situational disorders. Some children who murder their parents do so under the influence of a severe mental illness, such as schizophrenia. Still others simply have bad character, classifiable as an antisocial personality disorder (or, for especially young offenders, a conduct disorder). In Allentown, Pennsylvania, for example, two chronically delinquent brothers—ages 15 and 17—who fashioned themselves as white supremacist skinheads, killed their father when he refused to let them drive the family car. They also murdered their mother and 11-year-old brother. As another example of "bad" rather than "mad" offenders, 19-year-old Erik Menendez and his 22-year-old brother Lyle murdered their parents, Joseph and Mary, execution style as they slept in their posh Beverly Hills home. Joseph Menendez, a Cuban refugee, had built his fortune in the video distribution business, and the police suspected, based on the crime scene and the victim's business dealings, that the murder may have been a Mafia hit.

As the police tracked down leads in the case, the Menendez brothers had already split the first portion of their large inheritance and had begun to pursue the lifestyle of rich bachelors. After seven months, however, as the organized crime theory dissolved, the police scrutinized apparent inconsistencies in the Menendez brothers' alibis. The two brothers eventually broke down under police interrogation and admitted to the murders. Erik and Lyle Menendez were convicted of murder after two jury trials in which their claim of having been abused by their father seemed far less plausible than the motive of greed. The brothers are currently housed in separate prisons, and both are married. Erik married a longtime pen pal, Tammi Menendez, in 1999, and Lyle first married former model Anna Erickson in 1996 and then married his second wife, Rebecca Sneed, in 2003. Neither of the Menendez brothers are allowed conjugal visits.

It is not always so easy to determine in which of Heide's categories a case of parricide belongs. During the early hours of February 2, 2008, 15-year-old Nicholas Browning, who lived in suburban Cockeysville, Maryland, crept into his parents' bedroom and shot his sleeping father in the head. He then killed his mother and two brothers. At his sentencing, Browning's attorney argued that the defendant had, for years, been a victim of battering at the hands of his abusive and alcoholic father, whom he and his brothers had referred to as Hitler. In the defense version of events, Browning had been beaten so severely and often that his immature mind could think of no alternative for ending the brutality than to eliminate his abusive father.

At the same time, one of Nicholas's classmates, as well as students who rode the school bus with him, had quite a different take on the origin of the murders. Nicholas had recently begun talking to his friends about killing his wealthy parents in order to inherit their money. In addition, he bragged about beating his younger brothers, stealing from his parents' liquor cabinet, and taking the family car without permission or a driver's license. One student suggested that Nicholas was a "spoiled kid" who was known for mocking minorities and people with disabilities. After killing the members of his family, Nicholas disposed of his gun in close-by bushes and then spent the next day with friends. Accompanied by the same students, he returned to the scene of his crime and faked being shocked to find the bodies of his parents and siblings. When questioned by the police, he initially claimed that the murders were committed by armed robbers who had committed a home invasion. After six hours of being interrogated by investigators, however, Nicholas realized the futility of continuing to lie about his complicity in the murders and finally confessed. Browning was sentenced to four life terms and will be eligible for a parole hearing in 2032.

Although the media image of parricide may be the teenage killer who kills a parent, 83% of people who kill their parents are adults, and the reasons they kill may be very different. Adult children with a history of financial trouble, mental health issues, job loss, and substance abuse may return home, or parents with various issues may be forced to live with their adult children. One of the less common yet especially insidious forms of family homicide involves the victimization of elders who, because of advanced age, infirmity, or dependency, are vulnerable to family members. Sons, daughters, and other relations have been known to abuse elders for emotional reasons, or, as in the Menendez case, murder them greedily to hasten an expected inheritance. There have been several recent cases of caretaker killings of elderly men and women as middle-aged children either become overwhelmed by the caretaker role or want to speed up the reading of the will.

From 1976 to 1980, about 25% of homicides of elders were committed by a spouse or other family member of the victim. However, since 2010, the percentage has increased to 50%. Although nursing homes and assisted living facilities should lower the risk, some families can't afford these facilities and may try to do the caregiving themselves. And, of course, family members may keep elders at home just so they can cash their pension, social security, and/or disability checks and neglect their elders to death. John Latshaw, 57, and his girlfriend Dorothy Robinson, 53, were charged with murder after Robinson's 77-year-old mother was found dead in a room in their Schuylkill County, Pennsylvania, house. The victim, Elaine Latshaw, was dehydrated and malnourished; was soaked in feces, blood, and urine; and had bedsores and gangrene. Her son had checked her out of her nursing home a year before because he wasn't happy with the care she was getting or with the cost. Instead, he and his girlfriend allegedly locked her in a room to die and collected her $1,200 monthly social security check. They claim they were just observing her wishes. News stories are filled with horrific cases of dead and decaying elderly, trapped in rooms, starving, and suffering from infections and open wounds. As our population ages and more of us are caring for our elders, we will likely see increases in caretaker homicides.

FILICIDE

Murder is regarded as particularly heinous in cases of filicide, that is, when the perpetrator is a parent and the victim is a vulnerable child or infant. On average, about 500 victims, 400 of them children under age 18, are killed each year by their parents or stepparents.

Of course, numbers don't mean everything. The tendency to engage in epidemic thinking can easily give the public the false impression that the murder of children is vastly on the rise, of epidemic proportions, and in need of changes in public policy. Even a single act of child murder can have a tremendous impact on public opinion and criminal justice policy. In the United States, for example, the abduction and sexual murder of a young girl from New Jersey initiated a federal law requiring sex offenders who are released from prison to register with their local police. The kidnapping and murder of another child inspired a system called Amber Alert, whereby the media carry public service announcements containing details that might help to locate a young victim.

Many individuals believe that the greatest danger to children comes from strangers on the streets or from disaffected classmates in their schools. By contrast, the family is regarded as a crucible of love, not violence, and parents are seen as protectors, not perpetrators.[28] Thus, children are told, early on, not to trust strangers, not to take candy from people they don't know, and not to follow a stranger to his or her car, no matter what he or she promises to do. When American children go house to house collecting treats on Halloween, they are urged to stay in their own neighborhoods, as though none of the bad guys—the pedophiles, the serial killers, and the sexual predators—would be living on their own block. Many parents no longer allow their children to play outside, for fear that they will be kidnapped and killed.

Actually, the most dangerous period of the day begins when the school bell rings and youngsters are sent home. More than half of all child homicides in Canada, the United Kingdom, and the United States are committed not by strangers or classmates but by a child's own parents.[29]

Researchers have uncovered a range of possible motives for a parent's homicidal act. Some parents kill their children as a result of psychotic delusional thinking. They may hear voices commanding them to protect their children by taking their lives. More commonly, these murders involve parents without a conscience who come to see their children as obstacles to the fulfillment of their personal objectives. A young impoverished woman may take the life of an unwanted baby on its first day of life. A woman may kill her child to gain sympathy and attention from others, or a man may kill his child because he resents the attention the child is getting from the mother, or doesn't want to pay child support. Finally, some parents kill their children in response to a catastrophic loss, such as being fired from a job, experiencing a nasty separation or divorce, or dealing with a child's terminal illness. The parent who suffers a catastrophic loss may blame his spouse and decide to get sweet revenge by killing her and everything she loves, including her children. In certain cases of situational loss, however, a parent who murders a child with a debilitating illness seeks to relieve the victim of real or imagined pain and suffering. From the parent's viewpoint, the crime is altruistic, an act of love.

Some parents have killed their children inadvertently while administering physical discipline or as a result of severe neglect. Accidental homicide may occur during various forms of child abuse that unintentionally go to the point of causing death. The child is killed in an impulsive manner when the mother or father becomes intolerably frustrated and angry, which causes them to lose control. Although not a justification, the act is often victim precipitated, occurring when a child's behavior (e.g., constant and unmitigated crying or screaming) causes severe stress in the parent.

Of course, cases in which parents kill their children do not always involve young, vulnerable victims. Nearly 20% of sons and daughters murdered by their parents or stepparents are over age 18. In Connecticut in April 2017 a father, Mark Wilkinson, 55, shot and killed his daughter, Melissa, 33, and then himself at his daughter's home. He had been living on her couch for two years, and she had asked him to leave only hours before.

As discussed in Chapter 2, when women commit homicide, the nature of their offense tends to differ sharply from those perpetrated by men who dominate in the area of felony-murder, stranger killings, and, especially, sexual homicide. Women tend to kill intimates (husbands, boyfriends, sons, or daughters), whereas men more often attack strangers or mere acquaintances. Thus, the gender ratio narrows considerably in family homicides and especially the murder of young children.

Mothers are more inclined to kill their offspring during the first year of life. Fathers are more likely to kill their older children. Fathers are three times more likely than mothers to kill a child with a gun, while mothers are nearly four times more apt to kill a child with drugs, drowning, or smothering than are fathers. Mothers who commit filicide usually kill one child; fathers are more likely than mothers to take the lives of more than one of their children; fathers are also prone more to kill their partner as well. In addition, mothers who kill their children are more likely than fathers to suffer from a severe mental illness such as severe depression or psychosis. Whereas mothers are more likely to kill impulsively, fathers plan their attack and kill in a cold-blooded, methodical, and calculating manner. Finally, fathers who kill their children are also more likely than their female counterparts to commit suicide.[30]

The murder of a child by a parent is often preceded by other, less extreme forms of violence, including spanking. According to sociologist Murray Straus, children should never be spanked or subjected to any other kind of corporal punishment, no matter what the circumstances. First, spanking may have serious harmful side effects that do not show up until much later.[31] For example, children who are spanked tend to be more aggressive later on in life as compared with children who are not spanked. They are more likely to commit crimes as adults, and their rate of cognitive development and educational achievement is slower. Overall, spanking increases the risk of many behavior problems that parents would like their children to avoid. Second, spanking is no more effective in repressing bad behavior than other methods of correction and control. In fact, all methods of correction and control have a high failure rate with toddlers. In older children, spanking (just like other methods) may have an immediate effectiveness in stopping the offensive behavior, but over months and years, corporal punishment tends to make things worse, whereas noncorporal punishment seems to be quite effective. Third, spanking is in contradiction to the ideal of promoting nonviolence in the family as well as society as a whole. Sweden was the first country to ban the corporal punishment of children in 1979. Since 1979 an additional 51 countries have banned spanking including, most recently, France in 2017.

According to Richard Gelles, up to 50% of the children killed by their parents or caretakers had been previously identified as at risk by child welfare agencies but were either left in their homes or returned to their families after a short-term placement.[32] Programs that aim to preserve or reunify the family may serve to benefit the child but not when carried too far. There is a widespread belief that children are almost always better off with their biological parents. Yet, when such programs represent the only option and are based on blind faith rather than evidence, a child's life may instead be placed in jeopardy.

Gelles also underscores the fact that many excellent potential foster families are lost due to their fear of child welfare placing the child they have bonded with back in the arms of their abusers despite the foster parents' objections and, worse, despite the danger to the child's life. Parents who have no interest in parenting their child are often pursued relentlessly by case workers metaphorically shoving the child in their face and screaming affirmations, "You will love this child and be a family even though you cracked her ribs and have also caused her permanent brain damage!" Meanwhile, the foster parents who wait to care for the child stand on the sidelines wearing their heart on their sleeve, watching helplessly to see how it all plays out.

"Red flags" that might indicate a high probability of a parent turning violent are typically ignored or misunderstood at a time when they could be used constructively. During courtship and prior to fatherhood, a jealous and possessive man may be regarded in a positive light by a woman who is flattered by the attention she receives from her partner. She may feel complimented by his jealousy and be willing to tolerate his controlling behavior. But much later, when their relationship turns sour and a wife/mother seeks to separate from her sociopathic mate, she may find herself and her children in extreme danger. Warning signs in a distraught mother are therefore possible to identify long before the birth of a child. Rather than ignore such "red flags," medical practitioners and mental health professionals should be ready to monitor, assess, and intervene. Waiting for childbirth may be a fatal mistake. An angry and depressed mother may, out of shame and guilt, keep secret her potentially destructive feelings about her newborn. Moreover, friends and relatives may miss the warning signs, mistakenly assuming that all women are thrilled about the birth of their children. We are in need of safety nets that are strong enough to catch those mothers who suffer from profound depression and despair. Not only will we improve the quality of life of many women who are in need of help, but we might also save the lives of their children.

INFANTICIDE

Young children are at far greater risk of being murdered by their parents than are older children or teenagers. Among infants murdered before they reach the age of 1 year, 77% of their perpetrators are a parent (or stepparent). More than 60% of all homicide victims under the age of 5 are murdered by their parents, but only 14% of murdered 10- to 14-year-olds are murdered by a parent. Juveniles who are in late adolescence are more likely to be killed by someone in their own age cohort than by a parent. Indeed, the proportion of filicides declines sharply as children get older.

From 1976 to 2016, the number of murders of children under age 5 has changed considerably, with an upward trend followed by a downward one. As shown in Figure 4.5, approximately 550 children under age 5 were murdered in 1976, but this number soared to nearly 800 during the late 1980s and early 1990s, when homicide of nearly every type increased. As with other forms of homicide, murders of children under age 5 have declined in recent years, down to almost 500 by 2016.

Infanticide is a remarkably different event from most other forms of homicide. Because of the small stature and physical vulnerability of young children, firearms are rarely used—or needed—to kill them. Most commonly, victims of this tender age are killed with hands or fists through strangulation, suffocation, beating, or shaking. Infanticide typically occurs during a fit of anger by an adult against a defenseless baby or following a chronic pattern of child abuse that turns fatal.

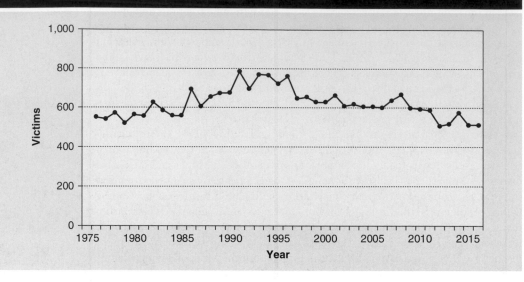

Figure 4.5 Homicide Victims Under Age 5, 1976–2016

After a mistrial and another overturned conviction, an Ohio mom, China Arnold, 26, was eventually convicted of and sentenced to life in prison without parole for murdering her 3-week-old baby by cooking her in the microwave in 2005. This is not the first mom to kill her child with a microwave. In 2002 a Virginia woman entered a guilty plea to involuntary manslaughter and was sentenced to 5 years in prison for killing her month-old son in the microwave, and more recently, a California mom, Ka Yang, 34, received a life sentence for the first-degree microwave murder of her infant daughter. There are also a number of sickening cases of both men and women killing cats and dogs in microwaves, ovens, freezers, and clothes dryers, but the punishments for these nonhuman murders are minimal.

As shown in Figure 4.6, the majority of the perpetrators of infanticide are parents or stepparents, not stranger abductors or intruders. Other than parents, the next largest category of perpetrators consists of male friends or acquaintances, very often the mother's boyfriend. Overall, less than 5% of infanticides are committed by babysitters or nannies.

The internationally publicized murder trial of 19-year-old English au pair Louise Woodward in the 1997 "shaken baby" death of 8-month-old Matthew Eappen of Newton, Massachusetts, gave many parents pause to think about the caretakers to whom they entrusted their young ones. Woodward was eventually convicted of involuntary manslaughter and was sentenced to time served, 279 days, in jail. She currently teaches dance in England. Babysitters have been known to murder children for reasons of ill temper and poor training, but these cases are few and far between. Although parents are wise to investigate fully those in whom they place so much trust, murder is generally the least of their concerns (especially compared with the much higher likelihood of accidental death).

For a parent, it can be tempting to blame the babysitter or nanny when bad things happen, perhaps even murder. In 2008, for example, Casey Anthony of Orlando, Florida, blamed a fictional nanny for the mysterious disappearance

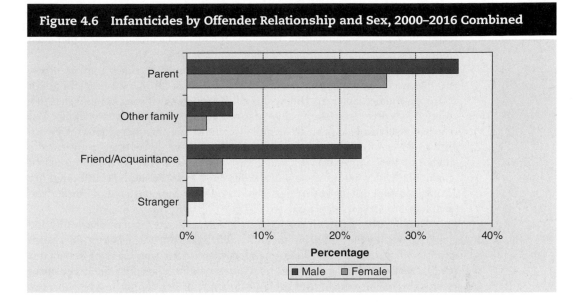

Figure 4.6 Infanticides by Offender Relationship and Sex, 2000–2016 Combined

of her 2-year-old daughter, Caylee. A full month after little Caylee had gone missing, Anthony's mother finally called the police. Anthony claimed that a nanny had kidnapped her child and that she had been too frightened to alert the authorities.

Social media postings showing Casey partying when she knew her daughter was missing (and dead) made Anthony one of the most despised women in America. When Caylee's body was finally discovered two months later in the woods near the Anthony home, it was too badly decomposed to determine the cause of death. However, evidence of duct tape on Caylee's remains allowed the medical examiner to rule the death a homicide.

Even before Caylee's body was found, Casey Anthony was charged with first-degree murder. Early speculation was that Anthony may have accidentally overdosed her daughter on chloroform, Xanax, or both. Given the paucity of evidence supporting a murder charge, Anthony was found not guilty of murder. She was, however, convicted of obstruction of justice for having lied to the police, although the conviction was later overturned. After the trial, it was discovered that Anthony may have researched suffocation deaths in advance of the little girl's death. Of course, then it was too late for authorities to pursue this new evidence because of the restriction against double jeopardy.

Anthony currently lives in Florida with one of the private investigators who had worked on the case and helps out with his business. In a recent interview, Anthony showed no sign of remorse. "I don't give a shit about what anyone thinks about me," said Anthony. "I never will, I'm OK with myself. I sleep pretty good at night."[33]

Neonaticide refers to the murder of infants during the first 24 hours of life. In the United States, most women who kill their newborn infants are young and impoverished. Typically, they never intended to get pregnant and struggle emotionally to accept motherhood. On the global level, neonaticide may reflect a cultural bias against girls. Recent coverage of births in India shows a sharp decline in the number of girls, and as many as 3 million baby girls are "missing," many of whom were likely the victims of infanticide or sex-selective abortions. This form of female gendercide has also been practiced in China for thousands of years, as boy babies are preferred to girls. Moreover, the incidence may have been increased following the establishment of China's one-child policy.

Sometimes older children are slain when a woman becomes convinced that her life would be far better without them. In August 2010, a 29-year-old South Carolina mother, Shaquan Duley, allegedly killed her two sons because she "just wanted to be free" from the burdens of parenthood. Initially, Duley told police that she had been involved in an accident, in which her car plummeted into the North Edisto River with her two sons trapped inside. Police divers later recovered the bodies of 18-month-old Ja'van and 2-year-old Devean. After being interrogated for hours, Duley admitted staging the accident and that she had suffocated her children before driving the car into the river. Duley was convicted of murder and sentenced to 35 years in prison.

Also in 2010, details emerged that Dominique Cottrez practiced a deadly and immoral, yet horribly effective, method of birth control. The 47-year-old woman from a village in northern France confessed to smothering eight of her infants over a period of almost two decades. Cottrez admitted keeping the pregnancies secret (her obesity made it possible to do so) and then killing her newborns at birth and hiding their remains in plastic bags, some in a garden and others in the garage of her home. Her husband and two older daughters were shocked when they discovered the truth about Dominique's murderous ways. She claimed that the babies were the product of an incestual relationship with her father, but DNA results determined that infants were instead her husband's. The woman later admitted to fabricating the incest story and was sentenced to 9 years in prison. She apparently did not suffer from postpartum psychosis or any other severe mental illness that would help to explain her actions. She just did not want more children but also did not want to visit a doctor about using contraception.

Because of the overwhelming statistical tendencies in cases of infanticide implicating parents, the focus of the investigation into the death of 6-year-old JonBenét Ramsey of Boulder, Colorado, during Christmas 1996 centered, rightly or wrongly, on the girl's parents, John and Patsy. When they refused to cooperate with the police, suspicion grew. And when Patsy could not be ruled out as the author of a ransom note found at the scene of the crime, many people became convinced that JonBenét's mother had murdered her young daughter. The JonBenét Ramsey case remains unsolved, and Patsy Ramsey has since died from ovarian cancer.

In August 2006, a mentally ill false confessor, John Mark Karr, claimed that he killed JonBenét, but, as is often the case in high-profile crimes, he only wanted to insert himself into the middle of a media circus. Karr desperately wanted the attention, and, unfortunately, for a few days, he got his wish. He has since slid back into obscurity. The 20th anniversary of the case generated a number of movies, docuseries, and conspiracy theories about who killed JonBenét. It was revealed in 2013 that a grand jury wanted to indict the parents, but the district attorney would not sign the indictment. Recent media coverage has pointed the finger at Burke, JonBenét's brother, and he has sued those who claim he was the killer.

Although child abductions by strangers sometimes do occur, in general, parents have a much greater range of motivations for committing infanticide than do acquaintances or strangers. Because of our steadfast belief that parents should be protectors rather than executioners, we tend to accept alternative explanations for child homicide, despite the strong statistical pattern favoring parents as suspects. This was what 23-year-old Susan Smith of Union, South Carolina, counted on when she and her estranged husband went before a national television audience in October 1994 and begged tearfully for the lives and safety of her two sons, 3-year-old Michael and 14-month-old Alex.

According to the distraught mother, a black stranger had jumped into her Mazda Protégé while she was stopped at a traffic light. The carjacker had reportedly ordered her out of the vehicle and then sped off with Smith's two boys still trapped in the backseat. The police were cautiously skeptical, however, because of some discrepancies in her description of the incident. Within days, after failing a polygraph test, Susan Smith confessed that she had rolled the car into a nearby lake with her children strapped helplessly inside. Smith had a very troubled childhood and had experienced the suicide of her father when she was a child. In addition, she had attempted suicide and had been molested by a stepfather as a child and continued to have a consensual sexual relationship with him when they were adults. Obviously, these factors do not justify Smith's actions, but they do help us to understand some of the factors that contribute to a mother's being capable of the murder of her two children. In the weeks that followed, Smith's motive for drowning her sons was revealed, and it certainly didn't place her in a sympathetic light. Smith had been told in a letter from her new boyfriend that he would not stay with or marry her because she had children. Smith apparently chose to sacrifice her offspring in the pursuit of romance. Two correctional officers have been fired for having sex with Smith while she has been in prison, and although she has had a number of other prison violations, including possession of drugs, Smith is still eligible for parole in 2024. Her ex-husband has since remarried and has two more children.

In some instances of infanticide, a young parent responds violently when unable to handle the pressure of a difficult, crying baby. Some instances may be aided by hormonal changes after childbirth, ranging from sleep deprivation to clinical postpartum depression or even psychosis. In recent years, some movement has even been seen in raising a postpartum defense to murder charges.

Andrea Yates of Houston, Texas, drowned her five children, ranging in age from 6 months to 7 years old, in a frenzied religious hallucination. Yates was spared the death penalty but was sentenced to life in prison with eligibility for parole after 40 years. Although she admitted planning the murders in advance, Yates pled not guilty by reason of insanity due to an obviously severe case of postpartum psychosis (PPP). She had a history of institutionalization, suicide attempts, and previous postpartum depression. Yet jurors believed that Yates knew what she was doing was wrong and therefore failed to qualify for insanity under Texas law.

In November 2005, the Texas court of appeals threw out Yates's murder convictions. During her trial, a prosecution expert witness had testified in error that Yates had been inspired to kill her children by an episode of the television program *Law & Order*. It was determined later that no such episode ever aired. Yates received a new trial, and in July 2006, she was found not guilty by reason of insanity. She will spend her time in a state mental hospital until she is no longer a threat. Yates's husband divorced her and remarried but has continued to stand by his former wife, asserting that she was severely mentally ill, but not criminal, at the time of the deaths of their children.

Occasionally, as in Susan Smith's case, the use of lethal force against a young innocent is far more selfish and reprehensible than just the inability to cope with parenthood. Sadly, children are sometimes exploited for a number of self-serving reasons, including for profit, for love, even for attention. In what is known as Munchausen syndrome, adults and children have been known to feign illness or even self-inflict sickness or injury for the sake of attention.[34] For some people who may otherwise feel insecure and unloved, the attention they receive from family, friends, even the medical professionals when they are sick can become psychologically addictive, so much so that the sympathy is worth the suffering. In Munchausen syndrome by proxy, the victims, typically the mother's children, are exploited as pawns to fulfill the perpetrator's emotional needs.

For Marybeth Tinning of Schenectady, New York, the sympathy afforded a grieving mother grew irresistible. Craving attention, she learned that the support given to a new mother only lasts so long. When her third child, baby Jennifer, died shortly after birth following a weeklong struggle with hemorrhagic meningitis, she also learned that the attention surrounding a death could be as sustaining as that surrounding a birth. In a span of some dozen years, Marybeth gave birth to eight children and adopted another. All of them eventually died, usually of what had been diagnosed as sudden infant death syndrome (SIDS) or "crib death." Marybeth responded routinely following each loss of another child. She called all her friends and relatives to announce the latest reduction in the Tinning family, expecting the customary round of pity and attention. Her death announcements had become as emotionally arousing for her as the birth announcements; both would make her the center of attention. Marybeth began theorizing, almost bragging, about a genetic defect that she was passing on to each of her babies. But as children numbers six, seven, and eight died, sympathy for Marybeth started turning into suspicion.

For 5 years after the death of their eighth child, Marybeth and her husband, Joseph, remained childless. After years with an "empty nest," the Tinnings were ecstatic over the birth of their ninth child, Tami Lynne, in August 1985. The baby girl was beautiful, healthy, and full of life, yet those closest to the Tinnings quietly predicted that there would soon be another funeral to attend.

According to Marybeth, early in the morning of December 20, she went to check on her baby and found her lying on her stomach, motionless and breathless. Despite efforts to restore her breathing, Tami Lynne was pronounced dead. No longer able to ignore what had become painfully clear, Marybeth's sister-in-law went to the police with her suspicions. Tami Lynne was autopsied carefully and thoroughly, with new and improved methods for distinguishing SIDS from induced asphyxiation. According to the coroner's report, the baby had not died of natural causes but instead had been suffocated. Despite the fact that implicating evidence from earlier deaths had long since been buried, there was enough direct and circumstantial evidence to charge and convict Marybeth with second-degree murder. In 1987, she was sentenced to prison for 20 years to life. Due to her lack of remorse about the deaths of her children, Tinning, now 74, was denied parole for the sixth time in 2017.

Infanticides, as we have seen in other cases, can also result from a desire for more practical rewards, such as profit, companionship, or even vengeance. On Father's Day in 1999, Amy Shanabarger of Franklin, Indiana, returned home from her job as a grocery store cashier only to find her 7-month-old son, Tyler, dead, lying face down in his crib. After an autopsy, the coroner determined that the cause of death was SIDS. Just hours after the funeral, however, the boy's father confessed to the police that he had suffocated the infant while his wife was at work, by wrapping his head in plastic. Ronald Shanabarger, 29, admitted his motive was revenge against his wife, planning the homicide even before the child was conceived. He was angry and resentful that in 1996, before they were married, Amy had refused to cut her vacation cruise short to comfort him following the death of his father. According to the confession, Shanabarger fathered the child, waited until his wife bonded with the infant, and then murdered him so that his wife could experience the same kind of pain she had insensitively ignored years earlier. Shanabarger currently resides in prison with a scheduled release date of December 2023.

In cases where one parent is aware that another parent or adult is abusing a child but takes no action, he or she can be charged under "failure to protect" laws. In this case, someone can be punished for an omission, a failure to do something they should have. These statutes, existing in at least 29 states, are controversial because sometimes, for example, the silent partner is a battered woman who cannot even protect herself. She may believe reporting the violence being committed against her or her children will further incite the batterer. In October 1994, Pauline Zile, 24, of Ft. Lauderdale, Florida, reported her 7-year-old daughter, Christina Holt, missing from a shopping mall. The girl's body was discovered five days later, and Zile confessed that she had lied about the abduction story. In fact, her husband, the girl's stepfather, had beaten Christina to death. Because she had witnessed the beatings and helped create the false kidnapping story to protect her husband, Pauline Zile was convicted of murder and sentenced to life in prison.

Although women are more likely than men to be charged in failure to protect cases, Lisa Holland, 33, of Michigan was convicted of first-degree murder and sentenced to life in prison for killing her 7-year-old adopted son, whereas her husband was sentenced to 30 to 60 years for allowing the abuse to continue for years. The boy had come into the Holland home as a foster child in 2000 (as did three of his siblings) and was dead by 2005. According to testimony by her husband, Holland had tortured and abused the boy for years and kept him tied in the basement. After she hit him in the head with a hammer, the youngster did not eat, drink, walk, talk, or have control of his bladder. When he finally died, the father dumped the body in the woods.

In many cases, women convicted of allowing their child to be abused, sometimes to death, receive far harsher sentences than do the men who abused both the mother and the child. Robert Braxton Jr. pled guilty to abusing his 3-month-old daughter by breaking her ribs and femur and was sentenced to two years in prison. The mother, Tondalo Hall, was found guilty of failing to protect her daughter and given a sentence of 30 years in prison. There was no evidence that Hall had ever hurt her daughter, but there was evidence that Braxton had abused the mother and all three children for months and she was afraid of him.[35]

In 2006, 21-year-old Arlena Lindley was sentenced to 45 years in prison after her boyfriend, Alonzo Turner, beat their 3-year-old son to death. Witnesses testified that Turner had beaten the mother and son on many occasions and had threatened to kill Lindley if she tried to protect the boy. The night of the murder Lindley grabbed her son and ran outside to escape, but Turner dragged the little boy back in and locked the door behind him. But she didn't call police. A recent *BuzzFeed News* investigation documented case after case of the failure of failure to protect laws as the women/mothers are often punished so much more than the actual batterer/murderer. They found 73 cases of mothers sentenced to 10 or more years for failure to protect but only four cases of fathers sentenced for failure to protect.[36]

Recent analysis also shows that other policy choices can affect the rate of infanticide. Economists Kalist and Molinari found a statistical connection between the availability of Medicaid-funded abortion and rates of infanticide. Specifically, their analysis indicated that the rate of infanticide is between 13% and 20% lower in states that provide public funding for abortion.[37] Regardless of one's moral position on the long-standing debate over state funding of abortion on demand, restrictions on a woman's right to terminate pregnancy—which opponents often call "murder"—could actually, if Kalist and Molinari are right, result in higher rates of infant homicide.

Most of the United States hasn't caught up to many other parts of the world that recognize the possibility of diminished capacity for women who have recently given birth. In England, the Infanticide Act of 1922 abolished the death penalty for a woman who murdered her newborn. Many European courts automatically reduce the charges against a mother for murder of a child under the age of 1 year to manslaughter in recognition of hormonal issues still present after birth. At least 30 countries, including Canada, Germany, and Australia, allow women who kill their children within a year of giving birth either to be charged with a lesser crime than murder or to be sentenced for a shorter period of time. In 2009, Texas made a significantly progressive move by passing legislation that set a maximum punishment of 2 years' incarceration for a new mother who murders her infant.

MOTHERHOOD BY PROXY

Whereas some women hide their pregnancy and childbirth by killing the newborn, others want so desperately to be a mother that they commit murder to "adopt" the victim's child. Infant abductions used to occur primarily in hospitals. But in an effort to prevent intruders from stealing newborns from nurseries, many maternity wards stopped relaying birth announcements and added multiple levels of security. As is true in other crime prevention arenas, however, so-called target hardening approaches sometimes only displace the crime, inadvertently forcing strongly motivated perpetrators to seek alternative means to fulfill their goal. In the case of baby stealing, many thieves have resorted to taking other women's babies before they are born or after they go home.

Although most of the several hundred infant abductions committed since 1983 do not involve the use of violence of any kind, more recently, a particularly heinous form of abduction—newborn kidnapping by cesarean section (C-section)—has emerged.[38] These are cases of women who abduct a pregnant woman and, typically by fairly primitive means (e.g., car keys), cut the baby from the mother's womb. These are desperate attempts at motherhood with varying motives. Some of the women want the attention that pregnant women enjoy—motherhood by proxy—but most are faking a pregnancy to trap a man. In some cases, these women may have been suffering from pseudocyesis, a false belief that they really are pregnant, and even have symptoms such as an enlarged uterus and missed menstrual periods.

Our analysis of open source records identified 26 U.S. cases of attempted or completed fetal abduction by C-section since 1987. In these cases, most of the mothers-to-be were murdered, but eight managed to escape their would-be murderers. These cases reflect a bizarre range of motives and tactics used by women desperate for a newborn of their own. One abduction by C-section—fortunately an unsuccessful one—demonstrates the extent to which some women will go to "become a mother." In February 2005, 9-months-pregnant Sarah Brady, 26, of Ft. Mitchell, Kentucky, received a call supposedly from Sarah Brody, who claimed to have baby gifts that had been delivered to her by mistake. Sarah Brody was actually Katie Smith, 22. The two women chatted by phone, and Sarah Brady then went to Smith's house to pick up the package. Sure enough, there was a box filled with baby items from Sarah's baby registry. As it turns out, Smith also appeared to be heavily pregnant. Later in the day, Smith called again and said another package had arrived. Brady returned to Smith's apartment to get the second package. On this visit, Smith attacked Brady with a knife, and the two women struggled for at least 20 minutes. As is often the case in knife fights, the assailant became a victim: Brady fought back, hit Smith on the head with an ashtray, wrestled the knife from her, and stabbed her three times.

When police arrived and took a close look at Smith's apartment, they found a fully decorated and stocked baby nursery and surgical tools for a C-section delivery. Smith had falsely claimed to be pregnant on at least three other occasions and had worked as a nanny in several homes, where she had stolen ultrasound pictures. Smith died from her injuries (ruled to be a justifiable homicide due to self-defense), and Brady delivered a healthy baby girl days later. Because of cases such as this, many stores that offer online baby registries are beginning to change their systems to hide detailed information about the prospective mothers. But mothers-to-be are still looking for baby items and other expecting moms on Facebook and Craigslist, again illustrating the hunting grounds of social media.

PREVENTION AND RESPONSE

To any casual observer of current events, the occurrence of intimate and family murder seems endless. Yet, despite the tragedies in so many households across the country, the number of intimate and family murders has actually declined, from nearly 6,000 victims annually in the late 1970s to just over 4,000 in 2016. The percentage of all homicides traced to familial relationships has dropped as well. Although the trend may be in the right direction, the thousands of instances each year when women, men, and children are murdered by people they love, be it for power, passion, or profit, offend our sense of the sanctity and safety of marriage and family.

As we have seen, a number of initiatives would help to curb domestic violence homicides. Providing resources to families with substance abuse issues and removing guns from homes with any history of domestic violence would limit the facilitators of domestic homicide. Additional resources for LGBTQ victims, more shelter space (especially in rural areas) and shelter space that allows for family pets, financial counseling and resources for domestic violence victims, GPS tracking on domestic violence offenders, and risk assessment and domestic violence screening by law enforcement, primary care physicians, and other medical personnel could save lives. Mental health treatment for both victims and offenders, greater sensitivity to postpartum depression in new mothers and traumatic brain injuries in domestic violence survivors, respite for stressed parents, parenting and conflict resolution training in our school curriculum, and support for elderly couples when the husband in put in the position of caretaker, all may help to reduce the horrific phenomenon of domestic homicide. The words "until death do us part" should be a loving promise, never a loathsome threat.

ENDNOTES

1. Sharon G. Smith, Kathleen C. Basile, Leah K. Gilbert, et al., *The National Intimate Partner and Sexual Violence Survey (NISVS): 2010-2012 State Report* (Atlanta, GA: National Center for Injury Prevention and Control, Centers for Disease Control and Prevention, 2017).

2. Judith M. McFarlane, Jacquelyn C. Campbell, Susan Wilt, Caroline J. Sachs, Yvonne Ulrich, and Xiao Xu, "Stalking and Intimate Partner Femicide," *Homicide Studies* 3 (1999): 300–316.

3. Lenore E. Walker, "Battered Women and Learned Helplessness," *Victimology: An International Journal* 2 (1977): 525–534.

4. Dee L. R. Graham, Edna Rawlings, and Nelly Rimini, "Survivors of Terror: Battered Women, Hostages, and the Stockholm Syndrome," in Kersti Yllo and Michele L. Bograd, eds., *Feminist Perspectives on Wife Abuse* (Newbury Park, CA: Sage, 1998).

5. Edward W. Gondolf and Ellen R. Fisher, *Battered Women as Survivors: An Alternative to Treating Learned Helplessness* (New York: Lexington Books, 1988).

6. Donald G. Dutton, *The Domestic Assault of Women: Psychological and Criminal Justice Perspectives* (Vancouver: University of British Columbia Press, 1995).

7. Kathryn E. Moracco, Carol W. Runyan, and John D. Butts, "Femicide in North Carolina: A Statewide Study of Patterns and Precursors," *Homicide Studies* 2 (1998): 422–446.

8. Ann Goetting, "Homicidal Wives: A Profile," *Journal of Family Issues* 8 (1987): 332–341.

9. See R. K. Thyfault, "Self-Defense: Battered Women Syndrome on Trial," *California Western Law Review* 20 (1984): 485–510.

10. "Something in His Whiskey," *Economist*, August 20, 2016.

11. Elicka S. Peterson, "Murder as Self-Help: Women and Intimate Partner Homicide." *Homicide Studies* 3 (1999): 30–46.

12. Carrie Underwood, vocal performance of "Church Bells" (2015) and "Blown Away" (2012).

13. Laura Dugan, Daniel S. Nagin, and Richard Rosenfeld, "Exposure Reduction or Retaliation? The Effects of Domestic Violence Resources on Intimate-Partner Homicide," *Law and Society Review* 37 (2003): 169–198; Laura Dugan, Daniel Nagin, and Richard Rosenfeld, "Do Domestic Violence Services Save Lives?" *National Institute of Justice Journal* 250 (2003): 20–25.

14. Ana Swanson, "144 Years of Marriage and Divorce in the United States, in One Chart," *Washington Post*, June 23, 2015, https://www.washingtonpost.com/news/wonk/wp/2015/06/23/144-years-of-marriage-and-divorce-in-the-united-states-in-one-chart/?utm_term=.30f08d34ffa3.

15. Arthur L. Kellermann, Frederick P. Rivara, Norman B. Rusforth, et al., "Gun Ownership as a Risk Factor for Homicide in the Home," *New England Journal of Medicine* 267 (1993): 1084–1090.

16. National Institute of Justice, "Batterer Intervention Programs Often Do Not Change Offender Behavior," 2011, https://www.nij.gov/topics/crime/intimate-partner-violence/interventions/Pages/batterer-intervention.aspx.

17. Marieke Liem, Jack Levin, Curtis Holland, and James Alan Fox, "The Nature and Prevalence of Familicide in the United States, 2000–2009," *Journal of Family Violence* 28 (2013).

18. Shervert H. Frazier, "Violence and Social Impact," in Joseph C. Schoolar and Charles M. Gaitz, eds., *Research and the Psychiatric Patient* (New York: Brunner/Mazel, 1975).

19. Frazier, "Violence and Social Impact."

20. George B. Palermo "Murder-Suicide—An Extended Suicide," *International Journal of Offender Therapy and Comparative Criminology* 38 (1994): 205–216.

21. Marieke Liem, "Homicide Followed by Suicide: A Review," *Aggression and Violent Behavior* 15 (2010): 153–161.

22. R. Dawn Comstock, Sue Mallonee, Elizabeth Kruger, Kim Rayno, April Vance, and Fred Jordan, "Epidemiology of Homicide-Suicide Events: Oklahoma, 1994–2001," *American Journal of Forensic Medicine and Pathology* 26 (2005): 229–235.

23. Violence Policy Center, *American Roulette: Murder-Suicide in the United States* (Washington, DC, October 2015).

24. Radoslaw Panczak, Michael Geissbühler, Marcel Zwahlen, Martin Killias, Kali Tal, and Matthias Egger, "Homicide-Suicides Compared to Homicides and Suicides: Systematic Review and Meta-Analysis," *Forensic Science International* 233 (2013): 28–36.

25. Julie E. Malphurs and Donna Cohen, "A Statewide Case-Control Study of Spousal Homicide-Suicide in Older Persons," *American Journal of Geriatric Psychiatry* 13 (2005): 211–217; Jane Koziol-McLain, Daniel Webster, Judith McFarlane, et al., "Risk Factors for Femicide-Suicide in Abusive Relationship: Results from a Multi-Site Case Control Study," *Violence and Victims* 21 (2006): 3–21.

26. Donna Cohen, "Homicide-Suicide in Older People," *Psychiatric Times* 17 (2000): 49–52.

27. Kathleen M. Heide, *Why Kids Kill Parents: Child Abuse and Adolescent Homicide* (Columbus: Ohio State University Press, 1992).

28. Margaret G. Spinelli, *Infanticide: Psychosocial and Legal Perspectives on Mothers Who Kill* (Washington, DC: American Psychiatric Publishing, 2003).

29. David Finkelhor and Richard Ormrod, *Homicides of Children and Youth* (Washington, DC: Office of Juvenile Justice and Delinquency Prevention, 2001).

30. Suzanne Leveillee, Jacques D. Marleau, and Myriam Dube, "Filicide: A Comparison by Sex and Presence or Absence of Self-Destructive Behavior," *Journal of Family Violence* 22 (July 2007): 287–295.

31. Murray Straus, *Beating the Devil out of Them: Corporal Punishment in American Children* (Edison, NJ: Transaction, 2001).

32. Richard J. Gelles, *The Book of David* (New York: Basic Books, 1997).

33. Mary Bowerman, "Casey Anthony Breaks Her Silence: 'I Sleep Pretty Good at Night,'" *USA Today*, March 7, 2017.

34. Charles V. Ford, "Munchausen Syndrome," in Claude T. H. Friedmann and Robert A. Faguet, eds., *Extraordinary Disorders of Human Behavior* (New York: Plenum Press, 1982); Richard Firstman

and Jamie Talan, *The Death of Innocents* (New York: Bantam Books, 1998).

35. Adam Banner, "'Failure to Protect' Laws Punish Victims of Domestic Violence," *Huffington Post*, February 3, 2015.

36. Alex Campbell, "Battered, Bereaved, and Behind Bars," *BuzzFeed News*, October 2, 2014.

37. David E. Kalist and Noelle A. Molinari, "Abortion and Infant Homicide" (unpublished manuscript, Shippensburg University of Pennsylvania, February 2004).

38. Ann W. Burgess, Timothy Baker, Cathy Nahirny, and John Rabun, "Newborn Kidnapping by Cesarean Section," *Journal of Forensic Science* 47 (2002): 827–830.

CHAPTER FIVE

THE YOUNG AND THE RUTHLESS

The decade of the 1990s may long be remembered for its technological advances—the expanding power of personal computers, the ubiquity of the internet, and the proliferation of wireless communications. Yet to those who closely monitor crime trends, the 1990s will be remembered as the decade when the murder rate fell.

After having peaked, the rate of killing in the United States had, by the end of the 1990s, sunk to levels not seen for decades. As citizens across the country celebrated New Year's 2000 with incredible fanfare and relief that the projected catastrophic Y2K computer bug was little more than a scare, police departments rejoiced in their own sense of victory.

Criminologists had warned of an impending juvenile crime wave created by a new breed of "superpredators."[1] Despite the dire forecast, as the 1990s drew to a close, city after city reported spectacularly low homicide rates. Boston closed out 1999 with as few as 31 murders, compared with 152 in 1990. Philadelphia's homicide toll reached below the 300 level for the first time in well over a decade. New York City, despite a slight increase in 1999, tallied 667 murders, substantially below its 1990 peak of 2,245. By 1999, Chicago's murder toll had dropped to 641, the city's lowest level in many years and about half what it was in 1991.

Although these reductions, as well as declines in many other cities, were worthy of celebration, the murder rate was not at a low point for all segments of the population. Only when we look much more closely into the trends do we begin fully to understand the great crime drop of the 1990s.

AN "EPIDEMIC" OF YOUTH HOMICIDE

The overall rate of homicide offending (the number of offenders per 100,000 population) for all age groups combined has experienced substantial fluctuations—peaks and valleys, ups and downs—over the past few decades. Similar to the pattern shown earlier in Chapter 2 for the rate of homicide victimization, the rate of offending per 100,000 rose in the late 1970s and peaked at 11.7 in 1980. Then the rate declined by roughly 25% during the first half of the 1980s, down to 8.6 in 1985. The late 1980s saw another surge in the offending rate, peaking at 11.2 in 1991. From that point on, as crime control became a national priority, the offending rate experienced a long-term drop down to 5.1 in 2014. Despite an uptick in 2015, the offending rate remained half what is was at the start of the 1990s slide.

Probing deeper into these trends by comparing different age groups uncovers a very different picture. As shown in Figure 5.1, the rate of murder at the hands of adults age 25 and older has declined slowly yet steadily since the 1980s, by

Figure 5.1 Homicide Offending Rate per 100,000 Population by Age, 1976–2016

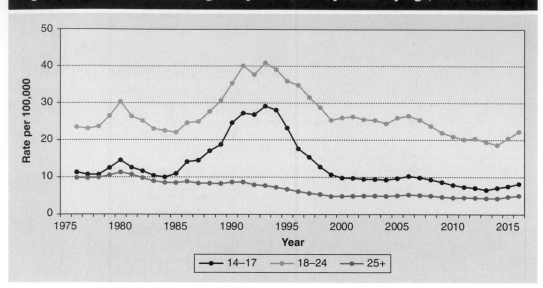

almost 60%, without any rise during the violence-filled years of the late 1980s. All of the swings in homicide rates were among younger offenders. From 1985 to 1993, the rate of killing among young adults aged 18 to 24 rose by almost 90% before dropping back down by more than a third by 2000 and then stabilizing through the new decade. Young adults have traditionally had the highest rates of offending, and this gap grew even wider in recent years. The most remarkable change, however, occurred among teenagers. Prior to 1985, teens committed homicide at the same low rate as their parents' generation. However, since the mid-1980s, the pattern of offending for adolescents has much more resembled that of their older siblings. From 1985 to 1993, the rate of murder committed by teenagers almost tripled, from 10.9 to 29.3 per 100,000, before its sharp decline in the latter half of the 1990s.

What happened in the mid-1980s that drove the youth homicide figures into record territory? Although many factors would underlie such a sharp trend as this, the most compelling and important was the emergence of crack cocaine as a popular street market drug in cities across the United States. Although the pharmacological effects of crack cocaine were worrisome, involving a lessening of impulse control as well as unpredictable effects on the body, the real damage to our society came from crime problems surrounding the dynamics of the crack drug market.[2]

When the crack market developed, the usual economic forces of supply and demand created fierce and violent competition for business. The demand for crack, which, unlike other street drugs, was sold in small single-hit quantities, was so great that dealers had to recruit large numbers of street merchants to distribute the contraband. In light of this intense demand, and that a fair number of adult sellers were being sent away to prison for long periods of time, teenagers were aggressively recruited and enlisted as street sellers. Not only were these brazen youngsters willing to take on the risks for some quick cash (and free drugs), but they also did so at a lower level of compensation. It was also perceived that, if caught, they would be treated more leniently by the courts.

Because of the violence associated with the drug trade, guns were an essential tool for survival. Youngsters trafficking in crack cocaine armed themselves for added muscle as well as for protection.[3] As soon as some teenagers were armed, their peers—even those uninvolved in crack as sellers or users—began to acquire guns as well.[4]

A virtual teen arms race spiraled out of control, instigated by, but not limited to, crack activity. Some kids carried guns for offensive purposes, others for self-defense, and still others for status among their friends and rivals. The arming of America's urban youth created a volatile mix of impulsivity and firepower, as trigger-happy adolescents used their weaponry for reasons both serious and trivial—from the elimination of a rival gang member to the execution of someone who "disrespected" them.

As shown in Figure 5.2, the entire surge in teen homicide offending was gun related. From 1985 to 1993, the number of teenagers who killed with a gun nearly quadrupled, before tailing off during the remainder of the 1990s and beyond. At the same time, there was no appreciable increase in juvenile homicides by other means. It has long been true that many teenagers are impatient, imprudent, and impulsive, willing to act spontaneously without fully thinking through the consequences of their actions. The availability of a gun in the hands of quick-triggered kids had a significant impact on the murder rate, both for their age group specifically and overall.

The trends in youth gun homicide are also related to gang activity. As shown in Figure 5.3, the number of homicides associated with street gangs soared in the late 1980s and early 1990s. In detailed analyses of homicide reports in Chicago and Los Angeles, Cheryl Maxson has shown that gang killings represented an increasing number and percentage of all murders from the mid-1980s to the mid-1990s.[5] During the 1980s, several national gangs (e.g., the Bloods, the Crips, and the Latin Kings) expanded their membership, as more and more youngsters were attracted to what these and other prominent gangs had to offer in terms of status, profit, and protection.

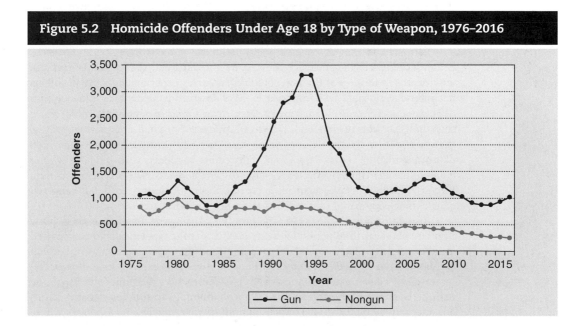

Figure 5.2   Homicide Offenders Under Age 18 by Type of Weapon, 1976–2016

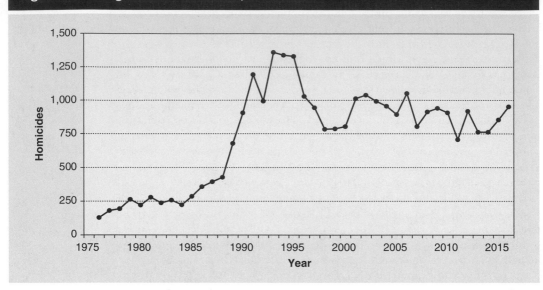

Figure 5.3 Gang-Related Homicides, 1976–2016

The definition of *gang*, not to mention *gang-related homicide*, can be problematic. For example, at what point does a group of kids involved in delinquent acts become gang activity? For our purposes, street gangs are to be distinguished from a host of other youth groups in which delinquent behavior occasionally flares, as well as prison gangs, organized crime groups, white supremacists, and terrorist cells. Most, but not all, street gangs consist of males from minority backgrounds— black, Latino, or Asian—who range in age from preteenagers to adults in their 30s (although sometimes older). Gang members typically live in proximity to one another and have strong neighborhood ties. Much of gang warfare erupts as a result of a shared desire to protect local territory from the encroachment of outsiders. But the antisocial behavior of gang members ranges widely from acts of vandalism and petty theft to incidents of assault and murder.

Estimates of gang membership and its impact come from a series of surveys of law enforcement agencies conducted by the National Gang Center (NGC). The results indicate that the percentage of agencies experiencing gang problems declined during the 1990s from nearly 40% down to roughly 25%, a major sign of success as city police departments were prioritizing antigang initiatives. Since then, however, cuts in city police resources appear to have had a negative impact, as the gang problem has rebounded somewhat. As of 2012 (the latest year for which data are available), almost 30% of law enforcement agencies reported having gang issues. Not surprisingly, prevalence estimates vary considerably by type of location. As of 2012, about 85% of agencies in cities with populations over 50,000 reported gang activity, compared to only 16% of agencies in rural areas.[6]

Also according to the NGC, the number of gangs and gang members grew over the five-year time period between 2007 and 2012. Specifically, the estimated number of gangs rose from 27,300 to 30,700, and the estimated total membership increased from 788,000 to 850,000. These figures translate to a significant toll in terms of gang-related killings. The NGC estimates that about 13% of the nation's homicides are gang related. The role of gangs in murder statistics varies considerably by type and size of jurisdiction. In Los Angeles and Chicago, where gang activity is most prevalent, as many as half of the murders are believed to be tied to gang activity.[7]

A more recent survey of law enforcement agencies across America by the FBI's National Gang Intelligence Center (NGIC) points to a persistent gang problem and violence associated with it. In a 2015 report, the NGIC found that over the previous two years, gang membership had increased in 49% of the jurisdictions, had remained relatively unchanged in 43% of the jurisdictions, and had declined in only 8% of the jurisdictions. Moreover, half of the responding agencies reported that gang-related violence had increased over the two-year time frame, while 36% saw no change and 14% indicated a reduced level of violence associated with local gang activity.[8]

There are several reasons why gang violence has reemerged, even if not nearly as extensively as in the past. First, many of the gang leaders who were sent away to prison in the 1980s and early 1990s are returning back to their old neighborhoods and their old gang affiliations. At the same time, young recruits who did not witness the bloodshed in those earlier years are attracted to the excitement, thrill, and status of gang membership. Finally, many cities have slashed their budgets for antigang initiatives, assuming, or perhaps just hoping, that the problem had been resolved.

Street gangs have changed dramatically over the past 40 years. They have proliferated not only in numbers but also in their ability to spread fear and terror throughout a community. During the 1950s and 1960s, gangs were noted for committing relatively minor offenses. They spoke about the need to protect their turf but rarely followed up by committing major crimes of violence. In sharp contrast, today's gang members are older, more likely to carry firearms, and more willing to be violent in pursuit of their objectives. Gangs often traffic in illicit drugs and stolen guns as a means of support, sometimes having connections to organized crime groups (e.g., Mexican drug cartels).

One of the most significant trends in gang activity during recent years involves the growth and spread of immigrant gangs around the country. Not unlike their European counterparts before them, recent newcomers to the United States from Latin American countries tend to be segregated in their residences by virtue of language and unemployment. In some Latino neighborhoods, gangs develop in order to provide vulnerable residents with the support and protection not available to them from the larger society.

The Salvadorian gang MS-13 (aka Mara Salvatrucha) first appeared in the Los Angeles area during the 1980s, but later spread throughout the country, especially to places where antigang efforts were less effective. The gang's criminal activities have included stealing and exporting automobiles, burglarizing houses and stores, selling illicit drugs, smuggling and selling firearms, carjacking, intimidating witnesses, and committing aggravated assault, rape, and murder.

Originally, members of MS-13 consisted almost exclusively of immigrants from El Salvador who had fled from the nation's civil war, settled in the city of Los Angeles, and formed a gang to protect themselves from the threatening activities of other, more established groups. Over the years, as MS-13 has become increasingly violent, the federal government has deported many of its members, only to see them return illegally and rejoin the gang. Since the 1980s, MS-13 has proliferated, becoming a loose network of essentially independent groups of immigrants and encompassing members from not only El Salvador but also Ecuador, Guatemala, Honduras, and Mexico.

Another influential Latino street gang, which operates in northern California, is known as SUR-13 (aka Sureños 13). Its members wear identifying red clothing to distinguish them from their principal rival, the Norteños, whose gang color is blue. Both gangs are especially active in Oakland and San Francisco. They are believed to be offshoots of Mexican prison gangs, although their members come from a range of ethnic groups. Like so many other gangs, the Sureños and Norteños express pride in their group by wearing their colors and tattooing gang symbols on their bodies. Teenage members steal from local liquor stores, while older members push drugs on the streets.

The West Coast is certainly not the only region of the country where immigrant gangs have flourished. In Miami, for example, Haitian gangs emerged in the 1990s comprised of poor immigrants who escaped to south Florida when a military regime seized control of their Caribbean homeland. Gangs in the Little Haiti section of Miami protected the community from area rival African Americans who were higher up on the social ladder. Among Miami's Haitian gangs, Zoe Pound stands out as the most ruthless, quick to enforce its rule and facilitate its illicit drug trade through whatever violent means were necessary.

Despite all the negative aspects (e.g., violent conflicts with rivals, intimidating citizens and business owners, selling contraband), street gangs offer several positive functions for their members.[9] Gangs provide an alternative socializing mechanism, especially as the institution of the family is weakened. By joining a gang, a young recruit can feel special, as if he belongs to something important, and be a member of a group that praises him. Moreover, it is a source of excitement and even economic resources. Where illicit drugs are sold, impoverished inner-city gang members gain not only a quick way to make money (tax free) but also a way to serve an apprenticeship in a growing business—the drug industry.[10] Finally, if not most importantly, gangs offer recruits virtually unlimited access to advancement. Unlike conventional paths to success—power and money—through school and career, a youngster can rise to the top of a gang no matter his or her skin color or background; all that's needed is a show of toughness and loyalty. For this reason, gangs may be more attractive to people who have fewer legitimate job opportunities.

Beyond the functions provided to their loyal participants, gangs can also benefit the communities that they are simultaneously inflicting with their strong-arm methods. A neighborhood gang can shield residents and business owners from outside threats, particularly posed by gangs from other neighborhoods and of other ethnicities. In addition, local gangs can promote locally embraced customs, values, and norms throughout its membership, including respect for elders and religious leaders. Law-abiding residents and gang members may, as Patillo puts it, "agree on goals, but disagree on strategies."[11]

The brutality of gang violence is often fueled by the more general phenomenon of group dynamics. As shown in Figure 5.4, not only are teen murderers significantly more likely to commit homicide with the help of accomplices, but also the percentage of juvenile murders involving two or more perpetrators has grown steadily.

It is well known that individuals, especially children, often act differently in a group setting than they do on their own. Sometimes peer pressure can encourage someone to conform to a prosocial norm, but frequently it can provide strong encouragement to do the wrong thing. In group settings, the activity may be secondary to interpersonal dynamics. A group leader may feel good that others are willing to follow his lead even into areas of behavior that are cruel and vicious. At the same time, the followers can feel good about the praise they receive from the leader (and other group members) for participating and showing allegiance. In group settings, so-called mob psychology can sweep participants into committing even horrible crimes that no one in the group really wants to do. In situations

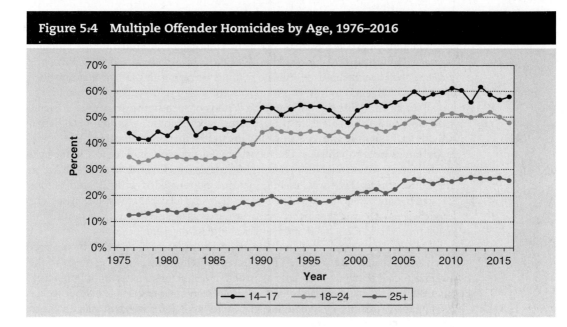

Figure 5.4 Multiple Offender Homicides by Age, 1976–2016

of a "shared misunderstanding," each group member wrongfully believes that everyone else but him actually desires to commit an offense.[12] Concerned about their reputation among friends, they all participate.

The group effect can operate within large mobs of people—such as in the widely publicized episodes of rioting or even lynchings—and in collections as small as a pair of accomplices. Following the arrest of two Vermont teenagers, 17-year-old Robert Tulloch and 16-year-old James Parker, for the January 2001 brutal murder of Dartmouth College professors Half Zantop and Susanne Zantop, numerous theories were proposed for a possible connection between the victims and the perpetrators. Some observers suggested that it may have been a hate crime related to the victims' German roots. Others speculated that they all had been members of the same hiking club. These and other proposed linkages proved wrong. The victims were selected just because they had something the assailants wanted—cash, to help fund their dream of traveling to Australia.

Rather than a connection between victims and offenders, it is instead the close bond between the two assailants that holds the key to understanding this tragic episode. Tulloch exalted in his leadership position, feeding off the admiration of his younger partner, while Parker sought the praise and approval of his older mentor. Had Tulloch and Parker been apart, arguably this crime would never have occurred. In tandem, they brought out the worst in each other.

Whereas the partnership of Tulloch and Parker facilitated their attack on the Zantops, countless youth follow a violent path through the support and encouragement of peers. The subculture of violence notion described in Chapter 3, if updated and modernized, is quite helpful in understanding the readiness for violence among many young urban dwellers. For inner-city youth, the American Dream, which appears absolutely unattainable, can be little more than a cruel nightmare. Alienated from mainstream society, minority youngsters instead often obey the code of the streets, in which respect is the fundamental and most vital commodity of daily life. Sociologist Elijah Anderson wrote that to earn respect and then guard against losing it, a youngster must comport himself at all times in a manner showing that he's ready and willing to be violent. According to Anderson, being disrespected is a fate worse than being murdered.[13]

On July 26, 2006, brothers Rasheem Dubose, 21, Terrell Dubose, 19, and Tajuane Dubose, 18, of Jacksonville, Florida, were challenged by Willie Davis Jr. Davis had nearly run over Tajuane with his car. Later in the day, Davis robbed Rasheem, held a gun to his head, and ordered him to remove his pants and dance in public. In another neighborhood, the victims of such transgressions and insults may have called the police. In the Duboses' world, anything short of retaliation would be a sign of weakness, would invite further victimization, and, most important, would rob them of their most precious possession—respect in the eyes of their peers. After fetching weapons and a ride, the Dubose brothers drove to the house where Davis was hanging out and pummeled it with 29 rounds, one of which ricocheted and killed Davis's 8-year-old niece, DreShawna, while she crouched down inside her bedroom to try and avoid the barrage of gunfire. All three brothers were charged and convicted of first-degree murder.

Another feature that strikingly distinguishes murders committed by younger assailants is the senseless nature of the underlying motivations. By contrast to the inspirations of profit, jealousy, and control that characterize most adult homicides, youthful offenders often, if not typically, kill for trivial reasons—a leather jacket, a romantic brush-off, a challenging glance, or no reason in particular. In a Los Angeles suburb, for example, two teenage girls murdered their best friend because they were jealous of her slender figure, waist-length auburn hair, good looks, and popularity with boys. In Miami, a 12-year-old boy killed a homeless man over a dispute involving a piece of pizza. In Independence, Missouri, a teenager murdered a Good Humor man because the vendor refused to give him a free frozen treat. And in Oklahoma, a 17-year-old, while riding around with a couple of friends, fatally shot a jogger purely as a break from boredom.

The limited capacity that juvenile killers have for appreciating the gravity of their crimes is stunningly illustrated by the remorselessness demonstrated by a Missouri girl after brutally killing a neighbor. In 2009, 15-year-old Alyssa Bustamante stabbed and strangled to death 9-year-old Elizabeth Olten. Bustamante then buried the body inside a grave she had dug days earlier in anticipation. Returning home afterward, the young killer scrawled this entry into her diary:

> I just f------ killed someone. I strangled them and slit their throat and stabbed them now they're dead. I don't know how to feel atm [at the moment]. It was ahmazing. As soon as you get over the "ohmygawd I can't do this" feeling, it's pretty enjoyable. I'm kinda nervous and shaky though right now. Kay, I gotta go to church now . . . lol.[14]

As shown in Chapter 2, since 2000, juveniles have constituted fewer than 10% of all homicide offenders. Even during the years of surging juvenile homicide rates, teenagers committed only about 15% of the nation's murders. However, you might not get that impression based on the news media. Based on a content analysis of news reports, for example, Pollak and Kubrin found juvenile offenders and juvenile victims are substantially overrepresented in crime coverage.[15] Part of the overexposure is likely a result of the unusual and bizarre reasons why kids commit murder, as with the cases just described. Crimes that seem to defy reason typically serve as prime fodder for journalists and reality crime shows. These stories leave Americans completely mystified, asking, "What's the matter with kids today?" to borrow a refrain from the classic musical *Bye Bye Birdie.*

Despite a widespread belief that kids today are indeed out of control, it absolutely remains the case that the vast majority of youngsters do not even come close to committing acts of serious violence, let alone homicide. Even among the highest rate group—young black males—for every youngster who commits homicide, literally hundreds never will.

Those adolescents who do commit homicide tend to differ from the rest in several important respects, besides demographics. Kenneth Busch and his colleagues, for example, studied the case histories of 71 juvenile murderers and compared them with similar data for a sample of 71 nonviolent delinquents, matched for age, race, sex, and social class. Overall, the young murderers were significantly more likely to have come from a violent family, to have abused alcohol, to have had severe educational deficiencies, and to have participated in gang activities.[16] More generally, the large body of research on violent youth has suggested a wide range of risk factors, including poor medical care and nutrition during early age as well as poor prenatal care; drug and alcohol dependency; inadequate supervision and ineffective parenting; emotional, physical, and sexual abuse; poverty; learning disabilities and academic problems; isolation from peers or contact with delinquent peers; and exposure to violent media and entertainment, among many others.[17] Yet none of these conditions, even in combination, are sufficient to produce homicidal behavior. Risk factors represent predispositions, not predestination.

EXPLAINING THE 1990s DECLINE

The precipitous decline in violence that thrilled Americans during the 1990s challenged criminologists to explain the sudden turnaround in lawlessness. Undoubtedly, such a sharp change in street crime would involve the coalescence of multiple factors, including demographic shifts by which the size of the most violence-prone segment of the population—teens and young adults—was shrinking relative to the total, increasing incarceration rates whereby dangerous felons were being kept behind bars for longer periods of time and innovative police strategies guided by constant monitoring of crime data and hot spots. However, arguably the most significant involved a reversal of the very factors that had pushed youth violence levels into record territories.[18]

Just as the increase in the U.S. homicide rate in the late 1980s and early 1990s can be linked to the crack epidemic, as described earlier, the subsequent decline can also be associated, at least in part, with a contraction or maturation of the crack market.[19] Typical of most fads in the marketplace, from fidget spinners to ripped jeans, the crack market passed through a natural evolutionary process. Although there had been street warfare over market shares in the early years of the drug, by the 1990s, the turf lines were being settled through survival of the fittest and the fiercest. Certain drug sellers were able to muscle or shoot out the competition—many of the losers had been incarcerated, killed, or had moved away from their neighborhood in a big city—and the crack frenzy began to dissipate. Also, by virtue of some widely publicized horror stories about the dangers of crack (e.g., the death of basketball star Len Bias), the demand for crack dissipated.

The crack market had largely devastated a particular cohort—those born from 1968 to 1974, especially blacks. When the crack market first hit the streets in the mid-1980s, these young people were old enough to be up to taking the risk but not old enough to know better. Thanks to what is known as the "big brother effect," those born after the early 1970s were scared away from crack by the devastation they saw in their older siblings and others in their communities. As a result, the rate of homicide by young black males in particular plummeted in the mid-1990s. As shown in Figures 5.5 and 5.6, although similar trends existed for white and black males, the rise and subsequent fall in homicide were especially steep among young black males.

On a statistical basis, murder by juveniles has fallen since 1993, but it fell from a level that was an all-time record when the crack epidemic wreaked havoc on youth, especially minorities in urban centers such as New York, Chicago, and

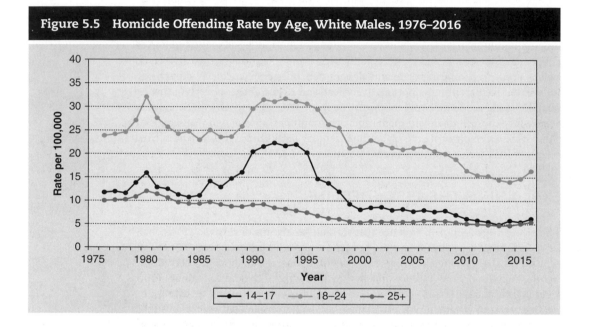

Figure 5.5   Homicide Offending Rate by Age, White Males, 1976–2016

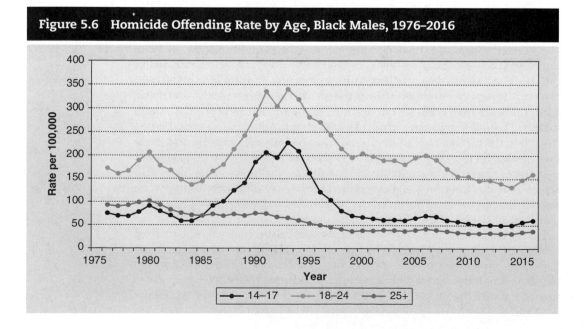

Figure 5.6   Homicide Offending Rate by Age, Black Males, 1976–2016

Baltimore. It would be a serious mistake, however, to frame the decline in crack-related violence as solely a market-driven trend that law enforcement passively watched from the sidelines. Rather, police agencies, in implementing community-oriented strategies, had much to do with curtailing the violence associated with crack, as well as guns and gangs. In Boston, for example, the police negotiated a cease-fire with warring gangs after getting everyone's attention by sending away to prison a major gang leader on federal weapons charges. The New York City police confiscated guns from the hands of teenagers through aggressive (aka "zero-tolerance") stop-and-frisk strategies.

It would also be a mistake to leave the impression that the reduction in youth murder was solely a result of the decline in the drug wars or due to police intervention. The level of youth violence subsided not only for murder but over a range of behaviors from simple assault to rioting, first in large cities but eventually in smaller cities as well. Perhaps precipitated by the incredible growth of violence associated with big-city drugs, many people around the country became desperate for solutions. Afraid to walk the streets in their own neighborhoods or go shopping downtown, they became sick and tired of feeling like victims. In urban centers across the country, residents sought to reestablish a sense of community as they began to recognize that they could make a difference in the lives of local youth. At the grassroots level, parents, teachers, psychologists, religious and business leaders, social workers, college students, and the police worked together in an effort to repair the moral, social, and economic damage done to young people over a period of 20 years and to take the glamour out of destructive behavior. Through myriad new programs, adults gave back to teenagers what they had lacked for more than two decades—supervision, structure, guidance, and hope for the future.[20]

Local schools were at the center of effective community efforts to reverse the scourge of teenage violence, often taking on responsibilities previously performed by the family. High school principals adopted a strict policy regarding students who carried weapons to school, making classrooms safer from the threat of gun violence. In addition, by means of effective conflict resolution programs built into the curriculum, many local schools began teaching their students what parents used to teach: to have empathy for victims, to control their anger, and to manage their impulsive behavior. Finally, through the 21st Century Schools initiative passed by Congress in 1994, schools provided what was lacking after the school day ended—adult supervision, guidance, and control through after-school programs.

Schools were not the only local institutions that stepped forward to fill guiding roles. Churches ran athletic and gun-buyback programs. Community policing placed more officers in strategic positions in high-crime areas. Probation officers rode in patrol cars to keep an eye on youthful probationers. Increasing numbers of local college students served as mentors, tutors, and peer mediators in neighborhood schools. Parents and teachers volunteered more to supervise after-school programs in athletics, drama, and the arts. Local businesses generated more summer jobs, at least some of which led to careers with the companies. More community centers opened their doors to local teenagers. Municipalities beefed up funds for community policing, with residents forming more partnerships with police.

In Boston, which was seen as a model in dealing with teenage crime, the murder count plummeted from 34 teen offenders in 1990 to only 3 in 1998.[21] Over the same period, the city saw a proliferation of programs geared toward at-risk teenagers. The wake-up call for Boston's community leaders came during a funeral service in 1992 at the Morning Star Baptist Church. As a crowd of mourners looked on in horror, a gang of local youths chased another teenager into the church, where they repeatedly stabbed him into submission. Shocked by this crime, a group of local Boston ministers decided that enough was enough and that it was time to act. Rather than wait for troubled youngsters to come to their churches, they decided to take their congregations to the streets and the gangs, working with the police to identify the most recalcitrant young offenders and to provide alternative programs for those teenagers whose lives could be turned around.

Boston's attack on juvenile violence during the 1990s was multifaceted, emphasizing prevention, tough and effective law enforcement, and formation of partnerships with local residents. The community policing effort increased communication between police and neighborhood youth. Perhaps taking their cue from Boston's churches, other local institutions—businesses, government, universities, schools, police, and parents—were suddenly more willing to get involved in the lives of local youth. The juvenile crime rate in Boston finally began to reverse direction, and sharply so.

The success of the Boston model influenced public policy nationwide. Although generating much political controversy concerning the separation of church and state, former president George W. Bush championed federal funding for faith-based organizations in an attempt to bring the church into the loop of providing services for at-risk youth as well as ex-offenders, the homeless, the hungry, substance abusers, those with HIV and AIDS, and welfare-to-work families.

It should be clear, then, that the range of explanations for the sizable and steady drop in homicide rates during the 1990s is extremely broad. Criminologists frequently cite changes in drug markets, the expansion of prison populations and community policing initiatives, intensified prevention and enforcement efforts, demographic change, and increased involvement of community leaders and ordinary citizens in grassroots crime-fighting campaigns as key contributors. However, a few other, less obvious and more controversial theories have also surfaced.

Anthony Harris and colleagues at the University of Massachusetts suggested, for example, that growth in medical technology and the spread of emergency medical services may have contributed to lessening the extent of carnage related to assaults with guns and other deadly weapons.[22] They attempted to show empirically that the lethality of criminal assault—the likelihood that aggravated assault victims survive rather than die from their injuries—can in part be linked to emergency care response.

On a very different tack, economists John Donahue and Steven Levitt proposed a rather hotly debated hypothesis, controversial both methodologically and politically, that declining rates of violence in the 1990s were a lagged or delayed effect of the legalization of abortion arising from the 1972 Supreme Court decision *Roe v. Wade*. "Teenagers, unmarried women, and African Americans are all substantially more likely to seek abortions," they wrote in a 1999 paper. "Children born to these mothers tend to be at higher risk for committing crime 17 years or so down the road, so abortion may reduce subsequent criminality through this selection effect."[23]

Their proposition, therefore, was that following *Roe v. Wade*, thousands of unwanted fetuses were aborted instead of being born into less-than-ideal environments, producing two decades later a reduction in the pool of at-risk, violence-prone individuals. Despite some persuasive logic, Donahue and Levitt appear to have overstated the impact of legalized abortion. The change in law, for example, cannot account for the steady decline in rates of homicide by adults, aged 25 and older, individuals who would have been born prior to the landmark abortion decision.

Even as the abortion–violent crime link was being debated in academic circles, the theory received a public airing through Levitt and Dubner's widely read book, *Freakonomics*.[24] Conservative talk-show host William Bennett, who had served as the secretary of education during the Reagan administration, confronted a firestorm of protest when he tried facetiously, and unwisely, to take the theory to an absurd extreme: that the rate of crime in America could be hugely curtailed if every conceived black baby were aborted.

Another fascinating hypothesis to explain the drop in youth crime—one that has nothing to do with funding for prevention programs, gang interdiction efforts by the police and the clergy, or shifts in drug markets—involves federal initiatives since the 1970s to remove lead from paint, gasoline, and drinking water. There is evidence that heavy exposure to lead, particularly in children, significantly impacts physical and psychological health and tends to increase the propensity toward aggressive behavior.[25] The reduction in childhood lead exposure in the late 1970s and early 1980s was, according to this theory, a key fact in the subsequent decline in violence in the 1990s and beyond.[26] That fewer children have toxic levels of lead would explain at least part of the decline in youth violence and homicide.[27]

Each of these novel hypotheses may contribute to our understanding of the 1990s crime drop, at least to some undetermined extent. However, each suffers from one major flaw. None—not advances in emergency medicine, changing access to abortion, nor regulations to address lead poisoning—can account for the steep rise in homicide rates beginning in the mid-1980s or for the fact that youth homicide rates plateaued in the early 2000s almost at the same level as they were prior to the mid-1980s surge. The rise-up then fall-back pattern is more consistent with transient factors than with a permanent policy change.

Whatever the actual causes for the downturn, it is clear that the widely reported and worrisome surge in youth homicide during the late 1980s and early 1990s has completely dissipated. In fact, the rate of homicide committed by teens and young adults since 2010 has remained lower than at any point in time over the past four decades. Criminologists who in the 1990s had wrongly predicted a continued rising tide of youth murder were sharply criticized for their part in scaring the public and for giving lawmakers the impetus for enacting stiff penalties for young killers.[28] To be fair, however, those same criminologists had advocated for increased funding for youth violence prevention, not increased punishment.

Although the youth homicide surge was fleeting, the aftereffects have been devastating and long-lasting. During those days of high crime rates, when fear was widespread in both black and white communities, the "superpredator" sound bite went as viral as things could go in an era before social media. Thousands of individuals who had been sentenced under the get-tough laws on juvenile murder enacted during that era remain incarcerated today, many of them for life. Although there has been some remediation, as discussed in this chapter (see section titled "Juveniles in the Adult System") and in Chapter 14, the juvenile justice system looks nothing like it was before youth killing became a matter of intense concern.

PRINCIPLES OF PREVENTION

Not all Americans are convinced about the value of prevention—especially early childhood enrichment efforts. Prevention strategies occur to keep kids from ever becoming involved in criminal activity; intervention strategies occur after a problem has begun. It seems that the public and policymakers alike would rather pay later than pay now. As a result, prevention initiatives are too often funded and implemented on a shoestring, and a rather short shoestring with a brief window of opportunity to show results. This is a recipe for failure and provides additional fodder for skeptics.

Smart crime fighting involves a balanced blend of enforcement (from community policing to identifying illegal gun markets), treatment modalities (from drug rehab on demand to community corrections and prisoner reentry services), as well as general and targeted crime prevention (from family support to summer jobs for high-risk youth). Regrettably, the prevention approach has at times been disparaged as "worthless" and as "soft on crime." Yet, this cynical perspective reflects gross misunderstanding of the process and goals of prevention, and a selective examination of outcomes. Simply put: Prevention programs can work; good prevention programs that are well implemented do work.[29]

Besides the matter of funding adequacy, there are five fundamental principles of crime and violence prevention that are critical to a successful investment:

1. No program is successful all the time or for all individuals.
   No matter how exceptional the initiative is, there will be failures, that is, those who recidivate despite our best efforts to prevent it. Rather than focusing on the failures (as the media tend to do in their "good news is no news; bad news is big news" posture), the goal should be a reasonable reduction in offending rates. In light of the enormous social and administrative costs associated with each criminal act, even modest gains are worthwhile.

2. Prevention should have an emphasis on the prefix *pre-*.
   Although it is unwise and inappropriate to "give up" on even a seemingly hardened offender, the greatest opportunity for positive impact comes with a focus on children—those who are young and impressionable and will be impressed with what a teacher, preacher, or some other authority figure has to say. It is well known that early prevention—during grade school if not earlier—can carry the greatest and longest-lasting impact before a youngster is seduced by gangs, drugs, and crime. It is far easier and considerably less expensive to build the child than to rebuild the teenager. It is more effective to "prehabilitate" early than to rehabilitate later.

3. Patience is more than a virtue; it is a requirement.
   Prevention is not a short-term strategy. Rather, it involves a continued effort, undaunted by setbacks. Unfortunately, many prevention programs are given short windows in which to show progress and are often terminated before the final results are in.

4. Prevention should take a multifaceted approach.
   Understandably, there is much temptation to target gang activity as perhaps the most visible and immediate threat to public safety. Although that is laudable and should be strengthened, there are many other points of intervention for successful crime reduction programming. For example, several proven and promising strategies are directed at at-risk families with young children. Rather than criticizing struggling underage mothers for their lack of parenting effectiveness, many programs support them in raising children who are less likely to become juvenile offenders. In addition, many school-based initiatives effectively and efficiently enhance the well-being of large numbers of children. Behavioral skills training at the elementary school level, antibullying curricula for middle school

students that recognize the link between bullying and later offending, peer mediation and mentoring programs in high school, and after-school activities targeted at the "prime time for juvenile crime," all have payoffs far greater than the investment.

5. Prevention is significantly cost-effective.
    Virtually all assessments of crime prevention confirm the adage that an ounce of prevention is worth a pound of prison time. It is, however, a political reality that sound investments in crime prevention can take years to reap the benefits. It takes a bold leader to earmark funds today for tomorrow's improvement for which his or her successor may derive credit.

DIAL M FOR MEDIA

Despite the highly successful effort in Boston and elsewhere to reduce the level of teenage violence, especially that relating to street gangs and guns, the problem has hardly been resolved. Although crack- and gang-related violence may have taken a nosedive, the nation must still contend with long-term issues, from supervision and television (too little of one and too much of the other) to adolescent angst and alienation.

It is easy enough to implicate the mass media—especially movies, television, video games, and YouTube—for the occurrence of hideous violence on a national level. Certainly, there is at least some evidence collected over several decades that a steady diet of media-depicted violence can help to desensitize young people, distorting their perceptions of social reality, and even inspiring heinous, brutal crimes in copycat fashion. The average child now grows up observing thousands of murders and tens of thousands of violent acts on TV and other forms of entertainment. Cumulatively, this has an effect, although the exact size and nature of the effect have been debated for almost as long as television has existed.

Communication research conducted for decades suggests that people who watch many hours of television every day tend to overestimate the percentage of the world population that is white and male, underestimate the level of poverty in our country, and exaggerate the amount of violence they are likely to encounter. Heavy viewers also tend to overestimate the proportion of jury trials in our courts and the number of miracle cures performed by doctors. They are socialized to accept a false view of reality because this is precisely what they see on TV every evening.

According to George Gerbner, children who view TV excessively tend to develop what he has labeled a "mean world view."[30] Wherever they look—in their neighborhood after dark, on the streets on the way to school, on the playground with their peers—they see violence and the threat of violence. They grow up feeling intimidated and vulnerable. In line with the television version of life, they exaggerate their likelihood of becoming a victim of violent crime.

Everywhere you turn on TV, you find violence. Because violence is entertaining, it sells; it keeps the ratings high; it keeps programs on the air.[31] The list of programs featuring violence seems endless—*Criminal Minds, CSI: Crime Scene Investigation, Major Crimes, Chicago P.D., Law & Order: Special Victims Unit*, almost everything aired on the Investigation Discovery network, not to mention local and network newscasts. The Lifetime Channel produces so many movies about murder that it belies the very name of the network.

Actually, our entire popular culture has increasingly become a culture of murder and violence. Gangsta rap lyrics often extol the virtues of shooting women and attacking whites, gays, and the police. Some heavy metal music expresses themes in which blacks, immigrants, gays, and women are brutalized. The entire genre of death metal, death rap, and horrorcore focuses on violent topics including murder, rape, mutilation, cannibalism, necrophilia, and suicide. White Power music calls for a racial holy war, one which white Christians would ultimately win.

Even more troubling, perhaps, are the new forms of hero worship, which has always been an integral part of the process whereby young people—adults in training—are socialized to internalize society's most cherished norms and values. Over the decades, we have celebrated members of society who have reached the pinnacle of success in their fields by honoring them in movies, documentaries, magazine profiles, and even on trading cards. More recently, we have extended our celebration to what some consider our new antiheroes, those who have distinguished themselves in the worst possible ways by reaching the pinnacle of "success" as murderers.

Celebrating evil and murder in popular culture, as described in Chapter 1, may be having a particularly profound impact on teenagers who want to feel important but often feel ignored by parents, peers, and teachers. The lesson for youngsters may be this: Behave yourself and adults won't notice; go on a rampage at school, and you become a big-shot superstar.

Magnifying the problem of a toxic culture, millions of children and teenagers lack adequate parental supervision, living with a single working parent or in a household where both parents hold full-time jobs. Although many youngsters may enjoy substitute forms of supervision provided by extended family, neighbors, or day care, far too many have no regular monitoring by adults. These children come home from school to an empty house, grab a snack from the refrigerator, and watch anything they want on television. If their television service lacks channels showing their choice of a grotesque movie, they can always stream some nasty R-rated or unrated movie on a mobile device. Or they can play a violent video game in which they rehearse—in a virtually realistic manner—stabbing, shooting, bombing, or running down other people. Or, they can roam the internet, visiting an array of pornographic, violent, and hate-filled websites.

In some respects, violence in television and film, which has been the focus of most of the debate over the decades, is relatively tame. It represents a passive form of entertainment, compared to the more active participation provided by video games. Rather than just lie on the living room couch and witness a massacre on television, children can cybernetically kill on demand—and learn to enjoy it—through one of many violent action games available to them in computer game stores or on the internet.

Critics often point to examples of mass killers to make the case that violent video game playing encourages violent behavior. It hardly went unnoticed that Adam Lanza, who killed his mother and then shot his way through the Sandy Hook Elementary School, killing 26 children and teachers, played violent video games incessantly while hiding in his basement away from the outside world. When he did venture outside, it was often to go to a nearby movie theater, where he spent hours playing a nonviolent video game, *Dance, Dance Revolution*. Of course, there were many other psychological factors that would have contributed to his murderous actions. As such, his obsession with video games was likely more a symptom of his infirmity and social anxiety than a cause of his behavior.[32]

The Pew Research Center has estimated that as many as 90% of children in the United States play video games, and that figure rises to 97% for adolescents between the ages of 12 and 17.[33] This is especially worrisome to children's advocates because the majority of games on the market feature violence, and many to an extreme level.

Moreover, the intrinsic incentives and rewards, such as accruing a top score from killing, advancing through game levels while developing homicidal mastery, and defeating an opponent in an internet-based competition, reinforce the will to kill, at least in the game setting. Although these games are fantasy, with surround sound and high-definition graphics, the line between virtual reality and stark reality can become rather thin. Moreover, role-playing games and virtual reality devices have taken gaming another step toward realism.

It has been a challenge for adolescent development scholars to keep their research agenda up to pace with the fast-changing world of gaming technology. Even so, some of the evidence, involving a range of methodological approaches, suggests that frequently playing violent video games tends to impact negatively on a youngster's attitudes and affect. The frequent gamer may become angry or desensitized, but not necessarily more violent. The extent to which violent games alter behavior is a wide-open question. After all, it would be unethical and hardly feasible to conduct a controlled randomized experiment that might definitively resolve the debate over whether playing violent games increases the propensity to commit serious acts of violence.

At the same time, an experimental study from the Indiana University School of Medicine has uncovered an impact of playing video games with violent themes on the gamer's brain activity. The researchers compared randomly formed groups of adolescents who played violent and nonviolent video games for a half-hour period. MRI scans of the area of the brain responsible for emotional arousal indicated significantly greater activity among subjects in the violent game–playing group than those in a comparison group.[34] Of course, it would be a leap to generalize these findings to actual behavior.

Reviewing the results of dozens of research studies on the effects of playing violent video games, psychologist Craig Anderson reported a statistically significant link between exposure to the games and increases in aggressive behavior, aggressive thinking, aggressive affect, and cardiovascular arousal, as well as decreases in helping behavior.[35] To whatever extent the evidence can implicate a causal connection, there are concerns, both in Congress and in living rooms across America, over the long-term impact of this thriving and relatively unregulated industry. However, most of the research that purports to find a link between violent video game playing and aggressive behavior is based on correlational evidence that cannot establish cause and effect.[36] It may just be that children predisposed to violent behavior are especially attracted to violent games (and other violence-filled forms of entertainment). The "chicken-and-egg" debate wages on and may never be settled conclusively.[37] In addition, some researchers have claimed that increased playing of video games, be they of violent or nonviolent content, keeps youngster safe in front of their screens, rather than hanging out where they can get into fights, or worse.[38] Still, even with some remaining ambiguity in interpreting the association between violent video games and aggression, both the American Psychological Association and the American Academy of Pediatrics have taken policy stands discouraging violent games for developing minds.

Of course, concern among pediatricians, parents, and politicians alike over the effects of violent entertainment of all forms on impressionable children is hardly new. As early as the 1960s, parents and child advocates were alarmed about exposing young viewers to unrealistic images of "cleaned-up violence." That is, because television programs and motion pictures of the day failed to depict the destructive aspects of punching, stabbing, and shooting, youngsters were growing up believing that violence didn't have consequences. To placate anxious parents, moreover, a voluntary code of the motion picture industry—movie ratings—was established to give them an opportunity to censor their children's viewing choices.

Beginning in the 1970s, the problem of sanitized film violence was replaced by a much more troubling phenomenon. To lure young people to the box office, producers frequently gave them exactly what they wanted—more graphic sex and violence. The movie rating system soon became a media version of "forbidden fruit"—more a guide for children in determining what they really must see than a guide for parents on what their children must not see. Experimental studies of factors influencing viewer selection have found that teenaged boys, in particular, prefer programs and films with an R rating or a parental warning, regardless of their content.[39] From the perspective of a young viewer, if you're not part of the mature audience, then you must be part of the immature audience, and what self-respecting, red-blooded American adolescent wants to be labeled that?

Parental warnings and violence ratings have been extended to television shows and video games under the assumption—or rather hope—that they will assist parents in choosing age-appropriate entertainment options. But as with films, the more mature ratings tend to boost the desirability of proscribed material among immature youngsters who are eager for adulthood.

Experiments have also shown that a steady diet of R-rated films in which violence and sex are fused together actually desensitizes youngsters to the plight of rape. For teenagers who are having trouble making the transition into adulthood, such films may also confuse them into believing that they cannot have sex without violence—that the one is inseparable from the other.[40]

The impact of media violence can be aggravated or mitigated, depending on the circumstances in which children grow up. It isn't that the mass media are so powerful; it is that our other institutions—our families, our schools, our churches and synagogues, our neighborhoods, our businesses, our political system—have become so weak with respect to raising children. Already-troubled kids with a host of biological, psychological, and social problems may be more susceptible to the messages in violent media, but the vast majority of consumers of violent media will never harm anyone. Violent media becomes the scapegoat if policymakers are unwilling to deal with the more important causes of violence.

In Japan, by contrast, television programs are much more violent than their American counterparts. Yet the level of street violence in Japan remains comparatively low. Part of the reason involves the continuing power of Japanese traditional values on its youth. But another important difference is that Japanese parents hardly use television as a babysitter the way that it is more typically used in the United States. In Japan, children watch television with an adult—a parent, a grandparent, a family friend—who monitors, guides, interprets, and explains. Thus, the fundamental issue is not just what children are watching but who is watching the children.

In the United States, rather than provide creative alternatives to parental supervision, politicians and entertainment industry leaders sought to develop a method for allowing parents to continue working full-time while still having remote control over their children's access to violent television. Under pressure to do something to shield children from shows that may be too disturbing for them, Congress enacted legislation mandating that, effective January 2000, all new televisions had to be equipped with a V-chip (V for violence), with which parents can theoretically filter out the most offensive programs from their children's after-school viewing options.

Although most parents are at least somewhat familiar with the television rating system, most don't make an effort to utilize any filtering tools. A 2016 survey found that only 36% of parents actually utilize either the television's V-chip or parental controls provided by their cable or satellite service.[41]

Even for parents who make use of the V-chip or similar device, it may be naïve to expect that unsupervised teenagers, left alone in front of their V-chip-controlled TV sets, will instead tune into National Geographic, read Shakespeare, or take up chess. More likely, they will bypass their parents' attempts at absentee censorship by streaming a grotesque film on their mobile device, playing a violent video game, or listening to the hate-filled lyrics of some rap and heavy metal. Or they might just go over to a friend's house whose parents didn't program their V-chip. The lesson is clear: Technology cannot adequately substitute for genuine attention and involvement from parents and other significant adults in the daily lives of children.

In the final analysis, even with enhanced rating systems and parental controls, it is important not to let the entertainment industry off the hook for its willingness to pander to and profit from the darker side of human behavior. At the same time, we should be careful not to place inordinate blame on the entertainment industry for violent acts perpetrated by children and teenagers. We should be similarly wary of single-issue critics who contend that the problem of kids today is the media, plain and simple. If anything is simple, it is the fallacy in such a simple-minded point of view.

It is true, of course, that experimental research has suggested a link between exposure to violent entertainment and attitudes tolerant of aggression. Yet we must also keep in mind that experiments are often limited in terms of real-world generalizability. Even if children are stimulated neurologically or appear somewhat desensitized in affect after viewing violent content or playing violent games, there are questions—and in the minds of some critics, lots of questions—whether this translates into lasting change in behavior. In addition, if violent entertainment were at the very root of the youth violence problem, as antimedia zealots claim, how can we account for the decline in rates of juvenile violence in the 1990s? Clearly, there was no reduction in the spread or popularity of violent entertainment. Perhaps if kids are spending their days and nights in front of video games, they aren't out committing crimes or being vulnerable to victimization by others?

The media have, at times, been used as a convenient scapegoat, and censorship has been proposed as an easy solution. Public concerns, political considerations, self-interests, and fear have often encouraged us to point fingers at a profitable industry, while ignoring some of the fundamental causes of violence that are much more difficult to resolve.

JUVENILES IN THE ADULT SYSTEM

Under the "infancy defense" from English common law, persons younger than age 7 could not be charged with crimes because of an irrefutable presumption that they lacked the ability to form criminal intent. For children between the ages of 7 and 14, the same presumption held, but it could be challenged or refuted based on evidence to the contrary. In common law, defendants older than 14 were considered no different than adults in terms of culpability or responsibility. By the end of the nineteenth century, children's advocates in the United States had become deeply disturbed about the treatment of minors by the criminal justice system, and understandably so. Children and adolescents were being prosecuted, convicted, and imprisoned in the same manner (and in the same institutions) as adults. Wanting to provide an alternative approach not just for young criminals but for incorrigible children as well, the so-called "child saving movement" successfully pushed for the nation's first juvenile court.[42] Established in Chicago in 1899, the new juvenile court was designed to take a therapeutic rather than punitive approach to handling youthful delinquents and status offenders. The process was to be paternalistic rather than adversarial.

The new approach to juvenile justice spread quickly, and through much of the twentieth century the juvenile court movement appeared to fare quite well. Over time, juveniles were afforded expanded rights (e.g., the right to an attorney), just like adults in criminal courts. By the 1980s, however, as rates of juvenile violence and murder, in particular, began to surge, politicians and the public alike questioned the role and appropriateness of juvenile court for these dangerous offenders of tender age.

A child found delinquent for committing a homicide or another serious crime would generally serve time within a juvenile detention facility until the age of majority (generally 18 years of age) or, in some states, a few additional years at the discretion of the judge. Under the assumption that wayward youths could be rehabilitated into law-abiding adults, juvenile sentences even for serious crimes were, for the most part, relatively short.

Even from the earliest years of the juvenile court system, the criminal courts were not completely willing to give up jurisdiction over all crimes committed by children. In part, the battle between the "kiddie courts" and the more prestigious and powerful adult courts was a political one over authority and turf.[43] More generally, in response to concerns that some youthful offenders were simply not amenable to treatment (as well as doubts about the efficacy of rehabilitation itself), waiver procedures allowed juvenile court judges to transfer particular defendants over to criminal adult court for prosecution and punishment. On a case-by-case basis, certain repeat, chronic, or violent youths were appropriately removed from the jurisdiction of juvenile court.

As the pressure on the juvenile court to take a harsher stance toward murder and other serious offenses mounted, however, judges began deciding the transfer question even for first-time offenders, less on the basis of treatment amenability and more to satisfy public opinion. In 1986, for example, 14-year-old Rod Matthews of Canton, Massachusetts, was arrested for the murder of his classmate, Shaun Ouillette; because of widespread outrage over the shocking and senseless crime, he became at that time one of the youngest children tried for murder in adult court.

Apparently, Matthews had made a hit list of possible victims, huddled with two buddies to determine the most deserving target, and then led his unsuspecting victim into the woods, where he bludgeoned the boy with a baseball bat. Afterward, Matthews brought his friends to view the body and to show off his courage. Despite his young age and lack of any criminal record, the juvenile court judge waived jurisdiction over to the adult court in the face of intense pressure from the victim's family and the local media.

In a closely watched Florida case, 12-year-old Lionel Tate was arrested in July 1999 for beating and stomping to death his 6-year-old neighbor, Tiffany Eunick. Tate claimed that her death was an accident, occurring during rough-house play in which he was imitating wrestling moves he had seen on television. Although old enough to be prosecuted as an adult, Tate was deemed too immature to have final say in whether to accept a plea bargain for a lesser penalty that had been offered by the prosecution. Instead, his mother insisted on a trial, a trial in which Tate was convicted and sentenced to life in prison.

Widespread concern for the harshness of the outcome, an outcome that was prescribed by Florida law, may very well have been considered when an appellate court in 2004 overturned his conviction. Tate subsequently accepted a plea deal for second-degree murder, receiving a term of incarceration equal to time already served and 10 years of probation. While the resolution was hailed by legal scholars, within 9 months Tate violated the terms of his probation by staying out after curfew and was returned to jail. Released once again in late 2004 with an extra 5 years of probation, Tate was unable to keep his nose clean. In May 2005, having by then reached the age of maturity, he was arrested for robbery and reincarcerated. Ending the long legal saga surrounding the troubled youngster, Tate was sentenced to 30 years in prison for violating his probation by possessing a gun and breaking a glass door at the Broward County Jail.

Unlike the judicial waiver strategy that many states had employed, the New York state legislature, reeling from a brutal double murder committed by a 15-year-old, decided to take matters into its own hands. In 1978, after 15-year-old Willie Bosket was sentenced to a maximum term of 5 years in Family Court for killing two men on the subway, the legislature passed the New York Juvenile Offender Law (aka the "Willie Bosket Law") mandating that all juvenile defendants as young as 13 who are charged with murder shall be processed in adult court and receive adult sentences unless there was compelling reason to move the case down to juvenile court.

How young is too young to hold children accountable? In New York, at least, 9-year-old girls who kill are handled with a sensible measure of compassion. During Memorial Day weekend in 2005, K. Shanine (identity protected) of Brooklyn fatally stabbed her best friend, 11-year-old Queen Washington, during an argument over a rubber ball. Although charged with murder, Shanine pled guilty to second-degree manslaughter and as a juvenile would serve a maximum of 18 months in a youth facility.

During the late 1980s and early 1990s, years after the Matthews and Bosket cases, juvenile murder rates rose sharply, and state legislatures responded with harsh measures. Rather than leave the waiver decision up to the judges, the wisdom of whose decisions was being questioned in the appellate court of public opinion, lawmakers generally proposed two alternative strategies: prosecutorial discretion and statutory exclusions. In the former, the determination as to whether to charge a youngster in juvenile or adult court is made by the prosecutor under the logic that this public official, elected by the citizenry, is more responsive to public mood than are judges, who in some states are appointed to the bench for extended terms. Alternatively, some state legislatures opted to write into the law exactly which offenses (e.g., homicides by offenders ages 14 and over) are excluded from juvenile court jurisdiction. Some states simply lowered the age of majority below the traditional 18 years old for all offenses. A few eliminated altogether the statutory lower limit on eligibility for criminal prosecution in adult court.

The 1990s saw rapid change in transfer laws across the country.[44] Between 1992 and 1997, amid the widespread panic over juvenile violence, 17 states expanded the range of offenses and lowered the eligibility age for judicial waiver. During these same years, 27 states expanded the list of crimes that were excluded from juvenile court jurisdiction, and 7 states reduced the age when these exclusions kicked in. Eleven states increased the range of crimes and reduced the age limits when prosecutors could opt to file charges in either juvenile or adult court.

These changes opened the floodgate wide for juvenile offenders to be charged and prosecuted in adult criminal courts. From 1985 to 1996, for example, the number of delinquency cases waived from juvenile to adult court, generally through decisions of the juvenile court judges, rose 47%, from 6,800 to about 10,000 annually. For violent offenses specifically, including homicide, the number of waivers more than doubled from about 2,000 per year to over 4,000 per year.[45] In addition to these more traditional transfers, many times more youngsters were being tried as adults arising from decisions by prosecutors to file cases in adult court or from statutory exclusions of cases away from juvenile court jurisdiction. As a consequence of the movement to prosecute juveniles as adults, the number of offenders under age 18 sentenced to serve time in an adult correctional facility also climbed, from 3,400 in 1985 to 7,400 in 1997.[46] As the rate of youth violence diminished during the latter half of the 1990s, so did the number of juveniles prosecuted in adult court and subsequently sent to state prisons. After peaking in the mid-1990s, the number of juveniles admitted to prison fell 45% from 1996 to 2002.

Despite the downturn in admissions, the youthfulness of certain offenders prosecuted as adults is still quite striking. In 2014, two 12-year-old girls in Waukesha, Wisconsin, were arrested for attempting to kill a classmate. The victim was stabbed nineteen times all across her body, yet managed to survive. The alleged assailants claimed that they planned and carried out the attack in order to appease Slender Man, a fearsome but fictional supernatural character. Despite their youth and the bizarre nature of the crime, the defendants were transferred to the jurisdiction of the adult court.

The two Wisconsin girls are far from the only preteens to experience the harsh realities of the adult criminal court. In 1999, Nathaniel Abraham of Pontiac, Michigan, was tried as an adult for murder surrounding an incident that occurred on October 29, 1997, when he was just 11 years old, making him one of the youngest children ever charged as an adult. Abraham reportedly shot a gun into some trees, hitting and killing 18-year-old Ronnie Greene Jr. Despite testimony from a defense witness that the defendant had the mental capacity of a 6-year-old at the time of the killing, Abraham was convicted of second-degree murder.

It is likely that the jurors had at least to some extent sympathized with the victim's family. To Ronnie Greene's relatives, in terms of their loss and anguish, it is largely irrelevant that the person who shot and killed him was a diminutive 11-year-old. To the families who lose a loved one, it matters not whether the perpetrator was 11 or 41; the victim is just as dead. In terms of this retributive notion of justice, juveniles and adults should arguably be treated no differently. Furthermore, there are indeed certain repeat, violent, chronic, ruthless juveniles who have proved through their recidivism that they are not amenable to treatment. They may have been through the juvenile justice system time after time but with little or no improvement in their character or behavior. As juvenile justice failures, these offenders can and perhaps should be sent to the adult system.

It could also be argued that not all juvenile offenders deserve adultlike punishment, even though they may commit an adultlike crime such as murder or rape. The inspiration for their vicious crimes often stems from their immaturity— for example, kids committing murder in order to impress their peers or even to fulfill a dare. We must fully consider the special nature of youthful offending— even murder. Teenagers may look like adults, dress like adults, act like adults, even shoot like adults, but they tend to reason like teenagers.

Some recent evidence from neurological studies supports the view that juveniles have a limited capacity for understanding consequences. According to Deborah Yurgelun-Todd, director of neuropsychology and cognitive neuroimaging at McLean Hospital, the frontal lobe portion of the brain, which controls the ability to think things through fully, does not tend to develop until late adolescence or young adulthood.[47] More recent research suggests that this portion of the brain may not fully develop until as late as 25 years of age. Indeed, it has long been recognized that teenagers are often impulsive—in a sense, "temporary sociopaths." Thus, leaving aside the purely retributive notion of justice, teenagers may not deserve the same punishment as adults given their limited capacity for considering consequences. Diminished capacity should mean diminished punishability, especially for nonhabitual offenders.

Making the juvenile justice system more just and punitive is one thing, but eliminating it, as some have proposed, is quite another. Expanding juvenile penalties and blending juvenile and adult sanctions for the most serious offenders will go a long way toward addressing public concern without entirely sacrificing young lives that could be salvaged. We need to be selective in how we prosecute juveniles, even juvenile murderers.

In a surprising and bold move, Judge Eugene Moore, on sentencing young Nathaniel Abraham following his adult conviction on a second-degree murder charge, chose not to follow through with an adult punishment. Rather than hand down a protracted term of incarceration, Moore sent the boy to a juvenile facility until the age of 21, at which time he would be released. With courtroom cameras rolling, the judge took time to articulate his concern for the snowballing trend in America toward trying juveniles as adults as well as his view that we should not forsake the rehabilitative goal, particularly when children are involved:

> The legislature has responded to juvenile criminal activity not by helping to prevent and rehabilitate but rather by treating juveniles more like adults. Is this the good option? Is our adult system successfully rehabilitating people, do our jails release productive, reformed citizens? We all know the answers to these questions. The real solution is to prevent an adult criminal population ever coming into existence. This only can be accomplished by taking advantage of the hope and promise of our youth and nurturing healthy adults.[48]

Quite apart from the question of rehabilitation, many proponents of the movement to try serious juvenile offenders as adults are hoping to send a strong deterrent message to other youngsters who might contemplate attacking a classmate or neighbor. Yet, we cannot deal effectively with teen violence through the threat of the criminal justice system. The threat of punishment, no matter how harsh, frequently fails to deter kids who face the threat of violence and death every day in their classrooms and their neighborhoods. As far as they are concerned, the criminal justice system can just take a number and wait in line with all the other enemies out to get them. Plus, tending toward impulsive action, adolescents do not fully weigh the costs and benefits.

Often these are juveniles who think little of and care even less about the future, who don't expect to live past their 21st birthday. The prospect of a long-term prison sentence will not dissuade them in the least. Criminologists Simon Singer and David McDowall, for example, conducted an assessment of whether the landmark and widely publicized New York Juvenile Offender Law of 1978 (the "Willie Bosket Law") had any impact on deterring youthful offenders. By comparing trends over time in New York and, as a comparison, Philadelphia, they found that the threat promised by the tough New York law did not have any impact in lowering rates of serious juvenile offending.[49]

Not only does the wholesale transfer of juveniles into the adult court make little sense theoretically, but also on a practical level it does little good in reforming offenders. Criminologists Bishop, Frazier, Lanza-Kaduce, and White compared a sample of Florida juveniles who were tried and sentenced as adults to a control group of juveniles retained in the juvenile system, matched on a variety of offense characteristics and risk factors. On follow-up, Bishop and her colleagues found that those who had passed through the adult system actually had a higher rate of recidivism than the control-group offenders.[50] Moreover, based on a review of a host of empirical studies on the impact of transferring juveniles to the adult criminal justice system, a distinguished group of scholars recommended that the practice be curtailed because of its tendency to increase rates of recidivism.[51]

As noted earlier, even the best criminal justice policies and practices will encounter failures. Despite Judge Moore's wisdom in sentencing Nathaniel Abraham so that he would be free at age 21 with a second chance to make a productive life for himself, he hardly took advantage of the break. Shortly after his release, Abraham was arrested on drug charges and given a sentence of 4 to 20 years, which he later compounded by assaulting a guard. After the arrest, Moore released a statement that he was "very disappointed and particularly sad for the hundreds of people who worked hard to rehabilitate [Abraham] for the nine years he was in the state training school and the wonderful mentors and volunteers and churches that stood by him."[52]

LOOKING AHEAD

Citizen concerns over the impact of television, motion pictures, video games, and the internet on children continue to be strong. Even so, some of the sense of urgency has faded as the violent crime rate plummeted well below levels reached during the bad old days of the early 1990s. Unfortunately, however, in the face of rosy crime statistics, many Americans may have come to believe falsely that we have won the war against youth violence.

Looking ahead, the population of at-risk youth, especially from disadvantaged backgrounds, is expected to expand. Given the social and economic strains that unevenly impact minority communities, growth in the population of at-risk youth signals the clear potential for recurring problems of homicide, violence, and other social ills associated with an expanding population of underclass youngsters. Although many cities have been successful in responding to the youth violence problem in years gone by, there is a new group of teenagers every few years. Today's teen will be tomorrow's young adult, and today's child will be tomorrow's adolescent, with each new cohort of teens looking to express its passion for rebellion and thirst for excitement. We must continue prevention efforts as the message of nonviolence is not passed from one generation of adolescents to the next. The problem of youth violence is never solved, but only controlled. Once we ease up on crime prevention and crime control efforts, trouble can rebound.

Even if youth and gang homicide were to increase in the years ahead, the overall murder rate may continue to decline or at least remain fairly level. This is because the fastest-growing segment of the population consists of senior citizens. The 65 million baby boomers, hardly babies anymore, are fast becoming card-carrying members of AARP, doing their part to bring down the crime rate just by aging. It is important, however, that we not be fooled by the graying of America and be blind to the problems of youth. The future of U.S. society may depend on our collective ability to reach unsupervised youngsters, to make them feel that someone besides a drug dealer cares about them.

ENDNOTES

1. John J. DiIulio, "The Coming of the Super-Predators," *Weekly Standard*, November 27, 1995.

2. Alfred Blumstein, "Youth Violence, Guns, and the Illicit Drug Industry," *Journal of Criminal Law and Criminology* 86 (1995): 10–36.

3. Joseph F. Sheley and James D. Wright, *In the Line of Fire: Youth, Guns and Violence in Urban America* (New York: Aldine, 1995).

4. David Hemenway, Deborah Prothrow-Stith, Jack Bergstein, Roseanna Ander, and Bruce Kennedy, "Gun Carrying Among Adolescents," *Law and Contemporary Problems* 59 (1996): 39–53.

5. Cheryl Maxson, "Gang Homicide: A Review and Extension of the Literature," in M. Dwayne Smith and Margaret A. Zahn, eds., *Homicide: A Sourcebook of Social Research* (Thousand Oaks, CA: Sage, 1999).

6. National Gang Center, "National Youth Gang Survey Analysis," http://www.nationalgangcenter.gov/Survey-Analysis.

7. National Gang Center, "National Youth Gang Survey Analysis, Measuring the Extent of Gang Problems," https://www.nationalgangcenter.gov/survey-analysis/measuring-the-extent-of-gang-problems.

8. National Gang Intelligence Center, *National Gang Report* (Washington, DC: Federal Bureau of Investigation, 2015).

9. Jeffrey Fagan and Deanna L. Wilkinson, "The Functions of Adolescent Violence," in Delbert S. Elliott, Beatrix A. Hamburg, and Kirk R. Williams, eds., *Violence in American Schools: A New Perspective* (New York: Cambridge University Press, 1998).

10. Felix M. Padilla, *The Gang as an American Enterprise* (New Brunswick, NJ: Rutgers University Press, 1992).

11. Mary E. Patillo, "Sweet Mothers and Gangbangers: Managing Crime in a Black Middle-Class Neighborhood," *Social Forces* 76 (1998): 755.

12. David Matza, *Delinquency and Drift* (New York: Wiley, 1964).

13. Elijah Anderson, *Code of the Street: Decency, Violence, and the Moral Life of the Inner City* (New York: Norton, 1999).

14. Associated Press, "Killer Teen Detailed Murder in Journal," *New York Daily News*, February 6, 2012.

15. Jessica M. Pollak and Charis E. Kubrin, "Crime in the News: How Crimes, Offenders, and Victims Are Portrayed in the Media," *Journal of Criminal Justice and Popular Culture* 14 (2007): 59–83.

16. Kenneth G. Busch, Robert Zagar, John R. Hughes, Jack Arbit, and Robert E. Bussell, "Adolescents Who Kill," *Journal of Clinical Psychology* 46 (1990): 472–485.

17. Rolf Loeber and David P. Farrington, eds., *Serious and Violent Juvenile Offenders* (Thousand Oaks, CA: Sage, 1998); David P. Farrington, "Predictors, Causes and Correlates of Male Youth Violence," in Michael Tonry and Mark H. Moore, eds., *Youth Violence* (Chicago: University of Chicago Press, 1998).

18. Alfred Blumstein and Joel Wallman, eds., *The Crime Drop in America* (New York: Cambridge University Press, 2000).

19. Andrew Lang Golub and Bruce D. Johnson, *Crack's Decline: Some Surprises Among U.S. Cities* (Washington, DC: National Institute of Justice, 1997); Alfred Blumstein, "Disaggregating the Violence Trends," in Alfred Blumstein and Joel Wallman, eds., *The Crime Drop in America*.

20. Jack Levin, "An Effective Response to Teenage Crime Is Possible—and Cities Are Showing the Way," *Chronicle of Higher Education* 35 (May 7, 1999): 14.

21. Janet Reno, *Youth Violence, a Community-Based Response—One City's Success Story* (Washington, DC: U.S. Department of Justice, 1996).

22. Anthony R. Harris, Stephen H. Thomas, Gene A. Fisher, and David J. Hirsh, "Murder and Medicine: The Lethality of Criminal Assault, 1960–1999," *Homicide Studies* 6 (2002): 128–166.

23. John J. Donahue and Steven D. Levitt, "Legalized Abortion and Crime" (Stanford Law School Working Paper, Stanford, CA, June 24, 1999).

24. Steven D. Levitt and Stephen J. Dubner, *Freakonomics: A Rogue Economist Explores the Hidden Side of Everything* (New York: Morrow, 2005).

25. Julie Wakefield, "The Lead Effect?" *Environmental Health Perspectives* 110 (2002): A574.

26. Jessica Wolpaw Reyes, "Environmental Policy as Social Policy? The Impact of Childhood Lead Exposure on Crime," *B.E. Journal of Economic Analysis & Policy Contributions* 7 (2007): 1–43.

27. Elise Gould, "Childhood Lead Poisoning: Conservative Estimates of the Social and Economic Benefits of Lead Hazard Control," *Environmental Health Perspectives* 117 (2009): 1162–1167.

28. Franklin E. Zimring, *American Youth Violence* (New York: Oxford University Press, 1998); Clyde Haberman, "When Youth Violence Spurred 'Superpredator' Fear," *New York Times*, April 6, 2014.

29. James Alan Fox, "Time to Reinvest in Prevention," *Connections*, Boys and Girls Clubs of America, Fall 2008.

30. George Gerbner, *Television and Its Viewers: What Social Science Sees* (Santa Monica, CA: Rand Corporation, 1976).

31. James T. Hamilton, *Channeling Violence: The Economic Market for Violent Television Programming* (Princeton, NJ: Princeton University Press, 1998).

32. James Alan Fox, "Banning Violent Video Games Would Do Little to Avert the Next Mass Murder," *New York Daily News*, March 24, 2013.

33. Amanda Lenhart, Amanda, Joseph Kahne, Ellen Middaugh, Alexandra Macgill, Chris Evans, and Jessica Vitak, *Teens, Video Games, and Civics* (Washington, DC: Pew Internet & American Life Project, 2008).

34. Yang Wang, Vincent P. Mathews, Andrew J. Kalnin, Kristine M. Mosier, David W. Dunn, and William G. Kronenberger, "Short Term Effects of Violent Video Game Playing: An fMRI Study" (Paper presented at the Annual Meeting of the Radiological Society of North America, Chicago, IL, November 26–December 1, 2006).

35. Craig A. Anderson, "An Update on the Effects of Playing Violent Video Games," *Journal of Adolescence* 27 (2004): 113–122.

36. Christopher J. Ferguson and Cheryl K. Olson, "The Supreme Court and Video Game Violence: Will Regulation be Worth the Costs to the First Amendment?" *Criminologist* 25 (July/August 2010): 18–21.

37. Craig A. Anderson, Akiko Shibuya, Nobuko Ihori, et al., "Violent Video Game Effects on Aggression, Empathy, and Prosocial Behavior in Eastern and Western Countries: A Meta-Analytic Review," *Psychological Bulletin* 136 (2010): 151–173; Christopher J. Ferguson and John Kilburn, "Much Ado About Nothing: The Misestimation and Overinterpretation of Violent Video Game Effects in Eastern and Western Nations: Comment on Anderson et al.," *Psychological Bulletin* 136 (2010): 174–178; Brad J. Bushman, Hannah R. Rothstein, and Craig A. Anderson, "Much Ado About Something: Violent Video Game Effects and a School of Red Herring: Reply to Ferguson and Kilburn," *Psychological Bulletin* 136 (2010): 182–187.

38. Scott A. Cunningham, Benjamin Engelstätter, and Michael R. Ward, "Understanding the Effects of Violent Video Games on Violent Crime" (ZEW Discussion Papers, No. 11-042, 2011).

39. Joanne Cantor and K. S. Harrison, "Ratings and Advisories for Television Programming," in *National Television Violence Study*, Vol. 1 (Thousand Oaks, CA: Sage, 1996).

40. Neil M. Malamuth and Edward Donnerstein, *Pornography and Sexual Aggression* (New York: Academic Press, 1984); Edward Donnerstein, Daniel Linz, and Steven Penrod, *The Question of Pornography: Research Findings and Policy Implications* (New York: Free Press, 1987).

41. Hart Research Associates, *Key Findings From 2014 TV Ratings Research Among Parents* (Washington, DC, 2016).

42. Anthony M. Platt, *The Child Savers: The Invention of Delinquency* (Chicago: University of Chicago Press, 1969).

43. David S. Tanenhaus, "The Evolution of Waiver in the Juvenile Court," in Jeffrey Fagan and Franklin Zimring, eds., *The Changing Borders of Juvenile Justice: Transfer of Adolescents to Criminal Court* (Chicago: University of Chicago Press, 1999).

44. Patricia Tourbet and Linda Syzmanski, *State Legislative Responses to Violent Juvenile Crime: 1996–97 Update* (Washington, DC: Office of Juvenile Justice and Delinquency Prevention, 1998).

45. Howard N. Snyder and Melissa Sickmund, *Juvenile Offenders and Victims: 1999 National Report* (Washington, DC: Office of Juvenile Justice and Delinquency Prevention, 1999).

46. Kevin J. Strom, *Profile of State Prisoners Under Age 18, 1985–97* (Washington, DC: Bureau of Justice Statistics, February 2000).

47. Deborah Yurgelun-Todd, "Functional Brain Changes in Adolescents" (Paper presented at the Whitehead Institute for Bio-Medical Research, Massachusetts Institute of Technology, Cambridge, MA, June 1998); B. J. Casey, Rebecca M. Jones, and Todd A. Hare, "The Adolescent Brain," *Annals of the New York Academy of Sciences* 1124 (2008): 111–126.

48. "Michigan Judge Sentences Nathaniel Abraham to Juvenile Detention," Court transcript, CNN.com, January 13, 2000.

49. Simon I. Singer and David McDowall, "Criminalizing Delinquency: The Deterrent Effects of the New York Juvenile Offender Law," *Law and Society Review* 22 (1988): 521–535.

50. Donna M. Bishop, Charles E. Frazier, Lonn Lanza-Kaduce, and Henry George White, *Juvenile Transfers to Criminal Court* (Washington, DC: Office of Juvenile Justice and Delinquency Prevention, 1998).

51. Centers for Disease Control and Prevention, "Effects on Violence of Laws and Policies Facilitating the Transfer of Youth From the Juvenile to the Adult Justice System: A Report on Recommendations of the Task Force on Community Preventive Services," *Morbidity and Mortality Weekly Report* 56 (2007): 1–16; Kareem L. Jordan, "Juvenile Transfer and Recidivism: A Propensity Score Matching Approach," *Journal of Crime and Justice* 35 (2012): 53–67.

52. Associated Press, "Nathaniel Abraham, Killer at 11, Sentenced in Unrelated Drug Case," September 28, 2009.

CHAPTER SIX

WELL-SCHOOLED IN MURDER

In the mid-1990s, just as the United States was beginning to enjoy plunging rates of youth violence and murder, a new phenomenon—school shootings—suddenly emerged, grabbing headlines around the country. On February 2, 1996, 14-year-old Barry Loukaitis entered his fifth-period math class at Frontier Junior High in Moses Lake, Washington, dressed in a long trench coat. Hidden inside were two pistols, dozens of rounds of ammunition, and a high-powered rifle. After executing his teacher and two classmates in cold-blooded fashion, Loukaitis calmly exited the classroom with a grin, and said dryly, "This sure beats algebra, doesn't it?"

Loukaitis's callous act prompted all sorts of questions about why he would commit such a singularly horrific crime. This wasn't just any multiple murder, but one at the hands of a youngster barely into his teenage years. Nor could the shooting be passed off as yet another episode of urban gang violence, the kind of incident that had become so tiresomely common in recent years. It was something incredibly unusual and stunning. No one knew at the time that Loukaitis, in his own way, would be a trendsetter in the worst sense of the term.

On October 1, 1997, 16-year-old Luke Woodham walked into a Pearl, Mississippi, high school just hours after having killed his mother. Pulling a gun out from under his trench coat, the chubby, bespectacled youngster immediately murdered two schoolmates and then sprayed bullets into a crowd of students, injuring seven more. His plan? To take over the school, kill all the students, and escape to Cuba. In the aftermath of the Moses Lake massacre and then the Pearl shooting spree, parents, teachers, and students around the country became extremely anxious about school safety.

Fears that schools had suddenly come under siege at the hands of dispirited and disgruntled students were more than confirmed by subsequent events. Exactly 2 months later, on December 1, 1997, 14-year-old Michael Carneal, a freshman at Heath High School in West Paducah, Kentucky, opened fire on an informal prayer circle held in the school's lobby, killing three girls and wounding five other students. Then on March 24, 1998, two boys, 11-year-old Andrew Golden and 13-year-old Mitchell Johnson, pulled the fire alarm at their Jonesboro, Arkansas, middle school and then began shooting at students and teachers as they filed out of the building for what they believed was a drill. When the gun smoke cleared, four students and a teacher (all female) were dead, and many more were injured. Because both boys were under age 14 at the time of the murders, they were imprisoned only until their 21st birthdays, as stipulated under Arkansas law.

Months after the Jonesboro shooting, it happened twice more and in the same week. On Tuesday, May 19, a Fayetteville, Tennessee, high school senior shot and killed a classmate over a romantic rivalry. Then on Thursday, May 21, Kipland

Kinkel, a 15-year-old freshman from Springfield, Oregon, armed with a .22-caliber semi-automatic rifle, turned his high school cafeteria into a battlefield, after having been suspended a day earlier for bringing a gun to school. At Thurston High, Kinkel killed 2 students and wounded 22 more. At home, he had killed his parents.

The next school year (1998-1999) saw fewer episodes of school-related homicide, yet featured the single event that burned deeply in the consciousness of the nation and virtually defined school terrorism. On April 20, 1999, Dylan Klebold and Eric Harris shot and killed 12 students and 1 teacher and wounded 23 others during a carefully planned siege on Columbine High School in Littleton, Colorado. They had wanted to detonate two large propane bombs inside the school cafeteria during a busy lunch period. But when they failed to explode, the backup plan involved shooting as many as possible before the police arrived.

By March 2001, following yet another multiple-victim shooting—this time at Santana High School, just outside of San Diego, California—the venerable Dan Rather, one of the nation's best-known and well-respected TV journalists, had declared school shootings to be an epidemic. While calling the spate of school shootings an "epidemic" may have been more hyperbole than reality, there is little question that the level of fear and anxiety over school safety was spreading wide and fast. With impressions heavily impacted by tragedies at Columbine High School and elsewhere, there was pervasive concern among school officials and parents of school-age children that school violence was definitely on the rise.

When the scourge of school shootings emerged, some criminologists speculated that it was just the next phase of the youth violence epidemic. What had started in the inner city, according to this view, had spread to middle-class America. Whatever the genesis, the issue of lethal violence inside of schools struck a nerve with the public.

Unlike crack and gang violence that had infested primarily minority neighborhoods in the urban core, school shootings occurred in suburbs and rural communities that had been largely immune from the urban bloodshed. Indeed, this may help explain why such extraordinary murders occurred where they did. The residents of towns like West Paducah, Springfield, Littleton, and Pearl felt impervious to crime and violence—what they regarded only as big-city problems. As a result, they never prepared for the possibility that teenagers in their town might become so alienated and marginalized as to go on a shooting spree at school in order to get even with parents, teachers, and classmates. Whereas urban schools had installed a variety of access controls and security measures and had initiated programs and policies in the areas of conflict resolution, peer mediation, and counseling, small-town and suburban schools tended to remain complacent and were caught off-guard, figuratively and literally.

Political observers capitalized on this uneven public response to youth homicide in cities versus elsewhere as a clear indication of racism. Most people, they said, seemed apathetic when, to an increasing extent, black kids were shooting each other on the streets of large cities, but once murder spread to the hinterlands, the demand for action was heard loud and clear. Although this allegation is likely valid—even today, gang-related shootings at school receive little media attention—there was another major change in the pattern of school violence that cried out for media and public attention: the emergence of multiple-victim shootings and mass murder.

Notwithstanding the unmitigated horror and outrage associated with the succession of high-profile school massacres over the five-year time span from 1996 to 2001, summarized in the first few entries of Table 6.1, schools were, in reality, not only safe relative to other settings in which children typically spend their time, but also growing safer—and not necessarily because of steps that were being taken to fortify them.

Table 6.1   Two Decades of Multiple-Victim School Shootings

| Date | School, Location | Shooter(s), Age(s) | Victims Killed | | | Victims Wounded | Total Victims |
			Students	Staff	Others		
February 2, 1996	Frontier Junior High School Moses Lake, WA	Barry Loukaitis, 14	2	1	0	1	4
February 19, 1997	Bethel Regional High School Bethel, AL	Evan Ramsey, 16	1	1	0	2	4
October 1, 1997	Pearl High School Pearl, MS	Luke Woodham, 16	2	0	1	7	10
December 1, 1997	Heath High School West Paducah, KY	Michael Carneal, 14	3	0	0	5	8
March 24, 1998	Westside Middle School Jonesboro, AR	Mitchell Johnson, 13 Andrew Golden, 11	4	1	0	10	15
May 21, 1998	Thurston High School Springfield, OR	Kipland Kinkel, 15	2	0	2	25	29
April 20, 1999	Columbine High School Littleton, CO	Eric Harris, 18 Dylan Klebold, 17	12	1	0	23	36
March 5, 2001	Santana High School Santee, CA	Charles "Andy" Williams, 15	2	0	0	13	15
March 21, 2005	Red Lake High School Red Lake Indian Reservation, MN	Jeffrey Weise, 16	5	2	2	5	14
October 2, 2006	West Nickel Mines School Nickel Mines, PA	Charles Roberts IV, 32	5	0	0	5	10
February 27, 2012	Chardon High School Chardon, OH	Thomas "T. J." Lane III, 17	3	0	0	3	6
December 14, 2012	Sandy Hook Elementary School Newtown, CT	Adam Lanza, 20	20	6	1	2	29
October 24, 2014	Marysville-Pilchuck High School Marysville, WA	Jaylen Fryberg, 15	4	0	0	3	7
September 28, 2016	Townville Elementary School Townville, SC	Jesse Osborne, 14	1	0	1	3	5
January 23, 2018	Marshall County High School Benton, KY	Gabe Parker, 15	2	0	0	14	16
February 14, 2018	Stoneman Douglas High School Parkland, FL	Nikolas Cruz, 19	14	3	0	14	31

Note: Incidents with 4+ victims and at least two deaths (not including the assailant); Cases through February 2018.

School violence is actually not a new phenomenon, and even incidents involving multiple victims have long been part of U.S. school history. In Michigan in 1927, Andrew Kehoe, a 56-year-old disgruntled school board member, murdered his wife and then launched several bombs in the small community, including at the local elementary school. Forty-five people were killed (more than three times the Columbine death toll), mostly elementary schoolchildren; another 58 were injured. Kehoe killed himself with a car bomb. He did not act solely out of impulse: Upset over taxes, his wife's poor health, and the loss of his farm, Kehoe had apparently planned the bombings for some time. After the incident, a sign was discovered on Kehoe's property, believed to have been a message of explanation from the mass murderer: "Criminals are made, not born."

THE RISK OF SCHOOL HOMICIDE

Unfortunately, no "official" (i.e., "known to the police") national data series for school crime exists. However, there are several sources of available data pertaining to school violence, based on student and/or staff surveys or news media reports, all of which vary with regard to their coverage, completeness, and accuracy. Arguably, the most accurate data available come from incident reports of school-associated violent deaths initially maintained by the National School Safety Center (NSSC), a private organization established in 1984 initially through federal funding directed by President Ronald Reagan. Then, in 2010, the data collection and reporting were assumed by the Centers for Disease Control and Prevention. Although these data are not exactly "official," school-related homicides are presumably always reported in some media outlet somewhere and thus relatively easy to identify.

The NSSC classifies a death as a school homicide if it occurs on the property of a public or private K–12 school (so any homicide that occurs on school grounds would be counted); while a student is on the way to or from a regular school session (e.g., bus stops, walking home from school); on the way to or from a school-sponsored event (e.g., athletic events, school dances); or as the "obvious direct result" of a school incident, function, or activity.[1] It is important to note that this definition includes many events that some people might not think of as school homicide, including adult domestic homicides (e.g., husband comes to a school to shoot his wife who works there), felony-murder robberies that occur long after a student has left school but is still technically on the way home (e.g., on the subway), and police action shootings (e.g., a fleeing felon is shot by police on school property during the weekend). This definition does not include homicides occurring at the nation's colleges and does not count the death of the offender if he or she commits suicide. Likewise, there are a number of school shootings each year that do not result in any deaths and will not appear on school homicide lists.

On August 30, 2006, for example, Alvaro Castillo, 19, of Hillsborough, North Carolina, shot and killed his father before driving to his former high school armed with smoke bombs, a shotgun, and a rifle, intending to open fire during lunchtime. Castillo had made a video after he shot his father, proclaiming, "Look at me. I'm not even crying. I just killed him, and I feel fine." The video shows the father's corpse, draped by a sheet. After killing his father, Castillo dropped the video into the mail on his way to the school. The recording showed Castillo watching violent movies, including *Scarface*, *The Predator*, *The Shining*, *Natural Born Killers*, and a documentary about the Columbine shootings.

Castillo was so obsessed with the Columbine shootings that he had his parents take him to visit the site of the horrific massacre. He often wore a black trench coat to emulate the killers and even named his gun "Arlene" after Eric Harris's weapon. Although he had designs on entering the school shooter "hall of shame," Castillo failed to kill anyone at his school, although two students were injured during his attempt.

Table 6.2 displays annual counts for several measures of school-related homicides (perpetrated by students or nonstudents). Between the 1992–1993 and 2016–2017 school years, there was a total of 361 fatal assaults at primary and secondary schools in the United States in which at least one victim was killed, of which 259 involved shootings. These included attacks by students (such as the Columbine massacre) as well as by assailants not directly connected with the school setting (such as the Sandy Hook mass murder). Overall, these shooting incidents claimed the lives of 323 victims, 222 of whom were students. Of course, Columbine, Sandy Hook, and several others claimed the lives of more than one victim. Over the 24 school years covered in Table 6.2, a total of 435 individuals were killed, of whom 308 were students. The remaining victims were administrators, faculty, or other school employees, as well as parents and individuals not connected with the school. Almost 70% of the incidents took place at a high school, and the remainder were about equally split between middle schools and elementary schools.

Along with the tallies of incidents and victims, the rate of homicide victimization per million students is calculated based on annual public and private school enrollment figures. Notwithstanding the extensive news coverage of school violence during the five-year span between the February 1996 Moses Lake massacre and the March 2001 shooting spree in Santee, and later surrounding the December 2012 massacre of 26 students and staff members at the Sandy Hook Elementary School, the number of incidents and the number of victims, both overall and students only, are appreciably lower than in the early 1990s, when school violence was hardly a major issue in America.

Part of the reason for the disconnect between incidence and awareness involves the changing nature of the offenses. Many of the homicides near the beginning of the 1990s reflected gang activity, interpersonal disputes, and arguments—violence unrelated to school issues spilling onto school grounds. There was certainly no lack of awareness regarding the youth crime problem in the early 1990s or alarm associated with the notion of young "superpredators" terrorizing the streets of urban America, but this problem was not particularly related to schools. Although some of the urban violence was occurring at school, the source of the conflict was located elsewhere.

Most school homicide incidents are still single-victim/non–mass murder events reflecting rival gang member fights, interpersonal disputes, domestic homicides, and robberies. On June 28, 2006, James Lamont Bagsby, 15, was arrested for shooting and killing Anthony Michael Ramirez, 11, and wounding his brother, Joseph Ramirez, 13, in the San Bernardino, California, schoolyard of the Dr. Martin Luther King Jr. Middle School. He was also charged with nine counts of assault with a deadly weapon for shooting at other children on the basketball court. Bagsby had been in a group home for juveniles in Victorville and had escaped. He allegedly approached the boys at the school and asked them if they were part of the San Bernardino gang. When they said they were not, he opened fire. Police say that the boys did not provoke the attack and were not part of any gang. Bagsby was tried as an adult and given a prison sentence of 107 years to life.

These sorts of events nearly disappeared during the 2001–2002 school year, and overall crime rates declined during this brief period as well. The "September 11 effect" for a short time brought people together and focused their attention on a much greater enemy than their own personal issues.

Table 6.2   School-Related Homicide Incidents and Victims

Academic Year	Number of Incidents		Number of Fatalities		Students Killed per Million
	Total	Shootings	Total	Students	
1992–1993	44	34	45	36	0.74
1993–1994	42	31	43	30	0.61
1994–1995	17	12	17	15	0.30
1995–1996	26	19	29	21	0.41
1996–1997	23	13	24	17	0.33
1997–1998	26	18	35	28	0.54
1998–1999	10	5	23	22	0.42
1999–2000	19	10	19	12	0.23
2000–2001	16	13	16	7	0.13
2001–2002	4	2	4	2	0.04
2002–2003	13	7	13	11	0.20
2003–2004	34	24	36	21	0.38
2004–2005	23	16	23	14	0.26
2005–2006	5	5	5	4	0.07
2006–2007	12	8	17	14	0.25
2007–2008	4	4	4	4	0.07
2008–2009	9	6	9	6	0.11
2009–2010	5	5	5	3	0.05
2010–2011	4	4	5	1	0.02
2011–2012	2	2	6	5	0.09
2012–2013	5	4	32	20	0.36
2013–2014	6	6	8	4	0.07
2014–2015	7	6	11	6	0.11
2015–2016	3	3	3	3	0.05
2016–2017	2	2	3	2	0.04
Total	361	259	435	308	0.24

Source: Adapted in part from National School Safety Center, *School Associated Violent Deaths.*

The trend in school homicides has been roughly parallel to the decline in youth killings more generally. The majority of school homicide incidents continue to be in large, inner-city schools and involve gang violence. James Tate and six others were charged with the April 14, 2003, New Orleans shooting death of 15-year-old

Jonathan "Caveman" Williams inside the school's gymnasium. In addition to the murder, three others were wounded. Tate pled guilty to manslaughter and conspiracy to commit second-degree murder, for which he received a 15-year prison sentence. This school shooting was actually more typical of most school homicides. It was basically an assassination, as the offenders thought the victim had murdered a cousin of one of the coconspirators.

Although homicides arising from a conflict between one victim and one perpetrator are newsworthy at the local level, these episodes rarely make national news, whether the participants are black, white, Asian, or Latino. Yet the events of the 1997–1998 school year got everyone's attention, all the way to the White House, which established a Presidential Advisory Committee in the wake of an episode in Clinton's home state of Arkansas. As the body counts grew larger, murder grabbed the attention of the nation.

It is not coincidental that shootings occurred at schools rather than at some other location. Notwithstanding the fact that most schools do not experience serious forms of violence, the school day itself can present certain risks. Not only do children congregate in large numbers while at school, thereby creating occasions for conflict, but also the school setting can sometimes breed feelings of inadequacy, anxiety, fear, hostility, rejection, and boredom. For most kids, the hazing rituals of school will make them feel sad, humiliated, and depressed. Some will find a group of outsiders to cling to, others will be suicidal, and some will develop substance abuse problems or find another way to cope until the humiliation of school is over. Most of them don't harm anyone. But, for some vengeful or alienated children, school can represent an ideal place, both logistically and symbolically, for getting even or settling a score. Just like the adults who turn their disappointments into rage and commit workplace massacres, some students (and some adults) blame the school for most of their disappointments and take their revenge there.

As shown in Table 6.2, the lull in the number of school-related homicides during the 2001–2002 academic year was followed by yet another dramatic increase in the number of incidents and victims from 2002–2003 through 2004–2005. For the remainder of the decade, however, the incidents and victims remained relatively few in number, except for a modest spike in 2006–2007. There were no multiple-victim homicides for several years following the October 2006 siege on a small Amish schoolhouse in Pennsylvania in which five girls were shot to death by a gunman who then took his own life. That relative lull was broken six years later with the catastrophic shooting spree at Sandy Hook Elementary School in December 2012.

Despite the well-publicized shootings, our nation's children are relatively safe, given the number of contact hours they spend at school. Comparing the dozens of schoolchildren killed each year in school-related violence with the millions who attend, there is now literally a 1 in 4 million chance that a child will be murdered while at school. Of course, when it does happen, especially when there are multiple victims, the repercussions spread far beyond the grounds of that school or the borders of that community.

COPYCAT SHOOTINGS

The rash of school shootings in the late 1990s raised questions about what's different about kids in modern society that would explain this kind of behavior. In many respects, kids today are no different than youngsters from earlier generations. Teenage alienation has existed as long as there have been teenagers, and school bullying has been around as long as there have been schools. What is different is today's culture and the weapons to which youngsters have access.

Generations ago, an angry high school student would not even have considered the idea of bringing a gun into the classroom. Instead, he might have had thoughts about breaking a few windows or spray painting graffiti in order to vent his rage. The notion of turning the school into a battleground would never have come to mind. Sadly, because of widely publicized school shootings around the country, youngsters have been given new deadly examples to follow. And getting a gun is not a problem. Although too young to purchase a deadly semi-automatic, a child can borrow, steal, or purchase one from a willing older friend.

In the aftermath of a highly publicized school shooting, most children identify with the pain of the victims. They grieve for the slain students whom they only knew through television reports, discuss their fears with parents and classmates, and hope that history will not repeat itself in their own school. More than a few students identify instead with the power of the perpetrators. This is the foundation for the copycat phenomenon. Although copycatting may not account for all or even most school-related homicides, there is some empirical evidence that a school shooting incident is "contagious," that is, produces an elevated likelihood of a similar event over a several-week time frame.[2]

Ever since it stunned the nation in April 1999, the Columbine High massacre has represented a watershed event in the chronicle of school and youth violence. And, given the extensive coverage (e.g., on magazine covers) afforded them posthumously, assailants Klebold and Harris instantly became "poster boys" for school-shooter copycats and other admirers. Fifteen-year-old Charles Andrew Williams told friends he wanted to "pull a Columbine" just before his March 2001 rampage at Santana High School in Santee, California. According to the police investigating the Sandy Hook shooting, gunman Adam Lanza was obsessed with the Columbine massacre. Brothers Robert and Michael Bever, ages 18 and 16 respectively, who in July 2015 teamed up to murder five of their family members in Broken Arrow, Oklahoma, had also intended to launch a nationwide killing spree to outdo Columbine and become more famous than their murderous idols.

Despite residing in different countries, several admirers of Klebold and Harris connected through social media and formed a "Columbiners" fandom. At least a few members of the club did more than just fawn over their heroes. In 2007, 18-year-old Pekka-Eric Auvinen fatally shot eight people at his high school in Tuusula, Finland, and then, like Klebold and Harris, killed himself with a single gunshot to the head. Although their plan was thwarted, several Columbiners conspired to carry out a mass shooting at a mall in Halifax, Nova Scotia, coincident with Valentine's Day 2015.

It is no coincidence that until very recently, nearly all episodes of multiple murders in schools have involved white teenaged boys from small towns. Although this may reflect lesser security preparedness in rural areas, the copycat effect is strongest when there is close similarity between hero and follower. A youngster from Tennessee might identify with the plight of a kindred spirit from Arkansas or Kentucky, whose shooting spree is covered in the news. By contrast, for a black youngster living in a Chicago project, the same episode may not resonate. Black teenagers are more likely to be involved in single-victim incidents stemming from interpersonal disputes and gang rivalries.

At the very least, the copycat phenomenon can determine the timing and form of a murderous attack. If the publicized killers strike a school, then they provide the idea to murder in the classroom rather than at a shopping mall or a law firm. If the killers use a firearm, then those who imitate are also likely to use a gun rather than a knife, explosives, or a hammer. Finally, the copycat effect is short lived, causing a number of similar attacks to be committed over a limited period.

Thus, many vicious murders cluster together in time. For example, in the 1997–1998 school year, when Kip Kinkel went on his shooting spree, there were eight multiple-victim homicides at U.S. schools compared to two during the previous academic year. For a few disturbed individuals, the media hype and publicity given to killers can provide a source of role models for their own behavior, even inspiring them to realize their dreams of stardom and grandeur.

Thirty years ago, a child might have imitated his or her friends down the block. Now, thanks to the pervasiveness of television and the internet, he is just as likely to follow the lead of teenagers in Pearl or Springfield. Like their adult counterparts, troubled teenaged killers can be inspired by other killers, but they may also be inspired by fictional portrayals in films and video games. Kip Kinkel, for example, had been fascinated with the popular movie version of Shakespeare's *Romeo and Juliet*. When the police searched his house where he had killed his parents, they encountered music from the film playing loudly and repeatedly on the home stereo by means of a loop.

It can be rather tempting to draw parallels between cases that would seem to suggest copycatting. Yet trying to prove the copycat effect through anecdotal evidence can be tricky. Many fine scholars have been misled, for example, by a tale about 14-year-old Barry Loukaitis's 1996 school shooting described at the outset of this chapter and the influence of the novel *Rage*, published two decades earlier by Stephen King using the pseudonym Richard Bachman. In King's story, a high school student takes his algebra class hostage at gunpoint after killing two teachers. Loukaitis, who owned the book and had read it several times, similarly barged into his math class dressed in a long trench coat and armed with two pistols and a high-powered rifle. After killing a teacher and two students, Loukaitis said sardonically, "This sure beats algebra, doesn't it?"—a line reportedly lifted straight from *Rage*.

This often-repeated illustration of copycatting is quite intriguing, but also not exactly accurate. Although Loukaitis did make the remark, no such line appears in King's book. The closest is when King's assailant makes the wisecrack, "This sure beats panty raids." In the way that rumors and legends often develop, the curious connection was first reported in a national news story published in the *New York Times*. Because of sharp criticism of the book, including allegations that it may have recklessly helped to inspire a wave of school shootings, Stephen King insisted that his publisher take *Rage* out of print. Since that time, many others have told the tale of "sure beats algebra" without checking the actual text of *Rage*. This does not mean, of course, that Loukaitis wasn't affected by King's writings in a more general way, just not exactly as rumored.

ADULT SCHOOL SHOOTERS

Mass murder at school by disgruntled pupils was a scary new wrinkle in the 1990s. A decade earlier, schoolyards were the targets of imbalanced adults looking to hurt society where it hurt the most. School snipers then were likely not to be teenagers but middle-aged adults such as Laurie Dann, the 36-year-old resident of Glencoe, Illinois, who, in May 1988, went on a rampage with a .22-caliber handgun in a Winnetka elementary school. Dann had a long history of mental illness and assaults against others. Clearly troubled, she had attempted to murder her husband with an ice pick, poisoned sorority members at Northwestern University, and mailed poisoned items to many other people over the years. Dann killed an 8-year-old boy at the school and injured five others. Dann also shot and injured another man at his house after the school shootings and took her own life at the home.

The contagion effect in murder can impact adults as well as children. In September 1988, 19-year-old James Wilson of Greenwood, South Carolina, went on a shooting spree at a local elementary school, killing two children. When the police searched his home, they discovered that Wilson had pinned to his wall a photo of his hero, Laurie Dann, taken from the cover of *People* magazine. There were 12 different school shootings from 1988 through early 1989, the last of which was Patrick Purdy's January assault on the Cleveland Elementary School in Stockton, California. He murdered five Southeast Asian children as they played at recess.

The prevalence of adult-perpetrated school massacres had all but disappeared—that is, until the mid-2000s. In 2006, a 53-year-old man, Duane Roger Morrison, lurked around the Colorado Platte Canyon High School grounds in Bailey, Colorado, not far from Littleton, Colorado, the site of the Columbine shootings. On the morning of September 27, he entered the school with a revolver and a semi-automatic pistol (and a backpack that he falsely claimed held a bomb) and took six female student hostages, whom he sexually assaulted. Morrison released four of the hostages later in the day but killed one girl when she tried to escape, and then killed himself. Morrison had asked about the whereabouts of specific girls, whom he may have researched on MySpace. An outdoor and gun enthusiast, Morrison was a carpenter who had also built and owned haunted houses. He had no connection to the town of Bailey and, according to law enforcement, was living out of his Jeep. Although his 14-page suicide note to his brother made no reference to his school shooting plans, he had clearly planned the assault in advance.

Only a week later, in another incident with a sexual motive, 32-year-old local milkman Charles Carl Roberts IV, the married father of two, took hostages at a one-room Amish schoolhouse in Lancaster County, Pennsylvania. Roberts sent the male students and adult females away and kept 10 young Amish girls in the schoolhouse. Roberts had a shotgun and handgun, tools, and equipment for binding the girls, barricade equipment, and candles, toilet paper, and other supplies indicating he planned to be there for a while. Roberts also brought tubes of sexual lubricant with him, and when he called his wife from the scene, he indicated that he had been dreaming about molesting girls for years. Police swarmed the schoolhouse sooner than Roberts had anticipated. Roberts did not get the chance to molest any of the 10 girls but he shot all of them at close range, killing 5 of them.

It is likely much more than coincidence that Roberts's planned sexual assault and multiple murder at the Amish schoolhouse were preceded one week earlier by Morrison's sexual assault on Platte Canyon High School. Both killers were adult males, both targeted girls, both had sexual assault on their minds, and both attacked in a rural schoolhouse.

Many Americans may have forgotten the school attacks of 2006. However, nearly everyone will long remember December 14, 2012, a "day of infamy" in terms of school violence, when 20-year-old Adam Lanza slaughtered 26 children and teachers at Sandy Hook Elementary School in sleepy Newtown, Connecticut, before taking his own life. The Sandy Hook massacre, and the issue of school shootings in general, dominated the news and the national discourse, so much so that the Associated Press named it the top news story of the year. The massacre at Sandy Hook eclipsed another Sandy, the devastating hurricane that stormed the eastern coast. Hurricane Sandy directly resulted in five times as many deaths of Americans than did the shooting with a similar name. However, unlike the

Table 6.3 Multiple-Victim Shootings in Schools Outside the United States, 2000–2016

Date of Rampage	Location	Shooter's Name, Age	Killed	Injured	Student	Victim Type
April 26, 2002	Erfurt, Germany	R. Steinhäuser, 19	16	6	Former	Staff and students
June 6, 2003	Pak Phanang, Thailand	A. Boonkwan, 17	2	4	Current	Students only
September 28, 2004	Carmen de Patagones, Argentina	R. Solich, 15	3	5	Current	Students only
November 7, 2007	Jokela, Finland	P. Auvinen, 18	8	0	Current	Staff and students
March 11, 2009	Winnenden, Germany	T. Kretschmer, 17	15	9	Former	Staff and students
April 7, 2011	Rio de Janeiro, Brazil	W. M. Oliveira, 24	12	20	Former	Students only
January 24, 2016	La Loche, Canada	Name withheld, 17	4	7	Current	Staff and students

storm, in which the victims averaged over 60 years of age, the Connecticut school massacre primarily claimed the lives of young children, causing it to have a decidedly different impact on the nation's consciousness.

Although Americans have obsessed over the safety of their schools for the past couple decades, the concern is hardly limited to this country. Parents around the globe have had their own worries about school-related homicides, and not just from terrorists who would target schoolchildren as a way of hurting society in a most profound way (as in the 2004 three-day siege at a Russian school by Islamic extremists, resulting in the deaths of 186 children). Table 6.3 presents a list of multiple-victim shootings at elementary or secondary schools outside of the United States that were committed by current or former students. Although none resulted in as many deaths as did the Sandy Hook massacre, several were devastating in their own right, claiming a dozen lives or more.

EXPLAINING SCHOOL MASSACRES

Based on in-depth case studies of 10 school shooters, psychologist Peter Langman has developed a three-class typology for understanding the mind-set and motives of youngsters who turn their schools into battle zones. Some schoolyard killers may be considered psychopathic, having a callous disregard for their human targets and enjoying the power achieved by gunning down their schoolmates. Others may be deeply disturbed to the point of being psychotic with a tenuous grasp on reality. Still others kill in response to their own traumatic background. Such trauma can reflect mistreatment by parents at home or even fellow students and peers at school.[3]

Several high-profile cases of school homicide have involved a victim of long-term bullying seeking payback with a gun. For example, 16-year-old Luke Woodham, who, as described earlier, murdered two female classmates (one of whom was his former girlfriend) and wounded seven other students at his Pearl, Mississippi, high school, was quite explicit in what drove him to the brink. In what apparently was meant to be a suicide note (were it not for the fact he lived), Woodham wrote, "I am not insane! I am angry. I kill because people like me are mistreated every day. I do this to show society—push us and we will push back. I have suffered all my life. No one ever truly loved me."

Woodham was not the only beleaguered student to have avenged repeated bullying with a counterassault. Lenhardt and her colleagues assembled case profiles of 15 young assailants involved in 13 episodes of school homicide in the United States between 1996 and 2005. She and her colleagues found that 73% of the 15 perpetrators had apparently been the victims of bullying and persecution. Of course, bullying itself is hardly sufficient to produce the level of rage seen in recent school rampages; it is usually harassment in combination with poor coping skills that produces this extreme response. Lenhardt's results show that 71% of attackers felt rejected and isolated by peers, 64% had poor coping skills, and 64% demonstrated an exaggerated need for attention and respect.[4]

To understand the horrific actions of schoolyard snipers, it is as important to examine friendships as it is to delve into family background. At Columbine, 18-year-old Eric Harris and 17-year-old Dylan Klebold were generally seen as geeks or nerds, from the point of view of any of the large student cliques—the jocks, the punks, and so on. Excluded from mainstream student culture, they banded together and bonded for mutual support and respect. The image they attempted to create was clearly one of power and dominance (the very characteristics of masculinity that all teenage boys pursue)—the gothic incivility, the forces of darkness, the preoccupation with Hitler, the celebration of evil and villainy. Harris and Klebold desperately wanted to feel important, and in the preparations they made to murder their classmates, the two shooters got their wish. They plotted and planned for over a year, colluding and conspiring to put one over on their schoolmates, teachers, and parents. One of their videotapes shows them talking about how the shootings would finally get them the respect they deserved. They amassed an arsenal of weapons, strategized about logistics, and made final preparations. Yet, until it was too late, not a single adult got wind of what Harris and Klebold intended to do. One can only wonder why not.

As is the case with some of our most heinous team serial killings, birds of a feather may kill together. Harris, the leader, would likely have enjoyed the respect and admiration from Klebold, who in turn would have felt uplifted by the praise he received from his revered buddy. In their relationship, the two boys got from one another what was otherwise missing from their lives: They felt special, they gained a sense of belonging, and they were united against the world. As Harris remarked while he and his friend made last-minute preparations to commit mass murder: "This is just a two-man war against everything else."

On April 20, 1999, after months of planning, preparation, and practice shooting, Klebold and Harris armed themselves with guns and explosives and headed off to their high school. By the time their assault ended with self-inflicted fatal gunshots, a dozen students and one teacher lay dead.

The vast majority of those who have committed school-related homicide are male. This is especially true for cases of multiple murders such as the Columbine massacre. Of course, girls (and female teachers) are included among the scores of youngsters (and adults) who have been slain in school-related murders. Some criminologists have suggested a strong gender component to school shootings (specifically, boys systematically targeting girls). For example, in *Rampage: The Social Roots of School Shootings*, Newman noted that "the predominant pattern in school shootings of the past three decades is that girls are the victims."[5] In addition, based on an analysis of a dozen school shootings between 1997 and 2002, Klein suggested that "nearly all the boys who killed in these shootings specifically targeted girls who rejected them, or minimally implied that they acted due to a perceived rejection by a girl."[6]

There have in fact been several lethal assaults inspired at least partially by romantic conflict—cases in which certain victims were specifically selected out of jealousy or spite. Mitchell Johnson, one of two boys who perpetrated the mass murder at their middle school in Jonesboro, Arkansas, reportedly told classmates that he was intending to shoot all the girls who had rejected him. Notwithstanding this and other illustrations of school homicides by lovelorn boys, there is relatively little evidence to confirm a prominent antifemale theme. Among the 429 victims of school-related homicides between the 1992–1993 and 2014–2015 academic years, only 27% were female. Focusing just on the 303 student victims, 25% were female. Of the 218 student victims killed with a firearm, 28% were female. Only when narrowing the victim pool to students murdered in a multiple-victim shooting by another student does the gender breakdown come close to even: Nearly half (25 out of 49) of these victims were female.

Whatever the victim–offender gender mix, some school rampages may be associated more with gender identity than with gender itself. Adolescence can certainly be a difficult life stage for many teens and preteens relation to issues of sex, sexual orientation, and gender. However, according to Kimmel and Mahler, these pressures and conflicts have been implicated in a good number of school shootings. In a careful analysis of 28 random school shootings, they uncovered substantial evidence that certain assailants acted in retaliation for frequent teasing and insults that challenged their masculinity. In essence, for these beleaguered and much-maligned students, violence served as the ultimate vehicle for proving their power and manhood.[7]

As with other forms of crime, it is unlikely that there is a single cause of school shootings or a single factor shared by all school shooters. However, research has isolated some risk factors. Recent work suggests that school shooters suffer a series of deprivations in their lives, such as lack of encouragement and self-esteem and that those marginalizing experiences finally explode in the highly competitive school environment. Many school shooters share a history of childhood instability and marginalization from caregivers and guardians, planting the seeds of neglect. These shooters—almost entirely white males—are often isolated and unpopular among their peers. They associate with other kids similarly marginalized, and their anger takes on a morally righteous tone. The school shooters lack any sort of cultural capital such as popularity, athletic abilities, physical fighting abilities, socioeconomic standing, or relationships with girls, so instead, they prove their masculinity through extreme violence. Boys are socialized to be aggressive, violent, and dominant; if they are the butt of harassment, bullying, taunts, and humiliation, they find someone to pick on, too. In some cases, they may even blame their parents for their miserable lives.

The hazing rituals of secondary schools in the United States are painful and brutal for those on the receiving end and are obviously too much to take for some kids who are already troubled. Childhoods filled with neglect, abuse, disappointments, and poor peer choices (if they even have any real friends); being shorter or heavier than the norm or having appearances perceived as effeminate; suffering neurological problems or school failures; and having access to weaponry—all of this may boil over and explode.

BLAMING PARENTS

The April 20, 1999, massacre at Columbine High School in Colorado sent shock-waves throughout the nation, with many Americans watching the horrific drama unfold on their living room television screens. In the aftermath, there was a tremendous outpouring of sympathy for the grieving families of the dozen students and one teacher killed by Dylan Klebold and Eric Harris before they took their own lives. Few people, however, had much compassion in their hearts for the parents of the two shooters. Few people thought much about their loss and the additional burden they had to bear for the actions of their sons.

In an interview with Oprah Winfrey a full decade after the shooting, Susan Klebold described the local reaction.[8] She was no victim in the eyes of her neighbors and associates. Instead, she was widely condemned as a perpetrator, an accomplice, a co-conspirator—as the person who had created a monster by virtue of her bad parenting. In this view, held by angry community members and outraged local elected officials alike, the parents of Eric and Dylan had failed to teach their sons the moral values that would have stopped them from committing a massacre and were therefore responsible for their murderous outburst.

Parents of school shooters hardly need us to cast blame; they struggle with the enormous weight of self-imposed guilt. This reaction came through loud and clear in Klebold's interview with Oprah. For months following the Columbine shooting, she was reluctant to use her last name when among strangers and avoided having eye contact with other members of the community. She confessed to her talk show host to being plagued by bouts of shame and humiliation.

Elevated juvenile crime rates and well-publicized episodes of school violence have prompted many Americans to question the role of family and parenting. Under the assumption that bad kids are products of bad homes—parents who are neglectful and psychologically or physically abusive—many communities have enacted parental responsibility laws in an attempt to threaten parents with fines or jail time into taking their job more seriously.

Certainly, the important role of parenting cannot be denied. There is often evidence of neglect, if not overt abuse, in the backgrounds of many school shooters. In his case histories of 48 school shooters, Peter Langman determined that 10 had experienced significant childhood trauma or loss within their families. Some were raised in dysfunctional homes with drug-abusing or violent parents, and some were victims of physical abuse at the hands of their parents.[9] Vossekuil and colleagues reported that over one-quarter of school shooters in their study lived in a single-parent or foster-parent home.[10]

Notwithstanding the troubled home life identified in certain instances, much of the time teenagers become violent despite the best efforts of parents. Until a child is 8 or 9 years of age, it is still realistic to expect the family to exercise a large measure of control over his or her behavior. By the time a youngster has reached the age of 10 or 11, however, adolescence has set in, making an already-troubled child incredibly susceptible to making bad and sometimes violent choices.

It would, of course, not be possible to hold Bill and Faith Kinkel legally responsible for their son Kip's violent outburst at his high school in Springfield, Oregon, just a short drive up Route 5 from Silverton, where the first parental responsibility law was passed. They were executed by their boy in stage one of his deadly assault, yet this has not prevented them from being charged in the court of public opinion. In the aftermath, public sentiment was accusatory: How could they have given their son permission to buy a gun—not one but several, including a semi-automatic rifle? Why didn't they instead get him some help?

The truth is that the Kinkels did try to get their son the help that he needed. For years, they tried to provide him with whatever was required to overcome his learning and social deficiencies. Throughout his childhood, Kip Kinkel never fulfilled his parents' hopes and expectations. Dyslexic and physically awkward, Kip struggled academically and socially. He surely wasn't as talented as his older sister, Kristin, and could never measure up in the eyes of his parents, both of whom were highly regarded schoolteachers. With each failed attempt to find activities and pursuits in which he could excel, Kip Kinkel's frustration only grew more intense. Regrettably, Kip did seem to have a passion for bomb making and guns, much of which he learned over the internet. His cyber contacts not only provided him with the inspiration but also reinforced his darkening character and mood. As the demands of high school and the perceived disappointment of his parents increased, Kinkel turned his attention to the school shootings in Pearl and Jonesboro. He yearned to feel important, to satisfy his parents' standards, and to be accepted by his classmates.

Although hardly a desirable alternative, the murder of Bill and Faith Kinkel at the hands of their son, if nothing else, did spare them the pain and humiliation of being held accountable, legally if not socially, for his rampage. Other families have experienced the trauma, not just of losing a son either to prison or suicide but also of feeling the scorn and self-imposed guilt for murders committed by their child prior to a final resolution.

Nancy Lanza suffered a similar double-whammy fate as the Kinkels—that is, being murdered by one's child prior to his school rampage and then being blamed for having contributed to the tragic event. Hours before massacring 26 students and staff members at the Sandy Hook Elementary School, Adam Lanza shot and killed his mother while she slept in her bed. The 20-year-old "borrowed" his mother's firearms to commit all 27 of his murders.

On December 14, 2013, the first anniversary of the shooting, Governor Dannel Malloy of Connecticut asked that churches across the state ring their bells 26 times, once for each victim of the massacre. This capped off a year of collective mourning that featured heart-wrenching gestures of support for the grieving families, including a vigil with 26 candles attended by President Barack Obama and moments of silence at sporting events around the country. The April 2013 Boston Marathon, before being eclipsed by its own catastrophe, was dedicated to Newtown, one mile of the race for each victim.

These and other tributes to Newtown apparently ignored Nancy Lanza as a victim. Worse than just being excluded from Newtown remembrances, public sentiment has treated her more as an accessory than as a victim. She is scapegoated, if not for creating a madman, then at least for failing to recognize and respond to telltale warning signs. In Adam Lanza's biography, there is much material for anyone looking, with the benefit of 20/20 hindsight, for possible red flags. Her son was noncommunicative and socially withdrawn, extremely anxious and intolerant of physical contact. He was diagnosed with Asperger's syndrome and had struggled with obsessive-compulsive disorder. In addition, he was fascinated with violent video games as well as news stories about mass murder, especially mass shootings.

For her part, Nancy Lanza has been disparaged for many of her parenting choices, from decisions she had made regarding school attendance to her ownership and storage of guns. "There was obviously a breakdown in terms of the parenting and the structure in that house," said Bill Sherlach, whose wife was the school's psychologist and was murdered in the Sandy Hook shooting.

Nicole Hockley, whose son was among the slain students, was particularly harsh in blaming Nancy Lanza: "It's clear that (Adam Lanza) had mental illness and intervention was not made," she said in an interview with CBS. "There was not responsible gun ownership, either, because there was access to weapons and firearms."

The PBS documentary *Raising Adam Lanza* focused squarely on the mother's supposed missteps. In the program, school administrators second-guessed Nancy Lanza for having withdrawn Adam from the high school where he was so miserable.

Nancy Lanza was distressingly aware of her son's mental health problems but would not have anticipated that he was dangerous. Notwithstanding his interest in guns and violence, Adam Lanza had never acted out in an aggressive manner. Even the mental health counselors who had seen him had had no indication that he was capable of such an awful crime.

When recounting the social and psychological history of someone who commits some extreme act of violence, we tend to look selectively for events consistent with the outcome while downplaying those that are inconsistent. Many have emphasized, for example, Adam Lanza's passion for playing violent video games, such as *Call of Duty*, but overlooked the many hours he spent at a local theater playing the dance simulation game, *Dance Dance Revolution*. Moreover, Nancy Lanza's willingness to take her son to the shooting range is easy to condemn, while ignoring her well-meaning attempt to find common ground with her increasingly reclusive son.

Nancy Lanza is not around, of course, to answer the accusations about her parenting. She couldn't defend her life from gunfire, and she can't defend her memory from the slings and arrows of public scorn. Out of fairness, however, we should assume that she had the best of intentions in raising her son Adam, unless and until there is definitive evidence to the contrary.

FEAR FACTOR

The series of school shootings that marked the late 1990s radically altered the face of public education and had many Americans questioning whether schools were safe places for children. Each episode (at least those that were featured in the national media) incited widespread fear and anxiety. Each recurrence of the seemingly same old story of some alienated adolescent running amok in the hallways of his school intensified concerns that school shootings were not just an occasional and frightening aberration but a new and persistent crime wave that should place schools everywhere on high alert.[11]

In reaction to the flurry of school shootings in the late 1990s, the Gallup polling organization incorporated school violence and safety as a regular theme in its ongoing program of research measuring changes in public opinion. Gallup had not examined the issue since 1977, when a quarter of parents surveyed across America indicated a concern for their children's safety at school. Twenty years later,

Gallup routinized its questioning regarding school violence and safety in surveys coinciding with the start of each school year, as well as at exceptional points in time immediately following certain widely publicized school rampages.

Figure 6.1 displays the results of the series of Gallup polls that asked parents if they feared for the safety of their oldest child while he or she was at school. Clearly, the Columbine shooting had a strong effect on the respondents' sense of security for their children, as the majority of respondents (55%) surveyed on the day following the April 20, 1999, massacre indicated feeling fearful.

As Americans faced new challenges during the decade after Columbine (precipitated by the 9/11 attack on America), the school-related fears of parents slowly subsided, despite a spike of 45% in the survey taken immediately after the multiple shooting at Santana High School in Santee, California. By the late 2000s, as the level of panic and media hype dissipated, the percentage of parents worried about their child's safety settled back to 26%, just about the same level as a decade earlier.

The December 2012 massacre at Sandy Hook (the deadliest school massacre in the United States except for the 1927 bombing of a Michigan elementary school that killed 45, including 38 children) produced only a modest jump in the percentage of parents expressing fear (increasing from one-quarter to one-third). It is possible that Americans have grown somewhat accustomed to, although certainly not tolerant of, the occasional incident of multiple fatalities of students.

Despite the relatively low statistical risk, the extensive, sensationalized, and ubiquitous news coverage of certain high-profile school shootings (particularly those in largely white, suburban communities) has raised the level of panic and fear. Because of advances in communications technology and the emergence of 24-hour news channels with fleets of satellite trucks, dreadful images of multiple murders of innocent children can be transmitted live to viewers far and wide, making it feel almost as if the horror is taking place in their own neighborhoods.[12]

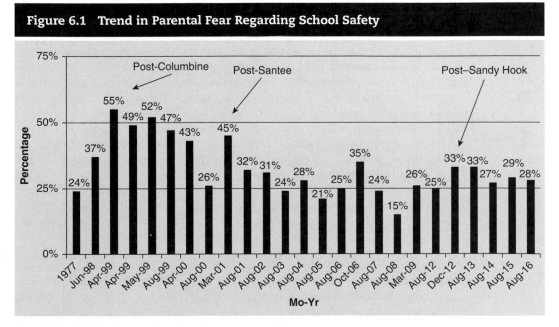

Figure 6.1   Trend in Parental Fear Regarding School Safety

Source: Gallup Poll.

Not only have rates of school homicide declined over recent years, but so have other violence-related behaviors as well. Compared with the 1990s, students are less likely today to report carrying a weapon at school and are less likely to report being threatened with a weapon. In addition, reports of physical fighting in school on school grounds have declined. Although schools are becoming safer, students and their parents do not always perceive that this is the case, and they are more likely to report staying home from school because of fear for their safety. The media hype and "breaking news" coverage of school shootings have a lingering effect and contribute to unreasonable levels of fear among many parents as well as students, teachers, and staff.

Even with the rate of serious school violence at a relative low point, as of August 2016, 28% of parents surveyed by Gallup remain concerned about school safety. Of course, perceptions of risk aren't always in step with reality. To the contrary, impressions are often resistant to change and typically lag behind the actual trends. Unfortunately, these fears, even if out of proportion with the risks, tend to force school administrators to invest scarce resources in unnecessary school security measures that might otherwise be better spent on the educational mission.

THREATENING WORDS AND WARNING SIGNS

In a seminal FBI study of school shooters, Mary Ellen O'Toole described the process of "leakage" in which a would-be assailant relays to others, close by or far away, the nature of his or her plan of attack:

> "Leakage" occurs when a student intentionally or unintentionally reveals clues to feelings, thoughts, fantasies, attitudes, or intentions that may signal an impending violent act. These clues can take the form of subtle threats, boasts, innuendos, predictions, or ultimatums. They may be spoken or conveyed in stories, diary entries, essays, poems, letters, songs, drawings, doodles, tattoos, or videos.[13]

A recent study of 28 cases of school shootings committed between 1988 and 2009 in six countries found similar evidence of leakage. Gerard and her colleagues found that 75% of the assailants had planned the incident in advance and 43% had made prior threats in advance.[14] Although there are indeed many instances in which school shooters have, implicitly or explicitly, tipped off their intentions, it is generally not until after the fact that these warning signs become crystal clear.

In the aftermath of the Columbine tragedy, much of the focus (and finger-pointing) was about warning signs that were reportedly missed or ignored. Following years of investigation, Jefferson County Sheriff Ted Mink released nearly 1,000 pages of documents associated with the shooting. These documents included the diaries of Harris and Klebold and the writings that Harris and Klebold left in each other's yearbooks. In the material the boys display intense levels of nihilism, anger, and contempt for their schoolmates. Their diaries explain that they felt like outcasts because they were different from everyone else. They also show that the boys tracked the provisions of state and federal gun laws to learn how to acquire weapons. Harris followed anti–gun control groups and even wrote a class paper that noted how easy it would be to bring a gun to school. Other documents also suggest that they dropped several clues before their attack. In fact, Klebold wrote a story for his English class depicting a man who kills nine high school students and expressed his personal sympathy for and understanding of this man. The boys' journals show that they both were preoccupied with guns, bombs, murder, and the Nazis, which explains their decision to carry out their shooting on Hitler's birthday.

Barry Loukaitis, who killed a teacher and two students during a February 2, 1996, shooting spree in his algebra class at Frontier Junior High in Moses Lake, Washington, did more than just consume stories of violence; he also wrote them. Before going on his deadly rampage, Loukaitis had submitted to his English teacher a poem about killing:

> Murder
> It's my first murder
> I'm at my point of no return
> I can't let him live now
> He'd go to the cops for sure
> So I finish
> I look at his body on the floor
> Killing a bastard that deserves to die
> Ain't nothing like it in the world
> But he sure did bleed a lot

Sometimes the warning signs are even more direct. Mitchell Johnson, Andrew Golden, and Luke Woodham all told friends in advance and in no uncertain terms that they planned to shoot classmates. As many as 39 people knew of Jeffrey Weise's plans to attack Red Lake High School on an Indian reservation in Minnesota. For two years, Weise had discussed his plans for the 2005 shooting with his friends and many others. Then, on March 21, 2005, after first killing his grandfather, a tribal police officer, and his grandfather's companion, Weise, then 16, took his grandfather's weapons and drove to Red Lake High School in a federally owned squad car. Once there, he launched his 10-minute rampage, wounding seven students and fatally shooting a security guard, five students, one teacher, and then himself.

Whether the confidantes took the shooters' words of warning seriously, the powerful code of silence obeyed by many teenagers may still have discouraged them from "snitching," even if it would have meant preventing a murder. It is also conceivable that many who were aware of Weise's plan considered him to be all talk, no action.

The mantra "see something, say something" failed miserably when Nikolas Cruz, 19, killed 17 students and teachers and wounded 14 others at the Marjory Stoneman Douglas High School in Parkland, FL, on Valentine's Day, 2018. Following the massacre, reports surfaced about the long-standing concerns that former classmates, teachers, and neighbors had about Cruz's behavior and potential for violence. Two worried citizens had gone directly to the FBI, but the authorities apparently did not take seriously his alleged threats to shoot up the school. In the absence of a criminal record, Cruz's history of animal abuse, violence against others, social media postings showing self-mutilation, firearms fixation, and school expulsion for fighting were not enough to prevent him from purchasing the AR-15 semiautomatic rifle that he used to perpetrate the bloodbath.

For every plan of attack that is brought to fruition, there are more situations in which a disgruntled student's plot to carry out a bloodbath is averted before any or most of the damage is done. In many instances, a third party—be it a student, staff member, or other individual—courageously intervenes by talking down or taking down the assailant. More often, a planned attack is thwarted when someone with knowledge of a would-be attacker's plans comes forward to warn a school resource officer or someone else in a position of authority before the assailant launches into action.

According to a study by Eric Madfis, the majority of averted school rampages were thwarted not by metal detectors or surveillance cameras but because students informed authorities about a threatening remark made by a schoolmate.[15] Examples of such interventions are not hard to find.

Nichole Cevario, an 18-year-old honor student at Catoctin High School in Maryland, wasn't really focused on her upcoming graduation or the year-end senior prom. She wasn't planning on living that long and wanted to make sure that others at her school would only receive their diplomas posthumously. For months, she had been preparing for an assault by assembling an arsenal of weapons, including a shotgun and materials for a pipe bomb, as well as by studying the safety and emergency response procedures employed at her school. However, 2 weeks before the April 5, 2017, target date, Nichole's father found her diary, which laid out in stunning detail the harm she was about to inflict on others and herself, and called the police.

Weeks later, on May 9, 2017, a girl in Thunder Bay, Ontario, happened to read a frightening message in an online chat room posted by a 16-year-old boy living a thousand miles away in North Carolina who apparently was planning a bloodbath at his high school. Taking no chances that it might be just words or a sick joke, the girl reported what she learned to her local police department, which in turn contacted the Union County, North Carolina, sheriff's office. Barely an hour after the initial tip, a school resource officer at Forest Hills High School found knives, fireworks, a bottle of flammable liquid, as well as a hit list of names in the student's backpack.

Similar to the thwarted assaults planned for Catoctin High School in Maryland and Forest Hills High School in North Carolina, each year there are countless reports of tragedies averted by an informant, typically a classmate brave enough to break the social norm against snitching. However, the so-called code of silence still tends to stifle many otherwise well-meaning students. Based on interviews at 11 schools where a planned rampage attacks had been averted, Madfis also found that many students who had had first-hand knowledge of a friend's deadly intentions chose to keep quiet. Moreover, some who ultimately did the right thing by telling someone in authority did so not out a sense of altruism but only because they were personally threatened or concerned about being held responsible as an accessory. Fortunately, in such cases, it only takes one to make the difference between death and survival.

RESPONSES TO SCHOOL SHOOTINGS

Even knowing that the chance of a school rampage is remote, many school administrators have chosen to be extra cautious and vigilant, especially in the aftermath of catastrophic incidents like the Columbine and Sandy Hook massacres. Better safe than sorrow.

After Columbine, schools around the nation went on red alert. Many heightened security, installing metal detectors, surveillance cameras, entry control devices, and even armed guards, to try to protect the school setting from the latest threat.

Although these responses to the school violence panic are quite understandable, they cost school districts hundreds of millions of dollars of scarce resources, and yet, most of this technology can do little to deter the truly motivated and determined student from seeking revenge. Metal detectors and other security measures are hardly foolproof; there are many ways in which a determined student can smuggle weapons past these devices. Jeffrey Weise fatally shot an unarmed security guard at Red Lake High School and then walked through the metal detector carrying the firearms he subsequently used to kill five students and a teacher. Of course, a vengeful student can still kill his victims in the schoolyard (as in Jonesboro,

Arkansas) or even on the bus. Security might even be regarded as a challenge to be overcome by a rebellious student who would like to show up the administration. Furthermore, an overreliance on target hardening can encourage a false sense of security, causing school officials to think that the problem has been resolved.

Administrators also responded with tough zero tolerance policies against weapons or even menacing words, putting students on notice that guns, knives, or threats of violence would not be tolerated. Applied rigidly, this resulted in the suspension of elementary schoolchildren in Georgia for making a list of people they wanted to hurt (including Barney, the purple dinosaur), a girl in Colorado who brought the wrong lunch bag to school (it contained an apple and a paring knife), and a second grader in Maryland who made a gun out of construction paper. On other occasions, this no-nonsense stance may have inspired additional feelings of alienation. Six months after the Columbine massacre, another student at the suddenly infamous high school in Littleton was overheard threatening to finish the job.

In light of the many instances in which explicit or implied threats were ignored in advance of a school shooting, various security consultants have promoted strategies for identifying the "few bad apples" before they attempted to wreak havoc on their classmates. In the wake of the 1990s string of multiple-victim shootings in schools around the country, the Bureau of Alcohol, Tobacco, and Firearms teamed up with a California software company to test out a computerized threat assessment program for violent students. High-tech right down to its name, the "Mosaic 2000" system purported to evaluate students on a scale from 1 to 10 to predict potential for violence.[16] This system was one of many in an array of checklists and guidebooks available from such prominent government agencies as the U.S. Department of Education and the Federal Bureau of Investigation to help school personnel profile potentially violent students.[17]

The prestigious American Psychological Association issued a set of warning signs for possible school violence, which included loss of temper on a frequent basis, frequent physical fighting, significant vandalism or property damage, increased use of drugs and alcohol, detailed plans to commit violent acts including threats or plans to hurt others, carrying a weapon to school, and violence toward animals. Unfortunately, we only recognize the risks after the damage has been done. We are not very good at predicting who will become a school shooter before the violent acts occur; rather, we engage in retrospective postdiction by doing postmortems of the cases.

Predicting violent behavior, especially in rare and extreme forms, is enormously difficult. In terms of the few bad apples theory, there are lots of apples that are not quite perfect in color, size, or shape but are fine just beneath the skin. There are lots of kids who look, act, or dress like our image of the schoolyard shooter—they might wear black trench coats, scary tattoos, or gang-associated baseball caps. Yet very few of them will translate their deviant adolescent attitudes into dangerous acts of violence. Checklists of warning signs typically cast a wide net and end up identifying a significant number of false positives, which could do further damage by labeling kids who likely would have never acted out.

In addition, any attempt to single out the potential troublemakers could actually do more harm than good, by stigmatizing, marginalizing, and traumatizing already troubled youth. "Don't hang with Johnnie—he's a bad apple." Already ostracized and picked on by his peers, Johnnie could sense that even the teachers and the administration were against him. The "bad apple" label could even become a self-fulfilling prophesy, encouraging doubly alienated children to act out in a violent manner.

Stressing how to identify characteristics of the individual troublemaker also lets schools off the hook. By turning the problem of schoolyard homicide into a lesson in abnormal psychology, the blame can be located outside of the school setting. From this perspective, students have to change, not the schools. A study of city schools found that school administrators who failed to institute antiviolence policies and programs were especially likely to take the "abnormal psychology" approach.[18] They regarded their troubled students as victims of inadequate upbringing, family conflict, excessive exposure to media violence, and parental abuse and neglect (i.e., bad apples not falling far from the tree).

Focusing on the individual child also ignores the fact that students often act far differently in group settings than when they are alone. To understand the course of events in Jonesboro, Arkansas, and Littleton, Colorado, for example, we must examine the relationships and interactions among the perpetrators as closely as we scrutinize their personal backgrounds and individual pathologies. To children, the expectations and approval of close friends can be all important, especially when parents and other adults are not around. The issue may not be one of a few bad apples but of a poorly tended orchard.

One of the best approaches to reducing the potential for violence through prediction is to reduce the caseload of teachers and guidance counselors.[19] Smaller classes and increased staffing allow school personnel to observe even subtle issues, which cannot be easily determined from a simplistic checklist, an anonymous phone call, or an elaborate computer algorithm. More important, our focus should not be on the potentially violent kid, but on the unhappy kid (although at times these may be one and the same). We should use warning signs, but use them to reach troubled youngsters, long before they become troublesome. If we wait until a student has murderous intentions, we have waited much too long.

Without destroying the civil liberties of young people and harming many innocent students with false accusations, we may never be able to identify each and every would-be assailant before he brings a weapon to school with deadly intentions. Even if reliable predictions were possible, we may not be able to intervene effectively in all cases. By contrast, focusing on changing schools and identifying troubled schoolchildren has much broader potential. In the process of improving the school climate, we can enhance the health and well-being of all children and, at the same time, hopefully avert murder.

OVERPROTECTION

In response to concerns over the potential for violence, many schools have invested heavily in security measures, including surveillance cameras, metal detectors, armed guards, simulation drills, and aggressive searches of students' clothing, backpacks, and lockers. According to the National Center for Education Statistics, two-thirds of public schools nationwide employ surveillance cameras; among secondary schools, the figure reaches over 80%. A majority of upper-level schools employ drug-sniffing dogs and school resource officers; more than 10% use metal detectors either daily or on a random basis.

Unfortunately, excessive emphasis on security can send a worrisome and counterproductive message to students by constantly reminding them that they need to be protected from impending harm. Security is supposed to alleviate fear, not create it.

Countless schools, voluntarily or by legislative mandate, have implemented and routinized active shooter simulation drills, sometimes with fake blood and blanks fired in the hallway for added realism. The hope is that students and faculty will be sufficiently prepared should some dispirited student or deranged intruder decide to turn the school into a battle zone.

Although well-intentioned, active shooter drills, first introduced after the 1999 Columbine massacre and now more prevalent since the 2012 Sandy Hook shooting spree, can do more harm than good. It is questionable whether children are indeed better prepared by participating in such charades. Many would likely not recall what they had learned during occasional lockdown drills, especially amid the panic associated with the real thing. But the downside is in needlessly scaring impressionable youngsters and reinforcing the notion that they are in constant danger.

Emergency drills are nothing new to the school day, of course. Drills to prepare students in the event of fire or other natural catastrophes are commonplace. Yet the aggressive nature of shooting drills staged in many schools makes them qualitatively different and exceptionally more traumatizing to children. The psychological harm that may come from these simulations is not warranted in light of the low probability that such an event will actually occur.

Notwithstanding the horror associated with these episodes, on a statistical basis, school shootings should be one of parents' least concerns when it comes to the safety of their children. The death toll, on average two dozen annually, pales in comparison to the hundreds of youngsters killed in drowning and bicycle accidents. Enhanced training in water and bicycle safety will go further to protect children than running them through school hallways while being stalked by a pretend bad man wielding a pretend gun or having them in lockdown while the SWAT team clears the building.

This is not to suggest that we should abandon all efforts to safeguard children while they are at school, only that security should be low-key rather than in your face. Cameras, lockdown drills, and armed guards roaming the halls can increase anxiety rather than alleviate it. Students shouldn't be made to feel that they are being watched minute-by-minute. That can create a climate counterproductive to learning.

Surveillance systems in school buildings should be as unobtrusive as possible. This is a lesson that architects of Sandy Hook's new school, built to replace the one where so many were slaughtered, incorporated into their plans. The new school's reconstruction uses landscape design to create natural and aesthetic separation between the school and visitors, including pushing the school back from the road to provide for more open space. Visitors must cross one of three bridges to the front entrance, and first-floor rooms are elevated from ground level. The open space and building configuration allow for easier means of entering and leaving should an emergency evacuation ever become necessary.

Apart from Sandy Hook, another promising covert security measure is the use of acoustic detection systems, technology developed for the military to identify gunfire. For example, the Guardian Indoor Gunshot Detection system employs small and well-disguised sensors throughout a school building that would immediately alert first responders of a shooting as well as the shooter's location and movements. It is, of course, extremely unlikely that the system would ever be triggered. Even so, it would be comforting to know that should the unthinkable in fact occur, the speed and efficiency of police response would likely save lives and reduce injuries. The objective is to prepare the school but not to scare the children.

HEALTHY AND SAFE SCHOOLS

Despite the school violence hype and panic, schools are exceptionally safe.[20] With structure and regular supervision, the rate of violence in schools is lower than on the street corner, at the shopping mall, and, for some kids, even at home.

Youngsters are more likely to be killed traveling to school than they are to be murdered at school by an armed classmate.

Yet concern with school violence is not completely misplaced and may even motivate much positive change. Garcia and Kennedy have noted that many school officials charged with developing safety plans have begun to recognize that costly weapon detection systems and cumbersome entry control devices are not the school violence panaceas that many had hoped they would be.[21] In fact, administrators now acknowledge that these technologies are fairly ineffective at preventing serious school violence and in some instances may violate students' rights. Since only about one-third of school shootings occur in the actual school buildings (many more occur in parking lots, breezeways, bus stops, and athletic fields), we would be misdirected to spend all of our capital improvement money on the actual school building.

Principals have looked to invest in other strategies, mainly school resource officers, security guards, mental health personnel, and prevention programs. For example, many high school and middle school principals have recognized violence prevention as a priority and adopted effective conflict resolution and peer mediation programs, have expanded after-school programs, have instituted antihate curricula, and have worked to bring community resources into the school in the form of tutors and mentors. Also, efforts are under way to bring about structural changes that would give more attention to children who desperately need it. Such measures include reducing the size of the schools and the size of the classes, extending the school day, providing meaningful alternative school programming for suspended and expelled students, reinstating extracurricular activities that have fallen victim to budget cuts, hiring more school psychologists and guidance counselors, expanding school resource officer programs, recruiting parents to help patrol crime-prone areas such as parking lots and athletic fields, and bringing other volunteers from the community to meet with needy students.

One of the most important strategies adopted by administrators around the country in the aftermath of the school slaughters is to respond directly and aggressively to bullying and cyberbullying. Rather than ignoring incidents of harassment and intimidation or recommending that victims stand up and fight back, educators are intervening in two ways to prevent bullying: by implementing programs designed to increase sensitivity and empathy among students and teachers to the plight of victims and by training staff to recognize even subtle forms of intimidation.

For too many years, schools often responded to reports of bullying by placing the blame on the shoulders of victims, implicitly assuming that they were somehow responsible for their own victimization, if only because they failed to stand up for themselves. In cases where a student had to be transferred from one class or homeroom to another to prevent further harassment, it was usually the victim and not the bully who was displaced.

In the past couple of decades, however, school administrators have come to take—or have been compelled to take—a more enlightened view of the causes of and solutions to bullying. Rather than focusing just on the victims and offenders, schools have had far greater success by addressing the broader school climate.

Despite the range of promising tools for bullying suppression, there are significant hurdles to their successful application in school settings. Most of all, the school climate must be amenable to changing norms surrounding intimidation and aggression. Intolerance for acts of bullying must be the perspective widely embraced and shared by both faculty and students, not something merely imposed on students by administrative decree.

Unfortunately, even when students and teachers appear, at least superficially, solidly unified against bullying, certain deeply rooted prejudices that favor bullies over victims remain somewhat resistant to change. A study of perceptions and attitudes among middle school students and teachers in Pennsylvania found relatively weak confidence in the utility of antibullying curricula and role-playing strategies.[22] Rather, both groups seemed to prefer an approach that encourages victims to be more assertive and to stand up for themselves. Apparently, the long-standing "blame the victim" viewpoint suggesting that victims are in some way responsible for their mistreatment remains somewhat impenetrable.

Notwithstanding the widespread adoption of various school-based antibullying curricula, the empirical evidence with regard to their preventive value is somewhat disappointing. An analysis of antibullying interventions implemented over a 25-year time period, from 1980 to 2004, concluded that the effectiveness of bullying prevention programs was modest at best, and mostly impacted knowledge and attitudes rather than actual bullying behavior.[23]

Regardless of the approach to prevention and enforcement, it remains extremely challenging to convince bullies that their actions are disadvantageous for themselves, besides being injurious to the targets of their abuse. All too often, bullies gain from their use of power over weaker classmates. Not only do they often acquire some tangible outcome, such as their victim's lunch or personal property, but also they are typically admired for their strength and supremacy.

Contrary to the common stereotype that bullies are unhappy, unsuccessful misfits attempting to compensate with their fists, those who rule the hallways are typically seen as cool and well-liked. Based on responses from nearly 400 middle school students, researchers at the University of Virginia observed that bullies were, based on peer nominations, overwhelmingly considered to be the more popular students in class.[24] The popularity of bullies was particularly pronounced among female students—the "Mean Girl" phenomenon. No matter what we say or do, the social and tangible benefits that some youngsters derive from harassing weaker and more vulnerable classmates can sometimes be too gratifying to be so easily discouraged.

The personal gratification experienced by bullies may not just be social but appears to have a biological basis as well. A University of Chicago study compared brain scans from teenage boys with aggressive conduct disorders along with a group of nonaggressive adolescents as they watched a video of someone inflicting pain on another person. The aggressive subjects responded with increased activity in the pleasure-sensing portion of the brain; the comparison group showed no such reaction.[25]

The solution to the problem of bullying and cyberbullying goes well beyond the walls of little red schoolhouses and the messages posted on social media sites. In our competitive culture, bullies frequently win. We worship athletes (from pee wee to pro) who taunt their opponents. In the workplace, managers are often rewarded for manipulating subordinates. And many of our political leaders capture votes by bullying ("challenging") their rivals with tough-sounding, "bring it on" rhetoric. Efforts to combat school bullying will be feeble so long as we admire brutes and pity pushovers. Sure, schools need to change, but so does society in general.

ON TO COLLEGE

On April 16, 2007, Seung-Hui Cho killed 32 students and faculty members on the campus of Virginia Tech in Blacksburg, before killing himself. He used a pair of semi-automatic firearms. The shooting spree took place in two separate incidents, two hours apart—the first in a residence hall and the second in a building that houses the School of Engineering.

The mass murder was not the first episode reflecting Cho's emotional and behavioral problems that had drawn attention, even though no one could have anticipated the extent of his dangerousness. In 2005, the 23-year-old senior had been accused of stalking two young women and was ordered by the court to receive outpatient mental health services. More recently, one of his instructors urged him to seek psychotherapy when he wrote violent passages in a couple of written assignments.

The scope of the Virginia Tech massacre may have been unprecedented, but the idea of a college student opening fire on his peers was hardly new. It was only a matter of time that high-profile shootings associated with middle and high school students would graduate to the college level. Many of the miseries suffered by students long before they matriculate have continued to influence their thinking about their peers and about themselves. The impact on a student who was bullied throughout his early years of schooling does not necessarily dissipate later in life.

Cho's single act of carnage—one that shocked the nation—had roots that started forming years earlier. He was an immigrant from South Korea whose family had relocated to the United States when he was 8. Apparently his lack of facility with the English language, his selective mutism (i.e., inability to communicate in social settings because of anxiety), and his extreme shyness were enough to make him the daily object of ridicule and scorn throughout his days in middle and high school. By the time he had moved into his room in a residence hall at Virginia Tech, Cho was already filled with hatred and resentment, perhaps toward his peers, Americans, or all of humankind. Cho had most of the characteristics discovered in younger school shooters. He had long suffered from depression, had been severely bullied, blamed all of his problems on fellow students, had few if any friends on whom he could depend for encouragement and support, and had access to semi-automatic weapons.

He also had a model for his massacre in the now legendary Columbine slayings. Although the slaughter in Littleton, Colorado, had occurred eight years earlier, Harris and Klebold had remained in the minds of alienated and marginalized students around the country—including Cho—as bullied students who fought back and achieved some degree of infamy.

In between his two killing sprees on campus, Cho anticipated his own demise. He had a two-hour period when he was able to mail a package of materials—his writings, photographs, and a video-recorded "manifesto"—to NBC News. The photographs showed Cho aiming his guns in a threatening pose. They depicted the killer as a strong and powerful individual who could not easily be ignored. The video consisted of a rambling, incoherent, and disjointed message in which he sought to justify his rampage as a rational response to those individuals who destroyed his life. They had many chances to change their ways, he offered, but chose not to do so. Therefore, the victims of his killing spree were, in Cho's mind, actually responsible for his angry mass shooting. Unfortunately, NBC released both the photos and the video, assuring that Cho's image would live in infamy and that the potential for copycatting would remain for years to come.

Whereas the 1990s witnessed a disturbing string of high-profile mass killings at middle and high schools around the country, a very different form of campus violence has commanded our attention in recent years—specifically, shooting rampages at colleges and universities, highlighted by massacres at Virginia Tech and Northern Illinois University less than 10 months apart. More recently, the sense of safety and serenity of college campuses has been shaken by several devastating killing sprees, including the 2012 massacre at Oikos University in which seven people were fatally shot; the 2014 rampage at the University of California, Santa Barbara, that claimed the lives of six victims; and the 2015 mass shooting at Umpqua Community College in which eight students and their professor were shot to death inside a classroom.

Although incidents at middle schools, high schools, and institutions of higher education all fall under the umbrella of "school shootings," there are, in fact, several characteristics of college campuses that make them unique. Security measures often adopted by middle schools and high schools (e.g., locks on building doors during school hours, random searches for contraband, visitor sign-in procedures, random metal detector checks on students) would hardly be feasible for most colleges and universities that feature sprawling campuses and multiple buildings. In addition, security measures for colleges and universities should in part be governed by the community's desire for a free and open campus. Colleges and universities present unique challenges to security because the nature of their existence depends on a free flow of individuals and expression. Care must be taken not to reinforce exaggerated perceptions of vulnerability. Indeed, it is critical not to promote fear and anxiety while attempting to reduce risk. Thus, whereas tight security measures might be appropriate for middle and high schools where students generally have no choice of attendance, the same approach on a college campus could create an environment so distasteful to student prospects as to encourage them to look for options elsewhere.

In addition, the issues that motivate campus shooters and their younger counterparts are vastly different. Shootings at high schools are often precipitated when students feel bullied or persecuted by their classmates and/or teachers.[26] However, as shown in Table 6.4, the perpetrators of multiple-victim shootings at colleges and universities are typically current or former graduate students; had been enrolled in professional schools for law, medicine, or nursing; or were faculty members hoping for tenure. Unlike Cho from Virginia Tech, they tend to be older individuals (with an average age of over 30) who turn to violence in response to what they perceive to be unbearable pressure to succeed or the unacceptable reality of failure.

In graduate, law, or medical school, students who had been at the top of their class through high school and college may come to find themselves struggling to get by with just passing grades. No longer supported financially by parents, they experience great pressure to juggle assistantship activities or outside employment with coursework and thesis research, with little time for attending to social networks. At some point, their entire lifestyle and sense of worth may revolve around academic achievement. Moreover, their personal investment in reaching a successful outcome can be viewed as a virtual life-or-death matter.

Unlike undergraduates, students in graduate and professional programs often lack balance in their personal lives, narrowly focusing on academic work and training to the exclusion of other interests and other people in their lives. They may even work in the lab to all hours of the night, subsisting on cold pizza and junk food, thereby jeopardizing their health and well-being. Although the role and responsibilities may differ, faculty pursuing tenure may face similar pressures to produce, as tenure denial can have profound impact on future employment prospects.

Pervasive media images of the mass shooting at Virginia Tech and elsewhere raised the specter of serious violence on college campuses. By any measure, however, the risk of serious violence on campus remains remarkably low, particularly in its most extreme form.[27] But should the unthinkable tragedy occur,

Table 6.4 Multiple-Victim Campus Shootings, 1990–2017

Date	School Name	Shooter(s), Age(s)	Victims Killed	Role at School
November 1, 1991	University of Iowa	Gang Lu, 28	5	Graduate student
August 24, 1992	Concordia University	Valery I. Fabrikant, 52	3	Faculty
December 14, 1992	Simon's Rock College	Wayne Lo, 18	2	Undergraduate student
January 26, 1995	University of North Carolina	Wendell Williamson, 26	2	Former law student
August 15, 1996	San Diego State University	Frederick Davidson, 36	3	Graduate student
January 16, 2002	Appalachian School of Law	Peter Odighizuwa, 42	3	Former law student
October 28, 2002	University of Arizona	Robert Flores, 40	3	Nursing student
September 2, 2006	Shepherd University	Douglas Pennington, 49	2	Parent of students
April 16, 2007	Virginia Tech	Seung-Hui Cho, 23	32	Undergraduate student
February 8, 2008	Louisiana Tech	Latina Williams, 23	2	Nursing student
February 14, 2008	Northern Illinois University	Steven Kazmierczak, 27	5	Former graduate student
October 26, 2008	University of Central Arkansas	Four teenagers	2	None
February 12, 2010	University of Alabama Huntsville	Amy Bishop, 45	3	Faculty
May 10, 2011	San Jose State University	Napoleon Lavarias Caliguiran, 54	2	None
April 2, 2012	Oikos University	One L. Goh, 43	7	Former nursing student
January 15, 2013	Hazard Community College	Dalton Lee Stidham, 21	3	Former nursing student
June 7, 2013	Santa Monica College	John Samir Zawahri, 23	3	None
May 23, 2014	Univ. of California, Santa Barbara	Elliot Rodger, 22	6	None
October 1, 2015	Umpqua Community College	Chris Harper-Mercer, 26	9	Undergraduate student

Note: Incidents with at least four victims and at least two deaths (not including the assailant).

the consequences can be devastating and long lasting. Understandably, college officials have responded proactively, as parents rightly expect a special level of care for their sons and daughters while they are away at school. At least in the short term, when the possibility for copycatting is not insignificant, it is prudent that colleges take reasonable steps to ensure the safety of students as well as faculty and other employees.

Unfortunately, some of the measures colleges and universities have undertaken, amid an atmosphere of fear, are beyond what is reasonable, undermining the carefree atmosphere of campus life. For example, many schools involve their undergraduates in staging active shooter simulations, which, like the drills forced on students in primary and secondary schools, can potentially be traumatizing and tend to suggest that the danger is truly imminent. In addition, expanded laws permitting carrying a concealed weapon on campus that have been enacted in several states in the years since the Virginia Tech massacre can create a secondary risk. Should there be a campus rampage, it could be difficult for first responders to distinguish the armed assailant dressed in blue jeans and carrying a backpack from others who are armed, dressed in blue jeans, and carrying backpacks. Mass confusion could potentially result in an increased victim count.

Finally, no matter how diligent and responsible academic and safety officials are in improving violence prevention efforts and security measures on campus, there can be no absolute guarantee that a tragedy like Virginia Tech will not occur. If any prospective student, undergraduate or graduate, requires iron-clad assurance of safety at school, then the only recourse might be to opt for an online degree.

ENDNOTES

1. James Alan Fox and Jack Levin, *Overkill: Mass Murder and Serial Killing Exposed* (New York: Plenum Press, 1994).

2. Sherry Towers, Andres Gomez-Lievano, Maryam Khan, Anuj Mubayi, and Carlos Castillo-Chavez, "Contagion in Mass Killings and School Shootings." *PLOS ONE* 10 (2015): e0117259.

3. Peter Langman, *Why Kids Kill: Inside the Minds of School Shooters* (New York: Palgrave Macmillan, 2009).

4. Ann Marie C. Lenhardt, Melissa L. Farrell, and Lemuel W. Graham, "Providing Anchors— Reclaiming Our Troubled Youth: Lessons for Leaders from a Study of 15 Targeted School Shooters," *Educational Forum* 74 (2010): 104–116.

5. Katherine S. Newman, *Rampage: The Social Roots of School Shootings* (New York: Basic Books, 2004).

6. Jessie Klein, "Cultural Capital and High School Bullies: How Social Inequality Impacts School Violence," *Men and Masculinities* 9 (2006): 53–75.

7. Michael S. Kimmel and Matthew Mahler, "Adolescent Masculinity, Homophobia, and Violence: Random School Shootings, 1982-2001," *American Behavioral Scientist* 46 (2003): 1439–1458.

8. Susan Klebold, "I'll Never Know Why," *O Magazine*, October 13, 2009.

9. Peter Langman, *School Shooters: Understanding High School, College, and Adult Perpetrators* (Lanham, MD: Rowman & Littlefield, 2015).

10. Bryan Vossekuil, Robert A. Fein, Marisa Reddy, Randy Borum, and William Modzeleski, *The Final Report and Findings of the Safe School Initiative* (Washington, DC: U.S. Secret Service and Department of Education, 2002).

11. Ronald Burns and Charles Crawford, "School Shootings, the Media, and Public Fear: Ingredients for a Moral Panic," *Crime, Law and Social Change* 32 (1999): 147–168.

12. Linda Heath and Kevin Gilbert, "Mass Media and Fear of Crime," *American Behavioral Scientist* 39 (1996): 379–386.

13. Mary Ellen O'Toole, *The School Shooter: A Threat Assessment Perspective* (Washington, DC: U.S. Department of Justice, 2000).

14. J. F. Gerard, K. C. Whitfield, L. E. Porter, and K. D. Browne, "Offender and Offence Characteristics of School Shooting Incidents," *Journal of Investigative Psychology and Offender Profiling* 13 (2016): 22–38.

15. Eric Madfis, "Averting School Rampage: Student Intervention Amid a Persistent Code of Silence," *Youth Violence and Juvenile Justice* 12 (2014): 229–249.

16. Lisa Richardson, "Schools Testing Threat Analysis," *Los Angeles Times*, December 18, 1999, p. B3.

17. Janet Bingham, "FBI Puts 'Risk List' Out for Schools: 60 Factors to Help ID Violent Students," *Denver Post*, November 9, 1999, p. A1.

18. Jack Levin and Heather Beth Johnson, "Youth Violence and the Urban Public School Response," *Journal of Research in Education* 7 (1997): 3–7.

19. Denise C. Gottfredson, *School Size and School Disorder* (Baltimore: Center for Social Organization of Schools, Johns Hopkins University, 1985).

20. Elizabeth Donohue, Vincent Shiraldi, and Jason Ziedenberg, *School House Hype: School Shootings and the Real Risks Kids Face in America* (Washington, DC: Justice Policy Institute, September 15, 1998).

21. Crystal A. Garcia and Sheila Suess Kennedy, "Back to School: Technology, School Safety and the Disappearing Fourth Amendment," *Kansas Journal of Law and Public Policy* 12 (2003): 273–288.

22. Laura M. Crothers and Jered B. Kolbert, "Comparing Middle School Teachers' and Students' Views on Bullying and Anti-Bullying Interventions," *Journal of School Violence* 3 (2004): 17–32.

23. Kenneth W. Merrell, Barbara A. Gueldner, Scott W. Ross, and Duane M. Isava, "How Effective Are School Bullying Intervention Programs? A Meta-Analysis of Intervention Research," *School Psychology Quarterly* 23 (2008): 26–42.

24. Peter Thunfors and Dewey Cornell, "The Popularity of Middle School Bullies," *Journal of School Violence* 7 (2008): 65–82.

25. Jean Decety, Kalina J. Michalska, Yuko Akitsuki, and Benjamin B. Lahey, "Atypical Empathic Responses in Adolescents With Aggressive Conduct Disorder: A Functional MRI Investigation," *Biological Psychology* 80 (2009): 203–211.

26. Vossekuil et al., *The Final Report and Findings of the Safe School Initiative*.

27. James Alan Fox and Harvey Burstein, *Violence and Security on Campus: From Preschool Through College* (Santa Barbara, CA: Praeger, 2010).

CHAPTER SEVEN

SERIAL KILLERS

Thanks in part to a fascination with anything that is "serial," whether it be murder, rape, arson, or robbery, there has been a tendency to focus a good deal of attention on the timing of different types of multiple murder. Thus, the Federal Bureau of Investigation (FBI) distinguishes between spree killers who take the lives of several victims over a short period of time without a cooling-off period and serial killers who murder a number of people over weeks, months, or years, but in between their attacks live relatively normal lives.[1] In 2008, for example, Nicholas T. Sheley, then 28, went on a killing spree across two states, beating as many as eight people to death over a period of several days in an effort to get money to buy crack. Sheley's victims ranged from a child to a 93-year-old man. At the time of these incidents, Sheley already had a long criminal history of robbery, drugs, and weapons convictions and had spent time in prison. Sheley is doing life in prison in Illinois for six of the murders and faces two additional homicide charges in Missouri.

Unfortunately, the distinction between spree and serial killing can easily break down. For example, over the course of 2 weeks in 1997, Andrew Cunanan killed two victims in Minnesota, then drove to Illinois, where he killed another person, and then on to New Jersey, where he killed his fourth victim. While evading apprehension, and on the FBI's 10 Most Wanted List, Cunanan was labeled a spree killer. He then disappeared from sight, although citizens far and wide called the FBI claiming to have spotted the fugitive, hoping for a cash reward. Two months later, the elusive killer turned up in Miami, where he shot to death fashion designer Gianni Versace. Cunanan's revised body count—five victims—was accumulated over a period of months, not days, and with a rather lengthy cooling-off period between the fourth and fifth murders. Should he be regarded as a spree killer or a serial murderer? Does it really matter all that much?

In 1990, Danny Rolling brutally murdered five college students in Gainesville, Florida, at three different crime scenes over a 72-hour period and thus appeared to be a spree killer. It turns out that Rolling had slaughtered a family of three in Shreveport, Louisiana, 8 months before his Gainesville attacks, making Rolling a serial killer. Again, does it really matter? Rigidly focusing on the timing of attacks, although interesting, is far less important to our understanding of multiple homicide than attempting to assess the killer's motivation.

Recently discovered serial killer Todd Kohlhepp, 45, kidnapped and kept a woman chained in a shipping container on his South Carolina property for months in 2016 after he lured the woman and her boyfriend to his home under the ruse of hiring them to clean for him. Kohlhepp murdered the boyfriend immediately in front of the woman. When police traced the last of her cell phone pings to

Kohlhepp's property, they heard her banging on the walls of the storage shed. After rescuing the distraught woman, the police searched the property and turned up two more bodies that appeared to have been killed months earlier. The authorities thought they were dealing with a serial killer, but Kohlhepp then confessed to an unsolved mass murder of four at a motorcycle shop in 2003. Kohlhepp, a successful real estate agent, avoided the death penalty by pleading guilty to seven murders. But if he's linked to the other murders under investigation, including a triple homicide and bank robbery in 2003, he may not be able to avoid the death penalty after all. Is Kohlhepp a mass killer, a serial killer, or a hybrid of both?

Another issue related to defining serial murder surrounds the minimum victim threshold. Several years ago, the FBI broadened its long-standing definition (assailants who killed at least three victims) to include repeat killers with just two victims to their name, claiming that it would be helpful in conducting homicide investigations.[2] Some criminologists who research the topic of serial murder have followed the FBI lead, whereas others have maintained thresholds of three or even four. In an effort to identify the optimal threshold based on empirical data, Fridel and Fox found that offenders with two victims differed significantly in terms of motive, partnership, and crime scene behaviors from their more prolific counterparts. Whereas law enforcement may find it useful to operate with a different definition for law enforcement purposes of investigative work, maintaining a somewhat higher threshold appears to be better for distinguishing this particularly deadly breed of killers from a large pool of two-timers and serial murder wannabes who stop killing or are apprehended before accumulating more victims.[3]

A commonly held view concerning repeat murderers, perhaps because of the widespread fascination associated with their crimes, is that they are always driven to kill by sexual urges, and indeed many of them are. Still, at least some appear to be motivated by material gain, and their homicides tend to be more instrumental than expressive. They rob, burglarize, steal cars, and often kill their victims not for some emotional or sexual release but primarily to acquire money and possessions. Murder is just a means of covering up their tracks.

For example, over a 3-week time span in October 2002, the D.C. Snipers—John Allen Muhammad and Lee Boyd Malvo—gunned down 10 strangers, all chosen randomly, from a "sniper's nest" situated in the trunk of their blue Chevy sedan. During this entire period, aside from eating and sleeping, their time was apparently consumed by planning, executing, escaping, and hiding from the police. Muhammad was executed in November 2009. His teenaged accomplice, Malvo, was not eligible for the death penalty because of this age and is serving life sentences without the possibility of parole. Malvo recently confessed that he and his murderous mentor were also responsible for an additional four killings, three of which were committed in the course of armed robberies. The motive for the D.C. area killings was profit: The killers attempted to extort $10 million from the authorities in exchange for a "cease fire."

Besides the spree–serial distinction, it is also valuable to distinguish full-time from part-time repeat killers. The D.C. Snipers devoted their full attention to selecting appropriate locations, killing victims, communicating with the police, and hiding out. For most serial killers, however, murder is a part-time hobby, thus the notion of "cooling off." They typically return to their normal activities (e.g., holding a job, attending classes, playing with their children) after each murder. But during these dormant times, they often plan their next murder, putting hundreds of miles on their cars as they troll and surveil potential victims, reliving their past murders with pictures and souvenirs, or even returning to bodies yet undiscovered.

Given the role that murder occupies in their actions and thoughts, serial killers typically can recall even the smallest details of their crimes, even years after being captured.

THE MANY FORMS OF SERIAL KILLING

There is a multitude of different motives that provoke serial killers and help them to justify their actions. Some, such as Marybeth Tinning discussed in Chapter 4, have slain a series of children to satisfy a pathological need for attention and sympathy. As described later in Chapter 12, some serial killings have occurred in the context of cult activity. A charismatic cult leader such as Charles Manson or Adolfo de Jesús Constanzo inspires his followers to commit homicides, often ritualistic or excessively brutal in nature, both to achieve some political or spiritual goal and to nourish the leader's excessive need to be in charge. A few serial killers are driven not by a charismatic cult figure but by the commandments of delusional forces that place them on a relentless mission of murder. Still other serial killings are expeditious cover-ups. Railway Killer Ángel Maturino Reséndiz, for example, was charged in 1999 with killing nine people in Texas, Kentucky, and Illinois, all near railroad tracks, in the process of robbery and burglary, primarily to eliminate potential witnesses.

By far, however, the most common form of serial murder surrounds the killer's quest to satisfy his own sadistic urges or excessive need for control. He exploits his victims as a means of satisfying personal, and often sexual, desires.[4] Interviews with serial killers reveal that some experience psychological relief after killings, rather than guilt and disgust. Although serial murder has been loosely described as "motiveless," there is indeed one motive—to satisfy an intense appetite for sadism, power, and control. Many serial murderers kill not for love, money, or revenge but just for the fun of it—because it makes them feel good.

We tend to overlook certain serial killers, even with large body counts, simply because their motives seem mundane. Most media attention and public fascination are focused on sexual sadists. Far less attention is given to mothers who kill their children, nurses who poison their patients, or armed robbers who repeatedly take the lives of their victims to eliminate all witnesses. Although most definitions of serial murder do include women who kill their family members for insurance money and the murders committed by medical professionals, many scholars ignore those series of murders committed as part of a criminal enterprise related to gangs, drugs, or organized crime.

Because of the massive publicity devoted to such crimes as the grisly slayings of at least 17 males by cannibalistic necrophile Jeffrey Dahmer, the term *serial murder* has become part of everyday vocabulary. Serial killers such as David Berkowitz (Son of Sam), Kenneth Bianchi (the Hillside Strangler), and Theodore (better known as Ted) Bundy are featured in prime-time TV docudramas and mass-market paperbacks, no longer just in obscure detective magazines. Serial murder is a profitable industry. Stretching the limits of decency, moreover, serial killers have, as described earlier, clearly become a fixture in our popular culture, featured on trading cards and in comic books as well as on T-shirts and in games. Further glamorizing and romanticizing their crimes, journalists and true crime writers often assign colorful monikers to their murderous activities (see Table 7.1). Curiously, most people can easily name nine serial killers, yet not so many can identify the nine justices of the U.S. Supreme Court.

Table 7.1   Selected Serial Killer Monikers

Killer(s)	Moniker
Charles Albright	The Eyeball Killer
Richard Angelo	The Angel of Death
David Berkowitz	The Son of Sam
Paul Bernardo & Karla Homolka	The Ken and Barbie Killers
Kenneth Bianchi & Angelo Buono	The Hillside Stranglers
Ian Brady & Myra Hindley	The Moors Murderers
Jerry Brudos	The Shoe-Fetish Slayer
Ted Bundy	The Lady Killer
David Carpenter	The Trailside Killer
Richard Chase	The Vampire of Sacramento
Andrei Chikatilo	The Rostov Ripper
Douglas Clark	The Sunset Strip Slayer
John Norman Collins	The Coed Murderer
Adolfo de Jesús Constanzo	The Godfather of Matamoros
Dean Corll	The Candy Man
Juan Corona	The Machete Murderer
Jeffrey Dahmer	The Milwaukee Monster
Albert DeSalvo	The Boston Strangler
Nannie Doss	The Giggling Granny
Larry Eyler	The Interstate Killer
Albert Fish	The Cannibal
Lonnie David Franklin Jr.	The Grim Sleeper
John Wayne Gacy	The Killer Clown
Carlton Gary	The Stocking Strangler
Ed Gein	The Ghoul of Wisconsin
Vaughn Greenwood	The Skid Row Slasher
John George Haigh	The Acid Bath Murderer
Keith Jesperson	The Happy Face Killer
Theodore Kaczynski	The Unabomber

Killer(s)	Moniker
Patrick Kearney	The Trash Bag Murderer
Edmund Kemper III	The Coed Killer
Bobby Joe Long	The Classified Ad Rapist
Pedro Lopez	The Monster of the Andes
George Metesky	The Mad Bomber
Ivan Milat	The Backpack Killer
John Allen Muhammad & Lee Boyd Malvo	The D.C. Snipers
Dennis Rader	The BTK Strangler
Richard Ramirez	The Night Stalker
Melvin David Rees	The Sex Beast
Gary Leon Ridgway	The Green River Killer
Danny Rolling	The Gainesville Ripper
Arthur Shawcross	The Genesee River Killer
Harold Shipman	Doctor Death
Anthony Sowell	The Cleveland Strangler
Timothy William Spencer	The Southside Slayer
Peter Sutcliffe	The Yorkshire Rapist
Carl Eugene Watts	The Sunday Morning Slasher
Wayne Williams	The Atlanta Child Murderer
Randall Woodfield	The I-5 Killer

The most prolific serial killers tend to be organized psychologically. They methodically stalk their victims for the best opportunity to strike so as not to be seen, and they smartly dump the bodies far away so as not to leave any clues. The discovery of a body in a dump site does not provide investigators with the crime scene where most of the forensic evidence—hairs, blood, fibers, semen—is located. In a sense, becoming a serial killer is a process of self-selection. A confused assailant who kills in a frenzied way cannot successfully plan, execute, and cover up the crime. The most dangerous, cunning murderers are a great challenge for law enforcement authorities. Notwithstanding advances in forensics, computerized offender tracking, and even behavioral profiling, when these crimes are solved, luck generally plays a significant role.

It may not be completely fair to law enforcement to characterize these apprehensions as lucky, because they still involve the police doing their job. Although killers like Theodore Bundy and Gary Heidnik may have been caught in routine traffic stops and Berkowitz was linked to the Son of Sam killings as a result of a parking ticket he received near one of the crime scenes, these obviously involved important police activities—even if not requiring tremendous technical skill—and highlight the significance of a police presence in our society.

There is also some evidence that the most organized killers can begin to deteriorate over time. Bundy began his killing career with a duffle bag filled with weapons, disguises, and tools and had several ruses he used to lure women (e.g., his arm was in a sling and he needed help loading something into his car). By the time he committed the Chi Omega sorority house murders at Florida State University, however, Bundy used a log he found at the crime scene as his murder weapon and left bite marks on his victim's body. Apparently, Bundy's transformation was from a highly organized to a quite disorganized killer.

The notion that serial killers subconsciously wish to be caught and for this purpose carelessly leave telltale clues at crime scenes or act impetuously and recklessly may hold in detective novels but has little validity when applied to most real cases. When spree/serial killer Andrew Cunanan traveled from the Midwest to the East in a series of stolen cars, killing his first four victims along the way, many law enforcement experts speculated that his incautious actions, such as using his victims' cell phones, indicated a latent desire to be apprehended. Despite this wishful thinking on the part of investigators, Cunanan remained hidden in plain sight before surfacing in Miami to kill again. Even as the police cornered him on a Miami houseboat, Cunanan still controlled when, where, and how the killing spree would end. On July 23, 1997, as police and media helicopters circled above him, the 27-year-old killer took his own life rather than be taken alive. Perhaps it was a death wish, but clearly not an arrest wish.

DECEIVING APPEARANCES

Several myths have long existed about serial killers, whereas other legends are rather recent in origin.[5] One of the oldest misconceptions is that of the serial murderer as a human monster, derived from and reinforced by Hollywood creations such as Jason in the movie *Friday the 13th*. In one thriller after another, screenwriters have portrayed serial killers as glassy-eyed lunatics whose entire existence is centered on satisfying their compulsion for human destruction.

Actually, it would be somewhat comforting if the Hollywood image were at all accurate. If serial killers indeed looked like crazed maniacs and acted in a patently bizarre fashion, they would be easily identified and avoided on sight. Unfortunately, in very many respects, most serial killers are extraordinarily ordinary, and, as such, extremely dangerous.

Quite opposite to the Hollywood thriller stereotype, a more modern characterization describes these killers as unusually handsome and charming, perhaps generalizing from one of the most celebrated cases of modern times, that of Theodore Bundy, who murdered dozens of women from Washington State to Florida and was indeed a "lady killer," in more ways than one. During his trial, a number of female admirers came to court, their hair styled to look like some of Bundy's victims, and sat gazing at the "dreamy" defendant. Similarly, Richard Ramirez, the so-called Night Stalker of Los Angeles, also was sought after by numerous adoring women during his trial. They attended his trial dressed all in black as an expression of support and devotion. In 1996, while locked away in a California prison, Ramirez married one of his adoring fans.

Several other serial killers, including Randall Woodfield, Ángel Maturino Reséndiz, Henry Louis Wallace, and Arthur Shawcross, found love and marriage after being convicted and imprisoned for vicious crimes. A few states—California, Connecticut, Mississippi, New Mexico, New York, and Washington—allow for conjugal visits from spouses. Bundy managed to become a father while in prison (semen was somehow smuggled out of the prison), and his then-wife had a daughter in 1982.

Aspiring to marry a convicted and imprisoned serial killer may say much more about the mental health of the bride-to-be than the charm of the killer himself. Marrying someone in prison is one way an insecure woman can be assured that her man is not cheating on her (at least with other women). He may be behind bars but not in the bars looking for a good time. She always knows where he is, even at 3 a.m. Women who are attracted to men who have committed atrocious crimes, referred to as hybristophiles, may suffer from their own mental health issues and seek attention as the wife or girlfriend of a notorious murderer.

It is tempting to focus only on the defects of killer groupies (e.g., their lack of self-esteem and their bad judgment) to explain their attraction to serial killers. Some of them find a mission in their relationship. They must attract the attention of the world and tell everyone that their man is innocent, that he is only a victim of injustice and not a vicious criminal. Still other women may feel special because their man shared his most personal and intimate thoughts. Only she sees his gentler side.

Aside from the needs of killer groupies, however, what deserves to be acknowledged as well is society's complicity in making these murderers into appealing celebrities. In some cases, serial killers have received more national publicity than many rock stars or rap artists. Moreover, most serial killers are extremely manipulative. They know exactly how to lure vulnerable women into a relationship, just as they understood how to lure their poor victims into a position of total vulnerability in order to take their lives.

It would be wrong, however, to characterize all, or even most, serial killers as charming, charismatic, and attractive. Some are, by conventional standards, decidedly undesirable in appearance, and still others suffer from intense shyness. Interestingly, shyness has been identified as a factor that may protect against delinquency, apparently as a trait that limits the number of peer contacts. However, shyness—and particularly shyness with women—is a characteristic that appears in many case histories of male serial killers.

For some serial killers, in fact, murder can be their only strategy for seeking sexual gratification and even "enjoying" the "company" of others. Leonard Lake, a middle-aged recluse who lived in the woods just east of San Francisco, was painfully aware of his limitations when he outlined on videotape, with chilling calmness and clarity, his motives for abducting women. Preparing to build an elaborate underground bunker in which to imprison young women as sex slaves, Lake described in logical, although patently selfish, terms why he felt the need to proceed with what he called "Operation Miranda":

> I am a realist. I am 38 years old, a bit chubby, with not much hair, and I'm losing what I have. I am not particularly attractive to women—or I should say particularly attracting to women. And all the traditional magnets— the money, the position/power—I don't have. And yet I am still very sexually active, and I am still very much attracted to a particular type of woman who almost by definition is totally uninterested in me.
>
> Dirty old man, pervert, I'm attracted to young women, sometimes even as young as 12, although to be fair certainly 18–22 is pretty much an

ideal range as far as my interests go. I like very slim women, very pretty of course, petite, small breasted, long hair, if I am allowed. And, such a woman, by virtue of her youth, her attractiveness, her desirability to certainly the majority of mankind, simply has better options. There is no particular reason why such a woman should be interested in me.

But there is more to it than that. It is difficult to explain my personality in 25 words or less, but I am in fact a loner, I enjoy the peace, the quiet, the solitude, I enjoy being by myself. And while all my relationships with women in the past have been sexually successful, socially they have almost always been a failure. I've gone through two divorces, innumerable women, 50–55, I forget exactly the count, I counted recently. I'm afraid the bottom line statement is the simple fact that I'm a sexist slob.

I enjoy using women, and of course women aren't particularly interested in being used. I certainly enjoy sex. I certainly enjoy the dominance of climbing on a woman and using her body. But I'm not particularly interested in the id, the ego, all the things that a man should be interested in to complement a woman's needs. Now I can fake these emotions, and I can fake them very well. In the past, I've been very successful at attracting fairly interesting and attractive women simply because I did fake fairly well an interest in their needs and their requirements. So momentarily I had what I wanted and they thought they had what they wanted. But in the long term I don't want to bother.

What I want is an off-the-shelf sex partner. I want to be able to use a woman whenever and however I want. And when I'm tired or satiated or bored or not interested, I simply want to put her away, lock her up in a little room to get her out of my sight, out of my life, and thus avoid what heretofore has always been the obligation to entertain or amuse or satisfy a particular woman or girlfriend's whims of emotional whatevers.

Such an arrangement, of course, is not only blatantly sexist, but highly illegal. There's no doubt about it. It violates all of the human rights and blah blah, blah blah blah. To spare posterity my concept of other people's morality, I'm explaining my morality—what I feel, what I want. And as of this moment I am going to try to get it.

With the help of his buddy Charles Ng, Lake constructed a holding cell inside a bunker next to his home in which he kept a steady supply of slaves. He used them as long as they were appealing and satisfying, and then violently discarded them as human trash. Surely, Lake could have hired prostitutes to fulfill his sexual needs and housekeepers to perform the other assorted chores. But there was much more to his fantasy: ownership. He sought to possess total power over his victims as if they were indeed his slaves. Leonard Lake committed suicide by taking a cyanide pill as soon as he was apprehended by police, and Charles Ng, whose shoplifting brought him and his partner to the attention of police, was convicted of 12 murders and is currently on death row in California. His trial was one of the most expensive in history.

Although Leonard Lake was as intelligent as he was self-absorbed, it is also part of the modern mythology that serial killers are typically brilliant—like the Hannibal Lecter character from Thomas Harris's novel, *The Silence of the Lambs*. Although some serial killers, such as Lawrence Sigmund Bittaker and Edmund Kemper, have genius-level IQs, many others clearly have sub-par intelligence.

Based on data drawn from the Homicide Investigation and Tracking System (HITS) database in Washington State, Godwin determined that only 16% of the 107 serial murderers he studied had attended college and only 4% graduated with a bachelor's degree. The majority were employed in blue-collar jobs working for other people.[6] Using a much larger database, Aamodt found that roughly 15% of serial killers attended at least some college. Although partially a result of a large amount of missing data on educational attainment, Aamodt reported that as many as 43% of serial killers had no academic degree at all, not even a high school diploma.[7]

Regardless of social class, IQ, or level of education, most serial killers—at least those who successfully remain at large for long time periods—typically possess a certain degree of cunning, criminal savoir faire needed to accumulate a significant body count. Many of them are exceptionally skillful in their presentation of self, so much so that they appear beyond suspicion and thus are difficult to apprehend. But many of them just target the most vulnerable and only have to offer drugs or money to trap a victim. They are hardly engaging in complicated art thefts or bank heists. Like terrorists, they mostly go after soft targets.

PREVALENCE AND TRENDS

It is difficult to gauge the full extent of serial murder. Because of complexities in linking murders committed by the same perpetrator but at different times and often different locations, no precise estimate of the prevalence of serial killers is even possible. Early estimates of serial murder suggested there was an emerging epidemic with hundreds of active killers and thousands of victims killed every year, but this was largely media hype and hysteria.[8] Although a large percentage of all killers featured in TV dramas, news magazine programs, and true crime books commit serial murder, most research places the death toll linked to known serial killers at about 1% of all murders in the United States, a couple hundred victims per year at most. However, there is also research that suggests there may be many more overlooked victims of serial killers. Some proportion of missing persons and unidentified dead are likely serial homicide victims, as well as deaths that are misclassified as natural deaths (as in the case of a medical murderer or deaths wrongly classified as sudden infant death syndrome [SIDS]). Additionally, some missing persons are never reported as missing by anyone. These "missing missing," including runaways, prostitutes, homeless persons, and drug addicts, are particularly vulnerable to serial killers. Including these typically undercounted victim pools could easily double or triple the known annual serial murder death toll.[9]

Notwithstanding these limitations in measuring the prevalence of serial murder, the best available source of information pertaining to serial killers and their victims is the Radford University/Florida Gulf Coast University Serial Killer Database (hereafter called the Radford/FGCU database).[10] The Radford/FGCU database includes information of offender demographics, childhood life events, family variables, education, military history, substance use, locations and dates of murders and other crimes, motives, types of victims, weapons, and sentencing outcomes on nearly 5,000 repeat killers (with at least two kills) and 14,000 victims from around the globe and dating as far back as the 15th century.

Rather than include all cases contained in the Radford/FGCU database, we focus on the most deadly serial predators—those who killed at least four victims.

Figure 7.1 Serial Killers by Decade of First Murder

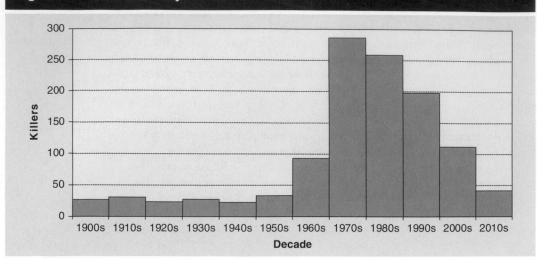

In addition, given the questionable reliability of data from cases outside the United States, we limit the analysis to those who stalked victims in the United States.

Figure 7.1 displays counts of serial killers operating in the United States whose first killing took place between 1900 and 2016 (members of serial killer teams are each counted as separate offenders). As shown, there were relatively few known cases during the first half of the twentieth century. The pattern emerging during the past few decades is radically different, however. The number of known serial killers grew rapidly from the 1960s into the 1980s. Following the 1970s peak, the number of cases declined somewhat in the 1980s, 1990s, and since 2000.

Although rapid growth into the 1970s and 1980s clearly suggests significant shifts in the prevalence of serial murder, these results are vulnerable, at least in part, to alternative explanations related to changes in data accessibility and quality of record keeping. As interest in serial murder increased, so did the likelihood that case histories would be published in some fashion. Additionally, as law enforcement became better equipped to identify linkages between victims slain by the same killer or killers, the detection of serial crimes and criminals became more likely. To some extent, therefore, the surge in serial murder may have been at least partially an artifact of increased reporting and improved detection. Notwithstanding these concerns, the trend in serial killings into the 1980s is quite consistent with a more general rise in violent crime, including homicide, in the United States as well as an increase in population size.

As the incidence and public awareness of serial murder grew through the 1980s, so did the sense of fear and panic. However, in recent decades the number of serial murderers has tapered off. Aside from mirroring the overall drop in homicide discussed in Chapter 2, a number of factors have contributed specifically to the decline in serial murder victimization, including the Amber Alert system, sex offender registries, GPS tracking, better insurance fraud detection, hospital death surveillance systems, DNA analysis, reduced prevalence of hitchhiking and broken-down cars on the road, and fewer free-range kids and more hovering parents.[11] These changes and technologies may also mean that some would-be serial offenders never killed anyone or killed only a few victims before being apprehended. Books such as Gavin de Becker's *The Gift of Fear* and the constant inundation of murder shows may have contributed to the decline by making people hypervigilant and less likely to take risks. Easy online access to hardcore pornography may also have given the sexually violent an alternative to acting out their fantasies on real victims.

Even though many technological advances have shielded potential victims from the clutches of serial killers, in certain ways technology may also make us more vulnerable. For example, social media such as Facebook and internet-based services such as Craigslist have been a boon for predators trolling online for victims. The convenience of online shopping also brings potential assailants to the homes of possible victims when packages are delivered. For example, using his part-time job at UPS to access records, 30-year-old Jason Thomas Scott murdered five women in Maryland, including two cases in which he killed both mother and daughter.

Whatever the reasons for the decline over the past couple of decades, the problem of serial murder remains a difficult and perplexing one for law enforcement and, of course, for the citizens concerned for their personal safety. Even with fewer than a dozen serial killers per year captured by the police plus an unknown number of others undetected or on the loose, the fear and suffering provoked by serial murderers is extraordinary, warranting an attempt to understand who these offenders are and why they kill.

CHARACTERISTICS OF SERIAL KILLERS

Much of what comprises "common knowledge" about serial killers is based on case studies of the most unusual and bizarre crimes as well as fictional accounts in books and film. For the longest time, there was little in the way of hard data on large numbers of cases to provide a reality check on the many widely held assumptions about the characteristics of serial killers, their crimes, and their victims. In recent years, however, several criminologists have assembled data sets on serial murder specifically to provide perspective. As mentioned, the most complete resource is the Radford/FGCU database.

In addition to focusing only on serial killers operating in the United States, for whom the data are more complete and reliable, we also limit our analysis to cases from the past several decades for the very same reason. Details on cases occurring long ago are rather difficult to obtain. Thus, the offender and victim characteristics to be provided in the tables to follow involve cases in the United States from the 1970s forward in which the assailant is confirmed to have murdered at least four victims spread over some period of time. Following these criteria, the Radford/FGCU database for the years 1970 through 2016 contains 897 offenders who were responsible for more than 4,600 killings (some of which are linked to two or more offenders acting as accomplices).

Determining the precise number of victims killed by these offenders is, unfortunately, next to impossible. Often, the full extent of their murder tolls can only be suspected, and the documented cases for which they are convicted or linked with a high degree of certainty may understate the extent of carnage. On the other hand, some offenders, grandiose in their self-image as killing machines, exaggerate their victim tallies as they boast to the press and even the police about how powerful and superior they are.

As shown in the top of Table 7.2, the 897 serial murderers fitting the stated criteria were implicated, on average, in 6.77 killings each over a span of nearly five years, with the 842 male assailants slightly deadlier than the 55 females (6.82 and 6.04 killings, respectively). Of course, the most notorious serial killers (e.g., Theodore Bundy, Gary Ridgway, and John Wayne Gacy, to name a few) can be linked to dozens of murders over much longer time frames. Since 1970 about 35% of serial killers had four victims, another 21% had five victims, and 12% had six victims. The remaining third had seven or more victims.[12]

In addition to these known serial killers, a number of unsolved cases across the nation continue to baffle investigators. Furthermore, despite recent advances

Table 7.2   Characteristics of Serial Killers, 1970–2016

Offender Characteristic	Offender Sex		Total
	Male	**Female**	**Total**
Number of cases	842	55	897
Average victim count	6.82	6.04	6.77
Average career length (yrs)	4.9	4.3	4.9
Killing rate (victims/yr)	5.3	5.6	5.3
Offender age at first kill			
Under 20	15.9%	9.1%	15.5%
20–29	51.7%	50.9%	51.7%
30–39	23.8%	27.3%	24.0%
40–49	7.2%	5.5%	7.1%
50+	1.3%	7.3%	1.7%
Total	100.0%	100.0%	100.0%
Average age	27.3	29.1	27.4
Offender race/ethnicity			
White	48.9%	72.7%	50.4%
Black	41.1%	18.2%	39.7%
Hispanic	8.0%	5.5%	7.8%
Asian	1.2%	3.6%	1.3%
Other	0.8%	0.0%	0.8%
Total	100.0%	100.0%	100.0%
Type of motive			
Profit	35.0%	40.0%	35.3%
Pleasure	44.0%	32.7%	43.3%

Offender Characteristic	Offender Sex		Total
	Male	Female	
Anger	12.3%	7.3%	12.0%
Other	8.8%	20.0%	9.5%
Total	100.0%	100.0%	100.0%
Scope of killing			
National	16.4%	14.5%	16.3%
Regional	12.7%	9.1%	12.5%
Local	70.9%	76.4%	71.2%
Total	100.0%	100.0%	100.0%

in technology and communication, law enforcement officials may still be unaware of the presence of many other serial killers. The unsolved or open cases and the undetected cases, taken together, could account for hundreds of additional victims.

Table 7.2 features information on the demographic and other key characteristics of serial killers, indicating that certain widely held beliefs about these assailants are not completely accurate. Overall, 93.9% of serial killers are male. The disproportionate involvement of males in serial homicide in part reflects, of course, their greater numbers in murder rates, generally. However, according to these statistics, the gender ratio among serial killers is slightly more pronounced than the 90% for murder overall, a finding that is consistent with the prevailing view among most researchers that almost all serial killers are men.

Even when the serial murders committed by women are heinous, cruel, and sexually predatory, the tendency is still to portray them as victims. Karla Homolka fully and willingly participated with her husband in the brutal rapes and murders of three girls, one of whom was her own younger sister, to satisfy her own sexual fantasies. Gwendolyn Graham and Catherine Wood, convicted of killing five elderly people in a nursing home (and suspected of as many as 10 deaths in total), used their murders as foreplay, sneaking away afterward into vacant rooms to have sex and discuss fondly their victims' dying moments. Aileen Wuornos, a Florida prostitute who murdered seven men, told the jurors during her trial that she hoped their daughters would be raped.

Dozens of women have murdered children, stepchildren, husbands, and parents for the benefit of collecting on their life insurance. Given the reluctance to label the most brutal female killers as serial predators, profiles of the female serial killers may be off the mark. Much more weight appears to be given to a female killer's past history of child and domestic abuse, portraying her as a victim, as mentally ill, and as not responsible for her actions.[13] Nevertheless, criminologists are beginning to recognize the existence of a female sexual predator. Women, like men, can develop deviant psychosexual needs. Women can only begin to achieve equality with men if their predatory, violent, and murderous behavior is acknowledged as a product of their free will to kill and be punished accordingly.

In terms of age, 51.7% of serial murderers started killing in their 20s and another 24.0% started in their 30s, with an average age of onset at about 27. Of course, most have killing careers that last years, and the average age at mid-career is 30 years old. It is not very common for a teenager to have acquired an insatiable taste for murder. It is equally uncommon for such a youthful offender to have developed the level of skill and cunning needed to carry out a prolonged career of killing without being caught after one or two murders or attempted murders. Typically, the toxic ingredients that create a serial killer take time to ferment.

Table 7.2 also shows that 50.4% of serial killers are white, less than the proportion of the population that is white and non-Hispanic (61.3%). The proportion of serial killers who are black (39.7%) is three times greater than their 13% representation in the general population but still below the substantial share (slightly more than half) of all homicides committed by blacks. However, at least historically, the involvement of black serial killers may have been understated. The percentage of serial killers who are black has increased with each successive decade, exceeding 50% among those who began killing since 2000 and nearing convergence with homicide in general.

Why were black serial killers overlooked for so long? In part, it was the serial killer stereotype, promulgated back in the 1980s by the FBI, of the white, middle-aged male with above-average intelligence. In addition, racism contributed to the greater media coverage of cases with white victims and a hesitancy to use the terms *monster* and *animal* when referring to black offenders. Moreover, serial killings of black victims, especially those who are impoverished and marginalized politically, are less likely to be connected, prioritized for investigation, and subsequently solved.

The delayed identification and apprehension of two recently captured serial murderers illustrate how the victims' race may play a role in how aggressively law enforcement responds. In both cases, moreover, many of the murdered women, living on the margins of society, were never reported as missing by anyone—examples of Quinet's "missing missing."

It took 25 years for Lonnie David Franklin Jr., a 57-year-old black male, to be arrested as the "Grim Sleeper" killer. Franklin's apprehension in July 2010 apparently closed the book on the unsolved murders of 10 black residents of Los Angeles. However, Franklin may not have been sleeping at all. Recently, the LAPD released 160 photos of unidentified women found in Franklin's possessions. Since the release of the photos, at least 20 women have been identified and are alive, but more than 100 of the photos have yet to be identified and may be additional victims of Franklin. Franklin was convicted of killing nine women, linked to at least 25 murders, and sentenced to death in 2016.

In October 2009, 51-year-old Anthony Sowell, also a black man, was convicted of 11 counts of murder after 10 bodies of black women and one human skull were discovered buried in the yard of his Cleveland, Ohio, home. Sowell was able to evade detection and arrest for years, despite the noticeable stench coming from the decaying remains. In addition to the 11 known victims, Sowell is also being investigated for several other missing person and unsolved homicides cases. Whatever the full extent of his crimes, Sowell remains on Ohio's death row.

Many other black serial killers, including Lorenzo Gilyard, John Floyd Thomas, and Chester Turner, were able to stay under the radar for lengthy periods of time because of the type of victims they targeted. The media focus far more attention on murdered or missing white females, which in turn impacts the level of pressure placed on the police to find the person responsible. This phenomenon, known as "the missing white woman syndrome," can certainly be seen in the extensive media coverage and law enforcement resources cases like Laci Peterson, Elizabeth Smart, Lauren Spierer, and Caylee Anthony received.[14]

The typical serial killer is someone like Hillside Strangler Kenneth Bianchi, who, along with his cousin Angelo Buono, raped, tortured, and murdered 10 young women in the Los Angeles area in the late 1970s. The Hillside Strangler moniker is quite telling. Although 40% of serial killers use a gun, that percentage is much lower than the 65% for murderers generally. When serial killers do employ guns, they often only use them initially for coercion and intimidation but then prefer a more hands-on method for the actual murder. Too easy, too clean, and much too distant, a gun would only rob the serial killer of his greatest pleasure: exalting in his victim's suffering.

Serial killers will often change their modus operandi (MO), or method of killing. They may change methods over time because they improve their techniques. Dennis Rader, the BTK Strangler, started out trying to strangle victims with leather shoe ties, but they broke so he then switched to stronger strangulation methods. Serial killers may also change their MO in response to actions taken by the victim or the presence of others nearby. Whereas they may prefer to strangle, a highly resistant victim could force them to use a firearm or another, more practical method. The serial killers may also change the MO in response to police investigations and media release of case details so as to make their crimes appear unconnected to one another. However, although they may alter their MO, the serial killers rarely change their signature—their personal sexual fantasies embedded into the crime scene. They may have a compulsion to display bodies in elaborate poses, insert foreign objects into the bodies, or cut, bite, or dismember the body. Analysis of U.S. serial killers active since 1970 finds 40% of serial killers raped their victims, 15% tortured their victims, and 4% engaged in cannibalism or necrophilia.[15]

It is well known that some serial killers keep totems, or souvenirs from their crimes. Joel Rifkin, for example, who in 1993 confessed to murdering 17 prostitutes in New York, kept his victims' underwear, shoes, sweaters, cosmetics, and jewelry in his bedroom. Jeffrey Dahmer, who was killed by a prison inmate in 1994, proudly displayed pictures of his victims on the walls of his apartment and kept body parts in his refrigerator. Missouri's Robert Berdella, a 40-year-old man who held captive six male sex slaves, had a particularly rich collection of souvenirs, including two human skulls and over 200 photographs of his victims in a variety of degrading poses before and after death, and with various vegetables inserted into their body cavities. He also chronicled his "human experiments" in a detailed diary of his tortures. But these cases may reflect the activities of a subset and a more Hollywood version of serial killers, as analysis of the Radford/FGCU data finds that only about 9% of serial killers kept some sort of memento.

A few serial killers feed their need to feel important and powerful by taunting the police and making the headlines. The self-named Zodiac Killer, who killed at least five people during the 1960s and 1970s in the San Francisco Bay area, sent several cryptic notes to newspapers. These notes contained a code that has never been broken, and the Zodiac case remains unsolved.

During the 1970s, a serial killer in Wichita, Kansas, phoned a local newspaper reporter directing him to a section of the public library where he located a letter claiming credit for the recent massacre of a local family. In his letter, the killer wrote: "The code words for me will be . . . Bind them, Torture them, Kill them." He signed the letter "BTK Strangler," for bind, torture, and kill. From that point on, the BTK moniker was commonly used by newspaper reporters in their articles about the killer's string of seven murders. In January 1978, BTK sent a poem to a reporter at the *Wichita Eagle-Beacon*, in which he wrote about a victim he had slain a year earlier. In February of the same year, BTK wrote a letter to a Wichita television station complaining about the lack of publicity he had received for his murders. "How many do I have to kill," BTK asked, "before I get my name in the paper or some national attention?" In addition, the killer compared his crimes with those of Jack the Ripper, Son of Sam, and the Hillside Strangler.

It was believed that BTK's killing spree had ended in 1991. Then, after more than 13 years, BTK surfaced once again to terrorize the Wichita community. In March 2004, he sent a letter to the Wichita newspaper in which he claimed credit for the unsolved death of Vicki Wegerle, who was killed in September 1986. As evidence of his complicity, BTK enclosed with his letter a photocopy of Wegerle's driver's license and photographs of her body.

BTK was again communicating with the police and the media. The killer's sudden reemergence indicated that he was feeling insecure about being out of the spotlight. He apparently hadn't taken anyone's life in several years and wasn't getting much attention from the public. When later asked about his hiatus, BTK said that he was too busy with his children's activities to have time for killing.

BTK turned out to be 59-year-old Dennis Rader, a church council president, former Cub Scout leader, and compliance officer who had terrorized the city of Wichita over three decades. Among the items that Rader sent to the media was a floppy disk, which, unknown to the killer, contained an electronic imprint that could be traced back to its source—a computer in the Christ Lutheran Church where he had served as president of the congregation. After learning that Rader had access to the church computer, police were able to gain access to Rader's daughter's DNA from Pap smear results performed at the local university clinic and link the DNA specimen to some of her father's crime scenes.

Because the state of Kansas had no death penalty at the time that Rader committed his crimes, he was able to escape execution. But on June 28, 2005, BTK was given the most severe sentence possible under Kansas law—10 consecutive life terms with no possibility of parole for 175 years.

Serial killers are often described as nomads, who roam from city to city, state to state preying on unsuspecting victims whom they encounter in their travels. Of course, pinpointing the geographic area in which serial killers operate can be somewhat challenging. They can have separate abduction, murder, and body dumping sites.[16] In addition, bodies dumped in one place, such as a river, can eventually be discovered somewhere far away. To complicate matters even further, a victim may be abducted and killed far from home (e.g., a prostitute who travels across the country), and the killer may live far from a kill site or dump site.

Notwithstanding the stereotypical drifter, most serial killers are fairly local in their pursuit of victims. Many have jobs, families, and various other responsibilities that would make it difficult to wander far and wide. In his analysis of U.S. male serial killers from 1975 to 2004, Hickey found that only 28% committed murders in more than one state, whereas 61% killed in a relatively limited area, and 11% murdered their victims all in the same location (e.g., their home or workplace). Female serial killers, according to Hickey's data, were even less likely to be nomadic.[17]

Our analysis of Radford/FGCU data revealed similar results. As shown in Table 7.2, 71.2% of serial killers are local, another 12.5% are regional, and only 16.3% are national serial killers. The location of serial killers by state typically mirrors the state populations; that is, larger states have more serial killers, and sparsely populated states have fewer. New Hampshire is frequently absent from lists of places trolled by serial killers, but recent developments in an unsolved string of murders have changed that. In January 2017, a Pennsylvania man known as Bob Evans, who had died several years earlier, was implicated in the murders of four people whose bodies were discovered stashed in barrels in a park in Allenstown, New Hampshire. Evans was somewhat of a chameleon, having used different aliases over the years. Besides linking him to the crimes, DNA analysis determined that Evans was the biological father of one of the four New Hampshire victims. As a final oddity surrounding the case, months later, DNA revealed Bob Evans's real name was Terry Peder Rasmussen.

VICTIMS OF SERIAL MURDER

Table 7.3 presents characteristics of victims slain by U.S. serial killers operating since 1970. As shown, nearly half (45.6%) of the victims are 20 to 39 years of age, most are white (64.1%), and, surprising to many students of serial murder, the primary method is gunshot (40.9%) followed by strangulation (28.4%).

One of the most striking dissimilarities between serial murder and criminal homicide generally is the nature of the offender–victim relationship. Unlike single-victim murder, which commonly arises from some dispute between partners, family members, or friends, serial murder is typically a stranger-perpetrated crime.[18] Specifically, as shown in Table 7.3, 64.2% of serial murder victims were

Table 7.3 Characteristics Victims of Serial Killers, 1970–2016

Victim Characteristic	Victim Sex		Total
	Male	Female	
Number of cases	1,953	2,647	4,600
Victim age			
Under 5	4.5%	2.0%	3.0%
5–19	18.6%	24.0%	21.8%
20–29	25.6%	30.0%	28.2%
30–39	17.1%	17.5%	17.3%
40–49	10.9%	9.6%	10.1%
50–59	8.8%	5.2%	6.7%
60+	14.5%	11.8%	12.9%
Total	100.0%	100.0%	100.0%
Victim race/ethnicity			
White	59.7%	67.2%	64.1%
Black	26.6%	25.4%	25.9%

(*Continued*)

Table 7.3 (Continued)

Victim Characteristic	Victim Sex		Total
	Male	Female	
Hispanic	10.3%	5.5%	7.5%
Asian	3.2%	1.4%	2.1%
Other	0.2%	0.6%	0.4%
Total	100.0%	100.0%	100.0%
Method by which killed			
Bludgeoned	5.8%	8.8%	7.5%
Poisoning	6.7%	3.3%	4.8%
Gunshot	57.2%	27.9%	40.9%
Stabbed	11.4%	14.5%	13.1%
Strangled	14.0%	39.9%	28.4%
Smothered	2.6%	2.5%	2.5%
Other	2.2%	3.2%	2.7%
Total	100.0%	100.0%	100.0%
Relationship to offender			
Family	5.1%	5.0%	5.0%
Acquaintance	42.6%	22.3%	30.8%
Strangers	52.4%	72.8%	64.2%
Total	100.0%	100.0%	100.0%

strangers to their offender. To some extent, the abundance of stranger victims reflects the predatory patterns of these killers as well as the greater ease with which stranger attackers can escape apprehension and, therefore, be free to amass a large tally of kills.

The gender characteristics of serial killer victims are quite different from those of homicide victims generally, as were described in Chapter 2. Given the strong sexual element in the motivations of many male serial murderers, their victims tend to be female—fully 67%. Despite the greater number of females slain, moreover, some serial killers are gay or bisexual and purposely target male victims for rape and murder.

Although some serial killers have targeted coeds, they are much more likely to prey on particularly vulnerable individuals—runaways, prostitutes, homeless people, or patients in nursing homes and hospitals. Serial killers rarely choose professional athletes, bodybuilders, or National Rifle Association (NRA) conventioneers as their victims. Some research in serial murder has suggested that the victim actually has a symbolic value for the killer; for example, Ted Bundy may have selected women who physically resembled a girlfriend who had dumped him. The problem with this line of reasoning is that so many of the women in high schools and colleges in the 1970s looked like his victims. It was popular to wear long, straight hair parted down the middle. Rather than a Norman Bates–like complex regarding their mothers or their girlfriends, serial killers more likely choose women in general because of their heterosexuality and the inability of most of them to defend themselves.

The marginality of prostitutes, drug addicts, and runaways gives the killer a special advantage. It may take considerable time for someone to report her as missing and even longer to recognize that a woman has become a victim of homicide. By the time the police locate a body, they are typically left with skeletal remains—no DNA, fingerprints, fiber, or hair from the killer. Indeed, they are lucky to be able to identify the victim, let alone the killer. In November 2003, Gary Leon Ridgway, the Green River Killer, in a plea bargain to avoid the death penalty, admitted to killing more than 49 prostitutes in the Seattle area over a 16-year period. In his statement, Ridgway said he targeted prostitutes "because I thought I could kill as many as I wanted without getting caught." According to the serial killer, "they were easy to pick up without being noticed" and "they would not be reported missing right away, and might never be reported missing." Most serial killers who prey on prostitutes do so because they are accessible and easier to dehumanize. Still, some repeat killers clearly hate women and especially detest prostitutes. Both Green River Killer Gary Leon Ridgway and John Eric Armstrong, for example, claimed to have loathed prostitutes. By choosing a vulnerable, transient victim pool, they expected their crimes would go unnoticed and, at the same time, would exact revenge against the gender that had rejected them in the past. When Robert Charles Brown, 52, was apprehended by the state of Colorado in 2006, he claimed his murders were triggered by his disgust for women and their lack of morality. Brown likely murdered as many as 48 women across nine states and two countries beginning when he was a 17-year-old medic in the U.S. Army stationed in Korea. He was successful for so long because, like many other serial killers, he had a lot of different jobs over the years that required travel; basically he was always a drifter. The son of a sheriff's deputy, Brown was characterized as a handsome, bright loner. One of his favorite pastimes was to wear a Halloween mask, with which he delighted in scaring women and children outside their homes. Ironically, Brown was born on Halloween in 1952.

In addition to their lack of a prior relationship with their assailants, serial murder victims also tend to share one important trait—their vulnerability. Although virtually anyone can be targeted, serial killers tend to prefer vulnerable victims, and this victim preference reflects the relative ease with which the offenders can abduct and slay certain targets. Pedophile Wesley Allen Dodd of Washington State encountered little difficulty in snatching children from parks and other public spaces. Arthur Shawcross made a habit of trolling Rochester's red-light district, not needing even an ounce of force to find sex workers willing to enter his web of control.

Like the serial killers who prey on them, at least through the decade of the 1990s, victims also tended to be white. Given the increasing detection of black serial killers and the intraracial nature of homicide, blacks are more likely than ever to be targeted. The age range of victims is quite broad, reflecting the disparate classes of favored victims. Perhaps most widely known are those serial killers who target prostitutes in their 20s and 30s. But some serial killers have targeted infants, as in the case of Texas nurse Genene Jones, while others such as Orville Majors of Indiana, have targeted primarily elderly hospital patients.

KILLING TOGETHER

Like Kenneth Bianchi and his favorite cousin and killing partner, Angelo Buono, many serial killers have accomplices. Nearly one-third of the male killers and about half of female killers in the Radford/FGCU database operated in teams of two or more (although this figure is naturally elevated because of the multiple counting of those who are part of a team).[19] The most common male serial killing team is comprised of two or three males, whereas when a woman is part of a team she is typically operating with a male. These male–female partnerships make up a small proportion (4%) of all teams. It is the two or more males working together that can create unimaginable horror. The folie à deux effect, otherwise known as the madness of two, suggests that one psychotic person can create psychosis in another. Although in many cases of folie à deux, two people may just think there are people living in the trees in their yard or they may begin planning against alien invasions, for serial killer teams, the notion is more about sadistic murder than sheer madness. They encourage each other to do the wrong thing and are more likely to torture their victims than are their counterparts who operate alone. For Lawrence Bittaker and Roy Norris, for instance, killing was a team sport. They called it the "birthday game," seeking to kill teenage girls of different ages (13, 14, 15, etc.), like trophies. Bittaker and Norris preferred blondes and tortured them in their specially equipped van, which they called "Murder Mac." The pair tape-recorded the torture sessions so they could relive them later in their spare time. Chapter 12 on cults suggests that shared madness can transfer from one charismatic leader to hundreds, even thousands of people.

Serial killer teams sometimes involve family members—spouses such as Karla Homolka and Paul Bernardo, cousins like Bianchi and Buono, and father–son pairs like the Kallingers. Joseph Kallinger, dubbed the "The Shoemaker," recruited his 13-year-old son, Michael, in a series of brutal home invasion robberies, sexual assaults, and murders. Joseph, who had experienced horrible abuse as a child and was beaten by his adoptive parents, had a long history of sexual assaults, arsons, and mental illness before he became a father. The father and son team brutalized a number of victims in several different families across three states, and three of the victims died as a result. The earlier death of one of his other sons was also later linked to Joseph. A cobbler by trade and diagnosed with paranoid schizophrenia, Joseph Kallinger was convicted and died in prison years later. Because his son was thought to have been under the control of his violent and twisted parent, Michael was held in a juvenile facility until he turned 21 and was then released.

Some of the more fascinating partnerships include men and women. Ray, 76, and Faye Copeland, 69, looking like the couple in the famous *American Gothic* painting, were the oldest couple ever sentenced to death in the United States. Ray had a long cross-country history of scams, swindles, and cons and by 1986 decided that the best way to silence the drifters and hitchhikers he had recruited to write bad checks for his cattle purchases was to kill them. Five men were killed by the Copelands before their apprehension in 1989. Faye was thought to have been a victim of her domineering husband. But when the jury saw the quilt she had made from the dead men's clothing, she also was convicted and sentenced to death. Ray died in prison in Missouri before he could be executed, while Faye, after suffering a stroke, was paroled to a nursing home, where she died a year later.

Although the Copelands' motive was financial, the most common male–female teams have a sexual motive. Doug Clark, the so-called Los Angeles Sunset Strip Killer, did the murdering and decapitating, while his girlfriend, Carol Bundy (no relation to Theodore), assisted. She even prepared the severed heads of victims for him to use as sex objects in the shower. She would do anything for her guy and for the sake of their love.

BEYOND U.S. BORDERS

It is hard to deny that the vast majority of ultra-notorious serial killers—the ones who have become household names (at least in American households)—are from the United States. Serial killers like Ted Bundy and Jeffrey Dahmer are as famous as the Hollywood actors who played them in films. Despite our focus here on patterns of serial murder in the United States, there are certainly many major cases occurring elsewhere around the globe. They simply do not receive the same level of attention in the media, at least not the American media.

Known as the Werewolf of Russia, former police officer Mikhail Popkov, 52, was convicted of 22 murders but recently admitted to killing more than 80 people. If true, Popkov's tally of victims would be third to Colombia's Luis Garavito (138 victims) and Pedro López (110 victims). Active for at least 20 years, Popkov, while in uniform, was able to lure often intoxicated victims into his police car, purportedly for rides home.[20] Although most of his victims were women leaving nightclubs and restaurants, Popkov thought of them all as prostitutes and claimed he was trying the cleanse the street of sex workers. Another Russian serial killer, Alexander Pichushkin, 43, who was called the Chessboard Killer, murdered at least 49 mostly homeless men and women from the 1990s until he was caught in 2006. His goal was to kill 64 people, one for each square on the chessboard.

Like the ploy used by John Wayne Gacy in Des Plaines, Illinois, Colombian Luis Garavito was able to attract and control young boys by offering them employment. Beginning in 1992, young males ranging in age from 6 to 16, many of them homeless street kids, were disappearing without a trace. But with the country steeped in political unrest, rather few of the disappearances resulted in missing person reports. After mass graves were discovered in 1999, an investigation led the authorities to Garavito's doorstep. Garavito was definitively linked to as many as 138 victims, but may have raped, mutilated, and killed more than 300. Nicknamed "The Beast," Garavito was convicted and sentenced to 1,853 years in prison.

A very different fate became of Pedro López, another Colombian citizen, who killed women and girls in the 1970s in Colombia, Ecuador, and Peru. Although convicted of 100 murders in Ecuador, he was released from prison and deported to his home country. In 1998, after a few years in a psychiatric facility, López was released on good behavior. As of this writing, his whereabouts are unknown.

Justice came swiftly for China's Yang Xinhai after he confessed to 67 murders and an additional 23 rapes from 1999 until 2003. Following his release from prison on an attempted rape conviction, Yang was dumped by his new girlfriend when she learned about his past. At that point, Yang turned from rape to murder. Breaking into the homes of unsuspecting families, he viciously bludgeoned his victims with axes, shovels, and hammers. Yang was convicted on murder charges on February 1, 2004, and was executed 2 weeks later.

South Africa's most prolific serial killer, Moses Sithole, was convicted of committing 38 murders in less than a 2-year time span, although he claimed to have actually killed twice that number. Released from prison in 1994 after serving several years on a rape conviction, Sithole began killing almost immediately. His access to victims came easily through his job at an agency designed to fight child abuse. He abducted women who came to interview for positions at the children's homes, and then beat, raped, and strangled them. He then scrawled the word *bitch* on their dead bodies before dumping them. Sithole was captured in 1995 and sentenced to a total of 2,410 years for the 38 murders and 40 additional rapes.

Using the full range of cases in the Radford/FGCU database (i.e., all repeat killers since the 15th century from around the globe), Aamodt found that over half the world's serial killers were located in the United States. In part, this is a function of population size. The United States is nearly three times the population of Japan and two times the population size of Russia, but it has 30 times the serial killers of Japan and 39 times the serial killers of Russia. Moreover, despite exceptionally large populations in India and China, Aamodt reports only 63 known Indian serial killers and 41 from China. However, rarely do serial killer scholars recruit translators for the world's non-English newspapers, and thus language barriers may explain the lack of information about serial killers in some parts of the world. It may also be possible that cultural differences make it less likely that serial killers in some other parts of the world will be featured and glorified in the mass media.

There are certainly other reasons why there is a disproportionate number of known serial killers in the United States. These include better law enforcement investigation techniques, better crime reporting by law enforcement, better reporting by media and the sheer number of media outlets, freedom of the press, and the freedom to move from one place to another (mobility). If bad childhoods play a role in the development of serial killers, there is no evidence that U.S. parenting is worse than parenting in China, Russia, or India.

THE MURDERING MIND

Many people assume that anyone who kills for fun, pleasure, or sport must be psychotic and out of touch with reality. Indeed, some serial killers have been driven by severe mental illness, such as Herbert Mullin of Santa Cruz, California, who killed 13 people in a span of 4 months in order to avert an earthquake—or at least that's what the voices told him.[21]

However, based on his analysis of more than 100 offenders, Godwin found little evidence that serial killers suffer from profound mental disorders. Only 28% of the murderers in his sample had a history of receiving any kind of treatment for mental illness; even fewer (20%) had a history of being treated for alcoholism or drug abuse. Most serial murderers are not insane in a legal sense or psychotic in a medical sense. Although they know right from wrong, know exactly what they are doing, and can control their desire to kill, they typically choose not to do so. Even the serial killers who remember childhood abuse, experience hallucinations, and "discover" multiple personalities at trial time may be suffering from mental disorders manufactured to support an attempted insanity plea as a last resort.

Psychologically, most serial killers are sociopaths (or antisocial personality types), a condition that was discussed in Chapter 3. They possess a disorder of character rather than of the mind, involving a lack of conscience and feelings of remorse, an inability to feel empathy for others, pathological lying, a manipulative style, impulsivity, and a total concern for maximizing their own pleasures in life.[22] Other people are seen merely as tools for fulfilling their own needs and desires, no matter how perverse or reprehensible. The serial killer is more bad than mad—simply put, he is evil.

Serial killers have often been characterized as suffering from low self-esteem. Although some killers are undoubtedly motivated by feelings of inadequacy, the relationship between low self-esteem and violence has little empirical support. Rather, anecdotal evidence suggests that many serial killers (including the medical murderers described in Chapter 8) may suffer from narcissism or "self-love." They have a very inflated sense of themselves and demand that the rest of the world recognize their greatness. They have a godlike complex and believe that the society's rules simply do not apply to them.[23] Whereas therapy and medication can help and even cure attention-deficit disorders, depression, anxiety, and obsessive-compulsive disorders, personality disorders are fairly intransigent. People suffering from antisocial, histrionic, and narcissistic personality disorders often fail to acknowledge that they even have a problem. Confronting the nurse who is murdering her patients, the Munchausen mom drawing attention to herself, or the boss who thrives on the misery and humiliation he causes in his employees rarely results in a confession or any insights about their behavior.

As noted, for many serial killers, murder makes them feel superior and feel good about themselves, as though they have actually achieved something important. Robert Berdella's collection of souvenirs served several important purposes. First, for a man who had otherwise led an unremarkable life, his treasures made him feel accomplished. They represented the one and only way in which he had ever distinguished himself "as a real pro." More important, the souvenirs became tangible reminders of the "good times" Berdella had spent with his "playmates." With the aid of his photographs, he could still get pleasure, even between captives, from reminiscing, daydreaming, fantasizing, and masturbating. In fact, serial killers have lasting memories as well as incredibly vivid and elaborate fantasies. Through murder and mayhem, they literally chase their dreams.[24]

Even though serial killers tend to be sociopaths, totally lacking in concern for their victims, some actually do have a conscience and the capacity for remorse but are able to neutralize or negate their feelings of guilt. There is a powerful psychological process—known as dehumanization—that allows many serial killers to slaughter scores of innocent people by viewing them as worthless and, therefore, expendable. By targeting marginalized groups—prostitutes, the homeless, runaways—they can rationalize (if they need to for their own sense of emotional comfort) that they are doing something good for society . . . or at least nothing that bad.

Jeffrey Dahmer actually viewed his crimes as a sign of love and affection. He told Tracy Edwards, his final victim, who managed to escape and led the police to Dahmer's apartment of horrors, that if he played his cards right, he, too, could give his heart to Jeff. He meant it literally of course, but, according to Edwards, he said it in an affectionate, not a threatening, manner. In a strange turn of events, Edwards, once the hero who helped catch Dahmer, was charged in relation to a drowning death in 2011.

Many serial killers skillfully compartmentalize the world into two groups—those whom they care about and everyone else. Kenneth Bianchi, for example, could be kind and loving to his wife and child as well as his mother and friends, yet be vicious and cruel to those he considered expendable. He and his cousin started with prostitutes, choosing victims for whom they had very little concern. Later, when comfortable with killing, he branched out to middle-class, more respectable targets. Angelo Buono died in prison of a heart attack in 2002, while Bianchi, having been denied parole multiple times, resides at Walla Walla State Penitentiary in Washington, awaiting his next hearing, which is not scheduled until 2025.

According to Stephen Giannangelo, serial killers are also eased into their murderous avocation by the clumsiness and impulsivity of their first kill.[25] He likens the first murder to the sexually inexperienced teenager who fumbles in the backseat of a car as he attempts to have sex with his date. For a serial killer, what might begin as a rape or an assault is transformed, in the excitement of the moment, into an act of homicide. Almost inadvertently, the killer crosses the threshold separating fantasy from fact. Whatever shame he may feel for having committed a serious offense is completely overshadowed by the "rush" that he acquires from finally discovering what he needs.

In addition to sociopathy, another critical ingredient to the profile of many serial killers is a strong tendency toward sexual sadism. More generally, these men have a craving for power and control. They tie up their victims in order to watch them squirm and torture their victims to hear them scream. They rape, sodomize, degrade, bludgeon, and mutilate their victims in order to feel powerful, dominant, and superior. One of Lawrence Bittaker's victims pleaded, "Please, if you're going to kill me, tell me so that I can pray first." Bittaker was exhilarated by his victim's begging. He assured her that she would not die and then slammed an ice pick in her ear. He just loved the control.

The sexual sadist derives intense pleasure through the pain, suffering, and humiliation of another person. In a pure sense, sexual sadists enjoy the act of inflicting pain on another, a nonconsenting victim. Yet the pleasure may also flow from the result—the screams and degradation of the recipient—rather than from just the act itself. Sexual sadists can also relish vicariously when another person (an accomplice or even an actor in a film) causes a victim to suffer. Thus, not only can a pair or team of serial killers enjoy personal satisfaction from raping and torturing a victim, but also their feeling of superiority can be enhanced by the power of the partnership.

The essence of the sadistic drive lies in the desire to achieve total domination and mastery over another person. From this point of view, the pleasure derived from killing depends, at least in part, on the sadist's role in having caused the victim to suffer. An alternative argument holds that the sexual or psychological pleasure that a sadistic killer derives from the act of torturing his victim may be more a result of observing the victim's agony than from the actual infliction of pain. This hypothesis appears to be supported by experimental research in which aggressive sex offenders become sexually aroused when shown simulated scenes of men inflicting pain on women.[26]

This begs the question, however, of whether the arousal stems from observing the victim's suffering or from identifying vicariously with the aggressor. Regardless of whether the critical component is the stimulus (the direct infliction of pain) or the response (the victim's suffering itself), the fundamental objective in the actions of the sadistic serial killer is to achieve complete mastery over his victims. In other words, humiliation, enslavement, and terror are vehicles for attaining total domination over another human being.

Power and control may be critical themes in the character of serial murderers, yet these traits are also common in many successful people in the worlds of business, politics, and even academics. The willingness to win at all costs, no matter who is hurt in the process, may insulate many winning individuals from looking back at those they exploit along the road to success. A vital difference between serial killers and those who backstab only figuratively may be access to legitimate opportunity.

At the same time, the sadistic sexual fantasies of the serial killer may also reflect his search for power. It appears that many serial murderers, from an early age, become absorbed deeply in a rich fantasy life involving images of sex and violence. As they mature into adolescence, their fantasies become more and more consuming, increasing in their power as internal drive mechanisms that motivate them to cross the line into murderous behavior.

Robert Prentky and his colleagues compared the nature and prevalence of sexual fantasy between groups of sexually motivated serial killers and single-victim murderers also with sexual motivation to their crimes. Self-report interview data showed the serial murderers were more apt to describe a strong and intrusive fantasy life involving violent themes and paraphilias.[27]

Paraphilias—unusual sexual attractions or practices—are common among sexually motivated serial killers. Rather than just a relatively harmless fetish (e.g., an attraction to nonhuman objects such as feces or shoes), some serial killers exhibit far more serious passions, including cannibalism, pedophilia, necrophilia, and, especially, erotophonophilia (i.e., becoming sexually aroused from mutilation and murder, or at least fantasizing about it).

The BTK Strangler, Dennis Rader, admitted to investigators that his attraction to violence and death began early in life. He recalled that at the age of 8 he would get aroused watching his grandmother kill chickens by strangling them with a leather shoestring. He also admitted to shoplifting issues of *True Detective* magazine as a kid. Rader had rich fantasies involving images of bondage and sexual violence. Even in high school, he wasn't sexually excited about girls unless he imagined tying them up.

Courts rarely view paraphilias as being beyond the perpetrator's control or a legitimate excuse for murder. For example, Jeffrey Dahmer's plea of insanity based on his necrophiliac and cannibalistic desires was rejected at his Wisconsin trial.

Not all children who fantasize about sadistic forms of violence grow up to be serial killers. The fact that most serial murderers do not initiate their murder sprees until well into their adult years indicates the important role of adult experiences—failures in relationships and at work—in the making of a serial killer. Many individuals who have suffered profoundly as children grow into healthy and nonviolent adults. They benefit later from positive experiences with peers, romantic partners, and coworkers who give them the support and encouragement that they lacked when they were young.

This was unfortunately not true of Danny Rolling, who turned to murder at the age of 36, killing three in his hometown of Shreveport, Louisiana, and five more in Gainesville, Florida. Not only had Rolling been the victim of an abusive parent, but also his adjustment and personal problems continued through adolescence into early adulthood. A brief marriage ended in divorce, his adult relationship with his parents continued to be severely strained, and he couldn't manage to hold a job. Instead, he drifted first from job to job, next from state to state, then from prison to prison, and finally from murder to murder.

Amazingly, given the abuse and horror in many of their childhoods, serial killers rarely kill themselves. Their own suffering is not internalized but rather externalized—they blame others. Occasionally, a serial killer will attempt suicide. Gary Heidnik, for example, tried to take his own life 13 times, and murdering nurse Charles Cullen also had multiple suicide attempts throughout his life. How can someone who is so skilled at killing others be so inadequate at killing himself? Clearly, the answer is that neither Heidnik nor Cullen truly wanted to die.

Herbert Baumeister, an exception to the rule, committed suicide in 1996, but only after the discovery of thousands of bone and teeth fragments on his family's estate in Westfield, Indiana. Although only 8 of Baumeister's victims were positively identified, the fragments were of at least 11 bodies. A father, husband, and businessman, he may have also been the so-called I-70 Killer who operated during the late 1980s, as work often took Baumeister from Indiana to Ohio over this highway. Baumeister's victims were gay men whom he had picked up in bars in Indianapolis. This case is also an example of how serial killers can remain undetected and uninvestigated for so long when their victim pool is a marginalized group. It is unlikely that Baumeister's murderous career would have been as lengthy had he elected to slay college students or other middle-class victims.

EXPLANATIONS FOR SERIAL MURDER

Isolating those factors that encourage someone to kill repeatedly has been the focus of a large body of research dating back many years. The ingredients in the metaphorical toxic soup include a combination of biological, psychological, social, and cultural factors that simmer inside the developing individual for decades until they boil over in the form of relentless and hideous brutality.

Whenever the case of an infamous serial killer is uncovered, be it a cannibalistic sadist or a not-so-merciful mercy killer, journalists and behavioral scientists alike tend to search for clues deep within the killer's biography that might explain his or her seemingly senseless or excessively brutal murders. Many writers, for example, have emphasized Theodore Bundy's concerns over having been born "illegitimate," and biographers of Hillside Strangler Kenneth Bianchi capitalized on his having been an adopted child.

Biological Factors

Researchers are not of one mind, however, in explaining what produces the psyche of the serial murderer. Some stress genetic or biological factors in accounting for such defects as sociopathy. Moffitt and Henry suggest, for example, that damage to the right hemisphere of the brain may be responsible for losses of "social sensibilities," including lack of empathy and difficulties with bonding.[28] Some neurologists and psychiatrists have suggested that many killers—especially killers who commit senseless acts of brutality—have incurred severe injury to the limbic region of the brain as a result of profound or repeated head trauma, generally during childhood. Dorothy Otnow Lewis and colleagues, for example, examined 15 murderers on Florida's death row and found that all showed signs of neurological irregularities.[29]

Recent research finds that a significant proportion of multiple murderers may have various neurodevelopmental disorders, including autism spectrum disorders (ASD) and head injury.[30] Obviously, most people with some form of autism never harm anyone, and some studies suggest people with autism are less likely to be aggressive or violent. However, a condition that has been called "criminal autistic psychopathy" reflects a particularly virulent form of Asperger's syndrome.[31] Several serial killers, including Danny Rolling and Andrei Chikatilo, had suffered significant head injuries as children (and sometimes additional head injuries as adults), and a number of serial killers had possible or probable autism, including Jeffrey Dahmer, Robert Berdella, and Keith Jesperson. For a few killers, there were indications of both autism and head injury.

Significant scientific progress has been made regarding the possible links between various neurobiological factors and violent behavior. A 2017 study of the development and current state of scientific knowledge about possible biological factors as pathways to serial murder has identified a number of different risk factors, including head trauma, brain damage and dysfunction, serotonin/adrenaline dysfunction, ASD, various childhood illnesses, in utero exposure to toxins, and birth complications.[32] Of course, none of these factors are present in the histories of all or even most serial killers. It is likely that these biologically based risk factors become associated with violence only in certain social contexts when combined with other psychological and social predisposers.

There is compelling reason to believe that traumatic brain injuries resulting from severe head trauma can potentially have dire effects on behavior, including violent outbursts, learning disabilities, and epilepsy. Henry Lee Lucas was reportedly beaten by his mother with lumber and broom handles. He later claimed to have experienced frequent dizzy spells and blackouts. Bobby Joe Long, who was convicted of a total of nine counts of murder, also appears to have endured several severe head injuries. In three different episodes, at the age of 5 or 6, Long fell off a swing, from a horse, and off his bicycle, suffering repeated brain concussions in the process.

There are important possible causal order problems with theories that connect brain damage and violent behavior. If the individual is a thrill seeker and engages in dangerous pastimes (e.g., reckless driving), then the same set of personality traits may also lead to head injuries. In the presence of other negative social contexts (e.g., physical and sexual abuse, substance use and abuse), the same thrill-seeking need may act as a predisposing factor to violence. Thus, in some cases, head injuries may be a result of aggressive and violent behavior rather than their cause.

Childhood Factors

While considerable attention has been paid to biological and neurological factors, other investigators point instead to early childhood experiences and repeated psychological trauma during development, such as insufficient bonding of the child to his parents as well as physical and psychological abuse. Children who are abused, neglected, or abandoned tend to grow into needy adults who have difficulty bonding with others, a so-called attachment disorder. Lacking control over their own lives as children, many remain insecure as they mature, continuing to possess an intense need to control their social environment. From an early age, they are unable to trust others and instead learn to manipulate people in order to fulfill their needs.

There is a long tradition of research on the childhood correlates of homicidal proneness. For example, John Macdonald long ago hypothesized a triad of symptoms—bed-wetting, fire setting, and cruelty to animals—which he viewed as reactions to parental rejection, neglect, or brutality.[33] Although the so-called Macdonald's triad was later refuted in controlled studies, and bed-wetting and fire setting appear to have no causal link with future violent behavior, the connection between animal cruelty and subsequent violent behavior remains a continuing focus of investigation.

A number of studies in the years since Macdonald's work have purported to support the hypothesis that violent individuals are also abusive toward animals.[34] For example, Kellert and Felthous found significantly more childhood animal cruelty among aggressive criminals than among either nonaggressive criminals or noncriminals.[35] Moreover, tracking the criminal records of 153 animal abusers compared with 153 nonabusers, sociologist Arnold Arluke and colleagues determined that the animal abusers were five times more likely to commit acts of human violence, including murder, rape, and assault.[36]

As described in the case studies of Steven Egger's *The Killers Among Us*, serial murderers don't just abuse animals but also torture and dissect them.[37] Egger's description of serial killer Jerry Marcus notes how the killer set pregnant cats on fire and poured hot water on hungry dogs and, after these sadistic acts, felt exhilarated and proud. Jeffrey Dahmer started his killing spree on neighborhood pets when he was a child. He had a pet cemetery and a long history of animal decapitation and vivisection. It appears that much more attention should be given to those who abuse animals, as there is ample evidence that in many cases, the "animals" just get bigger.

People of any age who derive pleasure from the suffering of living creatures may come to have a long future of child abuse, partner violence, rape, or murder. Of course, countless youngsters experiment with abusing animals, including birds, reptiles, and rodents, yet outgrow their morbid fascination to become decent, well-adjusted adults. Serial killers are qualitatively different, however. As children, they may have tortured dogs and cats—animals that are loved by others as pets—in a hands-on sadistic manner, long before shifting to human prey.[38]

It is often suggested that because of deep-rooted problems stemming from childhood, serial killers suffer from a profound sense of powerlessness, which they compensate for through extreme forms of aggression to exert control over others. But many people who suffer from a feeling of powerlessness go on to help others avoid this experience and work as volunteers, advocates, and philanthropists. The biographies of many serial killers reveal significant physical and psychological trauma at an early age. Based on in-depth interviews with 36 incarcerated murderers, Ressler and his colleagues found evidence of psychological abuse (e.g., public humiliation) in 23 cases and physical trauma in 13 cases.[39] Eric Hickey reported that among a group of 62 male serial killers, 48% had been rejected as children by a parent or some other important person in their lives.[40] Of course, these same types of experiences can be found in the biographies of many "normal" people as well. More specifically, although useful for characterizing the backgrounds of serial killers, the findings presented by Ressler and Hickey lack a comparison group drawn from nonoffending populations for which the same definitions of trauma have been applied.

Although many serial killers do have horrific childhoods, they are also very manipulative and may exploit the "child abuse syndrome" to their own advantage in an effort to receive a sympathetic ear. As a sociopath, the serial killer is a particularly convincing and accomplished liar. As a professional trained to be supportive and empathic, his psychiatrist may be easily conned. The case histories of such malingerers as Kenneth Bianchi and Arthur Shawcross, both serial killers who fooled mental health professionals with fabricated tales of child abuse, remind us to be skeptical about the self-serving testimony of accused killers eager to escape legal responsibility for their crimes.

As a related matter, more than a few serial killers—from David Berkowitz to Joel Rifkin—were raised by adoptive parents. In the "adopted child syndrome," an individual displaces his anger for birth parents onto adoptive parents as well as other authority figures. According to Kirschner, the syndrome is often expressed, early in life, in "provocative antisocial behavior" including fire setting, truancy, promiscuity, pathological lying, and stealing.[41]

The apparent overrepresentation of adoption in the biographies of serial killers has been exploited by those who are looking for simple explanations for heinous and senseless crimes. In reality, the way in which this link operates has not been completely explained. That is, possible triggering mechanisms might include the effects of rejection by birth parents, maternal deprivation during the critical first few months of life, poor prenatal care by the birth mother, or genetic deficiencies passed on from one or both biological parents.

It is often said that "hindsight is 20/20." This is definitely true in terms of explaining serial murder. Following the apprehension of a serial killer, we generally hear mixed reports that "he seemed like a nice guy, but there was something about him that wasn't quite right." Of course, there is something about most people that "isn't quite right." However, when such a person is exposed to be a serial murderer, we tend to focus on the red flags in his character and biography that were ignored. Even the stench emanating from Jeffrey Dahmer's apartment, which he explained to the neighbors as the odor of spoiled meat inside his broken freezer, was unexceptional until after the fact.

The methodological problems of predicting violence in advance are well known. For a category of violence as rare as serial murder, the low base rate and consequent false-positive dilemma are overwhelming. Simply put, there are thousands of white males in their late 20s or 30s who are sadistic, thirst for power, lack strong internal controls, tortured animals as children, and were adopted or abused, but the vast majority of them will never kill anyone. Although we might be able, after the fact, to explain why someone became a serial killer, we cannot predict in advance who will become one in the future. The best we can usually do is retrospective postdiction, looking back and seeing how all the risk factors come together.[42]

ENDNOTES

1. Robert K. Ressler, John E. Douglas, Ann W. Burgess, and Allen G. Burgess, *Crime Classification Manual* (Lexington, MA: Lexington Books, 1992).

2. Federal Bureau of Investigation, *Serial Murder: Multi-Disciplinary Perspectives for Investigators* (Washington, DC: Behavioral Analysis Unit, National Center for the Analysis of Violent Crime, U.S. Department of Justice, 2008).

3. Emma E. Fridel and James Alan Fox, "Too Few Victims: Finding the Optimal Minimum Victim Threshold for Defining Serial Murder," *Psychology and Violence*, 2017, doi:10.1037/vio0000138.

4. Janet Warren, Roy R. Hazelwood, and Park E. Dietz, "The Sexually Sadistic Serial Killer," in Thomas O'Reilly-Fleming, ed., *Serial and Mass Murder: Theory, Research and Policy* (Toronto: Canadian Scholars' Press, 1996).

5. James Alan Fox, Jack Levin, and Emma E. Fridel, *Extreme Killing: Understanding Serial and Mass Murder*, 4th ed. (Thousand Oaks, CA: Sage, 2018).

6. Grover Maurice Godwin, *Hunting Serial Predators: A Multivariate Classification Approach to Profiling Violent Behavior* (Boca Raton, FL: CRC Press, 1999).

7. Michael G. Aamodt, personal correspondence, July 30, 2017.

8. Kenna Kiger, "The Darker Figure of Crime: The Serial Murder Enigma," in Steven A. Egger, ed., *Serial Murder: An Elusive Phenomenon* (New York: Praeger, 1990).

9. Kenna Quinet, "The Missing Missing: Toward a Quantification of Serial Murder Victimization in the United States," *Homicide Studies* 11 (2007): 319–339.

10. Michael G. Aamodt, Radford/FGCU Serial Killer Database—2017, Radford, VA: Radford University.

11. Michael G. Aamodt and Michael A. Surette, "Is the Decline in Serial Killing Partially Explained by a Reduction in 'Free Range Kids?'" (Paper presented at the Annual Meeting of the Society for Police and Criminal Psychology, Ottawa, Canada, September 26, 2013).

12. Fox, Levin, and Fridel, *Extreme Killing: Understanding Serial and Mass Murder*.

13. Patricia Pearson, *When She Was Bad* (New York: Penguin Books, 1998).

14. Zach Sommers, "Missing White Woman Syndrome: It's NOT a Media Myth," *The Crime Report*, April 3, 2017.

15. Fox, Levin, and Fridel, *Extreme Killing: Understanding Serial and Mass Murder*.

16. Kim D. Rossmo, "Geographic Profiling," in Gerben Bruinsma and David Weisburd, eds., *Encyclopedia of Criminology and Criminal Justice* (New York: Springer, 2014).

17. Eric W. Hickey, *Serial Murderers and Their Victims* (Boston: Cengage Learning, 2013).

18. Kenna Quinet and Sam Nunn, "Establishing the Victim–Offender Relationship of Initially Unsolved

Homicides: Partner, Family, Acquaintance or Stranger?" *Homicide Studies* 18 (2014): 271–297.

19. Fox, Levin, and Fridel, *Extreme Killing: Understanding Serial and Mass Murder*.

20. Victor Ferreira, "In Prison for 22 Murders, Russian 'Werewolf' Serial Killer Admits Raping, Killing 59 More Women," *National Post*, January 11, 2017.

21. Donald T. Lunde, *Murder and Madness* (San Francisco: San Francisco Book Co., 1976).

22. Robert D. Hare, *Psychopathy: Theory and Research* (New York: Wiley, 1970).

23. Brad J. Bushman and Roy F. Baumeister, "Threatened Egotism, Narcissism, Self-Esteem, and Direct and Displaced Aggression: Does Self-Love or Self-Hate Lead to Violence?" *Journal of Personality and Social Psychology* 75 (1998): 219–229.

24. Robert A. Prentky, Ann W. Burgess, Frances Rokous, et al., "The Presumptive Role of Fantasy in Serial Sexual Homicide," *American Journal of Psychiatry* 146 (1989): 887–891.

25. Stephen J. Giannangelo, *The Psychopathology of Serial Murder: A Theory of Violence* (Westport, CT: Greenwood, 1996).

26. Orestes Fedora, John R. Reddon, and James W. Morrison, et al., "Sadism and Other Paraphilias in Normal Controls and Aggressive and Nonaggressive Sex Offenders," *Archives of Sexual Behavior* 21 (1992): 1–15.

27. Prentky et al., "The Presumptive Role of Fantasy in Serial Sexual Homicide."

28. Terrie E. Moffitt and Bill Henry, "Neuropsychological Studies of Juvenile Delinquency and Juvenile Violence," in Joel S. Milner, ed., *Neuropsychology of Aggression* (Boston: Kluwer, 1991).

29. Dorothy Otnow Lewis, Jonathan H. Pincus, M. Feldman, L. Jackson, and B. Bard, "Psychiatric, Neurological and Psychoeducational Characteristics of 15 Death Row Inmates in the United States," *American Journal of Psychiatry* 143 (1986): 838–845.

30. Clare S. Allely, Helen Minnis, Lucy Thompson, Philip Wilson, and Christopher Gillberg, "Neurodevelopmental and Psychosocial Risk Factors in Serial Killers and Mass Murderers,"

Aggression and Violent Behavior 19 (2014): 288–301.

31. Michael Fitzgerald, *Young, Violent and Dangerous to Know* (New York: Nova Science, 2013).

32. Sasha Reid, "Developmental Pathways to Serial Homicide: A Critical Review of the Biological Literature," *Aggression and Violent Behavior* 35 (2017): 52–61.

33. John M. Macdonald, "The Threat to Kill," *American Journal of Psychiatry* 120 (1963): 125–130; Daniel S. Hellman and Nathan Blackman, "Enuresis, Firesetting, and Cruelty to Animals," *American Journal of Psychiatry* 122 (1966): 1431–1435.

34. Alan R. Felthous, "Childhood Cruelty to Cats, Dogs and Other Animals," *Bulletin of the American Academy of Psychiatry and the Law* 9 (1981): 48–53.

35. Stephen R. Kellert and Alan R. Felthous, "Childhood Cruelty Toward Animals Among Criminals and Noncriminals," *Human Relations* 18 (1985): 1113–1139.

36. Arnold Arluke, Jack Levin, Carter Luke, and Frank Ascione, "The Relationship of Animal Abuse to Violence and Other Forms of Antisocial Behavior," *Journal of Interpersonal Violence* 14 (1999): 963–975.

37. Steven A. Egger, *The Killers Among Us: An Examination of Serial Murder and Its Investigation* (Upper Saddle River, NJ: Prentice Hall, 1998).

38. Jack Levin and Arnold Arluke, "Reducing the Link's False Positive Problem: The Link Between Animal Abuse and Human Violence," in Andrew Linzey, ed., *Animal Abuse and Human Violence* (Brighton, England: Sussex Academic Press, 2009).

39. Robert K. Ressler, Ann W. Burgess, and John E. Douglas, *Sexual Homicide: Patterns and Motives* (Lexington, MA: Lexington Books, 1988).

40. Hickey, *Serial Murderers and Their Victims*.

41. David Kirschner, "Understanding Adoptees Who Kill: Dissociation, Patricide, and the Psychodynamics of Adoption," *International Journal of Offender Therapy and Comparative Criminology* 36 (1992): 323–333.

42. Dwayne M. Smith and Margaret A. Zahn, *Homicide: A Sourcebook of Social Research* (Thousand Oaks, CA: Sage, 1999).

CHAPTER EIGHT

MEDICAL MURDER AND MUNCHAUSEN SYNDROME BY PROXY

In this chapter, we cover two different but overlapping types of murder that capitalize on the dependency of the victims in certain settings or situations: (1) medical murder and (2) killings linked to Munchausen syndrome by proxy. Medical murder, also known as healthcare serial killing, is committed by staff in a medical setting. Munchausen syndrome by proxy involves a caregiver who intentionally harms or fakes medical problems in their children or others in their care, sometimes resulting in murder.

It is a sad fact of life that hospitals, clinics, and nursing homes are places where some people go to die. More tragically, they are also places where some go to be murdered. Several different forms of homicide, serial in nature, can be grouped together because they occur in healthcare settings. It has become increasingly common to find medical professionals charged with homicides committed in the line of duty. For our purposes, medical murderers include nurses, doctors, nurse's aides, emergency medical technicians, nursing home aides, and other medical professionals or staff who intentionally kill their patients to satisfy a variety of personal desires or psychological needs.

Excluded from the classification of medical murder, however, are homicides that are committed by people employed as doctors, nurses, or other healthcare workers but that are not related to their professions. There are, without a doubt, many cases of doctors and nurses who kill a family member for profit or murder their spouse during a nasty separation or divorce. Also not included in a list of healthcare serial killers are people who claimed to be doctors and convinced naïve, desperate people to fall for their quack medicines. An untold number of people die every year from incorrect diagnoses and unscientific "cures." Many of these killers, some of whom actually have a medical license, starve their patients to death or expose them to toxic compounds, natural therapies, or herbal remedies. In addition, our definition of medical murder does not include the tens of thousands of patients who die each year because of medical incompetence, malpractice, or error.

Medical murderers have often been called Angels of Mercy and Angels of Death, but there is nothing angelic or merciful about their crimes. Although euthanasia and physician- or other assisted suicides (e.g., Kevorkian-style "medicides") are, according to law, considered criminal homicide in most areas of the United States, there are several states (Oregon, California, Colorado, Vermont, Washington, and Washington, D.C.) that have legalized physician-assisted suicide. This type of death of terminally ill patients, known as "death with dignity," implies willing participation by the patient—a wish to die. But the victims of medical murder are patients who not only had no wish to die but also, in most cases, had expected the medical staff to help them get well.

Emphasizing cases involving repetitive and deliberative acts, we do not focus on medical professionals who killed "only" one patient and either stopped on their own accord or were exposed by colleagues or a victim's family members who suspected foul play. Finally, also not included in the scope of medical murder are multiple killings in medical settings that are not connected to medical treatment. For example, in April 2003, a doctor went berserk in a hospital in Madrid, Spain, killing two and wounding six people with a knife. Her attack was aimed at colleagues and patients but had nothing to do with her role as a physician.

Most everyone is familiar with the names of serial killers like Theodore Bundy and Jeffrey Dahmer. But few can identify notorious medical killers who were responsible for much higher victim counts over longer periods of time. For example, few people recognize the name Efren Saldivar, a respiratory therapist in California who may have murdered as many as 200 patients between 1989 and 1998, or nurse's aide Donald Harvey, who killed as many as 80 people in Kentucky and Ohio between 1970 and 1987.

Also relatively obscure is Charles Cullen, a hospital-hopping nurse who confessed to killing 40 patients but may have killed as many as 300, ranging from 22 to 80 years of age, in New Jersey and Pennsylvania during a 16-year murderous career.[1] Before being convicted and given 17 consecutive life sentences, Cullen was an institutional drifter, committing murder in at least 10 different facilities. He was fired from five nursing jobs and resigned from two others. Although rumors and accusations about Cullen frequently surfaced, hospital administrators did not share their suspicions with other employers (in most states, hospitals can be sued for negative comments about current or former employees). Cullen has shown no remorse for his crimes, explaining that depression led him to kill. He claims to have attempted suicide more than 20 times during his lifetime—an amazing failure given how well he knows how to cause death.

Medical murder is certainly not a new phenomenon. From 1907 to 1912, for example, Amy Archer-Gilligan ran a home for the aged in Connecticut where she poisoned as many as 40 residents. Jane Toppan, a nurse's aide in turn-of-the-20th-century New England, confessed to killing at least 30 people but is suspected of having poisoned as many as 100. Toppan's motive involved, at least in part, the sexual excitement she derived from the murders. Rupert Furneaux's *The Medical Murderer* and John Camp's *One Hundred Years of Medical Murder* provide details of several cases of nurses and doctors who murdered patients during the 19th and early 20th centuries.[2]

In many early medical murder cases, the motive was profit. Thus, although there is a long history of certain medical professionals and nursing home staff members murdering patients in their care, it is only in the past few decades that medical murderers with motives other than financial gain have been identified and reported. Our interest here centers on medical professionals who kill for personal gratification derived from the act itself, as well as those whose enjoyment comes indirectly by the fruits of their nefarious labors.

COUNTING MEDICAL MURDERS

Medical murder is fundamentally different from other types of serial killing, and not just in terms of motivation. Whereas it becomes fairly clear when the bodies of prostitutes are discovered in close proximity of each other that a sexual predator is at large, it can take years to recognize the murders committed by a medical professional given the nature of the job. Occurring in a setting where infirmity and frailty are the norm, deaths ordinarily do not raise suspicions but are generally assumed to be related to the very reason the deceased was admitted to the facility. Even when suspicious circumstances do exist, either due to the manner of a patient's death or because of a curiously large number of deaths over a short time span, hospital administrators are extremely reluctant to admit what may be happening. They wish to avoid negative publicity if the suspicions are unfounded or may be concerned that insurance will not cover intentional homicides committed by staff members.

As a result, it is difficult to derive an accurate assessment of the number of medical murders that have occurred over time. Because of increased media interest in medical murders over the past several decades, many observers assume that this type of crime has indeed increased. Yet, we have no way of knowing for certain whether there has been a real increase in the occurrence of medical murder or whether the increased numbers are simply the result of improved reporting and detection.

Our review of known cases over the past 30 years indicates that many medical murder perpetrators killed several victims per month during their active phases. We can only assume that there are many more medical murders that go undetected, particularly when these institutional drifters work and kill in several medical settings over the course of their careers.

As illustrated by the long active periods of many of the offenders, medical murders are generally not revealed as homicides until long after the fact. As a result, official crime reporting sources, such as the FBI's *Uniform Crime Reports*, do not count these deaths in statistical tallies. Also, a number of hospitals have conducted investigations into suspicious deaths although no suspect was ever charged with murder. For example, an investigation of Springfield Community Hospital in Dayton, Ohio, which was launched in 1985 (but was halted and then resumed in 1993), discovered that as many as 30 patients may have been murdered. Empty bottles of Pavulon (a muscle relaxant) were found in various places around the hospital. Although there was a primary suspect, no one was arrested.

Similar to serial murder generally, the number of medical murder cases in the United States peaked in the 1980s, declining ever since then. During the 1980s, as many as six to eight cases were detected during any given year. If these offenders followed the pattern of one or two murders per month (as was the case for several medical murderers), then 16 deaths a month would result in nearly 200 deaths per year, and these only include the six to eight offenders who were identified. If only a small proportion of these murders were uncovered, or if the monthly average death toll per offender was as high as four (as in the Springfield, Ohio, case), then the number of medical murders each year could have easily reached 500 to 1,000. The near disappearance of medical murder in the United States over the past 10 years suggests our improved death surveillance systems, electronic records management, and drug control may be working.[3] For now, it appears that decades-long killing sprees in our hospitals, nursing homes, and hospice centers have subsided.

Although medical murderers to date were far more likely to have been nurses and nurse's aides than other types of medical workers, this may be somewhat of an artifact. Because nurses have formal ties to patients, their connections are more easily discovered and investigated. However, any number of other medical staff members (e.g., doctors, janitors, dieticians, therapists, administrative staff) are in and out of patient rooms at various and unrecorded times of day. Combined with less easily traceable methods of killings often used in these settings (e.g., suffocation with a pillow or pinching off oxygen flow), the number of cases of medical murder committed by ancillary medical staff may be especially undercounted. Not appearing on many lists of medical murderers, Anthony Joyner murdered six elderly women, aged 83 to 92, in a nursing home in 1983. The victims were strangled, smothered, or drowned, and Joyner admitted to raping at least one of his victims. Joyner worked in the kitchen of the nursing home, so, although he wasn't a medical professional, his murders occurred in a healthcare facility. Given our aging population, we might expect nursing homes and assisted living facilities to become a significant hunting ground for serial killers.

Recent coverage of patient abuse in Georgia's mental hospitals reminds us that there are several places a medical murderer can operate. Injuries resulting in death in a Georgia hospital did not lead to criminal charges or even the firing of employees suspected as the assailants (although the state has paid hundreds of thousands of dollars in civil damages to victims and their families). According to an investigative report in the *Atlanta Journal-Constitution*, as many as 115 state mental hospital deaths from 2002 to 2007 were ruled as suspicious. After a patient was beaten with a metal pipe in 2002, investigators found metal pipes stashed throughout one Augusta mental hospital. Rape accusations, beatings, and even homicides were slow to be exposed to the outside world.[4]

HEALTHCARE MURDERS GLOBALLY

Cases of medical murder have been reported in more than 20 countries. Detection is much more likely in industrialized nations, and thus the number of medical murders in other, less developed countries of the world is unknown.

In the definitive work on serial murder by healthcare professionals, Yorker and her colleagues analyzed 90 cases of healthcare workers in 20 countries who had been prosecuted during the time period 1970–2006.[5] Overall, 70% of the cases involved a hospital setting, 86% of the perpetrators were nurses or nurse's aides, and slightly more than half used drug injection as their primary means of killing.

In addition, 60% of the cases identified by the Yorker team were from outside the United States. Moreover, given that detection is far less likely in nonindustrialized countries, this observed percentage of non-U.S. cases is probably understated.

A recent case in Canada illustrates just how long (10 years in this instance) a nurse can continue to kill without being detected. Elizabeth Wettlaufer pleaded guilty to eight counts of murder and four counts of attempted murder, admitting to having injected 14 elderly people with lethal doses of insulin between 2007 and 2016. One murder occurred in a patient's home, but the other seven murders occurred in three different long-term care facilities. The fact that she was able to stay working as a nurse after being fired for "medication errors" caused public outcry. Wettlaufer was only caught after she confessed. Without that, her crimes likely would not have been detected. She received a life sentence with a chance at parole in 2041.

Some medical murderers are detected early on, as was the case with Benjamin Geen, 25, of Oxfordshire, England, a thrill-killing nurse who engaged in a three-month spree during 2004 and 2005. Geen killed 2 people but was also charged with harming 15. Geen injected the patients with muscle relaxants and insulin and has admitted that he loved the attention and the excitement of attempted resuscitations. Geen, who is suspected of being involved in other cases as well, was convicted and sentenced to 17 life terms in prison, where hopefully he won't be permitted near the prison infirmary.

Medical murder cases are extremely difficult to prosecute, as illustrated by the case of Italian nurse Daniela Poggiali, who was arrested in 2014 and convicted of murder in 2016. Poggiali came to the attention of authorities when she took a selfie with one of her dead patients and posted it on Facebook. Although she apologized and admitted that posting the picture was in bad taste, her defense team successfully argued on appeal that elevated potassium chloride levels in patients could not be tied to Poggiali and the fact that death rates were three times higher while she was on duty was based on nothing but speculation. Poggiali's conviction was overturned in 2017 and she was released.

A common strategy used by prosecutors in these cases is to establish a statistical probability based on the times of death and the shifts worked by a suspect, evidence that is sometimes challenged for accuracy and relevance. In 2004, a Dutch court sentenced nurse Lucy de Berk, 42, to life in prison for four murders, although she was suspected of at least 13 murders and five attempted murders from 1997 to 2001. De Berk's conviction was overturned in 2008 in part because of errors in the calculated likelihood that multiple murders occurred under one nurse's watch. In addition, witnesses retracted incriminating statements, and questions were raised concerning the role that certain substances (e.g., digoxin) played in patient deaths.

Rarely are medical murderers caught in the act, so establishing the chain of evidence is difficult at best, as many hospital staffers have access to patients and deaths occur that are assumed to be natural and thus not investigated properly at the outset. Several recent cases against nurses have been dismissed or have resulted in acquittal when facts could not establish that the nurse was actually the person who administered the lethal dose or that the medication given to terminally ill patients was done not for the thrill of it but to reduce patients' suffering. Thus, some cases originally believed to be cases of medical murder are overturned because of insufficient proof. Many of the medical murders that did not result in criminal convictions did, however, involve multimillion-dollar civil judgments against hospitals and other facilities.

As we saw in Chapter 7, serial killers occasionally work in teams, and medical murder is no exception. Between 1983 and 1989 four Austrian nurse's aides at the Lainz General Hospital killed at least 42 patients. The first murder, committed by one of the nurse's aides, was at the request of the suffering patient. But Waltraud Wagner decided she liked the rush and found three other nurse's aides to join her. No longer just killing terminally ill patients, they murdered patients who annoyed them or were difficult to care for. Doses of morphine also quickly lost their appeal, and the nurses switched to water boarding the patients by pinching of their nose and forcing water down their throats until they drowned. Rumors circulated throughout the hospital as death rates soared, but no one took any action. When the murder team got together one day after work for a drink, a doctor overheard them reminiscing about that day's murders and an investigation was finally launched. Wagner, the ringleader, was convicted of 15 murders and another one of the team was convicted of 5 murders. The two others were convicted of manslaughter and attempted murder. By 2008, all had been released from prison.

It is not just medical professionals who use medical facilities as their hunting grounds. Joan Vila Dilme was a security guard at a Spanish nursing home when, in 2010, one of the dead patients was found to have suspicious burns to the mouth and throat. When questioned, Dilme confessed to the murders of 11 elderly patients, insisting that he was just putting an end to their suffering. Dilme was sentenced to 127 years in prison.

The psychological benefits that medical murderers derive from playing God were reflected in the murders committed by Sonia Caleffi, a 34-year-old nurse in Milan, Italy, with a history of depression. Caleffi injected air into the veins of patients, causing embolisms, respiratory failures, and, ultimately, death. She admitted that she killed her patients to feel powerful and important, even keeping a diary about her victims. It appears that she may have been trying to create situations in which she could provide lifesaving resuscitation, but still the patients died. For the medical murderer, nothing feels more invigorating and exhilarating than controlling life and death. Caleffi was convicted of murdering 12 patients and received a 20-year prison sentence.

Stephan Letter, a 27-year-old nurse, was thought, until recently, to be Germany's worst serial killer, at least since World War II. Letter killed a minimum of 29 patients in 2003 and 2004 with injections of tranquilizers and muscle relaxants. More than 40 bodies were exhumed in the investigation of his activities, yet many other possible victims had been cremated. Letter had originally wanted to be a doctor and claimed that he was only trying to help some of his victims by freeing them from pain and suffering. However, he also admitted that he may have acted hastily in some cases when he injected people who had suffered only minor injuries.

Letter's death count was surpassed with some recent announcements about a fellow German medical murderer, nurse Niels Hoegel. Hoegel was convicted of two murders and two attempted murders in 2015 and was sentenced to life in prison. But investigations continued into other suspicious deaths, as the authorities reviewed the records of hundreds of his other patients' deaths. The exhumations of 130 bodies in three countries has linked at least 84 additional murders to Hoegel. The 40-year-old murderer injected his patients with at least five different types of drugs over the course of his killing years. He claims that he did it to display his resuscitation skills (a number of patients did survive) and because he was bored. Hoegel had worked at two different German clinics from 1999 until 2005 where staff became suspicious about his activities. In fact, several have been charged with failing to act on their suspicions. Hoegel claims he doesn't know exactly how many patients he killed, suggesting that he lost track.

Like other serial killers, medical murderers rarely kill themselves, but there are exceptions to every rule. Anne Grigg-Booth, 52, of Lancashire, England, worked the night shift, when staffing levels are lower. She was charged with three morphine overdose deaths and may have killed many more during her 25-year nursing career. In 2005, before she could be tried, Grigg-Booth overdosed on antidepressants and alcohol. Her death was ruled an accident, but she may indeed have overdosed intentionally. Grigg-Booth, known for her domineering personality, was estranged from her family. She had recently gone through a divorce and left behind a houseful of animals. Despite her approach to humans, Grigg-Booth was a rescuer of strays.

MOTIVES AND TYPES OF MEDICAL MURDERERS

Medical murderers are similar to other serial killers in that they often choose vulnerable populations as their victims—the sick, the elderly, and children. There are, however, some unique gender ratios for medical murderers. Criminologists have discovered relatively few females among serial killers. Eric Hickey's research, for example, found only 15% of serial murderers were female, but 54% of healthcare killers were females (including females alone and those who were part of teams). Thus, the unusually large proportion of females among medical murderers indicates that this type of crime may be quite different from most other serial homicides.[6] Even though more medical serial killers are female than is the case for serial killers in general, males are still overrepresented among medical murderers based on their employment representation, as males make up only approximately 6% of all nurses but account for nearly half (44%) of all serial killer nurses.[7]

We know that medical murders are more likely than most other types of homicides to be committed by females, in part because they are overrepresented in these professions. We also know that the typical murder weapon—poison—is most likely to be the method chosen by female serial killers (suffocation is the second most common method chosen by female medical murderers).[8] Thus, access to poisons and vulnerable populations creates more of the situational components needed to carry out these crimes.

Some medical killers use nonnarcotic or uncontrolled substances to kill their patients. In 2008, for example, Kimberly Saenz, 35, of Lufkin, Texas, injected bleach into intravenous tubes of several of her patients. Five survived to describe the excruciating pain from the cleaning solution, while another five died as a result. Saenz was convicted of five counts of capital murder (as well as five other charges of aggravated assault) and was sentenced to life in prison.

Although personal motives—power, control, or attention—predominate in medical murders, some cases appear to have been inspired by profit. England's Harold Shipman was a beloved doctor who made house calls to his many elderly patients. The last patient's death was not suspicious, but the forged will was. Shipman was the beneficiary, and the family demanded an investigation. Shipman was killing his patients with morphine at least as early as 1995 and continued through his apprehension in 1998. His own background was checkered, as he had become addicted to morphine early in his career and paid a fine after forging prescriptions. Although funeral home directors and other medical personnel were alarmed at the significant number of Shipman's dying patients, little was done. In the end, he was convicted of only 15 murders but very likely committed more than 200 over the course of his career.

Yardley and Wilson's recent work on a sample of 16 nurses (7 males and 9 females) who were convicted of killing in hospital settings makes several important points.[9] They identified five factors that often appear in these cases: a higher incidence of death on their shift, mental instability/depression, tendency to make colleagues anxious, possession of drugs at home or work, and having a personality disorder. Other presumed red flags were absent in most cases, including talking about death, lying about personal information, possessing books about poison or murder, and trying to prevent others from checking on their patients. Noting the nurse-murderers' motives of mercy/compassion, power, demanding patients and caseloads, and money, Yardley and Wilson's analysis, similar to most research on medical serial killers, neglects to consider a sexual component.

An analysis of the methods used in medical murders as well as the context in which the killing takes place suggests at least two primary types of perpetrators. One type, the "power killer," murders in silence, often works the night shift, and seems able to continue killing over a relatively long period of time. The opportunity to determine who lives and who dies provides the power and control that this offender craves. Although some medical murderers boast about their crimes, the power type often kills in relative obscurity. These nurses and nurse's aides bask in the power of having taken a life and seem to enjoy baffling physicians. They tend to prefer a subtle approach such as morphine injection, rather than the code blue–inducing Pavulon (which paralyzes the respiratory system while the patient remains conscious) or heart-stopping substances such as digoxin.

Because the power killers' activities take place under quieter circumstances, it may take years before anyone detects or responds to the extraordinarily high number of deaths occurring during their shifts. As is noted in Table 8.1, several of the more recent medical murderers have been power killers. Their offenses may also have a sexual component, but interviews with these killers have shed relatively little light on this dimension.

Donald Harvey, a nurse's aide and autopsy assistant, appears to fit the profile of a power killer. He poisoned or smothered patients, neighbors, family, and friends over a 17-year time period in and around Cincinnati. He also had a history of suicide attempts, burglary, and other thefts, as well as institutionalization for mental problems that included repeated electroshock therapies.

The other major type of medical murderer is the "hero killer," typically a nurse who craves attention. Hero killers attempt to create a life-or-death emergency with the goal of either watching others scramble to save the life of the victim or, more usually, thrusting themselves into the center of the dramatic crisis. Several of these murderers became known as nurses who functioned very well in code blue situations. It is unclear how many of the victims were intended to die. By definition, the nurse takes the victim to the edge of death and, in some cases, may have intended to save the patient's life skillfully and spectacularly rather than to take it.

Even when the patient does not survive, the murderer has still experienced the excitement of the emergency situation and of baffling other medical professionals as to why the patient died. The hero type may be praised by coworkers and the victim's family for their vigilant attempts to save the life. During the 1970s and 1980s, for example, licensed vocational nurse Genene Jones is believed to have murdered up to 60 infants and children during the 1970s and 1980s by injecting them with lethal doses of an antiseizure drug. She reveled in the attention and glory of bringing dying young patients back to life in front of their terrified parents.

Hardly suspecting foul play when their daughter Chelsea passed away despite Nurse Jones's extraordinary efforts to save her, the McClellans placed an ad in the local newspaper containing the following open letter:[10]

To All Our Friends in Kerrville:

Often we live our lives without a tendency to acknowledge those friends around us. Then something will happen which causes us to become aware of others. Such was the case in the loss of our little Angel, Chelsea Ann McClellan. The response from the people of Kerrville, many of whom we only knew in passing, was both heartwarming and most helpful in our grief. The many beautiful flowers, cards and letters we received made us realize the city of Kerrville has a heart.

A special thanks to Dr. Kathryn Holland and Genene Jones for extending Chelsea's stay longer by their caring in such a sensitive way. A care which extended beyond loss and helped us more than anyone could ever know.

Sincerely,
Reid & Petti McClellan

In 1984, Jones was charged and convicted of murdering young Chelsea, as well as attempting to kill a 4-week-old boy who survived, and was given concurrent sentences of 99 years and 60 years, respectively. As is often the case, prosecutors figured that Jones would be locked away forever. However, because of sentencing guidelines in place in Texas in the 1980s, Jones was scheduled for release in 2018, that is, until 2017, when prosecutors charged her with two additional murders from the 1980s.

Another medical murderer, Joseph Dewey Akin, was directly linked to 17 suspicious deaths but suspected of as many as 100. His killing marathon likely began in Georgia in 1983 and ended in North Fulton Regional Hospital in Alabama in 1990. Akin falsely claimed to have earned a 4-year nursing degree when he actually had only 2 years of training. He was also cited for his difficulty in getting along with others on the job. Exaggerated credentials, braggadocio, and difficulty with interpersonal relationships are characteristic of many of the "hero" medical murderers. Nurse Akin chose to kill his patients with drugs that induced cardiac arrest, setting the stage for his grand performance as the heroic lifesaving "super nurse." While insisting on his innocence, Akin accepted a plea agreement for manslaughter and was sentenced to 15 years in prison. However, he was paroled after serving only 6 years.

Interviews with medical murderers suggest that, in addition to the primary motives of power, control, or attention, they are encouraged secondarily by having dependent or demanding patients, heavy patient caseloads, and a need to cover up for other crimes on the job. They may be stealing drugs, money, or belongings from patients. Or, they may be inspired by pure hatred, as was Orville Lynn Majors of Indiana, who poisoned to death at least six patients. Majors stated that he simply "hated old people" and thought "they should all be gassed.[11]

Medical murderers typically suffer from a variety of personality disorders. Those who kill while attempting to achieve heroism are characteristically narcissistic, a personality type that includes a grandiose sense of self and a belief that the world needs to recognize their greatness. It is when their inflated sense of self is questioned by others that they become angry and aggressive.[12]

Power killers, despite an arrogant veneer, may have an overwhelming feeling of worthlessness and lack of control. As with serial murderers in general, many medical killers suffered childhoods filled with trauma, abuse, or neglect. Being different, feeling like an outsider, and suffering humiliation can also lead to feelings of powerlessness and rage. Robert Hale, focusing on the internal motives of offenders, suggested that serial killers have experienced some form of torment and humiliation early in life.[13] This humiliation turns to rage, and that rage becomes targeted at others—in many cases others who may remind the killer of someone who embarrassed them earlier in life. Erich Fromm viewed destructive aggression as a response to feelings of powerlessness. For the medical murderer, particularly the hero killers, their not always death-defying acts of endangerment and attempted rescue place them at the center of attention and make them feel important and dominant.

In the medical setting, staff members can be humiliated or embarrassed by others; for example, demanding doctors may snap at overworked nurses, or an incompetent nurse may be marginalized by coworkers. Some medical staff may even find the work itself to be humiliating (e.g., bathing the elderly in a nursing home or changing too many bedpans), and so they purposely target their workplace and its captive pool of potential victims in order to seek revenge for perceived mistreatment. Obviously, not everyone who has suffered humiliation and embarrassment turns their feelings into murderous rage, so we must also consider the contextual factors that help explain killings by medical staff.

Table 8.1 Selected Multiple Murder Cases in the United States

Name, Age, and Occupation of Offender(s)	Location	Years of Activity	Suspected Victim Count	Number of Convictions	Sentence	Method	Motive	Other
Joseph Dewey Akin, 32, Nurse	Georgia & Alabama	1983–1990	Over 100	1	Pleaded guilty to manslaughter; sentenced to 15 years in prison	Lidocaine and epinephrine	Hero	Fired for false credentials, difficulty getting along with others
Richard Angelo, 26, Nurse	New York	1987–1989	At least 10	4	Sentenced to 61 years to life in prison	Pavulon and Anectine	Hero	Former fireman and EMT
Charles Cullen, 43, Nurse	New Jersey & Pennsylvania	1987–2003	40	22	Pleaded guilty; sentenced to 11 life terms in NJ; sentenced to 6 life terms in PA	Digoxin, insulin, and other drugs	Power	Works with authorities on how to catch others; donated kidney to a friend in 2006
Robert Diaz, 46, Nurse	California	1971–1981	12–60 elderly	12	Sentenced to death; died of natural causes in 2010	Lidocaine	Power	Would predict patients' deaths
Jeffrey Feltner, 26, Nurse's aide	Florida	1990	7 elderly	1	Pleaded guilty; sentenced to life in prison with parole eligibility after 25 years; died in 1993	Smothered	Hero	Police received anonymous tips about unnatural deaths
Kristen Gilbert, 33, Nurse	Massachusetts	1996	4	4	Given four consecutive life sentences without parole eligibility	Epinephrine, ketamine, and acepromazine	Hero	Tried to impress boyfriend, a security guard at hospital; staff nicknamed her "Angel of Death"
Gwendolyn Graham, 23, Catherine Wood, 24, Nurse's aides	Michigan	1987	10	5	Graham given life without parole eligibility; Wood given 20–40 years in prison	Smothered	Power/ Sex	Kept trophies. Wood never actually killed, confessed when Graham began threatening babies
Jeanine Hannah, 55, Nurse	Wisconsin, California & Oregon	2000–2002	2	1 criminal, another civil	Sentenced to 99 years in prison	Insulin overdose	Money	History of fraud in home healthcare, killed to cover up theft
Donald Harvey, 35, Nurse's aide	Kentucky & Ohio	1970–1986	32–80	24	Given four life sentences; killed by another inmate in 2017	Smothered or hooked patients up to empty oxygen tanks	Power/ Sex	Suicide attempts, mental hospital commitments, 21 electroshock therapies 1983–1986, burglaries

Name	Location	Years active	Victims	Convictions	Sentence	Method	Motive	Notes
Vicki Dawn Jackson, 36, Nurse	Texas	2000–2001	20–24	Plead no contest to 10 murders	Sentenced to life in prison	Injected muscle relaxant, mivacurium chloride	Power	Killed demanding patients, including third husband's grandfather
Genene Jones, 33, Licensed vocational nurse	Texas	1978–1982	47 children	1, plus convicted of injuring child	Sentenced to 159 years; due for release in 2018 but indicted for additional murder in 2017	Anectine and Heparin	Hero	Needy, liar, and sexually promiscuous
Orville Lynn Majors, 38, Licensed practical nurse	Indiana	1993–1995	60–130 elderly	6	Given six consecutive 60-year sentences	Epinephrine and potassium chloride	Power	Hated the elderly
Randy Powers, 31, Nurse's aide	California	1984	12	Convicted of assault on a baby	Sentenced to 5 years in prison; released in 1987	Lidocaine	Hero	After release, enrolled in EMT program under false name; rejected when identity discovered
Brian Rosenfeld, 32, Nurse	Florida	1990	23-25	3	Sentenced to life in prison with parole eligibility after 25 years	Not located	Power	Targeted victims in geriatrics ward
Kimberly Saenz, 25, Nurse	Texas	2008	5	5	Sentenced to life without parole eligibility	Bleach injected into dialysis tubes	Power	10 dialysis patients injected with bleach, 5 of whom died
Efren Saldivar, 28, Respiratory therapist	California	1989–1998	100–200	6	Pleaded guilty; sentenced to life without parole eligibility	Pavulon, Anectine, or oxygen deprivation	Power	Claimed other nurses were doing the same thing
Michael Swango, 44, Doctor	Several states in the U.S. and also Zimbabwe	1983–1997	35–60	4	Pleaded guilty; sentenced to life in prison	Potassium chloride, epinephrine, Anectine, cyanide	Power	Suspected of poisoning coworkers' food
Bobbie Sue Dudley Terrell, 29, Nurse	Florida	1984	18	4	Pleaded guilty; sentenced to 95 year in prison; died in 2007	Insulin, asphyxiation, or strangulation	Hero	Schizophrenic, overweight, and shy

MUNCHAUSEN SYNDROME BY PROXY

Munchausen syndrome involves making oneself sick or faking illness, usually in order to attract attention or sympathy. The proxy variant of this disorder, introduced in Chapter 4, involves inducing or faking illness in someone else, typically a child. Many of the medical serial killers we've discussed in this chapter suffered from Munchausen syndrome by proxy (MSBP), including Benjamin Geen, Sonia Caleffi, Joseph Dewey Akin, and Genene Jones.

Both forms of the syndrome can be exhibited in the actions of the same individual, as illustrated in the case of nurse Beverly Allitt, who, at age 24, was convicted in Nottingham, England, on 13 counts of murder, attempted murder, and assault on children, many of them infants. Nurse Allitt's symptoms started appearing early in her life. Between 1987 and 1991, she sought treatment dozens of times for apparently self-inflicted injuries to her hands, legs, back, and head. It wasn't until a large number of young hospital patients under her care died or suddenly became critical that her activities were scrutinized. Autopsies on the children revealed that Nurse Allitt had been murdering the patients by suffocation or with injections of insulin or potassium.

When later examined by a court-appointed psychiatrist, Nurse Allitt confessed that she had been upset over not having been admitted to a nursing course and over having been chosen last for her nursing assignment. Allitt's scheme provided the validation that was otherwise missing in her life. By stealthily killing a child, she could outsmart the brilliant doctors and play God. As she told the psychiatrist, "I had to prove I was better than what people thought."[14]

Yorker notes that in most cases, nurses who kill patients do not have previous criminal histories, but some do have previous histories of Munchausen or MSBP, an earlier sign of their desperate need for attention and power.[15] The nurse or other caregiver who makes victims sick (and sometimes kills them) may manifest motives similar to people with MSBP—they do it to attract attention from parents, coworkers, doctors, friends, and family members. Unfortunately, these killers continue to get the attention they crave even after their crimes have been discovered, as some of them have been featured on news programs such as *Dateline NBC*, *48 Hours*, and *60 Minutes*.

Whereas there appears to be a welcomed hiatus in healthcare serial killers in the United States, there is no such pause in cases of MSBP. Most of the time, these involve parents, typically mothers, who fabricate symptoms in their children (e.g., apnea, seizures, and convulsions), fake illnesses by manipulating medical tests (e.g., adding blood to urine samples), or induce sickness or death by suffocating their children or exposing them to drugs and other toxic substances. In one case, a mother picked her child's wounds to the bones and filled them with animal feces and pet hair.

MSBP includes a mother who induces illness by poisoning her child or who falsely claims she witnessed the child having a seizure. Whereas faking or inducing an illness can be a powerful way to manipulate others or to shirk responsibilities, MSBP moms harm their children, sometimes fatally, for the sake of attention. Some experts argue that this psychological disorder is merely an excuse and that the assaultive behavior is nothing more than child abuse.

In *Patient or Pretender: Inside the World of Factitious Disorders*, Feldman and colleagues contend that many deaths initially diagnosed as sudden infant death syndrome (SIDS) may have actually been cases of MSBP.[16] At times, a parent's attempt to use illness for the sake of attention can inadvertently result in the death of the victim. Although most MSBP cases involve mothers who hurt (or kill) their children, some people attempt to gain similar attention by poisoning or otherwise hurting their pets.[17]

Long before the term *Munchausen syndrome by proxy* was coined in the 1970s, people with this factitious disorder were killing. From 1946 to 1969, Martha Woods killed three of her own biological children, a nephew and niece, a neighbor's child, and her adopted son. As an army wife, Martha capitalized on her frequent relocation to hide her murders. Wherever her husband was stationed, Martha would rush into the emergency room with an unconscious infant. Smothering was her method, and no one suspected anything until the last child, her adopted son Paul, died. She was convicted of murder and received a life sentence. As is often the case with MSBP, Martha was a pathological liar, claimed constantly about being stalked by strangers, and had one dramatic incident after the next.

Martha was certainly not a pioneer in performing this insidious form of child abuse. History reveals hundreds if not thousands of cases of women, dating as far back as the 1600s, who murdered one child after the next, pretending they were the grief-stricken parent. And there are many contemporary documented cases of MSBP: Waneta Hoyt killed her five children, Kathleen Folbigg killed her four children, and Diana Lumbrera killed her six children and a niece. All were diagnosed with MSBP and all claimed that their babies were the victims of SIDS, otherwise known as crib death or cot death.

Every once in a while, things don't go quite as planned for a Munchausen mom. As chronicled in the HBO documentary *Mommy Dead and Dearest*, Dee Dee Blancharde had been making her daughter Gypsy Rose sick for years, conning Gypsy's father, the medical community, neighbors, and virtually everyone she met into thinking Gypsy had innumerable health problems. Dee Dee's story was that, as the result of a premature birth, Gypsy suffered from brain damage, sleep apnea, a chromosomal disorder, leukemia, asthma, muscular dystrophy, and eating disorders. Dee Dee moved, switched doctors, claimed medical records were lost in Hurricane Katrina, changed their names and birthdates, and swindled from every charity she could find. She shaved her daughter's head to mimic chemotherapy, fed her through a feeding tube, made her use a wheelchair, had her saliva glands removed, had tubes put in her ears, and beat her.

Of course, Gypsy Rose hadn't been sick but became increasingly ill over time because of the medicine her mother forced on her. Dee Dee kept her isolated so the fraud wouldn't be discovered. But then Gypsy Rose found an online boyfriend with a history of indecent exposure, mental health issues, low IQ, autism, and an interest in bondage and sadomasochism. The two conspired to kill her abusive mother and run away together. In 2015, the boyfriend fatally stabbed Dee Dee, and the young couple fled. Eventually apprehended, Gypsy, now 25, pleaded guilty to second-degree murder and received a 10-year sentence in prison.

MSBP moms are similar to the hero-aspiring medical killers described earlier: Both seek attention through jeopardizing the lives of others, even if subsequent deaths are not specifically part of the plan. A Nebraska case from 2004 illustrates the tragedy that can result from MSBP. Andrea Yager, a 17-month-old girl, died in 2004 after being intentionally smothered by her mother. On no less than five separate occasions, Jodi Yager, 22, had rushed her baby daughter to the emergency room. On one trip to the emergency room, Andrea had reportedly swallowed oil from a lantern, and on others she apparently had suffered unexplained bouts of unconsciousness or seizures, episodes that curiously took place only when the child was alone with her mother. Sadly, baby Andrea never made it to her second birthday. Given the suspicious circumstances, Yager was prosecuted for murder.

She pleaded no contest to the lesser offense of intentional child abuse resulting in death and was sentenced to 46 years in prison.

Due to increased awareness (and hidden video surveillance) by the medical community, a sizable number of MSBP cases have been reported in recent years. In fact, there are more individual cases of homicide implicating MSBP than of medical murder, although the death toll associated with medical murder cases tends to be much higher. However, convictions are not always a slam dunk. In Missouri, Stephanie McMullen, 30, a former pediatric oncology nurse, was accused of poisoning her son with injections of feces while he was in the hospital. The prosecutor presented evidence that McMullen had been researching child poisonings on her home computer, while her defense attorney argued that any number of people could have been responsible for the boy's poisonings, including hospital staff. Given the circumstantial nature of the evidence, the jury could not reach a unanimous verdict, resulting in a mistrial.

When trials involving MSBP cases do result in a conviction, the sentences can vary wildly. Defendants whose victims survive the mistreatment can receive relatively short sentences and may be eligible for probation and counseling, whereas those whose selfish actions result in the death of their children may be sentenced to relatively long prison stays.

Tracie Fleck, whose attempt to inject her 21-month-old daughter's intravenous tube with fecal matter was thwarted when caught on video at an Indianapolis hospital, pleaded guilty in 2005 to two counts of battery and was sentenced to 6 years in prison plus 2 years' probation. That same year, Kimberly Austin, 37, of Houston, Texas, received a 99-year sentence for injecting one of her children with a fatal dose of insulin. Austin's four children had been to a doctor or hospital a stunning 235 times. Her techniques included smothering, poison, starvation, injections, unnecessary surgeries, and gagging her children with her fingers.

Like medical murder, the frequency of MSBP cases is virtually impossible to determine, although estimates have ranged from 200 to 1,200 cases annually in the United States.[18] Often the young victims are given a fairly obscure diagnosis of "failure to thrive." It is usually the most extreme cases that come to the attention of hospital staff. Schreier and Libow, in *Hurting for Love: Munchausen Syndrome by Proxy*, discovered several cases in one year in the same hospital. They found that approximately 10% of the victims of MSBP fail to survive, although others have suggested that the mortality rate may be as high as 25%.

MSBP offenders, again typically mothers and rarely fathers, may behave like serial killers, with cooling-off periods during which they are not making their child sick but still basking in the martyrdom of caring for a sick child.[19] These offenders, both mothers who make their child ill and nurses who poison patients and cause code blue situations, are similar in motivation (although far more dangerous) to people who falsely report crimes in order to gain the attention of others.

As is true with other types of homicidal offenders, it is unclear whether the source of the desperate need for attention among MSBP mothers and nurses is rooted in extremely low self-esteem or narcissism. Some research on the backgrounds of Munchausen moms has found that many are burdened by profound feelings of being ignored as children.[20] More specifically, many report having a physically or emotionally distant father (or husband), and some experts have suggested that the doctor may actually represent a father figure to the Munchausen offender.

As emphasized in Chapter 7, serial murderers tend to exploit vulnerable targets, and this is certainly true for children of Munchausen moms. In her book *Sickened*, Julie Gregory describes her own experiences as a victim of a MSBP mother. Gregory grew up in rural Ohio with a mother who starved her (so that she would appear sick), beat her, fed her matches, gave her medications that caused migraines, and dragged her from doctor to doctor demanding attention and painful tests. As a child, Gregory tried unsuccessfully to get help from school nurses as well as her father. Fortunately, she survived to tell her story.

Whereas society was once relatively ignorant about MSBP, today's greater awareness, sometimes bordering on hyperawareness, may cause some parents to be accused unjustly of wrongdoing. Babies who were thought to be cases of MSBP may have died as a result of other causes, such as neurological problems or reactions to prescribed medications. MSBP case histories have identified a number of risk factors and warning signs, including inexplicable illnesses, discrepancies in the medical history as given by a parent, events that only occur in the mother's presence (and cease when separated from the mother), a mother who is not appropriately worried about the child and is more interested in interacting with medical staff, and a mom with a medical background and an extensive history of her own illnesses. However, these involve subjective judgments that can produce many false positives and unfounded suspicions surrounding the actions of innocent parents.

Of course, no subjective judgments were needed in the case of Sarah Dillard-Lubin, 25, after she pleaded guilty to assault and was sentenced in 2010 to 7.5 years in prison with no possibility of early release or parole. Dillard-Lubin, a former Oregon medical assistant already on probation for a 2005 poisoning of her infant son, fed her infant daughter two opiate pills. In both incidents, she sought to create drama in order to gain the attention of the fathers of her babies. Like women who murder other women to steal their babies, the Munchausen moms are not dying, but killing, to get the attention of others.

ADMINISTRATIVE FACILITATORS AND FAILURES

While factors that may promote murderous impulses for those operating in medical facilities are similar to those for other serial killers (e.g., childhood neglect, abuse, or trauma), some special situational circumstances serve as facilitators for medical homicides. Most obvious is the easy access to drugs that are capable of killing patients. Routinely administering narcotics to patients, nurses can, as part of their routine, turn patients into victims. Nurse's aides, who do not have the same access to controlled substances, use other means, such as suffocation or poisoning.

In addition to providing medical murderers with access to possible victims and the means to kill them, hospitals and nursing homes may also facilitate murder through inadequate surveillance and even covering up suspicious deaths. It is fairly recent that hospitals have started conducting "mortality analyses" that might indicate an excessive number of deaths in a particular unit and/or shift. In some situations, there appears to have been a code of silence surrounding suspicions similar to the "don't snitch" custom that police often confront in trying to investigate street crime.

Coworkers had joked and gossiped about the deaths of patients under the care of respiratory therapist Efren Saldivar, but most did not bring their suspicions to the attention of hospital administrators. According to Saldivar, many others were doing what he did. Curiously, not only was Saldivar fired, but so, too, were four other respiratory therapists, and two managers resigned. Particularly troubling is that Saldivar even referred to himself as an "Angel of Death" before being apprehended.

Even when suspicions arise that there may be a serial killer working in a hospital or nursing home, staff may be reticent to contact the police. Instead, administrators may attempt to determine on their own whether the deaths were the result of incompetence, impairment, or intent. Given the documented cases of hospitals refusing to acknowledge nurse and physician impairment (e.g., drug and alcohol addiction) or failing to discipline incompetent doctors and nurses, it is easy to imagine similar inaction and concealment of intentional homicides by medical staff.

Another contributing factor is the occasional reluctance of medical professionals to admit that they do not know why a particular patient died. Rather, they may feel pressured to produce a cause of death, however inaccurate or incomplete. In the case of Munchausen moms, the doctors, nurses, and other medical staff are naturally inclined to believe that parents love their children and thus are apt to be sympathetic rather than suspicious of the parents with sick children.

The landmark 1999 study by the Institute of Medicine found that as many as 98,000 U.S. hospital deaths a year may result from error.[21] A more recent study suggests that the number is closer to 250,000, which would make medical incompetence the third leading cause of death behind cancer and heart disease.[22] Even unintentional incompetence on the part of a single doctor can result in the deaths of a significant number of people. Dr. Jayant Patel of Portland, Oregon, had been banned from surgery in Oregon and New York by 2001, so he took his skills to a hospital in Australia, where it is alleged that his incompetence led to the deaths of at least 87 patients. As is often the case in the United States, the disciplinary actions against him were not disclosed by any of his references when he applied to the Australian hospital, resulting in institutional blindness to his trail of bodies.

There are still other institutional facilitators that make lengthy medical killing sprees possible. Dr. Michael Swango was glaringly incompetent in medical school, but he managed to graduate, albeit near the bottom of his class. It was his sinister motivation, not his lack of medical skill, that ultimately placed patients in grave danger. Swango killed an untold number of patients over a period of almost 20 years as he worked in seven different hospitals. Swango's killings began during his internship at the Ohio State University Hospital, from which he was dismissed amid a frenzy of speculation about the deaths of a number of patients. When Swango applied for new jobs, almost no one called to check his references or background. Investigations took place in nearly every hospital where he was employed, but in most cases, no charges were ever filed. Finally, several different investigators and administrators spread the word about Swango, but not before he had killed at least 35 people, and probably many more. As illustrated by the Swango case, the disciplinary records of nurses and other medical professionals are confidential. Thus, it can be very difficult to track incompetent medical staff or, even worse, medical predators who switch jobs and move from state to state.

Medical murders are rather difficult to prosecute. Multiple people in a healthcare setting have access to the patients. Potentially incriminating evidence is often innocently and routinely discarded, and the deceased are buried or cremated often without an autopsy. In fact, the number of autopsies performed in the United States has been declining since the early 1970s. As of 2007, the percentage of deaths for which an autopsy was performed was at a historic low of about 9%, and the rate was even lower for the elderly or those known to have been suffering from a disease.[23]

A significant number of medical murderers have not been charged with homicide at all. For a number of reasons—including difficulty proving intent and a lack of proper medical documentation, forensic deficiencies, and a lack of hospital cooperation—many of these killers are instead convicted of some level of assault, neglect, or even something as trivial as distribution of a controlled substance. Some avoid a conviction altogether.

In August 2003, for example, the criminal complaint against Richard Williams was dismissed, surprising many observers close to the case. Williams had been charged with 10 counts of first-degree murder of patients in a Missouri veteran's hospital. The prosecutor was forced to dismiss the charges due to lack of hospital cooperation and incompetent procedures at the private crime laboratory that had handled the forensic evidence. Williams, who was originally suspected in more than 40 deaths, sued the lab for negligence, but the Eighth Court of Appeals dismissed the suit.

PREVENTION AND INTERVENTION

Monitoring all the activities in hospitals and nursing homes, much less in the home healthcare industry, would seem an impossible task. At a minimum, hospitals should initiate surveillance and mortality analysis systems. These can include data systems that document drug use, patient deaths, and so forth, by shift, staff, and unit. Obviously, by the time these systems could alert the hospital to an unusual number of deaths, a serial killer would already have enjoyed a significant period of activity at the deadly expense of several patients. Video surveillance may also be an asset for the prevention of both medical murder and MSBP cases, as many mothers continue to poison or suffocate their children even while they are in the hospital.

In addition, to the extent that nursing shortages and burdensome working conditions contribute to caregivers' desires to end a patient's life, hospitals should be required to maintain suitable staff–patient ratios. More reasonable staffing levels would also allow supervisors to monitor staff activities. In the event that hospitals and nursing homes mandate limits on staff hirings, patients may need to be prepared to be turned away when there are staffing shortages.

Obviously, greater attention should be paid to investigating the credentials and previous work histories of applicants for positions in medical facilities. Unfortunately, state regulations related to hiring practices and background checks vary considerably across the country. Recently, because of the Cullen case, New Jersey became one of the first states to allow healthcare facilities to report to other facilities when an employee has been disciplined. No longer will professional misconduct or incompetence be hidden for fear of lawsuits from the suspected offender. In addition, criminal history background checks are now required for all healthcare personnel, as a condition of professional license renewal. The National Practitioner Data Bank is also available, which can be used by all states to document incompetence and malfeasance.

Clearly, we have made progress, at least in the United States, where there have been very few healthcare serial killers detected in the past decade. But continued improvement in prevention and intervention strategies should include closer monitoring of narcotics and other drugs (even those that, although not controlled substances, can be lethal nonetheless) and significant penalties for hospital administrators who attempt to cover up suspicious circumstances. To track cases of MSBP, hospital registries for both patients and staff members (much like criminal history databases) may have merit in response to the mobility of perpetrators. Some MSBP parents take their children to different doctors or different hospitals when suspicions arise. Similarly, nurses and other health workers sometimes change jobs when rumors start to spread, only to resume their deadly treatments at a new location.

As is often true when female perpetrators are at work, the law underplays the seriousness of MSBP. In almost all states, mothers caught poisoning and otherwise intentionally harming their child in a MSBP scenario are typically charged with low-level misdemeanors. Until endangering the life and health of a child is handled more seriously, these offenders will continue to play out their selfish schemes with relative impunity.

Because the deaths of patients in hospitals and nursing homes are to some extent "expected," closer inspection of these deaths by medical examiners and/or coroners is warranted. Many states have created death review teams for the investigation of any child's death, and similar types of oversight may be needed in nursing homes.

LOOKING AHEAD

As hospitals in the United States became sensitized to the possibility of having a medical murderer in their employ, the number of known cases increased. However, then, in part because of aggressive surveillance and investigation of suspicious deaths, the incidence fell. Crime is a function of opportunity, and it is clearly possible that as our population ages and more people reside in nursing homes or are treated in some type of medical setting (including in-home care and hospice) where mortality surveillance systems are not in place, the problem could resurface.

The very deadly Dr. Harold Shipman did most of his work in patients' homes, murdering hundreds of people for financial gain. Even protocols for multiple physician signatures on death certificates did not stop Shipman. He had no trouble finding colleagues to sign the death certificates even though they knew his patient death toll was much higher than their own. Prevention of medical murder should include a system for monitoring mortality in general practice, nursing homes, and home healthcare.

Looking ahead, the next hunting ground for medical murder may be our nation's jails and prisons. It has been recently publicized that physicians who have been convicted of crimes and/or lost their medical licenses because of various forms of misconduct are being hired by some states faced with increasing jail and prison populations and growing healthcare demands.[24] Physicians who drugged and sexually assaulted former patients are now serving the inmate population. Who will believe the incarcerated felon over the word of a doctor when some form of medical misconduct occurs? Will anyone care about or investigate the unexpected death of a violent prison inmate?

ENDNOTES

1. Charles Graeber, "The Tainted Kidney," *New York Magazine*, October 24, 2007.

2. Rupert Furneaux, *The Medical Murderer* (New York: Abelard-Schuman, 1957); John Camp, *One Hundred Years of Medical Murder* (London: Bodley Head, 1982).

3. Joyce Frieden, "Healthcare Serial Killings Down in U.S. but Up Globally," *MedPage Today*, October 28, 2014.

4. Alana Judd and Andy Miller, "A Fatal Struggle but No Punishment," *Atlanta Journal-Constitution*, January 14, 2007.

5. Beatrice Crofts Yorker, Kenneth W. Kizer, Paula Lampe, A. R. W. Forrest, Jacquetta M. Lannan, and Donna A. Russell, "Serial Murder by Healthcare Professionals," *Journal of Forensic Sciences* 51 (2006): 1362–1371.

6. Eric W. Hickey, *Serial Murders and Their Victims* (Belmont, CA: Wadsworth, 2013).

7. Yorker et al., "Serial Murder by Healthcare Professionals."

8. Hickey, *Serial Murders and Their Victims.*

9. Elizabeth Yardley and David Wilson, "In Search of the 'Angels of Death': Conceptualising the Contemporary Nurses Healthcare Serial Killer," *Journal of Investigative Psychology and Offender Profiling* 13 (2016): 39–55.

10. Peter Elkind, *The Death Shift: The True Story of Nurse Genene Jones and the Texas Baby Murders* (New York: Viking, 1989), pp. 154–155.

11. *Indiana v. Orville Lynn Majors Jr.*, Probable Cause Affidavit, December 29, 1997.

12. Brad J. Bushman and Roy F. Baumeister, "Threatened Egotism, Narcissism, Self-Esteem, and Direct and Displaced Aggression: Does Self-Love or Self-Hate Lead to Violence?" *Journal of Personality and Social Psychology* 75 (1998): 219–229.

13. Robert Hale, "The Role of Humiliation and Embarrassment in Serial Murder," *Psychology: A Journal of Human Behavior* 31 (1994): 17–23.

14. R. Pendlebury, "Allitt Is Locked Away Forever," *Daily Mail* [London], May 29, 1993, p. 9.

15. Fred Bayles, "Nurse Gets Life in Prison for Killing 4: Veteran's Experts Explore Motives of Medical Murderers," *USA Today*, March 27, 2001.

16. Marc Feldman, Charles Ford, and Toni Reinhold, *Patient or Pretender: Inside the Strange World of Factitious Disorders* (Toronto: Wiley and Sons, 1994).

17. James A. Oxley and Marc D. Feldman. "Complexities of Maltreatment: Munchausen by Proxy and Animals," *Companion Animal* 21 (2016): 586–589; "Is Man's Best Friend in Trouble?" *Reuters Health*, September 6, 2002.

18. Herbert Schreier, "Munchausen by Proxy Defined," *Pediatrics* 110 (2002): 985–988; B. Vennemann, T. Bananowski, B. Karger, H. Pfeiffer, H. Kohler, and B. Brinkmann, "Suffocation and Poisoning—The Hard-Hitting Side of Munchausen Syndrome by Proxy," *International Journal of Legal Medicine* 119 (2005): 98–102; Herbert Schreier, "Munchausen by Proxy," *Current Problems in Pediatric Adolescent Healthcare* 34 (2004): 126–143; H. Schreier, "Error in Munchausen by Proxy Defined," *Pediatrics* 113 (2004): 1851–1852; Guy E. Brannon, "Munchausen Syndrome by Proxy," *E-medicine Specialties*, April 4, 2006.

19. Herbert A. Schreier and Judith A. Libow, *Hurting for Love: Munchausen Syndrome by Proxy* (New York: Guilford Press, 1993).

20. Ibid.

21. William C. Richardson, Donald M. Berwick, J. Cris Bisgard, et al., *To Err Is Human: Building a Safer Health System* (Washington, DC: Institute of Medicine, September 29, 1999).

22. Martin A. Makary and Michael Daniel, "Medical Error: The Third Leading Cause of Death in the US," *British Medical Journal* [online] 353 (2016).

23. Donna L. Hoyert, "The Changing Profile of Autopsied Deaths in the United States, 1972–2007" (NCHS Data Brief 67, National Center for Health Statistics, 2011).

24. Andrew A. Skolnick, "Critics Denounce Staffing Jails and Prisons With Physicians Convicted of Misconduct," *Journal of the American Medical Association* 280 (1988): 1391–1392.

CHAPTER NINE

RAMPAGE

Chapter 1 discussed in some detail the public's fascination with murder and the reasons behind it. Much of the voracious appetite that many people maintain for true crime is directed toward sexual sadists and serial killers, particularly the ones whose celebrity drives the murderabilia marketplace. By contrast, multiple murderers and those who perpetrate a violent rampage in some public setting also attract intense public interest, but for a very different reason: fear rather than fascination. In light of recent and widely publicized massacres in schools, churches, restaurants, and other public venues, the level of anxiety is clearly elevated.

The year 2012 appears to be the point in time when public rampages and mass shootings grabbed the full attention of the public, the press, and politicians alike. It was then that some really bad things came in threes: the April 2 mass shooting at a California university in which seven were killed and three others were injured; the July 20 massacre at an Aurora, Colorado, cinema resulting in 12 deaths and 70 nonfatal injuries; and the December 14 shooting at a Newtown, Connecticut, elementary school, which claimed the lives of 20 children and six adults. Suddenly, mass murder, mass shootings, and public rampages became a major area of concern, sparking public debate and scholarly research.

The hype and hysteria associated with tragic events of 2012 and several others since then have led to much confusion about terminology. For example, *mass murder* generally refers to an event in which an assailant or assailants kill four or more victims in a single explosion of violence, with mass shootings representing a large subset of cases that involve a handgun or rifle. More recently, some observers have suggested that mass shootings should include instances in which four or more are shot regardless of the severity of injury, which has given cause for headlines such as "How Often Do Mass Shootings Occur? On Average, Every Day, Records Show."[1] However, in nearly half of this "daily" variety of mass shootings, no one is killed. Unfortunately, when Americans hear wild claims about the incidence of mass shootings, they think of the well-known massacres that claimed dozens of lives—such as the large-scale, devastating attacks at Columbine High School, Virginia Tech, Sandy Hook Elementary School, and the Pulse nightclub in Orlando, Florida—and become overly alarmed.

Further muddying the waters, the FBI has promoted the relatively new term *active shooter*, defined as a gunman who is actively engaged in killing or attempting to kill people in a populated area.[2] In contrast to the mass murderer or mass shooter definitions, both of which rely on a minimum number of victims killed and/or injured, the active shooter concept focuses solely on presumed intent, not outcome.

The conflicting definitions employed by various agencies, media outlets, and researchers have created significant confusion. Here, we focus specifically on murder, not attempts or intentions. We also give particular attention to multiple homicides, the seemingly senseless killings that produce so much fear and anxiety.

MASS MURDER

As we suggested in Chapter 7, the victims of the typical serial killer are members of marginalized or vulnerable groups, such as prostitutes. By contrast, the victims of mass murderers tend to be students, teachers, coworkers, friends, and family. Whether it involves a distraught husband/father, a disgruntled former employee, an unhappy customer, or a dispirited student, we all bear some risk of becoming a victim.

We have chosen to discuss school shootings, hate-motivated murders, and terrorism in separate chapters due in part to their different causal factors and policy implications. In this chapter, we focus on mass killers and rampage shooters, especially those who target family, former and current coworkers, and total strangers, without any political motive.

It is informative first to examine the characteristics of mass killers, particularly across the major types of this extreme form of homicide: family massacres, felony-related murders, and public slaughters. For this, we accessed a database of U.S. mass killings of at least four victims spanning the years 2006 through 2016 that was assembled by staff at *USA Today* and expanded by Fridel.[3] Based on the FBI's Supplementary Homicide Reports as well as media accounts of missing cases, this database yields a total of 355 killers who were responsible for committing 317 mass murders (about 29 incidents a year) involving more than 1,600 victims. As indicated in Table 9.1, overall about 41% of these mass murderers were white, and more than 93% were males. About 70% of the assailants were in their 20s or 30s, but nearly one-quarter were older than age 40.

Almost half of the mass murders in the United States involve family members as victims, as opposed to the random shootings of strangers at a fast-food restaurant or a shopping mall or the targeting of a category of people. In most of these cases, the father murdered his wife (or ex-wife), children and/or stepchildren, and sometimes even the family pet. This, of course, accounts for the fact that about 70% of family mass killers are over 30 years old and nearly one-third are over 40 years old, a pattern very different from other forms of murder.

Of the remaining cases, there are about an even share of felony-related mass killings (e.g., murdering the witnesses to a robbery) and public massacres. Even though mass killings in public places, such as a church, a restaurant, or a school, are relatively rare, they are by far the most frightening. After all, these rampage killings can occur at any time and to anyone. Finally, other than a couple dozen cases that involve a variety of other motivations, less than 10% of mass murder cases are unsolved. Given the extensive evidence that tends to be associated with these outbursts of extreme violence, they are typically solved as soon as the police arrive, often because the perpetrator commits suicide at the scene.

Methodical and Selective

Mark Barton's exit line dripped with evil sarcasm. "I hope this won't ruin your trading day," said the 44-year-old stock investor as he wrapped up his July 29, 1999, bloody rampage in Atlanta's financial district. Armed with two semi-automatic

Table 9.1   Characteristics of Mass Murderers, 2006–2016

Characteristic	Family	Felony	Public	Other	Unsolved	Total	All U.S. Homicides
Mass Murder							
Incidents	156	49	57	28	30	317	
Victims	719	222	431	254	126	1,626	
Offenders	162	101	63	59	NA	355	
Offender Age							
Under 20	5.5%	7.8%	4.9%	13.8%	—	6.7%	18.6%
20–29	25.8%	48.5%	55.7%	37.9%	—	38.5%	40.9%
30–39	37.4%	35.0%	14.8%	17.2%	—	31.2%	20.0%
40–49	23.3%	6.8%	18.0%	13.8%	—	16.9%	11.7%
50+	8.0%	1.9%	6.6%	17.2%	—	6.7%	8.8%
Total	100.0%	100.0%	100.0%	100.0%	—	100.0%	100.0%
Offender Sex							
Male	92.0%	94.2%	93.4%	96.6%	—	93.3%	90.5%
Female	8.0%	5.8%	6.6%	3.4%	—	6.7%	9.5%
Total	100.0%	100.0%	100.0%	100.0%	—	100.0%	100.0%
Offender Race							
White	47.9%	22.3%	49.2%	53.6%	—	41.1%	42.9%
Black	30.7%	50.5%	31.1%	32.1%	—	36.6%	54.3%
Hispanic	14.1%	19.4%	8.2%	10.7%	—	14.4%	NA
Other	7.4%	7.8%	11.5%	3.6%	—	7.9%	2.8%
Total	100.0%	100.0%	100.0%	100.0%	—	100.0%	100.0%
Weapon							
Gun	78.3%	85.4%	93.7%	60.0%	88.9%	82.5%	69.0%
Nongun	21.7%	14.6%	6.3%	40.0%	11.1%	17.5%	31.0%
Total	100.0%	100.0%	100.0%	100.0%	100.0%	100.0%	100.0%

No information is available on the perpetrators in the 30 unsolved incidents.

pistols, a Colt .45 caliber and a Glock 9-mm, the gunman had navigated deliberately through two Atlanta investment offices, All-Tech and Momentum Securities, located just across Piedmont Road from each other. The afternoon shooting spree left nine dead and a dozen others wounded. By sundown later that evening, Barton had turned his gun on himself when cornered by police at a gas station several miles northwest of the scene of the crime.

What was it that caused Mark Barton to snap? And did he in fact snap? The widespread notion that mass gunmen like Barton erupt suddenly into an uncontrollable, murderous rage is deeply rooted in the popular vernacular frequently used to describe these events: expressions such as "going berserk," "going ballistic," or even "going postal" (a code word for workplace massacres coined after a string of post office shootings in the mid-1980s and early 1990s). Psychiatric research has also generally supported the idea that mass murderers "run amok"—they are totally out of touch with reality (i.e., psychotic) and select victims at random who happen to be "in the wrong place at the wrong time."[4]

A more careful examination reveals quite a different picture. On the contrary, most mass killers do not just snap and start shooting anything that moves. Typically, these murderers generally act with calm deliberation, often planning their assault days, if not months, in advance. Their preparations often involve assembling the arsenal of weaponry as well as the most effective means of ambush. In addition, mass murderers tend to be quite selective in targeting their victims. They aim to kill those individuals they are convinced are responsible for their miseries, frequently ignoring anyone not implicated in the plot against them.

Mark Barton surely didn't just wake up on that warm July day and spontaneously decide to perpetrate a bloodbath. His crime spree was hardly sudden and episodic. Two days earlier, Barton had rammed a claw hammer into the skull of Leigh Ann, his 27-year-old second wife, stuffing her body into a closet at their home in the Atlanta suburb of Stockbridge. The next morning, he took his two children, 12-year-old Matthew and 8-year-old Mychelle, to get haircuts. Later that night— the eve of his downtown shooting spree—Barton bludgeoned his son and daughter as they slept in their beds. He then held each child face down in the bathtub to ensure they would not wake up in pain. Once he was certain they were dead, he tucked them both into their beds and placed a favorite toy next to each of them—a Game Boy for his son and a stuffed animal for his daughter.

Barton was so deliberate in his actions that he left a note at his home explaining his motives. "I killed Leigh Ann because she was one of the main reasons for my demise," Barton wrote. "I killed the children to exchange them for five minutes of pain for a lifetime of pain. I forced myself to do it to keep them from suffering so much later. No mother, no father, no relatives." He also left several other notes around the house relaying whatever sentiments came to mind. Next to his son's body, Barton placed a brief message to God: "I give you Matthew David Barton— my son, my buddy, my life. Please take care of him."

There is considerable evidence, moreover, that Barton's murder string may have actually started 6 years earlier. He was a suspect in the untimely death of his first wife and her mother at his in-law's home in Alabama. Not only did this clear the way for him to be with his 21-year-old girlfriend/mistress Leigh Ann (who later became his second wife and next victim), but also the life insurance proceeds became invaluable for him to get a fresh start on his slumping career.

The popular image of a killer who shoots randomly at human targets without rhyme or reason would hardly characterize Barton's crimes or, for that matter, the actions of most mass killers. It was no accident or random choice that Barton selected the location for his vengeful shooting spree. The two day-trading centers were the very places where he had been ruined financially. He had failed miserably in the high-stakes, high-pressure occupation of day-trading in volatile technology stocks.

Barton lost $153,000 in a single day, forcing Momentum Securities to call in his credit. He turned next to All-Tech and pushed his losses to almost a half-million dollars. He also resented those around him who had profited so handsomely on trades of shares of internet stocks such as Amazon and Yahoo. As he wrote in his suicide letter, "I don't plan to live very much longer. Just long enough to kill as many of the people that greedily sought my destruction."

Barton's rampage is not the only example of a murder incident that began in the family and then spilled into the workplace. In April 2006, Herbert Chalmers took the life of Sylvia Haynes, 53, the mother of his child, at her apartment. A few hours later, he was overheard bragging about plans to kill his boss. He then drove to the catering service where he had once worked, a company located on the northwestern edge of St. Louis employing 50 workers, and shot to death an owner of the company and the owner's daughter (who operated the payroll office). Chalmers then committed suicide. A smart employee pushed the owner's wheelchair-bound husband into a cooler where he was out of Chalmers's sight and therefore saved his life.

According to his coworkers, Chalmers was a disgruntled former employee who had been fired after failing to come to work on the day before his rampage. The family connection involved his child support payments. Company employees told the police that Chalmers became enraged when he was told his wages would be garnished for child support. He apparently blamed the mother of his child as well as the catering company and decided to get even with both.

The Role of Firearms

As shown in Table 9.1, 82.5% of mass murderers kill their victims with a gun. Especially for a mass killer who carefully selects his victims, firearms play a key role in several respects. Most important, the gun corrects the perceived power imbalance between the employee and his or her superior. The gun is the Great Equalizer, as 28-year-old Gang Lu put it in a letter to the press just before his 1991 rampage at the University of Iowa in which he sought out and executed three professors who had overlooked him for an important dissertation prize. Actually, over a 12-minute period, the graduate student in physics shot to death five members of the university community. If he had had a knife or had used his hands, there is little chance that Gang Lu would have amassed such a large body count. Using explosives, he might have taken the lives of individuals who had nothing to do with his perceived mistreatment.

The gun, of course, is simply far more lethal than a knife, particularly if the avenger seeks to execute large numbers. Lankford has shown that accessibility to firearms predisposes a country to experience large numbers of mass killings, regardless of the mental health of its citizens.[5] Table 9.2, which lists the largest mass killings in the United States, illustrates the extent of carnage literally triggered with firearms. In 24 of the 30 mass murder incidents, guns were involved. The gun also psychologically distances the attacker from his victims. Although full of rage, he might be deterred were it necessary to kill with his hands. By contrast, a gun makes it very easy psychologically, and U.S. gun laws make it very easy for him to acquire what he needs to carry out his act of vengeance. Louisville's Joseph Wesbecker went into a gun shop, pointed to a semi-automatic weapon displayed under the counter, and asked "How much?" Surprised at the price, he responded, "That's all? I'll take two!"

Although Great Britain has far tighter restrictions on guns than does the United States, mass shootings have occurred there in workplaces, families, schools, and even public places. On June 2, 2010, a down-on-his-luck cabbie, Derrick Bird from Cumbria, a small town north of London, used two licensed firearms, a .22 rifle and a shotgun, to kill his brother, his lawyer, and nine others chosen largely

Table 9.2 Largest Mass Murders in the United States Since 1900

Name(s)	Victims	Year	Location type	Place	Weapon(s)
Timothy J. McVeigh	168	1995	Federal building	Oklahoma City, OK	Bomb
Julio Gonzalez	87	1990	Nightclub	New York, NY	Fire
Stephen Paddock	58	2017	Concert	Las Vegas, NV	Gun
Omar Saddiqui Mateen	49	2016	Nightclub	Orlando, FL	Gun
Andrew Kehoe	45	1927	School	Bath, MI	Bomb
Jack Gilbert Graham	44	1955	Airplane	Denver, CO	Airplane
David Burke	43	1987	Airplane	Cayucos, CA	Airplane
Seung-Hui Cho	32	2007	College	Blacksburg, VA	Gun
Adam Peter Lanza	27 (26+1)	2012	School	Newtown, CT	Gun
Devin Patrick Kelley	25	2017	Church	Sutherland Springs, TX	Gun
Humberto de la Torre	25	1982	Hotel	Los Angeles, CA	Fire
George Jo Hennard	23	1991	Restaurant	Killeen, TX	Gun
James Oliver Huberty	21	1984	Restaurant	San Ysidro, CA	Gun
Nikolas Cruz	17	2018	School	Parkland, FL	Gun
Charles Whitman	16 (14+2)	1966	College	Austin, TX	Gun
Ronald Gene Simmons	16 (14+2)	1987	Home	Dover, AR	Gun/Knife
Syed Rizwan Farook & Tashfeen Malik	14	2014	Workplace	San Bernardino, CA	Gun
Patrick Sherrill	14	1986	Post office	Edmond, OK	Gun
Eric Harris & Dylan Klebold	13	1999	School	Littleton, CO	Gun
George Banks	13	1982	Home	Wilkes-Barre, PA	Gun
Howard Unruh	13	1949	City street	Camden, NJ	Gun
Jiverly Wong	13	2009	Immigration center	Binghamton, NY	Gun
Nidal Malik Hasan	13	2009	Military base	Fort Hood, TX	Gun
Willie Mak, Benjamin Ng, & Tony Ng	13	1983	Nightclub	Seattle, WA	Gun
Aaron Alexis	12	2013	Navy yard	Washington, DC	Gun
James Eagan Holmes	12	2012	Movie theater	Aurora, CO	Gun
Mark O. Barton	12 (9+3)	1999	Office building	Atlanta, GA	Gun
James Ruppert	11	1975	Home	Hamilton, OH	Gun
Michael Kenneth McLendon	10	2009	Home	Geneva, AL	Gun
James Edward Pough	10 (8+2)	1990	Office building	Jacksonville, FL	Gun

Note: Cases through February 2018. Victim counts within parentheses represent those killed during and then prior to the mass murder.

at random. Although many Brits saw this as a failure of gun control to prevent assailants bent on destruction and others as justification for tighter restrictions, no set of laws can guarantee that mass shootings will never occur. Were it not for its strict gun laws, England could conceivably experience more episodes than it does.

In China, where gun control laws are extremely strict, a rash of mass slashings and hammer attacks singling out youngsters in elementary school classrooms began in March 2010 and continued into 2012. In April 2010, a 33-year-old knife-wielding former teacher wounded 16 students and a teacher at Hongfu Primary School. One month later, an unemployed 47-year-old man walked into Zhongxin Kindergarten, where he stabbed 29 students, two teachers, and a security guard. Most of the victims were only 4 years old. All of them survived the attack.

Terrorists tend to prefer explosives over guns or knives. The 1995 bombing of a federal building in Oklahoma City in which 168 men, women, and children lost their lives is more typical of terrorism than it is of nonpolitical acts of mass murder. Most mass killers are much more selective than terrorists in their choice of victims. Bombs might maximize the carnage, but firearms are also extremely deadly weapons, and they allow a killer to aim his violence at the particular targets he associates with causing his miseries in life—at certain family members, coworkers, classmates, or members of a despised outgroup.

Gun advocates have argued that gun-free zones issue an invitation to potential mass killers by assuring they will not be confronted by armed opposition. According to Lott, for example, James Holmes purposely selected the Century 16 Movie Theater in Aurora, because it alone advertised being a gun-free zone.[6] Moreover, advocates argue that civilians carrying concealed weapons would be able to stop a mass killer before he amasses a large body count. Yet Duwe and his collaborators have found instead that only 13% of mass public shootings perpetrated between January 2009 and July 2015 occurred in gun-free zones.[7] Phillips and his associates similarly concluded that concealed handgun licensing was independent of violent crime rates. It depends on where the line is drawn.[8] If the almost 50% of mass murders that happen in residences are included, then the influence of gun-free zones becomes sharply reduced. If schools and college campuses are included, then there will be a major increase in the presence of mass murder located in gun-free zones.

Rather than being deterred by an armed opposition, a dedicated gunman might even secure additional weapons from those victims who are carrying their own firearms. Days prior to his September 13, 2013, massacre of 12 people at a Washington, D.C., Navy Yard, Aaron Alexis test-fired an AR-15 assault rifle at a Lorton, Virginia, gun shop but was prevented from buying one because of a state law limiting the sale of such weapons to Virginia residents. According to the statute, an "assault firearm" refers to any semi-automatic rifle or pistol that is equipped with a 20+ round magazine or that can accommodate a silencer or a folding stock. As a result, the 34-year-old assailant entered the Navy Yard armed only with an 870 Remington pump-action shotgun that he carried unobtrusively in sections and then assembled in a men's room. Moving through the building, he apparently obtained a couple of semi-automatic 9-mm pistols and ammunition from two of his fallen victims. Many of the navy's employees at the yard were carrying authorized firearms, but their presence in large numbers did not discourage the amassing of a large body count.[9]

The October 1, 2017, massacre at a country music festival on the Las Vegas Strip injected a frightening new dimension into the gun debate. Fifty-eight of those in attendance were shot to death; hundreds more were injured. The killer, 64-year-old Stephen Paddock, a local professional gambler and former accountant who lacked a criminal record and had no formal psychiatric history, shot through the smashed window of his room on the 32nd floor of the Mandalay Bay Hotel, overlooking the packed open-air concert below. In a matter of just 10 minutes, the venue was transformed into a scene of death and despair. That's also how long it took for the police to reach the gunman's location, prompting Paddock to take his own life.

Audio recordings of the killer's rapid-fire onslaught suggested immediately that he had used an automatic weapon, such as a machine gun. The weapons found in his hotel room consisted of 23 firearms, including 12 semi-automatic rifles that had been outfitted with a "bump stock," an apparatus that replaces a rifle's standard stock, the part held against the shoulder. The bump stock permits a rifle to slide back and forth quickly, so that it fires almost at the rate of an automatic weapon. With the aid of thousands of rounds of ammunition and a bump stock modifying the two rifles he chose to fire on the crowd of concert-goers, Paddock was able to perpetrate the deadliest mass shooting in modern American history.

Just over a month following the Las Vegas massacre, the nation was stunned once again by another large-scale mass shooting. On Sunday, November 5, 2017, dozens of parishioners of a Baptist church in Sutherland Springs, Texas, were shot, 25 fatally (along with the fetus of one pregnant victim), by Devin Patrick Kelley, 26. Kelley's rampage is believed to be the result of an ongoing domestic dispute involving his former in-laws, who usually attended the church. Although his former mother-in-law was not present on the day of the massacre, his former wife's grandmother was present and was among those killed. After the shooting, Kelley fled from the church and then was pursued in a high-speed chase by two citizens. Kelley eventually crashed his car and used his handgun to take his own life.

Kelley's background included a failed stint in the military and a history of domestic violence. Just prior to his rampage, Kelley posted on Facebook a photograph of himself posing with a gun, and sent threatening texts to former in-laws. Kelley appears to reflect the usual pseudo-commando profile, an angry man who blamed everyone else for his own failings.

Indiscriminate Massacres

There are, of course, cases of mass murderers who do kill more or less indiscriminately, on average about five a year in the United States. On October 16, 1991, one day after he turned 35, George Hennard Jr. rammed his pickup truck through the plate glass window of Luby's Cafeteria in Killeen, Texas, and then randomly opened fire on customers as they ate their lunch. Hennard's crime would not necessarily have suggested a vendetta against any group in particular, but statements from his neighbors and his own written words clearly revealed that he blamed women, above all others, for everything that went wrong in his life and wanted to get even with them. Yet, getting out of his truck and positioning his two semi-automatic pistols, Hennard shot at anyone in his path, regardless of gender, and then ended his killing spree by shooting himself in the head. Including one victim who died a few days later, Hennard's murder toll at Luby's totaled 23. Nineteen others were wounded in the attack, some seriously.

Similarly, the Aurora cinema killer, 24-year-old James Holmes, in July 2012, directed gunfire indiscriminately at total strangers in the audience of a showing for a new Batman film. After leaving his PhD program in neuroscience at the University of Colorado in June 2012, he opened fire in a crowded cinema rather than on campus, where he might have taken the lives of the professors on his graduate committee. As indicated earlier, there have been other graduate students who blame professors for their loss of academic standing, but they usually aim their violence at faculty and students, not at dozens of strangers in a motion theater.

The Aurora killer's indiscriminate rampage provides a clue as to his mind-set. On campus, Holmes had seen a psychotherapist who specialized in schizophrenia.

The diagnosis of schizophrenia would explain a number of characteristics that depart from the profile of a typical mass killer. It would explain why Holmes dyed his hair red and then informed the police, "I am the Joker" when he was apprehended. If schizophrenic, he might really have believed it. It would explain why he booby-trapped his apartment with explosives in order to take the lives of police officers but then told the police about it before they entered the building. His original intention was to rig his apartment so that attention was diverted from his cinema attack. But he seemed to be profoundly confused, suffering from a serious thought disorder that prevented even more innocent lives from being taken by the bombs in his apartment. It would explain why he never intended to commit suicide. Many other mass murderers set out to take their own lives, even if they don't succeed. This killer went to the crime scene wearing protective body armor and then dropped his weapons and gave himself up without a struggle.

In some multiple homicides, the crime scene can move from place to place, because it consists of the killer's vehicle. We saw this phenomenon earlier in the murder spree committed in England by cab driver Derrick Bird, who shot many of his victims while seated in his taxi. In the United States, an Uber driver in Kalamazoo, Michigan, allegedly committed a series of random shootings in three locations: outside a restaurant, at a car dealership, and at an apartment complex nearby. On the night of February 20, 2016, Jason Dalton, the 45-year-old Uber driver, killed between transporting various customers from place to place. Dalton's motive was unclear: He claimed to have been controlled by an Uber app from the devil that took over his mind and body and forced him to take lives. He told the police that his iPhone directed him where to go and when to shoot people. Six people were shot to death and two others were injured. Dalton's trial was scheduled for the fall of 2017. His plea was a rare one: Not guilty by reason of insanity.

Targeting a Category of Victims

Holmes may have chosen a crowded cinema in order to maximize his body count. Yet more often, the location and even the particular victims are chosen because the killer sees them as responsible for his misfortunes. In May 2014, 22-year-old Elliot Rodger took the lives of six people and injured another 14 in Isla Vista, California. Rodger had felt profoundly rejected and decided to exact a deadly measure of revenge against females—especially the young and attractive females who ignored him—as well as the males they seemed to prefer over him.

First, he stabbed to death three young men who lived in his apartment complex. Then, driving to a nearby Starbucks, he ordered a triple vanilla latte that he consumed while seated behind the wheel of his black BMW. Along the way to waging his "war against women," he paused long enough to record and upload a chilling 7-minute YouTube video titled *Elliot Rodger's Retribution*, in which he expressed his frustration and anger in no uncertain terms. His plan was to punish women as well as the "obnoxious" men with whom they preferred to have sex.

"I'm 22 years old and still a virgin," Rodger confessed. "Never even kissed a girl. And through college, 2 1/2 years, more than that actually, I'm still a virgin. It has been very torturous," he said. "The popular kids, you never accepted me and now you will all pay for it. Girls, all I ever wanted was to love you, be loved by you. I wanted a girlfriend. I wanted sex, love, affection, adoration."

Rodger had made his intention very clear in a lengthy and rambling autobiography that he called his manifesto: "I will attack the very girls who represent everything I hate in the female gender: The hottest sorority of UCSB. I will kill every slut at the Alpha Phi sorority." Two hours later, he drove up to the

Alpha Phi sorority house, where he shot three women standing outside, injuring two and killing a third.

Rodger's next stop was a local deli. Inside, he took the life of a UC Santa Barbara student and then drove his BMW around the neighborhood near campus, where he opened fire randomly on pedestrians walking nearby. After being wounded in a gun battle with the police, Rodger's final act was to take his own life with a gunshot to his head. In a matter of hours, he had killed six and injured another 14, before committing suicide.

There are many mass killers like Rodger who target an entire category of victims, often expressing in the most extreme violence their disdain for one group or another. Twenty-five-year-old Patrick Purdy was a young man filled with resentment. Depressed and paranoid, Purdy was almost always alone, had no girlfriends, and seemed to dislike everyone. He was conspiratorial in his thinking. In the end, however, he singled out a particular group—Southeast Asians—as being especially blameworthy. On January 17, 1989, Purdy visited his former elementary school in what had become a predominantly Southeast Asian section of Stockton, California. He was hoping to kill as many Asian children as possible.

For some 5 years before opening fire at an elementary school, Purdy had drifted from place to place, along the way repeatedly getting into trouble with the law. In 1980, he was arrested in Los Angeles for soliciting a sex act from an undercover police officer. In 1982, he was arrested on charges of possession of hashish, and the next year he was convicted of possessing a dangerous weapon. A few months later, he was arrested on a charge of receiving stolen property. In October 1984, he did a 30-day stint in county jail in Woodland, California, for being an accomplice to a robbery. In 1987, he was arrested for indiscriminately firing a 9-mm pistol in the El Dorado National Forest. On top of this, he was charged with resisting arrest for kicking a deputy sheriff and shattering a window of the patrol car with his feet.

Purdy despised almost everyone, but especially people in positions of authority and especially his "enemies," the newcomers to America's shores. Purdy had a special hatred for Southeast Asians. He often bragged about his father's conquests in the Vietnam War. Purdy fantasized about following in his dad's army bootsteps, but it would have to remain a fantasy because Patrick was only 7 years old when the U.S. forces pulled out of the Vietnam conflict.

Purdy would fight his own war against Southeast Asians. He would try one more time to achieve something big, and this time, his mission would not fail. For weeks, Purdy had been living in Room 104 of the El Rancho Motel on the edge of Stockton, California, a riverfront agricultural city located some 80 miles east of San Francisco. He needed to concentrate, to plot his final assault on those who were to blame for his miserable existence. "General Purdy" spent hour after hour, day after day, in his "war room," manipulating the hundreds of toy soldiers, tanks, jeeps, and weapons that he had collected in order to simulate an attack and to develop an effective military strategy. There were toy soldiers everywhere: on the shelves, on the heating grates, even in the refrigerator.

On Tuesday morning, January 17, Purdy donned his military flak jacket, picked up a handgun and his AK-47 semi-automatic assault rifle, and drove his 1977 Chevrolet station wagon a couple of miles to the Cleveland Elementary School in Stockton—the same elementary school he had attended from kindergarten to third grade. But things recently had begun to seem different to him, and it wasn't just having grown older. When he had lived there as a child, the neighborhood was white; now it was predominantly Asian.

Arriving at the Cleveland School just before noon, Purdy could see hundreds of young children—most of them refugees from Cambodia, Vietnam, China, and

Mexico. Purdy preferred the term *boat people* when he spoke disparagingly of Asian refugees. Despite the chill in the air, the children played joyfully at recess on the blacktop in front of the brown stucco building, unaware of the war that would soon be declared.

As a diversionary tactic, Purdy parked his car and then set it ablaze with a Molotov cocktail in a Budweiser bottle. Then he eased through a gap in the fence surrounding the school building and walked onto the crowded school grounds, where he opened fire. Over a period of several minutes, Purdy sprayed 60 rounds from his AK-47 at screaming children, firing in a sweeping motion across the blacktop. He didn't stop until he heard the sirens of approaching police cars. No one would take him alive. He removed the handgun from his belt. He had saved this gun for one purpose.

Purdy died instantly from a single shot from the gun on which he had written the word *Victory*. Purdy's victory toll was high. Five children, aged 6 through 9, all from Southeast Asia, were dead, and 29 more, in addition to one teacher, were wounded.

Rodger hated women; Purdy despised Southeast Asians. In the early morning hours of March 25, 2006, 28-year-old Kyle Huff targeted ravers—young people who attend all-night dance parties where electronic and rave music are played. At a rave after-party in Seattle, Huff opened fire, killing six ravers ranging in age from 14 to 32. He then placed the gun in his mouth and pulled the trigger, taking his own life.[10]

Kyle and Kane Huff were twin brothers who had lived together in Seattle for almost five years, after leaving their home in Whitefish, Montana. While they were students at Whitefish High School, the twins looked and acted different—they wore trench coats, combat boots, and long hair and were pretty much ignored by most other students, who regarded them as outsiders. But the twins also had family members to give them the support and encouragement they needed. After graduation, Kyle was able to keep a full-time job.

After moving to Seattle, however, Kyle's employment picture became more and more sporadic. He had been working, off and on, as a pizza deliveryman, but was out of work at the time he went on his rampage. Two months earlier, he had worked at a nearby Pizza Hut. He also briefly delivered for Pagliacci Pizza. Two years before that, he was employed for a few days at a Domino's Pizza close to his apartment, but he was quickly fired for his unreliability. With every lost job he became more and more frustrated.

He then began to stalk ravers, perhaps seeing in their lifestyle everything lacking in his. They were sociable; he was not. They had sexual relationships and lots of friends; he did not. They were able to have fun; he was always deadly serious. But unlike many mainstream members of the Seattle community, the ravers were tolerant; they emphasized respect for differences and peace rather than competition and rivalry. Kyle was an outsider in the social and work scenes, but he was accepted—even if only peripherally—by the ravers.

Almost one month after the massacre occurred, the manager of an apartment complex about a mile from Huff's apartment inspected a nearby dumpster and discovered what he thought was a bomb but turned out to be only modeling clay and wires. Wrapped into the "bomb" was Huff's handwritten suicide note, dated three days before he committed mass murder and apparently meant to be read by his twin brother Kane.

In the following suicide letter, Huff explains that what he sees as the "hippie" preoccupation with "the world of sex" is destroying our country. "This is a revolution," he tells his brother. And he urges Kane not to kill himself but to help fight for the cause.

03/23/06

To Kane From Kyle

I hope that you will find this letter after the fact. Don't let the police or FBI keep you from haveing it, this is my last wish for you to see this. Don't kill yourself moron. That's the last thing I would want to happen, As long as your alive, so is part of me, ya know, I hate leaving you by yourself, but this is something I feel I have to do, My life would always feel incomplete otherwise. I can't let them get away with what they're doing, kids like me and you are seriously dying over this shit, I hate this world of sex that they think they are striving to make, this is a revolution brother, the most important thing to happen since Man began, to let it die out would be a crime. I will never able to "cum" with them, I will always see it as hell. The things they say "and do" they're rapeing us are just too disturbing to me to just ignore and try to live my life with. I know this is a short letter and might sound stupid, but it would take a book to properly explain this to you, I don't have the time for that, or the will. The basic jist of it is that they're fucking, next to us when we're really high to make us freak out. And trying to stop are heart by making it palpatate And they are doing it it's just a question of if were willing to be OK with it. And obviously im not. Maybe someday you'll be willing to help me kill this hippie shit. I know that its going to get worse now, but that's part of the . . .

Now kids Now!!! Bye Kane, I love you

GETTING EVEN THROUGH MURDER

Many rampages are much more selective than indiscriminate, occurring at the killer's workplace or residence where relationships that turn sour can have a profound impact on his self-esteem and hope for the future. Michael McDermott, in December 2000, killed seven of his coworkers at Edgewater Technology in Wakefield, Massachusetts, but he hardly shot indiscriminately at anything that moved. Blaming his dire financial position on certain offices of the company, McDermott selectively targeted his fellow employees only in payroll and human resources. Moreover, McDermott's rampage was anything but spontaneous. A day earlier, he had left a cache of weapons and ammunition under his desk, so as to be fully prepared for his murderous onslaught. In court, McDermott tried to convince the jury that he was a victim of severe mental illness—that he had been convinced that he was killing not coworkers but Hitler and six of Hitler's henchmen. Not believing the defendant, the jury gave McDermott a life sentence without parole eligibility. The sentencing outcome for McDermott is typical. For mass murderers who do not kill themselves or who are shot down by police, they can expect to spend the rest of their lives in prison or be executed.

We don't usually think of a military base as a workplace, but that is exactly what it is for hundreds of thousands of our service men and women. On November 5, 2009, at 1:30 p.m., a U.S. Army psychiatrist, Major Nidal Malik Hasan, opened fire at the Fort Hood Soldier Readiness Processing Center, located just outside of Killeen, Texas. The 39-year-old Muslim American shooter killed 13 people (12 soldiers and a civilian) and injured another 30, before being subdued by police officers from Fort Hood's Department of Emergency Services. Hasan had recently suffered a string of negative evaluations for his substandard performance. In addition, he may have felt harassed by fellow soldiers because of his Muslim faith. And, given his standoffish nature, he was not likely to have sought support from others.

The killer's mind-set had not always been so negative. Hasan had enlisted more than 2 decades ago, hoping to pursue his education and to express his loyalty as a proud U.S. citizen. This was long before the war in Iraq, the 9/11 attacks, and even the Gulf War. At this juncture, however, he dreaded going to war against Islam, as he reportedly viewed it. Despite attempts to gain a discharge from the U.S. Army, Hasan was facing deployment overseas. It was one thing to counsel returning soldiers here in the United States but quite another to support the war from the front lines.

It is no coincidence that Hasan's mass murder occurred outside his worksite, the Soldier Readiness Center, where soldiers receive routine medical treatment immediately before being deployed to war zones. His murderous rampage was probably an act of terrorism, as indicated by Hasan's Muslim affiliation, his Middle Eastern–style clothing, and reports of his having shouted out "Allahu Akbar," an expression of praise to God. He had also communicated by e-mail with an imam who declared Hasan a hero for shooting down 13 people.

At the same time, Hasan's rampage was also a classic case of workplace homicide, even though a military base would seem to be an unusual location. Such a crime would seem more likely to occur inside an office building or a factory. Despite its unique function, Fort Hood is indeed a workplace, the U.S. Army an employer, and Hasan a disgruntled worker attempting to avenge perceived unfair treatment on the job. Unlike terrorists generally, there is no evidence that Hasan's objective was to spread terror throughout the country or the armed services. His rampage was apparently selective, not indiscriminate. He chose the location—his workplace—and then apparently singled out certain coworkers for death. Revenge for perceived mistreatment may have inspired his rampage as much as any political or religious considerations.[11]

Apparently, Americans were split as to Hasan's motivation. When asked by pollsters in the days following the massacre whether the killer's actions were to be considered an act of terrorism or an act of murder, 47% responded "terrorism" and 45% responded "murder."[12]

More often than not, mass killers select particular victims to kill in order to avenge perceived injustices. In December 1987, after Ronald Gene Simmons executed his 14 family members for insult and insubordination, he then launched a 45-minute shooting spree through the town of Russellville, Arkansas, killing a woman who had spurned his romantic advances and a former boss and wounding several others at former worksites. As he surrendered, Simmons remarked, "I've gotten everybody who hurt me."

Despite a killer's selectivity, however, even in the most focused rampage, many innocent victims die in the crossfire or because they stand in the way of the killer's murderous swath. Frequently, however, they are killed because the gunman associates them with the primary target. The notion of murder by proxy (described earlier in Chapter 4) explains the carnage at many worksites. The mass killer seeks revenge by targeting a primary victim he holds responsible for his miseries as well as anyone associated with that primary victim, whether coworkers, fellow newcomers, service providers, customers, or the like. Problems at the workplace occasionally spill over onto related venues in the life of an angry and frustrated individual. In April 2009, Jiverly Wong, a 41-year-old Vietnamese immigrant, was despondent about having lost his job at a Shop-Vac assembly plant in Binghamton, New York. His anger was not directed toward the company, however, but toward the nonprofit American Civic Association, whose mandate involved helping immigrants in the Binghamton area with counseling and resettlement. Wong's facility with the English language was extremely marginal, and he seemed to blame the immigration service center.

Wong arrived at the association in downtown Binghamton as a citizenship class was in progress on a Friday morning. Barricading the back door so as to trap his potential victims, Wong shot to death 13 people, critically injured another 4, and then took his own life. The police arrived to find all of the bodies in a classroom and 37 terrified survivors hiding in closets and a boiler room on the premises.

During the 1980s and continuing through the early 1990s, a string of massacres occurred at post offices around the country (so many that the phrase "going postal" became part of the vernacular). Then, in January 2006, after a total absence of deadly postal shootings in the United States for a period of almost eight years, a former postal worker on retirement disability for psychological reasons opened fire at a mail processing facility in Goleta, California, killing six employees and then herself. It was later discovered that her body count was even larger than first thought: Just before driving to the postal facility, she had shot to death a former neighbor, with whom she had had a heated argument.

The killer was Jennifer San Marco, a 44-year-old woman who, because of serious long-term psychological difficulties, had not worked at the mail processing plant for more than 2 years. During her 6 years on the job, there were several reports that her behavior was increasingly strange, bizarre, or psychotic. She apparently heard voices, engaged in loud conversations with herself, stared at her coworkers, and made a number of racist remarks. The killer apparently believed that she was being threatened by a conspiracy involving workers at the mail processing plant, a local medical facility, and the Santa Barbara County Sheriff's Department. In addition, San Marco was reportedly hostile toward minorities. Only one of her seven victims was white. She shot to death three blacks, one Chinese American, one Filipino, and a Latino.

Her mental illness notwithstanding, San Marco had legally purchased her 15-round Smith and Wesson pistol and ammunition from a pawn shop. The required background check had turned up no problems. Curiously, most disgruntled workers and other mass killers would not even consider buying a weapon through illegal means. After all, they see themselves as law-abiding citizens, not criminals. They are just looking for some justice. To them, the murder is not a crime; it's simply just deserts. For example, 35-year-old Colin Ferguson, who on December 7, 1993, transformed the Long Island Railroad into a shooting gallery when he shot to death six commuting passengers, purchased his gun legally in California. Nine months before going on his killing spree, he checked into a cheap hotel and waited more than the necessary 2 weeks to qualify for a legal gun purchase.

LOSSES AND FRUSTRATIONS

Even though mass slaughters may not be sudden, there generally are still clear-cut events that precipitate the bloodshed. The most random crimes are often inspired by small and seemingly insignificant matters but that, in the killer's paranoid and sometimes psychotic view of the world, are important concerns. Most mass murderers experience acute life stressors and/or chronic strains before they turn to violence as a response.[13] In more typical cases, the gunman seeks to redress a personal slight, often real, usually involving a catastrophic loss—the loss of a relationship, a job, or even honor. In Chapter 4, we examined certain cases of mass murder within the family. One of the more common forms of mass killing involves a head of household who decides either to punish his wife and children for some transgression or, alternatively, to protect them from the misery of living in a cold, cruel world. However, one of the most frequent forms of mass murder, particularly in recent years, surrounds employment disputes—a firing, layoff, warning, or losing out on a promotion or award.

In January 2009, Ervin Lupoe, a medical technician and resident of Wilmington, California, sent a letter to a local television station's website complaining that both he and his wife had been fired unfairly from their jobs at Kaiser Permanente Medical Center in Los Angeles. According to Lupoe's letter, two days before being terminated, an administrator told the couple: "You should not even have bothered to come to work today. You should have blown your brains out." Lupoe added that he had given up hope when the medical center failed to offer him any assistance, even though they were aware that he and his wife had no sources of income and were supporting five children under the age of 8. Finally, Lupoe wrote that he planned to kill his children, his wife, and their children as "an escape for the whole family." After gunning down all the members of his family, Lupoe wrote a suicide note in which he explained that he had not wanted to leave their children with a stranger and then took his own life.

When love and family loyalty become a component in the mass killer's motivation, outsiders—neighbors, friends, and extended kin—are typically incredulous to learn that a seemingly loving and normal husband and father has slaughtered his wife and children before committing suicide. In July 2000, residents of the seaside suburban community of Barry, outside of Cardiff in South Wales, were shocked to discover a gruesome family annihilation in their midst. Forty-nine-year-old Robert Mochrie, often described as a "devoted family man," had hanged himself after bludgeoning to death his wife and four children as they slept in their middle-class, single-family home.

Mochrie had a 10-year history of severe depression and had seen a psychiatrist on a number of occasions. He and his wife of 23 years were no longer intimate, and one of their children was autistic. On top of everything else that went wrong, he had recently experienced a number of failed business ventures that left him in deep debt, unable to pay his bills, and faced with bankruptcy. Being a "loving father and good husband," Mochrie made sure that his family members died in their sleep with a blow to the head, minimizing their pain and suffering. He then covered each body with a blanket, as though trying to protect them.

Other than family annihilations, one of the more prevalent forms of mass killing involves employment disputes that are resolved violently in the workplace. Thirty-three-year-old Paul Calden said that he'd be back, and regrettably for the employees of the Fireman's Fund Insurance Company in Tampa, Florida, he was true to his word. On January 27, 1993, 8 months after being fired from his job, he returned to get his revenge. This time, however, he'd be the one to do the firing. Calden sat in the company cafeteria. He was as cool as the ice in the Diet Coke that he sipped while waiting patiently for his victims to arrive for lunch. Calden approached three of his former supervisors as they were seated together at the back of the lunchroom. Standing over the table and taking aim with his 9-mm semi-automatic pistol, Calden announced, "This is what you get for firing me," and calmly started shooting, methodically encircling the table with gunfire. By the time it was all over, Calden had killed his three former managers and had wounded two other employees. His next and final victim was himself.

Paul Calden was the quintessential disgruntled employee—the so-called coworker from hell. He had drifted from job to job, causing trouble wherever he worked. Just prior to his employment at Fireman's Fund, Calden had worked at Allstate Insurance, where he threatened his supervisor by deliberately displaying the butt of a gun inside his briefcase. This manager was so frightened by Calden that he offered him a severance package that he couldn't refuse.

During his 2-year employment at Fireman's, Calden had developed a reputation for being a belligerent hothead. He constantly challenged his supervisors' authority, at one point nearly coming to blows because of a reprimand. He threatened to sue the company for denying him a raise that he felt he deserved. He shouted obscenities at a female coworker who had taken his favorite parking place. He even filed a harassment complaint because a fellow employee displayed a bumper sticker on her car that offended him.

In contrast to Calden's spotty work record, other vengeful employees like Joseph Wesbecker come to feel invulnerable to job loss because of their long-term employment with the same company. From their perspective, they have given their best years to the boss, have unselfishly dedicated their careers to the organization, and resent that their hard work and loyalty are not being returned in kind by the company.

At the time that he walked into the office of Standard Gravure in Louisville to open fire on his coworkers, workplace avenger Joseph Wesbecker was on long-term disability. Out of work, the 47-year-old divorcé had plenty of time to follow events in the news. Wesbecker was particularly intrigued by Patrick Purdy's January 1989 shooting rampage at the Cleveland Elementary School in Stockton, California, which claimed the lives of five Southeast Asian children. Days after reading the news about Purdy's massacre of students in Stockton, Wesbecker purchased an AK-47 very much like Purdy's.

Just before massacring his coworkers, Wesbecker left behind, in the kitchen of his home, an issue of *Time* magazine whose cover story, "Armed in America," described Patrick Purdy's shooting spree at the Stockton elementary school. Wesbecker had folded back the pages so that a photograph of Purdy's AK-47 was open and facing up. Wesbecker was every bit as angry as the drifter in Stockton, but his enemy was closer to home. Rather than pin all of his problems on Southeast Asians, Wesbecker blamed his bosses at Standard Gravure for his despair. The Louisville printing plant had recently been sold to a new owner, and he felt strongly that the new management team didn't appreciate his more than 20 years of hard work. By all accounts, Wesbecker was an excellent pressman, and he always put in long hours of overtime and extra shifts, which had earned him the nickname "overtime hog."

Suffering from depression, Wesbecker had sought an exemption from a certain job task that was particularly stressful to him, a request that was endorsed by a government employment arbitrator but resisted by management. Wesbecker was so resentful that he told a coworker that he was going to get even with the company and even showed him the gun in his lunch bag with which he intended to carry out his plan of action. He also talked about his "hit list" of intended victims.

Months later, on September 14, 1989, Wesbecker made an unscheduled visit to work—he had a job to do. Roaming the corridors with an AK-47, Wesbecker systematically sought out his intended targets, killing eight and wounding a dozen others. He was so methodical in his assault that he purposely spared a friend: "Not you, John," Wesbecker said to the fortunate coworker who cowered in front of him, and sauntered on by.

PROFILE OF THE WORKPLACE AVENGER

A recurring theme underscoring rampage killers is anger and disgruntlement directed at a company, agency, or other type of workplace. They may be a worker or ex-worker who feels wronged by an employer or a customer or client who feels disregarded or mistreated by a retailer or service provider. Understandably, the most noteworthy examples of workplace-related murder are those in which large numbers of victims are killed or injured, such as the case used here for illustrative purposes. Of course, most workplace avengers do not kill as many as Mark Barton or Joseph Wesbecker killed. Still, the psychological impact on the workforce is significant even if just one person is killed. Even then, after all, there are typically many others who would have witnessed the murder and would have feared for their lives.

Table 9.3 displays information on the characteristics of workplace murderers, in particular those who murder one or more of their coworkers. Whereas teens and young adults are heavily overrepresented among all murderers generally (as was

Table 9.3   Characteristics of Workplace Murderers, 1976–2016

Characteristic	Percentage
Offender age	
Under 18	3.1%
18–24	20.2%
25–34	29.5%
35–49	29.3%
50+	17.8%
Total	100.0%
Average = 35.7	
Offender sex	
Male	91.6%
Female	8.4%
Total	100.0%
Offender race	
White	71.7%
Black	24.6%
Other	3.8%
Total	100.0%
Weapon	
Gun	61.5%
Knife	18.8%
Blunt object	10.3%
Brute force	5.1%
Other	4.4%
Total	100.0%

discussed in Chapter 2), workplace murder is a notable exception to the rule of youth. As shown, more than 47% (compared with 27% of homicide offenders generally) are at least 35 years old. Also as shown, whites represent some 72% of workplace killers, compared to the more even racial split for homicide offenders generally. In fatal workplace disputes, finally, the gender ratio is very close to that for murder in general, with more than 91% male perpetrators.

The overall profile of the typical workplace murderer then is that of a middle-aged white male, who feels that his employment problems signal the end of the world as he knows it. Despite changing gender roles, men—much more than women—still tend to judge their self-worth by what they do rather than who they are. If they aren't doing anything, then what good are they? Furthermore, men tend to regard violence as a means for establishing control, as an offensive move, whereas women see it as a last resort, as a defensive move. Thus, men who suffer psychologically because of the loss of a job are more likely to respond violently in order to "show them who's boss." Or perhaps, women are more content to exact their revenge in quieter ways, for example, by means of poisoning, assassinating someone's character, gossiping, or getting others to do their dirty work.[14]

There are relatively few female workplace avengers. Although women have been offenders in a number of mass murders (e.g., Jennifer San Marco, mentioned earlier), they typically massacre their families. Other women have gone on rampages but have shot to death only one or two victims and thus don't fit the widely accepted definition of a mass murderer. In a rare case of a woman targeting a number of strangers, Sylvia Seegrist, in 1985, randomly shot to death three people outside a shopping mall in Springfield, Pennsylvania. As women begin to focus on their careers in the way that men have traditionally done, they can be expected to face similar disappointments and may become more skilled in the use of firearms. If so, we might reasonably expect to see more female mass killers.

The murders committed by Amy Bishop might foreshadow the future state of the distribution of gender as represented in multiple homicide. The 45-year-old assistant professor of biological sciences was enraged about being denied tenure at the University of Alabama in Huntsville. On the afternoon of February 12, 2010, she attended a Friday faculty meeting armed with a 9-mm handgun. After sitting quietly for a short period of time, she reportedly rose from her chair and, with cool deliberation, immediately started shooting at her shocked colleagues.

Bishop apparently implicated the members of her own department in her failure to receive tenure and remain at the university. She chose to execute those accountable for what she regarded as an intolerable and unjust decision—an outcome that would leave her without much of a chance for a future in academics. When the faculty meeting ended, three faculty members lay dead, and three others were wounded.

Bishop's tenure review may very well have been handled carefully, respectfully, and consistent with due process. And, of course, even if the process was flawed, that would not justify mass murder. The assailant was a Harvard-trained neurobiologist who had accumulated a record of receiving grants and producing scholarly publications. In recent years, she had distinguished herself as one of the inventors of InQ, an incubator for human cell growth. Based on available student evaluations, her teaching was generally at least acceptable by conventional standards, although she also had detractors among the student population. Moreover, Professor Bishop was apparently also known on the campus as a troublemaker—as a thorn in the side of the university's administration. Months earlier, an appeal of her failed tenure application was turned down. According to several people around the campus quoted in news reports, Bishop was quite bitter and vocal about her plight, as the end of her employment at the university approached.

Many Americans take personal responsibility for their employment-related failures (e.g., "I should have tried harder to do what was expected by the boss. Next time, I will."). But workplace avengers typically externalize blame, locating it in the mistreatment by others who, perhaps undeservedly, hold unrestrained power over their fate. Should Professor Bishop, as a noted scholar with an Ivy League pedigree, have questioned the legitimacy of the tenure process or those who were in a position to judge her record of achievement?

Based on reports of Bishop's difficulty getting along with others on campus, it would be all too easy to dismiss this violent episode as just some "nut" who couldn't handle the pressures associated with academic life. Indeed, that seems to be the prevailing view of the hundreds who posted online comments in the days following the shooting. Although hardly justifying a violent response, it should not be overlooked that the prevailing economic climate, in which academic budgets are shrinking and tenure lines evaporating, has rendered the impact of the denial of tenure as catastrophic. For highly trained scholars who lose their jobs, the alternative opportunities can be rather slim. As Cary Nelson, president of the American Association of University Professors, told the *Huntsville Times*, "The most likely result of being denied tenure in this nonexistent job market is that you will not be able to continue teaching. . . . You probably can't get another job."

Some workplace murders involve youthful perpetrators, but most do not. To a younger employee, a job is often just a job, certainly not a career, and there is always another opportunity down the road. The middle-aged employee, however, views termination or the threat of termination as truly the end of the road. He or she sees few opportunities for alternative employment at the same wage, benefit, or status level to which he or she has grown accustomed. At this juncture, the middle-aged worker expects to be at the top of his or her career, not hitting rock bottom.

In part, the middle-aged worker responds desperately and violently, not just because of limited opportunities in the future but because of what has transpired in the past. The road to mass murder, particularly at the job site, is a long one, involving a good number of bumps along the way. Mark Barton, for example, had experienced years of disappointment, which likely eroded his ability to cope and intensified his feelings of persecution. After graduating from the University of South Carolina with a degree in chemistry, he seemed to fail at each and every turn. He was pushed out of an executive position at TLC Manufacturing in Texarkana, Texas, a company he helped to form. Moving next to Georgia, he tried his hand at chemical sales, another dead end financially. Finally, he used the profits from the insurance settlement from his first wife's death to invest in the stock market, a move that ultimately bankrupted him.

Of course, most disgruntled employees and ex-employees don't take out their anger on the company. Some may blame themselves, become depressed, and consider suicide as their only option. Others may take out their frustrations on their family. Workplace avengers are different. Many of them commit suicide, but not until exacting revenge for the wrongs they perceive have been committed against them. Almost without exception, workplace murderers feel as though they are the victims, and that others, especially the boss, have treated them unfairly. Were they to trace the job disappointments to their own inadequacies, they might turn aggression inward. Seeing everyone else to blame, however, they choose to execute those responsible, before taking their own lives.

Perceptions of racial discrimination involve placing responsibility for frustrating circumstances away from the individual employee and onto the company. At the core of an August 10, 2010, massacre at a Hartford, Connecticut, beer distribution plant, a gunman was convinced that he had been a victim of racism. At 7:36 a.m. on Tuesday, August 3, 2010, the police in Manchester, Connecticut, received an emergency call reporting that the gunman was shooting at the offices of Hartford Distributors in the Buckland Industrial Park. When officers arrived on scene, they discovered that eight workers had been slain and two more injured. Confined to a small space in the company office, the gunman, who was black, had taken his own life. But first, he had phoned his mother, explaining that he had shot some people at work, that he loved her and his girlfriend, and that he was sorry.

The killer was identified as 34-year-old Omar Thornton, a warehouse worker who had just been asked to resign (at the threat of being fired) after being caught on video stealing beer from his employer. Having calmly signed a letter of resignation, Thornton pulled out a handgun and started firing on his supervisors, the company president, and a union representative. He then ran through the warehouse and loading dock, shooting certain employees but ignoring others. The life of a disabled worker was spared, as she pleaded with the gunman, and he moved on to kill another victim.

Thornton believed that his perceived mistreatment at work was a result of racial discrimination. He had told a friend that a racial epithet and a noose had been scrawled on the wall of a bathroom in the warehouse. He apparently felt that his termination was just another example of racism. In fact, immediately after shooting his victims, Thornton himself called 9-1-1 to explain the rationale for his rampage. "They treat me bad over here," the killer complained in a calm voice. "They treat all the other black employees bad over here too." He said further, "I took it into my own hands, and handled the problem." Union representatives, however, claimed that Thornton had never filed a complaint about racial harassment. Nor was there any evidence that he had complained to state or federal agencies.

Many Americans, of course, suffer the kinds of catastrophic losses and letdowns endured by Thornton, Barton, and Wesbecker, yet they are able to lean on close friends and family to help them deal with life's disappointments. Most of the workplace avengers, however, are socially isolated. They are either like Paul Calden and live in seclusion or like Barton and don't feel sufficiently connected to family. Socially and psychologically alone, they regard work as the only meaningful part of their lives. When they lose their job, they lose everything. They lack not only the emotional support for their problems but also the healthy reality check as their feelings of paranoia and persecution build.

This is exactly how it was for Joseph Wesbecker. He was divorced for the second time, and his relationships with his children were badly strained. His job was the only thing in his life that was going well and that gave him some sense of purpose and satisfaction—a reason to get up in the morning. But that was taken away when management forced him to take long-term disability rather than to make a reasonable accommodation for his psychological impairment, which was to be exempted from performing a particularly stressful job function.

For a lonely employee, like Wesbecker, termination from a job means not just a loss of self-esteem and the loss of income but also the loss of his only source of companionship—his coworkers. Therefore, job loss carries a double burden: frustration and anger, on the one hand, and a severance of important social anchors, on the other.

Here, too, there is a trend in society that places more and more middle-aged men at risk. A high rate of divorce, greater residential mobility, and a general lack of community and neighborliness mean that, for many Americans, work is their only source of stability and companionship. And men, much more than women, often center all of their friendships on the job.

Finally, a worker may be frustrated and angry and lonely and isolated; he or she may blame the boss and feel that management is corrupt and unfair. But if he or she doesn't have access to a powerful weapon or know how to use it, the disgruntled employee may not be able to exact the kind of revenge that he or she seeks.

PREVENTING MURDERS BY DISGRUNTLED EMPLOYEES AND CUSTOMERS

Nationally, as many as six people are murdered every month at the hands of a coworker or former coworker. And for every tragic incident of workplace homicide, thousands of workers are assaulted or threatened by an associate on the job. Even less conspicuous are the countless numbers of angry workers who seek to sabotage their company's bottom line. They may spread ugly rumors to discourage sales or surreptitiously subvert the manufacturing process. In one case, an angry worker was caught on videotape as he secretly urinated into the company office coffeepot.

In response to concern over violence in the U.S. workplace, a wide range of books and pamphlets, seminars, and consultants have surfaced to help companies, large and small, cope with the growing threat of violence on the job. Some experts focus on security concerns, others on promoting effective Employee Assistance Programs (EAPs). Still others recommend processes to enhance employment screening techniques or channels of communication to alert management about troublesome workers before they explode.[15]

Although all these approaches may be useful, the overriding goal should be to make civility and decency in the workplace as critical a goal as profit. Companies need to upgrade and humanize the way they deal with all employees every day rather than just to focus narrowly on how to respond to the occasional worker who has made threats. Long-term planning to improve employee morale pays off in human terms. A study conducted for Northwestern National Life Insurance concluded that companies with effective grievance, harassment, and security procedures also reported lower rates of workplace violence.[16]

Decades ago, the bond between management and worker was far stronger. Most Americans believed that bosses had the best interests of workers in mind; managers felt that their workforce was loyal to the company. But the expectation of loyalty between worker and boss has gone the way of the dinosaur and has been replaced with an adversarial perspective on both sides. In an era of corporate takeovers, megamergers, skyrocketing salaries for the super-rich, and corporate CEO scandals, workers often feel that they are left with nothing while the corporate fat cats have multimillion-dollar homes and enormous savings accounts. This represents a lethal mix for disenfranchised, marginalized, mentally ill workers who have been demoted, passed over for promotion, or fired.

It isn't only workers and ex-workers who blame their problems on the company. Disgruntled customers, clients, patients, and even citizens sometimes seek to avenge perceived mistreatment by banks, loan offices, law firms, hospitals and clinics, schools and colleges, unemployment offices, courthouses, federal officials—in short, "the system"—through violence and murder. Each year, several dozen workers are killed at the hands of customers or clients.

Mental health workers are at particular risk of being attacked by the people they serve.[17] On occasion, a violent incident with a disgruntled patient results in the murder of a practitioner who works in a clinic, a hospital, or at a client's residence. In August 2004, for example, 26-year-old Teri Zenner, a social worker and graduate student at the University of Kansas, made a home visit to her 17-year-old mentally ill client. Without warning, the client became irate and pulled out a knife, stabbing the social worker to death. Since his wife's murder, Matt Zenner has worked tirelessly to bring to public attention the dangers faced by social workers. He established a scholarship in Teri's memory and has testified before Congress on the problem of violence perpetrated by clients.

In some cases, getting even with the system means targeting a number of individuals. For example, in a suburb of St. Louis, Charles Lee Thornton, age 52, had for years appeared regularly at city council meetings complaining of persecution, fraud, and cover-up by city officials. He was fined repeatedly for code violations, issued a number of unsuccessful lawsuits against the city, and filed a complaint with the Equal Employment Opportunity Commission (ultimately dismissed) alleging racial discrimination in the awarding of contracts he had wanted for his construction company. In 2003, he placed signs on the side of his van, indicating he would never again accept lies from city officials. On February 7, 2008, Thornton went on a shooting spree at a meeting of the city council in city hall, killing six, including a police officer, the head of public works, a reporter, two council members, and the mayor. Thornton was then shot to death by police.

In an earlier episode of a vengeful attack on the system, 45-year-old George Lott opened fire with a concealed 9-mm semi-automatic handgun during an appellate court proceeding in Ft. Worth, Texas, on the morning of July 1, 1992. It appeared to those present in the crowded fourth-floor courtroom that Lott was shooting wildly at anything that moved. The two attorneys who were slain and a third attorney and two judges who were wounded just happened to be at the wrong place at the wrong time. Lott escaped through the mass confusion, only to show up six hours later at a local television station to tell his side of the story. Speaking on-air with the news anchor, Lott detailed his deep-seated grudge against the judicial system that he believed had been unfair to him.

Similarly, in July 1993, eight people were slaughtered at a San Francisco law firm by a former client; in June 1990, eight others were shot to death at a General Motors financing office in Jacksonville by an embittered customer whose car had been repossessed. Four public employees were gunned down at the Schuyler County Courthouse in October 1992 by a "deadbeat dad" who questioned the legitimacy of the child support demands. In 1993, three doctors at the Los Angeles County Medical Center were shot by a patient who believed that the doctors weren't taking his chronic illness seriously enough.

On occasion, the vengeance of a killer is directed beyond the local level to attack representatives of the state and federal government. In January 2011, Jared Loughner, a 24-year-old distraught and angry loner, shot to death six and injured another 14 people outside a supermarket in Tucson, Arizona. Loughner's primary target was Gabrielle Giffords, a Democratic congresswoman who had voted for certain liberal policies that the shooter opposed (but who also supported Second Amendment rights). Giffords suffered serious injuries, but survived.

Another example of fighting the government through the barrel of a semi-automatic took place on the morning of June 14, 2017, when a man who was angered by the election of President Trump opened fire as Republican members of Congress practiced for their annual Congressional Baseball Game for Charity. The perpetrator, an American citizen living in Belleville, Illinois, shot five people, including the House Majority Whip and a Capitol police officer. In a confrontation with Capitol officers lasting almost 10 minutes, the assailant was shot to death.

Notwithstanding the uniqueness of the location and individuals injured, there is much about the ballfield shooting that is absolutely textbook, especially the assailant's deliberate selection of targets. Although he wasn't gunning for specific people, the gunman clearly sought to harm a specific group of people: Republican lawmakers whom he felt were destroying American society, favoring the rich over average folks like him. Rather than fight city hall literally, he sought to bring down officials at the federal level. Despite his intentions, the assailant fell far short of earning the dubious status of mass killer, thanks to the quick thinking and marksmanship of two Capitol police officers who, as luck would have it, were assigned that day to protect the Majority Whip, given his leadership role in Congress.

When we think of workplace murder, we might want to conjure up, first of all, an image of workers who feel betrayed by their boss and decide to get even. In the 1990s, an employee was more than twice as likely to be killed by an angry coworker than by a disgruntled customer. As suggested in Figure 9.1, however, the times have changed in a more deadly direction. Whereas the number of workplace murders committed by employees has remained more or less constant over the years, the number of dissatisfied customers or clients who seek revenge through murderous means has escalated beginning in 2003 and then stabilized at a level that rivals the number of homicides committed by employees. "Fighting city hall" has taken on a new and more ominous meaning. Economic resentment can be felt not only by vengeful employees but, just as frequently, by disgruntled clients and customers who desire getting even with the system—to win one for the little guy.

In a complex, bureaucratic society, more and more citizens are feeling powerless against the red tape and unresponsiveness of big business and government. Most, of course, will do little more than complain loudly about the injustice. But increasing numbers simply refuse to sit back and take it.

Like the disgruntled employee, the vengeful customer or client is typically an isolated, middle-aged man who, after a prolonged period of frustration, suffers a major financial or personal setback that he views as catastrophic. With no one to turn to for assistance or support, he deliberately decides to punish the institution

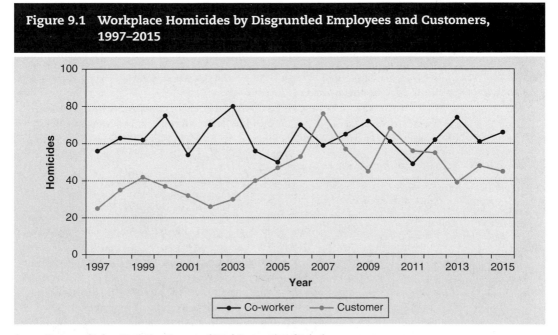

Figure 9.1 Workplace Homicides by Disgruntled Employees and Customers, 1997–2015

Source: Bureau of Labor Statistics, Census of Fatal Occupational Injuries.

that has caused him so much grief. Tending to externalize blame, he sees himself as a victim, not a criminal, who seeks justice through killing.

Part of the problem lies in the impersonal or ineffective response of customer relations in both public and private sectors. Increasingly, consumers are frustrated by automated phone systems with endless button pushes and lengthy holding queues, by poorly trained or overburdened customer relations representatives, and, of course, by computer glitches. In many companies, customer service has become customer disservice.

And now, with virtually every company having an internet site, getting help is even harder. They may have Web pages with Frequently Asked Questions, but they rarely seem to be the questions that the frustrated customer has in mind. For that, he might just have to connect to www.customerservice.com/dont-hold-your-breath.

When customers or clients deal with a small company, they can easily identify the right person to see in order to resolve a complaint. In large, impersonal bureaucracies, however, finding a responsible party is all but impossible. Some customers get mad, yet give up in frustration; a few decide to get even through sabotage or, worse, through murder.

Murder by dissatisfied customers or clients will likely never reach epidemic proportions, but these incidents reflect, albeit in the extreme, a more general problem in the United States today. In the face of growing alienation and cynicism, large companies and agencies must upgrade and humanize their customer relations efforts. They must always remember the adage: "The customer is always right, especially when he's holding a gun!"

ENDNOTES

1. Sharon Lafraniere, Sarah Cohen, and Richard A. Oppel Jr., "How Often Do Mass Shootings Occur? On Average, Every Day, Records Show," *New York Times*, December 2, 2015.

2. J. P. Blair and K. W. Schweit, *A Study of Active Shooter Incidents, 2000–2013* (Washington, DC: Federal Bureau of Investigation, U.S. Department of Justice, 2014).

3. Emma E. Fridel, "Mass Murder in the United States: 2006-2016" [Data file] (Boston: Northeastern University, 2017), adapted from P. Overberg, M. Hoyer, J. Hannan, B. Upton, E. Hansen, and E. Durkin, "Explore the Data on U.S. Mass Killings Since 2006," *USA Today*, 2016.

4. Joseph Westermeyer, "Amok," in Claude T. H. Friedmann and Robert A. Faguet, eds., *Extraordinary Disorders of Human Behavior* (New York: Plenum Press, 1982).

5. Adam Lankford, "Public Mass Shooters and Firearms: A Cross-National Study of 171 Countries," *Violence and Victims* 31 (2016): 187.

6. John R. Lott Jr., "Media Coverage of Mall Shooting Fails to Reveal Mall's Gun-Free Zone Status," *Fox News*, December 6, 2007.

7. Grant Duwe, Tomislav Kovandzic, and Carlisle E. Moody, "The Impact of Right-to-Carry Concealed Firearm Laws on Mass Public Shootings," *Homicide Studies* 6 (2002): 271–296.

8. Charles D. Phillips, Obioma Nwaiwu, Szu-hsuan Lin, Rachel Edwards, Sara Imanpour, and Robert Ohsfeldt, "Concealed Handgun Licensing and Crime in Four States," *Journal of Criminology* (2015): 1–8.

9. Jim Miklaszewski, Pete Williams, Richard Esposito, and Erin McClam, "Gunman Kills at Least 12 at Washington Navy Yard," *NBC News*, September 16, 2013.

10. James Alan Fox, Ann W. Burgess, Jack Levin, and Marleen Wong, "The Capitol Hill Murder Case," *Brief Treatment and Crisis Intervention* 7 (2007): 127.

11. *Newsweek*, "The Domestic Terror Threat," November 20, 2009.

12. CNN, "CNN Poll: Majority Think Fort Hood Shooting Was Preventable," November 19, 2009, http://www.cnn.com/2009/US/11/19/fort.hood.poll/index.html.

13. Samara McPhedran, "Australian Mass Shootings: An Analysis of Incidents and Offenders," *Journal of Interpersonal Violence* (2017): 1–24.

14. Anne Campbell, *Men, Women, and Aggression* (New York: Basic Books, 1993).

15. Mark Braverman and Richard V. Denenberg, *The Violence-Prone Workplace: A New Approach to Dealing with Hostile, Threatening, and Uncivil Behavior* (Ithaca, NY: Cornell University Press, 1999).

16. Northwestern National Life Insurance Company, "Fear and Violence in the Workplace: A Survey Documenting the Experience of American Workers," Minneapolis, MN, 1993.

17. Erika Harrell, *Workplace Violence 1993–2009* (Washington, DC: Bureau of Justice Statistics, 2011).

CHAPTER TEN

HATE HOMICIDES

In June 2017, a 48-year-old man plowed his van into a crowd of Muslims as they left the Finsbury Park Mosque in north London. One man died, two were treated at the scene by medical personnel, and eight others were hospitalized with injuries, some very serious. The assailant was arrested at the scene. A witness told police that he shouted, "I want to kill all Muslims."

It is likely that the attack on members of London's Muslim community was committed in response to a couple of recent terrorist episodes in London perpetrated by Islamic radicals. Whatever its precipitant, the episode constitutes a hate crime. According to the traditional FBI definition, hate or bias crimes, including homicides, involve "criminal offenses committed against persons, property, or society that are motivated, in whole or in part, by the offender's bias against a race, religion, disability, sexual-orientation, or ethnicity/national origin."[1]

Thus, the FBI definition specifies the motivation for committing the offense; it requires that a racial, religious, ethnic, or some other identified difference between victim and offender play at least some role in inspiring a criminal act. For example, someone who falsely considers immigrants from Latin America as polluting the stream of intelligence and culture in American society might assault Latinos as they exit a neighborhood restaurant. The perpetrator seeks to send a message to all newcomers from south of the border: Leave the United States now or you will be next. Or, an individual who illegally takes money to buy illicit drugs may decide to rob only Asians because of some stereotype the person holds regarding this group of people. If part of the motivation for the robbery involves the victim's Asian identity, then the offense can be regarded as a hate crime.[2]

The term *hate crime* was coined in the late 1980s in response to a racial incident in the Howard Beach section of New York City, in which a black man was killed while attempting to evade a violent mob of white teenagers shouting racial epithets. Although widely used by the federal government, the mass media, and researchers in the field, the term is somewhat misleading because it suggests incorrectly that hatred is invariably a distinguishing characteristic of this type of offense.[3] Although it is true that many hate crimes involve intense animosity toward the victim, many others do not. Conversely, many crimes involving hatred between an offender and a victim are not "hate crimes" in the sense intended here. For example, an assault that arises out of a dispute between two coworkers who compete for a promotion might involve intense hatred, even though it is not based on any racial or religious differences between them. Similarly, a love triangle may provoke intense emotions, having nothing at all to do with race or religion.

CHARACTERISTICS OF HATE HOMICIDE

Estimates of the prevalence of hate crimes vary widely. According to the FBI, there were some 7,321 bias offenses in 2016, including 4,720 involving some form of personal violence. Among the victims of hate-motivated violence, 41.3% were intimidated and 54.2% were assaulted. In 2016, 9 murders and 24 rapes were reported as hate crimes. Of course, the FBI count is based on a voluntary reporting system to which many local jurisdictions refuse to contribute, causing hate offenses of all kinds to be underreported. In 2016, almost 15,255 law enforcement agencies representing more than 289 million Americans, or 88% of the country's population, participated with the FBI's program, but only 1,776 agencies (or 12%) actually reported any hate crimes occurring in their jurisdictions. Some notable ostensibly cooperative but actually nonparticipating jurisdictions included the state of Mississippi, where no hate crimes were reported. Wyoming reported only two, Arkansas only five. Moreover, an offense may not be recorded as a hate crime because of lack of evidence that it was motivated by bias. The perpetrators might not have used a racial slur or written hate graffiti, might never have confided their intent to the police or an acquaintance, or might remain unknown to law enforcement. It is even less likely that a hatemonger will be prosecuted and convicted. Lack of evidence at the crime scene is only part of the problem. In many cases, victims who initially cooperate with the police to identify an assailant will become anxious and reticent about giving testimony in court.[4]

In October 2006, a mother of six wearing a hijab (the head scarf of a devout Muslim woman) and carrying a 3-month-old infant in her arms was gunned down while walking on an affluent residential street in Fremont, California. Because her assailant did not leave any indication of his intent at the crime scene, the motivation for this murder could not be definitively identified. Yet relatives of the victim as well as local Muslim leaders who have been able to rule out such other possibilities as robbery and revenge were convinced that the motive was hate.

Moreover, when it comes to determining whether a hate crime has occurred, perception trumps reality. In November 2016, a 42-year-old woman wearing a head scarf returned to her parked car in Fremont after hiking up Mission Peak only to find that her car windows had been smashed and her purse stolen. A note left by the assailants read: "Hijab wearing Bitch. This is our nation now. Get the f… out." Actually, the victim, who suffered from the autoimmune disease known as lupus, only wore a bandana to protect her head from the sun and not for any religious purpose. She was born in the United States, was not an immigrant, and was not of the Islamic faith. Still, that did not stop the police from classifying the episode as a hate crime. The perpetrators obviously believed they were attacking a Muslim newcomer to the United States.[5]

It is difficult to assess exactly, or even approximately, how many hate-motivated homicides occur each year in the United States because the underlying circumstances are often not especially clear-cut. In 2016, for example, the FBI, using federal criteria, reported only 9 hate-motivated homicides out of a total of more than 15,000 murders for the year. Without much doubt, the 9 homicides classified as hate crimes represent a significant undercount.

Part of the challenge in classifying homicides as hate-motivated is that a key participant in the crime—the victim—is not alive to tell his or her side of what transpired. For less serious forms of hate crime, we know that victim reports, based on confidential surveys, far outnumber official police statistics. Even victim reports probably underestimate the actual prevalence of hate offenses. It isn't only law enforcement personnel who are reluctant to report hate attacks. There are apparently numerous victims who also prefer not to inform anyone—and especially not the police—that they have been targeted. Also according to the Justice Department report, hate crimes involve much greater violence than other offenses. Some 84% of all hate attacks included robbery, sexual assault, aggravated assault, or murder.

According to a study by criminologist Jack McDevitt, many high school students refuse to report hate crimes to the police, a parent, or a teacher.[6] If they inform at all, it is more likely to a friend, which means that their report never gets official attention. Only 3% of the youthful victims of hate crimes reported their offense to the police. Moreover, immigrants may come from states where the police are seen as part of a repressive regime and not trusted. Racial minorities and the LBGT community may feel the police are the "enemy of occupation." Such victims never report hate crimes against them. One survey found that almost 80% of Shiite Muslims in the United States who were victims of post-9/11 discrimination failed to report the incidents to the police.[7]

After 9/11, hate crimes targeting Muslims (and anyone who might possibly have been a Muslim) increased some 1,600% from the year 2000, making them the second-most likely religious group (behind Jews) to be victimized. Many were victims of arson, vandalism, or assault. A few were murdered, not to rob them but simply because they wore a turban or spoke with an accent. In Mesa, Arizona, a 49-year-old Sikh Indian wearing a turban was shot down in front of his gas station. In Dallas, a Pakistani Muslim was found shot to death in his convenience store. In San Gabriel, California, an Egyptian Christian was killed in his grocery store.

The influence of group membership can hardly be exaggerated in the case of murders inspired by hate. As a cultural phenomenon, there may be literally millions of Americans who have adopted ethnocentric attitudes. They may tell racist jokes, use racial epithets, and verbalize their dislike of immigrants, gays, Jews, or people of color. Most Americans, however—notwithstanding their bigoted beliefs—would never dream of translating their hate into the commission of a crime, especially not murder.

But for someone who is angry and hate filled, membership in an organized group can make all the difference. For one thing, the hatemonger's group teaches him that he is not alone in his bigotry. He knows, perhaps for the first time, that other people share the depths of his concern and his revulsion about the state of the nation and the decline of his "heritage" or race. Joining up gives him the inspiration needed to translate his attitudes into activism, to risk his personal safety in order to take a strong stand against race mixing, communism, or the so-called Zionist conspiracy. Second, if a hatemonger works together with other members of a group, then there often is some sharing of tasks that weakens his sense of personal responsibility. He has only driven the car or gone along for the ride; he only kicked or hit the victim, but never delivered the fatal blow. Moreover, owing to what social psychologists call a group effect, he may also be able to take risks with his personal safety that he would have regarded as unthinkable before taking membership in a group of like-minded comrades. Finally, hate groups tend to be apocalyptic, preaching to their members that global war is inevitable. The battle cry of the racist and anti-Semitic Creativity Movement, for example, is "Rahowa"—standing for racial holy war. The bible for many hate groups is Andrew Macdonald's novel *The Turner Diaries*, a fictionalized account, written by a white supremacist (the late William Pierce) under a pseudonym, in which a bloody racial war is waged and won by the Aryan good guys.

TYPES OF HATE HOMICIDE

Hate homicides, not unlike hate crimes generally, seem to fall into one of four categories in terms of their perpetrators' motivations: thrill, defense, retaliation, or mission.

Thrill Hate Crimes

Thrill hate crimes are typically perpetrated by groups of teenagers or young adults who, bored and idle, decide to go out together looking for someone to attack. The sadism and excessive brutality involved in many thrill homicides suggest that at least some of the killers—perhaps the leaders of the group—have an excessive need to feel powerful at the expense of their victim. It takes only one sadistic bigot with power to exercise his will in a group of young people who are eager to please their peers and be accepted. Most thrill offenders might easily fit the label, offered by political scientist Meredith Watts, of "fellow travelers."[8] They may not harbor intense hatred toward their victim, but they also cannot bear the idea of being rejected by their friends. These are typically marginalized and alienated youngsters, whose thrill attack gets them little more than bragging rights and a vague sense of their own importance. And that is apparently enough to provide the inspiration for singling out a vulnerable victim. Almost half of all hate attacks can be regarded as thrill hate crimes.[9]

Most thrill attacks take the form of vandalism, desecration, and assault. Occasionally, however, a group of young people looking for some excitement will attack their victim with lethal force. It is no coincidence that many thrill hate crimes are committed by a group of friends who support and encourage one another in their quest for excitement.

An appropriate example is the tragic case of 37-year-old Marcelo Lucero, an Ecuadorean immigrant who came to the United States and settled in Long Island, New York, at the age of 21, only to be stabbed to death on a dark street in the town of Patchogue by seven teenagers who decided to go "beaner jumping," as they put it. For more than a year, the seven friends had, on a number of occasions, set out to locate a Hispanic to attack. Earlier in the day of Lucero's slaying, they had targeted another Hispanic man with a BB gun, shooting him from their passing car.

The state of New York sentenced Jeffrey Conroy, who was 17 at the time he plunged a knife into Lucero's chest, to 25 years for the crime of manslaughter and assault as a hate crime. Conroy's six companions received prison terms of up to 7 years each.

The vulnerability of people with disabilities tends to make them easy targets of thrill-seekers. According to anonymous victim accounts from the Bureau of Justice Statistics data, individuals with a disability (especially those with a developmental disability), in 2015 alone, were victims of about 47,000 rapes, 79,000 robberies, 114,000 aggravated assaults, and 476,000 simple assaults. The victimization rate of serious violent crime for persons with disabilities (12.7 per 1,000) was more than three times the rate for persons without disabilities (4.0 per 1,000).[10]

Over the years, police departments around the country have increased their sensitivity to hate crimes based on race, religion, or sexual orientation, but they still may not recognize disablist bias in the motivation for an assault. In 2015, only 88 of the 6,820 hate offenses reported by the police to the FBI targeted people with physical, emotional, or intellectual disabilities. Obviously, this represents a tremendous underestimate of the problem. In 2015, 20% of all disabled violent crime victims believed they were targeted because of their disability.[11]

Many hate crimes committed against victims who are intellectually or emotionally challenged are committed by a group of friends looking for a sadistic thrill. In February 2010, for example, Jennifer Daugherty, a 30-year-old intellectually disabled woman in rural Pennsylvania about 30 miles east of Pittsburgh, was stabbed to death allegedly by six individuals who were simply out to have some fun at her expense. But before taking Jennifer's life and dumping her remains in a garbage can, her killers first tortured her in the most sadistic manner imaginable. Pretending to be her good friends, they abducted Jennifer and kept her as a prisoner for several days. During this time, they forced her to ingest spices, vegetable oil, detergent, urine, and various medications. They shaved Jennifer's head, bound her with Christmas decorations, beat her with a towel rack, a vacuum cleaner hose, and a crutch. Then, after forcing her to write a suicide note, they stabbed her in the chest, neck, and side.[12]

Defensive Hate Crimes

In contrast to thrill offenses motivated by a need to be accepted and feel important, *defensive hate crimes* are, from the perpetrators' viewpoint, designed to protect their turf, territory, neighborhood, women, job, reputation, school, or campus—in general, their birthright. In some precipitating episode, the victims are perceived to threaten what the offender regards as belonging to him: members of a black family moving onto a previously all-white block, the first Asian student in a college dormitory, or a gay man attending a party. The attack is typically aimed at particular victims, those who dare challenge or threaten the security or well-being of the offender. When the threat subsides, so does the attack.

Defensive hate crimes may begin with relatively harmless acts designed to alert the victim that he or she is trespassing on private property. If, however, the original message is disregarded—if the black family remains on the block, if the Asian student fails to change residence halls, or if the gay man refuses to leave the party—then the offense may escalate into violence, until the desired result has been achieved.

During the 1990s, the majority of hate crimes could be characterized as thrill-motivated.[13] Since the September 11th terrorist attack on New York City, Washington, D.C., and rural Pennsylvania, however, hate crimes have become much more defensive from the hatemonger's point of view, targeting a particular group of outsiders in response to some threatening episode. In defensive hate crimes, the perpetrator tends to be somewhat older. Rather than operate in a group, he more often attacks alone. He feels as though he is a victim, someone whose economic well-being, cultural/religious identity, neighborhood, or very survival is being threatened by outsiders.[14]

Thus, there was a dramatic increase in hate crimes against Muslim and Arab Americans following the 9/11 terrorist attack in 2001 that killed almost 3,000 people, against gays and lesbians following the passage of the first gay marriage law by the state of Massachusetts in 2003–2004, against African Americans following the first election of President Obama in 2008, and against immigrants when the unemployment rate peaked in 2010. Moreover, an increase in hate-tinted rhetoric espoused by our national political leaders in the face of soaring income inequality across the decades has contributed recently to a substantial growth of hate crimes in the United States. According to Brian Levin at California State University in San Bernardino, in 2016, there were 1,037 incidents, a more than 23% increase from the previous year in the nine areas he researched: New York; Washington, D.C.; Chicago; Philadelphia; Montgomery County, Maryland; Columbus, Ohio; Seattle; Long Beach, California; and Cincinnati.[15]

On occasion, more than one stigmatized characteristic defines the identity of a hate crime victim, causing a perpetrator's defensive need to escalate to a fever pitch. In August 2010, a 21-year-old college student and aspiring film producer, apparently in a drunken stupor, allegedly slashed the neck, arms, and face of New York City cab driver Ahmed Sharif. While a customer in the cab, the college student engaged in what was initially a friendly conversation. He asked the cabbie where he was from and how many years he had been in the United States. Then he wanted to know whether Sharif was Muslim. When the driver responded that he was, his passenger attacked him with a utility knife.

The motive was not to rob the cabbie. Moreover, the two men—driver and passenger—had been total strangers, so personal issues were not involved. The college student was charged with attempted second-degree murder as a hate crime. The precipitant for the passenger's enraged attack was, at that time, constantly on the minds of New Yorkers. Observers suggested that the assailant had become angered by the national debate as to whether or not an Islamic community center and mosque should be erected on a site only two blocks from Ground Zero. Thus, the passenger wasn't looking for a thrill; instead, he felt a need to rid his community of what he perceived to be a threat to our country. Unfortunately, the assailant was not deterred by reason or logic. His victim had absolutely nothing to do with the tragic September 11 attack on the World Trade Center; he was, instead, a patriotic American.

Retaliatory Hate Crimes

In *retaliatory hate crimes*, a single hate-motivated attack is often followed by a number of follow-up attacks by members of the victimized group. Retaliatory attacks tend to have the greatest potential for fueling additional hate crimes on both sides. Unlike defensive hate crimes designed to eliminate a particular "outsider" from a neighborhood, a workplace, or a school, retaliatory offenses often target not the original offender but anyone from the offender's group. Thus, the victim of a retaliatory crime is selected at random, as long as he or she is perceived to belong to the perpetrator's group.

This was certainly the case with respect to Ronald Taylor. In a suburb not far from the city of Pittsburgh, the 39-year-old black resident of Wilkinsburg was at his wit's end. After a lifetime of suffering racial discrimination, insults, and slights, Taylor felt that he could no longer tolerate what he believed to be the continuing racist neglect by his white maintenance man, John DeWitt. The front door of Taylor's apartment unit had remained broken for some period of time without being repaired, and Taylor fixated on his white maintenance man as the source of the problem.

On March 1, 2000, racial revenge was on Taylor's mind. Leaving his apartment, he remarked to a black neighbor living nearby that he wasn't going to hurt any black people, that he was just "out to kill white people." Taylor was true to his word. Not finding John DeWitt, he instead fatally shot a carpenter who had been working in the building. Then, he walked to a fast-food restaurant in the Wilkinsburg business district, where he shouted, "White trash. Racist pig," and opened fire again, killing two and injuring two more.[16] At one point in his rampage, while waving his gun and making threatening gestures toward a group of people, he yelled at a black woman, "Not you, sister." All of Taylor's victims were white.

Mission Hate Crimes

Mission hate crimes are the rarest and also the most dangerous category of offenses. They are the most likely to involve the members of an organized hate group as well as severe mental illness on the part of the perpetrator. They are also the most likely to result in a murder. Mission hate offenses represent no more than 5% of all hate crimes but probably a much larger proportion of hate homicides.[17]

The mass murder at a Sikh temple in suburban Milwaukee on Sunday, August 5, 2012, was referred to as an act of "domestic terrorism" by the Oak Creek police chief, meaning that the attack was perpetrated by a resident of this country rather than a foreigner. The killer, Wade Michael Page, was a white army veteran approximately 40 years of age who committed suicide after taking the lives of six people and wounding another four. The Southern Poverty Law Center reported he participated in a neo-Nazi punk rock band and was a long-standing member of white supremacist groups in the local area.

Page's rampage was the first mass murder but hardly the first violent episode aimed at Sikh Americans during more than a decade after the September 11, 2001, attack on America. Hate can be quite diffuse, targeting a broad range of innocent victims, including those who are mistaken for other groups. Sikhs, for example, are often mistaken for Muslims because they wear turbans and have beards. Just four days after 9/11, Balbir Singh Sodhi, a 49-year-old immigrant from India who wore a turban and a beard, was shot down and killed while in front of his gas station in Mesa, Arizona. The gunman, Frank Roque, then opened fire on a man of Lebanese descent and an Afghan family nearby. He was angry about the terrorist attack on America and was looking to retaliate against anyone who might possibly have been Muslim or Middle Eastern, or who had dark skin and spoke with a foreign accent. His reward? Serving a life sentence in a maximum security prison.

Hate can remain dormant in a culture, emerging without warning from the darkness in response to some threatening episode. In the weeks after September 11, the FBI reported more than 40 anti-Arab and anti-Islamic hate crimes across the country. In addition, there were more than 300 reports of harassment and abuse filed with the Council on American-Islamic Relations. For several months after the attack on America, hate crimes directed against Muslim Americans increased by 1,600%, according to 2001 FBI statistics.[18]

Unfortunately, the tit-for-tat mind-set has not ended almost two decades after the horrendous 2001 attack on New York City, rural Pennsylvania, and Washington, D.C. The thinking is "You got us; now we will get you." Thus, one hate crime can inspire large-scale, ongoing violence between groups. As has happened repeatedly in Northern Ireland, Israel, Syria, and India, an act of violence committed by one side can easily escalate into multiple acts of terrorism on the other side. It can happen, and has happened, in the United States of America.

Unlike most other vengeful killers, when someone goes on a rampage based on hate against an entire group, he is not aiming to eliminate a particular set of individuals. Any Sikh American is at risk. Indeed, anyone who has dark skin, speaks with a foreign accent, or wears a turban is regarded as the enemy. The killer isn't interested in whether the victims are married or single, have children, follow a favorite baseball team, or have the same personal problems that he has. He has dehumanized his potential victims long before he arrives at his crime scene. To him, their only important characteristic is their cultural or physical difference.

The massacre in Wisconsin might not have targeted Sikh Americans, in particular. It is more likely the act of an individual who despises anyone who is not in the mainstream of American society. For a period of time, the police in Chicago and New York paid particular attention to Sikh temples, just in case another bigoted individual decided to settle a gripe through the barrel of a gun. Yet the next set of victims might just as easily have been Muslim, Jewish, Catholic, Hindu, or Buddhist.

Or African American. One of the most horrific hate-inspired mass murders in recent history occurred in the year 2015 at the historic Emanuel African Methodist Episcopal Church in Charleston, South Carolina. Twenty-one-year-old Dylann Storm Roof, a budding white supremacist, attempted to start a race war when he shot to death nine black congregants as they participated in a Bible study group at the church. For an hour, Roof had a conversation with his eventual victims, suggesting to them falsely that he had come to pray rather than kill. Then he stood up and announced to members of the group that he was there "to shoot Black people." All of Roof's victims were shot multiple times.

The killer had purchased a Glock handgun using the gift his parents had given him for his 21st birthday. He had practiced marksmanship in his backyard, where he also took numerous selfies with Confederate flags. Roof never joined a white supremacist group. Instead, he learned to hate online, by logging onto hate websites and researching crimes by blacks against whites.

Unlike thrill, defensive, and retaliatory attacks, mission hate crimes tend to be broad in scope and extend over time. Their perpetrators generally have no particular person or persons in mind to victimize; instead, they seek to destroy each and every member of a particular group. As a result, they may kill indiscriminately within a category, targeting a number of people simultaneously or going on a killing spree in a number of venues. For those who have made a career of bigotry, they might continue their killing spree until such time that they are finally apprehended by law enforcement.

In November 1995, four young men affiliated with the Nazi Lowriders of Lancaster, California, brutally murdered Milton Walker, a 43-year-old black homeless man in a vacant lot behind a fast-food restaurant. While shouting racial slurs at their victim, the young, white attackers repeatedly bludgeoned him with a wooden board, kicked him, and then smashed him in the face with a pipe. The assailants were at least partially inspired by a desire to impress other members of their group. All of the perpetrators were devoted to the cause of eliminating minorities from their town. But their motivation went far beyond the bragging rights bestowed on those who kill.

Indeed, the attack resulting in the slaying of Milton Walker was no isolated incident committed by dabblers, but one episode in a much larger series of offenses carried out by the Lancaster Nazi Lowriders, whose members had sought for years to eliminate minorities and create an all-white community. Their group had a long record of intimidating and attacking minorities for the purpose of leaving the impression that Lancaster was not safe for blacks, Latinos, or Asians. Members had taken part in a number of racially motivated beatings, stabbings, and threats.

Not every mission killer is connected, of course, with some organized hate group. Included in the mission category are also the relatively rare individuals who, acting out of severe mental illness, go gunning for victims who are representative of a group they despise. In 1989, for example, Patrick Purdy murdered five Southeast Asian children as they congregated on the playground at the Cleveland Elementary School in Stockton, California. Having drifted from place to place and unable to hold a steady job, his mental health deteriorated rapidly. In his distorted thinking, Purdy came to blame the immigrants who had recently moved into his community for all of his personal problems.

The extent of human destruction perpetrated by someone on a mission depends on his or her ability to avoid apprehension. Shortly after midnight on February 2, 2006, 18-year-old Jacob Robida walked into Puzzles Lounge, a popular gay gathering place in the city of New Bedford, Massachusetts, 50 miles south of Boston, and ordered a drink at the bar. Then, after having one more shot of whiskey, he walked to the back of the room near a pool table and removed a hatchet from his black trench coat. Two men were able to grab the hatchet from the assailant's hands, but not before Robida had slashed both of them in the face. He then pulled out a 9-mm pistol and shot a third man in the stomach. Next, he put the gun to his own head and squeezed the trigger, but when it failed to fire, Robida ran out the front door of Puzzles Lounge and into the night.

Robida's rampage had just begun. After escaping from the gay bar where he left three men seriously wounded, he drove to Charleston, West Virginia, and picked up 33-year-old Jennifer Bailey, a woman with whom he had previously lived. The couple drove to Gassville, Arkansas, where Robida confronted police officer James Sell, who asked him to pull over to the side of the road in a routine traffic stop. Robida first gunned down Sell, then shot to death his female companion, and finally turned the gun on himself, taking his own life as the police closed in on him.

It was no coincidence that Robida had initiated his rampage targeting gays. The first thing he had asked the bartender before slashing and shooting patrons was "Is this a gay bar?" According to those who knew him well, he hated gays and lesbians, but he also despised blacks and Jews. His Myspace website contained a photograph of Robida wielding a firearm; behind him, his bedroom walls were covered with anti-Semitic writings and swastikas. Robida had an extensive collection of Nazi memorabilia, including books about the Third Reich, Nazi flags, and a sword. Among his books was a copy of *The Turner Diaries*.

Murderous mission hate crimes are planned, sometimes far in advance. Typically, they are intended to maximize the loss of human life and to generate widespread publicity among a population. The killer has a message to send. He is angry and frustrated, he blames the members of a certain group, and he is willing to sacrifice his personal well-being for the sake of a larger cause. In July 2006, a 30-year-old Muslim American who had developed an intense anger toward Jews forced his way through the front door of the Jewish Federation in Seattle and opened fire with two semi-automatic handguns, killing a 58-year-old woman and injuring five others. The intruder blamed Jews for the war in Iraq and U.S. cooperation with the state of Israel. He had bought his weapons and ammunition days earlier and searched the internet for Jewish organizations before settling on the Jewish Federation as a target. Ending his rampage, the perpetrator was convinced by one of his wounded victims to phone 9-1-1. He told the operator that he had a gun to the head of a hostage and asked her to contact the media. Within minutes, the police arrived on the scene to apprehend the gunman, bringing an end to his deadly mission of hate.

ORGANIZED HATE GROUPS

In April 2014, 73-year-old neo-Nazi Frazier Glenn Miller went hunting for Jews. The former leader of the KKK-linked Carolina Knights and the White Patriot Party had been sentenced to 3 years in prison on weapons charges and participation in a plot to assassinate Morris Dees, the cofounder of the Southern Poverty Law Center in Montgomery. Now Miller, who carried a Remington 870 shotgun and a handgun for the task at hand, drove to the Jewish Community Center and a Jewish retirement home down the road in Overland Park, Kansas, where he parked and waited for Jewish victims to come his way. A few minutes later, the gunman had shot to death Dr. William Corporon and his 14-year-old grandson at the Jewish Community Center and 53-year-old Terri LaManno in the parking lot of the retirement home where her mother resided. Unknown to Miller, all three of his victims were Christians, not Jews: Corporon and his grandson were Methodists, and LaManno was a Catholic. At the end of August 2015, Miller was found guilty of capital murder. Two months later, he was sentenced to death.

Most Americans are at least somewhat acquainted with the objectives of white hate groups such as the Ku Klux Klan and neo-Nazis. Those who are familiar with U.S. history know that the Klan has risen and fallen time and time again in response to challenges to the advantaged position of the white majority. During a short period of post–Civil War Reconstruction, for example, many whites were challenged by newly freed slaves who sought some measure of political power and began to compete for jobs with white working-class Southerners. As a result, the Klan, responding with a campaign of terror and violence, lynched thousands of blacks. Klan-initiated violence increased again during the 1920s, as some Americans sought "protection" from an unprecedented influx of immigrants from eastern and southern Europe. During the 1950s and 1960s, uniformed members of George Lincoln Rockwell's American Nazi Party gave the Nazi salute and shouted, "Heil Hitler!" Over the same period, Klansmen in their sheets and hoods marched in opposition to racial desegregation in schools and public facilities.

By contrast, the more recently organized hate groups operating since 1990 aren't necessarily known for bizarre uniforms or strange rituals. Followers of such white supremacist groups as Tom Metzger's White Aryan Resistance (aka The Insurgent) have shed their sheets and burning crosses in favor of more conventional attire. They often disavow the Klan and the neo-Nazi movement in favor of a brand of "American patriotism" that tends to play better among average Americans.[19]

Metzger's suspicion about the declining appeal of the Klan seems justified. They now wear shirts and ties, not sheets or hoods. Some of their most influential followers are former KKK members who recognize the futility of looking deviant, perhaps even anti-American. The new groups talk in code words and phrases about the very issues that concern Middle America. They preach that the heritage (meaning race) of white Christians is being eroded by foreign (meaning Jewish/communist) influence; they lament the rise of government interference (meaning Jews in high places who supposedly force racial integration down the throats of white Americans) in the lives of average citizens (meaning white Christians); and they condemn welfare cheating (meaning blacks and Latinos), which they incorrectly perceive as being rampant. In addition to wearing business suits, some get facelifts (like former Klan leader David Duke did) or don hairpieces (Tom Metzger had one).

Several have run for public office. For example, Duke once ran for governor of Louisiana, and Christian Identity's former spiritual leader, Richard Butler, entered the race for mayor of Hayden, Idaho. Even in their support of bizarre-looking skinhead youth, they themselves are more concerned with projecting a respectable public image. They realize that younger people often reject the robes and ritual in favor of paramilitary dress. Concerned with the reaction of both the public and the police, some white-power skinhead groups have recently taken a cue from their mentors by wearing their hair conventionally and getting rid of their black leather jackets.

Even some Klan leaders have changed their tune, at least in the way it is played for recruiting purposes. The leader of the Knights of the Ku Klux Klan in North Carolina, for example, actually barred violent neo-Nazis from its meetings. The head of the Klan in Florida urged its members to become a group "known for hating evil, instead of being a group known for hating Negroes." He has repeatedly suggested that his group does not hate anyone but "loves the white race."

In 1978, after leaving his position as national director of the KKK, David Duke launched the National Association for the Advancement of White People. More recently, after spending a term of office in Louisiana's House of Representatives, Duke inaugurated a "civil rights group" for the purpose of fighting the "massive discrimination" against "European Americans" and in favor of blacks, Latinos, Jews, and gays. But, according to the Anti-Defamation League, Duke's organization represents nothing more than an obvious attempt on the part of a "leading racist" to pitch himself in a more socially acceptable manner as a civil rights leader. Then, on March 29, 2004, more than 300 white supremacists came together in New Orleans to celebrate the return of Duke, who was released from federal prison after serving time for fraud. Almost two years later, on December 11, 2006, Duke attended the Holocaust Denial Conference in Tehran, sponsored by the Iranian Foreign Ministry. More recently, he again made his presence known on national television in August 2017, when he condemned counter-demonstrators at the Charlottesville, Virginia, rally in support of maintaining confederate statues, calling the opposition "leftist terrorists."

According to the Southern Poverty Law Center, there may be no more than 50,000 members of white supremacist groups across the nation. Considering that the United States is a country whose residents number more than 320 million, this is a relatively small total. To place this figure in historical perspective, consider that during the 1920s 4 million Americans were members of the Ku Klux Klan.

On the other hand, the Southern Poverty Law Center estimates that the number of hate groups has been on the rise. Currently, this watchdog organization is tracking as many as 917 organized hate groups around the country, roughly a 50% increase over the number in the year 2000. At the same time, thanks to a vacuum of leadership, the influence of certain neo-Nazi organizations seems to have declined during the past few years. Several of the leading organizations in the hate movement—the National Alliance, David Duke's European-American Unity and Rights Organization, Matt Hale's Creativity Movement, and Aryan Nations— suffered setbacks of major proportions. By contrast, hard-core anti-immigrant groups whose members confront or harass suspected newcomers grew from 173 in 2008 to 319 in 2010. There have also been membership gains for such groups as the Ku Klux Klan, the National Socialist Movement, the Council of Conservative Citizens, and neo-Nazis.[20]

THE ROLE OF THE MILITARY

Twenty-year-old James Burmeister and his two buddies were soldiers stationed at the Ft. Bragg army base outside of Fayetteville, North Carolina. They were also racist skinheads who hated blacks, Latinos, and Jews. The three friends didn't belong to any nationally organized hate group. By day, they completely immersed themselves in the disciplined military training required of all recruits on base. But at night, they shed their military uniforms in favor of the steel-toed boots and green jackets associated with the Nazi movement.

During the early morning hours of December 7, 1995, the three soldiers drove their Chevrolet Cavalier into a black neighborhood located in the heart of town. They had spent the night drinking, playing pool, and watching topless dancers at a local sports bar.

All the while, Burmeister had made his intentions clear enough. He talked incessantly to his friends about wanting to find the enemy and have a little fun, about wanting to earn a badge of honor in the form of a spider web tattoo worn only by those members of the movement who had killed in order to further the Nazi cause. He liked the excitement, the thrill, and the bragging rights. Shortly after midnight, the three spotted the victims, Michael James, 36, and Jackie Burden, 27, who were walking together along a dirt road, totally unaware of the danger lurking just ahead. Burmeister jumped out of the car and, without warning, immediately opened fire on the black couple with his 9-mm Ruger handgun, killing them both. The three then sped away from the scene of the crime, leaving the bodies of their two victims to be discovered by passersby.

A 2008 FBI review identified 203 individuals in the white supremacist movement from October 2001 to May 2008 who had served in the military at some point during this period of more than 7 years. Compared against the almost 24 million veterans in the population of the United States in 2008, the number of hate group members with military experience is admittedly miniscule, even if you include those who never expressed their racist beliefs and remained beneath the radar while serving their country. Moreover, these 203 individuals who could be identified as white supremacists represent only a small percentage of the thousands of Americans who belong to hate groups.[21]

Yet the influence of hatemongers who have military backgrounds seems to be much greater than their small numbers suggest. Sociologist Pete Simi has suggested that the extremist strategy to infiltrate the military and law enforcement has existed "for decades." In a study they conducted of individuals indicted for far-right terrorism-related activities, Simi and Futrell found that at least 31% had military experience.[22] According to the FBI, most extremist groups have at least some members with military experience. They tend to hold leadership positions and have enormous prestige within the organization, owing to their knowledge of firearms and explosives and their access to weapons. White supremacists who have served in the military are widely regarded by their associates as playing an important role in preparing for an anticipated war against Jews, people of color, and the federal government.

There is reason to believe that the U.S. Department of Defense has recently increased its efforts to eliminate violent racists from its ranks. Yet the number of white supremacists in the military may have increased since the FBI review was reported. As enlistment rates have declined and the military has struggled to meet its recruitment objectives, the U.S. Army has loosened its recruiting standards. Veterans suffering from posttraumatic stress disorder have been ordered back to Iraq for an additional tour of duty. Americans with criminal records have been allowed to sign up. Lax recruiting standards have similarly opened the door to larger numbers of gang members, neo-Nazis, and other white supremacists. In August 2017, a white supremacist group known as Vanguard America rallied in Charlottesville, Virginia, where one of its members drove his vehicle through a crowd of counter-demonstrators, killing 32-year-old Heather Heyer and injuring dozens more. Vanguard's leader was Dillon Hopper, a military veteran who, until 2011, had served as a marine recruiter and also had been deployed to Iraq and Afghanistan during his term of service.[23]

CURRENT STATE OF HATE CRIME LAWS

It is not surprising that so many states have chosen to enact legislation that targets hate violence. Not unlike less serious hate offenses, hate-motivated homicides impact not just a particular individual but every member of a victim's group.

In a sense, they are crimes against society at large, causing intergroup hostility to increase and incivility to thrive and prosper at the expense of peace and tranquility. Even hate-motivated murders occurring decades earlier have become deeply entrenched in the collective memory of our country as well as its federal legislation.

The murder of James Byrd is an appropriate example. Three white supremacists met behind bars, where they joined the Aryan Brotherhood, a penitentiary hate group for white inmates who, after serving their time, are frequently recruited by white supremacist groups on the outside. The three perpetrators also had connections to the Ku Klux Klan. Indeed, they had planned to start a local chapter in the community of Jasper, Texas. In June 1998, after being released from prison, the three dragged Byrd, a black man, to his death behind their pickup truck for more than two miles down a rocky country road in Jasper, Texas. Whether intended or not, the killers sent an unmistakable message to every black American regarding their vulnerability.

Similarly, the vicious murder in October 1998 of 21-year-old gay college student Matthew Shepard by two young men in Laramie, Wyoming, was a warning to every gay person not to exercise their constitutionally guaranteed rights. For his "sin," Shepard was beaten into a coma and left tied to a fence in the desert. He died 5 days later.

The brutal murders of Byrd and Shepard foreshadowed a major change in federal law that continues in force to the present day. On October 28, 2009, President Obama signed an important federal bill named the Matthew Shepard and James Byrd, Jr. Hate Crimes Prevention Act, which expanded the protected categories to include not only race and religion but also sexual orientation, gender, gender identity, and disability status. This law also extended the areas that federal authorities are able to investigate and prosecute, and provided assistance in cases at the state level, even where local law did not protect the category of residents who were being victimized.

We have come a long way from the days when legislation at the federal level did nothing more than mandate the identification of incidents of hate crime. In 1990, the Congress of the United States passed the Hate Crime Statistics Act, which required the reporting of statistics on hate crimes nationally. When it comes to providing legal protection to vulnerable groups, however, until recently, the task was mostly left up to the states. Specifically, 45 states and the District of Columbia have statutes criminalizing various types of bias-motivated violence or intimidation. Each of these statutes covers bias on the basis of race, religion, and ethnicity; 30 cover disability; 31 cover sexual orientation; 26 cover gender; 9 cover transgender/gender-identity; 13 cover age; 5 cover political affiliation; and 5, along with Washington, D.C., cover homelessness.[24]

The question arises as to where you draw a line with regard to which groups deserve additional protection and which do not. Hate crime laws were originally designed to cover those groups whose members possessed extraordinary vulnerability as likely targets of violence. Recent events have inspired some changes in our thinking as to who should and should not be included in hate crime legislation. In July 2016, five white police officers were gunned down on the streets of downtown Dallas and three white police officers were shot to death in Baton Rouge, as "payback" for a string of unarmed African American men who were killed by local law enforcement in cities and towns across the country. Two months earlier, the state of Louisiana added police officers to its list of protected categories in its "Blue Lives Matter" hate crime legislation. Many other states debated doing the same but declined to make a change in the law. At the same time, it was widely known that most states already enhance the penalties for attacking a member of the police force. In New Hampshire, for example, the intentional killing of law enforcement personnel, including sheriffs, city police, state troopers, correctional officers, and probation officers, is punishable by death. The same criminal act committed against a civilian is likely to result in a prison sentence rather than an execution.

Notwithstanding their value in combating bias and bigotry, hate crime laws have been recently challenged by legal scholars and social scientists who suggest that by punishing speech, the statutes violate the First Amendment. Yet hate crime laws do not punish constitutionally protected hate speech. Most of these statutes only increase the penalty for behaviors that are already illegal—vandalism, harassment, assault, and the like. Moreover, using the words of a perpetrator who utters racial slurs or ethnic epithets to establish motivation is nothing new or unusual in criminal law. For example, the difference between killing someone in self-defense versus committing first-degree murder may rest largely on what a defendant has said. Criminal law has always taken into consideration the motivation and intent of the offender.[25]

The United States has chosen not to follow the lead of many European countries, where anti–hate speech legislation has been passed. Countries including Canada, France, Great Britain, and Germany have all passed laws prohibiting at least some forms of hate speech. In Germany, these forms of prohibition have been applied most broadly, particularly in the area of Nazi propaganda and symbols that are illegal to own or display. Consistent with its long tradition of free speech protections, the United States has, except on college campuses, decided not to develop similar legislation. Even in the area of campus speech codes, moreover, efforts in the United States to control offensive speech have been met with significant resistance and debate.[26]

Another argument often espoused in opposition to hate crime laws is that they apply only to "special groups." In reality, however, each and every American potentially receives protection from hate crime statutes that criminalize acts motivated by a characteristic of the victim. Thus, Christians who are targeted are as likely as Jews and Muslims to be protected by the law. Whites are as likely to be protected as blacks, Asians, and Latinos. Straights are as likely to be protected as gays and lesbians. In fact, some 20% of all racially motivated incidents reported to the FBI involve white victims targeted by members of another racial group.

When a bias crime results in murder, opponents of hate crime laws take the opportunity to emphasize that enhanced penalties are meaningless when applied to a crime for which a life sentence or the death penalty is already the only option. How is it possible, some argue, for hate crime legislation to have deterred the killers of Matthew Shepard or James Byrd?

The arguments surrounding hate crime legislation are much more complex than some have suggested. First, as noted earlier, most hate crimes do not rise to the level of murder; rather, they are intimidations, vandalisms, and assaults. Second, bias-motivated murders may be committed by several individuals, for example, a leader who possesses sadistic tendencies and fellow travelers who join in because they fear being rejected by their friends. Although hate crime laws may not discourage a sadist who plays a leadership position in a group, they might very well dissuade those who are on the fence about going along for the ride and helping out. In the beating death of Matthew Shepard, for example, the two perpetrators were accompanied by their girlfriends, who were accused of serving as accomplices by, among other things, helping to dispose of the killers' bloody clothes.

Finally, even if they fail to deter a single homicide, hate crime laws send a symbolic message of some importance, first, to members of vulnerable groups who are eager to know that not every American is a hatemonger and, second, to good people everywhere who disavow hate and intolerance but are not always so sure that they have company. In sum, from the perspective suggested decades ago by French sociologist Émile Durkheim, hate crime legislation plays a symbolic function by reflecting and reinforcing the values—tolerance and respect for diversity—that Americans claim to cherish.

ENDNOTES

1. Federal Bureau of Investigation, *Crime in the United States–2016* (Washington, DC: U.S. Department of Justice, 2017).

2. Jack Levin and Jack McDevitt, *Hate Crimes Revisited* (Boulder, CO: Westview Press, 2002).

3. Barbara Perry, *In the Name of Hate* (New York: Routledge, 2001).

4. Federal Bureau of Investigation, *Crime in the United States–2015*.

5. Sarah Ravani, "Woman Wearing Headscarf Targeted for Anti-Muslim Hate in Fremont," *San Francisco Chronicle*, November 17, 2016.

6. Michael Rosenwald, "Many Teens Silent on Hate Crimes, Study Finds," *Boston Globe*, January 28, 2002, p. B2.

7. Religion News Service, "In Brief," *Washington Post*, November 19, 2005, p. B9.

8. Meredith W. Watts, *Cross-Cultural Perspectives on Youth and Violence* (Stamford, CT: JAI Press, 199).

9. Levin and McDevitt, *Hate Crimes Revisited*.

10. Erika Harrell, *Crime Against People With Disabilities, 2009–2015* (Washington, DC: Bureau of Justice Statistics, 2017).

11. Ibid.

12. Edecio Martinez, "'Friends' Killed Disabled Woman, Forced Her to Write Suicide Note," *CBS News*, February 12, 2010.

13. Jack Levin and Jack McDevitt, *Hate Crimes: The Rising Tide of Bigotry and Bloodshed* (New York: Plenum Press, 1993); Levin and McDevitt, *Hate Crimes Revisited*.

14. Jack Levin and Ashley Reichelmann, "From Thrill to Defensive Motivation: The Role of Group Threat in the Changing Nature of Hate-Motivated Assaults," *American Behavioral Scientist* 59 (2015): 1546–1561.

15. NBC News, "U.S. Hate Crimes Up 20 Percent in 2016, Fueled by Election Campaign: Report," March 14, 2017.

16. Jack Levin and Gordana Rabrenovic, *Why We Hate* (New York: Prometheus Books, 2004), p. 55.

17. Jack Levin and Jim Nolan, *The Violence of Hate: Understanding Harmful Forms of Bias and Bigotry*, 4th ed. (Lanham, MD: Rowman and Littlefield, 2017).

18. Federal Bureau of Investigation, *Hate Crime Statistics–2001* (Washington, DC: U.S. Department of Statistics, 2002).

19. Levin and McDevitt, *Hate Crimes Revisited*.

20. Mark Potok, "The Year in Hate and Extremism," *Intelligence Report* (Southern Poverty Law Center, Spring 2017), https://www.splcenter.org/fighting-hate/intelligence-report/2017/year-hate-and-extremism.

21. FBI Counterterrorism Unit, "White Supremacist Recruitment of Military Personnel Since 9/11," FBI Intelligence Assessment, July 7, 2008.

22. Pete Simi and Robert Futrell, *American Swastika: Inside the White Power Movement's Hidden Spaces of Hate* (Lanham, MD: Rowman and Littlefield, 2010).

23. Daniel Trotta, "U.S. Military Battling White Supremacists, Neo-Nazis in Its Own Ranks," *Reuters*, August 21, 2012.

24. Anti-Defamation League, "Hate Crimes Defined—State Laws," 2017, https://www.adl.org/sites/default/files/documents/assets/pdf/combating-hate/Hate-Crimes-Law-The-ADL-Approach.pdf.

25. Samuel Walker, *Hate Speech: The History of an American Controversy* (Lincoln: University of Nebraska Press, 1994).

26. James B. Jacobs and Kimberly A. Potter, "Hate Crimes: A Critical Perspective," in Michael Tonry, ed., *Crime and Justice: A Review of Research* (Chicago: University of Chicago Press, 1997).

CHAPTER ELEVEN

MURDEROUS TERROR

S ome mission-oriented hate homicides can be regarded as acts of terrorism. Using the FBI's definition, these crimes involve "the unlawful use of force or violence against persons or property to intimidate or coerce a government, the civilian population, or any segment thereof, in furtherance of political or social objectives."[1] Clearly, there are violent mission hate offenses whose purpose is to send a message of coercion and intimidation. As noted in Chapter 10, for example, one of Dylann Roof's key objectives in shooting to death nine African American churchgoers was to help precipitate a race war that would be won by white Americans and lead to the total elimination of people of color from American soil.

According to specialists on the topic, terrorism is a premeditated act of violence that attempts to produce a climate of fear and anxiety. It is aimed, then, not just at a set of immediate victims, but at a much wider audience. The terrorist attacks are typically random and symbolic, targeting civilians and government officials. Because terrorism is widely regarded by society's members as an unacceptably deviant act, it causes a general sense of outrage.[2]

The September 11, 2001, attack on the United States has all of the elements associated with a terrorist act. Its perpetrators, the 19 suicide bombers who flew planes into the World Trade Center and the Pentagon, had planned their attack for years, hoping to maximize its impact in spreading anxiety across the United States. Thousands lost their lives in the assault, but almost every American was impacted as a secondary or tertiary victim. Afterward, millions refused to take a plane or travel abroad; for a period of time, they wished to stay close to home. Flag-waving became a national pastime. Almost everyone felt profoundly threatened.

In response, the George W. Bush administration moved to expand the power of federal law enforcement to detain, investigate, interrogate, and prosecute suspicious individuals in this country.[3] Congress, in immediately passing the Patriot Act, made it easier to conduct searches, wiretap telephones, and secure electronic records. Attorney General John Ashcroft approved of giving FBI agents increased powers to monitor the internet, political rallies, demonstrations, and mosques. Some 80% of Americans expressed their willingness to forfeit certain freedoms for the sake of security. Almost 2 decades after its enactment, a modified version of the Patriot Act remains in force until at least the year 2019.[4]

HATE HOMICIDE AND DOMESTIC TERRORISM

Not every terrorist act is a hate crime; not every hate attack is an act of terror; but the line between hate crime and terrorism is not always clearly drawn. At the Los Angeles International Airport (LAX) on the morning of July 4, 2002, Hesham

Mohamed Ali Hadayet waited patiently in line at the El Al airlines ticket counter, and then, without uttering a word, opened fire with his .45 Glock semi-automatic handgun. Before security guards could wrestle him to the ground, the Egyptian immigrant had managed to spray a dozen bullets into a crowd of people, killing two innocent victims, both Israeli citizens.

The 41-year-old assailant was an accountant who had migrated to the United States some 10 years earlier. Unfortunately, his personal life had recently fallen apart. The small limousine service he had been running out of his apartment in Irvine was mired in debt. And a few days before his deadly rampage at LAX, Hadayet's wife and two sons had left him to return to Egypt. Hadayet's grievances were political as well as personal. He was outraged by the policies of the United States toward Palestinians and had long argued that the government of his Egyptian homeland be overthrown. He had told an ex-employee that he despised all Israelis, and he had vented his anger at a neighbor for flying an American flag after September 11, 2001.

Somehow, Hadayet's political views and personal problems intersected in his mind, as he searched in vain for some reasonable resolution to the circumstances that had left his life in shambles. In the end, however, he solved his problems by committing murder. From the standpoint of the Israeli government, there was no doubt from the beginning that Hadayet had committed an act of terrorism. Rather than target Aer Lingus, Air Canada, or Alitalia, he had directly and exclusively attacked the Israeli national airline. Hadayet was an Egyptian who despised Israelis. His attack was designed to send a message around the world about the vulnerability of the country of Israel and its official airline. The terrorist message was clear: "This airline is unsafe; do not fly El Al if you value your personal safety." From the FBI's viewpoint, however, the assailant had more likely committed a hate crime. He had personal problems: His wife and children were gone, he had recently suffered financial disaster, and he hated Jews. Moreover, there was no evidence that Hadayet was a member of any organized terrorist group.

Almost one year after the assault at LAX, however, the FBI admitted that Hadayet's crime was an act of terrorism, even if it was also a hate crime. The two types of attacks are not mutually exclusive. An individual who, for personal reasons, incites terror among a civilian population can still be regarded as a terrorist, based on the consequences of his behavior. Moreover, even if he is not a member of a radical organization such as Islamic State of Iraq and Syria (ISIS) or al Qaeda, someone who hates Jews, Americans, Muslims, or any other group of people can be regarded as committing a terrorist act. Attacking as an individual rather than as a group does not disqualify a person from fitting the FBI's definition.

Indeed, a growing number of terrorist threats have recently consisted of "lone wolf" attacks by individuals or a couple of friends who have been inspired by an organized group (e.g., ISIS, al Qaeda, or a white supremacist organization in the United States) in which they do *not* hold active membership. In the early morning hours of June 12, 2016, for example, 29-year-old security guard Omar Mateen opened fire on the 300 customers—90% Latinos—inside Pulse, a gay nightclub in Orlando, Florida. Born in the United States to Afghan parents, the killer sought revenge against Americans for what he regarded as their mistreatment of Muslims in Syria and Iraq, but he especially despised gays and lesbians. He also hated Latinos.

It should be noted that Mateen had suffered a number of significant failures in his personal life, never achieving his goal of pursuing a career in law enforcement and suffering a nasty divorce from his first wife. Thus, acting alone, Mateen committed a terrorist act as well as a major hate crime. He amassed an incredibly large victim count: 49 dead and 53 injured, the second deadliest mass shooting by a single assailant in modern U.S. history. Before being able to escape the scene, he was shot to death by 11 officers who fired at least 150 bullets in his direction, hitting him multiple times.

In a more recent act of "lone wolf" terrorism, eight people were killed and almost a dozen injured when, on the day of Halloween 2017, a 29-year-old man in a rented pickup truck drove down a crowded bicycle path near the World Trade Center in New York City. The alleged killer was an immigrant from Uzbekistan in Central Asia who had been living in the United States since 2010. Authorities found a note near the killer's truck indicating that his attack was made in the name of ISIS.

Terrorism can also be a family affair, being perpetrated by close relatives who share the same ideological bias as well as a sense of outrage directed at a particular community or entire society. On the afternoon of April 15, 2013, near the finish line of the Boston Marathon on Boylston Street, two brothers who identified with the cause of radical Islam planted a couple of pressure cooker bombs among the spectators. Exploding seconds apart, the assailants' bombs killed three and injured at least 264. Later that day and still on the loose, 19-year-old Dzhokhar and 26-year-old Tamerlan Tsarnaev also shot to death an MIT police officer and, during an exchange of gunfire, wounded a transit police officer. Attempting to escape by automobile, Dzhokhar accidently ran over and killed his older brother and then fled into a nearby 20-block neighborhood, where he hid in a boat in the backyard of a resident. Thousands of police officers conducted a thorough manhunt, leading to his capture and arrest.

INTERNATIONAL TERRORISM

The worst act of international terrorism ever committed in the United States occurred on September 11, 2001. Coordinated by the al Qaeda terrorist network, the attack involved four jet hijackings by 19 terrorists: an American Airlines flight from Boston to Los Angeles that crashed into the North Tower of the World Trade Center in New York City; a United Airlines flight from Boston to Los Angeles that was deliberately flown into the South Tower of the World Trade Center; a United Airlines flight from Newark to San Francisco that crashed in Stony Creek Township, Pennsylvania; and an American Airlines flight from Washington, D.C., to Los Angeles that targeted the Pentagon in Arlington, Virginia. Almost 3,000 people— citizens of 78 nations—lost their lives in these coordinated terrorist attacks.

In response, President George W. Bush sought to eliminate the base of operations and training facilities for worldwide terrorism. On October 7, 2001, he initiated Operation Enduring Freedom, a military maneuver designed to destroy the al Qaeda training camps and Taliban military installations in Afghanistan, where, according to intelligence sources, Islamic extremists from around the globe had assembled. As a result, the Taliban governing body was forced from power and some 1,000 members of al Qaeda were arrested.

Unfortunately, these military actions were vastly inadequate. Even after the leadership of al Qaeda was decimated, terrorist activity continued in the form of small cells and lone wolf attacks. More generally, the violence in Afghanistan remained at an unacceptable level for years after 2001, causing the North Atlantic Treaty Organization (NATO), under the direction of the U.S. military, to become increasingly involved in combat operations until 2014, when it transferred all security obligations to the Afghan government. Following the date of withdrawal, however, an agreement between the United States and Afghanistan allowed NATO troops to remain in an advisory role.

To this day, U.S. armed forces remain in Afghanistan to protect the viability of its friendly government and secular institutions. The role of the American military consists mainly of conducting airstrikes and providing air coverage for Afghan military forces. In the meantime, the large-scale destruction of civilian populations has shifted to Syria and Iraq, countries that have become saturated with violence as perpetrated by the members of the extremist group ISIS in opposition to the established governments in their own countries, in oppositional Muslim nations, as well as in Western democracies. In the face of widespread unrest among the population, the decimation of al Qaeda left a power vacuum in the oppositional fringe, which was quickly filled by ISIS.

The Rise of the Islamic State (ISIS)

In recent years, ISIS has committed a number of brutal acts of violence, including the beheading of Americans, Canadians, and Japanese civilians. The first decapitation by ISIS occurred in August 2014. After being held prisoner for 2 years, American war correspondent James Foley's gruesome murder was perpetrated ritualistically, recorded by camera, and then circulated globally on the internet, causing the leaders of Western nations to voice their disgust with ISIS as a group lacking in any semblance of humanity.

Tens of thousands of civilians and government officials around the world have been killed each year by terrorists. In recent years, a number of the most deadly terrorist acts in Europe and, to a lesser extent, in the United States have been inspired by the propaganda and training of ISIS. In December 2015, a married couple opened fire during a holiday party held at the California Department of Health in San Bernardino, California. It took only 5 minutes for the two terrorists to shoot to death 14 employees and injure another 22. Later on, the two assailants were killed when they exchanged gunfire with the police. Both had been influenced by radical Islamic groups in Asia and the Middle East. Both blamed the United States for igniting the fires of death and destruction in the Middle East.

Terrorism in Europe

In European countries, the influence of ISIS extremists has been substantially more widespread than in the United States, causing the overall level of terrorist violence to escalate during the past few years. In March 2016, for example, two suicide bombings at Brussels airport and a third bombing at a metro station in the city by ISIS extremists took the lives of 32 people and injured another 300. Several months later, 86 people were killed and hundreds more wounded when a 33-year-old Tunisian man inspired by ISIS drove his rented cargo truck through a crowded pedestrian mall in Nice, France. In December 2016, a failed asylum seeker deliberately drove a truck into the crowded Christmas market in Berlin based on instructions from ISIS, leaving 12 people dead and 56 injured. Four days later, the perpetrator was killed in a shootout with police near Milan, Italy. At the end of March 2017, an assailant drove his rented SUV through a crowd of pedestrians on Westminster Bridge in London, killing five and then leaving on foot to stab a police officer to death on Parliament grounds. ISIS claimed responsibility. In April 2017, a 22-year-old suicide bomber from Kyrgyzstan who had trained with ISIS operatives planted explosives on the metro in St. Petersburg, Russia, killing 14 and hospitalizing at least 50. During the same month, ISIS took responsibility for a terrorist attack by a 39-year-old man who shot to death a police officer and seriously injured two others on the Champs-Élysées in Paris. In the same month, a self-admitted member of ISIS killed four people and injured another 15 when he drove his truck down a busy shopping street in Stockholm. In May 2017, 22 people (including a number of children) were killed and 119 injured when a suicide bomber associated with ISIS attacked in the lobby of a crowded concert in Manchester given by the popular American singer Ariana Grande. In June 2017, three men rammed their rented van into pedestrians on the London Bridge and then randomly stabbed patrons in pubs and bars in nearby Borough Market, killing 7 and injuring 18. Witnesses heard the assailants shout, "This is for Allah." Two months later, 14 were killed and another 130 injured in Barcelona when a 22-year-old man slammed his white Fiat van into a crowd as they walked on a busy pedestrian mall in the city. In claiming responsibility, the propaganda outlet of ISIS referred to the attackers as "soldiers of the Islamic State." Six members of the terror cell, including the driver, were shot to death by the police.

Notwithstanding the important role of Muslim extremism in spreading violence throughout the Western world, terrorist fatalities are vastly more likely to occur in Middle Eastern, Asian, and African countries than in Europe or the United States. According to the Institute for Economics and Peace, Iraq, Afghanistan, Nigeria, Syria, and Yemen accounted for more than 73% of all terrorist deaths in 2015—some 21,000—whereas there were only 40 in the United States (Figure 11.1).

HOMEGROWN TERRORISM

We focus so much on the huge death toll—almost 3,000—resulting from the September 11, 2001, attack on America that it is easy to lose perspective on long-term trends in homegrown terrorism. As indicated in Figure 11.2, the number of terrorist attacks in the United States has declined precipitously since the late 1970s and early 1980s, when more than 75 incidents yearly (and as many as 150) was the rule. By contrast, in more recent years (2004–2014), the nation has endured fewer than 20 terrorist acts annually.

Also, largely as a result of the September 11 attack, most Americans, when they envision terrorism, understandably conjure up the names of groups such as ISIS, al Qaeda, Hezbollah, and Hamas. To most Americans, terrorist murder arises not out of the warped and perverted psyches of their deranged, vengeful, or sociopathic friends and neighbors, but in the plotting and planning of bloodthirsty groups originating in the Middle East. Yet the Anti-Defamation League estimates for the period 2006–2015 that, on average, only 2.6 attacks annually were carried out in the United States by Jihadist-inspired foreigners (i.e., individuals who were foreign-born and dedicated to radical Islam) and only 2.4 yearly were committed by Jihadist-inspired terrorists born on American soil. During the same period, five attacks annually were carried out by right-wing extremists who were born in the United States. In sharp contrast, about 400 Americans drown each year while taking a bath, and over 1,000 choke to death on food. The so-called D.C. Snipers represent a form of terrorism that lacks a major political motivation but was designed to send a message of fear and anxiety. In October 2002, 10 innocent people lost their lives when John Allen Muhammad and Lee Boyd Malvo, two down-and-out criminals—one a U.S. citizen, the other a teenager originally from Jamaica—conspired to hold the Washington, D.C., area hostage to their demand for $10 million. Their 3-week killing spree was meant to intimidate or coerce

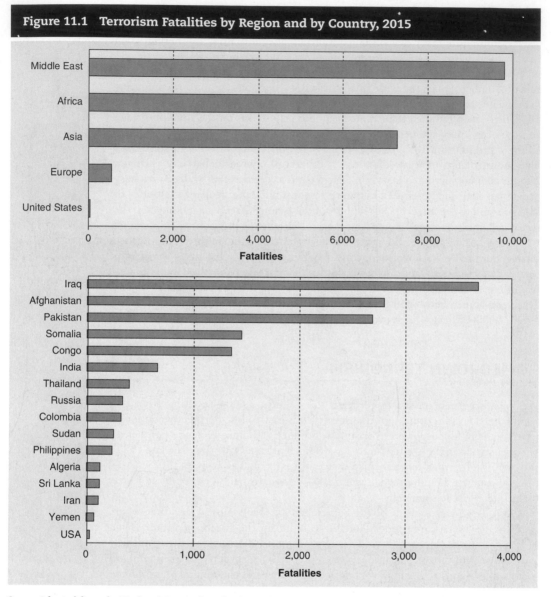

Figure 11.1   Terrorism Fatalities by Region and by Country, 2015

Source: Adapted from the National Consortium for the Study of Terrorism and Responses to Terrorism [START], Global Terrorism Database.

government officials. Their targets were not soldiers but civilians. Their motivation was apparently mixed: to extort a fortune from authorities, but perhaps also to get even with Americans for their treatment of immigrants and Muslims after 9/11, and to gain a sense of power by taunting the police and becoming celebrities. The D.C. Sniper episode reminds us, in a particularly chilling manner, that much of the terrorism in the United States is homegrown, originating as much in the psychopathology of the perpetrators as in their politics.

According to the FBI, only slightly more than one-third of all terrorist acts in the United States are international in origin. Most are instead perpetrated by U.S. citizens who hold a deadly grudge against the federal government, a particular category of people, or all humankind. The terrorists see social and

Figure 11.2 Terrorist Incidents in the United States, 1974–2014

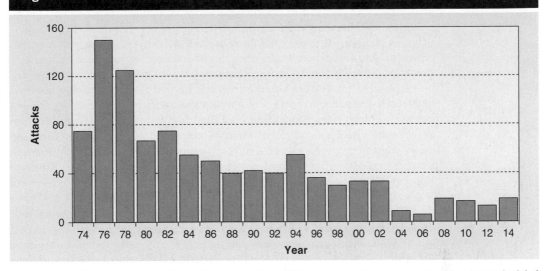

Source: Adapted from the National Consortium for the Study of Terrorism and Responses to Terrorism [START], Global Terrorism Database.

political issues in black and white terms and feel frustrated in their attempts to change society. They are self-righteous and utopian in their beliefs about the world. They are socially isolated, having no place to turn when they seek to confirm the validity of their ideas. Finally, they possess a coldblooded willingness to kill in order to secure not only a measure of sweet revenge through the barrel of a gun or a bomb but perhaps also a sense of their own power and importance.

The terrorists may elect to play a cat and mouse game with law enforcement, which they are convinced they will ultimately win. They may hope to terrify the community. They may seek to become celebrities, reading about their crimes in the headlines, on the 11 o'clock news, and on the cover of *Time* magazine. Or they may attempt to play God by deciding whether, and in what manner, their victims live or die. The terrorists might choose to strangle and mangle, torture and rape, bomb, or spray bullets at random targets. And, in the process, they get even with those they hold responsible for their miseries and wreak havoc throughout a community, a region, or an entire nation.

Since 9/11, citizens have felt very vulnerable. But many Americans are completely unaware that they were just as unsafe, perhaps more so, long before Middle Eastern terrorists decimated the Twin Towers in September 2001. FBI data indicate that almost 500 acts of terrorism occurred in the United States between 1980 and 2001. The unprecedented carnage of 9/11 can obviously never be ignored, but there have been numerous acts of terror committed against U.S. citizens long before al Qaeda and ISIS became household names. Indeed, the 1993 bombing of the World Trade Center in New York City took the lives of six people, a number that was apparently too small to make Americans pay attention.

Acts of domestic terror have been attempted by persons operating on their own, small groups of individuals, as well as the members of highly organized groups. In June 2006, seven men were charged with concocting a plot to blow up Chicago's Sears Tower and "kill all the devils we can." Most of the suspects were

U.S. citizens who, it was alleged by undercover FBI agents, had been organizing an Islamic army to wage a jihad in the United States. Prior to being arrested, their final act was to give an FBI informant a list of equipment they needed—boots, uniforms, machine guns, radios, vehicles, bulletproof vests, and $50,000 in cash.

The bombing offensive committed by the Unabomber, Theodore Kaczynski, represents one of the most deadly examples of domestic terrorism committed by a single individual. Not only was the Harvard-educated mathematician alone when he perpetrated his 18-year killing spree, but he was also a loner who despised high-tech society and, in order to communicate his message of destruction, decided literally to blow it up through the mail. Injuring 23 and killing 3 was as close as he came. The Unabomber had spent his days in an out-of-the-way Montana cabin, constructing bombs to be sent to his enemies and typing his manifesto, in which he railed against the evils of postmodern, technology-dependent America. Kaczynski's manifesto was printed in its entirety—just as he had demanded—in the *Washington Post*, where it accomplished its twofold purpose.

First, from the point of view of the killer, it made the Unabomber into some kind of folk hero, a high-tech Robin Hood, the image of a well-meaning if misguided humanitarian who had dedicated his life to saving us from ourselves. From the viewpoint of the FBI, however, printing the manifesto had a different result: It provided people with a set of clues to help identify the Unabomber and ultimately contribute to his apprehension. In the end, both objectives may have been realized: Americans organized Unabomber fan clubs and defense funds and wore Unabomber T-shirts while watching Jay Leno participate in Unabomber skits on his nightly TV show. At the same time, the Unabomber's brother, David Kaczynski, easily recognized certain idiosyncrasies in the syntax and substance of the Unabomber's manifesto, which, according to the FBI, led to Theodore's arrest. Thanks to a family that turned in one of its own in order to save the lives of people they didn't know, Kaczynski is presently serving a life sentence in a California prison.

In carrying out murderous terrorist acts, the number of perpetrators does not always come close to matching the number of victims. It is ironic indeed that an act of domestic terrorism resulting in a record-setting body count—168—would have been committed by perhaps only two individuals, who together concocted a plan to retaliate against the U.S. government for failing to respect the constitutional rights of citizens by blowing up a federal building and killing large numbers of government workers. But this is precisely what occurred in Oklahoma City in 1995, when Timothy McVeigh and his buddy Terry Nichols got even with Uncle Sam. They were convinced that the government was the enemy of white Americans; that a race war was inevitable; and that federal agents, being controlled by blacks and Jews, would scrap the Second Amendment and take all of their guns.

In a very real sense, students who seek to destroy their schools with gunfire or bombs can be considered homegrown terrorists. Many of the distinguishing features of terrorism (e.g., premeditation, creation of fear and anxiety, victimization of a civilian population larger than the death toll, and outrage) can be seen in episodes of school slaughter like those discussed in Chapter 7. In an odd but telling twist, the diary of Eric Harris, who teamed up with his buddy Dylan Klebold to perpetrate the Columbine massacre in April 1999, described their plans to crash a hijacked plane into the New York City skyline. What for millions of Americans seemed before September 11, 2001, to be absolutely unthinkable—to fly a jet into a skyscraper intentionally—had been conceived by a pair of Colorado teenagers more than 2 years prior to the actual attack.

American Muslims and Domestic Terrorism

Given the relatively large and growing number of terrorist inmates in the United States, it is important to note that the federal prison may have become an important recruiting center for radical Islamic terrorism. As of April 2016, there were 443 convicted terrorists incarcerated in U.S. federal prisons. Some of the more infamous convicts include Richard Reid, who attempted to ignite a shoe bomb while flying on an American Airlines flight from Paris to Miami; Ahmed Omar Abu Ali, who conspired to assassinate former president George W. Bush; Zacaria Moussaoui, who collaborated with al Qaeda to commit the 9/11 attacks on America; Najibullah Zazi, who engaged in an al Qaeda plot to bomb various targets in the United States; Daniel Patrick Boyd, who was charged with plotting to attack U.S. military personnel at the Quantico Marine Base; and Dzhokhar Tsarnaev, one of the Boston Marathon bombers.

At least 36 Americans who visited terrorist training camps in Yemen under false premises had converted to Islam in prison.[5] Many other terrorists may have received their inspiration behind bars. In May 2009, for example, three Americans and a Haitian immigrant were arrested by local and federal agents for planning to bomb synagogues in the New York City area and shoot down an aircraft with what they thought was a Stinger guided missile. Actually, the "missile" and "bombs" were all inoperative, given to the four would-be terrorists by federal agents posing as accomplices. The men had reportedly met in prison, where they converted to the Islamic faith and jointly developed plans for initiating acts of terrorism after their release.[6]

Terrorist activity perpetrated in the name of Islam has become a growing phenomenon in the United States. During the year 2015 and continuing into 2016, 37% of all domestic terrorist attacks—almost as many as the 38% attributable to white supremacists—were committed by Islamic extremists.[7] Still, it would be a mistake to suggest that American Muslims generally side with their radical religious fringe. As noted earlier, Islamic terrorism has been a much larger problem in Western Europe than in the United States. American Muslims have better integrated themselves into society than their counterparts in Europe, holding better-paid and more prestigious jobs and attaining higher educational achievements.

A 2017 Pew survey determined that most American Muslims are proud to be Americans, happy with their lives in the United States, and certain they can get ahead by working hard.[8] Moreover, American Muslims are extremely diverse, coming from many countries around the world and practicing a broad range of versions of Islam. As a result, they are much less likely than Muslims in Western Europe to form isolated and uniform Islamic communities apart from the mainstream. Since 9/11, the Muslim American community has helped security and law enforcement officials prevent nearly two of every five radical Islamic terrorist plots threatening the United States, and tips from the Muslim American community are the largest single source of initial information to authorities about these few plots.[9] At the same time, a majority of American Muslims report facing a lot of discrimination in their everyday lives and being treated unfairly by the mass media.[10]

Left-Wing Versus Right-Wing Terrorists

Domestic terrorism can also be linked to the operation of organized groups whose members plot and conspire to carry out the objectives of some violent master plan. For much of the twentieth century, and especially between 1960 and the mid-1980s, domestic terrorism came, for the most part, from political extremists on the left—from Marxist communists, socialists, militant minority groups, and Puerto Rican nationalists. Left-wing terrorists tended to be young, well-educated, upper-middle-class city dwellers. Many were African Americans and Latino Americans; almost one-third were women.[11]

In 1970, a group known as the Weather Underground declared war against the government of the United States. While preparing a bomb in a New York City safe house, three Underground members were accidentally killed. They later bombed the U.S. Capitol building, the Pentagon, police stations, and prisons.

Weather Underground members committed a number of murders in a series of bank robberies. In September 1970, revolutionary student Katherine Ann Powers and three companions set fire to a National Guard Armory in Massachusetts, stealing a truck and ammunition, which they supplied to the Black Panthers, a group of black militants. Three days later, the same Underground members robbed a branch of the State Street Bank in Boston, taking $26,000, with which they hoped to fund their revolutionary army. In the process, they murdered Walter Schroeder, a 42-year-old police officer who had responded to the bank's call for help. Although her four accomplices had long ago been apprehended and convicted, Powers remained a fugitive for 23 years before she surrendered to authorities. For her conviction of armed robbery and manslaughter, she was paroled in 1999 after serving six years in prison.

Another member of the Weather Underground, Kathy Boudin, participated in the 1981 robbery of an armored Brinks truck in suburban Nanuet, New York. During the holdup, Boudin and her friends shot and killed a security guard and two police officers. They made off with $1.6 million. For her part in the crime, Boudin was convicted of second-degree murder and served 22 years in prison. She was freed on parole in September 2003.

Left-wing terrorism has also come from the ranks of organizations dedicated to the cause of gaining independence for the Commonwealth of Puerto Rico. A small but obtrusive minority of Puerto Ricans have sought, through violent means, full and complete independence from the United States. In the 1970s and early 1980s, for example, the Armed Forces of National Liberation (FALN, after its Spanish name) was responsible for more than 100 bombings in New York City and Chicago, resulting in at least five deaths, 83 injuries, and more than $3 million in property damage. The most spectacular and deadly attack perpetrated by FALN occurred in New York City's crowded financial district on January 24, 1975, when a terrorist bomb ripped through Fraunces Tavern. Inside, dozens of Wall Street workers having lunch in the packed dining room were badly injured. Four died in the bombing; one was decapitated by flying debris. An hour later, wire service reporters received a phone call from an FALN representative, claiming responsibility for the terrorist attack. The caller explained the rationale for the deadly bombing: to retaliate for the CIA's killing of supporters of the Puerto Rican independence movement and to convince the U.S. government to abandon its "occupation" of the island of Puerto Rico.

Most of the terrorist murders committed from 1960 through the early 1980s involved left-wing revolutionaries in groups like the Weather Underground and the FALN. By contrast, Americans committing acts of organized domestic terrorism since the mid-1980s have tended to represent right-wing extremist causes, often involving white supremacy and/or hatred toward what they regard as a communist-controlled federal government. Typically, those Americans reputedly involved in right-wing terrorism are middle-aged, mostly white males who lack college degrees and are likely to be unemployed or impoverished. In the mid-1980s, a white supremacist militia group known as The Order sought to make good on its promise to spark revolution and to rid the nation of Jews, people of color, and liberals.

In 1985, the novel *The Turner Diaries* by William Pierce (aka Andrew Macdonald) about the inevitability of a global race war came to the attention of the U.S. Department of Justice, when members of The Order committed a number of robberies and murders in an effort to ignite the same kind of bloody war as depicted in the book. The group committed crimes ranging from robbing armored cars and counterfeiting to gunning down Jewish talk show host Alan Berg in the driveway of his Denver home.

In July 1996, Eric Rudolph caused the deadly pipe bomb explosion that ripped through crowded Centennial Olympic Park in Atlanta, Georgia, killing 44-year-old Alice Hawthorne of Albany, Georgia, and injuring more than 100. To maximize the damage, Rudolph had packed his 40-pound pipe bomb in a knapsack along with screws and nails. Later on, he justified his onslaught based on an ideology that considers all abortions as murder and gay rights as an abridgement of moral values.

Hiding in the hills of North Carolina, Rudolph was able to stay on the loose for 5 years until he was finally apprehended in 2003, while rummaging through a dumpster to find food behind a restaurant. Although typical of "lone wolf" terrorists who operate, for the most part, on their own, Rudolph was suspected by the FBI of having been assisted in securing food and shelter by local individuals who were ideologically friendly to the fugitive.

During his appearance in federal court in April 2005, Rudolph admitted committing the Olympic Park bombing as well as three others. During his 2-year series of attacks in the Deep South, he also injured four people in an explosion at the Otherside Lounge, a lesbian nightclub located on the northeast side of Atlanta, and killed 35-year-old Robert Sanderson at a women's health clinic in Birmingham. Rudolph also confessed to bombing a women's clinic that performed abortions in Sandy Springs, Georgia.

Having murdered two innocent people, Rudolph was definitely eligible to be executed by the federal government. Instead, he was sentenced in a plea bargain to four life sentences without parole, escaping death by, in return, confessing to his crimes and divulging to authorities the location of hundreds of pounds of dynamite he had stockpiled while hiding in the hills of North Carolina. Rudolph's motive? To anger and embarrass the federal government in the eyes of the world.

Right-wing terrorist activity has enjoyed a resurgence during the past few years, receiving much of its inspiration from supportive political rhetoric coming from our leaders in Washington, D.C., not to mention growth in the number of foreign-born Americans seen as competitors for jobs as well as the continuing decline in income among working-class Americans. During the summer of 2017, white nationalists and neo-Nazis battled demonstrators in the streets of several southern cities who were intent on seeing that long-standing statutes of Confederate soldiers were removed from public squares. In Charlottesville, Virginia, home of the University of Virginia, a densely packed crowd of antiracist protestors were mowed down by a speeding automobile as they walked on 4th Street. Heather Heyer, a 32-year-old paralegal, lost her life as she was struck from behind; dozens more received injuries. The driver, 20-year-old James Field, was photographed earlier attending a neo-Nazi rally with members of the white supremacist group Vanguard America. He was pictured posing among a group of Vanguard members, all of whom wore the organization's uniform consisting of a circular shield, white polo shirt, and khaki pants.

Sapp has identified three trends in the right-wing movement beginning in the mid-1980s.[12] The first involves Americans having group affiliations that read like a "Who's Who" of organizations promoting white supremacy—Aryan Nations,

Arizona Patriots, Ku Klux Klan, The Order, and Posse Comitatus. Their main objective in perpetrating terrorist acts is to prevent minority Americans from exercising their constitutional rights by sending them a message of fear and terror. The second trend noted by Sapp consists of survivalists who withdraw from conventional society in order to construct armed compounds in rural areas. They build bunkers, in which they stockpile weapons and food and await the demise of the federal government. The third and final trend in right-wing extremism involves the growth of Christian Identity, a set of religious tenets that provides a theological basis for believing that white Christians are intellectually and morally superior to people of color and other religions. White supremacist organizations often cloak their hatred in the aura and dogma of religion. Followers of the Identity Church are only "doing the work of God." At Sunday services, they preach that white Anglo-Saxons are the true Israelites depicted in the Old Testament, God's chosen people, while Jews are actually the children of Satan. They maintain that Jesus was not a Jew but an ancestor of the white, northern European peoples. In their view, blacks are "pre-Adamic," pre–Old Testament, a species lower than whites. In fact, they claim that blacks and other nonwhite groups are at the same spiritual level as animals and therefore have no souls.[13]

Members of this movement also believe in the inevitability of a global war between the races that only white people will ultimately survive. The survivalists among Christian Identity followers prepare for war by moving to communes where they can stockpile weapons, provide paramilitary training, and pray. According to the Southern Poverty Law Center, the number of Identity churches peaked in 2011 at 51 and declined to 21 churches in 2016.[14]

Stern has noted three important events and issues that were responsible for reinvigorating the extremist right beginning in the closing decade of the twentieth century.[15] First, federal gun control legislation (especially the waiting period initially included in the Brady law) caused white supremacist organizations to downplay their racist rhetoric in favor of espousing the belief—much more appealing to mainstream America—that the federal government was out to eliminate gun ownership. Second, the mishandled attempt on the part of Bureau of Alcohol, Tobacco, Firearms and Explosives (ATF) undercover agents in 1992 to arrest white supremacist Randy Weaver on firearm charges galvanized right-wing forces already convinced that the federal government was their enemy. During a prolonged standoff outside of Weaver's mountain cabin at Ruby Ridge, Idaho, U.S. marshals killed the white supremacist's pregnant wife and young son. Third, distrust of the federal government was further reinforced by the 1993 FBI siege of the Branch Davidian compound outside of Waco, Texas, which ended in a tremendous conflagration killing some 80 people, including two dozen children. These two highly publicized botched attempts on the part of federal agents to arrest extremists on weapons charges only added fuel to the fire of discontent among Americans who already doubted the competence and trustworthiness of the government. For a relatively few extremists, the incidents at Ruby Ridge and Waco inspired organized efforts to "defend the Constitution" and served to justify acts of terrorism. Membership in right-wing citizens' militias and survivalist groups together comprising the so-called Patriot movement has been estimated at between 15,000 and 100,000.[16]

The Southern Poverty Law Center suggests that these militia groups have declined every year since 1996, when the militia movement reached its peak with 858 groups. Evidence that Timothy McVeigh, just prior to his bombing of the federal building in Oklahoma City, had visited an Arizona chapter of the Patriot movement and had phoned a white supremacist compound in Oklahoma caused many Americans to turn away from right-wing extremist groups. The enormity of McVeigh's attack—taking the lives of so many men, women, and children—apparently disgusted potential members of the Patriot movement. By 2002, the number of groups in the Patriot movement had dropped to only 143.[17]

According to the Southern Poverty Law Center, many Patriot groups simply disappeared. Not unlike international terrorists around the world, Patriots organized themselves into small "cells" with no centralized leadership.[18] Although possibly limiting the ability of right-wing groups to amass resources, this lack of structure also restricts the effectiveness of any surveillance efforts on the part of federal security forces in their efforts to track political extremists.

The declining numbers of militia groups has recently reversed itself. According to the Southern Poverty Law Center, the number of antigovernment militia groups and Patriot organizations grew from 127 in 2009 to 330 in 2010 and peaked at 1360 in 2012. By 2016, the number of active antigovernment groups declined again to a still considerable but smaller 623.[19]

Many members of the Patriot movement are residents of rural and small-town America who experienced financial disaster beginning with the deep recession of the early 1980s, when ranchers, farmers, miners, and timber workers suffered profoundly. They were joined by blue-collar workers from major cities, who lost their jobs when the automobile industry went into severe decline. More recently, militia groups experienced a resurgence of interest and activism, once again among working-class white Americans, in response to growing income inequality and the massive exporting of jobs to workers in other countries.

The constitutionality of militia activities has been challenged by observers who regard them as illegal private armies.[20] In addition, there seems to be some degree of overlap in the memberships of white supremacy groups and militias, perhaps accounting for their shared conspiratorial thinking and hatred for the federal government. Following McVeigh's 1995 attack, some disillusioned militia members withdrew from the movement, abandoning any organized effort or joining a white supremacist organization instead. It took more than a decade after the Oklahoma City massacre to reestablish the Patriot movement as a viable political force at the margin of society.[21]

Single-Issue Terrorism

Acts of single-issue terror—for example, against environmental pollution, animal abuse, genetic engineering, abortion, company policies, or the like—may not be derived from some broad ideological position on the political left or right. Instead, single-issue terrorism is typically perpetrated by persons operating on their own or in groups who argue that the particular "evil" they hope to undermine has received the protection of society's legal system. They are therefore left having to go outside of the law.

The Earth Liberation Front (ELF) and the Animal Liberation Front (ALF) are the major organizations that have served to unite individuals in the United States who are willing to take illegal measures against environmental destruction or animal cruelty. Until recently, ELF and ALF were widely regarded as misguided but essentially benign organizations whose idealistic members had worked toward honorable goals—a cleaner environment and the humane treatment of animals. Representatives of ELF and ALF point out that their members have not injured or killed anyone in the United States. They did, however, break into a mink farm and free thousands of animals. They also have set fire to dozens of SUVs parked in the lots of automobile dealerships. In addition, the potential for injury and death seems to have increased, as the use of such tactics as firebombing property and spiking trees to prevent logging has been on the rise.

Radical environmentalists and animal rights activists have been responsible for 1,069 criminal acts in the United States between 1970 and 2007, including assassinations, armed assaults, bombings and explosions, facility attacks, and unarmed assaults.[22] From radical animal rights activists alone, between 2003 and 2010, a total of 5,578 criminal actions took place in the United Kingdom, Sweden, Italy, Germany, and the United States.[23] The targets of such terrorist acts have also broadened considerably, now including laboratories in which genetic engineering research is conducted.

Outside of the United States, ecoterrorism has taken a more dangerous tack. In 2003, less than 2 weeks before voters in the Netherlands went to the polls to elect a new government, animal rights activist Volkert van der Graaf shot to death a right-wing candidate for prime minister who had supported pig farmers in their battle against the animal rights movement.[24] In October 2012, Swedish ALF activists in the city of Kumla set fire to one of the cars of the owner of a fur store. Torching the car in front of the owner's home, ALF included the following message: "This is just a warning of what is coming if you don't end your involvement in the bloody skin trade NOW!!!"[25]

The escalation of violence by ecoterrorists may also have come to the United States. On the afternoon of September 1, 2010, 43-year-old James Lee, a radical environmentalist with a history of protesting the programs featured on the Discovery Channel, was shot to death at the Discovery company headquarters in Silver Spring, Maryland. Having taken three hostages (two employees and a security guard), Lee had strapped explosives to his chest and was holding a firearm. For hours, he spoke with negotiators. Then, as he raised his handgun in the direction of a hostage, Lee was felled by a police sniper who believed that the hostages' lives were in imminent danger. The gunman was convinced that the programs on Discovery had done more than their share to destroy the planet by encouraging global warming and animal extinction. On his website, Lee had posted a "manifesto," reminiscent of that of the Unabomber, containing his list of demands for the Discovery Channel—among other things, to stop encouraging the birth of more "parasitic human infants" and instead to encourage human sterilization and infertility. "All former pro-birth programs," he wrote, "must now push in the direction of stopping human birth."

THE IMPACT OF MURDEROUS TERROR

To the extent that a sizable number of Americans remain alienated and marginalized, acts of domestic terrorism cannot be expected to disappear entirely from the societal landscape. Depending on the state of our economy, the effectiveness of our government's foreign policy, and the ability of our society to reach residents who feel angry and ignored, there are bound to be violent and explosive outbursts from time to time, aimed at terrifying citizens or eliminating government officials.

International terrorism can similarly be expected to continue having an impact not only in the United States but also around the world. Wherever the peace process moves forward, extremist groups will predictably turn to violence. So long as terrorists believe that peace only robs them of their political and military clout, they will increase their efforts to destroy prospects for ending armed conflict.

This is precisely what has occurred from time to time between Israelis and Palestinians in the Middle East and, during an earlier period, between Catholics and Protestants in Northern Ireland, as well as between Muslims and Hindus in India. Terrorist attacks have continued to erupt in Iraqi cities, where local leaders have cooperated with the U.S. occupation or have sought to restore some semblance of normalcy to everyday life. The sectarian violence is often fueled by militant insurgents who are convinced that a large-scale civil war will promote their political and religious objectives. As of this writing, the group conflict in Syria has escalated into a hugely destructive civil war, causing millions of residents to migrate to more peaceful countries.

Almost 2 decades have passed since the September 11 attack on America, but we are only now beginning to assess the full impact of this tragic event on our way of life. Thousands lost their lives, including 60 police officers and 343 firefighters. The Twin Towers were crushed into nearly 2 million tons of burning concrete and steel. Many Americans have not put completely out of their minds the pain and suffering experienced by thousands of primary victims at the Twin Towers, the Pentagon, or in a doomed airliner over Pennsylvania, as well as tens of thousands of family members and friends and hundreds of thousands who knew a friend or the relative of a victim. In addition, there were millions of Americans in places like California, Arkansas, Michigan, and Massachusetts, who never had the opportunity of knowing the victims of 9/11 but nevertheless felt as though they had been robbed of a family member or a good friend.

Some Americans responded to the 9/11 attacks by directing their anger toward the 6 million Muslims in the United States. After 9/11, there was a 1,600% increase in hate crimes perpetrated against America's Muslim population. Most were acts of intimidation, but there were also numerous aggravated and simple assaults. Even in 2010, more than 4 in 10 Americans admitted feeling some degree of prejudice against Muslims. A Pew Research Center poll conducted in 2017 suggested that Americans do not see widespread extremism among the Muslim population, but still regard other religious groups—Jews, Catholics, mainstream Protestants, evangelical Christians, Buddhists, Hindus, and Mormons—in a more favorable light.[26]

In a 2014 study, researchers found a high prevalence of posttraumatic stress disorder (PTSD) and depression among nearly 30,000 persons who were rescue or recovery workers, lower Manhattan residents or area workers, or passersby on the morning of 9/11.[27] Of course, as the years pass, new generations of Americans will likely be able to distance themselves increasingly from the pain and suffering caused by the terrorist attacks on New York City and Washington, D.C. To those born around the turn of the century, 9/11 might feel like ancient history. They might very well experience a heightened fear of terrorism but be unaware of its source.

Moreover, notwithstanding the horrific carnage of 9/11 and its lasting impact on the collective psyche of America, not all of the news about 9/11 has been bad. In fact, nearly 60% claim that the attack on America has not made them more pessimistic about our nation's future. More than 80% are opposed to singling out Arabs or Muslims for questioning without probable cause. And more than a third of all Americans say that they coped with the horrors of September 11 not by purchasing a firearm or hiding in their homes but by reaching out and establishing a closer relationship, a tighter bond, with their families and good friends. Moreover, Americans' naiveté concerning the likelihood of being victimized by international terrorism has been replaced by a new collective awareness—vigilance—regarding the possibility of another major attack.[28]

September 11 gave us new heroes, including firefighters and other first responders, the New York City mayor, President George W. Bush, the volunteers at Ground Zero, the family members of victims, the passengers on Flight 93 who refused to allow terrorists to fly into the White House or the Capitol, and the U.S. military in Afghanistan and Iraq.[29] And after much controversy about whether to feature Osama bin Laden as its "Person of the Year" for 2001, *Time* magazine decided to look elsewhere for individuals to honor on its cover. Subsequent issues of *Time* continued mainly to feature virtuous individuals, for example, an Enron whistleblower, good Samaritans, and our troops in Afghanistan, until the year 2006, when the magazine chose to honor "you"—all Americans who use the internet.

In addition, September 11 brought out the generosity and compassion of Americans everywhere. In the months after the attack, much of the extreme hostility targeting Arabs and Muslims subsided, and grieving Americans found a more productive and healthier way to mourn our nation's loss—they volunteered at Ground Zero; donated money, time, or blood; and prayed for the victims. Following 9/11, the nation's charities were swamped with checks, cash, clothes, and even frequent flier miles. Some 36,000 units of blood was donated to the New York Blood Center. This was the biggest flood of donations that fund-raisers had ever seen. During the first two weeks alone, donations hit $500 million. By August 2002, the 10 largest charities claimed they had collected $2.3 billion. The sources of charity were diverse: race drivers donating their helmets, an all-star rock concert at Madison Square Garden, school bake sales in Wyoming, and a Massachusetts congressman's education fund to help the victims' families.

On September 11, 2001, Americans witnessed the most violent single incident of hate-motivated violence in our country's history. The attack on America was apparently inspired by an intense hatred of America and a desire to eliminate as many U.S. citizens as possible. This horrendous incident demonstrated the power and devastation that hate is capable of generating. One of the important lessons learned from the attack on America was that to ignore our vulnerability to murderous terrorism is to risk the potential for unimaginable tragedy.

REDUCING MURDEROUS TERRORISM

What can be done to reduce the scourge of terrorism besides alerting our citizens to be vigilant? Somehow, we must reinstate the credibility of our public officials—our president, our Congress, and our Supreme Court justices—so that alienated Americans do not feel they must go outside of the mainstream and radicalize their behavior in order to satisfy their goals.

There is, of course, no way of guaranteeing that another 9/11 will not occur on American soil. No matter how effectively we deal with the problem, it is impossible to reduce terrorist threats to zero. On the other hand, there is much that is within our control. In the past few years, our country has experienced relatively few terrorist acts in which lives were taken. Most of our extreme violent opposition has come from psychopathology, not politics. Aside from continuing to impose effective security measures, we should make sure that we do not treat millions of our citizens as though they are rubber stamps of one another, as though they are all a bunch of potential terrorists. Instead, we should seek to improve the quality of life for the alienated among us, even if they come from a different ethnic or religious group or from another country.

Bringing Americans back into the mainstream may be our most effective defensive weapon for preventing future acts of terrorism. All of us benefit when our fellow Americans do not feel they must go to the margins of society—to acts of extreme violence—for solutions to their personal problems.

ENDNOTES

1. Jack Levin, *Domestic Terrorism* (New York: Chelsea House, 2006).

2. Paul Wilkinson, "Current and Future Trends in Domestic and International Terrorism," in *Violence and Terrorism: Annual Editions* (Guilford, CT: McGraw Hill/Dushkin, 2004).

3. CNN.com, "House Approves Patriot Act Renewal," March 7, 2006.

4. Fox News, "Obama Signs Last-Minute Patriot Act Extension," May 27, 2011.

5. Julia Davis, "Convicted Terrorists Living Next Door, Deadly Terror Plot Devised Inside California Prison," Examiner.com, January 28, 2010.

6. Michael Daly, "FBI Arrest Four in Alleged Plot to Bomb Bronx Synagogues, Shoot Down Plane," *New York Daily News*, May 21, 2009.

7. Stav Ziv, "Right-Wing and Radical Islamic Terror Are Equally Serious Threats: ADL Report," *Newsweek*, May 20, 2017.

8. Jeff Diamant, "American Muslims Are Concerned—but Also Satisfied With Their Lives," Pew Research Center, July 26, 2017.

9. Kristina Cooke and Joseph Ax, "U.S. Officials Say American Muslims Do Report Extremist Threats," *Reuters*, June 16, 2016.

10. Emma Green, "How Much Discrimination Do American Muslims Face?" *Atlantic*, June 24, 2017.

11. Levin, *Domestic Terrorism*.

12. Allen Sapp, "Basic Ideologies of Right-Wing Extremist Groups in America" (Paper presented at the Annual Meeting of the Academy of Criminal Justice Sciences, Las Vegas, Nevada, 1985).

13. Southern Poverty Law Center, "Christian Identity," 2017, https://www.splcenter.org/fighting-hate/extremist-files/ideology/christian-identity.

14. Ibid.

15. Kenneth S. Stern, *A Force Upon the Plain: The American Militia Movement and the Politics of Hate* (New York: Simon and Schuster, 1996).

16. Jonathan Karl, *The Right to Bear Arms: The Rise of America's Militia* (New York: Harper, 1995).

17. Heidi Beirich and Bob Moser, "From Push to Shove," in *Violence and Terrorism: Annual Editions* (Guilford, CT: McGraw-Hill/Dushkin, 2004).

18. Southern Poverty Law Center, "Active 'Patriot' Groups in the United States in 2010," *Intelligence Report*, Spring 2011.

19. Southern Poverty Law Center, "Active Patriot Groups in the US in 2016," *Intelligence Report*, Spring 2017.

20. Thomas Halpern and Brian Levin, *The Limits of Dissent: The Constitutional Status of Armed Civilian Militias* (Amherst, MA: Aletheia Press, 1996).

21. Levin, *Domestic Terrorism*.

22. Jennifer Varriale Carson, Gary LaFree, and Laura Dugan, "Terrorist and Non-Terrorist Criminal Attacks by Radical Environmental and Animal Rights Groups in the United States, 1970–2007," *Terrorism and Political Violence* (March 2012): 295–319.

23. Sivan Hirsch-Hoefler and Cas Mudde, "Ecoterrorism: Threat or Political Ploy?" *Washington Post*, September 19, 2014.

24. M. S., "Did the Crime Fit the Time?" *Economist*, May 6, 2014.

25. Hirsch-Hoefler and Mudde, "Ecoterrorism: Threat or Political Ploy?"

26. Pew Research Center, "Americans Express Increasingly Warm Feelings Toward Religious Groups," February 15, 2017.

27. K. Caramanica, R. M. Brackbill, T. Liao, and S. D. Stellman, "Comorbidity of 9/11-Related PTSD and Depression in the World Trade Center Health Registry 10–11 Years Post Disaster," *Journal of Traumatic Stress* 27 (2014): 680–688.

28. Darren K. Carlson, "One Year Later, Concern for Civil Liberties Rising," Gallup Organization, September 10, 2002.

29. David W. Moore, "Firefighters Top Gallup's Ethics and Honesty List," Gallup Organization, December 5, 2001.

CHAPTER TWELVE

CULT KILLINGS

In popular culture, almost any bizarre or esoteric group one can imagine has been considered a cult. In this broad view, tens of millions of Americans have been involved for varying periods of time in one cult or another, whether organized around neo-Christian religious beliefs, Hindu and Eastern religion, the occult, witchcraft or satanism, Zen and other Sino-Japanese philosophical or mystical orientations, race, psychotherapy, politics, or self-improvement. Even broader in scope, the term *cult-like following* has been applied to include the inspired fans of certain rock groups, rap artists, movies, and sports teams, as well as the zealous followers of exercise or diet regimens. Similarly, referring to the cultlike characteristics of a group stretches the scope of inquiry to encompass almost any group—a gang, a fraternity, even a business enterprise—to which members are "slavishly devoted."[1] As a recent example, R&B artist R. Kelly has been accused of holding several women at his home in a cultlike state. The accusations include abduction, brainwashing, abuse, and physical confinement.

In this chapter, we have adopted a more limited view of what constitutes a cult, defining it as a loosely structured and unconventional form of religious group, whose members are held together by a charismatic leader who mobilizes their loyalty around some new religious cause. Typically, this cause is at odds with that of more conventional religious institutions. Using this definition, almost any new religious group that hasn't yet become institutionalized or widely accepted—whether benign or dangerous—could be regarded as a cult. From this perspective, then, early Christianity during Roman times was a cult, but so were the Branch Davidians, who in 1993 perished in the flames of Waco, Texas, orchestrated by their leader, David Koresh. Our definition would, at the same time, exclude from consideration here a wide range of groups that might have a strong influence on their members but are essentially secular rather than religious in their objectives.

As a force for social change, the cults or new religious groups of one generation may represent the conventional religious institutions and traditions of another. For example, the Church of Jesus Christ of Latter-Day Saints (aka the Mormons) began in 1830 as a small cult in an upstate New York village but now numbers more than 10 million church members around the world. Similarly, recently established cultural ideas and practices such as gender equality on the job, shelters for victims of domestic violence, and healthier diets all began as heretical or pioneering cult concepts (in this case, from the Oneidas, the Holy Order of MANS, and the Seventh-Day Adventists, respectively).

DANGEROUS CULTS

Of course, many people nowadays restrict the use of the term *cult* to refer only to new religious groups that they regard as destructive or dangerous. And there are many cults that give anticultists plenty of reason to despise them. Some cult members recruit in a deceptive way. They might, for example, lure unsuspecting students by promising them a party or a get-together at some out-of-the-way retreat while they fail to inform the students of their true intent, which is to convert them. Other cults are said to use methods of mind control or thought reform. And many groups regarded as cults require their members to become totally dependent on some authoritarian group leader who claims to have a special knowledge, gift, or talent. In extreme cases, the recruit is no longer allowed to make any important personal decisions of his or her own and must give up all relationships with old friends and family. The cult becomes a total and tyrannical institution.

Cult specialist Margaret Singer defines dangerous cults in terms of characteristics of its leaders, its leader–follower relationships, and its programs of persuasion. Based on these dimensions, she suggests that cults exhibit the following seven characteristics: (1) authoritarian leaders who claim a special mission and/or knowledge; (2) a charismatic, dominant leadership style; (3) leaders' claims to total allegiance; (4) claims to an innovative and exclusive answer to individual and societal problems; (5) an "ends justifies the means" logic that justifies manipulation of outsiders; (6) totalistic ideological and behavioral control over members; and (7) a major transformation of lifestyle.[2]

Most traditional religious organizations don't have a pressing need to use such tactics. Established Christian churches may, for example, recruit, but they can also depend on the process of socialization to attract new members—generation after generation of parents who teach their children the religious traditions they were taught at home. The last thing desired by conventional religious groups, in most cases, is to separate family members from one another—they are the most effective recruiters. Moreover, conventional religions can easily afford to lose members and still thrive and prosper with their remaining congregants.

But new religious groups typically don't have the luxury of being able to count on their beliefs and rituals being passed from parents to children in their congregations—not unless, of course, they are successful enough to stick around for more than one generation. And most of them don't. So it's either recruit from the ranks of the nonbelievers or perish as a religious group. As a result, the pressure for deception and unethical tactics of persuasion (also known as brainwashing) can become fierce. In addition, the extreme dependency often found among cultists can force members of a cult to abandon their relationships outside—relationships that might otherwise reduce their loyalty to their fellow cultists, to their cause, and to their charismatic leader as well. Therefore, there may be considerable pressure to give up old friends and reduce contact with family members. There are powerful forces within the cult to conform, comply, and go along with the program. At the extreme, such forces have occasionally been harvested by a deranged but convincing father figure who seeks to persuade his flock to follow him like sheep into practicing human sacrifice or committing murder. It should be noted that the all-encompassing popular culture definition of cults, although too broad for our purposes, also makes an important point. Even though gangs, fraternities, and exercise groups are not cults, their appeal may depend in part on certain of their cultish features—for example, their ability to isolate new members from former friends and relatives and an authoritarian decision-making structure.

Writing about the success of the Microsoft Corporation, reporter Bob Weinstein compared Microsoft with the Branch Davidians. He claimed that both organizations were cults, the only difference being that the Davidians were religious and Microsoft was a corporation. In both instances, members tend to be isolated from the outside world and are preoccupied with achieving their organizational mission as espoused by a charismatic leader. Corporate cults, he wrote, focus on the rules and regulations of the organization.[3]

Thus, even a major U.S. corporation can have cultlike characteristics. Indeed, the ability of a company to secure the unwavering loyalty of its workforce to corporate goals and leadership may help determine its long-term viability in the marketplace. Microsoft is certainly no cult applying the narrow definition of the term. It is not a religious organization, nor does it seek to eliminate relationships of workers with old friends and relatives. But Microsoft, just like many other successful corporations, can draw a lesson or two from the operation of those groups in society that have established themselves firmly as the cults in our midst by associating group objectives with spirituality and finding methods for maximizing the loyalty of their membership.

On occasion, even larger and more established religious groups have been accused of having cultlike characteristics. Scientology represents a contemporary example. Having an estimated membership between 25,000 and 40,000 and existing for decades, Scientology simply does not possess all of the characteristics associated with the small religious groups we call "cults." On the other hand, there have been allegations, over the years, that scientologists separate their congregants from friends and family and that some of their members are the victims of mind control.

THE APPEAL OF CULTS

Cults seem to become more attractive to the members of society during periods of rapid social change, at times when individuals are feeling a lack of structure and belongingness in their lives. Such new religious groups reflect tensions in society that make many citizens receptive to ideas originating outside of the conventional culture. In the second quarter of the 19th century, for example, as new technologies began having an impact throughout U.S. society, there was a dramatic upsurge in evangelical and communal organizations. During the tumultuous 1960s, as social and cultural change quickened its pace, cult activity once again swept across the country. These were periods during which the credibility of traditional institutions suffered, and many young people searched for an alternative lifestyle outside of the mainstream.[4] The rise of marginal groups such as cults also has at least something to do with the calendar. At the end of every century (not to mention every millennium), organized groups emerge to prophesize the end of the world. This millennial myth can be traced back to ancient biblical writings that predict that a cosmic cataclysm orchestrated by God will destroy the ruling powers of evil and raise the righteous to a new existence in a messianic kingdom lasting 1,000 years. This is the prophesied millennium.[5]

But not all contemporary millennialists sit back and wait for God to destroy the old system and usher in the new. Their vision of apocalypse goes far beyond any vision of a spiritual New Age metamorphosis. For some of these new apocalyptic thinkers, increasing income inequality since 1970 is the result not of abstract forces such as global competition and automation but of active behind-the-scenes covert manipulation by human beings with a purpose—international bankers, the United Nations, the federal reserve system, and one-world-order types who benefit at the expense of the average American. Their notion of apocalypse is just as active and just as physical—all-out war, nothing more, and nothing less.

Some apocalyptic thinkers have given death a helping hand. In March 1997, 39 members of the Heaven's Gate cult committed mass suicide in their rented mansion in Rancho Santa Fe near San Diego. Marshall Applewhite, the cult's leader, had convinced his followers—20 women and 19 men ranging in age from 26 to 72—that a spaceship traveling behind the Hale–Bopp comet was coming to pick them all up soon after they had shed their vehicles or containers (also known as bodies). The cult members were totally convinced that civilization on Earth was about to end and that they could enter a higher life form by getting rid of their bodies and boarding a spaceship to travel to what they called the next level. So they took lethal doses of poison after having positioned themselves in a ritualistic way. Each was dressed in black pants, dark socks, and new Nike sneakers; each was covered by a purple sheet that was neatly folded to resemble a diamond. When the bodies were found, each had a $5 bill and several quarters in his or her pockets. Applewhite had also demanded that his male followers castrate themselves, and they had all complied.

Not only did the Heaven's Gate suicide victims represent both genders and a wide range of ages, but they also consisted of blacks, Latinos, and whites who had come from all over the country—New Mexico, California, Texas, Utah, Colorado, Florida, Minnesota, Washington, Ohio, Massachusetts, Arizona, Missouri, Iowa, Wisconsin, New York, Idaho, and Nebraska. And these were not stupid or uneducated people. They were computer skilled, musically talented, and scholarly, but they were also needy, lonely, and depressed. Many had abandoned their families and friends months or years earlier and were completely on their own.

The Heaven's Gate cultists were hardly the first to commit mass suicide by poison. Over a 15-month period, beginning in October 1994, the bodies of 69 members of the Order of the Solar Temple were discovered in Switzerland, Canada, and France. Most of the charred bodies had been ritualistically positioned in a star formation and burned, with their feet facing the ashes of a campfire. Several handwritten notes found in homes and meeting places used by the cult suggested mass suicide. In one letter, the doomsday cultists explained that they were "leaving this Earth to find a new dimension of truth and absolution, far from the hypocrisies of this world." However, it was determined on closer inspection that most of the members of the Solar Temple had died methodically planned deaths—by shooting, poisoning, stabbing, or asphyxiation. Even if all of the adult members had consented to be killed, it would be hard to argue that the many children (as young as age 2) were anything more than murder victims. Incredibly, many of the Solar Temple cultists who died were wealthy, well-educated, and respected members of their communities—architects, nurses, and celebrated police officers—who were philanthropic, owned expensive property, or were regarded as intellectuals.

CHARISMATIC LEADERS AND THEIR FOLLOWERS

The body counts amassed by Heaven's Gate and the Solar Temple cultists are bad enough, yet they pale in comparison with the November 1978 mass suicide in Jonestown, Guyana, in which 913 Americans, all members of the People's Temple, perished. The complete domination of the People's Temple leader, 47-year-old Jim Jones, had a great deal to do with the effectiveness of the mass suicide. He had brought his followers from the United States to their new home in an isolated area in the jungle, thousands of miles from the influence of family or friends. Jonestown was located literally in the middle of nowhere.

Indeed, the one and only reality for the followers of Jim Jones was the power of Jones himself, whose charismatic sermons and rantings and ravings were the means by which he exercised control. Jones was convinced that the FBI and the

CIA were closing in on him and his flock. He decided to take everyone to a better life in the hereafter.

It is relatively easy to explain why a reportedly psychotic individual like Jim Jones might turn his paranoia and delusional thinking into destructive behavior. It is more difficult to understand how apparently normal, intelligent people can buy into a philosophy promising that they would achieve a better life in the hereafter and that their suicide would miraculously protect them from harm. As illogical and immoral as such beliefs may seem, however, many people could be made to accept these promises given the right set of circumstances.

According to social psychologist Philip Zimbardo and his colleagues, Jones may have acquired his ability to persuade from the classic novel *1984*, by George Orwell, in which a courageous individual attempts to resist the institutionalized techniques of mind control employed by government in order to control the masses.[6] Not unlike the procedures of thought reform described by Orwell in his fictional futuristic account, Jones assured the loyalty of his followers by demanding that they spy on one another and by keeping his presence in public consciousness through the messages he broadcast 24 hours daily over powerful loudspeakers. In both the novel and in Jonestown, "Big Brother" was constantly watching over the activities of community members.

In Orwell's novel, ordinary citizens were urged to kill themselves rather than to give up to the enemy who threatened to wage war on their society. Hundreds of Jonestown cultists were similarly persuaded that suicide would be a far better fate than to be killed by federal officials.

Thus, the members of Jonestown were rehearsed in the collective suicide procedure whereby they would take their turn to willingly drink a lethal dose of cyanide-laced Kool-Aid (a generic reference to what actually appears to have been a mixture of Kool-Aid and its competing brand, Flavor Aid). Men, women, and children stood in long lines, awaiting with faith and confidence their chance to sip the Kool-Aid and die with their comrades—thus, the origin of the idiom "drinking the Kool-Aid." But those who resisted and tried to escape were instead shot to death by Jones's armed guard. Others knew they had no realistic options and died taking the path of least resistance. During the mass suicide he had orchestrated, and knowing the end was near anyway, Jim Jones raised a pistol to his head and fired a single bullet through his brain.

Abnormal situations can make normal people do "crazy" things, especially if they perceive a strong self-serving purpose in doing so, such as profit, power, or protection. On April 12, 1989, the Mexican police unearthed a mass grave containing 15 victims of ritualistic human sacrifice—including many Americans— on an isolated ranch some 20 miles west of Matamoros, Mexico, just south of the Texas border. Within 24 hours, police had arrested four young men and sought several others, all members of a major drug ring, who allegedly were involved in the killings.

The police identified the spiritual ringleader of the drug-smuggling cult as Adolfo de Jesús Constanzo, a 26-year-old native of Cuba. His loyal followers called their charismatic leader "El Padrino" (the Godfather). Because of his spellbinding influence over his devotees, Constanzo allegedly was able to convince them that their drug activities could never be touched by the law so long as they obeyed his command to, among other things, kill for survival. His band of drug smugglers practiced Palo Mayombe. This black-magic derivative of Santería ("the way of the Saints"), a Caribbean voodoo belief, was blended with both satanism and Brujería, a form of witchcraft practiced by 16th-century Aztecs. Human and animal sacrifice was thought by the group to bring them immunity from bullets and criminal prosecution while they illegally transported 2,000 pounds of marijuana per week from Mexico into the United States.

Just as the disciplines of Jim Jones and Marshall Applewhite seemed within the range of psychological normality, the followers of Constanzo were hardly the crazed lunatics that many people associate with ritualistic slaughter and human sacrifice. Most of the cult members grew up in relatively affluent families and did not have histories of violence. Believed to be the high priestess or witch of the operation, for example, 24-year-old Sara María Aldrete Villareal was an honor student at Texas Southmost College, where she was listed in the college's "Who's Who" directory. In sharp contrast, Constanzo was the "Hitler" of his cult. Adolf Hitler, as a charismatic leader, had transformed ordinary German citizens into brutal SS (*Schutzstaffel*) killers through constant marches, all-day group singing of the party's anthem, and required cheering. Hitler capitalized on the promise of turning around Germany's terrible economy to help convince his followers of the urgency of his grand plan. Constanzo similarly capitalized on a powerful economic incentive, as well as on group pressure in order to foster obedience to his command. Like Hitler's marches and chants, Constanzo involved his followers in the elaborate and mysterious rituals of animal sacrifices and demonic incantations in order to achieve in his flock selfless devotion to the cause. Over time, they came to believe that they had been privy to a secret wisdom revealed only to their leader's disciples.

Constanzo's final command was to perform a death ritual—this time his own death. Several of his followers obediently shot Constanzo to death as police authorities closed in on them in Mexico City. Apparently, the practice of Palo Mayombe couldn't really protect Constanzo from bullets, nor could it immunize Aldrete and other cult members from prosecution for murder.

Part of the influence of a dangerous cult rests with the ability of its leader to convince his followers of his supreme, perhaps supernatural, wisdom. A veneer of religious doctrine and ritual is often employed in order to reinforce and encourage dedication to the cause, regardless of how deadly it may be. In many cases, the leader himself is convinced of his otherworldly talents. He sees himself as all-powerful, as possessing the ability to conquer all enemies.

Thirty-nine-year-old Jeffrey Don Lundgren of Kirkland, Ohio, was determined to do God's work. Having broken from a branch of Mormonism, the Reorganized Church of Jesus Christ of Latter-Day Saints, Lundgren was certain that the Creator was sending messages to him directly. It was his sacred duty, then, to carry out God's Will, no matter how distasteful or violent. After all, God's commandments transcend human laws.

Lundgren preached that the armies of Satan were about to strike. To save themselves, he and his flock would have to give up their worldly possessions (donating them to his church) and come together to live off the land until such time that Christ returned. In the meantime, there would be no electricity or shelter. And his followers would have to protect the temple by whatever means possible. For this purpose, Lundgren purchased semi-automatic rifles and handguns, along with tents, camping supplies, food, and hundreds of rounds of ammunition.

Early in April 1989, Lundgren had a vision in which God suggested that the enemy had already infiltrated his camp and must be eliminated. His victims were Dennis Avery and his family, followers who had given all of their worldly possessions to the divine cause but who also remained somewhat skeptical of the cult leader's legitimacy. On occasion, Dennis Avery had challenged Lundgren's divine authority.

On the evening of April 17, the self-appointed prophet led the members of the Avery family, one by one, into a red barn behind his farmhouse. Lundgren and five of his men had dug a deep pit in the barn's dirt floor. Each victim—Dennis, his wife Cheryl, and their three young daughters—was walked from the farmhouse to the barn, where their hands and legs were bound with duct tape. Then, Lundgren repeatedly shot his victims with hollow-point slugs from a .45 semi-automatic and threw their lifeless bodies into the pit.

On September 21, 1990, Lundgren's trial for first-degree murder concluded, when he was sentenced to death. Hearing the judge's decision, he told his attorney that everything was going according to God's plan and that his death sentence was predetermined. On October 24, 2006, Jeffrey Lundgren was executed at the Southern Ohio Correctional Facility.

The young children of cultists are often very vulnerable to the irrational demands of their spiritual leader. In 1999, 29-year-old Jacques Robidoux and his wife, Karen, living among the members of a small cult in North Attleboro, Massachusetts, complied with the demands of Jacques's sister, who insisted that God had instructed her that the couple's year-old son, Samuel, should live for an indefinite period only on his mother's milk. The cult was comprised of three interrelated families whose members shunned modern medicine and regarded the government as a "satanic system." Jacques and Karen's father-in-law served as leaders of the group.

This was not the first episode in which Jacques and his sister had claimed to receive direct instructions from God. First, they forbade eyeglasses; then, they prohibited cosmetics, shorts, photo albums, and books. When traveling, the group was forbidden from making any preparations in advance. They also were required to rid themselves of any relationships with relatives who were not members of their cult.

Then, Jacques Robidoux effectively ordered the execution of his own son. Over a period of 2 weeks, as Karen stopped producing milk and the effects of starvation set in, little Samuel's body weight dropped precipitously. Recognizing the dire consequences, Karen wanted to resume feeding her baby the solid food he needed to survive, but Jacques convinced her not to do so. He was convinced that medical doctors were satanic tools, and he prayed that God would see fit to allow Karen again to produce milk. Jacques also believed that if his son died, he would be able to bring him back to life. Instead, Samuel became totally immobilized and then, in this third week of starvation, permanently succumbed to malnutrition.

Seen by the court as a victim of cult influence, Karen Robidoux was eventually cleared of charges of second-degree murder. Her husband Jacques, however, who argued that he, too, had been "brainwashed" by other cultists, was convicted of first-degree murder and is serving a life sentence.[7]

In January 2007, another young child was executed by the members of a small cult, this time located in Baltimore. Queen Antoinette, the group's spiritual leader, was able to convince the victim's mother that her 16-month-old son Javon had a "rebellious and evil spirit" because he refused to say "Amen" before meals but that he could be cured by withdrawing his food.

Antoinette had secured her power over the cult members by demanding that they separate themselves from family and former friends. They were required to discard all of their possessions and to limit their social contacts to other members of the cult. On a daily basis, Antoinette made certain that they didn't wander far from her house and shunned all medical care. She even determined what they could and could not wear.

A Trinidad-born mother, Ria Ramkissoon, 23, believing in the supernatural powers of her cult leader, starved her son to death. Then, at the urging of Queen Antoinette, she prayed for his resurrection. For weeks, she remained with her son's body, dancing and singing to him. She even tried to give him water. When everything failed, Ramkissoon and her fellow cultists stuffed the dead boy's body into a suitcase and moved to Philadelphia, where it stayed for a year until the police eventually discovered it.

In court, a jury convicted Queen Antoinette of second-degree murder and sentenced her to 50 years in prison. Her daughter and another member of the cult were sentenced to 15 years behind bars. Javon's mother pleaded guilty to child abuse resulting in death. She received a suspended sentence, under the assumption that she had been brainwashed by the cult's spiritual leader. As a part of the court's agreement with the defendant, Ramkissoon's plea would be withdrawn should her son ever come back to life![8]

The increasing usage of the internet has expanded the reach of dangerous cult activity beyond the impact of interpersonal influence. In July 2017, Stephen Mineo, a 32-year-old man living in Coolbaugh Township, Pennsylvania, was apparently shot in the forehead at close range by his 42-year-old girlfriend. According to investigators, Mineo had asked his girlfriend to take his life after being harassed online by the satanic death cult to which he belonged. In recent days, the cult had warned its members about an impending invasion by alien intruders and the coming end of days. On Facebook, Mineo had posted about averting large-scale conspiracies and making preparations for the arrival of doomsday. According to his friends, he had wanted to get out of the cult, finding that it no longer met his needs. Mineo suggested that apocalyptic movies like *Resident Evil: Vendetta* gave him a view into the future.[9]

Europe has also experienced the operation of deadly and dangerous cults. In the city of Yaroslavl, a Russian city located some 160 miles northeast of Moscow on the Volga River, four teenagers—all 16 or 17 years of age—were murdered in June 2008 by the youthful members of a satanic cult. The eight killers, in their late teens, lured their victims, one at a time, to a secluded area, where they were forced to drink an excessive amount of alcohol before being stabbed 666 times. The bodies of the victims were cooked and eaten by the killers, who then disposed of their victims' hearts, arms, and scalps in a pit accompanied by satanic symbols.

In Argentina, the burned body of a 26-year-old woman was discovered in July 2017 off a highway near the town of Rincón de los Sauces. The victim, Fernanda Pereyra, was pregnant when she was stabbed to death and her remains burned using a large amount of gasoline. Authorities believe that Pereyra was ritualistically killed by the members of a satanic cult whose members were quite careful in choosing three sixes for determining their victim and the location of her murder—she was in her sixth month of pregnancy and her body was left at kilometer 6 on Route 6.[10]

NEEDS FULFILLED BY CULTS

Cults have historically had much drawing power with alienated youth. Teenagers who join satanic cults often suffer from mood disorders (e.g., depression and bipolar disorder), posttraumatic stress disorder, and personality disorders (including antisocial personality disorder).[11] Moreover, cults have a long history of recruiting lonely college students. Away from home for the first time and trying to make friends and fit in, college students may be particularly vulnerable to psychological manipulation. Colleges across the United States have banned from campus some of the more extreme religious groups known to prey on students (e.g., the International Churches of Christ and their sister group, HOPE Worldwide; University

Bible fellowship; Hare Krishnas; and the Boston Church of Christ). Like many of the hate groups discussed in Chapter 10, cults often hide behind a facade of Christianity.

Nowadays, certain terrorist organizations have taken on cultlike characteristics. Indeed, many disaffected young adults who might otherwise have assumed membership in a dangerous cult have instead joined terrorists who preach death and destruction of the "infidels" as their central mission. Not unlike Heaven's Gate or Jonestown, terrorist organizations may require their members to be prepared to commit suicide in carrying out an attack.[12]

Also, not unlike motivators of violent terrorist activity, important life stressors—a divorce or break-up, job loss, or deterioration in mental health—may all act as risk factors for the charismatic lure of a cult. Like serial killers, cult killers prey on the vulnerable, whether teenagers, adults, or senior citizens, whether females or males, whether educated and prosperous or uneducated and poor. In addition, there now exists a new hunting ground for cults—the internet. A perusal of virtually any chat room finds the cult recruiters proselytizing via instant messages to a wide range of potential recruits.

Adolescence is a stage of development frequently marked by a profound sense of marginality and powerlessness. Teenagers are neither children nor adults. They are expected to remain submissive to the demands of the older generation and, at the same time, achieve some sense of independence. For a youngster troubled in his search for belonging and personal meaning, a group that promises to provide both friendship and a sense of importance can be extremely attractive. As a result, cults organized around themes of vampirism and satanism may be particularly appealing to teenagers who feel thwarted in their quest for power and who are dissatisfied with their conventional peer relations.

In November 1996, a group of youngsters from in and around Murray, Kentucky, all members of a self-described vampire clan, traveled to Eustis, Florida, and the home of Richard and Ruth Wendorf, where they bludgeoned the couple to death with a crowbar. The victims were the parents of one of the murderous cult disciples—a 15-year-old girl who claimed to have been a demon in past lives. Along with her four fellow cultists, she fled the bloody scene in her parents' 1994 Ford Explorer, inside of which police later found a credit card belonging to the dead couple, a blood-drenched sheet, and books on ancient spells and vampirism.

The youthful members of the cult all believed they were vampires who possessed supernatural powers and who communicated with spirits while engaging in rituals in which they drank their own blood and that of mutilated animals. According to the 17-year-old leader of the cult, Rod Ferrell, as he gave his confession in court, slaying the Wendorfs was a necessary act that would "open the gates to Hell."

Satanic ritual and violence seem to be especially appealing to young people who have been easily influenced by the adults in their lives. The cult of Santa Muerte (Saint Death), a female deity who is often pictured as a skeletal figure, clad in a long robe and holding a scythe and a globe, has large numbers of followers (including many children) in Mexico and the southwestern United States. Santa Muerte cult members have, on occasion, been associated with violent criminal activities including mass murder. In March 2012, police in northern Mexico arrested eight Santa Muerte cultists in connection with the ritualistic killing and sacrifice of two 10-year-old boys and a woman. In May 2015, a 6-year-old Mexican boy was brutally tortured and killed by five other children, ages ranging from 12 to 15, all of whom revered Santa Muerte. Invited to play a "kidnap game" with the others, the victim's hands and feet were tied, and he was beaten with a club.

Then, he was hit repeatedly with stones and strangled to death. Finally, the older children buried the 6-year-old face down along with a dead animal in a shallow grave. Having confessed, the two 15-year-old boys were jailed while they faced criminal charges, but the other three were younger than 14 (the age of criminal responsibility in Mexico) and thus were kept under the custody of the state child services agency.

As vulnerable to cult influence as adolescents may be, alienation and marginality are hardly peculiar to the teenage years. Individuals from all age groups may be persuaded to commit even the most evil acts if they are also convinced of the righteousness of their cause. Those cults whose members are intensely hostile to conventional institutions have a potential for espousing and practicing violence.

According to Lifton, this potential for violent behavior has taken a much more dangerous turn for the worse. In fact, weapons of mass destruction in the hands of apocalyptic, paranoid cults pose a new—perhaps unprecedented—form of danger for citizens of countries around the world.[13]

The doomsday cult known as Aum Shinrikyo (Supreme Truth) is a case in point. In March 1995, its members killed 12 people and injured 5,500 more in a sarin nerve gas attack in the Tokyo subway system. The cultists left packets of frozen sarin on the trains, timing their assault so that the nerve gas thawed just in time to poison the rush-hour commuters.

Orchestrated by its 41-year-old charismatic leader, Shoko Asahara, the subway mass murder was part of a vastly larger plot designed to overthrow the Japanese government, establish a kingdom ruled by Asahara, and then ultimately to initiate a worldwide nuclear disaster that only he and his disciples would survive. Along the way, the cultists had committed murder and kidnapping, smuggled in firearms, and produced the Nazi-era nerve gas. Their deadly subway attack was designed to divert the attention of the police from an imminent raid on the cult's headquarters in the village of Kamikuishiki near the foot of Mt. Fuji. By the time they perpetrated the subway assault, the cultists were already under suspicion in a wave of violent acts, including the murder of a local lawyer and his family, the kidnapping and killing of a notary public, the explosion of a letter bomb in city hall, and the shooting of the chief of police. Their ultimate objective was world annihilation.

Many talented and wealthy people were attracted to the cause of Supreme Truth, including physicians and scientists who sincerely believed that Asahara possessed supernatural powers. In total, there were more than 9,000 members of Aum Shinrikyo, including 500 who lived in centers around Japan, many of whom donated their entire life savings and personal property to the cult. They were attracted by Asahara's Hindu and yogic teachings and powerful presence and were convinced by his promise to develop their supernatural talents.

Distraught or troubled people have an amazing capacity to rationalize their dangerous behavior. They don't need satanism or vampirism or even Heaven's Gate or Jim Jones, although such influences make a difference. At the same time, troubled people can take the most benign, even honorable idea and twist it into something hideous and evil.

In 1992, for example, five middle-class suburban New Jersey high school students murdered one of their classmates for kicks. The five youngsters ranged from 14 to 18 years of age; one was an altar boy and an Eagle Scout; another was a high school dropout who worshiped the Mafia. The victim, Robert Solimone Jr., was a perpetual outsider, a young man with a reputation around school as nothing more than a nerd. Then, one night, the victim sat with his "buddies" in the front seat of a car parked next to their high school. Everybody in the car convinced him to recite Hail Marys, and then suddenly, without warning, they took him from behind and strangled him to death with an extension cord. These youngsters had used religious ideas to give their evil deeds an aura of morality. They never constituted a cult in any formal sense, but they practiced a perverted version of mainstream religion that permitted them to commit murder with moral impunity.

As in the murder of Robert Solimone, it is sometimes difficult to conclude that violence is a consequence of participating in a cult. Both cult membership and homicidal (or suicidal) behavior may be a result of another set of factors—personality and mood disorders, sociopathy, and so on. So when cult membership and homicidal behavior occur in the same people, one of the factors is not necessarily a cause of the other.

NORMAL PEOPLE IN ABNORMAL SITUATIONS

It is all too easy to regard all cultists as crazy or naive. As we have seen, the truth is that normal but vulnerable individuals can do abnormal, even insidious, things. In August 1969, a number of young people under the guidance and direction of Charles Manson brutally murdered seven people in Beverly Hills. Manson was a charismatic leader who convinced his followers of his great power. If Manson had killed alone, it would have been understandable; he had grown up in the most horrific circumstances imaginable and had spent most of his life behind bars.

But his followers represented something else. Members of the so-called Manson family sincerely believed that Manson was Jesus Christ. Most of the Manson family members were white and middle class. Many were well educated; in high school, one had been voted most likely to succeed. Another had a master's degree in social work. You see, Manson's followers were given a cause—they really believed that through the race war they hoped to precipitate, they would assume the leadership of the country. This objective more than justified their staying together.

In fact, Manson cultists saw being part of the family and serving its cause as the ultimate solution to all of their problems. The Manson followers were as active as Manson himself in committing murder. None of them had been brainwashed into joining the family. Each was attracted to Manson by the promise of becoming a very important, extremely special person who was destined to make a mark on the world. They were profoundly influenced by Manson, but all of them made choices based on what they considered to be important in their personal lives. The Manson followers were hardly prisoners of war or inmates in solitary confinement. Instead, they were active participants.

At various times in their lives, many people can fall into vulnerable states. They may be lonely, hurting, having a hard time socially, having academic problems, or feeling overwhelmed or confused. During such temporary periods of misery and loss, another person can have a great deal of influence, especially another person who promises to point the way out of misery. Vulnerable people tend to be especially suggestible when they are flattered, deceived, lured, enticed, or are feeling very needy. Under such conditions, many people are more suggestible, more malleable, and more likely to be deceived. After all, when people are miserable, they are looking to change. Conformity and obedience become powerful forces under such conditions.

Psychologist Stanley Milgram long ago demonstrated that ordinary people from a broad range of occupations and social classes, both men and women, are willing to administer a severe, even lethal, electrical shock to a stranger, simply because they have been told to do so by an authoritative leader.[14] We shouldn't be surprised that vulnerable people are especially responsive to the demands of an authority figure—someone who is treated by fellow cultists as possessing special, perhaps even supernatural, knowledge, powers, or talents.

Once an individual joins a group, there are strong pressures to conform to its norms. Few people want to be left out, to be rejected by one's peers, and to look different in a negative way. Numerous psychological studies have shown that many otherwise healthy and normal individuals will give an incorrect answer to a simple and obvious question after observing other people give an incorrect response—not because they are confused but because they don't want to look different, even if it means being wrong.[15]

A classic study launched in 1971 by psychologist Philip Zimbardo and his associates at Stanford University may help shed additional light on the phenomenon of normal people doing abnormal, even horrific, things in order to fit in and belong to a group.[16] Zimbardo and his colleagues turned the basement of a building on campus into a mock prison. They created a number of cells by installing bars and locks on each room and then placing a cot in each one. Twenty student volunteers, all chosen for their mature and stable personalities, participated in the study. On a purely random basis (the flip of a coin), half of the students were assigned to play the role of guards and the other half were assigned to play the role of prisoners.

The experiment actually started at the homes of the 10 student prisoners. To increase the realism of the study, all of them were arrested, put in handcuffs, read their rights, and then driven to "jail" in police cars. They were then completely stripped, sprayed with disinfectants, issued prison uniforms, and placed into locked cells.

Everyone knew that the experiment was artificial and that it was supposed to end in 2 weeks. Nobody was really a prisoner; nobody was really a guard. It was make-believe; the roles decided purely by chance. Yet after only a few days, both the prisoners and the guards were playing their roles to the hilt.

Guards were told only to keep order. Instead, they began to humiliate and embarrass the prisoners, coercing them to remain silent on command, to sing or laugh in front of the other inmates, and to clean up messes made by the guards. In some cases, the guards verbally and physically threatened and intimidated the prisoners, apparently to assert their authority.

The prisoners became more and more passive and compliant. In accord with their assigned roles, the prisoners obeyed orders and accepted commands, no matter how unreasonable. They began to feel totally powerless to fight back. After only 6 days, four of the prisoners had to be excused from the study, having suffered serious episodes of anxiety, anger, or depression. In fact, the entire experiment was ended in less than a week when it became clear that the guards had become abusive and the prisoners were emotionally at risk.

Interviews conducted after the experiment ended were revealing. Both the prisoners and the guards told Zimbardo and his associates that they were both shocked and ashamed at how they had behaved. None of them would have predicted that they were capable of such cruelty, in the case of the guards, or obedience to authority, in the case of the prisoners. Remember that all of the student volunteers had been selected for their mature and stable personalities. Yet they all acted according to the roles created by the structure of prison life.

Zimbardo's prison experiment demonstrates the incredible power of situational factors to influence normal individuals, whatever their psychological makeup, to mistreat other human beings or to obey the cruelest sort of authority. The hopeful implication of Zimbardo's findings is that it is easier to change situations than to change individual predispositions. We can often structure the experiences of society's members in such a way that blind conformity to unhealthy norms of behavior is minimal.

Yet in most live-in cults, just about every detail of everyday life comes under the scrutiny of the group. In many, there are dress codes, restrictions on what the members can eat and drink, and enforced marriages and relationships. Most of the members work for cult-owned businesses. Of course, there are also cults whose members seem to belong only on a part-time basis. For example, they might work outside of the cult. But even when the control of a cult seems less than total, members are often restricted in terms of their friendships, what happens to the money they earn, where they are permitted to live, and whether they are allowed to raise their own children.

Because society romanticizes the teenage years, it may not be obvious that there are probably numerous students who are miserable enough to want to make profound changes in their lives. They hope to feel a sense of power and control; they want very much to be accepted and to have a sense of belonging. Some will lower their level of aspiration; others will change their goals to those that do not require an advanced degree; still others will find a source of satisfaction outside of their jobs, school, or family. A few who cannot adjust and remain miserable in their quest for acceptance and success may even choose an illegal alternative. Others will continue ritualistically to go through the motions of getting an education without knowing why.

Once a student is motivated to accept an alternative approach, however, instructors, advisors, friends, clergy, family members, resident assistants, and counselors have a special opportunity to become agents of change. This is when they ought to intervene to provide structure and support and, in some cases, to avert disaster. Students need inspired mentors and role models. Instead, they may seek peer counseling and involvement and perhaps an alternative point of view. Some will look for tutoring and advice. Others will want support and encouragement. If they find what they need, they may become productive, happy citizens. If not, they may remain miserable, whether or not they join some dangerous cult.

SUICIDE OR HOMICIDE?

Because of the tremendous influence of cult leadership, there can be a fine line between mass homicide and mass suicide. At the very least, the ritualized act of self-destruction of the Heaven's Gate cultists, for example, was encouraged by their charismatic leader. It is reasonable to speculate that most, if not all, of the 39 Heaven's Gate victims would still be alive today if they hadn't met up with Marshall Applewhite. The same probably applies to members of the Solar Temple. Out of loyalty to their spiritual mentor and to one another, cultists are especially vulnerable to commandments for self-destruction. The last thing they want is to be rejected by their deified leader and their cherished fellow cultists. The strong group processes in a cult—conformity, suggestion, obedience to authority—make it all but impossible for dedicated cultists to defy the collective will of the group and ignore an order, even if it means dying for the cause. This was apparently true of the Heaven's Gate victims.

Suicide bombers in the Middle East have been similarly encouraged to take their own lives. In some extremist Islamic groups, martyrdom is taught as a technique for furthering their religious and political agenda. Dedicated members are urged to strap on an explosive device and become a human bomb, killing as many civilians as possible. Recruits are typically young men and women who have been taught that self-sacrifice in the struggle against the infidels will ensure them a place of honor on Earth as well as in the hereafter. To encourage suicide, the photographs of bombers are placed on a wall of honor, in the way that the pictures of sports heroes and entertainment celebrities are featured in the Western world. They receive the respect and admiration of the people who mean the most to them—their fellow cultists. Much of the same logic seems to motivate the suicidal attacks perpetrated by a terrorist group such as ISIS or al Qaeda.[17]

If we claim that people under duress should not be held to the same level of responsibility for their criminal behavior, then people who have fallen under the "spell" of a tyrannical cult leader can be regarded as incapable of making a decision about taking their own lives. The abduction of 14-year-old Elizabeth Smart of Salt Lake City by a crazed, self-styled cultist and his wife—masters of religious persuasion—provides an appropriate illustration of this point. Smart was snatched from her bed in the middle of the night and held captive for more than a year, during which time she may have had, but didn't take, opportunities to escape her kidnappers. In a sense, she was a "prisoner of war" whose very survival depended on the mercy of her captors. Her life was constantly threatened, as were the lives of her family members. Fear was a powerful motivator. It eventually forced Smart to believe that her abductors had absolute control over her fate and the fate of her loved ones.

Basing his notion of cultic persuasion on the experiences of prisoners of war, Lifton has identified a number of characteristics of a thought reform (aka brainwashing) environment: (1) milieu control, which involves control over all communication and information, to prevent doubt about the omnipotence of the group from arising; (2) mystical manipulation, which involves a claim of higher authority that morally elevates the group's ends, justifies its practices, and undermines the individual independence of its members; (3) demand for purity, which involves a black-and-white worldview that allows leaders to control members through inculcation of guilt; (4) sacred science, which involves defining group ideology as ultimate truth and inhibits individuality of members; (5) loading the language, which involves use of insider jargon that constricts members' capacity for independent thought and feeling; (6) doctrine over persons, which involves denial of any self and reality that is independent of the group; and (7) dispensing of existence, which involves degrading outsiders and creating an us-versus-them mentality.[18]

Lifton's list of persuasive techniques and beliefs operates only to the extent that a recruit is virtually a prisoner whose total environment has been modified and controlled by his cult membership. In most cases of cultic influence, by contrast, it is pure myth to suggest the image of a totally passive recruit who lacks any power to resist while under the spell of a madman. Some social scientists have argued instead that cult recruits possess an element of free will that can only be manipulated so much. They regard affiliation with cultists as fundamentally voluntaristic. Some even refer to the groups not as cults but as "new religious movements," because they do not conclude that the group structure of recruitment processes undermine individual autonomy and voluntarism.[19]

As suggested by Bromley and Shupe, moreover, what appears to be extreme behavior may not actually represent a personal transformation but rather conformity to expected role behavior.[20] Even extremely vulnerable individuals possess an active self—they are typically not brainwashed into misbehaving, but comply willingly to the requirements imposed on their membership. From this viewpoint, there is a definite limit to the power of a charismatic leader to mold or shape the behavior and beliefs of his disciples. Most cult leaders are not in the category of a Jim Jones or Marshall Applewhite, even if they are extremely persuasive. When they do harm to others, cult followers might rationalize their criminal behavior by holding their leader responsible, but they actually have no one to blame but themselves.

ENDNOTES

1. Nicole Biggart, *Charismatic Capitalism* (Chicago: University of Chicago Press, 1989).

2. Margaret Singer, *Cults in Our Midst* (San Francisco: Jossey-Bass, 2003).

3. Bob Weinstein, "Be Wary of the 'Corporate Cult,'" *Newsday*, March 5, 2000, p. 12B.

4. Jack Levin, *Blurring the Boundaries: The Declining Significance of Age* (New York: Routledge, 2013).

5. Philip Lamy, *Millennium Rage: Survivalists, White Supremacists, and the Doomsday Prophecy* (New York: Plenum, 1996).

6. Philip C. Zimbardo, Craig Haney, and William C. Banks, "A Pirandellian Prison," *New York Times Magazine*, April 8, 1973.

7. John Ellement, "Jury Acquits Robidoux of Murdering Baby," *Boston Globe*, February 4, 2004, http://archive.boston.com/news/local/massachusetts/articles/2004/02/04/jury_acquits_robidoux_of_murdering_baby.

8. Edecio Martinez, "Cult Members Face Sentencing for Starving Toddler Javon Thompson to Death for Not Saying 'Amen,'" *CBS News*, May 18, 2010.

9. Fox News, "Pennsylvania Murder Tied to Online Cult, Police Say," July 16, 2017.

10. Fox News, "Murder of Pregnant Woman Linked to Satanism?" August 17, 2017.

11. Margaret Singer and Richard Ofshe, "Thought Reform Programs and the Production of Psychiatric Casualties," *Psychiatric Annals* 20 (1990): 188–193.

12. Adam Lankford, *The Myth of Martyrdom* (New York: St. Martin's Press, 2013).

13. Robert Jay Lifton, *Thought Reform and the Psychology of Totalism* (Chapel Hill: University of North Carolina Press, 1989).

14. Stanley Milgram, "Behavioral Study of Obedience," *Journal of Abnormal and Social Psychology* 66 (1963): 371–378.

15. Arthur Dobrin, "The Astonishing Power of Social Pressure," *Psychology Today*, April 14, 2014.

16. Zimbardo et al., "A Pirandellian Prison."

17. Adam Lankford, *The Myth of Martyrdom*.

18. Robert Jay Lifton, *Thought Reform and the Psychology of Totalism*.

19. Ibid.

20. David Bromley and Anson Shupe, "Affiliation and Disaffiliation: A Role Theory Approach to Joining and Leaving New Religious Movements," *Thought: A Review of Culture and Ideas* 61 (1986): 197–211.

CHAPTER THIRTEEN

CATCHING KILLERS

If one were to judge solely from television crime dramas like *Law & Order*, *CSI: Crime Scene Investigation*, *Major Crimes*, and *Criminal Minds*, crime doesn't pay. Almost without exception, TV criminals, and murderers in particular, are identified, arrested, and convicted, all in under an hour (unless it's a "two-parter," of course). Although these shows may frequently feature real stories that are "ripped from the headlines," the lesson that virtually no one gets away with murder is obviously more than a slight exaggeration. After all, this is television land, and the good guys usually prevail.

Hollywood distortion aside, the idea that murderers are usually apprehended is actually not so out of line with the facts. Of the seven so-called Part I offenses that comprise the FBI's collection of serious crimes, homicide has the highest clearance rate—that is, the percentage of offenses known to the police that are cleared or solved by law enforcement authorities. As shown in Figure 13.1, violent crimes (murder, forcible rape, robbery, and aggravated assault) have clearance rates that exceed those of the three property offenses (burglary, larceny-theft, and motor vehicle theft), and murder ranks at the top of the clearance rate list. In 2016, nearly three out of five homicides reported to the police were cleared by an arrest or some other exceptional means (e.g., suspect flees the country or commits suicide).

Recent investigative reporting has shown that murder prosecutions in situations where the victim's body has not been located are fairly rare. However, almost 90% of these cases still result in a conviction.[1] Other evidence, oftentimes circumstantial, can be used to convince jurors of the defendant's guilt. Motives, phone histories, witness statements, computer records, false alibis, histories of violence, and testimonies of codefendants all help to strengthen "no body" cases. For instance, the accused murderers of New York City socialite Irene Silverman were successfully prosecuted even though her remains were not recovered. The prosecution was able to show that the mother and son murder team, Sante and Kenneth Kimes, forged documents, had the victim's personal items in their possession, had guns, drugs, gloves, and other "murder kit" paraphernalia, and sold some of Silverman's property. Both defendants were convicted and sentenced to lengthy prison terms. Once convicted, Kenneth Kimes revealed to investigators that he and his mother had dumped Silverman's body in a New Jersey construction site about 60 miles from the Holland Tunnel.

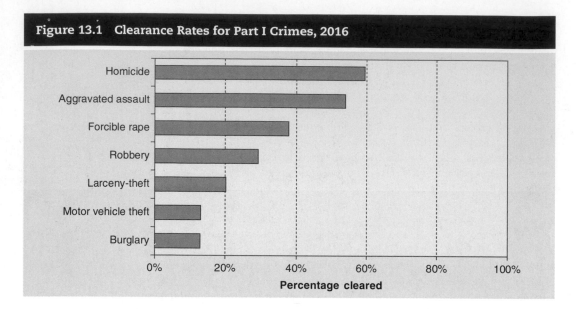

Figure 13.1 Clearance Rates for Part I Crimes, 2016

SCIENCE OF THE LAMBS

The greater success that police have in solving murders than other types of crimes may at first appear a bit surprising. After all, the victim isn't able to identify the perpetrator in a police line-up or describe to the detectives exactly what transpired leading up to the attack. Yet the victim—or at least the corpse—does "speak" in a sense through the wealth of forensic clues left under fingernails, on the skin, or within vital organs, all available to lab experts and medical examiners to exploit in their investigation. Indeed, it is the uniquely violent nature of the homicidal act that tends to produce a large volume of physical evidence for forensic specialists. In addition, many homicides are preceded by a sequence of events—an argument, a challenge, a business dispute, marital infidelity—that often allow the police to identify the perpetrator. Technology—cell phones, text messages, e-mail, and social networking sites—also adds to the trail that police can follow.

The work of forensics units begins as soon as the homicide (or suspicious death or disappearance) is discovered. The first officer to arrive at the location protects the crime scene, cordoning the area off in yellow police tape and keeping it free of intruders (including other police personnel) until a systematic search and record can be constructed. Photographs and video of the area are taken as soon as possible so that the body can then be sent for an autopsy before certain transient evidence (e.g., stomach contents) becomes compromised.

One of the first objectives for the medical examiner or coroner is to determine the approximate time of death, a window of time when the murder would have occurred, which helps ultimately to assess which possible subjects could or could not have had contact with the victim during this time frame. A rough estimate of time of death, the postmortem interval (PMI), can be derived from the body temperature. Algor mortis, the rate at which a dead body cools, can be modeled mathematically, factoring in climate and atmospheric conditions. This process yields an interval of hours when death would likely have occurred. In addition to body temperature, the presence of rigor mortis, stiffness in the muscle tissues, can help narrow down time estimates. Rigor first appears in the small muscles of the hands and jaw within 2 to 4 hours, progresses to larger muscle groups within 4 to 6 hours, and becomes fully developed in about 12 hours. This stiffness then begins to taper off as the body starts decomposing.

Victims discovered after several days, if not longer, pose greater challenges. For forensic entomologists, the human corpse is viewed as a welcoming host for insect ecosystems or life cycles that are governed by predictable time patterns. Forensic entomology has delivered a wealth of information about the activities of various insects on a corpse. A variety of flies are attracted quickly to moist areas of a cadaver (e.g., open wounds, mouth, nostrils, and eyes) as a place to deposit their eggs. In about a day, the eggs hatch into maggots and begin feeding off the human remains. During this process, the maggots shed their casings (pupae) and eventually transform into flies. By examining the type and progress of insect infestation and the presence of pupae, the entomologist can assess time of death and possibly location (if the body was moved). Researchers at the University of Tennessee Anthropological Research Facility, also known as "the body farm," have analyzed the rate of decomposition in all kinds of habitats (e.g., in cool forests and on hot sand), particularly as indicated by insect activity. Bodies used for the research include unclaimed bodies donated by medical examiners as well as people who have donated their bodies in advance of their deaths.

Just as critical, if not more so, the medical examiner attempts to isolate the cause and manner of death—to discern if, in fact, the case is a homicide, rather than an accident or a suicide. Causes of death can include asphyxia, gunshot wound, stabbing, drug overdose, as well as malignant neoplasms (cancers) and several specific causes related to heart disease, diabetes, and stroke. The medical examiner or coroner will also establish a manner of death within the categories of natural, accident, homicide, suicide, or undetermined. Obviously, these determinations have great impact on future criminal and civil proceedings.

The presence of lividity, or livor mortis, reflected in dark purple discoloration of the skin often yields clues about the final moments prior to death. Once the heart stops functioning to circulate blood throughout the body, blood cells pool and settle by force of gravity to the lowest points of the body as it rests against the floor or other objects. A purplish discoloration of the skin at the low points sets in within 30 minutes and becomes fixed in about eight hours. Furthermore, the shade of discoloration can help to indicate cause of death. For example, carbon monoxide poisoning results in a cherry-red hue to the skin affected by livor mortis. On the other hand, death resulting from heart failure or asphyxia causes a particularly deep-purple tinge. In addition, if lividity is at all visible on discovery of the corpse (i.e., if the discoloration of the skin is not face down), then the body would have to have been moved or turned over following death. Examination of the skin also reveals much about the assault. The extent of bruising around injuries can suggest whether they were inflicted pre- or postmortem, because bruising can only occur while the heart is pumping blood to the affected area. Also, some bruising takes time to appear and therefore may only become evident after the victim is dead.

Bodies that are not discovered for weeks, or even longer, pose additional problems for forensics specialists to determine time and cause of death, as well as the identity of the victim. A body left exposed to the elements starts the long process of decomposition or putrefaction. After death, bacteria begin to escape from the gastrointestinal tract, specifically the bowel, compromising the entire vascular system. The body swells from internal gases and the skin discolors. Putrefaction distorts facial features and fingerprints, often complicating identification of the deceased.

Depending on atmospheric conditions, the corpse will experience additional kinds of transformation. If lying in a damp area, a greasy soap-like substance—known as adipocere—will form on the skin as body fats go through chemical changes. In especially dry and airy conditions, however, the corpse will mummify rather than decompose as the skin darkens and hardens to a leathery texture.

Corpses undiscovered for longer time spans, particularly when exposed to carnivorous animals, eventually dissolve to skeletal remains. Even then, certain markers can be used to identify the victim. A forensic anthropologist can discern not only whether bones are human in origin but also the age, race, and sex of the victim. The size, development, and wear of bones indicate certain age ranges. Additionally, race can often be classified based on the shape of the skull. Furthermore, through the process of "elaboration," the shape of the skull can also be used to project an image of what the victim may have looked like and can often hint at the geographical area of the victim or his or her ancestry. Gender may be evident from the structure of hip, pubic, and other bone structures. If all else fails, of course, forensic odontologists can examine teeth as a means of identifying victims through comparison with dental records (usually by examining cavity fillings, dental work, wear on the teeth suggestive of age, etc.). These and other means of victim identification (including DNA, as described later) may only provide an answer to the victim's identity, yet say little about who the perpetrator was.

The medical examiner routinely performs toxicological tests to identify poisonings and drug overdoses. Rather than just blood and urinalysis, medical examiners often use vitreous humor, the fluid of the eyeball, for their toxicological analyses, because this fluid maintains substances longer than do other bodily fluids. Inspection of knife wounds, blunt trauma, lacerations on bones and organs, as well as gunshot wounds all offer clues, not just to cause of death but often to the exact nature and size of the weapon and possibly the stature and approach of the assailant. Also, the examiner relies on a range of circumstantial evidence, such as the kind of ligature used and the absence or presence of a note, to distinguish a suicidal hanging from an autoerotic asphyxiation fatality (accidental death while inducing suffocation to enhance sexual arousal). Similarly, a psychological autopsy of an apparent victim of sexual homicide may be needed to rule out an accidental death that occurred as the victim was staging his or her sexual bondage fantasy. In attempting to establish cause and manner of death, recent medical advances help medical examiners and coroners discern purposeful acts of infanticide (e.g., shaken baby and suffocation) from crib death or accidental falls. Until recently, medical professionals were easily fooled by deceitful parents and caretakers who attempted to cover up a baby murder by claiming sudden infant death syndrome (SIDS). Still today, it is not always possible to distinguish at autopsy between SIDS and accidental or deliberate asphyxiation with a soft object without circumstantial evidence that the infant had been intentionally victimized.

Also in the realm of investigating possible cases of infanticide, medical examiners are sometimes confronted with distinguishing accidents from actions when a young child dies as a result of physical injury. Was head trauma produced by an accidental fall or by purposeful abuse? In February 1997, for example, 9-month-old Matthew Eappen fell into a coma and died from a fractured skull and subdural hematoma. He showed signs of previous injuries, including a broken wrist. An ophthalmologist at the Boston Children's Hospital noticed retinal hemorrhages, an indicator of possible shaken-baby syndrome. Nineteen-year-old Louise Woodward, a British au pair employed by the Eappens, was arrested, charged, and convicted of second-degree murder carrying a life sentence with parole eligibility after 15 years. Woodward's defense team immediately filed postconviction motions in challenging what, to many, including supporters back home in England, seemed like an excessively harsh penalty for the inexperienced, overwhelmed nanny.

Agreeing with the sentiment, the judge reduced the conviction to involuntary manslaughter and the sentence to time already served—279 days in total.

Forensic Applications of DNA

DNA (deoxyribonucleic acid), the genetic basis for all inherited traits, has undoubtedly been the single greatest advance for law enforcement in solving cases and bringing criminals to justice, as well as freeing the wrongly convicted. The first murder case solved with DNA evidence was that of British serial rapist and murderer Colin Pitchfork in 1987. After the rape and murder of two young girls in 1983 and 1986, the police had the offender's DNA and conducted a mass DNA sweep of more than 5,000 men who lived or worked near the murder scenes. Initially, Pitchfork was clever and convinced a friend to give a sample on his behalf. But this fraud was eventually reported to police and Pitchfork was arrested, convicted, and sent to prison for nearly 3 decades.

With the exception of identical twins, everyone has a unique DNA blueprint, which can be extracted from samples of human cells in saliva, skin, sweat, bone, and follicles of hair but more commonly in blood and semen. DNA genotyping can be used, therefore, not only to implicate a suspect but also to exclude someone whose DNA does not match the DNA found in crime scene evidence.

DNA molecules contain a genetic code, consisting of a lengthy sequence of four letters—A, T, C, and G, representing the four nucleotides (adenine, thymine, cytosine, and guanine). The molecules occur in base pairs: A is always associated with T, and C with G, and the pairs are arranged along a spiral-shaped structure known as the double helix.

Genetic samples come in two types: nuclear and mitochondrial DNA. Typically, *DNA* refers to the set of genes unique to each person (except in the case of identical twins) that is inherited from both the mother and the father. This DNA is contained within a cell compartment called the nucleus, hence its name as nuclear DNA. In contrast, the cell's energy powerhouses, the mitochondria, also have copies of DNA, but this is inherited only from the mother (and thus is only unique to a maternal lineage rather than a single individual). These two types of DNA have different uses in forensic analysis. Nuclear DNA, for example, is a unique identifier for each person and thus can be matched to national databases. In some cases, however, nuclear DNA is difficult if not impossible to extract—as the cell contains multiple mitochondria, and therefore multiple copies of its DNA, mitochondrial DNA is a valid alternative. Hair strands without the root, for example, can only provide mitochondrial DNA, which can link the sample only to the maternal relatives of a suspect.

In short, DNA from the nucleus of a human cell provides a unique genetic code, but it cannot be extracted from certain human matter, such as hair. Mitochondrial DNA may not be unique but still can provide an ancestral match. The probative value of a DNA match is unparalleled, especially in the opinions of jurors, who give great weight to its scientific authority. Of course, this has also meant that more than 350 falsely convicted defendants (many of them for murder) have been freed after retesting old crime scene evidence with new technology.[2] The ability to identify genetically an unknown killer through DNA left at the murder scene does not, of course, guarantee that the donor will be identifiable from available records and DNA data banks. Launched in 1990, a computerized DNA database, known as the Combined DNA Index System (CODIS), is maintained by the FBI. With all states submitting information to the national DNA index system, as of February 2017, genetic profiles of over 12 million offenders, 2 million arrestees, and 700,000 samples from cases were included in the database. Nearly all states have passed legislation permitting DNA data storage associated with convicted murderers and sex offenders; some states have broadened the guidelines to include other violent felons, nonviolent criminals, and all of those in the prison population.

Many states go one controversial step further by routinely taking DNA samples of all persons arrested. In 2010, President Obama expressed support for making DNA testing of arrestees a standard practice nationwide, despite concerns expressed by civil libertarians about privacy rights of individuals who are not as yet convicted of a crime. In 2013, the U.S. Supreme Court, in *Maryland v. King*, ruled 5–4 that taking a cheek swab of the arrestee's DNA is not intrusive and, like fingerprinting and photographing, a legitimate procedure not in violation of Fourth Amendment protections against an unreasonable search and seizure.

Despite the singular value of DNA genotyping and matching, there remains a danger to civil liberties that will play out in years to come. The appellate courts will need to deliberate on constitutionally acceptable methods for using this compelling evidence. Investigating the murders of five women between 2001 and 2003, for example, the Baton Rouge police performed a rather controversial DNA dragnet in an attempt to locate the unknown serial killer. Hundreds of potential suspects were asked "voluntarily" to allow a swab to be taken from the inner cheek for the purpose of comparison with DNA recovered at the crime scenes. They were advised of their right to decline, of course, but also were informed that such refusal would result in not only a court order for the sample but also public notification of their failure to cooperate. After Derrick Todd Lee was arrested and charged with the crimes, at least one innocent subject sued the police in attempt to have his DNA returned rather than have it saved in the state police DNA data bank.[3]

State legislatures are hurrying to catch up with technology. There are thousands of inmates in prisons in at least seven states whose DNA has never been collected or submitted to CODIS. Inmates who were incarcerated before states passed laws regarding DNA collection were not retroactively processed. Thousands of inmates in Nevada, Montana, Nebraska, Rhode Island, Georgia, Tennessee, and Delaware have fallen through the cracks. States are scrambling to pass new laws that allow for retroactive collection of DNA for people incarcerated before the DNA collection laws became popular in the late 1990s and early 2000s. We may see a boom in cold case solves as offenders doing life or sitting on death row are finally submitted to CODIS.[4]

The capture of serial killer Lonnie David Franklin Jr. demonstrates the increasing power and potential of DNA, specifically, the application of familial DNA matching. Dubbed the "Grim Sleeper," because of a 1988–2002 hiatus in the killing period, this case baffled California detectives since it began in 1985. They had had genetic evidence belonging to the unidentified assailant, but they came up empty when searching through the California DNA data bank for a hit. However, newer developments in the forensic analysis could potentially find a link to a close relative based on partial genetic matching. As it happened, an apparent familial link was identified to the DNA of a Christopher Franklin who had recently been convicted. The police then began surveillance of the subject's father, Lonnie Franklin. Retrieving DNA from a piece of pizza he had eaten in a restaurant, they finally had a full match to DNA from one of the 11 suspected homicides. Lonnie Franklin was convicted of 10 counts of murder and 1 count of attempted murder. On August 10, 2016, precisely 31 years from the date of his killing, the notorious Grim Sleeper was sentenced to death.

DNA can also enable law enforcement to clear up cold homicide cases from a long time in the past. In 1984, 9-year-old Mei Leung was murdered in

San Francisco by an unidentified assailant. At that time, homicide detective Holly Pera would not have had the benefit of DNA analysis, as this was still years before DNA was being used for crime solving and well before the California DNA data bank even existed. But in 2009, after reopening the case, Pera was ecstatically surprised when a genetic match was found to Night Stalker Richard Ramirez, who was arrested in 1985 for a string of murders around Los Angeles. Apparently, his path of destruction extended well beyond southern California.

Although the match was to a defendant who had already died, police in Decatur, Illinois, solved the 1984 Halloween murders of 12-year-old Sherry Gordon and her 9-year-old cousin, Theresa Hall, also by the retrospective application of DNA. Melvin Johnson, who had a history of crimes against children, died in a Texas prison in 2003. However, crime scene evidence from the 1984 double murder had been maintained and was finally submitted to a DNA database, linking Johnson to the Halloween murders. In the same way, Johnson was also posthumously connected to the 1985 sexual assault and murder of 25-year-old Sandra Hopson and the death of John Woods, 46, in May 1988.

Familial DNA helped the authorities in Boston finally resolve a half-century-old debate over the identity of the infamous Boston Strangler. Albert DeSalvo, while incarcerated on an unrelated charge, voluntarily confessed to being the man responsible for sexually assaulting and murdering 13 women in and around Boston between 1962 and 1964. DeSalvo was never formally charged with the murders and was himself the victim of homicide at the hands of a fellow inmate in 1973. Many observers insisted that DeSalvo was a fraud. Although correctly describing some of the unreported details about the crime scenes, he had certain key facts wrong. In 2013, cold case investigators trailed a nephew of DeSalvo, recovering a water bottle that he discarded. DNA analysis of the saliva revealed a fairly close match to a semen-stained cloth that had been saved from the Strangler's last victim, Mary Sullivan. That was enough evidence to obtain a court order to exhume DeSalvo's remains, from which a direct DNA match was obtained. The mystery of the Boston Strangler's identity was finally solved.

Currently, only 11 states are doing familial DNA searches as part of their criminal investigations, and other states are scrambling to pass legislation and procedures allowing for familial searches. Familial DNA searches are fairly common, however, in most of Europe, Australia, and New Zealand. Newer testing methods (e.g., eAllele) significantly reduce the number of DNA inconclusive results, and cutting-edge technological advances (e.g., "touch DNA" and the M-Vac System) allow investigators to gather DNA from places and materials never thought possible, even with DNA evidence that is decades old.

Technological Advances

Whereas DNA data banks catalog information about offenders, other repositories store and index data associated with offenses. For more than two decades, for example, the Bureau of Alcohol, Tobacco and Firearms (ATF) has maintained a gun tracing initiative in which firearms recovered in the process of criminal investigations can be traced through manufacturer, distributor, and dealer records back to the first point of retail sale. Of course, what may have happened to the firearm after reaching the street (such as private resale or transfer through theft) is beyond the scope of the gun tracing program.

Representing another avenue of firearms examination, so-called ballistics fingerprinting is predicated on the fact that every gun is unique in the inner surface of its barrel, arising from the particular tool marks left during the manufacturing process as well as imperfections in the metals used. As a result, microscopic examination of fired bullet casings can potentially link not just two spent casings to each other, as in traditional ballistic work, but also shell casings to an exemplar from the gun coded into a database shortly after production.

Launched in 1999, the National Integrated Ballistic Information Network (NIBIN) contains images of nearly 3 million shell casings from crime scenes and test-fired guns. Despite its great potential for solving gun crimes, only a few hundred of our nation's 18,000 law enforcement agencies use the NIBIN system. Over $300 million has been invested in the program, yet 11 states still have no means of entering information and nearly 20 others only have one or two terminals for inputting images of the shell casing and identifying possible matches. Although the usual budget shortfalls and understaffing leave the NIBIN potential unrealized, there have been nearly 75,000 matches and an unknown number of offenders and guns taken off the streets.[5] Some critics still argue that criminals can alter the gun barrel and that a certain degree of change in barrel surface occurs with each firing of a gun. However, the three-dimensional imaging now available in NIBIN has enhanced the ability to make definitive matches.[6]

A more novel approach to investigating gun crimes involves acoustic sensors that can alert police departments within seconds of a gunshot and pinpoint the location of the incident. Presumably a speedy police response would then increase the possibility of apprehending the shooter or even saving a gunshot victim with swift medical treatment. More than 90 cities across the United States, including Washington, D.C., Baltimore, Newark, St. Louis, Chicago, Indianapolis, Boston, and Oakland, have invested in this technology, sometimes referred to as "ShotSpotter." Jurisdictions are spending millions of dollars on the ShotSpotter technology, but even after years in use, it has yet to be evaluated for its effectiveness.[7] At a minimum, this technology may be best paired with surveillance cameras, enabling crime analysts to distinguish quickly between gunshots and, for instance, an engine backfiring and to be able to immediately review closed-circuit television (CCTV) footage for possible offender identification.

Forensic Error

Whereas the scientific theory underlying DNA is unimpeachable and the methods of extracting genetic material from limited trace evidence is improving every year, the testing process is still performed by human beings, who are not exactly infallible. Overburdened labs, poorly trained technicians, as well as mistakes in maintaining the integrity of DNA samples and record keeping have unfortunately resulted in more than a few erroneous results, from mislabeling of samples in Kansas to falsified records at a Florida lab. Errors and false reporting uncovered in 2003 at the overloaded and understaffed Houston crime lab were so bad that several employees were suspended or terminated and hundreds of tests were ordered to be redone. In another recent case, Shawnnon Hale, 26, sued a Denver crime lab after analysts mistakenly labeled DNA samples causing him wrongly to be held in jail for two months on a rape charge.

The Massachusetts State Crime Lab was rocked by scandal when it was revealed that an experienced DNA examiner, besides maintaining shoddy records, had falsified DNA results, leading to the conviction of numerous defendants. Not only did this necessitate retesting of evidence and retrials of defendants, but it also placed into question the extent to which juries can trustfully rely on such scientific evidence.

In 2009, the National Academy of Sciences published a damning report concluding that, with the exception of DNA analysis, traditionally accepted forensic techniques are substandard in terms of scientific rigor.[8] Convictions based on hair, bite marks, and handwriting comparisons are suspect, and may not be truly linkable to a single person or object. In the same way that eyewitness testimony must be taken with a grain of salt, analyses of fibers, blood spatters, and even fingerprints are of questionable probative value. These methods may be excellent for generating or eliminating suspects. However, they require subjective interpretations by experts, which can differ widely and thus are not sufficiently reliable to meet the legal standard of proof "beyond a reasonable doubt." In addition, some forensic laboratory equipment is out of date, and personnel may not be adequately trained or certified. Simply put, errors are made.

A study of the firearms unit of the Detroit Police Lab found missing records, unsecured and missing property, contamination, faulty equipment, and untrained and unqualified examiners. Other cases have included not just incompetence but also fraud, including false fingerprint identifications by a fingerprint analyst in the Los Angeles Police Department, slanted testimony by FBI lab technicians to help prosecutors, and fraudulent testimony by an Oklahoma chemist, Joyce Gilchrist, that sent innocent men to prison and two men to death row. Fred Zain, chief serologist at the West Virginia State Police crime lab, committed fraud on hundreds of cases, sending innocent people to prison; he left West Virginia and went on to work in Texas, where he died before he could be tried for perjury. Clearly these cases point to the need for crime labs to be completely separate entities from police departments and the need for oversight and control of the field of forensic science.[9]

None of these mistakes and miscarriages of justice should imply that scientific evidence is necessarily unreliable. Rather, all forms of evidence—forensic tests, psychiatric diagnoses, and eyewitness testimony—are subject to human error.

CLEARANCE RATES

Despite the rapid improvement in forensic techniques, the success rate in clearing homicide cases has dropped in recent years, especially in large cities, a trend that has put law enforcement under a certain degree of scrutiny from politicians and the media alike. As shown in Figure 13.2, the homicide clearance rate has declined since the mid-1970s, especially so in cities with populations of at least 250,000. Clearance rates vary widely by city, of course, with some police departments achieving clearance rates that exceed 80%, while others clear less than 30% of their homicides.

The Murder Accountability Project (MAP), formed in 2015 and operated by Thomas Hargrove, uses algorithms to detect clusters of similar unsolved homicides within a geographic area. The algorithm identified a cluster of unsolved killings in Gary, Indiana, in 2010, four years before the arrest of serial killer Darren Deon Vann. During filming for the recent A&E docuseries *The Killing Season*, Hargrove's team used their serial victim search algorithm to find other clusters of unsolved killings in Cleveland. MAP's initial focus was to draw attention to the more than 220,000 unsolved homicides across the United States, and now it also presents information about homicide clearance rates across the United States. Their recent analysis compared clearance rates from 1996–2005 to those of 2006–2015 and found 54% of the departments experienced declining homicide clearance rates while 46% reported improved clearance rates. The MAP efforts suggest that a number of factors may be related to increasing clearance rates in certain areas, including decreases in the number of homicides, the aggregation of

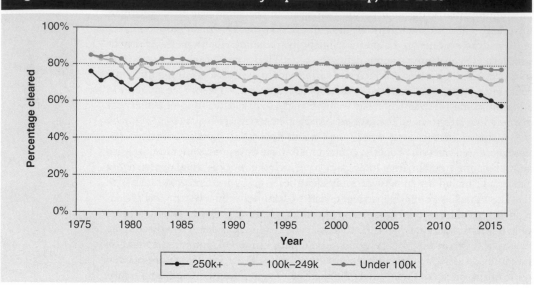

Figure 13.2 Homicide Clearance Rates by Population Group, 1976–2016

investigators in one location, the availability of DNA recovery and analysis, and the availability of both public and private CCTV.[10]

Having multiple experienced investigators assigned to a case and for longer periods of time can certainly improve the clearance rate, as can the use of case management systems that allow quick retrieval of suspect information. Of course, some of the factors affecting clearance rates do not involve police policies and procedures but are a result of the nature of the homicides. The perpetrator's efforts and skill in avoiding detection, the location of the homicide, the presence of eyewitnesses, and whether the homicide was drug-related or gang-related can all affect the likelihood of clearance in positive or negative ways.[11]

Some observers have questioned whether police personnel are doing a poorer job today or if they are just overwhelmed by heavy caseloads. The slippage in clearance, however, has much more to do with the changing nature of the caseload, not the sheer number of cases. As discussed in Chapters 4 and 5, there have been dramatic shifts in the pattern of homicide during several decades—specifically, fewer spousal homicides and more gang-related killings. Within the mix of cases that detectives must confront each year, there are simply fewer easy cases and more challenging ones.

Although surely there are exceptions, spousal murders are frequently solved as soon as the perpetrator calls the police to report the incident and, oftentimes, to surrender. Or, if there is any attempt to escape justice, typically a telltale pattern of precipitants points directly to the current or former spouse or lover—a history of abuse or recent conflicts that friends and neighbors report. There may be a recent affair or a newly secured life insurance policy that gives the police all they need to determine the motive and thus the suspect.

When 27-year-old Laci Peterson of Modesto, California, 8 months pregnant with her first child, disappeared on Christmas Eve, 2002, many of these same suspicious factors prompted the police, as well as a fascinated nation, to look squarely at her husband, Scott, as the prime suspect. The 30-year-old fertilizer salesman had been romantically involved with an attractive massage therapist from whom he had concealed his marriage. In addition, Peterson had recently purchased a $250,000 life insurance policy on his wife and was away on an all-day solo fishing trip on Christmas Eve, without an alibi witness, when his pregnant wife reportedly vanished. Each of these implicating factors in isolation could be explained away as innocent; after all, many men have extramarital affairs without resorting to murder, and many decide to upgrade their insurance policies right before the birth of a child. But the confluence of these and other circumstantial factors was just too much for law enforcement authorities to ignore. Even without a "smoking gun," Scott Peterson was arrested in April 2003 and charged with double homicide as soon as DNA testing on the remains of a woman and a baby that had washed ashore in San Francisco Bay, not far from the location of his Christmas Eve fishing jaunt, were positively identified as Laci and her son Conner. A year later, in a closely watched and widely publicized murder trial, Peterson was convicted of first-degree murder in the deaths of his wife and unborn son.

At the other extreme, murders committed by strangers frequently have no clear-cut motive. If there are no witnesses to the attack, the pool of potential subjects of an investigation can be hopelessly endless. In addition, the gang-related and drug-related crimes among youthful offenders and victims, the kind that surged in the early 1990s, were shrouded within a "Don't snitch" code of silence. Although there may have been many accomplices and witnesses who knew exactly the one responsible for a drive-by shooting or a "sending a message" execution-style slaying, no one was talking to the police. Moreover, the notion that snitches would be dealt with tended to limit the cooperation that the police could expect.

Not only are the old and infirm particularly vulnerable to the malicious and self-serving misdeeds of murderous caretakers, as described in Chapter 8, but also medical murders and hospital homicides pose special problems in terms of detection of foul play, suspect identification, and collection of probative evidence. Death among the elderly and terminal patients is more the norm than the exception, and so suspicions are slow to surface. Moreover, should an unusually high volume of deaths occur in a particular ward or on a particular shift, hospital administrators— charged with managing not just the well-being of patients but also the financial health of the institution—are in a quandary. They may be reluctant to blow the whistle prematurely and without sufficient cause, not so much out of concern for a staff member whom they might suspect is up to no good, but out of fear of a lawsuit against the facility for negligence or just reluctance to stir up doubts surrounding the management of the hospital or clinic. Furthermore, when there is sufficient cause for an investigation, the physical evidence may be long buried, requiring the delicate task of seeking family permission for exhumation without any certainty that a criminal act had occurred. In addition, some of the remains may have been cremated and along with them any evidence of poisoning.

INVESTIGATING CHALLENGING HOMICIDE CASES

One particular class of offenders, featured in Chapter 7, that has challenged the skills of homicide detectives, is the serial killer. It is not that these murderers are particularly intelligent, as suggested by fictional characters such as Hannibal Lecter in the film *The Silence of the Lambs* (and its sequels) or Dexter Morgan in the television series *Dexter*. It is more a certain degree of cunning—cleverness and carefulness—rather than brilliance that distinguishes these repeat and often prolific murderers from the rest.

A long-standing myth, commonplace in popular films and mystery novels, holds that serial murderers, at least at some level, wish to get caught. According to this view, serial killers, even the most sociopathic, actually do have a conscience strong enough to affect their behavior; they subconsciously leave clues to their crimes in order to get punished for their transgressions against humanity. This popular theme dates back years, at least to the 1946 case of William Heirens, the so-called Lipstick Killer, who scrawled a message for the Chicago police on the apartment wall of one of his victims, "For Heaven's sake, catch me before I kill more. I cannot control myself." Heirens spent over 60 years in prison as a model prisoner and may have been an innocent man. An admitted burglar, Heirens was convicted on coerced confessions, faulty evidence, confused eyewitnesses, and misinterpreted fingerprints, handwriting, and polygraphs. He was denied parole in 2007 and passed away in 2012 at the age of 83.

Unlike Heirens, most serial killers do everything they can to avoid getting caught. They are clever and careful; when it comes to murder, they are fiercely resourceful. They methodically stalk their victims for the best opportunity to strike so as not to be seen, and they smartly dump the bodies far away so as not to leave any clues. The cool and calculating manner in which many sociopaths cover their tracks arises out of the fearlessness that characterizes this personality type. They respond unemotionally and without panic to the prospect of capture, undeterred by the risk of apprehension. A self-selection process—a survival of the fiercest—operates to separate the coolheaded men from the hot-tempered boys. If sexual predators such as Jeffrey Dahmer or Theodore Bundy were not so good at killing and covering their trails, they would never have remained on the streets long enough to qualify as serial killers. They pick vulnerable victims such as prostitutes, runaways, and drug addicts, rather than NFL linebackers.[12]

Murders committed by a serial killer, at least the methodical ones, are typically difficult to solve because of a lack of an instrumental motive and useful evidence. Unlike the usual homicide that involves an offender and victim who know one another, sexually motivated serial murders are almost exclusively committed by strangers. Thus, the usual police strategy of identifying suspects—boyfriends, neighbors, or coworkers—by examining their possible motive, be it jealousy, revenge, or greed, generally helps very little. With no such clear-cut motive, there are no immediate suspects.

In Gainesville, Florida, for example, a large task force investigating the murders of five college students in August 1990 had a wealth of crime scene evidence for the lab to analyze, including pubic hairs and semen. For months, the task force operated a "pubes and tubes" strategy, collecting hair and blood samples from hundreds of "donors," just about anyone who possibly could have had a connection to the crime. But when seeking a stranger who had no prior relationship to the victims, this hunt for a killer was like searching for a needle in a haystack. The high-profile character of the Gainesville murders, furthermore, made for a particularly huge haystack of "suspects," as well-intentioned citizens from around the country phoned in the names of unscrupulous or sleazy people they thought might be involved.

Whereas the Gainesville investigation team was fortunate to have plenty of clues, perhaps more than they needed, other serial murder investigations have very little evidence of a tangible nature to go on. The more successful serial killers transport their victims from the scene of the murder to a remote dump site or makeshift grave. The police may never locate the body and thus never determine that a homicide has occurred. Even if the bodies of the victims eventually turn up at a dump site, most of the potentially revealing forensic evidence remains in the killer's house or car where the victim was slain; but without a suspect, the police do not know its location. Moreover, any trace evidence, such as semen within the vagina and skin beneath the fingernails, left on the discarded body tends to erode as the corpse is exposed to rain, wind, heat, and snow.

In 1988, for example, the police in New Bedford, Massachusetts, were stymied by a profound lack of physical evidence in their hunt for a killer of at least nine prostitutes and drug users. The unidentified predator had abducted his victims from the crime-ridden Weld Square area of town and discarded their remains along highways in southeastern Massachusetts. By the time the decomposed bodies were finally discovered, the police had enough trouble identifying the skeletal remains, much less the killer. After 3 decades, this case remains unsolved; with the trail growing colder with each passing year, it will likely remain unresolved permanently.

In Gainesville and New Bedford, like many other serial murder sites, the police had little difficulty detecting the work of a serial killer from an alarming increase in similarly patterned murders or disappearances. Despite the fact that the police, alerted to a serial murderer operating in the area, may heighten levels of surveillance, the killer may continue to tempt fate, believing arrogantly that he can outsmart the police. He persists in killing close to home or his workplace, staying within his comfort zone, knowing where he can best find and dump his victims as well as the best escape routes to avoid detection.

Many other serial killers, however, are able to obfuscate the serial pattern underlying their attacks by modifying the style of killing, by changing the type of victim, or by spacing the murders over time and distance. They can kill and dump one victim in Ohio and then be in Indiana stalking the next victim by the time the police uncover any evidence of the previous murder. With the murderous carnage distributed far and wide, law enforcement, by virtue of its decentralized nature, may never discern the wide-ranging work of a single murderer. Even if the killings are consistent in style (similar victim type or method of killing), so-called linkage blindness (being unaware of linkages to other crimes separated by space or time) becomes a significant barrier to solving serial homicides.[13]

ViCAP

To aid in the detection of serial murder cases, and specifically to address the linkage blindness problem, the FBI's Behavioral Sciences Unit in 1985 launched its Violent Criminal Apprehension Program (ViCAP). ViCAP is a computerized database for the collection and collation of information pertaining to unsolved homicides around the country. It is designed to flag similarities in unsolved homicides that might otherwise be obscured.[14]

ViCAP was used successfully, for example, in identifying unsolved homicides linked to Ángel Maturino Reséndiz, the "FBI's Ten Most Wanted" fugitive who, in 1999, traveled state to state by train committing robbery-murders along his route. Once it was determined that two Texas cases were linked to the same serial offender, the ViCAP database was searched for similar incidents in other jurisdictions, leading analysts to a 2-year-old Kentucky case that was eventually tied to the "Railway Killer" by DNA tests.

Although an excellent idea in theory, ViCAP has encountered significant practical limitations over the past three decades. According to former ViCAP manager Gregory M. Cooper, "[the system is] potentially a very effective tool. . . . As in any database, it's only as good as the amount of information in it."[15] Because of complexities in the lengthy and detailed data collection forms, even after launching a more convenient web-based version in 2008, cooperation from local law enforcement in completing ViCAP questionnaires has been far less than satisfactory. Most states do not require the police to submit cases to ViCAP, and fewer than 1,500 of the approximately 18,000 police agencies participate.

In addition to the missing data problem, pattern recognition is not as easy or straightforward as some may believe, regardless of how powerful the computer or sophisticated the software is. Serial killers often vary their targets or method of killing, sometimes just to experiment with new approaches or even purposely to throw off the authorities. Because of these factors and despite a healthy dose of funding from the U.S. Congress, ViCAP has failed to reach its potential. Lamenting the fact that police agencies often fail to communicate and coordinate information, Ritchie Martinez, former president of the International Association of Law Enforcement Intelligence Analysts, said, "The need is vital. But ViCAP is not filling it."[16]

As a case in point, the series of crimes perpetrated by D.C. Snipers John Allen Muhammad and Lee Boyd Malvo was not limited to the Washington Beltway but included Washington State, Arizona, Louisiana, Georgia, and Alabama. None of the earlier crimes elsewhere was linked by ViCAP to the October 2002 killing spree in Maryland, Virginia, and the District of Columbia.

The ViCAP model rests on the assumption that offenders follow a specific pattern or signature—consistency in victim type, sexual rituals, style of killing, and so on—and that this can be discerned from a preset list of categories describing the victim, offender, and crime scene. Case similarities, however, cannot necessarily be adequately reduced to a set of questionnaire-type items. During the 1990 investigation of the five grisly slayings in Gainesville, the task force was compelled to look out of state for help as the investigation dragged on for months without any of a large pool of potential subjects successfully tied to the crime scene through lab tests of blood and hairs. The critical lead eventually came from 800 miles away when a Shreveport, Louisiana, detective alerted the task force to a potentially related triple murder that occurred almost a year earlier. On November 4, 1989, 55-year-old Tom Grissom, his 24-year-old daughter Julie, and her 8-year-old nephew Sean were found bound and stabbed to death. Julie Grissom, a college student, had been raped and her body posed in a sexually provocative manner, possibly for shock value. Her body was washed with vinegar, and the killer had apparently spent considerable time cleaning the crime scene of potential evidence.

Many experienced investigators inside and outside of the task force discounted this lead, focusing on certain dissimilarities. To them, the cases were as different as day and night, literally: The Grissom murders in Shreveport had occurred in the late afternoon, unlike the early morning hours of the Gainesville attacks. Also, the Grissom murders did not reveal anything close to the level of brutality found in the mutilation and decapitation of the Gainesville victims.

Based on visual comparison of the crime scene photos, however, the Grissom murders appeared as if they very well could have been committed by the same assailant as the Gainesville slaughters. The task force was impressed with the similarities—the use of duct tape to control the victims, cleansing of victims following sexual penetration, attempts to destroy evidence, and similar provocative posing of bodies. As it happened, it was this link that directed the task force to consider 36-year-old Danny Rolling, hometown Shreveport, who was jailed in Ocala, Florida, on a robbery charge.

Needing more than just a Shreveport address to elevate Rolling to a high-priority suspect, the task force sought physical specimens to compare with evidence recovered from the Gainesville crime scenes. Because Rolling was in custody, however, rules pertaining to search and seizure prohibited him from consenting to investigators' requests for blood and hair samples. By virtue of the coercion implicit by their confinement, jail and prison inmates cannot consent to searches. Further complicating matters was that the Shreveport address was insufficient to convince a judge to issue a warrant for a body search. By a stroke of good fortune, however, Rolling needed to have an impacted wisdom tooth removed by the dentist. The bloody tooth, once discarded as trash, was no longer in Rolling's possession and could be submitted to the lab for DNA testing, an analysis that ultimately implicated Rolling as the Gainesville murderer.

Despite the problems encountered by the ViCAP initiative, computers are clearly an indispensable tool in managing homicide investigations. Large-scale investigative task forces rely on them for information storage and retrieval. In a case that drags on for weeks or months, particularly when there are multiple victims and multiple crime scenes, the volume of information is unmanageable without the use of technology. This is especially true in high-profile cases when the public is encouraged (often with promise of reward) to call information into a tip line. The annals of law enforcement reveal many instances in which a large-scale investigation failed because certain key pieces of information were difficult to access, lost, or not relayed to the appropriate detectives. In recent years, software for indexing investigative data (including witness statements, tips, and field reports) was created and now allows detectives to query a database to link, for example, forensic analysis of tire tracks with a witness's statement about observing a truck leaving the scene of a crime.

NamUs

Whereas ViCAP can be accessed only by law enforcement, the National Missing and Unidentified Persons System (NamUs), which became a reality in September 2008, can be used by the public, law enforcement, medical examiners, and coroners. Whereas ViCAP and the National Crime Information Center (NCIC) are tools for solving cases for law enforcement only, NamUs houses information about unsolved missing persons and unidentified remains for the entire country. The NamUs system looks for matches between the two databases, linking the missing with the unidentified. Anyone can search the NamUs database, virtually anyone can enter a missing person case, and medical examiners and coroners enter cases of the unidentified dead. Sensitive case data can still be locked from public view so law enforcement agencies can communicate sensitive information without risk. Searches on a variety of key identifiers including tattoos, DNA, clothing, scars, jewelry, and dental identifiers can link missing person cases to unidentified remains.

As of mid-year 2017, more than 30,000 missing person cases have been reported to NamUs. About 13,000 of these have been resolved, nearly 1,700 of them with a direct assist from NamUs itself. As for unidentified remains, nearly 15,000 have been reported to NamUs. Roughly 3,000 of these have been resolved, about 1,100 directly through a match within NamUs.

Of course, the computer can only do what police ordinarily do (i.e., track down leads and compare information), but the computer can do it at lightning fast speed. Recent advances in information database matching and artificial intelligence have assisted law enforcement in drawing critical clues from seemingly disparate and incomplete sources. Designed by an Arizona-based software firm and now owned by IBM, a program called Coplink searches and matches arrest records, emergency calls to 9-1-1, motor vehicle registration files, tattoos, nicknames, and other existing databases to help police track down information in a timely fashion. Coplink was installed late in the D.C. Sniper investigation, in fact on the very day when the police closed in on the two suspects in their blue Chevrolet Caprice at a rest stop off Route 95. Using a query about any person or vehicle identified within an hour of the shooting sites, Coplink flagged the fact that the same blue Caprice was stopped by police in multiple post-shooting roadblocks.

Behavioral Profiling

In addition to the ViCAP clearinghouse, the FBI provides technical assistance to local law enforcement in attempting to solve open cases of suspected serial murder and other extraordinary crimes. On request, the FBI assembles an investigative profile of the unknown killer based on psychological clues left at crime scenes, autopsy reports, and police incident reports. Typically, these profiles speculate on the killer's age, race, sex, marital status, employment status, sexual competence, possible criminal record, relationship to the victim, and likelihood of committing future crimes.

At the core of its profiling strategy, the FBI distinguishes between "organized non-social" and "disorganized asocial." Based on an FBI study of 36 killers (25 serial and 11 nonserial), typically the organized killer is intelligent, is socially and sexually competent, is of high birth order, is a skilled worker, lives with a partner, is mobile, drives a late-model car, and follows his crimes in the media. In contrasting tendency, the disorganized killer is unintelligent, is socially and sexually inadequate, is of low birth order, is an unskilled worker, lives alone, is not particularly mobile, drives an old car or no car at all, and has minimal interest in the news reports of his crimes.[17]

According to FBI analysis, these two types tend to differ in terms of crime scene characteristics. Specifically, the organized killer uses restraints on his victims, hides or transports the body, removes the weapon from the scene, molests the victim prior to death, and is methodical in his style of killing. In contrast, the disorganized killer tends not to use restraints, leaves the body in full view, leaves a weapon at the scene, molests the victim after death, and is spontaneous in his manner of killing. The task of profiling involves, therefore, drawing inferences from the crime scene as to what the behavioral characteristics of the killer are.

Profiling has contributed to the successful apprehension of several infamous serial murderers, including the Atlanta Child Murderer Wayne Williams, the Sacramento Vampire Richard Trenton Chase, and the Genesee River Killer Arthur Shawcross. However, there are many more cases in which profiling had no or limited impact, and a few cases in which a profile did more harm than good by leading investigators in the wrong direction.

In Baton Rouge, months after the police had linked several murders to a serial killer, the task force released details of an FBI profile of the unknown assailant. The profile described the killer as a strong, 25- to 35-year-old man who would be awkward in interacting with attractive women. The task force also speculated that the killer would be white or Hispanic because of the race pattern in his victim selection. Derrick Todd Lee, a muscular 34-year-old, was eventually arrested for the crimes. Friends and neighbors described him as "disarmingly charming" and "easy to get along with." And Lee is black.

The FBI's Unabomber profile, which guided the investigation of a series of bombings during the 1980s and 1990s, suggested that the perpetrator was in his mid-30s or early 40s, was a blue-collar worker with possibly some college education, and had resided in or around Chicago and, later, San Francisco. When Theodore Kaczynski was eventually captured, he was in his 50s, held a doctorate degree, and lived as a hermit in Montana.

Profiling is more an imprecise craft than an exact science. Behavioral inferences from the crime scene are speculative, at best, and have a low rate of success in leading to the identity of a killer.[18] Thus, whereas psychological profiles work wonderfully in fiction and in TV crime dramas, they are much less than a panacea in real life, even when constructed by the most experienced and skillful profilers such as those at the FBI Behavioral Analysis Unit. Nevertheless, profiles are not designed to solve a case but simply to provide an additional set of clues in cases found by local police to be unsolvable. Moreover, one should not expect a high success rate in any event; only the most difficult and "unsolvable" cases ever reach the attention of the FBI. Profiles are best used as interview strategies—suggesting, for instance, how to push the buttons of a certain type of suspect—and certainly not to limit the types of people who will be investigated.

It is critical, therefore, that we maintain some perspective on the investigative value of psychological profiles. Simply put, a psychological profile cannot identify a suspect for investigation, nor can it eliminate a suspect who doesn't fit "the mold." Rather, a profile can assist in assigning subjective probabilities to suspects whose names surface through more usual investigative strategies (e.g., interviews of witnesses, canvassing of neighborhoods, and "tip" phone lines).

The craft of profiling came squarely under the spotlight in autumn 2002, when full attention of the print and electronic media was focused on the D.C. area snipings. Although all media outlets monitored the unsolved case, the cable networks in particular covered the case virtually around the clock, examining every possible angle in excruciating detail. Each network had its team of experts—criminologists, psychologists, former law enforcement personnel, and so on—to speculate, pontificate, and interpret each new wrinkle of the unfolding real-life murder mystery.

Among the many topics examined on-air was what kind of person could carry out the deadly assaults and so successfully evade the police. Unlike the usual process of profiling, in which a wide variety of information is examined (crime scene photos, autopsy reports, investigative reports, etc.), for the TV profilers there was very little on which to base their speculations. The on-air profilers were not privy to much of the actual evidence, which the task force kept under wraps; yet there were certain statistical patterns among sniper cases that generally helped to shape their speculations. Although each of the analysts had his or her own unique perspective, there were some strong commonalities among their assessments. According to the experts, the shooter was likely a middle-aged, white male, possibly with a military background, and likely a loner. With no connection to the victims, who were targeted only because they happened to be at the wrong place at the wrong time, the sniper was likely expressing a grudge against all of society.

When the sniper case was finally solved, the media had a field day in scoring and second-guessing the accuracy of the very hunches they had solicited. Although many features of the statistical profile were accurate, one glaring error was scrutinized: Not only were there two snipers, not one, but also John Allen Muhammad and Lee Boyd Malvo were black, not white.

Some critics even suggested that the task force and the public at large were misled by the speculations of TV commentators.[19] "The important question is, was the orgy of speculation harmless—or was there a very dangerous undercurrent to it?" asked *Washington Post* reporters Paul Farhi and Linton Weeks following the suspects' arrest.

By saturating the public's consciousness with phantom images of thirty-something white men, did the media profilers distract attention from a more general and possibly open-minded search for the perpetrators? . . . If so, the media's performance raises a chilling possibility: that the suspects might have evaded detection for so long because witnesses were focusing too intently on media-created "profiles" that didn't come close to the real thing.[20]

At no time, of course, did the profilers rule out the possibility of the killer(s) being black. In fact, one analysis of statistical patterns published in the *New York Times* noted that even though a majority of snipers are white (55%), as many as 43% are black.[21] Thus, statistically it was more likely that the sniper was white than black, but it was hardly a certainty. More importantly, there is no evidence whatsoever that the task force focused only on white suspects or that the public in any way patterned their daily lives to avoid white men.

If anything, it was the white van theory, not the white man theory, that slowed and sidetracked the hunt for the D.C. Sniper. For weeks the police had alerted the public to a white van driven by the sniper, even distributing and posting on the internet composite sketches of a white panel truck. Given the power of suggestion, eyewitnesses to subsequent sniper strikes reported seeing a white van speeding away following the attacks. Of course, there are so many such vehicles on the road that it is hard not to see one in any finite span of time. Plus, the mind can easily be tricked by preconceptions and prejudices—in the moonlight, gray, tan, yellow, and beige can all appear white when a person is expecting to see white. As it happened, the narrow focus on identifying the white van was a significant hindrance to the investigation. When apprehended, John Allen Muhammad and Lee Boyd Malvo were resting inside their blue sedan.

The FBI no longer prefers the term *profiling* to identify their serial offender tracking positions. The bureau has had to contend with the negative connotation associated with racial profiling (e.g., getting pulled over by the police because of "driving while black"), Hollywood's distortion of the job of a profiler (e.g., in *The Silence of the Lambs*), and perhaps, most importantly, the fact that an analyst cannot offer expert testimony in court as a profiler. Agents can, however, offer expert testimony regarding crime scene staging—hence the new moniker, criminal investigative analysts, who identify the personality and behavioral elements of the individual killer by looking at the crime scene. More often than not, elements of the crime scene are present in a killer's lifestyle (soliciting prostitutes, patronizing gay bars, surfing porn on the internet, etc.).

Also contrary to some media portrayals, profilers (or criminal investigative analysts) typically work as a team, not as individuals. To build a profile, their analysis will include a visit to crime scenes (or photographs since, at the actual crime scene, law enforcement may not recognize the work of a serial killer), autopsy and crime lab results, investigative interviews and reports, descriptions and maps of the area around the killing, items taken by the killer, and dump sites.

Geographic Profiling

A more recent profiling strategy, one that has not been featured as frequently in TV crime drama, involves the examination of crime locations rather than crime scenes. In geographic profiling, the various addresses of a serial killer's crime sites, as well as body dumpsites, if any, are analyzed quantitatively as a pattern to predict where the unidentified assailant might live or work.[22]

As noted in Chapter 7, most serial killers prey on victims within a localized area. As creatures of habit and convenience, they tend to target victims encountered along their usual routes near home or work. Many prefer to operate in areas with which they are familiar, except for the immediate proximity to maintain a protective "buffer zone" against easy detection. Knowledge of the landscape is especially important should they need a quick escape route to avoid capture. Assuming these tendencies, a map of probable home bases can be constructed to guide police in canvassing a neighborhood for witnesses or conducting surveillance.

Geographic profiling computer programs apply various mathematical algorithms involving distances among locations of interest along with details about the terrain (e.g., roadways and physical barriers such as rivers) to produce what is called a "jeopardy surface"—a three-dimensional display of probabilities where a serial offender may reside within the overall hunting area.

A number of evaluation studies have been conducted by retrospectively comparing a geographic map of location probabilities against the actual residence of a serial offender who had previously been captured. Using a sample of 70 serial killers who had operated in the United States, David Canter and his colleagues reported just over half resided within the 5% area with the highest predicted probability, and nearly 90% had lived in an area with the highest 25% likelihood.[23] Of course, this is not quite the same as prospectively pinpointing a neighborhood or street in which an unidentified killer can be found.

Geographic profiling has been used sporadically in actual investigations with some success. With further work on software development and wider acceptance by law enforcement, the utility of this approach should grow. Of course, no matter how sophisticated the algorithm or how detailed the spatial data, geographic profiling should not be expected to solve cases directly. Rather, it can serve as a means of guiding an investigation toward a successful outcome.

In light of the tremendous acceleration in recent years in the power and reach of technology, including social media and crowd-sourced databases, it is likely that the tools for identifying and apprehending murderers will improve as a result.

SIGHTINGS AND VISIONS

The fallibility of eyewitnesses has been the subject of much research. Seeing may mean believing for the eyewitness, but one must always take the accuracy of these observations with a healthy grain of salt. In an emotional state of panic, expectations and prejudices about what criminals look like can color perceptions. The mind tends to fill in missing information using whatever is available—what others at a crime scene report (collective recollections), what the police suggest through their questions, what the papers publish, and so on.

As an experiment of the effect of external validation on eyewitness confidence, Luius and Wells asked a group of subjects who had witnessed a staged theft to identify the perpetrator in a photo lineup.[24] After their identification, some of the eyewitnesses were told that another witness to the crime had picked out the same perpetrator, some were told that another witness had identified a different individual, and some were told nothing about the other witness. As expected, the degree of confidence that subjects claimed to have about their lineup identification was greatly impacted by the positive, negative, or neutral feedback they received. More surprising is that those subjects whose confidence in their ability to identify the thief was enhanced or diminished by learning about another's recollection maintained their position even after being told that the information about the second eyewitness was incorrect because of a recording error. That is, their belief in what they saw, conditioned in part by external validation or invalidation, persisted even after learning that the validation was groundless. According to analysis by the Innocence Project, eyewitness misidentification has played a role in 70% of the convictions overturned by DNA. In the slight majority of eyewitness misidentification cases, the misidentification was not intentional; rather, it was simply a mistake. But in other cases, the misidentification was a lie due to some sort of self-interest.[25]

There are recommended strategies for enhancing the reliability of eyewitness identification in either a physical lineup or one using photographs. For example, to avoid subtle or even inadvertent hinting, the officer administering a physical or photo lineup should be unaware of which person is the suspect. And, of course, the "fillers" should match the suspects in as many respects as possible. Finally, witnesses should be instructed that the investigation will continue if no one in the lineup is familiar so that they don't feel pressure just to guess.

At times, hypnosis has been used in an attempt to improve memory and recall, particularly when a traumatic experience of witnessing a crime may have compelled the mind to repress memory. But, although hypnosis may be able to uncover recollections shrouded in pain, it cannot improve the lighting, improve line of sight, or remove prejudice and bias in stored images.

Whereas the therapeutic uses of hypnosis are well documented and widely accepted, forensic applications are much more controversial. Research on hypnosis indicates that the so-called "hypnotic trance" is little more than accepting the suggestions of a highly credible source.[26] More important is that hypnosis increases the level of confidence but not accuracy in recalling events. For example, under hypnosis, witnesses to a crime involving a masked gunman have been asked to mentally remove the criminal's disguise and describe his face. Filling in the details on their own, these hypnotized subjects become convinced about the description they give. It may be a figment of their imagination, but it is one of which they are absolutely sure. In the same way, psychologists studying hypnosis have compared age regression with age progression. After first taking their subjects back several years in life to recall events at that time, they then take them forward into the future and ask them to describe what they are doing. Subjects tend to recollect the future in as much detail and certainty as they recall the past.

While the use of hypnosis to enhance memories of eyewitnesses, victims, and even perpetrators remains controversial, so does the use of psychic visions in homicide investigations. Rarely do investigators like to admit seeking or relying on the input of psychics, but in more than a few instances their input has been valuable.

Perhaps owing to the high-profile nature of the case, the Gainesville student murder task force received more than a few tips from self-professed psychics, most of which were delegated with great skepticism to the lowest priority level. Early on in the investigation, the police received a call from a resident of Harrisburg, Pennsylvania, who claimed that she had had a powerful premonition, prompted by a television report of the crimes, that the killer's name was "Rollings." It wasn't until months later, when Danny Rolling catapulted to the top of the suspect list because of a DNA match between his blood and semen at the crime scenes, that the investigators, tracking back through their computerized records for any mention of the suspect name, took note of this lead.

"I literally jumped up and said I know who it is," recalled Sharon Carroll, a 45-year-old office manager. "I really don't think they believed me." Carroll was later investigated for any possible connection to the murders. No alternative explanation for her uncanny accuracy was ever found except, of course, the obvious one—a sheer coincidence.

The Gainesville case notwithstanding, the investigative value of psychic visions is more the material for fictional accounts (as in Patricia Arquette's character in the TV series *Medium*) than reality. A number of self-styled crime psychics have made exaggerated, if not outlandish, claims of being able to locate missing bodies or help solve major crimes. Yet, on closer scrutiny, many of their correct insights about various crimes appear to be a retrofit of vague psychic clues to actual details.[27] Psychics have joined the era of reality television, and dozens of channels feature the latest celebrity psychic looking for their 15 minutes of con and coincidence. Although ghost stories, psychics, mediums, witches, and werewolves may make for entertaining television viewing, there is no science to their paranormal claims.

WORKING A HOMICIDE IN THE MEDIA SPOTLIGHT

As noted in Chapter 1, homicide cases receive an inordinate amount of attention in the mass media, especially so when a killer, possibly "armed and dangerous," remains at large. Growth and competition in the news industry has caused media saturation of certain breaking or continuing crime stories. At the extreme, during the nearly month-long investigation of the D.C.-area sniper case in October 2002, the task force headquarters in Montgomery County, Maryland, became a makeshift media village. Virtually every major news organization was in residence, equipped with satellite trucks, tents, and power generators, as well as reporters and technicians, ready to go "live" with each new development in the case.

The task force, headed by Chief Charles A. Moose, obliged the information-hungry reporters and an anxious public with routine news conferences about the progress of the sniper manhunt. Not only was this relationship between the media and the investigation extraordinary in its closeness, but it also marked a significant break for the usual guarded interactions between police and journalists.

Much of the time, exchanges between law enforcement handling a high-profile case and the media attempting to respond to public fear or fascination are strained, if not distrustful. The police typically attempt to control the spread of information, especially certain details of the crime that are withheld for the purpose of validating confessions or interrogations of suspects. Seeking an advantage in covering a major story, reporters have been known to cultivate and even bribe inside sources in order to scoop the competition, although these scoops often turn out to be lacking in accuracy. The much-maligned police investigation into the death of 6-year-old JonBenét Ramsey, who was found on the morning after Christmas, 1996, in the basement of her Boulder, Colorado, home, suffered significantly from constant pressure of politics and publicity. As Colorado and national media speculated endlessly about the case, and especially the role of her parents, John and Patsy Ramsey, as well as her brother, the local authorities had great difficulty managing the investigation under the constant media spotlight.

The tremendous pressure on the authorities to identify and capture JonBenét's killer, combined with the continuing and intense media focus on the unsolved case, created a "perfect storm" for some obscure false confessor to seize the limelight and enjoy his 15 days of fame.

In 2006, John Mark Karr, 41, became a household name and suspect of the fortnight by professing his love for the slain girl and confessing his role in her death. With little more than the man's word, District Attorney Mary Lacy flew Karr first class from Bangkok to Boulder to face interrogation. On scrutiny, there were numerous holes and inconsistencies in Karr's tall tale, embarrassing the authorities and subjecting them to further charges of incompetence. Karr continues desperately to try to attract any sort of attention he can get.

Notwithstanding the often-contentious relations between cops and reporters, the media have on more than a few occasions been exploited by police to their advantage. In Sarby County, Nebraska, for example, the sheriff was able to challenge the killer through the media. Talking to reporters about the murders of two local boys, Sheriff Pat Thomas referred to the unidentified killer as "sick, spineless, [and] a coward" who didn't have the guts to pick on someone his own size. Little did Sheriff Thomas realize that the killer was closely following the progress of the investigation in the newspaper. Insulted by the sheriff's remark, 19-year-old John Joubert decided to prove he was more of a man than the sheriff had surmised. His next victim was a female adult who managed to break away from her assailant, take note of his license plate, and thereby help the police in making an arrest.

In the D.C. Sniper investigation, the use of the media to further the police effort was more purposeful. Chief Charles Moose spoke directly to the perpetrators through his televised press conferences. At one point, he attempted to earn the trust of the killer by slamming the media for printing part of a note left at one of the shooting sites. Actually, his outrage was a good job of acting designed to make him appear like the killer's ally.

For their part, killers oftentimes reach out to the police and public through the mass media. Son of Sam frequently sent letters to *New York Daily News* columnist Jimmy Breslin, and these messages were then printed in the newspaper. The Zodiac Killer, who terrorized the citizens of San Francisco during the 1960s and 1970s and was never caught, sent dozens of taunting letters to the police.

The police have often published written or verbal communications from an unknown perpetrator in the hope that someone will recognize the author. The most dramatic case was the Unabomber. After more than a dozen years of serial bombing, the Unabomber went public. Perhaps feeling invincible after fooling the police for so long, the unknown bomber apparently wanted to send a message that would advance his antitechnology agenda. It began with letters sent to the *New York Times*, which were eagerly excerpted in the paper.

Emboldened by his continuing elusiveness, the Unabomber then sent to the press a 35,000-word manifesto, titled "Industrial Society and the Future," insisting that it be published in a prestigious paper worthy of its content—the *New York Times* or the *Washington Post*. If his demand was not met, he would strike again: an odd and literal twist on the academic phrase "publish or perish."

Much hand-wringing ensued at the *Times* and the *Post* about how to respond to the bomber's threat. Ostensibly for the purpose of public safety, the joint decision of the editors of the two papers, in consultation with the FBI, was to start the presses. On September 19, 1995, the *Washington Post* published a special section with the document in full. This set a potentially dangerous precedent. Would others in the future decide to threaten violence unless their letters or manuscripts were published? Of course, reasoned the paper, this was not the typical offender, but someone who had terrorized the nation for almost 2 decades. They only hoped that someone would read the text and recognize its author.

The curious decision was to print the manifesto in the weekday edition of the *Washington Post*, attempting to satisfy the killer's demands in the most minimal way. The *Post* has far less circulation than the *Times*, and the daily substantially less than the Sunday edition. However, in the early internet days of 1995, the choice of location virtually guaranteed that very few people in the San Francisco or Chicago metropolitan areas—where the FBI believed the Unabomber had lived—would get hold of the daily edition of the *Washington Post*.

As the story unfolded, David Kaczynski did notice some similarity between the manifesto and his brother's ranting and raving about the evils of modern technology. Kaczynski contacted the FBI, leading to the eventual arrest of Theodore Kaczynski for the serial bombings. In the minds of many observers, the happy ending justified the controversial means. But David Kaczynski was actually tipped off long before the *Post*'s publication of the manifesto by reading the letters excerpted earlier in the *New York Times*. Even if the *Post* had not published the manifesto, David Kaczynski would, in all likelihood, still have responded to the FBI's invitation for anyone to examine the manifesto, denying the killer his undeserved platform.

Although forensic investigation, psychological profiling, and ViCAP all play integral roles in trying to apprehend killers, there is no substitute for old-fashioned detective work and a healthy dose of luck. In some cases the police get lucky because the killer slips up. He may begin to feel after a while that he is invincible and that the cops cannot match his skill or cunning. By becoming complacent, lazy, and sloppy, he starts to cut corners and take chances, which leads to his ultimate demise.

In June 1993, the police in Mineola, Long Island, indeed got lucky. Stopping a motorist in the middle of the night because of a missing license plate, state troopers discovered a woman's body in the back of the gray pickup truck. The driver, 34-year-old Joel Rifkin, was en route to dump the body of his 17th victim.

London's Colin Ireland thought he had all the bases covered, but ultimately he, too, hadn't worked out every important detail. Spanning several months in 1993, the 39-year-old Briton stalked and killed members of London's gay community without leaving so much as a clue. All of his five victims were gay men who engaged in sadomasochistic sex, enabling Ireland to bind and gag them at will. Hence, they were completely at his mercy.

Ireland was methodical. Before each and every murder, he emptied his pockets so that nothing would fall out and implicate him. Afterward, he spent hours wiping away the evidence, even destroying the clothes he wore at the scene of the crime. Despite his preparation and planning, however, Ireland made a major blunder. A security camera captured his presence as he walked behind his fifth and last victim at a subway station just prior to the murder. Seeing his photo reprinted in the newspaper, Ireland panicked and came forward to confess.

Frequently murderers are apprehended after being linked to crimes or violations having little apparent connection to their killings. Serial killer Theodore Bundy was captured after being stopped in Florida on a traffic violation, and New York's Son of Sam killer, David Berkowitz, was identified because of a parking ticket tagged on his car near one of his shooting sites. Although in these and other cases the police appear to have capitalized on some degree of luck, they benefited because of their attention to detail. Bundy's arrest resulted from the good work and alertness of an officer simply doing his job. Similarly, the lucky ticket associated with Berkowitz's vehicle would not have surfaced had the detectives not decided to track down all violations issued near each of the Son of Sam homicides. As in many areas of life, you make your own luck.

ENDNOTES

1. Thomas A. DiBase, "No Body Murder Trials in the United States," www.nobodymurdercases. com; Samantha Henry, "No Body? No Problem Convincing 90 Percent of the Time," *Washington Post*, April 11, 2010; Keith L. Alexander and Dan Morse, "Murder Cases Without the Victim's Body Are

Difficult, Prosecutors Say, but Winnable," *Washington Post*, April 17, 2017.

2. Innocence Project "DNA Exonerations in the United States," https://www.innocenceproject.org/dna -exonerations-in-the-united-states.

3. Susan Finch, "Baton Rouge Man Sues for His DNA," *New Orleans Times-Picayune*, June 3, 2001.

4. Seth Augenstein, "Hidden in Prison: 7 States Have Thousands of Inmates Not in DNA Databases," *Forensic Magazine*, July 17, 2017.

5. Beth Schwartzapfel, "This Machine Could Prevent Gun Violence—If Only Cops Used It," Marshall Project (in collaboration with the *Washington Post*), October 6, 2016.

6. Seth Augenstein, "NIST Launches New 3-D Ballistics Database," *Forensic Magazine*, July 11, 2016.

7. Matt Drange, "We're Spending Millions on This High-Tech System Designed to Reduce Gun Violence. Is It Making a Difference?" *Forbes*, November 17, 2016.

8. National Research Council, *Strengthening Forensic Science in the United States: A Path Forward* (Washington, DC: National Academies Press, 2009).

9. David A. Moran and Samuel R. Gross, "Put Scientists, Not Cops in Crime Labs," *Detroit Free Press*, November 8, 2008.

10. Eric Witzig, "Murder Clearance Rates Decline at Most Major Police Agencies," Murder Accountability Project, June 12, 2017.

11. Charles Wellford and James Cronin, "Clearing Up Homicide Clearance Rates," *National Institute of Justice Journal*, April 2000.

12. Kenna Quinet, "The Missing Missing: Toward a Quantification of Serial Murder in the United States," *Homicide Studies* 11 (2007): 319–339.

13. Steven A. Egger, "A Working Definition of Serial Murder and the Reduction of Linkage Blindness,"

Journal of Police Science and Administration 12 (1984): 348–357.

14. J. B. Howlett, K. A. Haufland, and R. K. Ressler, "The Violent Criminal Apprehension Program—VICAP: A Progress Report," *FBI Law Enforcement Bulletin* 55 (December 1986): 14–22.

15. Steve Ritea and Stephanie A. Stanley, "Why Didn't They Put the Pieces Together Sooner?" *New Orleans Times-Picayune*, June 1, 2003, p. 1.

16. T. Christian Miller, "The FBI's Flawed ViCAP Database," *Atlantic*, July 30, 2015.

17. Robert K. Ressler and Ann W. Burgess, "Violent Crime," *FBI Law Enforcement Bulletin* 54 (August 1985).

18. Institutional Research and Development Unit, *Evaluation of the Psychological Profiling Program* (Quantico, VA: FBI Academy, Quantico, 1981).

19. Rachel Smolkin, "Off Target," *American Journalism Review*, December 2002.

20. Paul Farhi and Linton Weeks, "A Surprise Ending," *Washington Post*, October 25, 2002, p. C1.

21. Jeffrey Gettleman, "The Hunt for a Sniper," *New York Times*, October 15, 2002, p. A19.

22. Kim Rossmo, *Geographic Profiling* (Boca Raton, FL: CRC Press, 1999).

23. David Canter, Toby Coffey, Malcolm Huntley, and Christopher Missen, "Predicting Serial Killers' Home Base Using a Decision Support System," *Journal of Quantitative Criminology* 16 (2000): 457–478.

24. C. A. Elizabeth Luius and Gary L. Wells, "Eyewitness Identification Confidence," in David Frank Ross, J. Don Read, and Michael P. Toglia, eds., *Adult Eyewitness Testimony: Current Trends and Developments* (New York: Cambridge University Press, 1994).

25. Kaitlin Jackson and Samuel Gross, "Tainted Identifications," National Registry of Exonerations, September 22, 2016.

26. Theodore X. Barber, *Hypnosis: A Scientific Approach* (New York: Van Nostrand Reinhold, 1969).

27. Joe Nickell, ed., *Psychic Sleuths: ESP and Sensational Cases* (Buffalo, NY: Prometheus, 1994).

CHAPTER FOURTEEN

GETTING AWAY WITH MURDER, OR NOT

"**P**rison is too good for them." "He'll be out on parole before the victim's body is cold." "The juvenile courts let kids get away with murder."

These are just a few of the kinds of allegations about the failures of the U.S. justice system that not only have become frequent fodder for radio talk show hosts, bloggers, and Twitter users alike but also are used by aspiring politicians who wish to characterize their opponents as soft on crime. Donald Trump, for example, received a significant bump in the polls following his heavy on "law and order" speech at the 2016 Republican National Convention, a theme of his populist candidacy that helped him win the White House on Election Day.

It is not surprising that Trump's stand on crime control resonated with millions of Americans. According to a Gallup poll taken in early October 2016, one month before the election, 45% of Americans felt that the criminal justice system isn't tough enough on criminals, while only 14% indicated that the system is too tough (the rest believing that the level of toughness is about right or offered no opinion).[1] The "need to get tougher" sentiment is not nearly as pervasive as it was in the crime-rampant early 1990s when over 80% surveyed by Gallup felt that the justice system was too soft on crime. Nevertheless, that nearly half of those surveyed in 2016 wanted tougher penalties in an era when crime rates are at a 50-year low reflects an insatiable appetite for harsh punishments.

At times, of course, the "criminals get away with murder" perception may indeed be accurate. In an effort to protect the rights of the accused, criminals have on occasion received unreasonably lenient treatment from the courts, including the acquittal of apparently guilty defendants because of procedural irregularities. The important question, however, is whether this is the exception or the rule.

It is undeniable that public attention is drawn to the absurd and the extreme. When the criminal justice system fails, it becomes a big news story and an opportunity for millions of Americans to stand in righteous indignation and to demand reform. It is not so newsworthy when cases follow the course that is intended by lawmakers. Yet one can surely trace the development of criminal justice as a piecemeal effort to respond to the latest high-profile cases, regardless of how common or representative they are.

THE INSANITY DEFENSE

Many of the recent legislative changes in the criminal code have surrounded an attempt to prevent criminals from getting away with murder. On occasion, these reforms have enabled the law to stay in touch with a fast-changing society.

For example, the historical traditions of English common law could hardly have anticipated regulations needed in the area of drunken driving or cybercrime. Similarly, allowances for conditions like posttraumatic stress disorder or the battered woman syndrome have been responses to medical and sociological knowledge as well as public opinion.

Unfortunately, in many aspects of criminal law, legislative reforms have come in response to perceived loopholes or deficiencies, which, in fact, were imagined or exaggerated. The law pertaining to the insanity defense and the associated not guilty by reason of insanity (NGRI) plea is surely a leading case in point.

Most people would agree that certain criminal acts committed by deeply impaired individuals may indeed be beyond their responsibility. If a parent stabs an infant daughter, acting under a hallucination that the girl is being smothered by the family dog (which is actually a stuffed animal), then neither has the parent any intent to kill nor is he or she a negligent caretaker. The homicide is excusable because it arises from a diseased state of mind.

Even English common law recognized madness as a defense against criminal responsibility. The first insanity trial occurred in 1724 England when Edward Arnold was charged with shooting Lord Onslow, whom Arnold had perceived was inside his "belly and bosom" and causing imps to keep him awake at night.

Over the past 300 years, legislatures and appellate courts have struggled with the meaning and definition of madness and have attempted various solutions to this elusive issue. Much of the time, however, these changes have been motivated by a perceived injustice in which insanity is seen to have allowed a defendant to get away with a crime. Perhaps it is more in theory than in practice that most people accept the validity of the insanity defense.

The historic McNaughtan rule, still used in some form in a majority of U.S. states, was more a response to public outcry than an attempt to fine-tune the law. In 1843, Daniel McNaughtan, a Scottish wood burner who was overwhelmed by delusions of political persecution by the Tory Party, attempted to assassinate English Prime Minister Robert Peel, instead mistakenly shooting to death his secretary, Edward Drummond. McNaughtan was found insane and thus not criminally responsible for the homicide, which so incensed Queen Victoria that she formed a panel of experts to rewrite the insanity law. The McNaughtan rule was designed to narrow the defense, especially for use by political "crazies" like McNaughtan.[2]

The McNaughtan rule is often called the "right–wrong test." To be criminally responsible under this standard, a defendant must both understand the nature of his act and also know that it was wrong. Despite its widespread adoption, many legal experts were uncomfortable with the strictly cognitive dimension of the McNaughtan defense. That is, the McNaughtan rule considered exclusively what the defendant was thinking, but nothing of his or her affect or emotional state.

As an alternative, the Irresistible Impulse Test considers whether the defendant was deprived of the mental power or capacity to control his or her actions. This approach was developed in 1883 and was first used in Alabama 3 years later.

During the 20th century, significant advances were made in the development of psychiatry and the understanding of human behavior (and misbehavior). Recognizing that mental illness could potentially affect the control mechanisms in ways poorly captured in existing definitions of legal insanity, the federal courts adopted the broadest definition embodied in the Durham rule, first formulated in New Hampshire in 1871. According to this approach, a defendant is not responsible if his or her criminal conduct was the product of a mental disease or defect. This rule was so broad and poorly defined that the number of insanity claims, including successful ones, rose precipitously. Defendants were alleging that their conduct resulted from depression or even character disorders.

The turning point in American public opinion arguably came on March 30, 1981, when 25-year-old John W. Hinckley Jr. attempted to assassinate President Ronald Reagan as he exited the Washington Hilton Hotel, a shooting that was captured on videotape and replayed on TV for weeks. Hinckley was so obsessed with actress Jodie Foster that he contrived the assassination plot to get her attention and win her affection for his courage. Just prior to taking a taxicab to the assassination site, Hinckley mailed a letter to Foster outlining his plans and motivation:[3]

> I will admit to you that the reason I'm going ahead with this attempt now is because I cannot wait any longer to impress you. I've got to do something now to make you understand, in no uncertain terms, that I'm doing all of this for your sake! By sacrificing my freedom and possibly my life, I hope to change your mind about me. This letter is being written only an hour before I leave for the Hilton Hotel. Jodie, I'm asking you to please look into your heart and at least give the chance, with this historical deed, to gain your love and respect.

Perhaps because of the patent absurdity of his motivation, John Hinckley was successful in raising an insanity defense. Yet an *ABC News* poll taken the day of the NGRI verdict found that 76% of Americans felt that justice had not been served by the outcome. The U.S. Congress and a number of state governing bodies apparently agreed and moved quickly to reform the law of insanity. Many legislatures adopted an approach contained in the American Law Institute's Model Penal Code, which took the best elements from both the McNaughtan and Irresistible Impulse rules and explicitly excluded character disorders, such as sociopathy.

The Model Penal Code definition of insanity states: "A person is not responsible for criminal conduct if at the time of such conduct as a result of mental disease or defect he lacks substantial capacity either to appreciate the criminality of his conduct or to conform his conduct to the requirements of law." The Model Penal Code approach was used in a majority of American states until the late 1980s; since then, the narrower McNaughtan definition has returned to favor. More importantly, through recent reforms to federal and many state statutes, the burden of proof was transferred to the defense. Rather than forcing the prosecution to prove the defendant sane, the defense would have to demonstrate insanity with clear and convincing evidence.

These changes have severely limited the scope of the insanity defense, although many Americans still fear that legal insanity is a gaping loophole through which thousands of cunning criminals walk their way to freedom. This perception could not be further from the truth. For example, a 1991 study funded by the National Institute of Mental Health of felony cases in eight states determined that less than 1% of defendants attempted the insanity plea as a defense, and only 26% of these were successful.[4] In addition, in those rare instances when NGRI pleas are successfully invoked, most of the time they occur through a plea agreement between the prosecution and defense counsel, not from a jury verdict.

The Insanity Defense in Practice

Even in the strongest of cases, the insanity defense is a hard road for the defense. Juries are extremely reluctant to return an insanity verdict, especially in homicide cases. Average Joes and Josephines often deliberate with a distorted perception of the ramifications of an insanity verdict. Many jurors labor under the false notion that the insanity defense is tantamount to a pardon, and thus are reluctant to vote for an insanity verdict even in cases that most observers declare open and shut. Jurors often suspect that a dangerous defendant can "beat the system" and "get off" on an insanity claim, soon to be free to prey on future victims. However, a "not guilty by reason of insanity" verdict means the defendant is dispatched to a secure mental health facility for an indefinite period of confinement. Even when jurors are instructed about the consequences of an insanity verdict, their fears about the impact and duration of that result can linger.

In 1994, for example, John Salvi murdered two receptionists during armed assaults on two Brookline, Massachusetts, abortion clinics in what appeared initially to be a politically motivated crime. Yet as his trial approached, it became clear to virtually everyone that Salvi's motivation for murder had more to do with mental illness than with any real desire to save the lives of unborn infants. He sincerely believed that he was the victim of a large-scale conspiracy to destroy Catholics. He told his parents that he had seen an evil bird in the family room of their home, and that he would stay up all night guarding against the presence of evil. He claimed to have watched a friend turn into a vampire. He ranted and raved about international plots to rob Catholics of jobs, to commit genocide against white people, and to destroy the Catholic Church. Despite the rather compelling evidence surrounding his severe illness, the jury was unwilling to acquit by reason of insanity. After his conviction, Salvi was sent to state prison, where he later committed suicide, apparently by asphyxiating himself with a plastic trash-can liner.

In another closely watched trial impacted by juror confusion, a Massachusetts jury found Philip Chism guilty of raping and murdering his high school math teacher in 2013 when he was a 14-year-old freshman. The evidence showed that Chism had attacked Colleen Ritzer, 24, with a box cutter in the school restroom and then dragged her body inside a large recycling bin into the woods, where he violated her with a tree branch and left a note saying he hated everyone. He then wandered aimlessly while still covered in his victim's blood and was spotted the next day walking in the middle of a busy two-lane roadway miles from home. When asked by the police about the blood on the box cutter inside his backpack, Chism indicated that it belonged to a girl who was buried in the woods.

The defense conceded at the outset that Chism had committed the acts. The case rested on his mental state: Did he have a mental disease that could excuse his conduct? Despite fairly compelling evidence of psychosis, including auditory hallucinations (i.e., hearing voices) and bizarre behavior in the aftermath of the murder, plus a family history of mental illness, the jury—not unexpectedly—rejected his insanity plea.

Immediately after the Chism verdict, one of the jurors explained to a *Boston Globe* reporter that "[insanity] just wasn't proven." However, in Massachusetts, after a defendant establishes an insanity claim, the burden falls on the prosecution to prove beyond a reasonable doubt that the defendant should not be absolved of criminal responsibility because of mental disease or defect.

Regardless of whether the Chism verdict was appropriate, the process for reaching the decision is worrisome. A jury is ordinarily equipped to evaluate most forms of evidence, including eyewitness testimony, crime scene photos, and even some scientific evidence. But whenever a plea of insanity is raised, the trial's emphasis shifts from "Did he do it?" to "Why did he?" and the jury's task becomes more challenging.

In most instances, jurors are able to set aside whatever preconceptions and biases they may have to keep an open mind. But an open mind may not be enough to evaluate experts from both sides as they debate medical diagnoses and their impact on criminal responsibility. Many jurors have difficulty understanding much of the complex and jargon-filled testimony delivered by psychiatric expert witnesses. Unfortunately, the appeal and authoritativeness of the expert witnesses—rather than the merits of the underlying psychiatric evidence—often carry the day. Moreover, when unable to weigh the conflicting conclusions reached by prosecution and defense experts, jurors may simply vote with their gut feelings and prejudices: "He did the crime, so how can he be not guilty even by reason of insanity?"

Legal scholars have periodically recommended professional juries for the most demanding cases—a panel comprised of doctors, psychiatrists, criminologists, and other scientists whose job is to make judgments about medical, psychiatric, and other technical evidence. Such juries are popular in many European countries. In Norway, for example, the determination of legal insanity is left to the experts—to its Forensic Board of Medicine.

For one thing, a professional panel of arbiters would overcome the difficulties that citizens often have in suspending their distrust of the insanity defense. During jury selection, prospective jurors who admit to believing that insanity is a legal loophole for criminals to avoid responsibility are dismissed; others may think similarly but dare not articulate their beliefs for fear of being perceived poorly before the judge, the attorneys, the press, and other onlookers in the gallery.

Ironically, cases in which the defendant's extremely dysfunctional background and hideous behavior leave little doubt about mental illness can be so disturbing for jurors that they choose punishment (including the death penalty) over hospitalization and treatment. In 1979, for example, a California jury found Richard Trenton Chase, the so-called Vampire of Sacramento, guilty of murdering six people, despite his having previously been institutionalized and diagnosed as schizophrenic. The jurors heard evidence of how he mutilated his victims and drank their blood. Prior to his month-long murder spree, Chase had consumed blood from rabbits, dogs, cows, and birds as replenishment for his own that, according to his delusions, was slowly draining from his head. None of this dissuaded the jurors from recommending death, and may even have encouraged it. Chase did in fact die a few months after his conviction, not in the state's gas chamber, but by his own hand.

In part, the low success rate in insanity claims stems from the misalignment between mental illness in the medical sense and insanity in the legal sense. That is, legal and medical definitions are not consistent in assessing the forces that influence aberrant behavior. It is quite possible for a person to be truly mentally ill yet legally responsible. Kip Kinkel, who killed both of his parents before his shooting rampage at Thurston High School in Springfield, Oregon, was, according to psychiatrists, deeply disturbed and possibly psychotic. The young murderer left this note near the bodies of his parents:[5]

I have just killed my parents. I don't know what is happening. I love my mom and dad so much. I just got two felonies on my record. My parents can't take that. It would destroy them. The embarrassment would be too much for them. They couldn't live with themselves. I am so sorry.

I am a horrible son. I wish I had been aborted. I destroy anything I touch. I can't eat. I can't sleep. I didn't deserve them. They were wonderful people. It's not their fault or the fault of any person or organization or television show. My head just doesn't work right. Fuck these voices inside my head.

I want to die. I want to be gone. But I have to kill people. I don't know why. I am so sorry.

Why did God do this to me? I have never been happy. I wish I was happy. I wish I made my mother proud, but I am nothing. I try so hard to find happiness, but you know me: I hate everything. I have no other choice. What have I become? I am so sorry.

In his taped confession to the police, Kinkel described voices in his head that encouraged him to kill. He was also suicidal, having taped a bullet to his chest just in case he needed one more round to take his own life. Shortly after his arrest, Kinkel rushed a police officer in a failed attempt to provoke him to shoot (suicide by cop).

Kip Kinkel initially entered an insanity plea but then withdrew it in favor of a plea of guilty as charged. During sentencing hearings, a defense psychiatrist testified that Kinkel had heard voices imploring him to kill. A neurologist also testified that Kinkel had holes in his brain, consistent with research findings into schizophrenic children. Notwithstanding the medical evidence, Kinkel was given a life sentence. It was clear that he knew what he was doing and that it was wrong.

Perhaps the insanity defense is infrequently attempted because defense attorneys are well aware of what the public likely misunderstands: that is, that an NGRI verdict, whether negotiated by opposing sides or determined by judge or jury, is hardly a free walk for the defendant. In fact, defendants committed to a psychiatric facility for an indefinite period of time following an insanity finding often spend more time in confinement than they would have had they been convicted of the criminal charge. Although they avoid prison (where they don't belong), they don't "get away" with anything at all.

John Hinckley Jr., for example, remained institutionalized at St. Elizabeth's Hospital, a federally operated psychiatric hospital in Washington, D.C., for 3.5 decades after a not guilty by reason of insanity verdict for his unsuccessful assassination attempt against President Reagan in 1981. For years, despite several bids to win his freedom by claiming he is no longer ill, Hinckley was only allowed occasional furloughs to visit home. Not until the age of 61 was Hinckley, one of America's most notorious nonmurderers, finally released to live free with his elderly mother in Virginia. Inarguably, Hinckley's fate was not the kind of lenient treatment that many misinformed citizens screamed about following his trial. As a historical note, moreover, the infamous Daniel McNaughtan didn't get off as easily as the Queen of England had suggested. He died in an asylum some 20 years after he was spared the death penalty for his crime.

Finally, the insanity plea is also eschewed by some defendants because it stigmatizes them as crazy. Some offenders would far rather be considered bad than mad. This is especially true for criminals who act to further their own political cause. Being labeled insane signals that their point of view has no credibility and is just the product of a diseased mind. This is the reason perhaps that the Unabomber Theodore Kaczynski rejected his attorney's attempts to plead insanity. He may have felt that a claim of insanity would negate his antitechnology ideology, articulated in his lengthy manifesto published in the *Washington Post* under threat of continued bombings.

Unlike political fanatics who reject insanity as an option, in cases of murdering moms, the defense is often employed in an attempt to excuse infanticides committed in the throes of postpartum psychosis. At times, the strategy has been successful, as in Andrea Yates's Texas retrial for drowning her five children. Apparently, juries are not as reluctant to spare a defendant with whom they may sympathize, notwithstanding the defenselessness of her young victims.

Despite the limited usage of the NGRI defense overall, many Americans call for its elimination, and some state legislatures have complied. Four states (Idaho, Kansas, Montana, and Utah) have abolished the defense. More than a dozen states have instituted the guilty but mentally ill (GBMI) alternative. The GBMI option ensures that the defendant is confined in custody, yet because of the mental illness, he or she serves time in a psychiatric facility rather than a correctional facility.

Some legal scholars have also argued for the elimination of NGRI, but not for the same knee-jerk emotional reasons that seem to underlie the popular viewpoint. According to Norval Morris, for example, the NGRI defense is simply unnecessary. If a mental disease is so profound that the defendant cannot form criminal intent, then he should not be convicted of a crime but should instead be civilly committed to a psychiatric facility.[6]

At the end of the day, the GBMI alternative may do little more than give jurors a comfortable alternative when struggling over what to decide with regard to a mentally ill defendant whom they believe committed the crime. There is essentially little difference between a defendant who is found guilty and then transferred to a psychiatric facility until well enough to return to prison and a defendant found GBMI who goes immediately to a psychiatric facility until well enough to be transferred to prison to serve the remainder of the sentence.

In April 2010, a Massachusetts jury rejected an insanity plea from defendant John Odgren in connection to his fatal stabbing of James Alenson in a bathroom at Lincoln-Sudbury Regional High School. Despite Odgren's psychiatric history—involving Asperger's syndrome, ADHD, bipolar disorder, and depression—the jury convicted Odgren of first-degree murder, leading to a mandatory sentence of life without parole eligibility. Because of his significant and long-standing mental illness, Odgren didn't spend even an hour in prison but was immediately transferred to a psychiatric facility for evaluation and treatment, where he would remain until such time that he could be moved to prison. Had Massachusetts used GBMI, the jury may very well have settled on this option. In the end, however, it would not have made any practical difference.

Revelations Under Hypnosis

The problems associated with using hypnosis to improve the recall of eyewitnesses to crimes, described in Chapter 13, are compounded when applied to defendants in trials involving the question of legal insanity. The fact that hypnotized subjects can confidently recall, create, or alter their biographies casts doubt on the accuracy of memories. On the one hand, it is quite possible that a hypnotized subject will reveal painful yet accurate memories. On the other hand, subjects can fabricate events in their past if it suits the occasion, the context, or some ulterior motive.

Forensic psychiatrist Dorothy Otnow Lewis, for example, was hired by defense counsel in the Arthur Shawcross case to reveal his motivation and to support a plea of insanity in his trial for the murders of prostitutes in Rochester, New York. Based on sessions of hypnosis in which she age-regressed Shawcross for early memories of mistreatment, Lewis testified that Shawcross suffered from posttraumatic stress disorder brought on in part by experiences of abuse during his childhood. At first, he recalled having a normal upbringing and failed to reveal any abusive experiences. After lengthy and persistent probing under hypnosis, however, Shawcross finally "remembered" being sodomized by his mother with a broomstick and being forced to perform oral sex with her.

Did Lewis's discovery of suppressed and painful memories of abuse in Shawcross's background reflect an uncompromising effort to uncover the truth about deeply hidden secrets? Or did Shawcross finally give his examiner exactly what he figured she expected to hear? Either way, Shawcross's mother called her son a liar, and, given his attempt to save himself through the insanity plea, he certainly had very good reason to fabricate or exaggerate bad childhood experiences. We really can't know for certain.

In forensic work, the hypnotist deals with a subject who may have a stake in faking a hypnotic trance and divulging inaccurate information about himself and his past. The hypnotist can actually create the information through subtle and perhaps not-so-subtle suggestions to the subject. Thus, it is possible for an individual who may indeed have felt intimidated as a child to recall under hypnosis experiences of abuse, particularly if the hypnotist solicits such recollections and the subject has a self-serving interest in providing them.

The case of serial murderer Kenneth A. Bianchi provides another revealing example of how hypnosis has been exploited to find support for the child abuse explanation for murderous impulses. In 1977 and 1978, Bianchi and his cousin Angelo Buono abducted, tortured, raped, and murdered 10 young women, whose bodies they dumped along roadsides in the Los Angeles area. Kenneth Bianchi's insanity defense was centered on the theory that he suffered from a multiple personality disorder, a psychiatric condition that has since been predesignated as dissociative identity disorder. As discussed in Chapter 3, this disorder is characterized by the presence of two or more distinct personalities sharing the same body and is believed to stem from a history of severe child abuse. An abused child escapes from cruel parental treatment by developing a fantasy world of pleasure and kindness. At the same time, the angry and hateful feelings toward the abusive parent are stored in a reservoir that the child suppresses. In later life, the two perspectives—the loving and the hateful—split into their own personalities, which compete for control. The angry "person" takes turns with various alter egos for dominance over the same body.

If Bianchi in fact had this psychiatric condition, it could easily explain and reconcile how someone as seemingly nice as Bianchi was able to commit the heinous crimes with which he was charged. Through hypnosis, a second personality surfaced—that of "Steve," a hostile, crude, impatient, and sadistic character who proudly claimed responsibility for the slayings. "Killing a broad doesn't make any difference to me," bragged Steve. Everything now made sense to the psychiatrists. Bianchi was advised by his hypnotist that his medical history failed to include the kind of documentation of child abuse that would be needed to support his insanity defense. Hypnotized once more, Bianchi then recalled a dream about "a woman putting his hands over a kitchen stove fire while he was young." Finally, the psychiatrists had the evidence of abuse that was lacking!

As the court hearings on Bianchi's sanity approached, the proposed diagnosis and the hypnotically included evidence began to crumble when subjected to external validation. Bianchi's mother did confess that she had threatened her boy, "See this fire? If I catch you stealing once more, I'll hold your hand over this stove." But she denied ever going further than a threat. Moreover, there was no evidence of burns or scarring in Bianchi's detailed childhood medical file. At best, the hypnotically included recollection was just a fearful memory transformed into an imagined event. At worst, it was the attempt of a pathological liar to escape justice.

CAPITAL PUNISHMENT

There are few issues that seem to create as much rancor, disagreement, and divide as the death penalty. Some Americans insist that killing for any reason, even under lawful state authority, is simply immoral. Other opponents of capital punishment argue that it is wrong to kill in order to send the message that it is wrong to kill. Still others express concerns over cost, racial bias, and the possibility of error.

More Americans, however, maintain a different view, supporting the use of capital punishment as an appropriate measure of justice, whether or not it deters others by example. Some advocate capital punishment for a broad array of murderers, whereas others more selectively would restrict its use to those who might be considered "the worst of the worst." Many proponents are especially incensed that some murderers can ever be released on parole or following commutation, given the fact that for their victims, there is no reversal, parole, or commutation from death.

The debate over the appropriate penalty for those who take a life often fails to distinguish, unfortunately, between the various kinds of homicides discussed in Chapter 1 (i.e., first- and second-degree murder, voluntary and involuntary manslaughter). Although most states do indeed allow parole, early release, good time, furloughs, and so on, for lesser forms of homicide, statutes on first-degree murder in most jurisdictions are hardly lenient.

Table 14.1 summarizes the penalties available state by state for first-degree murder convictions. As shown, nearly two-thirds of the states currently have a death penalty in place, although this represents three fewer states than just five years ago. However, most states use the death penalty sparingly. In fact, 65% of all executions carried out in the United States since 1976 were under the jurisdiction of just five states: Texas, Virginia, Oklahoma, Florida, and Missouri. As an alternative to capital punishment, all states but one (Alaska) can and do incarcerate at least certain first-degree murderers for life without the possibility of parole.

The public, it appears, is grossly misinformed about the life without parole sentence. Citizens hear about killers released on parole (generally those convicted of manslaughter or second-degree murder) and assume that this is the norm for all convicted killers, even first-degree murderers. Criminologist William Bowers, for example, conducted a telephone survey of 603 residents of Massachusetts, a state that has mandatory life without parole for first-degree murder. Only 3% of those interviewed were aware of the lack of parole eligibility for first-degree murderers.

A U.S. Department of Justice report on sentencing patterns for felony defendants provides some information on how homicide defendants are actually handled by the state criminal courts.[7] Of the 8,467 defendants convicted in 2006 of homicide (murder and nonnegligent manslaughter), 93% were sent to prison, one-quarter of them with a life sentence. Of the remaining defendants who received

Table 14.1 State Capital Murder Penalties

		Life Without Parole	
		Yes (N = 49)	No (N = 1)
Death Penalty	Yes (N = 31)	AL, AZ, AR, CA, CO, FL, GA, ID, IN, KS, KY, LA, MS, MO, MT, NE, NV, NH, NC, OH, OK, OR, PA, SC, SD, TN, TX, UT, VA, WA, WY	
	No (N = 19)	CT, DE, HI, IL, IA, ME, MD, MA, MI, MN, NJ, NM, NY, ND, RI, VT, WV, WI	AK

some term of years in prison rather than life (or death), the average maximum sentence exceeded 20 years.

In addition, life sentences are increasingly coming to mean that a defendant will indeed remain locked up for life. In 2012, 28% of lifers were serving life without parole eligibility, compared to 26% in 2003 and 18% in 1992. As of 2012, the number of prisoners serving life sentences in the state and federal prisons reached a new record of close to 160,000; nearly 50,000 without parole eligibility.[8] These offenders cannot be released, except in the unusual instance of a commutation or pardon.

Fueled by a widespread misunderstanding of the penalty structure for murder convictions, as well as by concern over rising homicide rates, public support for the death penalty mounted steadily over the final quarter of the 20th century. With this encouragement from the populace, the number of prisoners put to death increased as well. As shown in Figure 14.1, the number of executions rose fairly steadily from 1980 until 2000 but then declined thereafter. Whereas in the mid-1970s, the public opinion in this country was virtually evenly split on the appropriateness of capital punishment, by the mid-1990s support for the death penalty was overwhelming, with nearly 80% of Americans in favor of it. Apparently, some citizens simply view an execution as the only absolute guarantee against a convicted killer being released on parole, being commuted, or even escaping over the prison walls. In one national poll, only 4% of respondents believed that criminals sentenced to life incarceration would actually spend their lives in prison.

Arguably, no other aspect of the criminal law receives as much attention as capital punishment, despite its relatively minimal utilization. Even at its peak level of use in 1935, when nearly 199 convicts were put to death, murderers under a death sentence represented a tiny fraction of convicted killers and an even smaller portion of convicted criminals generally.

Notwithstanding its limited application, capital punishment is an issue that has been used as a litmus test for what kind of public officials we elect to office. For example, a case can easily be made that Democratic presidential nominee

Figure 14.1 Executions in the United States, 1930–2017

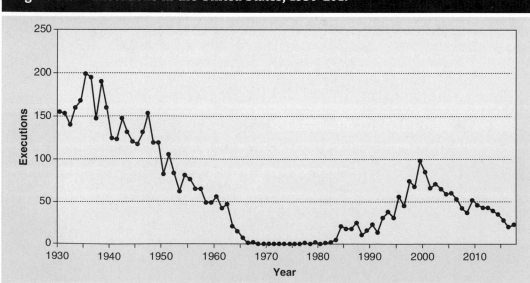

Michael Dukakis lost to Republican George H. W. Bush in the 1988 campaign because of his stand on capital punishment. Even though most death penalty cases (nearly 99%) fall within state, rather than federal, jurisdiction, the voting public was concerned about Dukakis's liberal anti–death penalty ideology.

Bill Clinton eased his way into the White House with a pro–death penalty stand. As the governor of Arkansas, Clinton signed the death warrant for an inmate executed under less-than-ideal circumstances. Candidate Clinton left the presidential campaign trail in 1992 to be present in Arkansas for the execution of Ricky Ray Rector, a severely brain-damaged black man who had killed a white police officer (and then shot himself in the head). Rector was obviously intellectually impaired and/or mentally ill. He routinely howled like an animal in the days leading up to his execution and did not understand what was about to happen to him. Rector even saved the cake from his last meal for a later that would never come. Although a decade too late to spare Rector's life, the U.S. Supreme Court in 2002 ruled unconstitutional the execution of prisoners who are intellectually disabled (or, as described at that time, "mentally retarded").

Over the past couple of decades, as homicide rates and executions have declined, public support for capital punishment has waned. Even with shifting public sentiment, a majority of most sociopolitical segments of the population still support the use of the death penalty. As shown in Table 14.2, a majority of Americans of both sexes, of all age groups, of all education levels (except for the most highly educated), residing in all regions, and of all religions favor capital punishment. Opponents outnumber proponents only among nonwhites, liberals, those with graduate degrees, and Democrats. No wonder that very few politicians who are opposed to the death penalty can get elected to public office, regardless of the strength of their record in other areas.

Table 14.2 Public Opinion on the Death Penalty for Murder, 2016

Category	Number of Respondents	Favor	Oppose	No Answer
All Respondents	2,867	57%	37%	6%
Sex				
Male	1,296	63%	33%	4%
Female	1,571	53%	40%	7%
Race				
White	2,108	62%	33%	5%
Black	463	39%	53%	8%
Other	296	50%	39%	10%
Age				
18–29	555	54%	41%	5%
30–49	978	58%	36%	6%
50–64	793	59%	35%	7%
65+	529	58%	36%	6%

(*Continued*)

Table 14.2 (Continued)

Category	Number of Respondents	Favor	Oppose	No Answer
Highest Degree				
Graduate	300	46%	49%	5%
Bachelor	525	51%	42%	6%
Associate	215	65%	29%	6%
High school	1,481	62%	33%	5%
Less than high school	340	54%	39%	8%
Region				
East	483	53%	41%	7%
Midwest	667	63%	33%	4%
South	1,073	57%	37%	6%
West	644	55%	38%	7%
Political Party				
Democrat	926	45%	49%	5%
Republican	647	74%	21%	5%
Independent	1,182	58%	36%	7%
Political Ideology				
Liberal	788	42%	54%	4%
Moderate	1,027	61%	32%	7%
Conservative	947	68%	27%	5%
Religion				
Protestant	1,348	60%	33%	6%
Catholic	668	56%	38%	5%
Jewish	56	48%	46%	5%
Other	149	56%	36%	7%
None	618	54%	42%	4%

Source: National Opinion Research Center, General Social Survey.

It is important to view these opinion levels with a grain of salt. Although the sampling and data collection approaches are quite sound, the wording of such questions as "Do you favor or oppose the death penalty for first-degree murder?" may not fully elicit an accurate picture of public sentiment. First, public opinion varies considerably based on the exact nature of the first-degree murder. Whereas the rape, torture, and murder of a child may fully arouse the public's thirst for the supreme penalty of death, felony-murders in which robbery victims are shot to death do not quite spark the same level of vehemence and vengeance.[9] More important, Americans may change their opinion depending on the alternatives— that is, the death penalty compared to what other punishment? Several polls have shown that when presented a choice of death penalty or life without parole, public support is fairly evenly divided. For example, the 2015 American Values

Survey from the Public Religion Research Institute found that 52% of the 2,695 respondents preferred life without parole, while 47% preferred the death penalty.[10] Moreover, opinions varied by political affiliation. Nearly two-thirds of Republicans voiced a preference for the death penalty over the alternative of life without parole, whereas about the same percentage of Democrats expressed a preference for a life sentence without the possibility of parole.

Curiously, whereas much of our criminal law pertaining to homicide developed 200 years ago in an attempt to limit those offenders who could face the penalty of death, in recent years most changes in homicide statutes have been introduced to expand the number of capital crimes. Following years of protest and disfavor during which a majority of Americans actually opposed the death penalty, a virtual moratorium on capital punishment started in the late 1960s and was formalized in 1972 when the U.S. Supreme Court struck down the death penalty. Based on arguments that minorities and the poor were more likely to be sentenced to death, the Court held (in *Furman v. Georgia*) that the death penalty was being applied in a capricious, arbitrary, discriminatory, and therefore unconstitutional manner. Importantly, the U.S. Supreme Court did not hold that capital punishment was inherently cruel and unusual but instead set out a process for how the death penalty could be administered in a fair and constitutional manner.

The Supreme Court also added in a later decision that the application of the death penalty must be in proportion to the seriousness of the crime: Only the most grievous acts should qualify for the supreme penalty. Because of the proportionality notion, it could be ruled unconstitutional to execute rapists. There is, however, another more practical reason for eliminating rape as a capital crime. Despite the historical practice, executing a rapist may even encourage murder by removing any disincentive for the offender to kill his victim in order to prevent her from testifying against him.

In the wake of this landmark 1972 *Furman* decision, more than three dozen states hurried to redraft their murder statutes to include a death penalty consistent with the Supreme Court's framework. To pass constitutional muster, the guidelines for sentencing a defendant to death would have to be clearly defined. A first-degree murder conviction was not sufficient. To limit the potential for bias, states had to identify those aggravating factors that would warrant it and mitigating factors that would disqualify it. In addition, the trial would need to be bifurcated so that the fact-finding guilt phase of the trial would be separate from the penalty phase. Thus, should a jury find a defendant guilty of capital murder (murder in the first degree with one or more special or aggravating circumstances), the trial would then proceed to hear testimony about the most appropriate sanction, usually either death or life imprisonment.

The Deterrence Debate

Volumes have been written debating the utility and appropriateness of the death penalty. One controversy that has received the most attention is that of its general deterrence—that is, whether the existence of the death penalty discourages potential murderers from following through with the act. Could life be so precious even to hardened criminals that the ultimate penalty might dissuade them more than any other sanction?

Much of the early research on this topic, conducted through the mid-1970s, suggested that the deterrence argument was little more than wishful thinking. Comparative studies showed that death penalty states did not have lower homicide rates than similar neighboring states without such a law.[11] In 1975, however, economist Isaac Ehrlich surprised the criminological community and changed the legislative debate by claiming to have demonstrated through a sophisticated statistical analysis that each execution deters about eight homicides.[12]

On the wings of Ehrlich's provocative study, several states rushed to enact death penalty legislation. Death penalty supporters seemed finally to have some hard evidence with which to defend their point of view. It was not until several years later that critics of Ehrlich's research were able to identify the fatal flaws in his work. The most important was that Ehrlich's analysis mainly hinged on the fact that during the late 1960s and early 1970s, when the death penalty was rarely used (only three executions were staged from 1966 to 1976), the homicide rate soared. Yet, other crimes soared as well, even those such as auto theft, which had little to do with capital punishment. Clearly, other factors were responsible for the growth in crime during the 1960s and 1970s, including a homicide rate that doubled from 1963 to 1973.

By the time that Ehrlich's work and a few similar studies by a handful of his disciples were refuted, the United States had seen renewed support for capital punishment. By then, the pro–death penalty movement had gained so much momentum that the deterrence argument was no longer vital to undergird the pro–death penalty position.

Despite a prevailing view over the past 2 decades that the death penalty is not a deterrent to murder, a handful of studies have appeared offering new evidence of a deterrence effect. Hoping to resolve the controversy, a 2012 panel of the National Academy of Sciences closely reviewed the existing body of research and concluded that studies claiming that the death penalty is a deterrent were methodologically flawed. The panel further concluded that overall there was no solid evidence that capital punishment tended either to increase or to decrease homicide rates.[13]

On balance, therefore, the scientific evidence is fairly clear in showing that the death penalty fails to deter murderers—that is, any more than life imprisonment does. Those offenders who are not dissuaded from committing a murder by the prospect of being locked up for life are also not likely to be discouraged by the prospect of death. Thus, although the death penalty may deter in an absolute sense (even murderers fear death), in a relative sense it is no more of a deterrent than the life imprisonment alternative. The key term is *prospect*, or the perceived probability that the penalty will be applied. Those who act with deliberation, planning, and premeditation generally view their risk of apprehension as low. If one is not caught, there can be no punishment, regardless of what penalty is on the books.

Although life imprisonment may be virtually as powerful a deterrent, many Americans are concerned about their tax dollars being used unnecessarily and wastefully to house and feed convicted murderers for the rest of their lives. Yet economic analyses have shown that the cost savings associated with removing a prisoner from a cell and executing him or her have been grossly exaggerated. Given the fixed overhead costs of incarceration—utilities, salaries, and maintenance— relatively little is saved by staging an execution. On the other side of the fiscal ledger, moreover, the cost of capital trials tends to be rather high. Given the life-and-death stakes, the necessary procedural safeguards in place in some states in an attempt to avoid a wrongful execution provide capital defendants with the best defense that the taxpayers can buy. Capital murder trials tend to be many times more costly than noncapital murder trials, given the complexity and length of these prosecutions. For example, the trial of Night Stalker Richard Ramirez cost California $1.8 million, and that was before any appeals were filed. Florida ended up spending more than $5 million on Ted Bundy's two trials, multiple appeals, and 9.5 years on death row until his execution, whereas incarcerating him under a life sentence would have cost less than 10% as much. The process could be streamlined, of course, but at a very different cost—the possibility of executing an innocent person.

Still, for many people, according to polls, the defining issue is justice or vengeance—an eye for an eye, a tooth for a tooth. According to a series of Gallup polls taken between 1991 and 2014, supporters of capital punishment overwhelmingly tend to cite retribution as the primary reason for their position, well ahead of any other justification.[14] Many supporters insist, despite the lack of deterrence and the costliness, that it is the just punishment, not to mention a surefire way of preventing the offender from repeating his offense, outside or even inside prison.

Race and the Death Penalty

The concern about racial discrimination, which motivated the 1972 moratorium on executions, no longer appears to sway public opinion or even the fairly conservative composition of the Supreme Court over the past three decades. In *McCleskey v. Kemp* (1987), the justices reviewed and debated the results of a statistical study, offered by University of Iowa law professor David Baldus, based on more than 2,000 murder cases in Georgia during the 1970s.[15] Baldus concluded that, even while controlling for a host of relevant factors, black defendants who killed white victims had the greatest likelihood of receiving the death penalty. Even so, the Supreme Court's majority dismissed the statistical correlation between race and sentencing, indicating that a defendant on appeal would need to demonstrate racial prejudice in his or her particular trial, not a statistical pattern in cases generally.

Under current operating procedures, there are actually more whites sentenced to death than blacks, both in absolute numbers and in relation to the homicide offending rates. As shown in Figure 14.2, the gap between the number of white

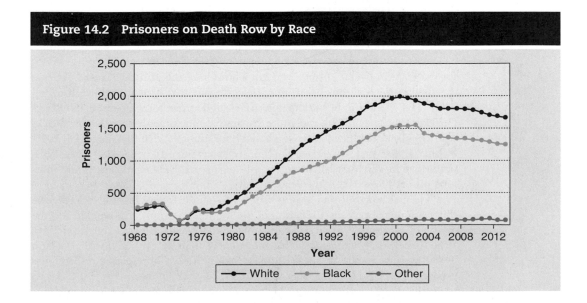

Figure 14.2 Prisoners on Death Row by Race

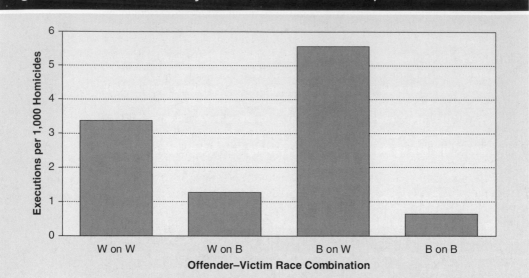

Figure 14.3 Execution Rates by Race of Victim and Offender, 1977–2015 Combined

and black prisoners sitting on death row nationwide has widened over the past 40 years since capital punishment was restored.

The pattern of racial discrimination is much subtler, however. Figure 14.3 shows rates of execution (executions per 1,000 cases) for offender–victim race combinations, by comparing solved homicides from 1976 through 2015 with executions through the end of 2016. Overall, regardless of race combination, there were 2.4 defendants executed per 1,000 known murderers. The differences according to race are, however, quite provocative and have different implications when probing below the surface. The execution rate for white killers (3.2 per 1,000 offenders) is double that for blacks (1.5 per 1,000 killers). Furthermore, those who kill whites are five times as likely to be executed as those who kill blacks (specifically 3.8 executions per 1,000 killers of white victims as compared with 0.7 executions per 1,000 murderers of blacks).

But when examining the race combinations of offenders and their victims, an apparent injustice emerges. As Baldus found for Georgia cases from the 1970s, for the country overall, blacks who kill whites have the greatest chance of being executed (5.6 executions per 1,000), much higher than that for whites who kill whites (3.4 executions per 1,000), four times higher than for whites who kill blacks (1.3 executions per 1,000), and, more disparately, nine times higher than for blacks who kill blacks (0.6 per 1,000). It is telling, for example, that on August 24, 2017, Florida, a state that has carried out 93 executions since 1977 and 289 since 1924, performed its very first execution of a white person for killing a black victim in its long history of exercising the death penalty.

Thus, although it may appear that black murderers are less likely to receive the death penalty, this is a function of the intraracial nature of homicide and the racism of a criminal justice system that places less value on black murder victims. When blacks kill whites, they are more likely than any other offender–victim dyad to receive the death penalty. Indeed, a long history of scientific research has exposed the racial bias associated with the use of capital punishment.

Other Issues Surrounding the Death Penalty

The death penalty is less likely to be carried out against women than men. From 1977 through 2016, 1,426 men and only 16 women have been put to death in the United States. Clearly, the gender ratio for executions is far more lopsided than that for murder. Women account for roughly 10% of all homicide offenders and only about 1% of executions.

Until fairly recently, the issue of age—specifically whether juveniles should be eligible for the death penalty—was hotly debated. But on March 1, 2005, abolitionists cheered when the U.S. Supreme Court announced, in *Roper v. Simmons*, that the death penalty for juveniles was unconstitutional, in violation of the Eighth Amendment's ban on cruel and unusual punishment. The decision ended a capital punishment practice in 19 states and took 72 minors off death row.

The rapid growth in the number of executions performed in this country during the 1990s was followed by a sharp downturn, specifically, from 98 executions in 1999 to just 23 in 2017. The number of prisoners on America's death rows has declined as well, from a high of about 3,600 in 2000 down to fewer than 3,000 in 2016. The relative dearth of executions over the past several years and the declining death row population stem from a variety of factors.

The precipitous drop in the nation's homicide rates in the 1990s and beyond reduced the number of new death sentences and death row admissions. In addition, the range of offenders who are eligible for the death penalty has been progressively narrowed through appellate action. As shown in Table 14.3, the U.S. Supreme Court has, over the past few decades, delivered a host of decisions that exclude certain classes of defendants—the legally insane, the mentally ill, the intellectually disabled, as well as the young—from being subject to the death penalty.

An additional reason for the sharply lowered number of executions in the United States is purely a matter of logistics. In recent years states have struggled to obtain the appropriate sedation drugs for the three-drug protocol used in lethal injections. Several countries prohibit drugs to be exported to the United States if the purpose is to carry out an execution. In addition, drug manufacturers, whose core mission is to promote health and healing, refuse to allow their products to be employed for such nefarious purposes. Further complicating matters, medical professionals keep as much distance as possible from the procedure out of their ethical commitment to doing no harm. As a result, correctional officials are fumbling and bumbling to find the right solution.

Table 14.3   U.S. Supreme Court Decisions Limiting Use of the Death Penalty

Year	Supreme Court Case	Type of Exclusion
1977	*Coker v. Georgia*	Offenders who rape an adult woman
1982	*Enmund v. Florida*	Offenders who are minor participants in felony
1986	*Ford v. Wainwright*	Inmates who are insane
1988	*Thompson v. Oklahoma*	Offenders who kill while under age 16
2002	*Atkins v. Virginia*	Intellectually disabled defendants
2005	*Roper v. Simmons*	Offenders who kill while under age 18
2008	*Kennedy v. Louisiana*	Offenders who commit crimes not involving death

Without the appropriate mix of drugs, the condemned can experience excruciating and prolonged pain during a process that is supposedly more humane than the electric chair, the gas chamber, and a variety of more archaic methods. It took nearly 2 hours for the state of Arizona to execute Joseph Rudolph Wood, during most of which time the 55-year-old double-murderer appeared, according to witnesses, to be gasping for breath and grunting in pain. Botched executions have also been reported in other states, horrifying death penalty opponents and many proponents as well. The punishment is supposed to be death, not torture.

In April 2017, the state of Arkansas attempted to execute as many as seven convicted murderers over a span of 11 days because its precious supply of midazolam was due to expire at the end of the month. Despite legal challenges about the effectiveness of the midazolam to avoid undue suffering, the state managed to execute four convicted murderers before the clock ran out.

Besides the reduced number of admissions, hundreds of inmates have been removed from death row because of a determination of innocence or procedural irregularities. Spearheaded by attorneys affiliated with the Innocence Project, at least 20 condemned men were freed after new DNA testing of old crime scene evidence proved their innocence before the death sentence could be carried out. Even more prisoners have been freed or retried based on revelations of police or prosecutor misconduct (e.g., planted incriminating evidence or suppressed exculpatory evidence) as well as perjured testimony by witnesses. Between 1973 and 2016, a total of 156 condemned prisoners had their charges dismissed, were pardoned, or were acquitted on retrial.

It remains a matter of considerable debate, however, whether and how many executed prisoners were in fact innocent (as opposed to merely improperly or unfairly convicted). A wrongful conviction is not the same as a conviction wrongfully obtained. The former reflects an innocent person who is convicted, whereas the latter describes a possibly guilty person who is convicted through improper means.

Growing awareness of overturned capital cases has made many observers extremely nervous about the finality of the death penalty. In 2000, Governor George Ryan of Illinois, a state that has traditionally been willing to execute murderers, made history and headlines by calling a moratorium on executions until the reliability of capital prosecutions could be determined. On announcing this move, he noted that the 13 condemned prisoners removed from death row in recent years based on innocence was one more than the number of executions that the state had performed since the restoration of capital punishment. Then, just prior to leaving office, Governor Ryan commuted the death sentences of all 156 inmates on the Illinois death row (along with 11 others). Most of the sentences were reduced to life without parole. Subsequently, in 2011, the state of Illinois formally abolished capital punishment largely out of concern for the possibility of executing the innocent. Ryan was, in a sense, a trendsetter. In recent years, the governors of four other states with the death penalty on the books (Oregon in 2011, Colorado in 2013, Washington in 2014, and Pennsylvania in 2015) imposed a moratorium on executions for various reasons, including concern for errors.

In a nation whose system of jurisprudence honors and protects the rights of the innocent over all else, growing concern for wrongful executions may signal that the days of the death penalty are numbered. For years, the United States has stood alone among Western nations in the practice of executing murderers. Our foreign peers—countries such as Australia, Canada, Finland, France, Germany, Italy, the Netherlands, New Zealand, Norway, and the United Kingdom—abolished capital punishment. Others, such as Mexico and Greece, have retained the penalty of death, but only for military crimes and high treason. Even the Russian Federation has imposed a moratorium on executions, although the provision for capital punishment remains on the books. Meanwhile, the United States is conspicuous among the list of nations imposing the death penalty for common murderers, a collection that includes the countries of Afghanistan, China, Cuba, Iran, Iraq, and Saudi Arabia.

At this juncture, there remains little chance that the U.S. Supreme Court will do much in the years ahead to change the law on capital punishment, especially with the conservative imbalance in its current membership. The Court has repeatedly held that, in general, the penalty does not violate the Eighth Amendment prohibition against cruel and unusual punishments or the Fourteenth Amendment's equal protection clause.

JUVENILE INJUSTICE

The administration of juvenile justice combines two processes: the circumstances under which juveniles are transferred to the adult criminal court for prosecution and the range of punishments that are available should they be convicted. In recent years, the U.S. Supreme Court has forged significant change in how states may punish violent juveniles. In a pair of decisions, the Court ruled against executing those whose crimes were committed before the age of 16 (*Thompson v. Oklahoma*, 1988) and then those whose crimes were committed before the age of 18 (*Roper v. Simmons*, 2005).

The Supreme Court was especially impressed and persuaded by the scientific evidence regarding brain development that was described in Chapter 5, specifically the slower development of the frontal lobe portion of the brain that controls judgment and decision making. In ruling against capital punishment for minors, the majority saw a clear and important distinction between juvenile killers and their older counterparts:

> The reality that juveniles still struggle to define their identity means it is less supportable to conclude that even a heinous crime committed by a juvenile is evidence of irretrievably depraved character. From a moral standpoint it would be misguided to equate the failings of a minor with those of an adult, for a greater possibility exists that a minor's character deficiencies will be reformed. (*Roper v. Simmons*, 543 U.S. 551 [2005], p. 16)

Even before the abolition of capital punishment for juveniles, very few convicts were executed for crimes they had committed as a minor. With or without the death penalty, a vast array of sentencing options exists for punishing young killers—everything from a short period of years for those retained in the juvenile court system to life sentences without parole eligibility for many of those prosecuted as adults.

As indicated earlier in Chapter 5, waiver procedures vary from state to state; some allow discretion by judges or prosecutors, whereas others require transfer under certain conditions based on age and offense characteristics. States also differ in terms of the sentences that juvenile murderers may receive, if convicted.

The elimination of the death penalty for juveniles as a result of U.S. Supreme Court decisions did not mean that the criminal justice system would suddenly go soft on punishing juveniles. With adult sentencing for juvenile murderers a common practice around the country, thousands of minors were still being condemned in a sense—condemned to die a natural death behind bars. By 2010, over 2,500 prisoners were serving life sentences without the possibility of parole for crimes committed before age 18.[16]

There was more to be done to reform the nation's exceptionally harsh sentencing patterns for juveniles, beyond just taking the death penalty off the table. In 2010, the U.S. Supreme Court in *Graham v. Florida* abolished the use of juvenile life without parole for nonhomicide cases, a decision that affected the fate of 123 prisoners nationwide, 77 from Florida. Although a modest advance, the Court signaled a much more significant move was potentially just around the corner, awaiting the right test case to challenge laws sentencing juvenile murders to a lifetime behind bars. In his majority opinion, Justice Anthony Kennedy concluded:

> *Roper* established that because juveniles have lessened culpability they are less deserving of the most severe punishments. 543 U.S., at 569. As compared to adults, juveniles have a "lack of maturity and an underdeveloped sense of responsibility"; they "are more vulnerable or susceptible to negative influences and outside pressures, including peer pressure"; and their characters are "not as well formed." These salient characteristics mean that "[i]t is difficult even for expert psychologists to differentiate between the juvenile offender whose crime reflects unfortunate yet transient immaturity, and the rare juvenile offender whose crime reflects irreparable corruption." Id., at 573. Accordingly, "juvenile offenders cannot with reliability be classified among the worst offenders." Id., at 569. A juvenile is not absolved of responsibility for his actions, but his transgression "is not as morally reprehensible as that of an adult." Thompson, supra, at 835 (plurality opinion). (*Graham v. Florida*, 560 U.S. 48 [2010], pp. 16–17)

Just two years following *Graham*, the U.S. Supreme Court ruled by a narrow 5–4 margin in *Miller v. Alabama* (2012) that laws mandating life without parole for juvenile murderers constituted cruel and unusual punishment in violation of the Eighth Amendment. Such a rigid approach to punishing juveniles failed to consider factors that might mitigate a young murderer's culpability for his or her crimes. "Mandatory life without parole for a juvenile precludes consideration of his chronological age and its hallmark features—among them, immaturity, impetuosity, and failure to appreciate risks and consequences," wrote Justice Elena Kagan in speaking for the majority. "It prevents taking into account the family and home environment that surrounds him—and from which he cannot usually extricate himself—no matter how brutal or dysfunctional."

Miller instantly invalidated sentencing statutes in the 28 states not allowing for mitigating factors and special circumstances that might warrant parole eligibility. The Court did not go as far as to rule against life without parole for juveniles altogether, just situations in which judges were not given any other option following a first-degree murder conviction. However, many state legislatures, as they took up the task of reformulating their juvenile murder statutes, went the next step by banning nonparolable life sentences. Specifically, as shown in Figure 14.4, 19 states have completely banned such sentences for juvenile murders no matter how reprehensible and atrocious the circumstances surrounding the crime. An additional four states modified their laws to eliminate juvenile life without parole except in limited situations. Some other states whose mandatory penalties were overturned by *Miller* took a different route, simply replacing a life sentence with a fixed term of 50 years or more, a virtual life sentence.

An important related issue that *Miller* left unanswered was whether such reforms should be retroactive. Although states could no longer mandate life without

Figure 14.4   Juvenile Life Without Parole (JLWOP) Sentencing by State

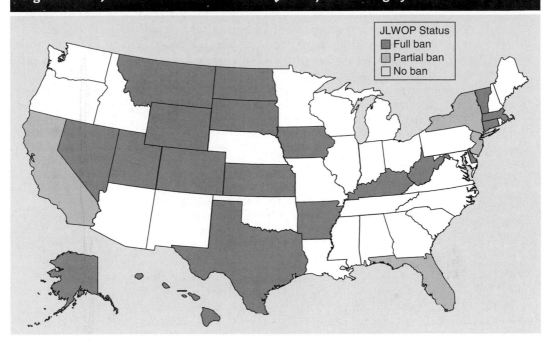

parole for juveniles, would prisoners currently serving life terms necessarily have their sentences modified? This was not a trivial matter, not just because it would require resentencing hundreds of offenders. The families of the victims had been assured that the person who had killed their loved one would never walk free. Some jurisdictions, through legislative action or state appellate court decision, boldly moved in favor of retroactivity. Then, in 2016, the U.S. Supreme Court resolved the matter, ruling in *Montgomery v. Louisiana* that *Miller* should extend to defendants whose crimes were committed in prior years.

Of course, in over half the states, juveniles can still be sentenced to prison for the rest of their lives as long as the determination is made with consideration of aggravating and mitigating circumstances. At this point, over 2,000 prisoners remain under life sentences or virtual life sentences for murders committed before their 18th birthday, making the United States the only nation that sentences juveniles to prison without hope of ever tasting freedom. For advocacy groups such as the Campaign for the Fair Sentencing of Youth, there is still more work to be done to achieve the goal of completely eliminating this cruel but all too usual practice.

ENDNOTES

1.   Gallup Organization, "Crime," http://www
     .gallup.com/poll/1603/crime.aspx.

2.   Richard Moran, *Knowing Right From
     Wrong: The Insanity Defense of Daniel McNaughtan*
     (New York: Simon and Schuster, 2000).

3.   John Hinckley's Letter to Jodie Foster Written
     Immediately Before Assassination Attempt, http://
     www.famous-trials.com/johnhinckley/533-letter.

4.   L. A. Callahan, M. J. Steadman, M. A. McGreevy,
     and P. C. Robbins, "The Volume and Characteristics

of Insanity Defense Pleas: An Eight-State Study," *Bulletin of the American Academy of Psychiatry and the Law* 19 (1991): 331–338.

5. "The Killer at Thurston High," directed by Michael Kirk, *Frontline* documentary, PBS, January 18, 2000.

6. Norval Morris, *Madness and Criminal Law* (Chicago: University of Chicago Press, 1982).

7. Sean Rosenmerkel, Matthew Durose, and Donald Farole Jr., *State Court Sentencing of Convicted Felons, 2006: Statistical Tables* (Washington, DC: Bureau of Justice Statistics, 2010).

8. Ashley Nellis and Jean Chung, "Life Goes On: The Historic Rise in Life Sentences in America," Sentencing Project, 2013.

9. James Alan Fox, Michael Radelet, and Julie Bonsteel, "Public Opinion on the Death Penalty in the Post-Furman Years," *New York University Review of Law and Social Change* 18 (1990–91): 499–528.

10. Robert P. Jones, Daniel Cox, Betsy Cooper, and Rachel Liene, *Anxiety, Nostalgia, and Mistrust* (Washington, DC: Public Religion Research Institute, 2015).

11. Thorsten J. Sellin, *Capital Punishment* (New York: Harper and Row, 1967).

12. Isaac Ehrlich, "The Deterrent Effect of Capital Punishment: A Question of Life and Death," *American Economic Review* 65 (1975): 397–417.

13. National Research Council, *Deterrence and the Death Penalty* (Washington, DC: National Academies Press, 2012).

14. Art Swift, "Americans: 'Eye for an Eye' Top Reason for Death Penalty," Gallup Poll, October 23, 2014.

15. David C. Baldus, Charles Pulaski, and George Woodworth, "Comparative Review of Death Sentences: An Empirical Study of the Georgia Experience," *Journal of Criminal Law and Criminology* 74 (1983): 661–753.

16. Equal Justice Initiative, *Human Rights Watch Reports, 2008–10* (Washington, DC: Amnesty International).

EPILOGUE: EPIDEMIC THINKING AND OVERRESPONSE

Whatever the current climate of public opinion, perceptions and attitudes are quite volatile and can easily be altered by high-profile events, regardless of their statistical prevalence. Crime rates may be at their lowest point in several decades, yet a particularly heinous episode of senseless violence, if covered extensively by the mass media, can quickly renew demands for tougher sanctions for criminals.

To suggest that the news media are overly reactive to extraordinary episodes is perhaps an understatement. Constantly seeking to increase their market shares, local and syndicated news outlets often treat the latest shocking murder case like a national catastrophe. Moreover, there is a clear tendency to hype their coverage by declaring the crime as the latest epidemic to confront the American public. The logic seems to be that if it isn't a raging epidemic, then no one will pay attention.

Almost every year, the news media contribute to constructing a new crime growth curve. Very few Americans realize that the current crime rate is lower than it has been in 30 years. The mid-1980s witnessed a serial murder panic fueled by outlandish reports that as many as 5,000 Americans were killed annually by these sexual predators. Next came a media-hyped scare in relation to carjackings, then home invasions, then sexual molestation in day care centers, then workplace killings, then road rage, then school shootings, then child abductions, and, most recently, active shooters. Many of the episodes on which the media focused their attention and their cameras were real in their impact on victims, yet statements concerning the risk to others were often exaggerated.

High-profile cases of missing children illustrate exactly how these so-called epidemics are invented. In February 2002, 7-year-old Danielle van Dam was snatched from her bedroom during the middle of the night, prompting a massive search of her San Diego neighborhood, as well as a nationwide appeal by her parents on the *Today Show* pleading her safe return. Three weeks later, however, the girl's charred and decomposed body was found near a small grove of trees east of San Diego. She had been abducted, molested, and murdered by her neighbor, 50-year-old David Westerfield.

"Bad things come in threes," it is said, and numbers 2 and 3 came in quick succession. In June, 14-year-old Elizabeth Smart was abducted from her bedroom while her younger sister watched in horror; 9 months later, Smart resurfaced alive and well after having roamed with a nomadic husband and wife team of religious zealots. Her abductor, who called himself Emmanuel, was a self-styled prophet with a long history of delusions that included fantasies of multiple child brides. In July 2002, a month following Smart's disappearance, 5-year-old Samantha Runnion was kidnapped as she was playing with a friend in the yard next to her home; her body was found the following day with evidence that she had been sexually molested and asphyxiated. Alejandro Avila, age 27, was arrested and subsequently convicted in Runnion's murder.

Eager to jump on the latest and scariest crime trend, the news media declared kidnapping the newest epidemic. One media outlet dramatically labeled the long, steamy months of 2002 as the "Summer of Abduction." Having considered the possibility that these abductions signaled a new and ominous trend, journalists and news directors began searching news wires far and wide for any story of a disappearance or attempted abduction to fit and confirm the epidemic theory. On Fox News Channel, Bill O'Reilly, formerly the host of *The O'Reilly Factor*, cited an erroneous statistic that 100,000 children are abducted each year by strangers. Hurriedly doing the math, he also miscalculated there to be more than 30 such kidnappings a day. Actually, the mathematically correct calculation would place the daily count at about 300 children, the host being off by an "O'Reilly Factor" of 10. If it were indeed the case that 100,000 children annually fall victim to stranger abduction, we would all likely be personally familiar with at least one such unfortunate child. Among a national population of 50 million youngsters under the age of 13, this prevalence of stranger abduction would translate to 1 out of every 500 children. At this rate, an average-size grade school would endure one stranger abduction each year. Stated in this way, the statistics seem more than a bit preposterous. Unfortunately, once these blatant exaggerations are stated as "facts" on one of the many 24-hour news channels, they are repeated and continue to contribute to uninformed policymaking.

Amid the tremendous media hype about child abductions by strangers, some sober perspective on the scope of the problem would surely have calmed some nervous parents and outraged politicians. The most reliable and trustworthy estimates of stranger–child abductions are in the hundreds, not hundred thousands. David Finkelhor and his colleagues place the stranger abduction figure at about 115 per year. Furthermore, the majority of these youngsters are eventually found alive. The less fortunate victims who are slain by their abductors number about 50 per year.[1]

Of course, the thought of any child being kidnapped, raped, and murdered is horrible, but in statistical terms it is hardly one of the greatest perils that children face on a daily basis—even if a serial predator is operating in the neighborhood. A child is more likely to be killed in a fall off of a bicycle than by being grabbed off the bike by a rapist or murderer; still, some parents are more apt to keep their children at home in protective custody than to enforce the use of the helmets. More children are killed each year by playing with their parents' loaded gun; yet some parents are more apt to lock up their children for safekeeping than their firearms.

With 50 million children in the United States under the age of 12, the likelihood of anyone ending up like Samantha Runnion is literally one in a million. For Samantha's family, of course, it matters not that her case is statistically exceptional. But for the rest of us, it matters a lot.

For the well-being of children, it is important that parents not pass along a sense of paranoia to their kids. Youngsters should not be made into prisoners of fear, constantly looking out for the boogeyman in a parked car. For society, it also matters—it matters that we resist the temptation to rush to enact legislation and public policy that is not well conceived.

As with other imagined epidemics, the intense focus on the issue of child abductions faded somewhat by the close of 2002, as Americans moved on to the next issue of the day. But in so many of these instances, also left behind is some poorly conceived policy response hurriedly crafted amid a climate of hysteria. Talk of an epidemic of workplace homicide with scores of disgruntled employees "going postal" may have enhanced efforts to support laid-off workers, but it also led to misguided efforts to profile unhappy workers rather than respond to their grievances. Widespread concern that our schools were populated by armed misfits who might "do a Columbine" may have forced educators to take issues such as bullying seriously, but it also resulted in serious infringements on the rights of many innocent students caught up in zero-tolerance policies.

In 2012, Americans witnessed, at least on their television screens, a series of shocking massacres, including deadly shooting sprees at a Colorado cinema and a Connecticut elementary school. By year's end, politicians, the press, and the public alike were obsessing over what some claimed to be a raging epidemic of random bloodshed. Many observers muddied the statistics by choosing to count cases in which multiple people were shot, but not necessarily killed, confusing the public by confounding mass casualty events with mass murders. Some media reports claimed there to be an average of one mass shooting a day in the United States, without any long-term data to discern whether the risk was increasing, decreasing, or remaining unchanged.[2] State legislatures and Congress felt compelled to respond to the apparent surge in random killings by debating new laws and procedures concerning guns, mental health, and security. However, the hard data on mass killings, as discussed in Chapter 9, confirmed that there was no significant increase in risk, only an increase in fear.

In the final analysis (literally, for this book at least), there is a lesson in our tendency to think in epidemic terms. It is important to view with healthy skepticism any public policy proposed in the wake of extraordinary and ghastly episodes of murder and mayhem.

ENDNOTES

1. David Finkelhor, Heather Hammer, and Andrea J. Sedlack, "Nonfamily Abducted Children: National Estimates and Characteristics," *NISMART Series Bulletin* (2002).

2. James Alan Fox and Jack Levin, "Mass Confusion Concerning Mass Murder," *Criminologist* 40 (January/February 2015): 8–11.

INDEX